Haematology Dept
Singleton Hospital.   Nov 1985

Recent Advances in
HAEMATOLOGY

A. V. HOFFBRAND MA, DM, FRCP, FRCPath
Professor of Haematology and Honorary Consultant, Royal Free Hospital and School of Medicine, London, UK

Recent Advances in
HAEMATOLOGY

EDITED BY

A. V. HOFFBRAND

NUMBER FOUR

CHURCHILL LIVINGSTONE
EDINBURGH LONDON MELBOURNE AND NEW YORK 1985

CHURCHILL LIVINGSTONE

Medical Division of Longman Group Limited

Distributed in the United States of America by
Churchill Livingstone Inc., 1560 Broadway, New York,
N.Y. 10036, and by associated companies,
branches and representatives throughout
the world.

First edition 1985

ISBN 0 443 03126 6
ISSN 0143-697X

British Library Cataloguing in Publication Data
Recent advances in haematology — No. 4
    1. Blood — Diseases
    616.1'5   RC636

Printed in Great Britain at The Bath Press, Avon

Preface

It is only three years since the third volume of Recent Advances in Haematology was published but it became apparent that increased knowledge, particularly resulting from the applications of molecular biology and monoclonal antibody technology to haematological disorders, warranted a new edition. These techniques are not only helping to unravel the cause of some blood diseases but are also being widely applied clinically, both for diagnosis and treatment. We have therefore included a chapter to help clinical haematologists understand the language, techniques and applications of recombinant DNA technology to genetic and acquired blood disorders.

In order to cover the field as comprehensively as possible and keep the book to a reasonable size, some chapters were allocated only half the length of others, and authors were advised to keep references (which might indeed take up a whole volume in themselves) to essential key papers and reviews, as far as possible.

Nevertheless, it is difficult to achieve a multi-author book which encompasses all major advances at the time of publication. Some authors inevitably submit manuscripts well before others and updating at page-proof stage is limited. While the book has been in preparation, the virus causing AIDS and the genes for Factor VIII and protein C have been sequenced. An increasing number of genetic defects causing thalassaemia has been described and the relations of qualitative or quantitative cytogenetic abnormalities and translocations of oncogenes to leukaemia or lymphoma initiation or progression have been widely explored. The editor hopes, however, that within the topics covered, the text encompasses major developments up to the end of 1984 and will provide a suitable basis for understanding new information in these areas which will undoubtedly appear in 1985 and subsequently.

As in the previous volume, the book is written by authors from Britain and North America. The spelling has been left in the style of the original manuscript. The editor wishes to thank all the contributors for the high standard of their contributions, despite very heavy commitments. It is also a pleasure to thank Miss J. Allaway and Mrs M. Evans for secretarial help at the Royal Free and the staff of Churchill Livingstone for their unstinting help and forebearance, without which this book would not have appeared.

London, 1985   A.V.H.

Contributors

EDWARD J. BENZ Jr MD
Associate Professor of Medicine and Human Genetics, Yale University School of
Medicine, New Haven, Connecticut, USA

JOHN CAIRNS MD FRCP(C)
Professor, Department of Medicine, Hamilton General Hospital, McMaster
University, Hamilton, Ontario, Canada

GENOVEFFA FRANCHINI MD
Laboratory of Tumor Cell Biology, National Cancer Institute, National Institutes of
Health, Bethesda, Maryland, USA

GILLIAN E. FRANCIS MBBS, MSC, MRCPath
Wellcome Senior Research Fellow in Clinical Sciences, Department of Haematology,
Royal Free Hospital and School of Medicine, London, UK

ROBERT C. GALLO MD
Chief, Laboratory of Tumor Cell Biology, National Cancer Institute, National
Institutes of Health, Bethesda, Maryland, USA

JOYCE E. GARDINER PhD
Research Fellow, Department of Immunology, Scripps Clinic and Research
Foundation, La Jolla, California, USA

JOHN H. GRIFFIN PhD
Associate Member, Department of Immunology, Scripps Clinic and Research
Foundation, La Jolla, California, USA

ALISON H. GOODALL BSc, PhD
Lecturer, Academic Department of Immunology, Royal Free Hospital and School of
Medicine, London, UK

JEROME E. GROOPMAN MD
Assistant Professor of Medicine, Harvard Medical School; Attending Hematologist-
Oncologist, New England Deaconess Hospital, Boston, Massachusetts, USA

IAN M. HANN MD, MRCP, MRCPath
Consultant Haematologist, Royal Hospital for Sick Children and Queen Mother's
Maternity Hospital, Glasgow, UK

KATHERINE A. HIGH MD
Research Associate, Yale University School of Medicine, New Haven, Connecticut, USA

JACK HIRSH MD, FRCP(C), FACP
Professor and Chairman, Department of Medicine, McMaster University, Hamilton, Ontario, Canada

A. VICTOR HOFFBRAND MA, DM, FRCP, FRCPath
Professor of Haematology and Honorary Consultant, Royal Free Hospital and School of Medicine, London, UK

ARMAND KEATING BSc, MD, FRCP(C)
Haematologist-Oncologist, Toronto Western Hospital; Assistant Professor of Medicine, University of Toronto, Canada

JOHN H. Kersey MD
Professor of Pediatrics, Laboratory Medicine and Pathology, University of Minnesota Medical School, Minneapolis, Minnesota, USA

LUCIO LUZZATTO MD
Professor of Haematology, Royal Postgraduate Medical School, University of London; Consultant Haematologist, Hammersmith Hospital, London, UK

PHILIP B. McGLAVE MD
Associate Professor of Internal Medicine, University of Minnesota Medical School, Minneapolis, Minnesota, USA

DAVID Y. MASON DM, MRCPath
University Lecturer and Honorary Consultant in Haematology, Department of Haematology, John Radcliffe Hospital, Oxford, UK

ROBYN M. MINCHINTON PhD, FAIMLS
Research Assistant, Department of Haematology, St Bartholomew's Hospital and Medical College, London, UK

FRED OFOSU PhD
Assistant Professor, Department of Pathology, McMaster University, Hamilton, Ontario, Canada

H. GRANT PRENTICE MB, FRCP, MRCPath
Senior Lecturer and Honorary Consultant, Department of Haematology, Royal Free Hospital and School of Medicine, London, UK

NORMA K. C. RAMSAY MD
Associate Professor of Pediatrics, University of Minnesota Medical School, Minneapolis, Minnesota, USA

GRAHAM R. SERJEANT CMG, MD, FRCP
Professor in the Faculty of Medicine and Director, Medical Research Council
Laboratories (Jamaica), University of the West Indies, Kingston, Jamaica

JACK W. SINGER MD
Chief, Oncology Section, Associate Professor of Medicine, Veterans Administration
Medical Center, Seattle, Washington, USA

HARALD STEIN MD
Professor and Head, Institute of Pathology, Freie Universität Steglitz, Institut für
Pathologie, Berlin, Germany

EDWARD G. D. TUDDENHAM MBBS, MRCP, MRCPath
Senior Lecturer, Department of Haematology, The Royal Free Hospital and School
of Medicine, London, UK

JAMES S. WAINSCOAT MRCP, MRCPath
Consultant Haematologist, John Radcliffe Hospital, Oxford, UK

ALAN H. WATERS PhD, FRCPath, FRACP, MRCP
Professor of Haematology; Honorary Consultant Haematologist, St Bartholomew's
Hospital and Medical College, London, UK

DAVID J. WEATHERALL MA, MD, FRCP, FRCPath, FRS
Nuffield Professor of Clinical Medicine, Director, MRC Molecular Haematology
Unit, John Radcliffe Hospital, Oxford, UK

THOMAS N. WIGHT PhD
Chief of Electronmicroscopy Laboratory, Department of Pathology, University of
Washington, Seattle, Washington, USA

Contents

1. The human haemopoietic microenvironment *J. W. Singer*
   A. Keating   T. N. Wight   1

2. The ABCs of molecular genetics: a haematologist's introduction
   K. A. High   E. J. Benz   25

3. The molecular pathology of thalassaemia *D. J. Weatherall*
   J. S. Wainscoat   63

4. Sickle cell disease *G. R. Serjeant*   89

5. Malaria and the red cell *L. Luzzatto*   109

6. Immunological analysis of tissue sections in diagnosis of lymphoma
   H. Stein   D. Y. Mason   127

7. Allogeneic and autologous bone marrow transplantation
   P. B. McGlave   N. K. C. Ramsey   J. H. Kersey   171

8. The prophylaxis and treatment of infections in patients with bone
   marrow failure *H. G. Prentice   I. M. Hann*   199

9. Viruses, *onc* genes and leukaemia *G. Franchini   R. C. Gallo*   221

10. The myelodysplastic syndromes and preleukaemia *G. E. Francis*
    A. V. Hoffbrand   239

11. Protein C and the regulation of thrombosis and haemostasis
    J. E. Gardiner   J. H. Griffin   269

12. Monoclonal antibodies and coagulation *E. G. D. Tuddenham*
    A. Goodall   285

13. Immune thrombocytopenia and neutropenia *A. H. Waters*
    R. M. Minchinton   309

14. Advances in antithrombotic therapy *J. Hirsh   F. Ofosu   J. Cairns*   333

15. The acquired immunodeficiency syndrome (AIDS) *J. E. Groopman*   369

Index   389

1. The human haematopoietic microenvironment

J. W. Singer   A. Keating   T. N. Wight

INTRODUCTION

The haematopoietic microenvironment (HM) is a poorly characterised structural arrangement of cells and their biosynthetic products that allow, and perhaps influence, the proliferation and commitment of haematopoietic progenitors (Trentin, 1971; Wolf, 1983). The importance of an environmental component of haemato-poiesis is suggested by the following in vivo observations:

1. Under normal conditions, haematopoiesis is restricted to specific sites such as the bone marrow in man and the spleen and bone marrow in mice despite the presence of circulating haematopoietic progenitors.

2. When mice are lethally irradiated and rescued by infused marrow cells, multipotent haematopoietic colonies formed from single cells grow only in the spleen and bone marrow (Till & McCulloch, 1961).

3. When marrow is ectopically implanted, haematopoiesis is reconstituted only after the stroma has developed (Tavassoli & Crosby, 1968).

4. When cultured marrow 'fibroblasts' are implanted under the renal capsule, bone formation occurs and is followed by haematopoietic cell infiltration (Friedenstein et al, 1974).

5. Marrow stroma transplanted to spleen exerts its own local effect on haemato-poietic colony growth (Wolf & Trentin, 1968).

6. A genetically anaemic mouse strain, the Sl/Sl^d has decreased numbers of CFU-S and cannot be rescued from irradiation by normal marrow cells. Spleen colonies do not form. However, when spleen or marrow from a normal mouse is implanted into the Sl/Sl^d, the normal stroma became actively haematopoietic but has not effect on the adjoining Sl/Sl^d stroma (Bernstein, 1970).

7. Histologic studies show that haematopoietic cells always arise in intimate relationship with poorly characterised cell populations which include adventitial reticular cells, endothelial cells and macrophages. Adipocytes, thought to be derived from reticular cells, are often associated with granulopoietic areas of marrow (Lichtman, 1981).

Despite these in vivo observations suggesting the importance of the HM, only the development of an in vitro system containing microenvironmental cells has made it possible to study its composition and function. Dexter reported that when mouse marrow cells were placed in suspension cultures in a medium containing horse serum, an adherent layer formed that was capable of supporting CFU-S proliferation for many months (Dexter et al, 1977). The adherent layer, unlike marrow fibroblasts (Friedenstein et al, 1974), contained cells of a diverse morphology including endothelial cells, reticular cells, fat cells, and macrophages. Thus, the Dexter system not only contained the cells thought to be important in the microenvironment from

1

the in vivo morphologic studies, but provided an in vitro system which propagated both multipotent stem cells and microenvironmental cells. It is therefore possible using the Dexter system to examine the structure and function of the HM.

The major emphasis of the present review is on studies applying the Dexter culture system to the human HM under physiologic and pathologic conditions. Since this system was only successfully adapted to human marrow in 1980 (Gartner & Kaplan), many of these studies are recent and some must be considered preliminary.

TERMINOLOGY

There is, as yet, no standardisation of either terminology to describe or methodology to culture microenvironmental cells. Dexter (1982) described murine stromal cell layers as consisting of epithelial cells, endothelial cells, macrophages, fat containing cells, reticular cells, and more recently, a cell he terms a 'blanket cell' that is intimately associated with maturing haematopoietic elements. However, these terms are only descriptive, although some preliminary biosynthetic and antigenic character-isation of these cells has been reported and will be discussed subsequently. For the purposes of this review, the term marrow stromal cells will be used generically and applied to the cell populations forming the adherent layer in actively haematopoietic long-term cultures. Other defining characteristics of stromal cells include biosynthesis of collagen, laminin, complex proteoglycans and their transplantability. (Discussed in subsequent sections.)

Friedenstein and others use the term 'fibroblast' to describe cultured marrow cells capable of transplanting a microenvironment (Friedenstein et al, 1970, 1974, 1978; Greenberg et al, 1981). However, these cells are not capable of supporting in vitro proliferation of CFU-S (Lubennikova & Domaratsky, 1976). Moreover, marrow fibroblasts serially passaged four or more times do not synthesise type IV collagen[1] (Keating et al, 1982a) and are not transplantable in either murine or human systems (Friedenstein et al, 1978; Golde et al, 1980). An assay has been described for the culture of marrow fibroblast colony forming cells (CFU-F) (Castro-Malaspina et al, 1980). The haematopoietic function and relationship to stroma of these cells has not been demonstrated. However, a recent report suggests that CFU-F also may be transplantable (Piersma et al, 1983) and thus may include some precursors of stromal cells. Colonies derived from CFU-F produce fibronectin, and types I, III, and V collagen (Castro-Malaspina et al, 1982). Type V collagen is not usually associated with fibroblasts but recently has been detected in stromal cells from long-term cultures (Keating & Singer, 1983). Thus, the relationship of fibroblasts and CFU-F to stromal cells remains uncertain.

Until the component cells of the in vitro microenvironment can be cloned and their characteristics rigorously defined, we suggest the generic term marrow stromal cells be used. Stromal cells can be functionally defined as those cells necessary to propagate haematopoietic progenitor cells in vitro. Therefore, since fibroblasts do not support

---

[1] Collagen is a major constituent of the extra-cellular matrix. At least five major types of collagen (referred to as types I, II, III, IV and V) are present in man, differing in their structure, function and distribution. Types I, II and III have a fibrillar structure and are predominantly extracellular, imparting support to connective tissues. Types IV and V do not form fibrils and are predominantly pericellular with type IV a major constituent of basal laminae.

long-term haematopoiesis, they are not stromal cells, although they may constitute a minor population of the stroma in long-term marrow cultures.

Continuously growing lines with preadipocyte characteristics derived from marrow stroma have been developed (Lanotte et al, 1982). Such lines contain cells of an epitheloid to fibroblastoid morphology that become adipocytes in the presence of hydrocortisone but not in the presence of insulin. Murine stromal lines are aneuploid and have not been reported to support the proliferation of CFU-S. Therefore, it is also not valid to consider them as more than a transformed component population of the normal stroma.

IN VITRO TECHNIQUES FOR STUDY OF THE MICROENVIRONMENT

'Fibroblastic' cell cultures and CFU-F

When bone marrow light density cells are cultured in the presence of either fetal calf serum or homologous serum without hydrocortisone, a confluent layer of 'fibroblastic' cells appears by 3–4 weeks. Evidence for haematopoietic function of these cells resides in experiments by Friedenstein who showed that guinea pig or rabbit 'fibroblastic' cells initiated the development of a haematopoietic organ when transplanted under the kidney capsule (Friedenstein et al, 1974). Despite these intriguing experiments suggesting that 'fibroblastic' cells have the ability to transfer at least the stimulus for development of a haematopoietic organ, they do not support CFU-S proliferation in vitro (Lubennikova & Domeretsky, 1976). Several studies examining these cells in man have been published and are referred to later (Castro-Malaspina et al, 1980; 1982; Gordon & Gordon-Smith; Kaneko et al, 1982).

CFU-F or 'fibroblast' colony-forming cell was a term originally used by Frieden-stein and co-workers (1974) to describe 'fibroblastic' cell precursors. When marrow cells were placed in flasks, at 3–5 days, colonies of 'fibroblastic' cells appear which approach confluence by day 14 and consist of up to several thousand cells. Colonies formed only when marrow cells were plated at high density and were found to have a frequency of between one and three colonies/10^5 marrow cells. The D_0 for murine CFU-F was found to be between 215 and 230 R by Werts et al (1980). The clonality of CFU-F colonies was assumed on the basis of a linear cell/dose response but has not been rigorously proven. Castro-Malaspina et al (1980) demonstrated that most CFU-F were less dense than $1.070 \, \text{g/cm}^3$ and did not express Ia antigen. They also showed that 'fibroblastic' cells derived from CFU-F reacted with antibodies to collagen types I, III, and V and fibronectin but did not express factor VIII associated antigen (Castro-Malaspina et al, 1980, 1982). When hydrocortisone was added to CFU-F cultures, fat-containing cells appeared. Fibroblastic cells from tissues other than bone marrow require insulin rather than hydrocortisone for adipocyte generation (Green-berger, 1978). However, the relationship of CFU-F to the complex stromal cell compartment in long-term cultures is uncertain. CFU-F may constitute either a minor cell population of stromal cells in long-term culture or could be an undifferentiated precursor cell population capable of forming the heterogeneous mesenchymal elements of the long-term culture stroma under appropriate conditions. Recent murine data indicating that CFU-F become partial donor-derived after marrow transplanta-tion (Piersma et al, 1983) suggest that CFU-F are a precursor population that can give rise to cells other than 'fibroblastic' cells which retain a host phenotype after transplantation (Friedenstein et al, 1978). Werts et al (1980) showed that murine CFU-F can migrate to re-establish haematopoiesis in a heavily irradiated site.

Long-term marrow culture (Dexter culture)

When mouse marrow cells are placed in suspension cultures containing a medium supplemented with horse serum and hydrocortisone, an adherent cell layer forms which supports proliferation of multipotent and committed haematopoietic progenitors for many months (Dexter, 1977). Unlike 'fibroblastic' cells, the adherent cell layer of long-term marrow cultures contain cells of varying phenotypes including endothelial-like cells, reticular cells, macrophages, and fat-containing cells. The most immature stem cells are intimately involved in the stromal cell layer and it is within this in vitro microenvironment that they proliferate, differentiate, and release more mature progenitors into the loosely adherent and free-floating compartments of the culture (Allen & Dexter, 1982; Dexter et al, 1980; Coulombel et al, 1983a). Thus, with refeeding, these cultures can be examined for the continued production of committed erythroid (BFU-E), granulocyte/macrophage (CFU-GM), and multipotent (CFU-S; CFU-GEMM) (Till & McCulloch, 1961; Fauser & Messner, 1979) progenitors. This system adds significantly to the colony-forming cell assays and provides a better in vitro model of in vivo haematopoiesis. Examination of the stromal cell layer in these cultures may yield an understanding of the organisation and function of the in vivo microenvironment. The importance of the stroma in in vitro haematopoiesis in these cultures can be easily demonstrated. If siliconised flasks are used to inhibit stromal cell attachment, stem cell proliferation does not occur (Dexter, 1982). Moreover, murine stromal cells from other organs do not support haematopoiesis (Reimann & Burger, 1979). Additional support for the adequacy of the Dexter culture as a model system for in vivo haematopoiesis comes from the observation that the system can reproduce the environmental and stem cell defects of genetically anaemic mice; the Sl/Sl^d and W/W^v, respectively (Dexter & Moore, 1977).

Partial success in adaptation of the Dexter system to human marrow was achieved by Gartner & Kaplan (1980). Using a combination of fetal calf serum and horse serum supplemented with hydrocortisone, CFU-GM could be maintained for up to 20 weeks in a flask culture system. The system was dependent on the formation of a confluent stromal cell layer containing mesenchymal cells and macrophages. Subsequent data have demonstrated that fibroblasts comprise only a minor component of the stroma in man (Keating et al, 1982a; Singer & Keating, 1983). The production of CFU-GM is suboptimal compared to the murine system, and it is rare to demonstrate BFU-E or CFU-GEMM beyond 8 weeks (Coulombel et al, 1983a; Powell et al, 1983). It should be noted, however, that some mouse strains such as NIH-Swiss only produce CFU-GM for about 20 weeks and that the success of the murine long-term culture is based on the use of genetically pure mice selected for forming an optimal culture system (Greenberger, 1980). Thus, it is not surprising that significant variation occurs in human cultures, some producing CFU-GM for over 22 weeks and others for less than 10 weeks. One possible explanation for the relatively poor performance of the human system may reside in the low number of stem cells with repopulating ability placed in each flask. For example, if cells such as the most immature CFU-S or preCFU-S are needed for murine culture maintenance and occur with a frequency of $1–2/10^6$ unseparated marrow cells in human marrow, then most human flask cultures which are initiated with 2×10^7 cells would have fewer than 40. These cells may not adhere to plastic and cannot enter the stromal cell layer until it becomes established at week 3–4. Therefore, 3–4 demipopulations of this compartment may occur prior to effective stem cell trapping leaving only 2–5 stem cells with repopulating ability. These may be insufficient to sustain long-term haematopoiesis. The low concentration of such cells may itself lead to terminal differentiation (Schofield, 1978). It is also probable that the conditions used for generating human long-term cultures are suboptimal. Nevertheless, an active human haematopoietic system can be sustained for up to several months and has been used to study haematopoietic cell-microenvironment interactions in normal and abnormal conditions.

EVIDENCE THAT MARROW STROMAL CELLS FUNCTION AS AN IN VITRO MICROENVIRONMENT

In vivo haematopoiesis does not occur in the absence of site-specific structures that both support and modulate multipotent stem cell expression. The cellular elements of the in vivo microenvironment include endothelial-lined sinusoids which are coated by adventitial reticular cells (Lichtman, 1981). Maturation of haematopoietic cells takes place in the intersinusoidal spaces closely associated with reticular cell processes. Few, if any, 'free fibroblasts' were noted in ultrastructural studies of mouse marrow. Adipocytes are thought to arise from adventitial reticular cells (Lichtman, 1981). Each of these in vivo microenvironmental cells has an in vitro counterpart in the stromal cell layers of long-term marrow cultures.

Since the function of the in vivo microenvironment is to sustain haematopoiesis, perhaps by providing stem cell 'niches' that can immortalise stem cells by preventing terminal maturation (Schofield, 1978), this may also be true of its in vitro counterpart. Although there is unequivocal data in the mouse that the stromal cells can support long-term haematopoiesis, data on the human system is less convincing due to the rapid decline in the production of progenitor cells.

To amplify and examine the effect of stromal cells on haematopoiesis, a series of experiments were done to deplete human marrow of the majority of measurable progenitor cells including CFU-GEMM by the use of a monoclonal anti-HLA-DR (Ia) antibody (7.2) and complement (C'). Washed 4-week-old marrow stromal cells or 4th passage marrow fibroblasts were irradiated with 800 R and then refed with media containing allogeneic marrow cells treated with $7.2 + C'$. Cultures were demipopulated and refed weekly. Control cultures contained media without a stroma. As shown in Table 1.1, by day 14, cultures placed in flasks with irradiated normal

Table 1.1 Ratio of CFU-GM detected in day 14 supernatant cells from irradiated flasks containing stromal cells or fibroblasts overlaid with marrow cells treated with an anti-HLA-DR monoclonal antibody (7.2) and complement to control flasks

Normal marrow stromal cells	Marrow stromal cells from CML patients	Marrow fibroblasts
6.37 ± 1.87 (mean $\pm$ s.e.m.; $n = 5$)	1.17 ± 0.17 ($n = 4$)	1.77 ± 0.34 ($n = 4$)

The mean ($\pm$s.d.) loss of CFU-GM in marrows treated with 7.2 and complement was $62 \pm 6\%$. 10^7 Ia-depleted marrow cells were placed over irradiated (800 R) stromal cells from normal donors, donors with CML or 4th passage normal marrow fibroblasts. Supernatant cells were harvested and cultured for CFU-GM growth. Results were compared to flasks containing no stromal cell layers. Irradiated stromal cell layers alone failed to produce any detectable CFU-GM.

stromal cells generated approximately five times the number of CFU-GM as did the fibroblast and media controls. This difference was sustained at 21 days and suggested that stromal cells have at least a permissive effect on generation of CFU-GM from a presumably less differentiated, Ia-negative precursor cell population. Since marrow fibroblasts did not exert this effect, the data suggest that the complex cell mixture present in the stromal cell layer of an active culture is needed and that as in the mouse, fibroblasts do not fulfill the requirements for a complete in vitro microenvironment. Thus, although the human long-term culture system is suboptimal, its stromal cell layer appears to fulfill some of the functional requirements for an in vitro microenvironment.

ORIGIN OF THE MICROENVIRONMENT

Transplantation studies

There have been two hypotheses regarding the origin of the stromal component of haematopoiesis in vivo. The first propounded by Maximow (1924) and also by Sabin (1920) who, on the basis of embryologic observations, suggested that haematopoietic cells originated from mesenchymal elements. The second hypothesis (reviewed by Fliedner & Calvo, 1978) and currently favoured, suggests that marrow stroma has an independent origin from perichondrial mesenchyme and that it is secondarily populated by circulating haematopoietic stem cells. Although attempts to clarify the origin of stromal cells using the in vitro methods described earlier have resulted in some conflicting data, two recent reports have indicated that under certain circumstances, both human and murine stromal cells may constitute a transplantable population (Keating et al, 1982a; Piersma et al, 1983). These results are not surprising in view of the data obtained by Werts et al (1980) showing migration of murine CFU-F from a shielded femur following 1000 R total body irradiation.

Other data suggesting migration of mesenchymal cells have been reported. Some intimal cells in plaques in a human cardiac allograft distant from the anastomotic sites were found to be of host origin. This suggested that there was a circulating progenitor for spindle-like cells capable of attaching to the endothelial surface, entering the vessel wall and proliferating (Kennedy & Weissman, 1971). In a murine system, Kearns & Lala (1982) demonstrated the bone marrow origin of stromal-like decidual cell precursors in the pseudopregnant mouse uterus.

Keating et al (1982a) showed, using fluorescent Y bodies to identify host or donor origin, that stromal cells in long-term marrow cultures initiated after allogeneic marrow grafting from donors of the opposite sex, become increasingly donor-derived with time. Specimens cultured from marrow aspirates taken more than 45 days after marrow infusion were nearly 100% donor-derived.

Piersma et al (1983), using chromosomal markers in mice, demonstrated that 3 months after transplantation approximately 50% of CFU-F were donor in origin. Feiner et al (1983) demonstrated the donor origin of 25–30% of adipocytes in mouse radiochimeras prepared by total lymphoid radiation. This percentage is similar to that determined previously by these workers for marrow mononuclear cells using a similar transplantation protocol. In an earlier study, Friedenstein et al (1978), transplanting mice with 75% fewer cells than were used by Piersma were unable to demonstrate donor CFU-F in radiochimeras. Bentley (1982) found that radiochimeric mice transplanted with only 10^5 marrow cells had host stromal cells in long-term culture. However, the mice did not obtain a sustained haematopoietic graft.

In humans, Golde et al (1980) showed that cultured fibroblasts remained host in origin after allogeneic marrow transplantation. Unlike the Keating study, Golde performed his analyses on 5th passage fibroblasts maintained without horse serum or hydrocortisone. A single patient study also demonstrating host origin of marrow fibroblasts after marrow grafting was reported earlier by Wilson et al (1978).

Origin of stromal cells in patients with clonal neoplasia originating in multipotent stem cells

The X-linked enzyme glucose-6-phosphatase dehydrogenase (G6PD) has been a useful marker system to determine clonality and cell lineage relationships in neoplasia (reviewed in Fialkow, 1983). Females heterozygous for G6PD type B (Gd^b) and a variant such as Gd^a have two populations of cells, one expressing type B G6PD and the other type A. If a neoplasm starts in a single cell, neoplastic cells will express only a single enzyme type, whereas normal cell populations will express both enzymes. Four relevant patients were studied. Studies on one patient were reported previously (Singer & Keating, 1983a). Clinical details and G6PD data on direct cell preparations, adherent cell layers and non-adherent cells from long-term marrow cultures are shown in Table 1.2. Both adherent and non-adherent cells from long-term cultures manifested only the single G6PD of the leukaemic clone. This finding was surprising in view of the non-haematopoietic appearance of the stromal cell layers from these cultures. An estimate of haematopoietic cell contamination using the 9.4 monoconal antibody (an antibody to T200, a surface protein present on all haematopoietic cells (Omary et al, 1980) to distinguish haematopoietic cells (see below, Characterisation of stromal cells) suggested that close to 70% of the stromal cells in patients 2, 3, and 4 were non-haematopoietic. Additional studies have shown that the G6PD content of normal stromal cells is approximately equivalent to that of the haematopoietic non-adherent cells and suggest that the G6PD activity of stromal cells was not overwhelmed by that of contaminating haematotropic cells. Further characterisation of these clonal stromal cell layers showed that some cells (<25%) expressed factor VIII associated antigen (patients 1 and 2), that stromal cell layers synthesised both interstitial and basal lamina collagens (patients 1 and 2), and that 40% of stromal cells recultured from patient 2 reacted with a monoclonal antibody against smooth muscle actin, the CGA-7 (see below, Characterisation of stromal cells). Thus, the stromal cells shown by G6PD to have originated from the neoplastic clone appeared to include a substantial number of cells with non-haematopoietic characteristics. The data suggest that these cells were derived from a neoplastic stem cell that also gave rise to haematopoietic cells.

Marrow fibroblasts from patients with chronic myelogenous leukaemia (CML) contain equal amounts of A and B G6PD demonstrating that they are non-neoplastic cells (Fialkow et al, 1977). The sensitivity of the G6PD system is such that if 5–10% of the stromal cells were fibroblasts, they would have been detected by their G6PD expression. These data then indicate that fibroblasts constitute only a minor population in stromal cell layers of long-term marrow cultures from these patients. In support of this conclusion, several other studies have examined the nature of 'fibroblastic' cells and CFU-F in Philadelphia chromosome (Ph[1]) positive CML.

Table 1.2   Studies of long-term cultures from four G6PD heterozygotes with multipotent stem cell leukaemias

Patient number	Diagnosis	G6PD %A/%B activity Uncultured tissues					Long-term marrow culture	
		Red blood cells	Granulocytes	Platelets	Skin	Marrow fibroblasts	Non-adherent cells	Stromal cells
1	Ph¹-positive CML	0/100	0/100	0/100	50/50		0/100	0/100
2	Ph¹-negative CML	90/10*	100/0	100/0	60/40		100/0	100/0
3	ANLL	0/100	0/100	0/100	60/40		0/100	0/100
4	Ph¹-positive CML	100/0	100/0	100/0		60/40	100/0	100/0

Hentel & Hirschlorn (1971) found the Ph[1] in 14/100 bone marrow fibroblasts cultured from a CML patient. Moreover, they reported finding 68/100 cells with a C-group trisomy in fibroblast cultures from a patient with acute leukaemia and a C group trisonomy. A later study by Greenberg et al (1978) failed to find Ph[1] in 'fibroblastic' cultures from 6 patients with Ph[1]-positive CML. Studies of CFU-F in a series of patients with myeloproliferative disorders including CML by Castro-Malaspina et al (1982) found that the biosynthetic and physical properties of CFU-F and their progeny were normal. Cytogenetic analyses showed absence of Ph[1].

In summary, the data support the concept that marrow stromal cells and marrow fibroblasts constitute separate cell populations. Stromal cells are transplanted following successful marrow transplantation, whereas fibroblasts remain host-derived. Stromal cells are derived from the neoplastic stem cells in certain clonal haematopoietic neoplastic disorders and thus may share a common origin with other haematopoietic cells. Fibroblasts originate from non-neoplastic cells in these disorders. CFU-F may constitute a mixed population; some may be stromal cell progenitors, while others give rise to fibroblasts.

Antigenic and physical characteristics of marrow stromal cell progenitors

We have undertaken a series of studies to examine some of the characteristics of progenitor cells giving rise to human long-term marrow cultures. Keating et al (1983) have shown that most stromal cells express the common acute lymphoblastic leukaemia antigen (CALLA) using two monoclonal antibodies (J-5 and 24.1). However, treating marrow cells with J-5 and complement (C') did not prevent the subsequent establishment of a long-term culture and the appearance of normal, J-5-positive stromal cells. Similarly, treating marrow cells with 7.2 and C' (7.2 is an antibody against HLA-DR (Ia) that is cytotoxic to CFU-GM, BFU-E, and GFU-GEMM) did not abrogate formation of a complete long-term culture system. The effect of 7.2 + C' was to decrease CFU-GM generation for 2–3 weeks. Thereafter, antibody-treated marrows generated an equivalent number of CFU-GM and BFU-E when compared to the control cultures (Keating et al, 1984).

To determine the physical properties of the progenitors for long-term cultures, marrow buffy coat cells were separated on discontinuous Percoll® gradients with $0.05\,g/ml$ density cuts between 1.050 and $1.080\,g/ml$ and individual fractions established in suspension culture with complete media. Using this system, the modal density for both CFU-GM and BFU-E is $1.065\,g/ml$. Somewhat surprisingly, although no single fraction used to generate long-term cultures produced CFU-GM beyond 12 weeks, all developed stromal cell layers. Those cultures started from cells with densities of 1.070 and 1.075 produced CFU-GM for the longest period of time (Table 1.3). The data suggest that interacting cell populations of several densities may be needed to establish successful human long-term marrow cultures and that the stem cells with the greatest capacity to produce CFU-GM as well as some cells that give rise to stromal cells lie within the denser fractions of the gradient. Moreover, both of these progenitor populations are physically separable from the majority of committed progenitor cells that form colonies in semisolid agar media.

In summary, progenitors for the haematopoietic and stromal cell elements of the human long-term culture system do not express CALLA or HLA-DR and both are present in the higher-density mononuclear cell fractions of a discontinuous gradient.

Table 1.3   Granulopoiesis in long-term marrow cultures initiated with cells of a single density (three experiments)

Density of starting cells (g/ml)	Duration of CFU-C production (>50 CFU-C/flask) (weeks)
1.050	2
1.055	2
1.060	3
1.065	6
1.070	12
1.075	11
1.080	9

Marrow cells were applied to discontinuous density gradients using Percoll® (Singer et al, 1980). Individual fractions were collected, established in long-term culture, and demi-depopulated weekly. Non-adherent cells were plated for CFU-C growth. All fractions produced confluent stromal cell layers.

REGULATORS OF MARROW STROMAL CELL PROLIFERATION: STUDIES WITH PLATELET-DERIVED GROWTH FACTOR (PDGF)

Stromal cells from normal human 4-week-old long-term marrow cultures were examined for the presence of PDGF receptors. Saturation binding of a highly purified iodinated PDGF (Bowen-Pope & Ross, 1982) to many cells in the stromal cell layer was demonstrated by autoradiographic and biochemical methods when primary stromal cells were regrown after trypsin treatment. The readherent stromal cells showed a strong mitogenic response to highly purified PDGF as measured by tritiated thymidine uptake. The dose-dependent binding of the iodinated PDGF was observed in the same range in which highly purified non-labelled PDGF stimulated incorporation of tritiated thymidine. Bone marrow fibroblasts were also shown to bear PDGF receptors and were responsive to highly purified PDGF. In several experiments, however, the number of PDGF receptors per cultured marrow fibroblast was substantially less than for autologous stromal cells derived from long-term marrow cultures (Rosenfeld et al, 1985).

A number of cultured cell types have shown responsiveness to PDGF including dermal fibroblasts, arterial smooth muscle cells and NIH 3T3 cells, but not vascular endothelium or epitheloid cell lines (Bowen-Pope & Ross, 1982). It is possible that PDGF functions as a mitogen in vivo also. PDGF released from activated platelets may locally stimulate the growth of connective tissue cells. Possible roles for PDGF in the pathogenesis of myelofibrosis in myeloproliferative disorders (Groopman, 1980) as well as in conditions with a platelet α-granule defect (Breton-Gorius et al, 1982) have been suggested.

Evidence that PDGF acts as a mitogen to cells of the in vitro haematopoietic microenvironment suggests that this factor may be indirectly involved in the regulation of haematopoiesis. The recent observation that marrow erythroid progenitor cell proliferation is augmented by PDGF (Daniak et al, 1983) may be explained by its action on marrow stromal cells. This is supported by the work of Delwiche et al (1983) who demonstrated that BFU-E growth from non-adherent marrow cells was augmented by PDGF only in the presence of underlayers of mesenchymal cells. They also showed that this enhancement was abrogated with antiprostaglandin agents. The potential importance of PDGF in myeloproliferative abnormalities was recently underscored by the finding of sequence homology between PDGF and the product of the Simian sarcoma virus oncogene (Waterfield et al, 1983; Doolittle et al, 1983; Deuel et al, 1983).

CHARACTERISATION OF HUMAN MARROW STROMAL CELLS

Stromal cells from normal human long-term marrow cultures were studied by indirect immunofluorescence with a variety of antibodies. The cells were examined in both untreated layers and as single cell suspensions formed by mechanical disruption. Most cells were found to bear HLA antigens, $\beta2$ microglobulin, fibronectin and the common acute lymphoblastic leukaemia antigen (CALLA). A minority of elongated cells and most small rounded cells were positive with 9.4, a monoclonal antibody recognising the pan-haematopoietic cell antigen, T200 (Omary et al, 1980). The overall frequency of 9.4-positive cells in the stromal layer varied between 5 and 30% from culture to culture. Non-adherent cells harvested from 4- and 8-week-old long-term cultures were nearly all 9.4-positive. Less than 20% of stromal cells reacted with 7.2, a murine monoclonal antibody recognising the Ia determinant.

Common acute lymphocyte leukaemia antigen (CALLA)

It is now clear that CALLA is not confined to haematopoietic cells (Metzger et al, 1981). Normal cultured skin and marrow fibroblasts also express CALLA (Braun et al, 1983). The finding of an antigenic determinant associated with CALLA on most human marrow stromal cells (Keating et al, 1983) is of interest because of the recent use of an anti-CALLA antibody in the treatment of patients with acute lymphoblastic leukaemia (Ritz et al, 1981, 1982). When marrow stromal cells were incubated with an anti-CALLA antibody (J-5 or 24.1) and complement, most of the flat, angulated cells and many of the fat-containing cells were lost. Nevertheless, long-term cultures could be generated with marrow cells similarly treated with anti-CALLA antibody and complement. The stromal cells in these cultures were also CALLA positive. These studies suggest that the CALLA-bearing stromal cells arose from CALLA-negative progenitors and that CALLA is a differentiation antigen acquired on mature marrow stroma.

Factor VIII associated antigen

Human stromal cells have been shown to compromise between 5 and 20% of cells that stain positively for factor VIII associated antigen by indirect immunofluorescence using an affinity-purified rabbit antibody (Keating et al, 1982a). Striking variation in the frequency of these positive cells is seen both within a normal stromal cell layer and from culture to culture. Whether these are true endothelial cells or are unique cells expressing endothelial-like characteristics is the subject of debate. Some marrow stromal cells synthesise type IV collagen and possess junctional complexes (Keating et al, 1982a), both characteristics of endothelial cells, but Weibel–Palade bodies, another endothelial cell hallmark (Weibel & Palade, 1964), have not been reported. Further studies with specific endothelial cell markers such as antilaminin antibodies, monoclonal antifactor VIII antibodies and fluorochrome-labelled Ulex europaeus I lectin (Holthofer et al, 1982), as well as the use of double immunofluorescence with non-endothelial cell markers, would be of interest. In the murine system, some workers have failed to identify factor VIII positive cells (Bentley & Tralka, 1982), while others found them in high frequency (Zuckerman & Wicha, 1983).

Cytoskeletal proteins

Human stromal cells from 1-month-old normal long-term marrow cultures were examined with a panel of monoclonal antibodies directed against cytoskeletal proteins (Gown, unpublished data). All stromal cells reacted with 43βE8 (Gown & Vogel, 1982), a monoclonal antibody recognising vimentin, an intermediate filament protein of mesenchymal cells. Surprisingly, 40% of the stromal cells in confluent cultures reacted with CGA-7 (Gown et al, 1983), an antibody specific for the α actin of smooth muscle cells. However, passaged marrow fibroblasts and human endothelial cells were negative. Double immunofluorescence studies with CGA-7 and an affinity-purified rabbit antibody directed against factor VIII associated antigen demonstrated that the cells in the stromal cell layer positive for factor VIII associated antigen and for smooth muscle actin represent separate subpopulations. All stromal cells were negative with an anticytokeratin antibody, 35βH11 and an antineurofilament antibody 31All (antibodies described in Gown & Vogel, 1982).

BIOSYNTHETIC FUNCTIONS OF MARROW STROMAL CELLS

Collagen

Recent studies have shown that interstitial and basal lamina collagen types are synthesised by marrow stromal cells (Keating et al, 1982a; Keating & Singer, 1983). Radiolabelled media and human stromal cell layers were analysed for pepsin-resistant collagenous proteins using polyacrylamide gel electrophoresis. Collagen types I, III, IV and, more recently, type V were identified. Most of the collagen and particularly types IV and V were found in the layer rather than in the medium. Conflicting results have been found with the murine long-term culture system. Bentley (Bentley & Foidart, 1980; Bentley & Tralka, 1982) failed to detect biosynthesis of collagen types IV and V in murine long-term cultures, while Zuckerman & Wicha (1983), using the same system, showed extensive deposition of type IV collagen by indirect immunofluorescence. Nonetheless, when Bentley et al (1981) examined sections of normal human bone marrow, they found type IV collagen associated with sinusoidal epithelium as well as both intracellular and extracellular collagen types I and III throughout the marrow. The role of the collagen matrix in human long-term cultures has yet to be defined and should be studied further since collagen is known to affect cell growth and differentiation in other systems (Reddi, 1979; Gospodarowicz & Vlodavsky, 1982).

Proteoglycans

Acellular components of the haematopoietic microenvironment that have been implicated in haematopoietic regulation are the proteoglycans and their constituent glycosaminoglycans. Proteoglycan is a relatively new term which replaces the older term 'acid mucopolysaccharides' to describe a group of macromolecules that together with collagen and other glycoproteins are present throughout the extracellular matrices of both hard and soft tissues (Hascall & Hascall, 1981). These macromolecules consist of carbohydrate polymers (glycosaminoglycans) covalently linked to a protein core. Different classes of glycosaminoglycans exist which depend upon the nature of the monosaccharides that constitute a specific disaccharide repeat pattern in the glycosaminoglycan chain. The disaccharides consist of a hexosamine and either a carboxylate and/or sulphate ester providing linear arrays of anionic charge to the molecule. The major type of glycosaminoglycans present as proteoglycans and found in most mammalian tissues include chondroitin-4 and -6 sulphate, dermatan sulphate, heparan sulphate and keratan sulphate. Hyaluronic acid is also a glycosaminoglycan but is not sulphated and unlike other glycosaminoglycans is not believed to be covalently linked to protein.

In addition to glycosaminoglycans, proteoglycans may also have various proportions of sialic acid containing oligosaccharides attached to their protein core. There are two major oligosaccharides associated with most proteoglycans and these can be distinguished from one another by 1) the nature of their covalent linkage to the protein, 2) presence or absence of N-galactosamine, and 3) presence or absence of mannose. Thus, proteoglycans are complex macromolecules exhibiting wide heterogeneity, encompassing different core proteins as well as different types, sizes and numbers of glycosaminoglycan and oligosaccharide chains. Another property that distinguishes some families of proteoglycans from others is their ability to interest with hyaluronic acid to form large multimonomer aggregates (Hascall & Hascall, 1981). The structure of a typical proteoglycan is depicted in Figure 1.1.

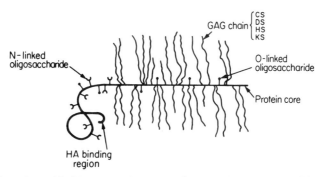

Fig. 1.1   A schematic model of the proposed structure of a proteoglycan monomer. The molecule consists of a central protein core to which are attached side chains of glycosaminoglycans (GAG) and various proportions of O-linked and N-linked oligosaccharides. Usually one type of GAG chain is associated with a single protein core. One end of the protein core may be specialised so that it interacts with hyaluronic acid (HA binding region). HA = hyaluronic acid; CS = chondroitin sulphate; DS = dermatan sulphate; HS = heparan sulphate; KS = keratan sulphate.

Proteoglycans are present as part of the extracellular matrix in all tissues and may either be found within the interstitial connective tissue space bound to collagen and other matrix glycoproteins and/or present in the pericellular environment associated with specific structures such as basal or external laminae of epithelial, endothelial and mesenchymal cells (Farquhar, 1981). In addition, proteoglycans may be integral components of cell membranes or associated with cell membranes in a receptor-like fashion (Höök et al, 1982). This dual localisation suggests that proteoglycans not only function as structural components capable of dissipating stress and maintaining tissue turgor but also as potential 'modifiers' of cell behaviour.

Early clinical and experimental studies of defective haematopoiesis due to prolonged starvation revealed excessive accumulation of proteoglycans within haemato-poietic organs (Pearson, 1967; Tavassoli et al, 1976). Histochemical studies using genetic models of anaemia (Sl/Sl^d mice) (McCuskey et al, 1973) and biochemical studies of experimentally induced polycythaemia in mice (Schrock et al, 1973) demonstrated that erythropoietically suppressed spleens contained elevated levels of proteoglycans compared to spleens of normal mice. These early studies led to the hypothesis that proteoglycan accumulation within haematopoietic organs suppressed haematopoiesis. Additional support for this hypothesis was obtained by Pleomacher et al (1978) who demonstrated inhibition of erythropoietic differentiation in vitro by treating marrow cultures with elevated levels of several different glycosaminoglycans including chondroitin sulphate, dermatan sulphate and heparan sulphate. These studies are contrasted by more recent analysis of erythropoietically suppressed spleens from experimentally induced polycythaemic and anaemic mice which failed to demonstrate increases in sulphate glycosaminoglycans (Noordegraaf & Pleomacher, 1979). Thus, uncertainty exists as to the nature of the proteoglycan change associated with defective haematopoiesis.

The possible importance of cell surface glycosaminoglycans in stem cell maturation has been considered by Del Rosso and his colleagues (1981) who have demonstrated that only mature granulocytes and not immature blast cells or peripheral blood leukocytes from leukaemic patients (Vannuchi et al, 1980) possess chondroitin-4-sulphate on their cell surface. Furthermore, immature haematopoietic cells only adhere to marrow stromal cells in vitro, whereas mature cells do not (Del Rosso et al, 1981). Yet, removal of chondroitin-4-sulphate from the surface of haematopoietic cells with specific glycosidases allows these cells to adhere to the stromal multilayer. Additionally, removal of heparan sulphate from the surface of stromal cells prevents the adherence of haematopoietic cells. These studies indicate the potential importance of glycosaminoglycans in stromal cell-haematopoietic cell interaction—an interaction that appears essential for in vitro haemopoiesis to occur.

To date, the majority of studies implicating proteoglycans and their constituent glycosaminoglycans in haematopoiesis have been indirect (i.e. examining glycosami-noglycan content in systems exhibiting defective haematopoiesis). A more direct approach has been taken by Dexter and his colleagues using the mouse long-term marrow culture system. Long-term active mouse bone marrow culture have been shown to synthesise and secrete hyaluronic acid and chondroitin sulphate into the culture medium (Gallagher et al, 1983). When these cultures were treated with β-D-xyloside, chondroitin sulphate synthesis was increased 30-fold, and these cultures exhibited elevated haematopoiesis (Spooncer et al, 1983). Xylosides substitute for the core protein acceptor for glycosaminoglycan synthesis and divert glycosami-noglycan synthesis from the core protein onto the xyloside. Since xyloside is not only known to stimulate free-chain chondroitin sulphate synthesis (see review, Hascall & Hascall, 1981) but also decrease the synthesis of the intact proteochondroitin sulphate, it is difficult to know the exact nature of the proteoglycan effect on haematopoiesis in this system. It may be that this 'modified' microenvironment is simply more conducive to stem cell proliferation. This work indicates an association between stimulated glycosaminoglycan synthesis and increased capacity for long-term marrow cultures to maintain haematopoiesis. Yet, it still remains to be shown whether a 'cause and effect' relationship exists.

Virtually all previous studies of haematopoietic systems both in vivo and in vitro have focused on glycosaminoglycan content and composition of haematopoietic microenvironments and have failed to consider the nature of the entire proteoglycan molecule. Since the intact molecule may be more important than its component parts in determining biological activity, it would seem essential to obtain information on the structure and types of proteoglycans present in the haematopoietic microenvironment if their role in haematopoiesis is to be clarified. Our laboratory has begun to examine the nature of the proteoglycans produced in active human long-term bone marrow cultures using combinations of DEAE ion exchange chromatography, molecular seive chromatography, density gradient ultracentrifugation, and electron microscopy.

Labelling cultures with ^{35}S-sulphate and ^{3}H-glucosamine, it is possible to demonstrate that they synthesise at least three populations of proteoglycans as well as hyaluronic acid (Fig. 1.2). The major sulphated proteoglycans synthesised by the marrow cultures can be divided into two size classes based on their elution position on molecular sizing columns. The largest class contains condroitin-4 and 6-sulphate

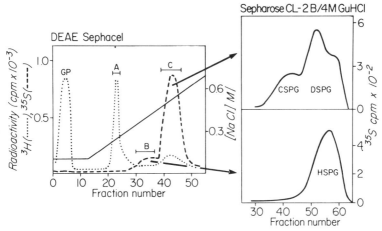

Fig. 1.2   The left panel represents a typical DEAE-Sephacel ion exchange chromatographic profile of ^{35}S-sulphate and ^{3}H-glucosamine material synthesised and secreted by human long-term bone marrow cultures. Peak A (labelled with ^{3}H) has been shown to contain hyaluronic acid. Peaks B and C were pooled and rechromatographed on molecular sizing columns (right panel). It was shown that peak B contained a small sulphated proteoglycan monomer (kav = 0.82 on Sepharose CL-2B) containing heparan sulphate. Peak C contained two populations: a large monomer (kav = 0.31 on Sepharose CL-2B) which contained chondroitin sulphate and a small monomer (kav = 0.62 on Sepharose CL-2B) containing dermatan sulphate.

while the smaller class contains dermatan sulphate. In addition, a small amount of a small proteoglycan containing heparan sulphate can also be isolated from these cultures using ion exchange chromatography (Fig. 1.2). The contribution of non-adherent cells to total proteoglycan synthesis was found to be minor. This pattern of proteoglycan synthesis differs from the pattern of proteoglycans isolated from cultures of serially passaged marrow fibroblasts. Fibroblasts appear to synthesise only a small class of proteoglycan monomer and do not synthesise the larger of the two species (Fig. 1.3). Previous studies of fibroblasts cultured from bone marrow indicate that heparan sulphate is a major sulphated glycosaminoglycan produced by these cells (Del

Rosso et al, 1979). We have not analysed the proteoglycans from marrow fibroblasts further but if they do synthesise a large amount of heparan sulphate, this would be markedly different from the long-term bone marrow cultures since heparan sulphate constitutes such a minor component of the total glycosaminoglycans in these cultures.

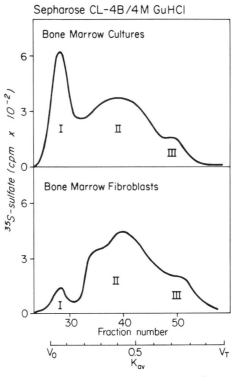

Fig. 1.3   A gel chromatographic profile (Sepharose CL-4B) comparing ^{35}S-labelled proteoglycans synthesised by haematopoietically active human long-term marrow cultures and haematopoietically inactive marrow fibroblasts. Note that the synthesis of the larger monomer (I) is greatly reduced in the fibroblast cultures.

Scanning and transmission electron microscopy of cultured marrow stromal cells reveal a mat-like layer of acellular material covering the adherent stromal cells (Fig. 1.4a–d). This overlying material could only be identified if the cultures were fixed in the presence of ruthenium red, a cationic dye known to retain proteoglycan (Luft, 1971). Immature haematopoietic cells were observed within this layer as well as in contact with the adherent stromal cells (Fig. 1.4e,f). The exact identity of this 'mat-like' material is not known, but its fine structure resembles combinations of hyaluronic acid and proteoglycans identified in other systems (Wight, 1980). These observations indicate that stem cells in vitro interact with components of their microenvironment. It remains to be shown whether this interaction involves specific proteoglycans. Studies of proteoglycans in long-term cultures from patients with haematopoietic disorders such as CML and aplastic anaemia in man and in the Sl/Sl^d mouse may help determine the functional effects of these macromolecules on haematopoiesis.

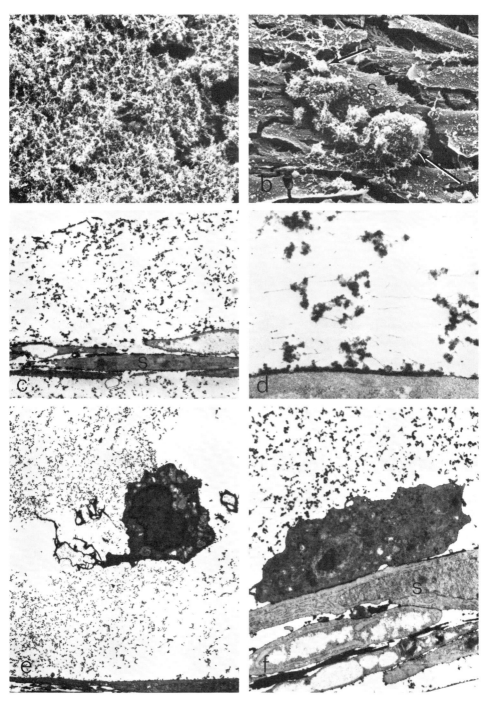

Fig. 1.4 An electron microscope composite of extracellular matrix in long-term marrow cultures fixed and processed in the presence of ruthenium red. **a:** A low magnification scanning electron micrograph demonstrating the presence of a layer of amorphous material lying on the surface of adherent stromal cells (×550); **b:** in some areas, this material is seen associated with round cells (arrows) associated with flattened stromal cells (S) (×100); **c:** a transmission electron micrograph of a cross-section of these culture demonstrating the extensiveness of this layer on top of stromal cells (S) (×4000); **d:** a higher magnification of this material demonstrating its filamentous and granular nature (×25 000); **e:** frequently, macrophage-like and immature haematopoietic cells are observed within this amorphous layer (×3 750); **f:** similar cells were also observed in close association with adherent stromal cells (S) (×7600).

Colony-stimulating factor

Colony-stimulating factor (CSF) was initially not detected in mouse long-term cultures (Dexter et al, 1977). Also, the addition of CSF to murine cultures failed to affect granulopoiesis (Dexter and Shadduck, 1980; Williams & Burgess, 1980). A recent study, however, employing bilayer agar cultures, indicates that CSF is both produced and consumed by murine stromal cells (Heard et al, 1982). Oblon et al (1983) showed that a murine stromal cell subpopulation of monocytes and/or endothelial cells was responsible for CSF production. Other workers have detected a colony-promoting factor in murine long-term marrow culture supernatant which augments CFU-GM formation in the presence of CSF (Izumi et al, 1983). Quesenberry & Gimbrone (1983) recently showed that human umbilical vein endothelial cells are potent producers of colony-stimulating activity.

The role of CSF in human long-term marrow cultures remains to be established. Preliminary data indicate that bioassayable CSF is present (Powell et al, 1983). In one experiment, CSF levels in the supernatant increased with time after culture initiation to 39% of maximum stimulation in an haematopoietically active 8-week-old culture.

Prostaglandins

Prostaglandin E (PGE) has been shown to stimulate haematopoiesis (Feher & Gideli, 1974) as well as suppress CFU-GM proliferation by affecting responsiveness to CSF (Broxmeyer & Moore, 1978; Kurland et al, 1978). The addition of PGE_1 to murine long-term cultures results in a dose-dependent decrease in CFU-S and CFU-C and an increase in CSF levels (Motomura & Dexter, 1980). In human long-term cultures, both CSF and PGE_1 levels increase in the supernatant with time in culture. The addition of indomethacin or acetyl salicylic acid (ASA) suppressed PGE_1 and reduced CFU-GM production in cultures (Keating, unpublished data). Whether indomethacin or ASA suppression of CFU-GM in long-term marrow cultures is a specific anti-prostaglandin effect remains to be established.

Interferon

Production of interferon by human long-term marrow cultures has not been studied, but Shah et al (1983) have demonstrated the production of high levels of β interferon and low levels of α interferon by a human marrow stromal cell line (Lanotte et al, 1981). However, the physiological significance of this is unclear. Addition of pharmacologic levels of α interferon (>500 i.u./ml) to human cultures resulted in decreased CFU-GM proliferation in the cultures but left the stromal cell layer morphologically unaffected (Keating et al, 1982b). Lower concentrations of interferon had no detectable effect on culture longevity or production of CFU-GM.

THE MICROENVIRONMENT IN HUMAN DISEASE

Any discussion of the role of the microenvironment in human haematopoietic diseases is of necessity speculative. Unlike the Sl/Sl^d mouse, where a microenvironmental defect can be demonstrated in vitro and in vivo and 'cured' by an in vitro as well as an in vivo microenvironmental transplant (Dexter & Moore, 1977), only a single case of human hypoplastic anaemia with evidence of a microenvironmental defect has been reported (Ershler et al, 1980). In that case, bone fragments from the patient were found to markedly inhibit haemoglobin synthesis, although red cell precursors appeared to be normal. The factor or cells responsible for the inhibition were not further identified. In the following discussions, clinical and in vitro data regarding the role of the microenvironment in aplastic anaemia and certain myeloproliferative disorders are summarised. It is anticipated that further use of the Dexter system will yield a better understanding of the role of the haematopoietic microenvironment in these disorders.

Aplastic anaemia (AA)

It has been speculated that some cases of AA are due to microenvironmental failure (Stohlman, 1972). This hypothesis declined in popularity with the success of syngeneic marrow infusions in curing most patients with AA who had an identical twin donor. However, in several well-studied recent cases, patients failed to engraft following an unprepared syngeneic marrow infusion but subsequently had haematopoietic reconstitution when the infusion was preceded by cyclophosphamide (Applebaum et al, 1980). Moreover, the recent demonstration that marrow stromal cells are transplanted with allogeneic marrow grafting in a non-irradiated patient with AA as well as in irradiated leukaemic recipients, suggests that the graft may be capable of reconstituting a damaged microenvironment (Keating et al, 1982a).

Gordon & Gordon-Smith (1983) reported that cultured 'fibroblastic' cells from three of six patients with AA had subnormal colony-stimulating factor-enhancing activity when compared to similar cells from normal donors. A patient who underwent marrow grafting subsequently normalised this function. The use of cultured 'fibroblastic' cells rather than stromal cells and the failure to characterise the cells tested make it difficult to draw conclusions from this intriguing observation. Studies of stromal cells from AA patients are needed. In particular, the ability of AA stromal cells to allow proliferation of normal HLA matched marrow would be of interest. Studies of biosynthetic functions of AA stroma should be done including an examination of matrix proteins and proteoglycans since it has been suggested that there are proteoglycan abnormalities in the Sl/Sl^d mouse (see Proteoglycans, above).

Studies in myelofibrosis

The normal marrow spaces are obliterated in primary or secondary myelofibrosis by an exuberant proliferation of fibroblasts. Studies with both G6PD and cytogenetics have shown in CML (Fialkow et al, 1977), and agnogenic myeloid metaplasia (AMM) (Jacobson et al, 1978) that the fibroblasts are not derived from the neoplastic clone. The fibroblasts in effect replace the normal haematopoietic environment and thus make studies of stromal cell abnormalities difficult.

Both fibroblasts and stromal cells have receptors for platelet-derived growth factor (PDGF) (see Regulators of marrow stromal cell proliferation, above). Thus, an haematopoietically derived factor is capable of stimulating proliferation of both normal (stromal cells) and abnormal (fibroblasts) microenvironmental cells. However, normal stromal cells appear to have more receptors per cell than do marrow fibroblasts. In the three cases of CML in G6PD heterozygotes described earlier, stromal cells were derived from the neoplastic stem cell. Thus, they may have or develop intrinsic regulatory abnormalities such as a change in PDGF receptor number or affinity. Fibroblasts might then have a growth advantage over abnormal stromal cells and cause myelofibrosis. Such hypotheses remain speculative pending further studies of stromal cell regulation in conditions that lead to myelofibrosis.

The microenvironment in myeloproliferative disorders

Clinical data suggesting there are microenvironmental abnormalities in several myeloproliferative disorders include the occurrence of myelofibrosis in AMM, CML and in some cases of acute non-lymphocytic leukaemia (ANLL). Data presented on pages 7–9 suggest that stromal cells in CML and in certain cases of ANLL may arise from neoplastic progenitors. Furthermore, preliminary results indicate abnormalities in proteoglycan biosynthetic patterns in long-term cultures derived from CML marrow (Wight, unpublished data).

The influence of CML stromal cells on committed progenitors was assessed in a recent study where it was found that with time, an increasing frequency of Ph^1-negative BFU-E grow from long-term marrow cultures established from patients with Ph^1-positive CML (Coulumbel et al, 1983b). Although this suggested that there is a selective advantage for normal progenitors in long-term marrow cultures, it is still possible that the Ph^1-negative colonies were derived from the CML clonal progenitor (Fialkow et al, 1981). Further studies using the G6PD system together with cytogenetic markers are needed to determine if the Ph^1-negative colonies were derived from normal stem cells.

Preliminary data show that irradiated CML stromal cells are less effective than normal stroma in allowing recovery of normal marrow CFU-GM following treatment with anti-Ia antibody (7.2) and C′ (Table 1.2). Whereas normal stromal cells increased the number of CFU-GM generated at day 14 to five times the control value, neither CML stromal cells nor normal marrow fibroblasts were effective. This suggests that CML stromal cells are defective in their ability to support normal haematopoiesis.

Although these studies are preliminary they serve to illustrate some uses of the long-term marrow culture system in examining stem cell-microenvironment relationships in normal and abnormal states. It is probable that additional information about the pathogenesis of haematopoietic neoplasia and the role of the microenvironment will result from further applications of long-term marrow cultures to clinical disorders.

REFERENCES

Allen T D, Dexter T M 1982 Ultrastructural aspects of erythropoietic differentiation in long-term bone marrow culture. Differentiation 21: 86–94

Applebaum F R, Fefer A, Cheever M A, Sanders J E, Singer J W et al 1980 Treatment of aplastic anemia by bone marrow transplantation in identical twins. Blood 55: 1033–1039

Bentley S A, Foidart J M 1980 Some properties of marrow derived adherent cells in tissue culture. Blood 56: 1006–1012

Bentley S A, Alabaster O, Foidart J M 1981 Collagen heterogeneity in normal bone marrow. British Journal of Haematology 48: 287–291

Bentley S A, Tralka T S 1982 Characterization of marrow derived adherent cells. Scandinavian Journal of Hematology 28: 381–388

Bentley S A, Knutsen T, Whang-Peng J 1982 The origin of the hematopoietic microenvironment in continuous bone marrow culture. Experimental Hematology 4: 367–372

Bernstein S E 1970 Tissue transplantation as an analytical and therapeutic tool in hereditary anemia. American Journal of Surgery 119: 448–451

Bowen-Pope D F, Ross R 1982 Platelet-derived growth factor II. Specific binding to cultured cells. Journal of Biological Chemistry 257: 5161–5171

Braun M P, Martin P J, Ledbetter J A, Hansen J A 1983 Granulocytes and cultured human fibroblasts express common acute lymphoblastic leukemia-associated antigens. Blood 61: 718–722

Breton-Gorius J, Bizet M, Reyes F, Dupey E, Mear C, Vannier J P, Tron P 1982 Myelofibrosis and acute megakaryoblastic leukemia in a child: Topographic relationship between fibroblasts and megakaryocytes with an α-granule defect. Leukemia Research 6: 97–110

Broxmeyer H E, Moore M A S 1978 Communication between white cells and the abnormality of this in leukemia. Biochimica et Biophysica Acta 516: 129–166

Castro-Malaspina H, Gay R E, Resnick G, Napoor N, Meyers P, Chiarieri D, McKenzie S, Broxmeyer H E, Moore M A S 1980 Characterization of human bone marrow fibroblast colony forming cells (CFU-F) and their progeny. Blood 56: 289–296

Castro-Malaspina H, Gay R E, Thanwar S C, Hamilton J A, Chiarieri D R, Meyers P A, Gay S, Moore M A S 1982 Characteristics of bone marrow fibroblast colony-forming cells (CFU-F) and their progeny in patients with myeloproliferative disorders. Blood 59: 1046–1054

Coulombel L, Eaves A C, Eaves C J 1983A Enzymatic treatment of long-term marrow cultures reveals the preferential location of primitive hemopoietic progenitors in the adherent layer. Blood 62: 291–297

Coulombel L, Kalousek D K, Eaves C J, Gupta C M, Eaves A C 1983B Long-term marrow culture reveals chromosomally normal hematopoietic progenitor cells in patients with Philadelphia chromosome-positive chronic myelogenous leukemia. New England Journal of Medicine 308: 1493–1498

Dainiak N, Davies G, Kalmanti M, Lawler J, Kulkarni V 1983 Platelet-derived growth factor promotes proliferation of erythropoietic progenitor cells in vitro. Journal of Clinical Investigation 71: 1206–1214

Del Rosso M, Cappelletti R, Vannuchi S, Ramagnani S, Chiarugi V 1979 Selective exposure of mucopolysaccharides is involved in macrophage physiology. Biochima et Biophysica Acta 586: 512–517

Del Rosso M, Cappelletti R, Dini G, Fibbi G, Vannucchi S, Chiarugi V, Guazzeli C 1981 Involvement of glycosaminoglycans in detachment of early myeloid precursors from bone marrow stromal cells. Biochima et Biophysica Acta 676: 129–136

Delwiche F, Raines E, Powell J S, Ross R, Adamson J W 1983 Platelet-derived growth factor (PDGF) enhances in vitro erythroid colony growth via stimulation of mesenchymal cells. Blood 62: suppl 1, 121A

Deuel T F, Huang J S, Huang S S, Stroobant P, Waterfield M D 1983 Expression of a platelet-derived growth factor-like protein in Simian sarcoma virus transformed cells. Science 221: 1348–1350

Dexter T M, Moore M A S 1977 In vitro duplication and 'cure' of haemopoietic defects in genetically anaemic mice. Nature 269: 412–414

Dexter T M, Allen T D, Lajtha L G 1977 Conditions controlling the proliferation of haemopoietic stem cells in vitro. Journal of Cell Physiology 91: 335–344

Dexter T M, Spooncer E, Toksoz D, Lajtha L G 1980 The role of cells and their products in the regulation of in vitro stem cell proliferation and granulocyte development. Journal of Supramolecular Structures 13: 513–524

Dexter T M, Shadduck R K 1980 The regulation of haematopoiesis in long-term bone marrow cultures. Role of L-cell CSF. Journal of Cell Physiology 102: 279

Dexter T M 1982 Stromal cell associated hemopoiesis. Journal of Cell Physiology suppl 1: 87–94

Doolittle R F, Hunkapiller M W, Hood L E, Davare S G, Robbins K C, Aaronson S A, Antonaides H N 1983 Simian sarcoma virus oncogene, V-SIS, is derived from the gene (or genes) encoding a platelet-derived growth factor. Science 221: 275–277

Ershler W B, Ross J, Finlay J L, Shahidi N T 1980 Bone marrow microenvironment defect in congenital hypoplasic anemia. New England Journal of Medicine 302: 1321–1327

Farquhar M G 1981 The glomerular basement membrane — a selective macromolecular filter. In: E Hay (ed) Cell biology of extracellular matrix. Plenum Press, New York, p 375–378

Fauser A A, Messner H A 1979 Identification of megakaryocytes, macrophages and eosinophils in colonies of human bone marrow containing neutrophilic granulocytes and erythrocytes. Blood 53: 1023–1026

Feher I, Gideli J 1974 Prostaglandin E_2 as stimulator of hematopoitic stem cell population. Nature 247: 550–551

Feiner B H, Strober S, Greenberg P L 1983 Murine granulopoiesis after fractional total lymphoid irradiation and allogeneic bone marrow transplantation. Experimental Hematology 11: 410–417

Fialkow P J 1983 Hierarchical hematologic stem cell relationships studied with glucose-6-phosphate dehydrogenase enzymes. In: Killman S A, Cronkite E P, Muller-Berat C N (eds) Haemopoietic stem cells, characterization, proliferation, regulation. Munksgaard, Copenhagen, p 1–7

Fialkow P J, Jacobson R M, Papayannopoulou T 1977 Chronic myelocytic leukemia: clonal origin in a stem cell common to the granulocyte, erythrocyte, platelet, and monocyte/macrophage. American Journal of Medicine 63: 125–131

Fialkow P J, Martin P J, Najfeld V, Penfold G K, Jacobson R J, Hansen J A 1981 Evidence for a multistep pathogenesis of chronic myelogenous leukemia. Blood 58: 158–163

Fliedner T M, Calvo W 1978 Hematopoietic stem cell seeding of a cellular matrix: A principle of intiation and regeneration of hematopoiesis. In: Clarkson B D, Marks P A, Till J E (eds) Differentiation of normal and neoplastic hemopoietic cells. Cold Spring Harbor Laboratory, NY, p 757–773

Friedenstein A J, Chailakhyan R K, Lalykina K S 1970 The development of fibroblast colonies in monolayer cultures of guinea pig bone marrow and spleen cells. Cell Tissue Kinetics 3: 393–403

Friedenstein A J, Chailakhyan R K, Latsinik N V, Panasyuk A F, Keiliss-Borok I V 1974 Stromal cells responsible for transferring the microenvironment of hematopoietic tissues. Cloning and retransplantation in vivo. Transplantation 17: 331–340

Friedenstein A J, Ivanov-Smolenski A A, Chailakhyan R K, Gorskaya U F, Kuralesoua A I, Latznik N I, Gerasimow U W 1978 Origin of bone marrow stromal mechanocytes in radiochimeras and heterotopic transplants. Experimental Hematology 6: 440–444

Gallagher J T, Spooncer E, Dexter T M 1983 Role of the cellular matrix in haemopoiesis. 1. Synthesis of glycosaminoglycans by mouse bone marrow cultures. Journal of Cell Science 63: 155–171

Gartner S M, Kaplan H S 1980 Long-term culture of human bone marrow cells. Proceedings of the National Academy of Sciences of the USA 77: 4756–4761

Golde D W, Hocking W G, Quan S G, Sparkes R S, Gale R P 1980 Origin of human bone marrow fibroblasts. British Journal of Haematology 44: 183–187

Gordon M Y, Gordon-Smith E C 1983 Bone marrow fibroblast function in relation to granulopoiesis in aplastic anemia. British Journal of Haematology 53: 483–489

Gospodarowicz D, Vlodavsky I 1982 The role of the extracellular matrix and growth factors in the control of proliferation of anchorage-dependent cells. In: Moore M A S (ed) Maturation factors and cancer. Raven Press, New York, p 73–104

Gown A M, Vogel A M 1982 Monoclonal antibodies to intermediate filament proteins of human cells: unique and cross-reacting antibodies. Journal of Cell Biology 95: 414–424

Gown A M, Gordon D, Vogel A M 1983 Analysis of smooth muscle cell-specific cytoskeletal antigens with monoclonal antibodies. Federation Proceedings 42: 502

Greenberg B R, Wilson F D, Woo L, Jenks M H M 1978 Cytogenetics of fibroblastic colonies in Ph[1]-positive chronic myelogenous leukemia. Blood 51: 1039–1044

Greenberg B R, Wilson F D, Woo L 1981 Granulopoietic effects of human bone marrow fibroblastic cells and abnormalities in the 'granulopoietic microenvironment'. Blood 58: 557–564

Greenberger J S 1978 Sensitivity of corticosteroid-dependent insulin-resistent lipogenesis in marrow preadipocytes of obese-diabetic (db/db) mice. Nature 275: 752–754

Greenberger J S 1980 Self-renewal of factor dependent hematopoietic progenitor cell lines derived from long-term bone marrow cultures demonstrates significant mouse strain genotype variability. Journal of Supramolecular Structures 13: 501–511

Groopman J E 1980 The pathogenesis of myelofibrosis in myeloproliferative disorders. Annals of Internal Medicine 92: 857–858

Hascall V C, Hascall G K 1981 Proteoglycans. In: Hay E (ed) Cell biology of extracellular matrix. Plenum Press, New York, p 39–63

Heard J M, Fichelson S, Varet B 1982 Role of colony-stimulating activity in murine long-term bone marrow cultures: evidence for its production and consumption by the adherent cells. Blood 59: 761–767

Hentel J, Hirschorn K 1971 The origin of some bone marrow fibroblasts. Blood 38: 81–86

Holthofer H, Virtanen I, Kariniemi A L, Hormia M, Linder E, Miettinen A 1982 Ulex europaeus I lectin as a marker for vascular endothelium in human tissue. Laboratory Investigation 47: 60–66

Höök M, Robinson J, Kjellen L, Johanson S 1982 Heparan sulfate: On the structure and function of cell associated proteoglycans. In: Hawkes S, Wong J L (eds) Extracellular matrix. Academic Press, New York, p 15–23

Izumi H, Tsurusawa M, Miyanomae T, Kumagai Mori K J 1983 Role of humoral factors in granulopoiesis: colony promoting factor (CPF) and its target 'pre-CFU-C' in long-term bone marrow culture. Leukemia Research 7: 155–165

Jacobson R J, Salo A, Fialkow P J 1978 Agnogenic myeloid metaplasia: A clonal proliferation of hematopoietic stem cells with secondary myelofibrosis. Blood 58: 189–194

Kaneko S, Motomura S, Ibayashi H 1982 Differentation of human bone marrow-derived fibroblastoid colony forming cells (CFU-F) and their roles in haemopoiesis in vitro. British Journal of Haematology 51: 217–225

Kearns M, Lala P K 1982 Bone marrow origin of decidual cell precursors in the pseudopregnant mouse uterus. Journal of Experimental Medicine 155: 1537–1554

Keating A, Singer J W, Killen P D, Striker G E, Salo A C, Sanders J, Thomas E D, Thorning D, Fialokow P J 1982a Donor origin in the in vitro haematopoietic microenvironment after marrow transplantation in man. Nature 298: 280–283

Keating A, Myers J, Singer J W 1982b Effect of bacterial and leukocyte derived interferon on human long-term bone marrow cultures (LTBMC). Clinical Research 30: 419A

Keating A, Singer J W 1983 Further characterization of the hematopoietic microenvironment. Experimental Hematology II Suppl 14: 6

Keating A, Whalen C K, Singer J W 1983 Cultured marrow stromal cells express common acute lymphoblastic leukaemia antigen (CALLA): Implications for marrow transplantation. British Journal of Haematology 55: 623–628

Keating A, Powell J, Takahashi M, Singer J W 1984 The generation of human long-term marrow cultures from marrow depleted of Ja (HLA-DR) positive cells: Blood 64: 1159–1162

Kennedy L J, Weissman I L 1971 Dual origin of intimal cells in cardiac–allograft arteriosclerosis. New England Journal of Medicine 285: 884–887

Kurland J I, Broxmeyer H E, Pelus L M, Bockman R S, Moore M A S 1978 Role for monocyte–macrophage derived colony-stimulating factor and prostaglandin E in the positive and negative feedback control for myeloid stem cell proliferation. Blood 52: 388–407

Lanotte M, Allen T D, Dexter T M 1981 Histochemical and ultrastructural characteristics of a cell line from human bone marrow stroma. Journal of Cell Science 50: 281–297

Lanotte M, Scott D, Dexter T M, Allen T D 1982 Clonal preadipocyte cell lines with different phenotypes derived from murine marrow stroma: factors influencing growth and adipogenesis in vitro. Journal of Cell Physiology 111: 177–186

Lichtman M A 1981 The ultrastructure of the hematopoietic environment of the marrow. A review. Experimental Hematology 9: 391–410

Lubennikova E I, Domaratsky E I 1976 Changes in the number of stem cells during cultivation of mouse bone marrow on a bed of fibroblast like cells. Byull Eksp Biological Medicine 81: 718–719

Luft J H 1971 Ruthenium red and violet. II. Fine structure localization in animal tissues. Anatomical Record 171: 369–389

Maximow A A 1924 Relation of blood cells to connective tissues and endothelium. Physiology Revue 4: 533–564

McCuskey R S, Meinke H A 1973 Studies of the haemopoietic microenvironment. III. Differences in the splenic microvascular system and stroma between SL/SL^d and W/W^v anemic mice. American Journal of Anatomy 137: 187–198, 1973

Metzgar B S, Borowitz M J, Jones H H, Dowell B L 1981 Distribution of common acute lymphoblastic leukemia antigen in non-hematopoietic tissues. Journal of Experimental Medicine 134: 1249–1254

Motomura S, Dexter T M 1980 The effect of prostaglandin E_1 on hemopoiesis in long-term bone marrow cultures. Experimental Hematology 8: 298–303

Noordegraaf E M, Pleomacher R E 1979 Studies of the haemopoietic microenvironment. II. Content of glycosaminoglycans in murine bone marrow and spleen under anaemic and polyethaemic conditions. Scandinavian Journal of Haematology 22: 327–332

Oblon D J, Castro-Malaspina H, Broxmeyer H E 1983 The production of colony-stimulating activity by monocyte enriched fractions from murine continuous bone marrow culture adherent layers. British Journal of Haematology 54: 291–299

Omary M B, Trowbridge I S, Battisfora H A 1980 Human homologue of murine T200 glycoprotein. Journal of Experimental Medicine 152: 842–852

Pearson H 1967 Marrow hypoplasia in anorexia nervosa. Journal of Pediatrics 71: 211–215

Piersma A H, Ploemaker R E, Brockbank K G M 1983 Transplantation of bone marrow fibroblastoid stromal cells in mice via the intravenous route. British Journal of Haematology 54: 285–290

Pleomacher R E, Van't Hull E, Van Soest P L 1978 Studies of the hemopoietic microenvironments: effects of acid mucopolysaccharides and dextran sulfate on erythroid and granuloid differentiation in vitro. Experimental Hematology 6: 311–320

Powell J, Keating A, Singer J W, Adamson J W 1983 Analysis of hematopoiesis in human long-term marrow cultures. Experimental Hematology II Suppl 14: 261

Quesenberry P J, Gimbrone M A 1980 Vascular endothelium as a regulator of granulopoiesis: Production of colony stimulating activity by cultured human endothelial cells. Blood 56: 1060–1067

Reddi A H 1979 Collagen and cell differentiation. In: Ramachandian G H, Reddi A H (eds) Biochemistry of collagen. Plenum Press, New York, p 449–478

Reimann J, Burger H 1979 In vitro proliferation of haemopoietic cells in the presence of adherent cell layers II. Different effect of adherent cell layers derived from various organs. Experimental Hematology 7: 52–58

Ritz J, Pesando J M, Sallan S E, Clavell L A, Notis-McConarty J, Rosenthal P, Schlossman S F 1981 Serotherapy of acute lymphoblastic leukemia with monoclonal antibody. Blood 58: 141–152

Ritz J, Sallan S E, Bast R C, Lipton L M, Clavell L A, Feeney H, Tercend T, Nathan D G, Schlossman S F 1982 Autologous bone marrow transplantation in CALLA positive acute lymphoblastic leukemia following in vitro treatment with J-5 monoclonal antibody and complement. Lancet ii: 60–62

Rosenfeld M, Keating A, Bowen-Pope D F, Singer J W, Ross R 1985 Responsiveness of the in vitro hematopoictic microenvironment to platelet-derived growth factor. Leuk Res (in press)

Ross R, Glomset J A 1976 The pathogenesis of atherosclerosis. New England Journal of Medicine 295: 369–377

Sabin F R 1920 Studies in the origin of blood-vessels and of red blood-corpuscles as seen in the living bloodstream of chicks during the second day of incubation. Contributions to Embryology 9: 213–268

Schofield R 1978 The relationship between the spleen colony-forming cell and the haemopoietic stem cell. Blood Cells 4: 7–25

Schrock L M, Judd T J, Meineke H A, McCuskey R S 1973 Differences in concentrations of acid mucopolysaccharides between spleens of normal and polycythemic CF_1 mice. Proceedings of the Society for Experimental Medicine 144: 593–595

Shah G, Dexter T M, Lanotte M 1983 Interferon production by human marrow stromal cells. British Journal of Haematology 54: 365–372

Singer J W, Adamson J W, Ernst C, Lin N, Steinmann L, Fialkow P J 1980 Polycythemia vera: physical separation of normal and neoplastic committed granulocyte progenitors. Journal of Clinical Investigation 6: 730–735

Singer J W, Keating A 1983 Studies on the in vitro microenvironment in man. In: Neth R, Greaves M F, Moore M A S, Winkler K (eds) Modern trends in human leukemia V. Springer-Verlag, Berlin, p 351–354

Spooncer E, Gallagher T J, Kriza F, Dexter T M 1983 Regulation of haemopoiesis in long term bone marrow cultures. IV. Glycosaminoglycan synthesis and the stimulation of haemopoiesis by β-D-xylosides. Journal of Cell Biology 96: 510–514

Stohlman J R F 1972 Aplastic anemia. Blood 40: 282–286

Tavassoli M, Eastlund D T, Yam L T, Neiman R S, Finkel H 1976 Gelatinous transformation of bone marrow in prolonged self-induced starvation. Scandinavian Journal of Haematology 16: 311–319

Tavassoli M, Crosby W H 1968 Transplantation of marrow to extramedullary sites. Science 161: 54–56

Till J E, McCulloch E A 1961 A direct measurement of the radiation sensitivity of normal mouse bone marrow cells. Radiation Research 14: 213–222

Trentin J J 1971 Determination of bone marrow stem cell differentiation by stromal hemopoietic inductive microenvironments (HIM). American Journal of Pathology 65: 621–627

Vannucchi S, Fibbi G, Cella C, Del Rosso M, Cappelletti R, Chiarugii V 1980 Cell surface glycosaminoglycans in normal and leukemic leukocytes. Cell Differentiation 9: 71–81

Waterfield M D, Scrace G T, Whittle N, Stroobant P, Johnsson A, Wasteson A, Westermark B, Heldin C H, Huang J S, Deuel T F 1983 Platelet-derived growth factor is structurally related to the putative transforming protein p28[sis] of simian sarcoma virus. Nature 304: 35–39

Weibel E R, Palade G E 1964 New cystoplasmic components in arterial endothelia. Journal of Cell Biology 23: 101–112

Werts E D, Gibson D P, Knapp S A, DeGowin R L 1980 Stromal cell migration precedes hemopoietic repopulation of the bone marrow after irradiation. Radiation Research 81: 20–30

Wight T N 1980 Vessel proteoglycans and thrombogenesis. In: Spaet T (ed) Progress in haemostasis and thrombosis. Grune & Stratton, New York, p 1–39

Williams N, Burgess A W 1980 The effect of mouse lung granulocyte–macrophage colony-stimulating factor and other colony-stimulating activities on the proliferation and differentiation of murine bone marrow cells in long-term cultures. Journal of Cell Physiology 102: 287–295

Wilson F D, Greenberg B R, Konrad P N, Klein A K, Walling P A 1978 Cytogenic studies on bone marrow fibroblasts from a male–female hematopoietic chimera. Transplantation 25: 87–88

Wolf N S 1983 The hematopoietic microenvironment: current status. In: Torelli U, Bagnava G P, Brunelli M A, Castaldini C, Di Prisco A V (eds) Frontiers in experimental hematology. Serono Symposia, Rome, p 233–251

Wolf N S, Trentin J J 1968 Haemopoietic colony studies. V. Effect of haemopoietic organ stroma on differentiation of pluripotent stem cells. Journal of Experimental Medicine 127: 205–214

Zuckerman K S, Wicha M S 1983 Extracellular matrix production by the adherent cells of long-term murine bone marrow cultures. Blood 61: 540–547

2. The ABCs of molecular genetics: a haematologist's introduction

K. A. High   E. J. Benz Jr

STRUCTURE AND EXPRESSION OF GENES: DNA, RNA, AND PROTEINS

Introduction

The terms 'molecular biology' and 'molecular genetics' refer to an experimental approach which attempts to understand the chemical basis for the inheritance and regulated expression of genetic information. Molecular genetics combines the techniques of the geneticist, the biochemist, the cell biologist, and the microbiologist in an effort to define both the structure and the functional behaviour of the macromolecules which control gene expression: DNA, RNA, and protein. Molecular genetics, in particular that part of molecular genetics known as recombinant DNA technology, has had a revolutionary effect on biomedical research because the technology allows one to isolate and characterise the genes which control haematologic processes. For that reason, it is now imperative that haematologists master the concepts and language of the molecular geneticist.

The purpose of this review is to introduce the haematologist to the tenets of molecular genetics, and to illustrate the application of this powerful experimental approach to the study of major haematologic problems.[1] We shall first discuss the basic structural features of DNA, RNA and proteins; we shall then consider the experimental methods which allow isolation and analysis of specific genes and their RNA products, and conclude with a brief survey of some applications of these methods to the study of haematologic problems.

The chemical basis of inheritance

Virtually all organisms (except a few RNA viruses) utilise deoxyribonucleic acid (DNA) for the storage, expression, and transmission to later generations of genetic information. In other words, genes consist of DNA. DNA is a linear (i.e. unbranched) polymer consisting of a sugar-phosphate backbone and four nitrogenous (purine or pyrimidine) bases which protrude from the backbone of the polymer (cf. Fig. 2.1).

The sugar portion of DNA is deoxyribose, and the four bases are adenine, guanine, cytosine, and thymidine. The fundamental unit of the DNA polymer is the nucleotide, which consists of one molecule of deoxyribose bound to a phosphate group at its $5'$ carbon position, and one of the nitrogenous bases bound at the $1'$ carbon. Adjacent nucleotides are linked together by phosphodiester bonds between the $5'$ carbon of the deoxyribose moiety of one nucleotide and the $3'$ carbon of the

[1] See Freifelder, 1983; Maniatis et al, 1982; Watson, 1976; Wu, 1979 for excellent surveys of the primary literature documenting the established facts discussed in this section.

next. Note that a DNA polymer linked in this fashion has polarity. That is, the two ends are recognisably different: at one end, called the 5' end, the terminal nucleotide has a free (unbound) phosphate at the 5' position; at the 3' end, the 3' phosphate is free. This is important because it allows the cell (or the molecular biologist!) to know in which direction events occur along a particular DNA strand.

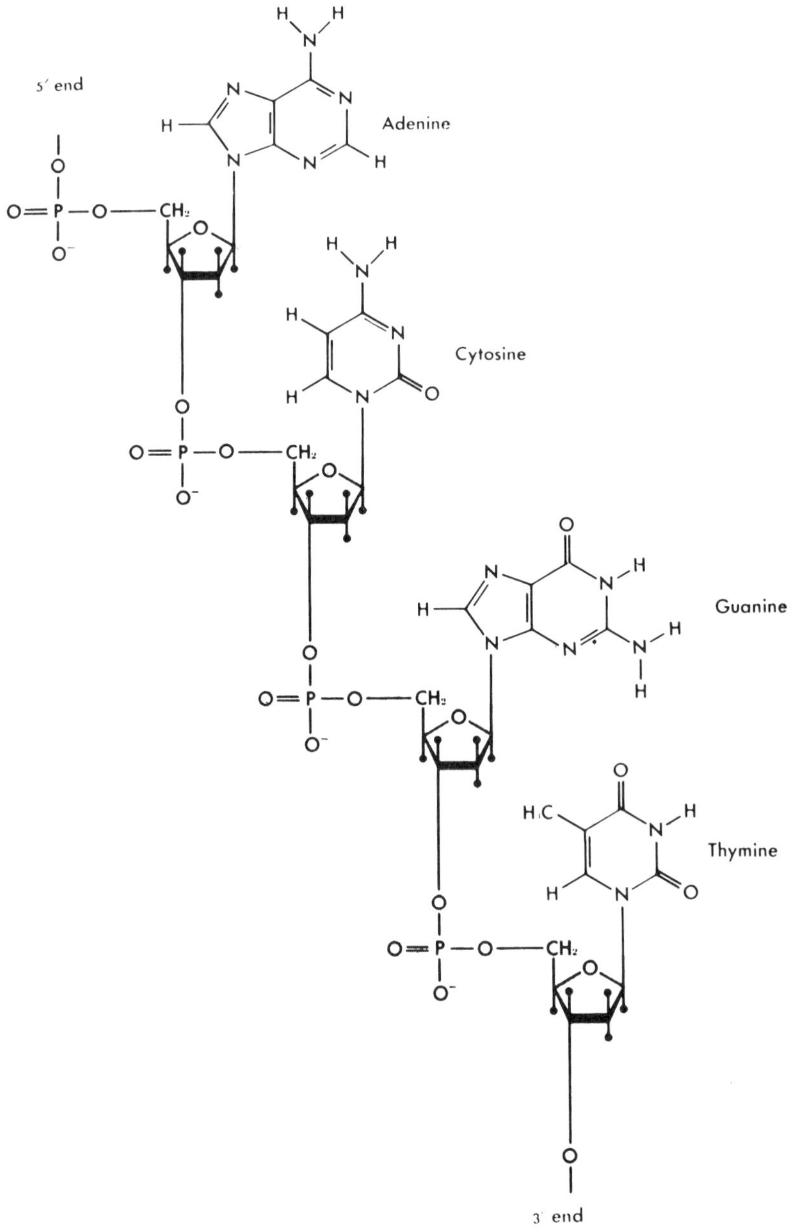

Fig. 2.1   Chemical structure of deoxy ribonucleic acid. Nitrogenous bases protrude from a sugar-phosphate backbone. (See text.) (From Watson J D 1970 Molecular biology of the gene, 2nd edn. W A Benjamin, Menlo Park California.)

The length of a DNA molecule is described in terms of how many nucleotides are contained in a linear chain. Since, as will be evident shortly, the critical informational component of the nucleotide is its nitrogenous base, the nucleotide chain length is usually referred to as length in bases. For example, a single-stranded DNA molecule containing 120 nucleotides is said to be 120 bases long. As discussed later, DNA is most frequently encountered as a double-stranded molecule; chain lengths of double-stranded DNA are thus expressed in base pairs (bp). Since many DNA molecules are thousands of bases or base pairs long, a shorthand designation, 'kilobases' is often used. These terms are often abbreviated as kb. Thus, a single-stranded DNA molecule 12 000 bases long is said to be 12 kb long, while a double-stranded molecule of the same length is 12 kbp long.

The 'base sequence' of a DNA strand is the order in which the nitrogenous bases appear as one 'reads' along the strand. In Figure 2.1, for example, the base sequence of the molecule shown is 5′–ACGT–3′. Note that the polarity of DNA molecules renders this sequence stereochemically (and genetically) unique. Thus, the sequence 3′–ACGT–5′ has an entirely different biological meaning even though it is identical to the first sequence except for its 3′ — >5′, rather than 5′ — >3′ direction.

DNA molecules are thermodynamically most stable in a double-stranded form, but the double-stranded form of DNA exists only if the sequence of bases on one strand is 'matched' by a 'complementary' sequence of bases on the opposite strand. Complementary bases are those which form hydrogen bonds with each other. Each of the four bases will form stable hydrogen bonds to only one of the four bases on an opposite strand. Thus, adenine will hydrogen bond only to thymidine, while guanine will bond only to cytosine (Fig. 2.2). These bonds are called base pairs; thus, one may have A–T and G–C base pairs, but, under ordinary circumstances, one does not encounter A–C or A–G base pairs, etc. The biological consequences of these base pairing rules are immediately apparent: the sequence of bases on one strand immediately dictates the sequence of bases which may occur on the opposite or

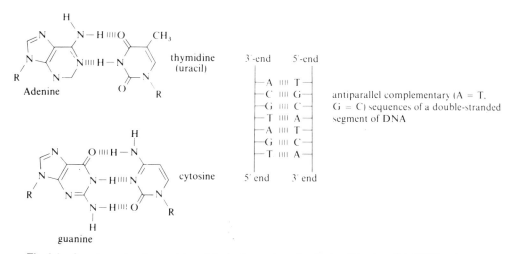

Fig. 2.2 Complementary base-pairing. Adenine base pairs only wih thymidine (uracil in RNA) and guanine only with cytosine. By these Watson–Crick rules of base pairing, if the sequence of one stand of a double standard DNA is known, the other is specified. (See text.)

'complementary' strand. Thus, the sequence 3'–ACGTAGT–5' on one strand of DNA will form double-stranded structures only with a complementary DNA strand containing the sequence 5'TGCATCA–3'. Note that the two strands form a stable double-stranded DNA helix only when they are arranged in an anti-parallel fashion. In other words, one strand in the 3'–5' polarity is bound to its complementary strand with a 5'–3' polarity.

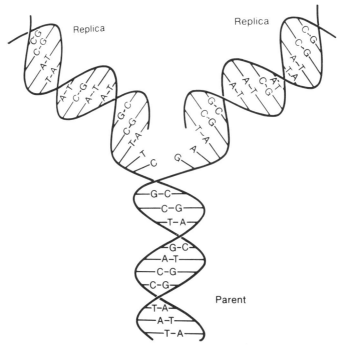

Fig. 2.3   The semiconservative nature of DNA replication. The double-stranded molecule separates and each strand becomes a template for the synthesis of a complementary DNA sequence. The result is two double-stranded daughter molecules, each identical to the parent.

Given the above chemical rules for formation of double stranded DNA molecules, the ability of DNA to carry information in the form of a base sequence and transmit it to subsequent generations of cells becomes clear. If the two strands of DNA, having complementary base sequences, are separated and each strand is 'copied' by the appropriate polymerase enzymes, the rules for stable base pairing dictate that each of the newly formed daughter strands be complementary in base sequence to the parent strands used as template (Fig. 2.3). Since the two parent strands were originally complementary to each other, the final result is two double stranded DNA molecules, each identical to the other.

Conversion of genetic information in DNA into phenotypically useful biochemical properties — the genetic code

The genetic information contained in the base sequence of a strand of DNA is 'expressed' first by synthesis (transcription) of a molecule of RNA called messenger RNA. RNA is also a linear polymer containing nucleotide subunits comprised of sugar, phosphate, and nitrogenous bases. Its structure is quite similar to DNA except that the sugar is ribose rather than deoxyribose, and the nitrogenous pyrimidine base uracil is used in RNA in place of the thymidine base in DNA. The ability of a base sequence of DNA to affect the properties of the cell is based on what has come to be known as the 'central dogma' of molecular biology. That is, a DNA molecule is copied into an RNA molecule (messenger RNA or mRNA), and the base sequence in the mRNA molecule is translated into the amino acid sequence of a protein. The proteins thus produced possess the enzymatic or structural capabilities which determine the phenotype of a cell. This central dogma of genetic information flow or gene expression can be summarised DNA → RNA → protein. The rules by which the base sequence of a DNA strand is converted into the amino acid sequence of the protein are summarised by the term 'genetic code' (Table 2.1). The base sequence of the mRNA copy, or transcript, of the DNA coding strand is read as a series of consecutive,

Table 2.1   The genetic code. Messenger RNA codons for the amino acids

Alanine	Arginine	Asparagine	Aspartic Acid	Cysteine
GCU	CGU	AAU	GAU	UGU
GCC	CGC	AAG	GAC	UGC
GCA	CGA			
GCG	CGG			
	AGA			
	AGG			
Glutamic Acid	Glutamine	Glycine	Histidine	Isoleucine
GAA	CAA	GGU	CAU	AUU
GAG	CAG	GGC	CAC	AUC
		GGA		AUA
		GGG		
Leucine	Lysine	Methionine	Phenylalanine	Proline†
UUA	AAA	AUG*	UUU	CCU
UUG	AAG		UUC	CCC
CUU				CCA
CUC				CCG
CUA				
CUG				
Serine	Threonine	Tryptophan	Tyrosine	Valine
UCU	ACU	UGG	UAU	GUU
UCC	ACC		UAC	GUC
UCA	ACA			GUA
UCG	ACG			GUG
AGU				
AGU				

Chain Termination Codons
UAA
UAG
UGA

* AUG is also used as the chain initiation codon.
† Hydroxyproline, the 21st amino acid, is generated by post-translational modification of proline.

non-overlapping, triplets (group of three bases). For example, the mRNA sequence 5'–AUGUGGUUU–3' specifies the incorporation of three amino acids: N–methionine-tryptophan-phenylalanine-C. The specificity which allows a particular triplet, called a codon, to direct incorporation of only one type of amino acid at that position is mediated by the tRNA molecule. For 61 of the 64 (4^3) possible codons which can be formed from a triplet of the 4 nitrogenous bases, there is a specific tRNA molecule which, at the appropriate position along its nucleotide sequence, contains the complementary triplet, called the anticodon. For three codons, UAG, UAA, and UGA, there is no corresponding tRNA; these three codons serve as 'stop' or 'termination' signals used to designate the position at which assembly of the protein chains stops. These three codons are sometimes called nonsense codons.

There are 64 possible codons and only 21 amino acids utilised for protein synthesis; thus, for some amino acids there are several codons. In this sense the code is degenerate. For example, there are six codons specifying the incorporation of leucine, but only one specifying the incorporation of methionine. Therefore, knowledge of the amino acid sequence of the protein does not immediately reveal the nucleotide sequence of the DNA and RNA molecules responsible for its production. However, knowledge of the nucleotide sequence of the relevant DNA and RNA molecules immediately predicts the amino acid sequence, since in no case does a single codon specify the incorporation of more than one type of amino acid. The genetic code is thus degenerate but not ambiguous.

Organisation of DNA molecules into genes; the pathway of gene expression

Up to this point, we have reviewed the basic tenets of genetic information storage and flow in the form of chemical information stored in DNA base sequences. We have introduced the essential vocabulary by which nucleotide sequences are converted into amino acid sequences of proteins. In this regard, virtually all species are identical. However, eukaryotic and prokaryotic species differ significantly in the manner in which DNA sequences are organised into functional units which we call genes. From this point forward, we shall consider only that system which apples to most eukaryotic genes.

Eukaryotic cells contain their DNA within the nucleus in the form of nucleoprotein complexes called chromosomes. For example, human cells contain 23 pairs of chromosomes. All available evidence suggests that each chromosome consists of a single, incredibly long molecule of DNA. The total number of base pairs present in the human genome is approximately three billion, existing in the form of 46 long molecules or chromosomes. Yet, most proteins are only a few hundred amino acids long, so that genes coding for them are, on the average, only a few thousand bases long. Thus, the sequence information in DNA must be organised along these very long molecules in the form of discrete units which we call genes separated by long stretches which do not code for protein.

The functional boundaries of the gene on each side have been elucidated. They are best introduced in the form of a prototype example, the human beta globin gene. In most of its structural aspects, the human beta globin gene is similar to other genes which have been characterised as a result of application of the techniques of recombinant DNA discussed later in this communication.

As shown in Figure 2.4, the human beta globin gene, like other eukaryotic genes, has a surprisingly complex 'microanatomy'. The nucleotide sequences which code for the actual globin protein do not exist as a single unbroken mRNA coding sequence. Rather, the mRNA coding sequences, called exons, are broken up into three discrete segments separated by two segments called intervening sequences or introns. While most eukaryotic genes have introns, the number and size of the introns vary

FUNCTIONAL ANATOMY OF A HUMAN β GLOBIN GENE

A. TRANSCRIPTION SIGNALS

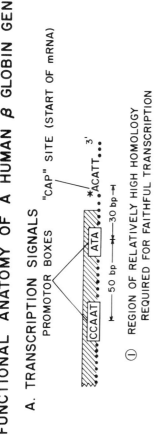

PROMOTOR BOXES   "CAP" SITE (START OF mRNA)

CCAAT   ATA   *...ACATT... 3'

← 50 bp → ←30 bp→

① REGION OF RELATIVELY HIGH HOMOLOGY
   REQUIRED FOR FAITHFUL TRANSCRIPTION

B. mRNA PROCESSING SIGNALS

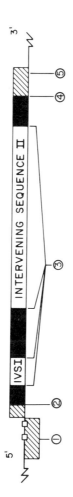

IVSI   INTERVENING SEQUENCE II

5'   3'

③ SPLICE SITES: 5'   GU...IVS...AG   3'

⑤ POLYADENYLATION SIGNAL   5'...AUAAA...GC 3'*

|← 20 bp →|

SIGNAL   SITE OF POLY(A) ADDITION

C. mRNA TRANSLATION SIGNALS

② INITIATOR CODON (AUG IN mRNA)
   (START OF TRANSLATION)

④ TERMINATOR CODON (UAA IN mRNA)
   (END OF TRANSLATION)

Fig. 2.4 The three exons are shown in black and the two intervening sequences in white. The cross-hatched areas show 5' and 3' flanking regions which contain signals necessary for accurate and efficient transcription and translation.

considerably. Some genes have only one intron, while others have many, some of which are considerably longer than the toal exon DNA in the genes. The function of intervening sequences remains unknown.

As shown in Figure 2.5, the entire gene, including the introns, is transcribed into a large mRNA precursor. The intervening sequences are subsequently excised and the

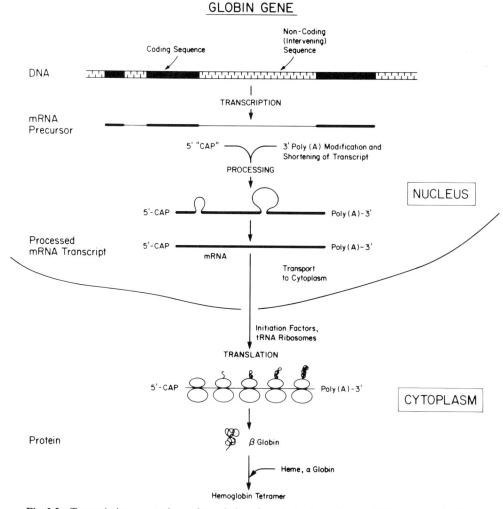

Fig. 2.5   Transcription, processing and translation of a typical eukaryotic gene. DNA is transcribed into a precursor mRNA molecule. The details of events during processing and translation are described in the text.

mRNA coding regions or exons are ligated together to form mature mRNA. Figure 2.5 depicts transcription beginning at the 5′ 'CAP' site or initiation site, and terminating at the last nucleotide at which a 3′ polyadenylic acid 'tail' is added after transcription. As indicated in Figure 2.4, the CAP site and the polyadenylation site are fixed by complex but well characterised nucleotide sequence signals. Recent studies suggest that some genes are transcribed well beyond the polyadenylation site on the 3' end of the RNA transcripts, but the extra sequences are excised early during post-transcriptional processing of the mRNA precursor. In any event, the mature mRNA molecule consists of the exons sutured together during processing out of the introns, marked at each end by the CAP site and the poly(A) tail.

Specific signals must exist at the 5' flanking region of the gene in order for transcription to occur. These sequence signals are called 'promotors'. As shown in Figure 2.4, at least two flanking regions are important. One, called the TATA box, is located about 30 bases upstream from the gene, whereas the second region, a GC rich sequence between -80 and -115, is also present in most genes. In many genes, this region contains a so-called CCAAT transcription box. However, some genes are effectively transcribed without this specific oligonucleotide signal.

The microanatomy of the eukaryotic gene can thus be summarised as follows: the informational component of the gene consists of mRNA coding segments, or exons, which are separated into 'blocks' by intervening sequences or introns. Signals for the entrance and binding of mRNA polymerase (promotor regions) are required to start transcription at a specific 'CAP' site, and transcription proceeds through the entire gene, including introns, to, and frequently beyond, a 3' polyadenylation signal. The nascent transcript of mRNA precursor is processed in the nucleus in such a manner that intervening sequences and excess 3' transcribed regions are removed, a CAP structure is added at the 5' end and a poly(A) tail at the 3' end. The mature RNA is then transported to the cytoplasm, where it binds to ribosomes and is decoded into the amino acid sequence of the protein according to rules discussed earlier.

Figure 2.4 shows the oligonucleotide signals utilised to indicate the beginning and the end of intervening sequences which must be removed. Although some flexibility is permitted for sequences surrounding these 'splicing signals', the GT at the 5' end of an intervening sequence and the AG at the 3' end appear to be absolute requirements. These splicing signals are relevant to the study of human disease, since abnormalities of mRNA splicing are responsible for at least one common group of genetic disorders, the thalassaemias.

The basic chemistry of the nucleic acids accounts for their ability to contain, convey and express genetic information. We have discussed the fundamental vocabulary and rules by which this information is utilised, and examined a prototypical gene which reveals the organisation of base sequences into specific units of information required for its own expression. The fact that so many statements can be made about the organisation and expression of a specific gene which comprises less than one millionth of the human genome is attributable to the development of recombinant DNA technology. This technical tool of the molecular geneticist has permitted the chemical isolation and quantitative analysis of genes. Before considering recombinant DNA however, it is necessary to review the concept of molecular hybridisation, the laboratory technique which permits exploitation of recombinant DNA technology.

Laboratory exploitation of base pairing specificity for the analysis of DNA and RNA molecules — molecular hybridisation

The immunologist's fundamental tool for analysis of the immune system has been the antigen–antibody reaction. The specificity with which a particular antibody molecule interacts with the antigen against which it was raised provides the basic assay needed to analyse and quantitate both the antibody and the antigen. For the molecular geneticist, the analogous fundamental technique is molecular hybridisation. The conceptual analogy to the antigen–antibody reaction is quite useful for considering the use of molecular hybridisation techniques. Since each strand of the DNA or RNA molecule contains a base sequence which will form a double-stranded structure only with the DNA or RNA molecule having the complementary base sequence by the base pairing rules discussed earlier, one can utilise a characterised DNA or RNA molecule as a 'probe' to detect and quantitate DNA and RNA molecules of complementary base sequence in a cellular extract containing a complex mixture of many sequences.

If one has a purified probe containing the base sequence (i.e. gene, mRNA, intergenic region, etc.) one wishes to analyse, molecular hybridisation assays can be developed rather easily. One simply prepares total DNA or RNA by standard techniques from the cells one wishes to study. The molecules are denatured to single-stranded form by heating and mixed with the denatured radioactive probe. When incubated under the appropriate conditions the radioactive probe will form stable double-stranded 'hybrid' DNA–DNA or DNA–RNA molecules only with those molecules in the mixture which have a complementary base sequence. A variety of techniques are available for distinguishing the double-stranded from the single-stranded forms of the radioactive probe after the hybridisation reaction. By analogy to antigen–antibody reactions, one can use the probe for detection, such as in situ hybridisation to fixed cells, for quantitation, via titration assays, for mapping of regions within the DNA or RNA molecules of interest via blotting techniques (by analogy to the use of antibodies to detect antigenic sites in tryptic digests of proteins), etc. Indeed, the major difference between molecular hybridisation techniques and immunochemical techniques is that, in general, the sensitivity and specificity of molecular hybridisation techniques far exceed those of antigen antibody reactions. The methods in subsequent sections of this review are frequently capable of detecting picogram amounts of DNA or RNA of a given base sequence even though the cellular mixture being studied may contain millions or tens of millions of other sequences.

There are many variations of the basic molecular hybridisation assay. One is limited only by access to a sufficiently pure and specific DNA or RNA probe. Exploitation of molecular hybridisation techniques far exceed those of antigen-antibody reactions. limited to a few special cases, such as red cell development and haemoglobinopathies, until techniques became available for the isolation and characterisation of any DNA sequence, regardless of its abundance within a given cell type. This has been the major contribution of recombinant DNA technology to the field of molecular genetics. The remainder of this report describes the ways in which recombinant DNA technology permits isolation of specific gene and mRNA sequences, and the exploitation of this availability for studies of important biological and clinical phenomena.

INTRODUCTION TO MOLECULAR GENETICS — THE ISOLATION OF INDIVIDUAL GENES BY MOLECULAR CLONING

Introduction

The single most important capability resulting from the development of modern molecular genetics is the ability to isolate genes by the process of molecular cloning. Virtually all of the improvements in investigation, diagnosis, and treatment of haematologic problems already realised or promised by this technology depend on this ability to obtain any desired gene in abundance and in pure form. We shall thus introduce the techniques and concepts of molecular genetics by describing the process of molecular cloning of genes.

Gene purification by molecular cloning is possible because of the development of an experimental armamentarium which has come to be known as 'recombinant DNA technology'. This 'technology' represents, in reality, the synthesis of a number of diverse technical advances in nucleic acid enzymology, microbial genetics, and polymer chemistry. Indeed, the term recombinant DNA refers to the fact that these advances permit one to join together (recombine) DNA isolated from two diverse biological sources. For example, human DNA can now be digested to yield manageable fragments, modified, and joined together with similarly treated molecules of DNA from microbes. Since the latter, as discussed later, possess experimentally useful biological properties, the formation of the recombinant DNA molecule allows one to manipulate the human DNA fragment in microbial host cells in ways which are not achievable in intact eukaryotic cells or tissues. The essence of recombinant DNA technology is this ability to insert DNA from complex eukaryotic genomes into simple microbial genomes, where one can take advantage of the many elegant and effective techniques of microbial genetics for the purification and harvesting of eukaryotic DNA sequences.

Enzymatic in vitro manipulation of DNA

Restriction endonucleases and DNA ligase — cutting and joining DNA molecules
Restriction endonucleases are remarkable bacterial enzymes which recognise and cut specific sequences of DNA. In bacteria, they are thought to serve as a host defence mechanism, recognising, cleaving, and thus inactivating foreign DNA. For the molecular biologist, they have provided the means of site-specific cutting and splicing of a complex DNA genome into a series of smaller reproducible fragments. They thus allow one to 'cut and paste' unrelated sequences of DNA in a controlled fashion. Nearly 400 restriction endonucleases have now been isolated, purified and characterised. By convention, they are named by the bacteria from which they derived. Some of the most commonly used, along with their recognition sequences, are listed in Table 2.2.

Table 2.2 Some commonly used restriction endonucleases and their recognition sequences

Name of enzyme	Microorganism	Recognition sequence and cleavage site
Eco RI	Escherichia coli	↓ GAATTC CTTAAG ↓ ↑
Bam HI	Bacillus amyloliquifaciens H	GGATCC CCTAGG ↓ ↑
Hind III	Haemophilus influenza	AAGCTT TTCGAA ↑
Sau 3A	Staph aureus	↓ GATC CTAG ↑

DNA ligases are enzymes which catalyse the joining together of two DNA molecules. They thus permit one to join together restriction endonuclease digested DNA fragments prepared from two diverse sources (e.g. human and microbial plasmid). These two steps, restriction enzyme digestion followed by ligation of two disparate DNA molecules, form the essence of gene cloning.

TYPES OF CUTS MADE BY RESTRICTION ENZYMES

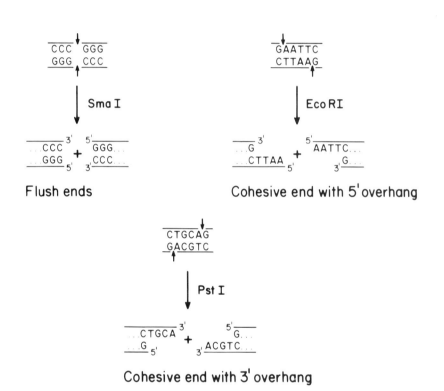

Fig. 2.6 Types of DNA termini generated by restriction enzymes. Restriction endonucleases generate molecules with either flush or cohesive ends. Endonucleases producing cohesive ends can generate either 5′ (e.g. *Eco RI*) or 3′ (e.g. *Pst I*) single-stranded ends.

The recognition sequences of most restriction endonucleases are generally four, five or six nucleotides long. These enzymes scan DNA, attach to each recognition sequence encountered, and catalyse the cleavage of both strands of a double-stranded DNA molecule at each point containing the recognition site. Some restriction endonucleases cleave in the centre of the site at the axis of symmetry, to generate what are called flush or blunt ends (Fig. 2.6). Most, however, do not cut at the centre of symmetry, but rather at positions several nucleotides apart on the two strands, yielding fragments with protruding single stranded tails, called cohesive ends (Fig. 2.6).

A DNA fragment with a cohesive end can, through complementary base pairing, be linked to other fragments with a cohesive end produced by the same endonuclease, to yield a new recombinant molecule. The base pairs can then be 'glued' by treatment with DNA ligase, which seals the short hybridising ends by forming covalent phosphodiester bonds. Thus, by the use of restriction endonucleases and DNA ligase, it becomes possible to engraft any DNA sequence to any other one. Use of other available techniques allows joining of DNAs even if they lack complementary cohesive ends. A discussion of these techniques is beyond the scope of this review but it is important to realise that any two DNA sequences can, through appropriate modification of their termini, be joined together to produce a recombinant molecule.

Restriction enzymes are extensively used in analysis as well as cloning of genes. Just as trypsin digestion of proteins reduces them to a collection of smaller polypeptides more amenable to analysis, so restriction endonuclease digestion of a gene yields a set of *restriction fragments* of shorter lengths which render them more suitable for nearly every type of DNA analysis.

A restriction endonuclease will cleave a genome into a unique set of restriction fragments; for DNA from any source (e.g. human bone marrow), the number and size of restriction fragments generated will be reproducible for each endonuclease. Following cleavage with a restriction enzyme these restriction fragments can be analysed by agarose gel electrophoresis, since the fragments are separated according to chain lengths (size) on such gels. By digesting any genome with various restriction endonucleases, one can generate a restriction 'map' of any gene one wishes to study. By comparing the map obtained with several enzymes used individually and in combinations, one can begin to decipher the fine structure of a particular gene around the various restriction sites within or near it. The reasoning used is entirely analogous to that used for peptide mapping of proteins after digestion by specific proteases.

Restriction enzymes reduce the extraordinarily long strands of chromosomal DNA to fragment sizes that are manageable for purposes of genetic manipulation. Recall that the human genome is approximately three billion base pairs long, packaged in the form of 23 chromosomes. Each chromosome is thought to consist of a single, long, double-stranded DNA molecule several hundred million base pairs long. For all practical purposes, such DNA cannot be handled chemically. Restriction enzymes reduce the size of these DNA fragments into the range of hundreds to a few tens of thousands of base pairs long. In this size range DNA can be chemically manipulated, inserted into biologically active microbial DNA molecules, and purified.

The availability of many different restriction endonucleases allows great flexibility in the choice of restriction sites one may use to clone genes or gene fragments for various applications. The 'art' of the molecular geneticist often lies in the innovative and effective use of these enzymes to generate the 'perfect' gene fragments for a particular application.

Reverse transcriptase — synthesis of DNA from messenger RNA
In an earlier section, we noted that the expression of genes occurs in the form of synthesis of a messenger RNA molecule which is then transported to cytoplasm, where it is translated into the amino acid sequence of a protein. We have also pointed out that it is well known that most messenger RNAs represent transcripts of only a portion of the genes from which they were derived, the transcripts of the intervening sequences having been excised during mRNA processing in the nucleus. There are many reasons why an investigator might wish to purify and establish the nucleotide

sequence of individual mRNA species within this population. However, chemical purification and analysis of most mRNAs is prohibited by the same constraints which we had discussed earlier with respect to chemical purification of individual genes. Molecular cloning of the individual mRNA species would thus be a very useful solution of this problem. Unfortunately, no widely applicable system exists for direct cloning of RNA molecules. Rather, one takes advantage of a fundamental advance in molecular biology which occurred in the late 1960s and early 1970s, the isolation of the enzyme reverse transcriptase.

Reverse transcriptases (often called RNA-dependent DNA polymerases) are enzymes present in RNA tumour viruses. Reverse transcriptases have the extremely useful property that they can accept either a single-stranded DNA or single stranded RNA molecule as a template for synthesis of a complementary DNA strand. Reverse transcriptases thus 'reverse' the flow of genetic information. By using reverse transcriptase to convert the population of mRNAs from a particular cell type into a population of single-stranded DNA molecules, one can accomplish the first step for converting the mRNA into a double-stranded DNA molecule capable of manipulation by all of the techniques useful for genomic DNA.

Reverse transcriptase will sythesise a complementary DNA strand (cDNA) on a messenger RNA template only if initiation of the reverse transcription reaction is 'primed' by a short double stranded region. In other words, one must hybridise or anneal a small DNA oligonucleotide to a complementary region of the mRNA molecule one wishes to copy. Fortunately, one can copy virtually the entire population of mRNAs from any cell by using a commercially available synthetic oligonucleotide 12–18 nucleotides long, oligo dT, as primer. As we have noted earlier, virtually all mRNAs in the cytoplasm of eukaryotic cells possess at their 3' ends a polyadenylic acid (polyA) 'tail'. This allows one to use oligo dT as a 'universal' primer.

When reverse transcriptase completes synthesis of a cDNA strand, it has a tendency to 'read back' along the newly sythesised DNA strand; in other words, the reverse transcriptase starts to copy a second DNA strand from the newly sythesised cDNA template. By so doing, the cDNA forms a terminal hairpin loop (Fig. 2.7); this is very useful, since the loop region serves as a 'self-priming' initiation site for synthesis of a second strand from the cDNA. As shown in Figure 2.7, one can use additional reverse transcriptase, or DNA polymerase I from *E. coli* to complete this second strand and thus create a double-stranded 'hairpin' molecule in which the two strands are joined at one end by the loop. Using another DNA modification enzyme called S1 nuclease, one can specifically excise the loop without damaging the double-stranded regions of the molecule. S1 nuclease digests only single-stranded DNA, leaving double-stranded regions intact. As shown in Figure 2.7, the mRNA has been converted into a double-stranded DNA fragment which is very similar to fragments one can generate from genomic DNA. By appropriate modification of termini, one can now recombine this double-stranded cDNA with DNA from a microbial vector for the purposes of molecular cloning.

The brief description just outlined illustrates the fundamental role of reverse transcriptase in the cloning of populations of mRNAs. Of equal importance is the ability of reverse transcriptase to synthesise single-stranded DNA probes from mRNA templates. If one had available primers capable of annealing to only one mRNA or a given region of one mRNA, one could use reverse transcriptase to synthesise specifically only a single cDNA species from a highly complex mixture of mRNAs. In other words one could obtain specific extension from the primer only of the cDNA of interest. Since specific primers can be obtained, these so-called primer extension techniques have proved to be extraordinarily important in both the cloning and analysis of many genes and will be discussed later.

PREPARATION OF cDNA FOR MOLECULAR CLONING

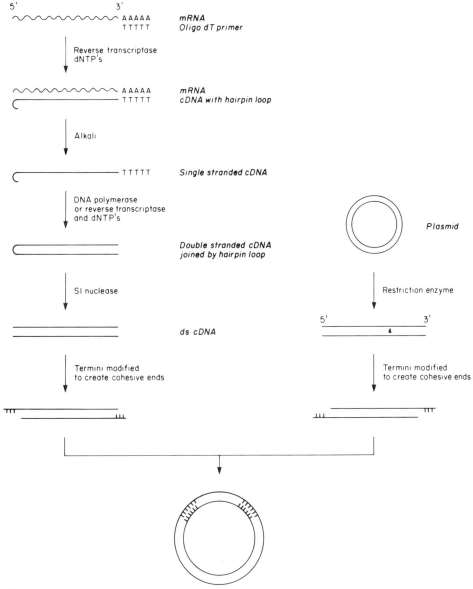

Fig. 2.7 Synthesis of double-stranded cDNA by reverse transcriptase and insertion of the ds cDNA into a plasmid. (See text for details.)

Cloning vehicles

The development of nucleic acid enzymology permits one to digest and modify DNA from mRNA, in such a way that the genome of an organism or the population of mRNAs in a particular cell type can be joined in vitro to DNA molecules from a different source; in other words, the discovery of these enzymes allows one to form recombinant DNA molecules. For our purposes, the importance of this capability lies in the fact that bacteria carry certain types of infective biologically active non-chromosomal or extrachromosomal DNA molecules. Recombinant DNA molecules formed between the eukaryotic DNA or cDNA mixture and the extrachromosomal microbial DNA, confer upon the eukaryotic sequences the biological capability of infecting bacterial host cells. This capability is of fundamental importance, since, once in the bacterial host cells, the eukaryotic DNA fragments can be manipulated and harvested like any other microbial gene.

Certain extrachromosomal DNA elements from bacteria have been developed which are particularly suited for recombination with foreign DNA and reintroduction into bacterial host cells. These are called cloning vehicles or cloning vectors because they permit one to separate the complex mixture of DNA fragments resulting from the aforementioned enzymologic manipulations into its component parts by the process of 'molecular cloning'. Molecular cloning refers to the fact that one incubates the population of recombinant DNA molecules with an excess number of bacterial host cells so that each host cell receives, on the average, only one recombinant DNA molecule. If one then spreads the suspension of bacteria onto petri plates at low cell densities so that each individual cell occupies a separate spot on the plate and grows into a distinct separate colony, one then has a large population of colonies, each derived from a single cell containing a single eukaryotic fragment embedded in the cloning vehicle. Thus, the mixture of DNAs has been converted to a mixture of bacterial clones, each containing a DNA fragment from the eukaryotic cells of origin; each fragment is thus purified from all other DNA fragments derived from the original source. A means for identifying the bacterial cell containing the gene of interest is all that is required for isolation of the cloned DNA species.

The sum total of all bacterial cells containing cloned DNA fragments from an experiment of the above type is called a 'library' of cloned DNA. The screening of such libraries to identify the gene of interest is discussed later. For the moment, we shall focus on the properties of the extrachromosomal DNA elements which allow one to introduce DNA from other tissues into bacteria for the purpose of cloning.

Plasmids

Plasmids are small, extrachromosomal, self-replicating circles of DNA which occur naturally in many strains of bacteria. Plasmids of interest to the molecular geneticist have been selected for several properties that they exhibit:

1. They possess their own origins of DNA replication and are capable of replicating relatively independently of the bacterial host genome.

2. Because of their self-replicating ability, these plasmids are amplifiable; that is, these plasmids can accumulate to levels of about 100–200 copies per host cell. This amplification ability allows one to harvest relatively large amounts of recombinant plasmids carrying cloned genes from relatively modest volumes of host cell culture medium.

3. Useful plasmids contain genes which modify the host cell phenotype so as to provide genetic markers for their presence in the host, e.g. antibiotic resistance.

4. A plasmid useful for cloning experiments must be capable of efficient uptake into the host cells from the appropriate culture medium. Plasmids must be biologically active in transfection of host cells; mixture of the host cell and the plasmid DNA in medium containing calcium phosphate causes uptake of the DNA by the cells.

Many different plasmids useful for a variety of molecular cloning purposes have been designed and engineered by molecular geneticists. The development of cloning vectors from naturally occurring plasmids represents one of the early successes of molecular genetics. Figure 2.8 for example illustrates the construction of a plasmid containing two antibiotic resistance genes. The essential DNA sequences present in these plasmids (DNA replication signals and the antibiotic resistance genes) comprise only a small proportion of the genomes of naturally occurring plasmids. By digesting these plasmids with restriction endonucleases and religating the mixtures, investigators created a whole series of novel, rearranged, plasmid circles of differing sizes. By transfecting host cells with these plasmids, selecting for the presence of the plasmids via antibiotic resistance and reisolation of the plasmid DNA, one could identify the small proportion of enzymatically rearranged molecules which retain biologic viability. By performing this experiment repeatedly, it was possible to delete from the plasmids nearly all of the non-essential DNA. These non-essential regions can then be replaced with DNA fragments containing useful sequences such as restriction enzyme recognition sites, viral or bacterial promotors, etc.

Plasmids are most useful for cloning small DNA fragments (less than 5–10 kilobases), since transfection efficiency declines as plasmids become larger than 10 kilobases. Plasmids are also preferred as cloning vehicles when one wishes to obtain large amounts of the cloned DNA sequence, because high copy number is attainable in host cells. When one must obtain large libraries with more than 10 000 members, or clone very large fragments (> 10 Kb), phage are preferred.

Bacteriophage
Bacteriophage are viruses which infect bacteria. Phage lambda, which infects certain strains of *E. coli*, is the virus from which most bacteriophage cloning vectors have been derived. Lambda is an extraordinary well-characterised organism consisting of a double-stranded genome approximately 50 kilobases long and a protein 'coat' which surrounds the DNA and contains the components needed for attachment to, and infection of, the host cells. If a suspension of lambda bacteriophage is spread on top of a 'lawn' of host cells growing on the surface of the petri plate, each phage will infect a single cell, replicate within it, and lyse it; the progeny will then infect adjacent cells and the cycle will be repeated until a clear plaque, representing the absence of bacteria from that spot, is generated. Each plaque represents a 'clone' of phage which are the progeny of a single parent, and is thus analogous to a bacterial colony.

Cloning vectors engineered from bacteriophage lambda are designed to accommodate larger fragments of DNA. The ability of the phage genome to be 'packaged' into a viable phage particle depends to some degree on size. Molecules less than 38 kb or greater than 52 kb tend to be non-viable because they cannot be packaged. Some lambda phage cloning vehicles have been engineered so that they are at their lower limits of packaging size, and, therefore, capable of accepting a recombinant insert

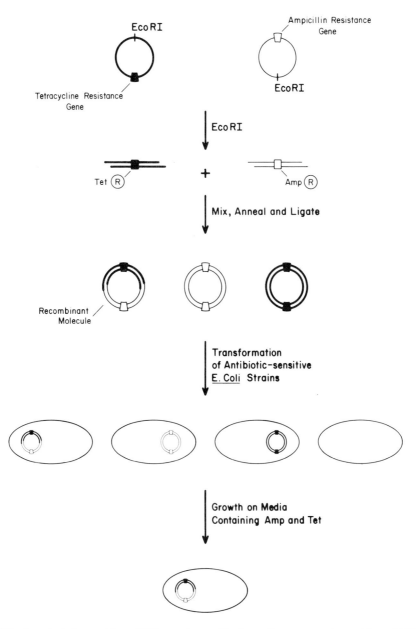

Fig. 2.8   A protypical recombinant DNA experiment. The figure diagrams use of recombinant DNA methods to engineer a novel plasmid vector containing two antibiotic resistance genes. Two plasmids, each containing a single Eco RI site and a single antibiotic resistance gene, are linearised by treatment with Eco RI. The two plasmids are mixed and allowed to anneal. Through base-pairing of complementary cohesive ends, new recombinants are formed. Some simple carry two copies of a single antibiotic resistance gene; others however carry one ampicillin and one tetracycline gene. These can be selected by growth of transformed bacteria in media containing both ampicillin and tetracycline.

10–15 Kb long; others contain non-essential DNA in the middle of the genome between two strategic restriction endonuclease sites. This 'stuffer' fragment can be removed by restriction endonuclease digestion and replaced by a cloned insert, so that only the recombinant phage are of viable size.

To utilise bacteriophage lambda vectors, one digests the phage with the appropriate restriction endonuclease, and, if necessary, removes the 'stuffer' piece by electrophoresis or sucrose gradient separation. A digest of genomic DNA with complementary cohesive ends is then simply ligated to the bacteriophage to generate the recombinant DNA molecules of viable size. A major advance that has made cloning with bacteriophage feasible has been the development of cell free extracts from certain strains of *E. coli* capable of promoting in vitro packaging. The recombinant DNA genomes are added to these packaging extracts, which produce viable phage particles with highly efficient infectivity. By using in vitro packaging techniques, more recombinant plaques per microgram of eukaryotic DNA are generated than can be obtained with plasmids. Using currently available cloning vectors and in vitro packaging extracts, one can prepare 'libraries' of cloned genomic DNA fragments 7–20 Kb long which represent essentially the entire human genome.

Cosmids and single-stranded bacteriophage
'Cosmids' are vectors designed to provide some of the advantages of plasmids and bacteriophage in the same molecule. A cosmid contains sufficient portions of phage genome that it can be packaged in vitro and can accommodate very large fragments of DNA, but retains sufficient plasmid features to enjoy the advantage of high intracellular copy number. M13 is a single-stranded bacteriophage which has gained wide use for subcloning of fragments from cloned genes for use as hybridisation probes or in nucleotide sequence analysis. Since M13 clones contain the insert in a circular single-stranded molecule, highly radioactive single-stranded DNA complementary to the clone can be prepared for these purposes by using primer extension techniques (see p. 49).

Identification of specific genes in cloned libraries — 'screening'
DNA modification enzymes provide the means for fusion together of eukaryotic and microbial DNA molecules. The biologic properties of the microbial DNA molecules used as cloning vehicles allow one to clone and 'grow' eukaryotic DNA sequences, each in its own microbial host cell. The entire population of recombinant bacterial colonies or bacterial phage plaques constitutes a representation of the whole genome or messenger RNA population, and is called a 'library'. The crucial step which must be accomplished next is the identification of the gene one wishes to isolate within this library. Since genomic and cDNA libraries routinely contain several hundred thousand members, of which a gene of interest comprises only one or a few members, the 'screening' of such libraries requires methods of exquisite sensitivity and specificity. In this section, we review some of the strategies which have been employed for identifying specific genes or cDNAs within complex libraries.

Although many strategies have been designed to construct and screen libraries for specific purposes, the general approach derives from a few basic theoretical and methodologic tenets. The chances of identifying a specific gene in a cloned library are clearly maximised if one can enrich the population of mRNAs, cDNAs, or genomic

DNA fragments for the gene of interest by physicochemical or, as discussed later, immunologic means prior to cloning. Libraries constructed from these enriched populations will contain a higher percentage of the desired gene, thus increasing the ease with which such libraries can be screened. Also required are methods for obtaining sufficiently pure and stringent probes to screen either an enriched or an unselected library. Clearly, the degree of stringency and purity required are greater if one must screen a totally unselected library.

These considerations are best illustrated by considering the 'easiest' genes to clone, the globin genes, and then contrasting the situation encountered for other genes.

By the time the erythroid precursor cells have reached their late (reticulocyte) stages, globin chains are virtually the only proteins still being synthesised. Globin messenger RNAs comprise over 90% of the messenger RNA molecules remaining at these late stages. Thus, by purifying poly (A)+ mRNA from reticulocytes, one can obtain a virtually 'pure' preparation of globin mRNAs. Conversion of this mRNA into double stranded cDNA, and cloning into plasmid vectors yield a library in which over 90% of the members are globin sequences. By the same reasoning, a radioactive single-stranded cDNA probe transcribed from such an mRNA preparation would also be over 90% pure for the gene of interest. This is sufficient for screening cloned libraries, since, for technical reasons, the most abundant cDNA species in a mixture of radioactive cDNAs yields the strongest molecular hybridisation signals. Indeed, in this case there is no need to screen the library by hybridisation techniques, since 'brute force' techniques, that is, actual isolation and DNA sequence analysis of 10 or 15 recombinant plasmids would almost certainly identify globin clones. It is not surprising that globin cDNAs were among the first to be cloned. Once a recombinant cDNA containing plasmid has been identified for the globin genes, it then becomes an ideal pure probe for screening genomic DNA libraries for the chromosomal globin genes. Indeed, this approach is very similar to that which was actually used for globin gene cloning in the late 1970s.

Unfortunately, globin genes are almost unique in that a cell exists which expresses them to the virtual exclusion of all other genes. Even highly specialised cells which synthesise large amounts of specific products (e.g. plasma cells sythesising immuno-globulin, fibroblasts synthesising collagen, etc.) rarely devote more than 5–10% of overall protein synthesis to the production of these products. In these situations, in vitro translation techniques can be used to identify the molecular weight of the mRNA after physical separation by density gradient or gel electrophoresis methods. If this mRNA originally comprises more than 1–5% of the total mRNA, this approach will provide a sufficiently enriched source of mRNA for synthesis of a specific cDNA hybridisation probe. However, these examples still apply to only a minute fraction of the genes one might be interested in cloning. Consider, for example, beta 2 microglobulin, a protein whose expression is essential to expression of histocompata-bility antigens, or adenosine deminase, an enzyme whose production is linked both to integrity of red cell physiology and immune competence. These proteins are produced in normal cells as only 0.01% of the total protein. Thus, on the average, only one out of one hundred thousand recombinant clones from a cDNA library will contain the mRNA for these proteins. Clearly, one must devise strategies to create probes capable of detecting these rare clones. We shall illustrate a few representative examples that have gained acceptance.

Immunochemical purification of specific mRNAs

Most proteins of haematologic interest have been studied by immunochemical techniques. In other words, highly specific antibodies have been prepared against these proteins for a variety of structural and functional studies. The usefulness of these antibodies for cloning of the gene is not immediately apparent, since the antibodies react to the protein rather than the nucleic acid sequences coding for them. Fortunately, newly synthesised proteins begin to fold and assume their three-dimensional conformation as they are being assembled on ribosomes. In a suspension of polyribosomes incubated with the antibodies, antigen–antibody complexes form only with those polyribosomes which are producing the desired protein. By using staphylococcal protein A affinity chromatography, one can isolate the polysomes which are bound to the antibody, and then isolate the mRNA from the polyribosomes. This method has proven to be surprisingly powerful. For example, Kraus & Rosenberg (1982) have utilised this approach to isolate an mRNA for ornithine trans-carbamylase, an enzyme representing only 1/100000 of the total protein population in liver cells.

In order to verify that a putative clone identified by the immunopurified mRNA is indeed the clone of interest, two basic approaches are available. The first, and most direct is establishment of the DNA sequence and comparison of the amino acid sequence encoded by the DNA sequence with the amino acid sequence of the protein. This is clearly a method of choice if one knows sufficient amounts of the amino acid sequence of the desired protein to have a standard for comparison. The second approach is more indirect, but allows one to utilise the specific antibodies to protein in lieu of amino acid sequence information. The putative clone is isolated in the form of its plasmid DNA, and affixed to a solid support (usually nitrocellulose filters). The filter bound DNA is denatured to single-stranded form and incubated with mRNA from a cell expressing the protein. The specific mRNA should hybridise to the recombinant plasmid, and be recoverable by recovering the nitrocellulose filter. The mRNA can be eluted from the filter and translated into protein in any one of a number of available in vitro translation systems. The translation products can then be identified as the protein of interest by immunoprecipitation of the radioactive proteins produced in the translation mix, using methods entirely analogous to those used to immunoprecipitate proteins from an cellular extract. This approach is called hybrid selected translation. A related method, called hybrid arrested translation, involves incubation of the mRNA preparation with denatured plasmid DNA in solution. The specific mRNA, by virtue of being bound into double-stranded mRNA-plasmid DNA hybrids, becomes inaccessible for translation so that the specific immunoprecipitable band disappears.

Immunochemical screening methods are elegant in principle, but quite difficult in actual practice. Nonetheless, in lieu of amino acid sequence data or a cellular source of highly enriched mRNA, the immunochemical approach remains the method of choice.

HYBRID SELECTED OR HYBRID ARRESTED TRANSLATION SCREENING

In general, immunochemical approaches to isolation of cDNA clones now follow the protocol described above. However, there are some situations for which the source of the desired mRNA is available in such small amounts that one cannot obtain preparative scale amounts of immunoprecipitated polysomes. Rather, in these situations a technique called subculture dilution is used to identify the clone of interest by means of the hybrid selection or hybrid arrested translation assay (Parnes et al, 1981). The library of cDNA clones is prepared and arbitrarily subdivided into a manageable number of 'pools' (cf. Fig. 2.9). The DNA from each pool is affixed to filters and incubated with mRNA. Each of the filters is then separately recovered and

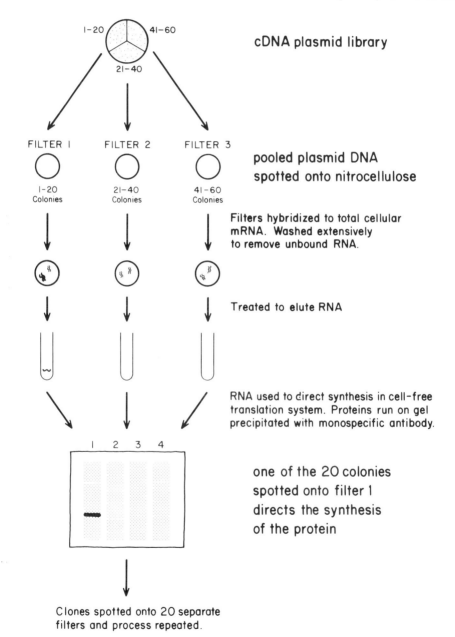

Fig. 2.9   Isolation of cDNA clone by subculture cloning and hybrid selected translation.

the mRNA eluted and translated. As shown in Figure 2.9, one or more of the pools should contain the desired cDNA and thus select the mRNA for detectable translation products. That pool is then further sudivided and the process repeated. As shown in the Figure, one eventually identifies one or a few clones with the capacity to select the mRNA for translation.

IMMUNOCHEMICAL IDENTIFICATION OF PROTEINS PRODUCED IN BACTERIA CARRYING RECOMBINANT PLASMIDS

In general, cloned eukaryotic genes are not expressed in their bacterial host cells, since significant differences exist in the structure of ribosomes, initiation factors, etc. required for protein synthesis in the two types of organisms. However, a number of cleverly engineered 'expression vectors' have been designed which allow bacteria to synthesise and translate mRNAs which encode a portion of the eukaryotic protein being cloned. A typical expression vector contains the promotor region, the mRNA initiation site, and the amino terminal coding portion of the gene for the bacterial enzyme beta galactosidase. This iducible gene has been very well characterised, and its expression can be manipulated and readily detected by many elegant techniques. The gene has an *Eco Rl* site within the coding portion. By attaching synthetic *Eco Rl* linkers to the termini of cDNAs, one can clone the cDNAs into the beta galactosidase gene. The host cell will express the beta galactosidase gene even when it is fused to the inserted DNA. Moreover, the fused protein which results (beginning as beta galactosidase, and ending as a portion of the protein specified by the cloned cDNA) is sufficiently stable in *E. coli* that it can be detected immunologically. Thus, direct identification is possible for any protein if a specific antibody is available.

Direct immunochemical screening of an expression vector library is generally conducted by approaches very analogous to molecular hybridisation screening, except that an antibody is used instead of a nucleic hybridisation probe. A circular nitrocellulose filter is pressed onto the petri plate on which the recombinant bacterial colonies or bacteriophage plaques are growing, thus yielding on the filter a replica of the petri plate. The filter represents a replica of the master plate. The filters are then treated with a variety of agents such as chloroform, to remove bacterial membrane lipids and other debris, incubated with the specific antibody and, after stringent washing to remove non-specific background, reacted with radiolabelled staphylococcal protein A or 'second antibody'. Autoradiography of the filters reveals those radioactive colonies or plaques which represent candidates for each specific clone desired.

Screening of libraries by differential molecular hybridisation

Whenever possible, the use of molecular hybridisation approaches to the screening of cloned libraries is preferred, because several powerful, sensitive, and precise filter hybridisation screening methods are available. These methods involve the generation of a replica of the petri plates containing the growing plaques or colonies on a nitrocellulose filter, as discussed above for immunochemical screenings of expression vectors. The filters are then incubated with a radiolabelled single-stranded hybridisation probe which has been selected to be specific only for the gene of interest.

Screening by hybridisation requires a pure and specific hybridisation probe. As noted earlier, this problem is simplified for a few genes and cell types such as globin and reticulocytes, or immunoglobulins and plasma cells, since relatively high degrees of enrichment are available as a result of specialisation of the cell and/or distinctive size of the mRNAs. Alternatively, one can utilise cDNA derived from mRNA prepared from immunoprecipitated polysomes, as discussed earlier. In lieu of these strategies, some workers have cloned genes by an approach known as 'differential hybridisation'. These approaches are particularly suitable in those situations for which one has two cell types very similar in all respects except for expression of the desired gene. For example, some leukaemia cell lines can be 'induced' to mature along specific myeloid, monocytic, or lymphoid pathways by pharmacologic agents. If one wished to clone the unique species of mRNA whose expression is induced as part of the phenotypic induction, one could prepare cDNA libraries from both the induced and uninduced cells, as well as preparing radioactive single-stranded cDNAs from these two cell types. By then hybridising replicas of the two cloned libraries with each of the probes, one can identify those clones hybridising only to the induced or uninduced cell derived cDNAs. These clones would presumably represent sequences expressed specifically in the induced or uninduced cell type.

Molecular hybridisation screening using synthetic oligonucleotides
In the early sections of this review, it was noted that the genetic code is degenerate but unambiguous. In other words, for any given amino acid there may be several codons; however, each codon uniquely specifies a single amino acid. The implication of these facts is that knowledge of a protein's amino acid sequence does not predict the single mRNA sequence which codes for it in vivo. Rather, the amino acid sequence predicts only that a large but finite number of mRNA sequences could specify it. For example, for each leucine in the protein there are six possible codons, etc. Nonetheless, it is possible to exploit amino acid sequence information about a protein to prepare a synthetic short DNA molecule (synthetic oligonucleotide), usually 12–20 nucleotides long, which can be utilised as a molecular hybridisation probe for screening libraries. The availability of these synthetic oligonucleotides has occurred as the result of advances in solid state polymer chemistry whereby, using phosphite or triester synthesis methods on solid-state matrices, one can now prepare oligonucleotides up to 20–25 nucleotides long in reasonable yield and with a great deal of sequence accuracy.

Synthetic oligonucleotides are gaining acceptance as the method of choice for cloning genes which code for proteins about which some amino acid sequence information is known. This is particularly true in view of recent advances which allow one to determine at least partial amino acid sequences rapidly for almost any protein that can be isolated in picogram–nanogram amounts.

A typical application of the oligonucleotide approach, which has been applied to cloning of genes such as interferon, is as follows: one scans the available amino acid sequence information and searches for a region 5–10 amino acids long which best matches two criteria:

1. Carboxy terminal regions of the protein are preferred to amino terminal regions, since cDNAs are synthesised from the 3' end of the mRNA template which is closest to the region coding for the carboxy terminus. Since reverse transcriptase often sythesises only incomplete copies of the mRNA, the regions coding for the carboxy terminus of the protein are more likely to be represented in the library, particularly if the protein is a rather long one.

2. The most desirable amino acid sequence is the least degenerate one. That is, regions rich in amino acids specified by only one or two codons are preferred. For example, methionines and tryptophans are favoured since each is specified by only a single codon. There are nine other amino acids which are also useful because for each there are only two codons. Clearly, amino acids such as leucine and arginine, for each of which six codons exist, are best avoided.

When the amino acid sequence has been selected, one then knows how many possible oligonucleotides could be complementary to that region of the mRNA. For example, for the sequence Met-Trp-Phe-Phe, the possible mRNA coding sequences would be AUG-UGG-UUU/C-UUU/C. A mixture of four oligonucleotides, accommodating the ambiguity of the two positions indicated, would cover all possibilities. If the next amino acid in this sequence were proline (encoded by CCN, where N is any of the four bases), one would require 16 oligonucleotides differing at each of the three ambiguous positions, in order to provide a sequence exactly complementary to each of the 16 possible mRNA coding regions. Clearly, an impossibly large number of oligonucleotides can code for relatively short amino acid sequences if degenerate codons are encountered. Fortunately, one can take advantage of a phenomenon called 'wobble' to simplify the number of oligonucleotides one needs to produce. Wobble refers to a phenomemon by which, using appropriate incubation conditions, one can 'bend' the rules of Watson–Crick base pairing. For example G–U as well as A–U base pairs can be formed. The pattern of more flexible base pairing rules under wobble has been well established. One can reduce the number of oligonucleotides by using a single base in the primer to hybridise to either of two bases in the degenerate position of the codon. For example, for the phenylalanine codons UUU/C, the complementary oligonucleotide AAA/G can be simplified to AAG.

By judicious selection of an amino acid region as close to the 3' end of the mRNA as possible, containing as little degeneracy in the coding sequence as possible, and by application of the rules of wobble one can usually devise an oligonucleotide usable as a molecular hybridisation probe for screening an unselected library for the gene of interest. The probes can be used in two ways (Fig. 2.10); first, for direct screening with the oligonucleotide, one incubates the probe with radioactive ATP and polynucleotide kinase which attaches the radioactive phosphate to the 5' end of the oligonucleotide and renders it highly radioactive. One simply detects the radioactive colonies or plaques which have hybridised to the radioactive oligonucleotide. The other approach involves the use of the oligonucleotide as a primer after incubation with the total mRNA preparation and reverse transcriptase. The cDNA synthesised from such a primer is, in theory, complementary only to the mRNA against which the primer was directed. One can either use the cDNA as starting material for preparation of an enriched library, or use highly radioactive cDNA prepared by this primer extension technique as a hybridisation probe for screening an unselected library.

'Cloning phenotypes' into foreign host cells
By analogy to the use of antibiotic resistance genes as selective markers for the presence of plasmids, one can sometimes exploit the selective advantage of a eukaryotic gene one wishes to clone for the purposes of isolating the gene. For example genes involved in purine metabolism have been selected from recombinant cells by growing the recombinants in the presence of purine antimetabolites. Under

these conditions only cells that have taken up the gene one wishes to isolate can survive. These methods are difficult to use because expression of the eukaryotic genes in microbial hosts cannot always be assumed. Cloning of genes in eukaryotic host cells by these techniques is feasible in some cases, but limited by the fact that one obtains very few recombinants compared to typical cloning experiments with microbial vectors.

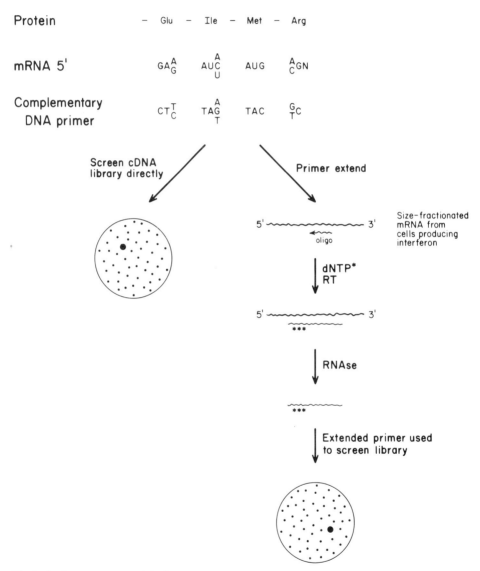

Fig. 2.10 Synthetic oligodeoxynucleotides. In this example, a short amino acid sequence from human leukocyte interferon was selected as a template for oligomer synthesis because it contains methionine, with only one codon, and glutamic acid, with only two (Goeddel et al, 1980). Based on the deduced mRNA sequences, a mixture of 12 oligomers was synthesised. Note that the oligomer is only 11 bases long since inclusion of the 12th base (the 3rd in the triplet for arginine, where N = any of the 4 bases) would have necessitated synthesis of a mixture of 48 oligomers. The use of the oligomer to screen the library directly or to direct primer extension is discussed in the text.

It has recently been shown that large fragments of human genomic DNA can be transfected directly into mouse fibroblasts, and often expressed therein. Those genes which code for certain proteins expressed on the cell surface, such as T cell specific antigens, have been identified on the transformed mouse fibroblast membrane by fluorescent antibody screening of the cell population. By using preparative fluorescent activated cell sorting techniques, one can obtain a population of cells enriched for those clones of cells expressing these surface markers. In principle, this can be exploited for cloning surface phenotypes even if one is not certain about the exact structure of the responsible proteins.

Summary

This portion of the review was intended to outline the principles and methodological approaches applied to the problem of isolating genes from eukaryotic cells. Clearly, the major requirements are the availability of enzymes which convert cellular DNA or mRNA into forms suitable for cloning, the availability of microbial vectors which allow the transfer of DNA into microbial host cells where one can exploit the ease of manipulation (in both genetic and biochemical terms) for isolation of the gene, and the availability of screening techniques which take advantage of either molecular hybridisation probes or immunochemical probes. What may not be immediately obvious from the foregoing is the uses to which these genes can be put for the study of haematologic problems. The remainder of the review deals with this issue.

USES OF CLONED GENES FOR THE STUDY OF GENE STRUCTURE AND EXPRESSION

A cloned gene sequence provides three advantages which are otherwise unattainable: First, the cloning process allows procurement of enough pure material for chemical determination of the nucleotide sequence of both the gene and its flanking regions. Second, the cloned DNA provides large amounts of exquisitely pure and specific molecular hybridisation probes for analysis of the gene's restriction endonuclease map in vivo, its copy number, chromosomal localisation and its mRNA transcription, processing, stability and function. Probes can be chosen to include the entire gene, regions within it, or any flanking region which has been cloned, by physical isolation or subcloning of the appropriate restriction endonuclease fragments. Third, the cloned gene can be subcloned into expression vectors derived from animal virus genomes (e.g. SV 40). These allow expression of the cloned genes in *eukaryotic* foreign host cells. This gene transfer capability allows studies of mRNA metabolism, effects of in vitro generated mutations on gene function, etc.

Nucleic acid sequencing

Our current understanding of the functional microanatomy of the gene, described at the beginning of the chapter (exons, introns, splice sites, promotor boxes, etc.) is derived from a precise knowledge of the nucleic acid sequences of genes. The delineation of normal base sequences, and the characterisation of changes that constitute the molecular basis of various inherited disorders (e.g. thalassaemia) have yielded information about the processes governing expression of normal eukaryotic genes. The techniques which allow rapid determination of the base sequences of DNA were first described by Maxam and Gilbert, and Sanger et al, in 1977 (Maxam & Gilbert, 1977; Sanger et al, 1977). The amount of sequence data that has been generated in the subsequent seven years is so vast that computers are necessary for the storage and analysis of this information.

DNA sequencing techniques are conceptually straightforward. The Maxam–Gilbert procedure (Fig. 2.11) for example, may be described as follows: a single-stranded length of DNA is radiolabelled at the 5' end, using polynucleotide kinase,

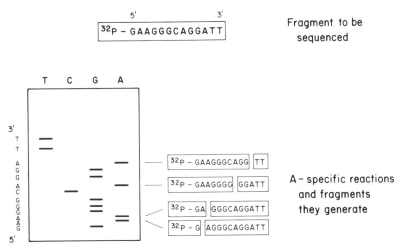

Fig. 2.11   Maxam–Gilbert sequencing. Fragments generated by the A-specific reactions are shown in detail to the right of the gel diagram. Note that the chemical treatment removes the A residue which was present at each cleavage site. Although each reaction generates a pair of fragments, only the 5' ³²P-labelled fragment will be visible with autoradiography. The gel diagram also includes lanes for T, C, and G illustrating the sequence 'ladder' obtained by performing entirely analagous reactions with reagents cleaving the DNA strand only at G, C, or T.

another useful DNA modification enzyme. The labelled DNA is then divided into four aliquots. Each aliquot is subjected to a series of mild chemical treatments, each specific for the cleavage of the strand at one of the four bases, i.e. one set of reactions is specific for eliminating As, another for Cs, etc. The conditions chosen are so mild that, on the average, only one nucleotide is attacked in each molecule. The result is a set of fragments specifically 'broken' at a single A,C,G or T residue, depending on the chemical reaction used. However, in the aggregate, the reaction mix contains molecules broken at each A,C,G, or T (cf. Fig. 2.11). If one 'scanned' the population of molecules in the A cleavage reaction one would see some molecules cleaved only at the first A encountered along the strand, others cleaved only at the second A, still others, only at the third A, etc. (cf. Fig. 2.11). These fragments can then be resolved by high resolution gel electrophoresis, which can separate fragments that differ by only one nucleotide in length. If the base-specific reactions are carried out in parallel and the resulting digests run side by side on a gel, the base sequence of the DNA can be read from the gel directly. The correct translational reading frame is readily identified as the only one without frequent stop codons. Using Maxam–Gilbert techniques it is routinely possible to sequence about five hundred bases in a week.

DNA and RNA analysis

Cloning and sequencing have proven to be extremely powerful tools in the study of human disease. By the use of cloning techniques it has been possible to generate milligram amounts of DNA probes which would have been available in only picogram amounts by non-recombinant methods. With theses cloned DNAs as probes, extensive mapping of genes and their transcriptional products (mRNAs) has been carried out. A brief survey of these methods follows.

Blotting techniques

Blot hybridisation is a technique which permits the identification and characterisation of a specific DNA or RNA species within a complex mixture of DNA or RNA fragments. Introduced in 1975 by E. M. Southern as a DNA analysis method, this general approach has been used extensively to map the coding and flanking regions of genes for which probes are available. Mapping by 'Southern' blotting has revealed polymorphisms in restriction sites within and adjacent to all genes studied so far; these polymorphic restriction sites have provided a new means for performing linkage analysis in the diagnosis of inherited disorders. Southern blotting has also been used to establish the absence of genes (e.g. in those thalassaemias which are due to globin gene deletions), and for measurement of gene copy number.

The 'Southern' technique is illustrated in Figure 2.12. First, total genomic DNA is extracted from the cells to be studied and digested with a restriction enzyme. The

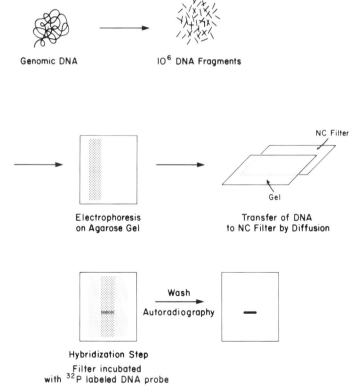

Fig. 2.12   Southern blot hybridisation. (See text for details.)

resulting mixture of fragments is separated by gel electrophoresis; due to the large number of fragments (in the range of one million for a human genome) generated by most endonucleases, the gel appears as a continuous 'smear' rather than as a series of discrete bands. After in situ denaturation of the fragments by incubation of the gel in

A. S₁ NUCLEASE ANALYSIS OF β GLOBIN mRNA

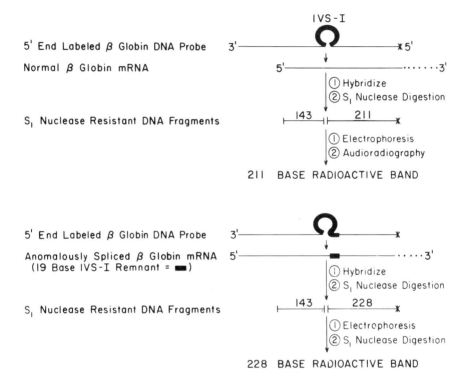

Fig. 2.13A Use of S1 nuclease analysis to map a splice site mutation in a patient with β^+ thalassaemia. The DNA probe spans the first intervening sequence and includes 211 bases from the second exon and 143 bases from the first exon. When this probe is hybridised to *mature* normal β globin mRNA and then treated with S1 nuclease, fragments 211 and 143 bases in length are protected, although only the radioactive 211 base fragment is visible on autoradiography. The lower diagram shows results expected from a form of β thalassaemia due to a single nucleotide substitution within IVS–1 which creates an alternate acceptor (3') splice site.

alkali, transfer of the DNA fragments to a nitrocellulose filter is accomplished by diffusion (thus, the term 'blotting'). The nitrocellulose filter is incubated in buffer containing a cloned radiolabelled DNA probe for the gene of interest. The probe hybridises only to the complementary DNA sequences on the filter; excess probe is then removed by washing. The bands identified by autoradiography represent the fragment size(s) generated by that enzyme. Restriction mapping of the gene by blotting can then be achieved by methods analogous to those described in part two.

By means of simple modifications, blot hybridisation has been adapted for analysis of RNA and proteins as well. 'Northern' blotting permits the identification of a specific *mRNA* species; in this procedure, a mixture of the cell's RNA (rather than DNA) is run on a gel and transferred to nitrocellulose. A DNA probe is used to identify the band of interest; hybridisation conditions are controlled to favour

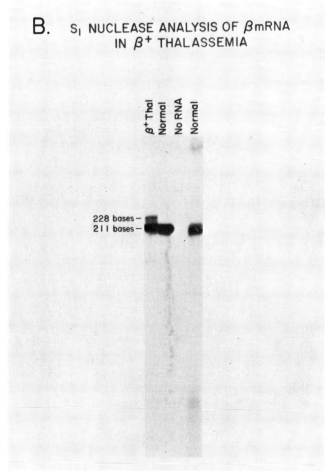

B. S₁ NUCLEASE ANALYSIS OF βmRNA IN β⁺ THALASSEMIA

228 bases —
211 bases —

Fig. 2.13B Both splice sites are used generating two processed mRNA's: (1) normal β mRNA; (2) alternately processed mRNA which retains 17 bases at the 3′ end of IVS 1 and thus protects 17 additional bases of the exon 2 portion of the probe.

formation of DNA–RNA hybrids. In 'Western' blotting, *proteins* are run on the gel and transferred to a solid matrix; the probe used in this case is a labelled antibody.

S1 nuclease analysis
Blotting techniques allow detection of genes and mRNAs and establishment of number and size of the DNA fragments or mRNAs species. However, fine structure mapping of the mRNA products of a gene requires an alternative approach. One powerful method called S1 nuclease mapping is illustrated in Figure 2.13.

To begin S1 nuclease mapping one labels a cloned DNA fragment at the 5′ end or 3′ end with appropriate DNA modification enzymes. The probe is chosen to span (Fig.

2.13) an informative region of the gene and its mRNA, such as a splice site, the 5' end cap site, etc. The end labelled probe is hybridised to the RNA mixture, then digested with S1 nuclease which destroys all non-hybridised (single-stranded) regions of the DNA probe. The length of the S1 resistant end labelled (radioactive) fragment is determined by gel electrophoresis and autoradiography. This length represents the distance over which the mRNA is complementary to the probe.

S1 nuclease allows one to identify mRNA precursors, splicing intermediates, 5' and 3' mRNA termini, etc. by use of a panel of strategic end labelled probes which span these regions in the gene. For example, a probe containing an intervening sequence will yield short fragments when hybridised to mature mRNA lacking introns, but longer fragments when annealed to mRNA precursors. In a total mRNA mixture, these different RNAs are recognised as a series of bands in the gel lane. An example showing presence of both normally and aberrantly spliced beta globin mRNA in a thalassaemic reticulocyte mRNA preparation is shown in Figure 2.13.

REPRESENTATIVE APPLICATIONS OF RECOMBINANT DNA METHODS TO THE STUDY, DIAGNOSIS, AND TREATMENT OF HAEMATOLOGIC DISORDERS

Molecular genetic technology provides the capacity for isolating genes; the cloned genes permit direct analysis of the structure of the gene, its surrounding DNA, and its mRNA and protein products. This analytical capability can be conducted at unprecedented levels of sensitivity and precision. Thus, it is hardly surprising that major advances have already occurred in the application of these methods to the clinical arena.

Students of globin gene expression during erythropoiesis, and of pathologic globin genes in the thalassaemia syndromes have experienced the dramatic impact of recombinant DNA technology on the investigation of haematologic diseases. Just prior to the advent of gene cloning techniques, it was known that thalassaemia syndromes arose from deficiencies in the amount and/or function of the relevant globin messenger RNAs. A few syndromes had been tentatively shown to be due to gene deletions, but the majority were apparently due to fine structure mutations further definition of which was impossible with existing methods. At about that time, gene cloning and gene blotting strategies became available. The discovery of intervening sequences, and the attendant requirement for mRNA processing events, followed shortly thereafter, as did actual cloning of a human beta globin gene. The information provided by these advances, such as the nucleotide sequence of the normal genes, the location of splice sites and intervening sequences, etc., allowed investigators to focus their efforts on these strategic functional regions. The availability of gene cloning technology rapidly led to the isolation of the thalassaemic genes, establishment of the nucleotide sequence, and identification of the responsible mutations. As elegantly summarised by others in this volume, recombinant technology has allowed such rapid progress that over 50 distinct forms of thalassaemia have now been described at the level of the precise mutation, its effect (often multiple and unexpected) on globin gene function, and the molecular genetic milieu (gene-framework) in which the mutations occur. None of this would have been possible without the ability to isolate genes.

Studies of globin genes also serve as the strongest example of the emerging importance of recombinant DNA technology as a source of novel diagnostic and therapeutic strategies. The details of advances in these areas are summarised by others in this volume. It is now possible to diagnose sickle cell anaemia and most of the common forms of thalassaemia early in gestation by gene blotting analysis, which requires only a small amount of amniotic fluid obtained by routine amniocentesis.

A. Mst Ⅱ cleaves normal, but not sickle β gene:

Codon:
Normal β^A globin: - p r o - g l u - g l u
Normal β^A gene: · C C T · G A G · G A G   Cleaved

Mst Ⅱ recognizes: C C T   N A G   G

Sickle β^S gene: · C C T · G T G · G A G
Sickle β^S globin: - p r o - v a l - g l u   Not cleaved

B. Different fragments are generated from sickle and normal β genes by Mst Ⅱ

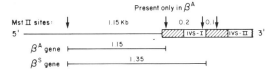

C. Diagnosis by gene blotting:

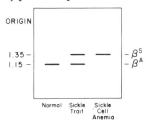

Fig. 2.14 MstII analysis for antenatal diagnosis of sickle cell anaemia. The normal nucleotide sequence through codon 6 contains an MstII recognition site which is abolished by the mutation. Thus an MstII digest of DNA isolated from fetal amniocytes yields different fragment sizes depending on the fetal genotype.

Since fetal amniocytes contain the same complete genome as found in other fetal tissues, gene blotting allows one to investigate inherited diseases without requiring access to a tissue expressing the affected gene. As shown in Figures 2.14 and 2.15, one can take advantage of restriction endonuclease site alterations created by mutations (e.g. sickle cell anaemia), or exquisite advances in oligonucleotide chemistry and molecular hybridisation technology which permit one to prepare specific oligonucleotides hybridising only to the normal or mutant genes (Fig. 2.15). Neither the required background information nor the necessary reagents would be available for these tests without cloned globin genes.

Exploitation of recombinant DNA technology for therapeutic purposes has already begun. Obvious examples include the use of human interferon and human insulin prepared by bacteria expressing recombinant DNA clones of these genes. Growth hormone derived from recombinant DNA methods is undergoing clinical trial, and a number of other therapeutically active proteins prepared by these strategies will be available within a few years. Perhaps less obvious applications are growing out of improved knowledge of gene physiology. For example, modification of DNA bases,

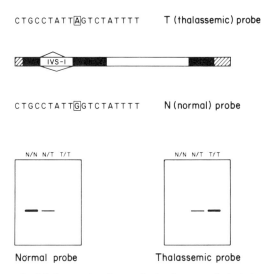

Fig. 2.15   Antenatal diagnosis of thalassaemia using synthetic oligomers. A single base change $(G \rightarrow A)$ within the first intervening sequence results in an alternate splice site and a thalassaemic phenotype. The 19-base synthetic oligomers span the site of the mutation and are identical except at position 10. Under stringent hybridisation conditions, each oligomer hybridises *only* to its exact complement. The Southern blot diagrams the results obtained for each possible fetal genotype.

such as methylation of cytosine residues, has long been suspected as a parameter influencing regulation of gene activity. Recombinant DNA technology permitted precise delineation of the location and physiologic relevance of methylated cytosines in and near genes active in a variety of systems. It became clear that some genes were exquisitely sensitive to methylation of cytosine residues in the region of their promotors. Among these was the gamma globin gene. In the fetus, the gene was active and not methylated, whereas in the adult, the gene was inactive and methylated (Fig. 2.16). The drug 5 azacytidine, a well-known chemotherapeutic agent, had been shown to lead to hypomethylation of DNA. Based on the improved understanding of parameters regulating gene activity, the hypothesis was made that hypomethylation of DNA in vivo by 5 azacytidine would induce gamma chain activity, and increase haemoglobin F synthesis. Increased haemoglobin F synthesis had long been regarded as a therapeutically desired goal, since gamma chains could replace beta chains in patients with beta chain haemoglobinopathies. The predicted effects were, indeed, observed in trials, first in animals and subsequently in human patients with thalassaemia or sickle cell anaemia. Although the use of 5 azacytidine is limited by unacceptable toxicity and long-term risk, the rationale developed for its use has, for the first time, led to controlled and predictable molecular manipulation of gene expression in vivo. The possibility for still other new strategies based on continually

RATIONALE FOR USE OF 5-AZACYTIDINE

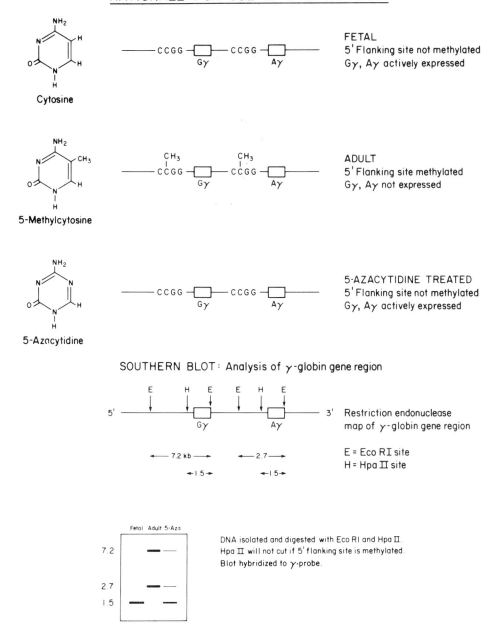

FETAL
5' Flanking site not methylated
Gγ, Aγ actively expressed

Cytosine

ADULT
5' Flanking site methylated
Gγ, Aγ not expressed

5-Methylcytosine

5-AZACYTIDINE TREATED
5' Flanking site not methylated
Gγ, Aγ actively expressed

5-Azacytidine

SOUTHERN BLOT: Analysis of γ-globin gene region

5'   3'   Restriction endonuclease
map of γ-globin gene region

E = Eco RI site
H = Hpa II site

7.2 kb   2.7
1.5   1.5

Fetal Adult 5-Aza

7.2
2.7
1.5

DNA isolated and digested with Eco RI and Hpa II.
Hpa II will not cut if 5' flanking site is methylated.
Blot hybridized to γ-probe.

Fig. 2.16 Rationale for the use of 5-azacytidine. The chemical structures in the left panel show that the carbon at position 5 in the pyrimidine ring is methylated in 5-methylcytosine, but replaced by a nitrogen in 5-azacytidine. Because 5-azacytidine inhibits methylation, DNA synthesised in its presence is hypomethylated at the 5' flanking region, and γ-globin expression occurs. The Southern blot diagram demonstrates the use of a methylation sensitive restriction enzyme to analyse the methylation status of cytosine residues. Because HpaII will not digest the DNA if the cytosine in its recognition sequence is methylated, the fragment sizes generated by a HpaII-EcoRI double digest will differ depending on whether the site is methylated or not.

evolving knowledge of gene physiology is thus extremely exciting, as is the prospect for actual gene transplantation or replacement experiments. The latter are technically and ethically not feasible at the present time. However, the rate of knowledge acquisition in this field has been so high that a viable strategy for gene surgery will undoubtedly develop soon.

The application of molecular genetic technology to haemoglobinopathies is prototypical rather than atypical. The past few years have witnessed the cloning and analysis of genes relevant to many haematologic disorders: clotting factors, immunoglobulins, glucose-6-phosphate dehydrogenase and other intermediary metabolic enzymes, immunoregulating substances such as adenosine deaminase, etc. Conditions as diverse as haemophilia B and antithrombin III deficiency are beginning to be characterised as specific molecular defects. Cytogenetic abnormalities are beginning to be associated with molecular genetic phenomena which may provide the critical clues as to the relationship between these abnormalities and haematologic neoplasia. For example, the Philadelphia chromosome has long been recognised as a diagnostic finding in patients with chronic myelogenous leukaemia. The rearrangement of chromosomes 9 and 22 seen in these disorders has now been shown to occur within an immunoglobulin locus, and, moreover to result in translocation of a cellular proto-oncogene. Oncogenes, as most readers are aware, are DNA segments homologous to viral genes which transform their target cells to neoplastic growth. No unifying hypothesis is currently available to relate the rearrangements of oncogene, immunoglobulin gene, and chromosomes in CML to the cause of the disease, but the association is too strong to be coincidental. Activation of other *onc* genes has been documented in a variety of leukaemias and lymphomas. These advances are discussed elsewhere in this volume. No clear-cut causality between *onc* gene rearrangement or expression and neoplasia in bone marrow tissue has been established. However, the rapid rate at which staggering amounts of information about these genes are being accumulated promises very soon to provide important keys about the neoplastic state.

This very superficial survey of only a few of the applications of molecular genetic technology should convince the reader that molecular genetics provides one of the most powerful tools given to haematologists by the basic sciences in this century. Traditionally, haematology has been the interface speciality for the application of basic science advances to clinical practice. The unique accessibility of blood cells, their distinctive and well-characterised differentiation patterns, and the wealth of information available about inherited and regulatory diseases of the bone marrow have allowed development of a rational pathophysiology amenable to study by new basic science techniques. Because so many haematologic disorders are so well characterised with respect to the specific proteins and biochemical pathways involved, haematology should be particularly well suited for the use of recombinant DNA methods. It is thus advantageous for haematologists to become conversant with the basic language and techniques of the molecular geneticist. We are confident that the same terms and concepts will become the language of the haematologist as well.

REFERENCES

Freifelder D 1983 Molecular biology. Science Books International, Portola Valley, California.
    (Comprehensive basic textbook.)

Goeddel D V, Yelverton E, Ullrich A, Heyneker H L, Miozzari G, Holmes W et al, 1980 Human leukocyte interferon produced by *E. coli* is biologically active. Nature 287: 411–416

Kraus J, Rosenberg L 1982 Purification of low-abundance messenger RNAs from rat liver by polysome immunoadsorption. Proceedings of the National Academy of Sciences of the USA 79: 4015–4019

Maniatis T, Fritsch E F, Sambrook J 1982 Molecular cloning: a laboratory manual. Cold Spring Harbor Laboratory, New York. (Brief discussions of theory, but primarily a detailed procedure manual for cloning and screening. Invaluable for beginners.)

Maxam A M, Gilbert W 1977 A new method for sequencing DNA. Proceedings of the National Academy of Sciences of the USA 74: 560–564

Orkin S H 1984 Prenatal diagnosis of hemoglobin disorders by DNA analysis. Blood 63: 249–253

Parnes J R, Velan B, Felsenfeld A, Ramanathan L, Fenini U, Appella E, Sidman J G 1981 Mouse β_2 microglobulin cDNA clones: A screening procedure for cDNA clones corresponding to rare mRNAs. Proceedings of the National Academy of Sciences of the USA 78: 2253–2257

Sanger F, Nicklen S, Coulson A R 1977 DNA sequencing with chain-terminating inhibitors. Proceedings of the National Academy of Sciences of the USA 74: 5463–5467

Southern E 1975 Detection of specific sequences among DNA fragments separated by gel electrophoresis. Journal of Molecular Biology 98: 503–517

Watson J D 1976 Molecular biology of the gene, 3rd edn. W A Benjamin, Menlo Park, California. (Introduction to fundamentals of nucleic acid chemistry and gene structure and function. A classic work.)

Wu R (ed) 1979 Methods in enzymology: recombinant DNA. Academic Press, New York. (Extensively referenced treatises about cloning and screening techniques.)

3. The molecular pathology of thalassaemia

D. J. Weatherall   J. S. Wainscoat

Since the last edition of *Recent Advances in Haematology* spectacular progress has been made in unravelling the molecular basis of the thalassaemias. Hence, we shall restrict ourselves to an account of the molecular pathology and phenotypic diversity of these disorders and how this information is being used to develop methods for their prevention by prenatal diagnosis. For more extensive coverage of the clinical and genetic aspects of thalassaemia, and its management, the reader is referred to several recent monographs and reviews (Weatherall & Clegg, 1981, 1982; Bank, 1981; Spritz & Forget, 1984; Higgs & Weatherall, 1983; Wood & Weatherall, 1983).

THE GENETIC CONTROL OF NORMAL HUMAN HAEMOGLOBIN

General arrangement of the globin genes

The human haemoglobins all have a tetrameric structure made up of two different pairs of globin chains. Adult and fetal haemoglobins have α chains combined with β chains (Hb A, $\alpha_2\beta_2$), δ chains (Hb A$_2$, $\alpha_2\delta_2$) or γ chains (Hb F, $\alpha_2\gamma_2$). In embryos, α-like chains called ζ chains combine with γ chains to produce Hb Portland ($\zeta_2\gamma_2$), or with ε chains to make Hb Gower 1 ($\zeta_2\varepsilon_2$), and α and ε chains combine to form Hb Gower 2 ($\alpha_2\varepsilon_2$). Fetal haemoglobin is heterogeneous; there are two kinds of γ chains which differ in their amino acid composition at position 136 where they have either glycine or alanine — those with glycine are called $^G\gamma$ chains and those with alanine are called $^A\gamma$ chains. The $^G\gamma$ and $^A\gamma$ chains are the products of separate ($^G\gamma$ and $^A\gamma$) loci. Recently, a detailed picture of the arrangement of the globin genes has been obtained (see Figs 3.1 and 3.2). The non-α globin genes on chromosome 11 form a linked cluster which is spread over approximately 60 Kb (Kb = 1 kilobase or 1000 nucleotide bases); they are arranged in the order $5'$-ε-$^G\gamma$-$^A\gamma$-$\psi\beta1$-δ-β-$3'$. The α-like globin genes are also in a linked cluster, in this case on chromosome 16 in the order $5'$-$\zeta2$-$\zeta1$-$\psi\alpha$-$\alpha2$-$\alpha1$-$3'$. The $\psi\beta1$, $\psi\zeta1$ and $\psi\alpha1$ genes are pseudogenes, that is they have sequences which resemble the β, ζ or α genes but contain mutations which prevent them from functioning as structural loci.

The globin genes have one or more non-coding inserts called intervening sequences (IVS) or introns at the same position along their length. The non-α globin genes contain two introns of 122 to 130 and 850 to 900 base pairs between codons 30 and 31 and 104 and 105 respectively. Similar though smaller introns are found in the α genes. The primary RNA transcript of the globin genes contain both introns and coding regions (exons). While in the nucleus the transcripts from the introns are removed and those from the exons spliced together. The exon/intron junctions all conform to the Chambon rule ($5'$-GT/AG-$3'$) which appears to be a requisite for normal splicing. The mechanisms involved in excision and splicing are reviewed by Lang & Spritz (1983) and Mount & Steitz (1983).

At the 5' non-coding (flanking) region of the globin genes there are two blocks of homology which are found in analagous positions in many species (see Maniatis et al, 1980). The first is AT-rich, a sequence originally found in the histone gene cluster of *Drosophila* and called the Hogness box. The second, called the CCAAT box, is found about 70 base pairs to the 5' end of the genes. These regions are involved in the initiation of transcription and hence play an important role in gene regulation. The 3' flanking regions of the globin genes all have the sequence AATAAA which is believed to be the signal for poly(A) addition to RNA transcripts.

The α globin gene cluster

The structure of the α globin gene complex is shown in Figure 3.1. Each gene is located in a region of homology approximately 4 Kb long, interrupted by two small non-homologous regions (Orkin, 1978; Lauer et al, 1980; Liebhaber et al, 1981b). It is thought that the homologous regions have resulted from gene duplication and that the non-homologous segments may have arisen subsequently by insertion of DNA into the non-coding region round one of the two genes. The exons of the two α globin genes have identical sequences. The first intron in each gene is identical but the second intron of α1 is nine bases longer and differs by three bases from that in the α2 gene (Liebhaber et al, 1980; Michelson & Orkin, 1980; Proudfoot & Maniatis, 1980).

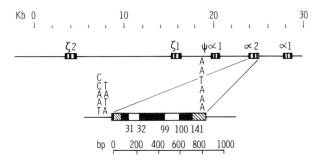

Fig. 3.1   The α globin gene cluster. The α2 gene has been enlarged to show the non-coding regions (hatched), the exons (dark shading), and introns (unshaded).

Despite the high degree of homology between the two genes, the sequences diverge in the 3' untranslated regions, 13 bases beyond the TAA stop codon. These differences provide an opportunity to assess the relative output of the two genes (Orkin & Goff, 1981a; Liebhaber & Kan, 1981). It appears that the production of α2 mRNA exceeds that of α1 mRNA by a factor of 1.5–3.0. The ζ1 and ζ2 genes are also highly homologous. The introns are much larger than those found in the α globin genes and, in contrast to the latter, IVS 1 is larger than IVS 2. In each ζ gene, IVS 1 contains several copies of a simple repeated 14 bp sequence which is similar to sequences located between the two ζ genes (see below) and near the human insulin gene. There are three base changes in the coding sequence of the first exon of ζ1, one of which gives rise to a premature stop codon. Thus it appears that ζ1 is an inactive pseudogene (Proudfoot et al, 1982).

The regions separating and surrounding the α-like structural genes have also been analysed in detail. These sequences, which make up about 90% of the gene cluster, may play a role in the regulation of gene expression. One particular family of repeats (named Alu after the restriction enzyme used for their demonstration) has been found in the intergenic regions. These sequences, which are represented about 300 000 times in the entire genome, are found on either side of the α globin genes. There are two hypervariable regions in the α gene cluster, one downstream from the $\alpha 1$ gene and the other between the $\zeta 2$ and $\zeta 1$ genes (Higgs et al, 1981a). These regions are highly polymorphic; in any individual their size usually varies from one chromosome 16 to the other. Hence they are of particular value for structural and genetic analysis of the α globin gene cluster. Recently, the inter-zeta hypervariable region from the α gene complex has been cloned and sequenced (Goodbourn et al, 1983). The basic structure consists of a directly repeating 36 nucleotide sequence — 5–GGGGCACAGG-CTGTGAGAGGTGCCCGGGACGGCTTTTGT-3′. This falls into two domains which show considerable homology both with each other and with the repeat sequences in the ζ gene introns and the hypervariable region near the human insulin gene. Recent studies indicate that this sequence also has strong homology with a sequence in one of the myoglobin gene introns (Weller et al, 1984). It is likely that rearrangements involving these repeats form the basis for the restriction fragment length polymorphisms generated in these regions (Goodbourn et al, 1983). In addition to the hypervariable regions, several bases have been found to be polymorphic within the α gene cluster and hence to give rise to restriction length polymorphisms (Wainscoat et al, 1983b).

The β globin gene cluster

The complete sequence of the ε, γ, δ and β genes and their flanking regions has been determined (Fritsch et al, 1980; Spritz et al, 1980; Barelle et al, 1980; Slightom et al, 1980). So far, no hypervariable regions have been found but at least six Alu repeat regions have been identified. Like the $\alpha 1$ and $\alpha 2$ gene pairs, the $^G\gamma$ and $^A\gamma$ genes appear to be virtually identical, suggesting a mechanism for gene matching during evolution. The $^G\gamma$ and $^A\gamma$ genes on one chromosome are identical in the region 5′ to the centre of the large intron, yet show greater divergence 3′ to that position. At the boundary between the conserved and divergent regions there is a block of simple sequence which may be a 'hotspot' for the initiation of recombination events which lead to unidirectional gene conversion (Slightom et al, 1980).

The non-α globin gene cluster has single base polymorphisms scattered along its entire length which create new restriction enzyme sites. Hence they generate a series of restriction fragment length polymorphisms (RFLPs) which can be used as markers for linkage analysis of mutations in the cluster (Jeffreys, 1979; Antonarakis et al, 1982a). It appears that there is a relatively small number of common RFLP haplotypes in this gene cluster (used in this sense the term 'haplotype' refers to the presence or absence of polymorphic restriction enzyme sites spread throughout the entire ε-γ-δ-β gene complex and its flanking regions). The haplotypes seem to fall into two domains (marked A and B in Fig. 3.2). On the 5′ side of the β gene, spanning about 32 Kb from the ε gene to the 3′ end of the $\psi\beta$ gene, there are three common patterns of restriction site polymorphisms; those found in Mediterranean and Asian populations are similar. In the region contained in about 18 Kb to the 3′ side of the β

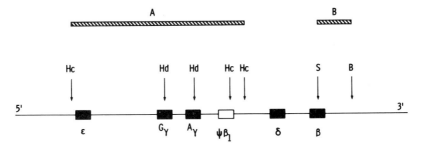

Fig. 3.2   The β globin gene cluster showing the position of the various restriction endonuclease polymorphic sites. The sites are grouped into A or B as shown by the cross-hatching. **Hc**, Hinc II; **Hd**, Hind III; **S**, Sau 96A; **B**, Bam H1.

gene there are three common patterns in Mediterraneans and Asians. Between these regions there is a DNA sequence of about 11 Kb in which there is randomisation of the 5′ and 3′ domains and hence in which a relatively high rate of recombination may occur (Fig. 3.2). Since the association between 5′ and 3′ domains is random, this region may be the only part of the β-gene cluster in which recombination occurs frequently. We shall return to consider the importance of these observations in the molecular analysis of β thalassaemia later in the chapter.

CLASSIFICATION OF THE THALASSAEMIAS

The genetic disorders of haemoglobin are divided into the structural haemoglobin variants and thalassaemias. The thalassaemias are characterised by a reduced rate of synthesis of one or more of the globin chains, and are classified into the α, β, $\delta\beta$ and $\gamma\delta\beta$ types. The α and β thalassaemias are further subdivided into α^0 and β^0 forms in which no α or β chains are produced, and α^+ and β^+ forms in which some α or β chains are synthesised but at a reduced rate. The defective synthesis of one pair of globin subunits leads to imbalanced globin chain production; the characteristic abnormalities of red cell maturation and survival are caused by precipitation of the chains which are produced in excess (see Weatherall & Clegg, 1981). In addition there is a group of mutations which interfere with the switching of fetal to adult haemoglobin production, known collectively as 'hereditary persistence of fetal haemoglobin'. Although of no clinical significance, these conditions are interesting models for studying the regulation of gene switching.

Like all biological classifications this approach to dividing up the haemoglobin disorders is not entirely satisfactory. For example, some structural haemoglobin variants are synthesised at a reduced rate and hence produce the clinical phenotype of thalassaemia; the most important of these is haemoglobin E, probably the commonest abnormal haemoglobin in the world population.

THE α THALASSAEMIAS

Classification and nomenclature

There are two important clinical forms of α thalassaemia, the Hb Bart's hydrops syndrome and Hb H disease (see Weatherall & Clegg, 1981). These conditions result from the interaction of two types of α thalassaemia determinants. Until recently it was customary to call the more severe type, which can be readily identified in heterozygotes, α thalassaemia 1, and the milder determinant, which is either silent or causes only mild red cell changes in heterozygotes, α thalassaemia 2. However, because haemoglobin synthesis and direct gene analyses have shown that the α thalassaemia 1 determinant is characterised by absent α chain synthesis from the affected chromosome it is logical to call this condition α^0 thalassaemia. Similarly, since α thalassaemia 2 causes only a reduced output of α chains from the affected chromosome, it is better to call it α^+ thalassaemia. This nomenclature has the advantage of conforming with that used for the β thalassaemias.

The simplest way in which these two classes of α thalassaemia might arise is shown in Figure 3.3. In this model, α^0 thalassaemia results from the loss (deletion) of both linked α globin genes, whereas α^+ thalassaemia results from the deletion of only one of the pair. It turns out that all the α^0 thalassaemias are due to deletions which remove both α globin genes. However, the α^+ thalassaemias are more complicated. In some cases the genes are deleted whereas in others they are intact but have mutations which inactivate them, either partly or completely. Hence, we can classify α^+ thalassaemia into deletion and non-deletion types. As will be apparent from Figure 3.3, when we talk about 'α thalassaemia genes' or 'determinants' we are describing the α gene products of one of a pair of chromosomes 16. It is much easier to use this approach in describing the α thalassaemias because their phenotypes depend on the relative activities of each of *two* linked α globin genes. In other words, the terms α^0 and α^+ thalassaemia describe *haplotypes* rather than specific lesions at individual α1 or α2 genes.

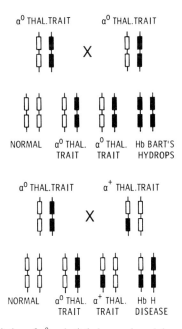

Fig. 3.3   Models for the transmission of α^0 and α^+ thalassaemia and the production of the Hb Bart's hydrops syndrome and Hb H disease. Normal α loci are shown by the open boxes and deleted or otherwise inactivated α genes by the shaded boxes.

α⁰ thalassaemia

The common Southeast Asian (SEA) or Mediterranean (Med) α^0 thalassaemias are caused by different deletions of the α globin gene cluster which start downstream from the $\alpha 1$ globin genes (Fig. 3.4) and extend upstream through the α globin gene cluster, removing the $\alpha 2$ gene, the $\psi\alpha$ gene, and, in one case, one of the ζ globin genes (Pressley et al, 1980c). Each of these deletions leaves the functional ζ gene ($\zeta 2$) intact.

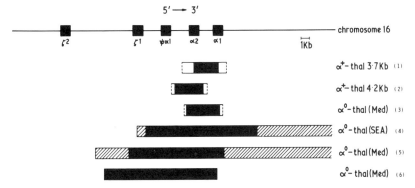

Fig. 3.4   The various α gene deletions responsible for α^+ and α^0 thalassaemia. (1) Orkin et al (1979a), (2) Embury et al (1980), (3) Pressley et al (1980a), (4) and (5) Pressley et al (1980c), (6) Nicholls et al, 1985. **SEA**, Southeast Asian; **Med**, Mediterranean.

Presumably this is why infants with the haemoglobin Bart's hydrops syndrome, who usually are homozygous for these determinants, can produce haemoglobin Portland ($\zeta_2\gamma_2$) and hence survive to term (Pressley et al, 1980c). Two rare α^0 thalassaemias, identified in patients with haemoglobin H disease, involve partial deletions of the $\alpha 1$ gene. In one case, a deletion of 5.2 Kb removes the whole of the $\alpha 2$ gene and the 5' end of the $\alpha 1$ gene; the remainder of the complex is intact (Pressley et al, 1980a). The other deletion was originally described as involving both ζ genes and the $\psi\alpha 1$ and $\alpha 2$ genes together with codons 1–56 of the $\alpha 1$ gene (Orkin & Michelson, 1980). However, reanalysis of this deletion has shown that it does not extend so far upstream as was originally thought; it ends between the two ζ genes thus leaving the $\zeta 2$ gene intact (Nicholls et al, 1985). It is not clear how these deletions have arisen. They may result from unequal crossing over but the reciprocal arrangements have not been observed. It is possible that major rearrangements of this type are lethal, and therefore selected against, or that they are very rare.

α⁺ thalassaemia

As mentioned earlier, the α^+ thalassaemias are of two types, deletion and non-deletion. The latter are so-called because no major deletions can be defined by gene mapping. In the deletion forms, different-sized deletions (3.7 and 4.2 Kb) remove one α globin gene and leave one functional α gene per haploid genome ($-\alpha$) (Fig. 3.4). These lesions are thought to have arisen by unequal crossing over between homologous pairs of chromosomes 16, leaving one α globin gene on one of the pair and three on the other. A 3.7 deletion may involve both α genes and leave a single composite α gene, while the other, 4.2 Kb, removes the $\alpha 2$ gene (Orkin et al, 1979a; Embury et al, 1980). Individuals with three α globin genes on one chromosome and two on the other, i.e. five α globin genes in all have been found in many different populations. The three α globin genes may represent the anti[3.7] or anti[4.2] crossover chromosomes (see below).

Several different 'non-deletion' α^+ thalassaemias have been characterised (Fig. 3.5). One involves the first intron of the $\alpha2$ gene and is characterised by abnormal splicing of the $\alpha2$ globin messenger RNA. It results from the loss of five bases (TGAGG) following the G of the invariant G–T within the donor splice site. This removes a Hph 1 site and so it can be identified by restriction enzyme analysis (Orkin et al, 1981a; Felber et al, 1982). In another, there is a single base mutation which produces a highly unstable α chain variant, Hb Quong Sze, which is rapidly destroyed and hence results in an α thalassaemia phenotype. In this case a leucine codon (CTG) in the $\alpha2$ gene is changed to CCG, which codes for proline (Goossens et al, 1982).

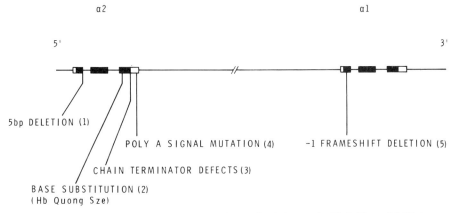

Fig. 3.5   A summary of the different non-deletion forms of α thalassaemia. (1) Orkin et al (1981a), (2) Goosens et al (1982), (3) Weatherall & Clegg (1975), (4) and (5) Higgs et al (1983).

Another group of non-deletion α thalassaemias result from single base mutations in the $\alpha2$ chain termination codon (Weatherall & Clegg, 1975; Hunt et al, 1982). Instead of reading 'stop', the point mutation allows an amino acid to be inserted at what is normally the position of the stop codon, and then sequences at the 3' end of the α globin messenger RNA which are not normally utilised are translated. This results in the production of an α globin chain variant with 31 additional amino acid residues at the C terminal end; the prototype is Hb Constant Spring. In this case the change in the termination codon, UAA to CAA, is reflected by the first amino acid in the elongated α chain which is glutamine, the codon for which is CAA. For reasons which are still not clear, the translation of this extra RNA makes it unstable (Hunt et al, 1982). Hence Hb Constant Spring is produced in very low quantities and is associated with the phenotype of α^+ thalassaemia. In fact, Hb Constant Spring is one of a family of chain termination mutants, all due to single base changes in the α chain termination codon (Weatherall & Clegg, 1981).

Recently, a form of α^+ thalassaemia has been found in eastern Saudi Arabian populations (Pressley et al, 1980b; Higgs et al, 1983). Homozygotes have Hb H disease. This is in contrast to homozygotes for other types of α^+ thalassaemia who have the clinical phenotype of heterozygous α^0 thalassaemia (see below). Hence, the

Saudi Arabian α^+ thalassaemia determinant must be more severe; despite there being four intact α genes, globin chain synthesis studies and messenger RNA analyses suggest that the output of α globin chains and messenger RNA in homozygotes is the equivalent of about one α gene's worth. The molecular basis for this defect has been defined recently (Higgs et al, 1983). One of the linked pair of α globin genes ($\alpha 1$) has a frame-shift mutation which totally inactivates it, while the other ($\alpha 2$) has a mutation in the highly conserved AATAAA sequence in the 3′ non-coding region of the α globin messenger RNA (AATAAA–>AATAAG). This lesion reduces the output from this gene, both in vivo and in vitro, probably because it interferes with polyadenylation of the α globin messenger RNA.

Genotype/phenotype relationships in the α thalassaemias

It is now possible to start to explain the genetic basis for at least some α thalassaemia phenotypes in different populations. For example, since the Hb Bart's hydrops syndrome and Hb H disease usually result from the homozygous or compound heterozygous inheritance of α^0 thalassaemia, they will only be found in populations in which this determinant occurs. Until recently it was difficult to explain the absence of these syndromes in African populations, because a clinical phenotype identical to heterozygous α^0 thalassaemia is found quite frequently in this racial group. The reason is now clear; Africans who appear to be α^0 thalassaemia heterozygotes are in fact homozygous for α^+ thalassaemia. The clinical and haematological results of the loss of two α globin genes are the same whether the two genes are lost from the same chromosome (genotype $--/\alpha\alpha$) or from different pairs of homologous chromosomes (genotype $-\alpha/-\alpha$) (see Higgs & Weatherall, 1983).

Since Hb H disease can result from the interaction of α^0 thalassaemia with either a deletion or non-deletion form of α^+ thalassaemia, or in the case of Saudi Arabs from the homozygous inheritance of a haplotype with two non-deletion forms of α^+ thalassaemia, it is clear that this condition is very heterogeneous at the molecular level (Higgs et al, 1981b). Can the clinical phenotype be related to these different molecular interactions? Although the clinical picture associated with different molecular forms of Hb H disease does not appear to differ significantly, compound heterozygotes for α^0 thalassaemia and non-deletion forms of α^+ thalassaemia have higher levels of Hb H than those who have α^0 thalassaemia and deletion types of α^+ thalassaemia; the reason is not yet clear (see Higgs & Weatherall, 1983).

Another curious anomaly is the variation in the clinical phenotype of individuals who are homozygous for different molecular forms of α^+ thalassaemia. Homozygotes for the deletion forms of α^+ thalassaemia (genotype $-\alpha/-\alpha$) have hypochromic red cells and mild anaemia; their blood picture is similar to heterozygous β thalassaemia. On the other hand, homozygotes for Hb Constant Spring (genotype $\alpha^{CS}\alpha/\alpha^{CS}\alpha$) have a moderately severe haemolytic anaemia and splenomegaly with relatively well haemoglobinised red cells (see Weatherall & Clegg, 1981). Since the haemoglobin Constant Spring mutation reduces the output of α chains to almost zero, there is no a priori reason why these phenotypes should be so different. Recently it has been found that the mechanism by which excess β chains are handled in the two conditions is completely different and that there is very rapid destruction of newly made β chains in haemoglobin Constant Spring homozygotes (Derry et al, 1984). However, it is still not clear why this leads to a more severe phenotype.

α thalassaemia carrier states (see Higgs & Weatherall, 1983)

Alpha^0 thalassaemia carriers have a marked reduction in MCH and MCV values, and approximately 5–10% Hb Bart's in the neonatal period. On the other hand, α^+ thalassaemia heterozygotes have almost normal blood pictures; as a group they have only slightly reduced MCV and MCH values. Although some of them have 1–2% Hb Bart's at birth this is not always the case (Higgs et al, 1980b). These observations have important implications for diagnostic haematology. An inherited hypochromic anaemia with a reduced MCH and MCV and a normal haemoglobin A$_2$ level may result from either the heterozygous state for α^0 thalassaemia or from the homozygous state for α^+ thalassaemia (or occasionally from the heterozygous state for β thalassaemia with a normal Hb A$_2$ level). Globin chain synthesis ratios are the same in the two α thalassaemia disorders and the only way they can be distinguished with certainty is by a family study or gene mapping. It is impossible to identify the heterozygous state for α^+ thalassaemia by haematological criteria, either at birth or in adult life, although the diagnosis can be suspected by globin chain synthesis studies. It can only be identified with certainty by α gene mapping, and then only if it is a deletion type.

Interactions of α thalassaemia with the sickling disorders

It has long been suspected that the coexistence of α thalassaemia can ameliorate sickle cell anaemia. However, earlier reports of this interaction were conflicting. In a recent study the clinical and haematological features of 44 individuals with sickle cell disease and the $-\alpha/-\alpha$ genotype were compared with 44 ($-\alpha/\alpha\alpha$) and 88 ($\alpha\alpha/\alpha\alpha$) age and sex-matched controls with the same disease. The $-\alpha/-\alpha$ group had significantly higher red cell counts and haemoglobin levels and lower MCV and MCH values than the other groups. They also had lower Hb F and higher Hb A$_2$ levels. Although there were no differences between the groups in the incidence of painful crises, the acute chest syndrome and chronic leg ulceration appeared to be less common in the $-\alpha/-\alpha$ group who also had a higher incidence of splenomegaly (Higgs et al, 1982). Essentially similar results were obtained in a smaller study (Embury et al, 1982). More recently it has been found that the red cell survival is significantly prolonged in patients with sickle cell anaemia who also have α thalassaemia (de Ceulaer et al, 1983) but α thalassaemia has little effect on the severity of retinal vascular changes (see also Ch. 4).

Other interactions of α thalassaemia with structural haemoglobin variants

Gene mapping studies have also clarified some previously puzzling observations on the haemoglobin constitution of individuals who are heterozygous or homozygous for α chain variants. For example, it was never clear why homozygotes for Hb J Tongariki have no Hb A if there are two α globin genes per haploid genome. Similarly, it was difficult to understand why some individuals who have inherited α thalassaemia together with Hbs Q, G Philadelphia or Hasharon have the clinical picture of Hb H disease with no haemoglobin A. It is now clear that each of these α chain structural variants can occur on a chromosome from which the other α globin gene is deleted. This explains the absence of Hb A in individuals with Hb Q–H disease ($-\alpha^Q/--$) and in Hb J Tongariki homozygotes ($-\alpha^J/-\alpha^J$). These interactions are discussed in detail by Higgs & Weatherall (1983).

The triplicated α gene arrangement

As mentioned earlier, the $-\alpha^{3.7}$ and $-\alpha^{4.2}$ haplotypes have arisen by unequal crossing over, leaving one α gene on one chromosome 16 and three on the other. Chromosomes carrying triplicated α genes corresponding to the 4.2 Kb $(\alpha\alpha\alpha^{anti4.2})$ and 3.7 Kb deletions $(\alpha\alpha\alpha^{anti3.7})$ have been described (Goossens et al, 1980; Higgs et al, 1980a; Trent et al, 1981). In most cases it appears that the third α gene is functional. Presumably because the slight degree of α globin chain excess can be easily dealt with by proteolysis there are no haematological abnormalities in persons with five α genes. Individuals with sickle cell anaemia and five α genes show no significant differences from those with four α genes. The level of HbS or C is higher in carriers with five α globin genes than in those with four (Higgs et al, 1984). Surprisingly, some triplicated α globin gene arrangements seem to be associated with reduced α chain synthesis (Kanavaakis et al, 1983). It seems likely that one or more of these triplicated α genes carry non-deletion α thalassaemia defects. The homozygous state for the triplicated α gene arrangement has been observed in associated with β thalassaemia; the clinical phenotype is β thalassaemia intermedia (Thein et al, 1984b).

Population genetics and dynamics of the α thalassaemias

The distribution of the α thalassaemia haplotypes has been reviewed recently (Higgs & Weatherall, 1983). The deletion forms of α^+ thalassaemia are widespread and are found in about 35% of some West African populations and in up to 70–90% of certain parts of India and Melanesia. Interestingly, the triplicated α gene arrangement has been found in every population examined so far and occurs in up to 2% of some African populations. Single and triplicated ζ gene arrangements also occur in several populations (Winichagoon et al, 1982). These observations suggest that unequal crossing over at the α or ζ gene complexes may be a fairly common event. Perhaps α globin gene sequence matching occurs by expansion and contraction of gene number by such a process (Maniatis et al, 1980) and that the single gene chromosome has come under strong selection in some populations. The cellular mechanisms whereby this might occur are unknown; it is interesting that the very high frequencies for the single α gene arrangement are always seen in populations where malaria is, or was, common. Thus it is possible that the deletion forms of α^+ thalassaemia have arisen as part of an evolutionary mechanism for α globin gene matching and that selection for the single α gene chromosomes has been much greater than for the triplicated arrangements.

We know even less about the mechanisms underlying the deletion forms of α^0 thalassaemia. It is possible that they have arisen by unequal crossing over. Preliminary data, in which the relationship between different length polymorphisms in the inter-ζ gene hypervariable region is matched with specific α thalassaemia deletions, is compatible with the notion that the unequal crossover which produces the deletion form of α^+ thalassaemia has happened on many occasions, whereas the production of an α^0 thalassaemia lesion is an uncommon event (Winichagoon et al, 1984).

Thus, it is becoming increasingly clear that the α globin genome is by no means fixed. Some of the remarkable variability in the size of the α gene cluster is summarised in Figure 3.6.

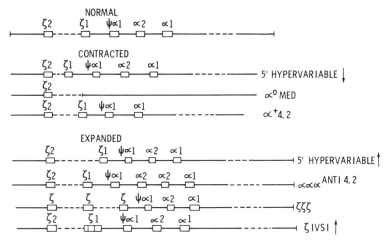

Fig. 3.6 A summary of some of the variations in size of the α globin gene cluster. The mechanisms include length polymorphisms in the hypervariable regions, deletions, triplicated α or ζ genes, and variation in the size of the introns of the ζ genes.

β THALASSAEMIA

The β thalassaemias are characterised by reduced (β^+) or absent (β^0) synthesis of β globin (Weatherall & Clegg, 1981). Recent sequence analyses of cloned β genes has demonstrated more than 30 different β thalassaemia mutations. Paradoxically, the clinical phenotypes associated with many of these lesions are not yet defined.

The first β thalassaemia genes to be analysed were unselected other than that they came from patients with β^0 or β^+ thalassaemia. However, the discovery of the association of specific patterns of restriction enzyme polymorphisms in the β globin gene cluster within populations (RFLP haplotypes, as defined earlier in this chapter) now allows a more direct approach to the problem of selection of genes for examination (Orkin et al, 1982a). It has been found that these haplotypes tend to be linked to specific β thalassaemia mutations within a particular population. Thus, cloning genes from different 'haplotype backgrounds' appears to be an efficient way of finding new mutations. A list of mutations which cause β thalassaemia, as known at the time of going to press, is shown in Table 3.1.

β^0 thalassaemia (Fig. 3.7)

Gene deletion
A 619-nucleotide deletion extending from the 3' third of the second intervening sequence through 209 bases of 3' flanking DNA has been demonstrated to be a common cause of β^0 thalassaemia in some Indian populations (Orkin et al, 1979b; Thein et al, 1984a).

Nonsense mutations
Two types of β^0 thalassaemia are caused by nonsense mutations. The first, originally found in a Chinese patient, is characterised by a mutation in codon 17 which causes

Table 3.1 β Thalassaemia mutations (from Orkin et al 1984, Collins & Weissman 1984)

Deletion
619 bp at 3' end of β gene
Chain termination mutations
Codon 15
Codon 17
Codon 39
Frameshift mutations
Codon 6 (−1 bp)
Codon 8 (−2 bp)
Codon 8 (+1 bp)
Codon 16 (−1 bp)
Codon 41/42 (−4 bp)
Codon 44 (−1 bp)
RNA processing mutations
Splice junction
   Donor   *IVS-1* GT → AT or TT. *IVS-2* GT → AT
   Acceptor *IVS-1* 25 bp deletion. *IVS-2* AG → GG
Consensus region
  IVS-1 donor (CAGGTTɢGт) G → C. T → C
Internal IVS
  IVS-1   110 G → A
  IVS-2   705 T → G
  IVS-2   745 C → G
Cryptic splice site in exon
  Codon 24 T → A (Silent)
  Codon 26 G → A (Hb E; Glu → Lys)
  Codon 27 G → T (Hb Knossos; Ala → Ser)
Poly A addition site   AATAAA → AACAAA
Transcription mutations
  −87   C → G
  −88   C → T
  −29   A → G
  −28   A → C
  −28   A → G

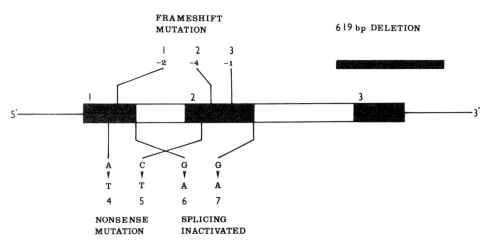

Fig. 3.7 Some of the mutations responsible for β^0 thalassaemia (see Table 3.1). The specific mutations are numbered and are found in the following references: **1** Orkin et al (1981b), **2** Orkin S H, personal communication (1983), **3** Kinniburgh et al (1982), **4** Chang & Kan (1979), **5** Orkin & Goff (1981), Trecartin et al (1981), Moschonas et al (1981), **6** Orkin et al (1982a), **7** Baird et al (1981).

premature termination of the β globin chain at this position (Chang & Kan, 1979). The second is caused by a mutation in codon 39 (Moschonas et al, 1981; Orkin & Goff, 1981b; Trecartin et al, 1981). This is the common form of β^0 thalassaemia in Sardinia, and occurs widely throughout the Mediterranean.

Frameshift mutations
Triplets of three bases code for individual amino acids. Loss or insertion of one or two bases, or more than three, throws the reading frame out of sequence and may generate premature chain termination codons. Hence, frameshift mutations of this type give rise to β^0 thalassaemia. The first of these lesions to be reported has a dinucleotide deletion in the codon for amino acid 8 which produces a new termination codon at the position of the new 21st codon. Such mutations appear to be relatively common causes of β^0 thalassaemia. They have all occurred in regions of short, direct repeats, consistent with their origin by replication slippage mechanisms (Efstratiadis et al, 1980; Orkin et al, 1982a).

Splicing inactivation
In addition to mutations within the protein coding sequences, β^0 thalassaemia is caused by base substitutions in the intervening sequences (IVS1 and IVS2) of the β chain gene (Baird et al, 1981; Orkin et al, 1982a; Treisman et al, 1982, 1983). In each case a G→A transition at position 1 of IVS1 and IVS2 have been found. These mutations change the GT sequence which, as mentioned earlier, is invariant at all 5′ splice sites. Hence they completely inactivate normal splicing. The IVS2 mutation is one of the few β thalassaemia mutations that is directly detectable by restriction enzyme analysis—in this case with the enzyme Hph 1 (Baird et al, 1981).

β^+ thalassaemia (Fig. 3.8)

Aberrant splicing
Abnormal processing of some of the β globin mRNA precursor may result in a deficiency of functional β globin mRNA and hence a β^+ thalassaemia phenotype. This usually arises from the generation of a cryptic splice site so that a variable amount of β globin messenger RNA is abnormally spliced. Hence it contains intron sequences

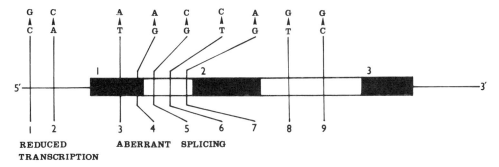

Fig. 3.8 Some of the mutations responsible for β^+ thalassaemia (see Table 3.1). The specific mutations are numbered and are found in the following references: **1** Orkin et al (1982a), **2** Ponz et al (1982), **3** Goldsmith et al (1983), **4** Orkin et al (1982b), **5** Treisman et al (1983), **6** Orkin et al (1982a), **7** Spritz et al (1981), Westaway & Williamson (1981), **8** Spence et al (1982), **9** Orkin et al (1982a).

which make it useless as a template for globin synthesis. The overall deficit of β chains reflects the relative amounts of normally and abnormally spliced β globin messenger RNA.

Several β^+ thalassaemia genes have been studied by analysing the expression of the cloned mutant gene after its introduction into cultured cells using a suitable vector (Busslinger et al, 1981; Fukumak et al, 1983; Treisman et al, 1983). For example, the molecular basis of a form of β^+ thalassaemia in which there is a $G \rightarrow A$ substitution 21 nucleotides from the 3' splice junction of intron 1 (Spritz et al, 1981; Westaway & Williamson, 1981) has been analysed by studying its expression in HeLa cells. The first intron of the variant globin gene is incorrectly spliced in about 90% of the mRNA because an additional 3' splice site is created by the point mutation. The remaining 10% of the mRNA is correctly spliced and can therefore be translated to synthesise normal β globin (Fig. 3.9). Mutations at IVS1 positions 5 and 6 interfere with splicing by activating three cryptic splice sites. An IVS2 position 745 mutation creates a new GTdinucleotide and hence a sequence that produces a new 5' splice site; this in turn leads to the activation of a cryptic 3' splice site at IVS2, position 579. Hence the principle RNA produced by this gene contains extra sequences, comprising IVS2 nucleotides 580–744 inserted between exons 2 and 3.

Mutations in the coding sequences may also cause abnormal RNA processing. It has been known for some time that the common structural variant, Hb E, produces a mild form of β thalassaemia (see Weatherall & Clegg 1981). Sequence analysis of a β^E gene revealed only the expected $GAG \rightarrow AAG$ change in codon 26, but no other mutations (Orkin et al, 1982b). However, expression of a β^E gene in HeLa cells showed abnormal RNA processing characterised by slow excision of IVS1 and

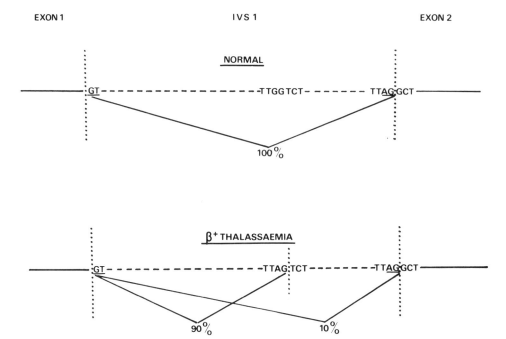

Fig. 3.9   The mechanisms of normal splicing and the abnormal splicing which occurs in one form of β^+ thalassaemia.

alternative splicing into exon 1 at a cryptic donor sequence within which the codon 26 nucleotide substitution resides. Similarly, a T→A change in the third position of codon 24 of a β thalassaemia gene activates a 5' splice site and results in a 75% decrease in the accumulation of normally processed β globin mRNA, thereby causing a β^+ thalassaemia phenotype (Goldsmith et al, 1983).

Reduced transcription
So far, two β^+ thalassaemia mutations have been reported which seem to affect the rate of transcription of the β genes. Mutagenesis studies of eukaryotic genes have identified 5' DNA regions necessary for normal levels of transcription: the ATA box sequence at -30 base pairs relative to the cap site and more distal sequences at -70 to -90 (see earlier section). Two β thalassaemia mutants have been found in these regions. The first involves a C→G change at position -87 leading to decreased RNA production when studied in an in vivo cell expression system (Orkin et al, 1982a; Treisman et al, 1983). The homozygous state for this mutation has not yet been reported; as judged by findings in compound heterozygotes, the clinical phenotype is a mild form of β^+ thalassaemia (Wainscoat et al, 1983d). The second, an A→C change at position -28, was reported in a Kurdish Jew; no information about the phenotype was given (Ponz et al, 1982).

THALASSAEMIA INTERMEDIA

The term thalassaemia intermedia describes clinical phenotypes which are more severe than the thalassaemia traits, but are milder than transfusion-dependent major forms of the illness. There are many different types of thalassaemia or interactions between thalassaemia and structural haemoglobin variants which can produce this clinical picture (see Weatherall & Clegg, 1981). However, because prenatal diagnosis programmes for β thalassaemia are being widely applied, the most important type of thalassaemia intermedia is the unusually mild form of homozygous β thalassaemia, i.e. individuals who have a moderate degree of anaemia, splenomegaly, haemoglobin findings compatible with homozygous β thalassaemia, and whose parents both have elevated levels of Hb A_2.

Since the anaemia of homozygous β thalassaemia is caused by imbalanced globin chain synthesis and the effects of precipitated α chains on red cell maturation and survival, there are several ways in which the condition might be ameliorated. The coexistence of α thalassaemia would reduce the magnitude of the excess of α chains and lead to more effective erythropoiesis. A relatively mild defect in β chain production would also cause less globin chain imbalance. The same effect could be mediated by particularly efficient γ chain production after birth, or by an unusually active proteolytic system in the red cell precursors, capable of removing relatively large amounts of precipitated α globin chain. Recent studies in Cyprus indicate that the majority of cases of homozygous β thalassaemia intermedia can be explained by the coinheritance of α thalassaemia or by the interaction of unusually mild forms of β thalassaemia (Wainscoat et al, 1983d).

The association of α thalassaemia and homozygous β thalassaemia
In a small pilot study using globin gene analysis it was found that a group of Cypriots with homozygous β thalassaemia intermedia all had either deletion or non-deletion

forms of α thalassaemia (Weatherall et al, 1981). To extend these observations, two larger controlled studies have been carried out (Wainscoat et al, 1983a, 1983c). The first, in Cypriots, showed that 14 out of 27 patients with β thalassaemia intermedia had coexistent α thalassaemia, in contrast to only four out of 30 thalassaemia major patients. A similar study in Sardinian patients demonstrated α thalassaemia in six out of eight patients with β thalassaemia intermedia compared with six out of 17 patients with β thalassaemia major. Therefore, in both populations the coinheritance of α thalassaemia ameliorates homozygous β thalassaemia but the effect is less marked in Sardinians. The most obvious explanation for this difference is that the predominant form of β thalassaemia in Cyprus is β^+ whereas in Sardinia it is β^0. A further large study correlating the clinical findings of patients homozygous for β thalassaemia with their α genotypes has confirmed that the deletion of two α genes may convert severe homozygous β^0 thalassaemia to milder forms, ranging from a later-presenting but still transfusion-dependent type to a non-transfusion-dependent variety (Furbetta et al, 1983). This study also showed that patients with deletion of two α genes had significantly higher Hb A_2 levels than those with either a normal α genotype or those with deletion of a single α gene.

The association of α thalassaemia with heterozygous β thalassaemia

Are there any haemotaological changes in β thalassaemia carriers which indicate that they may also have one or more α thalassaemia genes? This question has been studied by determining the α globin genotypes of 55 β thalassaemia heterozygotes (Kanavakis et al, 1982). A comparison of the haematological and haemoglobin synthesis findings of individuals with normal α genotypes ($\alpha\alpha/\alpha\alpha$) with those with one ($-\alpha/\alpha\alpha$) or two ($-\alpha/-\alpha$) α genes deleted showed that the latter groups have more balanced globin synthesis, higher haemoglobin levels, and larger better haemoglobinised red cells. This suggests that the degree of globin chain imbalance is a significant factor in determining the red cell characteristics in heterozygous β thalassaemia. Furthermore, screening programmes for β thalassaemia based only on the detection of a low MCV could miss cases of the interaction of α and β thalassaemia. The diagnosis should be suspected in an individual with a raised haemoglobin A_2 level and relatively normal red cell indices. In patients heterozygous for β thalassaemia with three α genes deleted ($-\alpha/--$) the haemoglobin level and red cell indices are significantly lower than in the other α-genotype groups. This finding presumably reflects not only a limitation of α chain production to one quarter of normal, but also that the cell is once more in chain imbalance, albeit in the opposite direction, with excess β chains.

It is probable that interactions of heterozygous β thalassaemia with α thalassaemia account for at least some of the reported cases of 'isolated high Hb A_2'. In a study of 10 Sardinian β^0 thalassaemia heterozygotes, all of whom presented with normal red blood cell indices and increased Hb A_2 levels, eight were found to have the α genotype $-\alpha/-\alpha$, and the remaining 2 had single α gene deletions, $-\alpha/\alpha\alpha$ (Melis et al, 1983).

'Mild' β thalassaemia

Recently, a mild form of β thalassaemia has been defined in Mediterranean populations. The initial observation was a description of 14 patients in 10 families, all originating from a small area of northern Portugal (Tamagnini et al, 1983). Clinically, the homozygotes ranged from asymptomatic (diagnosed on account of anaemia in pregnancy) to moderately anaemic and they were all found to have low levels of Hb F (~20%), indicating a relatively mild deficit in β globin production. All the patients were found to be homozygous for a particular RFLP haplotype which had been previously associated with a $T \rightarrow > C$ substitution at position six of IVS1 (Orkin et al, 1982a). In view of the origin of the patients it was suggested that this form of β^+ thalassaemia should be called the Portuguese type. Subsequently, this same haplotype has been found in patients with β thalassaemia intermedia characterised by low Hb F levels from other Mediterranean countries. The DNA of similar patients of Cypriot, Portuguese and Turkish origin has now been shown by hybridisation with a synthetic olignucleotide probe to have the same IVS1 mutation (Wainscoat et al, 1983d).

THE $\delta\beta$ AND $\gamma\delta\beta$ THALASSAEMIAS AND HEREDITARY PERSISTENCE OF FETAL HAEMOGLOBIN (HPFH)

With the exception of the rare $\gamma\delta\beta$ thalassaemias, this group of disorders are much milder than the β thalassaemias and hence are of less clinical interest. However, they provide models for studying the genetic control of the switch from fetal to adult haemoglobin.

Notation and classification
The notation and classification of this group of conditions is confusing and needs revision. Hitherto, it has been customary to categorise them as $\delta\beta$ thalassaemia or HPFH depending on the haematological changes, globin chain synthesis ratios and intercellular distribution of Hb F, and to further divide them, according to the structure of the Hb F which is produced, into ${}^G\gamma$, ${}^A\gamma$ or ${}^G\gamma{}^A\gamma$ varieties. Using gene mapping techniques, it has been possible to further subdivide them into deletion and non-deletion types.

It is now apparent that division of conditions which result from long deletions of the $\gamma\delta\beta$ globin gene cluster into $\delta\beta$ thalassaemia and HPFH is artificial; in effect they form a spectrum of disorders in which there is a variable (but never complete) compensation for absent δ and β chain production by ${}^G\gamma$, or ${}^G\gamma$ and ${}^A\gamma$ chain production. Hence, if we define thalassaemia as a disorder characterised by imbalanced globin chain synthesis, they are all forms of $\delta\beta$ thalassaemia. Furthermore, it is illogical to designate them by the type of Hb F that is produced. ${}^G\gamma$ $\delta\beta$ thalassaemia should be called $({}^A\gamma\delta\beta)^0$ thalassaemia; it is the ${}^A\gamma$, δ and β genes which are inactive (i.e. thalassaemic) and the ${}^G\gamma$ genes which remain active! Similarly ${}^G\gamma{}^A\gamma$ $\delta\beta$ thalassaemia should be called $(\delta\beta)^0$ thalassaemia. Perhaps the term HPFH should be restricted to those conditions in which there is no globin chain imbalance in homozygotes. Hopefully, as the molecular basis for more of these disorders is worked out it will become possible to classify them more logically.

In the brief summary which follows we shall retain the notation which is in current use in the literature (see Weatherall & Clegg, 1981).

Deletion forms of $\delta\beta$ thalassaemia and pancellular HPFH
The $\delta\beta$ thalassaemias are milder than the β thalassaemias because there is efficient compensation for the absence of β chain synthesis by γ chain production. Homozygotes have the clinical phenotype of thalassaemia intermedia with 100% Hb F;

heterozygotes have hypochromic microcytic red cells and between 5 and 15% Hb F. The condition is currently subdivided into $^G\gamma$ and $^G\gamma^A\gamma$ $(\delta\beta)^0$ forms according to the structure of the Hb F. They all result from deletions which remove the β and δ globin genes (Fig. 3.10). In the case of $^G\gamma$ $\delta\beta$ thalassaemia the deletions also involve the $^A\gamma$ genes. In one form of $^G\gamma$ $\delta\beta$ thalassaemia most of the region between the $^A\gamma$ and δ globin genes is inverted and there are small deletions involving the $^A\gamma$ and δ genes (Jones et al, 1980). $^G\gamma^A\gamma$ HPFH is very similar to $^G\gamma^A\gamma$ $\delta\beta$ thalassaemia except that heterozygotes have higher levels of Hb F and homozygotes have a haematological picture and a degree of globin chain production similar to heterozygous β thalassaemia; like $\delta\beta$ thalassaemia homozygotes they have 100% Hb F. $^G\gamma^A\gamma$ HPFH is also heterogeneous. Each type results from a different-length deletion of the $\gamma\delta\beta$ gene cluster (for references see Wood & Weatherall (1983) and the caption to Fig. 3.10).

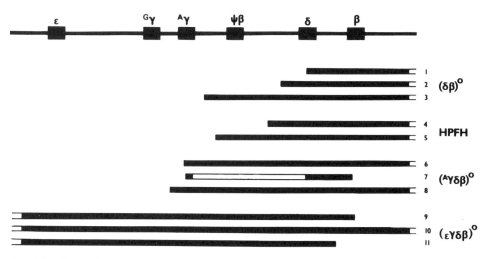

Fig. 3.10   Some of the deletions responsible for $\delta\beta$ thalassaemia and hereditary persistence of fetal haemoglobin. The nomenclature is discussed in the text. The specific mutations are numbered and are found in the following references: **1** Ottolenghi et al (1979), **2** Ottolenghi et al (1982), **3** Wainscoat et al (1984), **4** and **5** Tuan et al (1980), **6** Jones et al (1980), **7** Jones et al (1981), **8** Fritsch et al (1979), **9** Orkin et al (1981b), **10** Piratsu et al (1983b), Fearon et al (1983), **11** Van der Ploeg et al (1980).

The particular interest of these conditions is that they are all associated with relatively effective γ chain synthesis in adults. The reason why long deletions of the β and δ globin genes are associated with persistent γ chain synthesis is still not clear. Based on the observation that, as a group, the HPFH deletions (i.e. those with a relatively higher output of γ chains) tend to extend further upstream than those which produce $\delta\beta$ thalassaemia, attempts have been made to define putative regulatory regions in the β globin gene cluster which may or may not be involved in the deletion. One approach has been to compare the 5′ ends of the HPFH and $\delta\beta$ thalassaemia deletions which are closest together. It has been found that the two deletions end in a pair of Alu 1 repeats 5′ to the δ gene (Jagadeeswaren et al, 1982; Ottolenghi et al, 1982). The HPFH deletion ends in the 5′ Alu 1 repeat of the bipolar pair and the $\delta\beta$ thalassaemia in the 3′ Alu 1 repeat. Thus the two deletions have endpoints which are within 500 nucleotides of each other; the larger deletion causes a significantly higher output of γ chains than the smaller one. Hence, unless the different phenotypes are due entirely to differences in the DNA sequences at the 3' end of the deletions, the 5' Alu 1 repeat and the non-repetitive DNA connecting it to the 3' Alu 1 repeat must be considered to have an important regulatory role. Recently, Tuan et al (1983) have shown that the deletions which cause HPFH are situated at least 52–57 Kb from the 3' extremity of the β globin genes, while those which cause $\delta\beta$ thalassaemia are shorter and located no more than 5–10 Kb from the β gene. They suggest that the nature of the DNA brought into the vicinity of the γ genes by these deletions may be an important factor in determining the phenotype. On the other hand, three $^G\gamma$ $\delta\beta$ thalassaemias have been shown to have different 3' sequences yet their phenotypes are essentially the same (Trent et al, 1984).

A newly characterised form of $\delta\beta$ thalassaemia (Wainscoat et al, 1984) apparently breaks the rule that the putative 'regulatory region' is absent from all deletion types of HPFH but is present in the $\delta\beta$ thalassaemias. Heterozygotes show characteristics intermediate between $\delta\beta$ and HPFH (20% Hb F, almost normal red cell indices, and $\alpha/\text{non}-/\alpha$ globin chain synthesis ratios of 1.3), but compound heterozygotes with β^+ thalassaemia have the clinical picture of thalassaemia intermedia, much more typical of a patient with the $\delta\beta/\beta^+$ thalassaemia genotype. The tentative explanation for these findings is that there has been a deletion of the same regulatory region that is responsible for the HPFH phenotype (i.e. relatively high γ chain production), but that the proximity of the deletion 3' to the $^A\gamma$ gene has down-regulated this locus; this idea is supported by the $^G\gamma:^A\gamma$ ratio of the Hb F of 3:1. Using a similar argument it has been suggested that an individual with $^G\gamma$ $\delta\beta$ thalassaemia would have had the HPFH phenotype (due to loss of the presumptive regulatory region) if it were not for the loss of the $^A\gamma$ gene; the $^G\gamma$ gene, even if fully active, may not be able to compensate fully for the lack of β chain production (Jones et al, 1980). It appears, therefore, that deletion forms of $\delta\beta$ thalassaemia and HPFH form a continuous spectrum of conditions in which there is a variable level of persistent γ chain production which may depend on the precise length of the particular deletion.

$\gamma\delta\beta$ thalassaemia

The $\gamma\delta\beta$ thalassaemias have only been observed in heterozygotes. They are characterised by neonatal haemolysis and haematological changes of β thalassaemia with a normal haemoglobin A_2 level in adults (Weatherall & Clegg, 1981). Four deletions have now been described in this condition, all originating 5' to the $\gamma\delta\beta$ gene complex. Two of these (Piratsu et al, 1983a, Fearon et al, 1983) remove the entire complex; the other two end within the complex, in one case including the 5' end of the β gene and hence inactivating it (Orkin et al, 1981b), in the other case ending 2 Kb upstream from the β gene (Van der Ploeg et al, 1980). Interestingly, in the latter case the β gene does not function in vitro, although when cloned and expressed in vivo it appears to function normally (Kioussis et al, 1983). This may mean that a normally inactive locus has been brought into contact with the intact β locus on the affected chromosome, thus altering its expression, possibly by a local change in chromatin configuration.

Non-deletion forms of HPFH

So far, this section has dealt with conditions which result from major deletions of the $\gamma\delta\beta$ globin gene cluster. Because of the major changes in the structure of this region of the genome which must result from deletions of this magnitude, the value of these conditions as models for analysing the regulation of globin gene switching may be limited. However, there are forms of HPFH in which there appear to be no major deletions in the $\gamma\delta\beta$ globin gene cluster.

It is now apparent that non-deletion HPFH is extremely heterogeneous (see Weatherall & Clegg, 1981; Old et al, 1982a). Formal genetic studies have shown that at least three of these conditions, the Greek and British forms of HPFH and $^G\gamma\beta^+$ HPFH result from lesions which lie nearer to or within the $\gamma\delta\beta$ gene cluster. However, detailed gene mapping studies and sequence analysis of extensive regions of the cluster have failed to reveal any consistent changes. Furthermore, it has been found recently that determinants for some non-deletion forms of HPFH are definitely not linked to the $\gamma\delta\beta$ globin gene cluster (Gianni et al, 1983; Thein et al, 1983, unpublished data). This is the first indication that gene loci outside the globin gene cluster are involved in their regulation. Clearly, the definition of these 'distant' regulatory loci offers a new approach to analysis of the regulation of the human globin genes during development.

PRENATAL DIAGNOSIS

Currently, prenatal diagnosis of the haemoglobin disorders is carried out by fetal blood sampling and estimation of the relative rates of globin chain synthesis by radiolabelling. This method, which directly measures the product of the mutant globin genes, has been used successfully over the last few years (see Alter, 1981). However, fetal blood sampling is not possible until about the 18th week of pregnancy. This means a long period of uncertainty for the mother and, if required, a relatively difficult therapeutic abortion. Prenatal diagnosis has also been performed by restriction enzyme analysis of fetal DNA from cells obtained by amniocentesis (Kazazian et al, 1980). Amniocentesis cannot be done early in pregnancy, and it is difficult to obtain sufficient cells for gene analysis without first growing them in culture; again this means a late termination of pregnancy. Recently, however, techniques have become available for obtaining fetal DNA from biopsies of trophoblastic villi in the first trimester of pregnancy (see Williamson et al, 1981), and it is possible to obtain up to 100 μg of pure fetal DNA between the 6th and 10th week of pregnancy (Old et al, 1982b). If further experience shows that this procedure is safe for the mother and fetus, it may revolutionise the prenatal diagnosis of the haemoglobin disorders and other single-gene conditions.

Currently, only a few types of thalassaemia and structural haemoglobin variants are amenable to direct identification by restriction enzyme mapping (Weatherall & Old, 1983). This is possible only if a base change alters a restriction enzyme site, or if there is a major gene deletion or rearrangement. Hence, this approach is only feasible for identifying sickle cell anaemia, a few β thalassaemia mutations, the haemoglobin Lepore thalassaemias and the deletion forms of α thalassaemia. Most of the β thalassaemias and haemoglobin E, globally the most common structural haemoglobin variant, cannot yet be diagnosed directly by restriction enzyme analysis. Hence, another approach is required.

There are at least 13 polymorphic restriction enzyme sites scattered among the β globin gene cluster (see Antonarakis et al, 1982a, 1982b). The restriction fragment length polymorphisms (RFLPs) generated by these sites can be used as linkage markers for antenatal diagnosis of the β globin disorders. There are two main types of RFLPs in the β gene cluster. First, there are allele-linked RFLPs, i.e. polymorphisms linked in *cis* to specific globin gene mutations. However, linkage disequilibrium of this type is uncommon, and so far only two examples have been found; a Hpa I polymorphism and the β^S mutation in West Africans and a Bam H1 polymorphism and β^0 thalassaemia in Sardinia (Kan & Dozy, 1978; Kan et al, 1980). Thus, in most populations it is necessary to establish linkages between a particular β globin gene mutation and a RFLP in the β globin gene cluster by carrying out a family study before prenatal diagnosis. Hence, RFLP linkage analysis cannot be used for prenatal diagnosis of many firstborn children of 'at risk' parents. Furthermore, even if family members are available they may not have an appropriate RFLP for establishing linkage with a particular globin gene mutation. Recent studies in the UK indicate that RFLP linkage analysis will be feasible in about 50% of Cypriot families and 80% of Asian families (Old et al, 1984).

Despite these problems, first trimester diagnosis of β thalassaemia or sickle cell anaemia by analysis of fetal DNA obtained by trophoblast biopsy has been carried out recently (Old et al, 1982b). Since that publication we have performed over 50 successful prenatal diagnoses on trophoblast DNA, including one set of twins.

Recently, it has been possible to construct short oligonucleotide probes which will identify single point mutations in DNA by hybridisation under carefully controlled conditions. Probes for the sickle cell and common Mediterranean β^+ thalassaemia mutations have been used successfully to identify these lesions in genomic DNA (Conner et al, 1983; Orkin et al, 1983; Piratsu et al, 1983a). If these probes can be used to identify specific β thalassaemia mutations in heterozygous parents, the development of a battery of probes against the various point mutations responsible for the common β thalassaemias should make first trimester prenatal diagnosis of these conditions feasible for first pregnancies. This approach, together with the development of biotin-labelled probes, may make the global approach to the prevention of thalassaemia a possibility.

POSTSCRIPT: MOLECULAR THERAPY

Although great progress has been made in defining the molecular pathology of thalassaemia, and in applying this information to its prenatal diagnosis, no major advances in therapy have arisen from this work. Specific gene therapy is still a long way off. In the meantime, attempts are being made to reactivate the γ globin genes as an approach to the management of sickle cell anaemia and β thalassaemia.

Recently, 5-azacytidine has been used to 'stimulate' γ chain production in β thalassaemia and sickle cell anaemia (Ley et al, 1982, 1983). This approach was based on the observation that baboons who are made acutely anaemic increase their fetal haemoglobin level quite dramatically and this effect is augmented if they are given 5-azacytidine. The latter is a demethylating agent and it was reasoned that, since active genes are demethylated, the drug might be working by demethylation of the γ globin genes in adults. Ley and his colleagues reported a modest increase in fetal haemoglobin following the use of this agent and suggest that further clinical trials are justified. There is considerable controversy as to whether the drug works by demethylation or by killing some of the later red cell precursors. Its effect becomes evident within 24 to 48 hours of administration, suggesting that it is acting on late, differentiated erythroid precursors and that demethylation could be at least one mechanism involved in the increase of γ chain synthesis (Charache et al, 1983). On the other hand, hydroxyurea, which is not a demethylating agent, also augments γ chain production in anaemic monkeys (Letvin et al, 1984). Thus it is also possible that these agents cause increased γ chain production by killing more mature erythroid progenitors, thus leaving earlier progenitors, in which γ globin gene expression is more highly retained, to undergo premature terminal differentiation.

The observation that it is possible to reactivate γ chain synthesis, albeit to a modest degree, by pharmacological agents is encouraging. On the other hand, 5-azacytidine is a toxic drug and has well-defined tumour-producing properties (Harrison et al, 1983). There seems little place for developing clinical trials with this agent, although clearly this general approach to reactivation of γ chain synthesis must be investigated further.

Acknowledgement
We thank Mrs Janet Watt for her help in preparing and typing this manuscript.

REFERENCES

Alter B P 1981 Prenatal diagnosis of haemoglobinopathies: a status report. Lancet ii: 1151–1155

Antonarakis S E, Boehm C D, Giardina P J V, Kazazian H H 1982a Non-random association of polymorphic restriction sites in the β globin gene cluster. Proceedings of the National Academy of Sciences of the United States of America 79: 137–141

Antonarakis S E, Orkin S H, Kazazian H H et al 1982b Evidence for multiple origins of the β^E-globin gene in Southeast Asia. Proceedings of the National Academy of Sciences of the United States of America 79: 6608–6611

Baird M, Driscoll C, Schreiner et al 1981 A nucleotide change at a splice junction in the human β-globin gene is associated with β-thalassemia. Proceedings of the National Academy of Sciences of the United States of America 78: 4218–4221

Bank A 1981 Globin gene structure in disorders of hemoglobin. Progress in Hematology 12: 25–42

Barelle F E, Shoulders C C, Proudfoot N J 1980 The primary structure of the human ε-globin gene. Cell 21: 621–626

Busslinger M, Moschonas N, Flavell R A 1981 β^+-thalassemia: aberrant splicing results from a single point mutation in an intron. Cell 27: 289–298

Chang J C, Kan Y W 1979 β^0 thalassaemia, a nonsense mutation in man. Proceedings of the National Academy of Sciences of the United States of America 76: 2886–2889

Charache S, Dover G, Smith K, Talbot C C, Moyer M, Boyer S 1983 Treatment of sickle cell anemia with 5-azacytidine results in increased fetal hemoglobin production and is associated with nonrandom hypomethylation of DNA around the γ-δ-β-globin gene complex. Proceedings of the National Academy of Sciences of the United States of America 80: 4842–4846

Collins F S, Weisman S M 1984 The molecular genetics of human hemoglobin Progress in Nucleic Acids Research in a Molecular Biology (in press)

Conner B J, Reyes A A, Morin C, Itakura K, Teplitz R L, Wallace R B 1983 Detection of sickle β^S-globin allele by hybridization with synthetic oligonucleotides. Proceedings of the National Academy of Sciences of the United States of America 80: 278–282

De Ceulaer K, Higgs D R, Weatherall D J, Hayes R J, Serjeant B E, Serjeant G R 1983 Alpha thalassemia reduces the hemolytic rate in homozygous sickle cell disease. New England Journal of Medicine 309: 189–190

Derry S, Wood W G, Pippard M et al 1984 Hematologic and biosynthetic studies in homozygous hemoglobin Constant Spring. Journal of Clinical Investigation

Efstratiadis A, Posakony J W, Maniatis T et al 1980 The structure and evolution of the human β-globin gene family. Cell 31: 653–668

Embury S H, Dozy A M, Miller J et al 1982 Concurrent sickle-cell anemia and α-thalassemia: effect on severity. New England Journal of Medicine 306: 270–274

Embury S H, Miller J A, Dozy A M, Kan Y W, Chan V, Todd D 1980 Two different molecular organisations account for the single α-globin gene of the α-thalassemia-2 genotype. Journal of Clinical Investigation 66: 1319–1325

Fearon E R, Kazazian H H, Waber P G et al 1983 The entire β globin gene cluster is deleted in a form of $\gamma\delta\beta$ thalassaemia. Blood 61: 1273–1278

Felber B K, Orkin S H, Hamer D H 1982 Abnormal RNA splicing causes one form of α thalassemia. Cell 29: 892–902

Fritsch E F, Lawn R M, Maniatis T 1979 Characterisation of deletions which affect the expression of foetal globin genes in man. Nature 279: 598–603

Fritsch E F, Lawn R M, Maniatis T 1980 Molecular cloning and characterization of the human β-like globin gene cluster. Cell 19: 959–972

Fukumaki Y, Ghosh P K, Benz E J et al 1982 Identification of an abnormally spliced messenger RNA in erythroid cells from patients with β-thalassaemia and monkey cells expressing a cloned β^+ thalassemia gene. Cell 28: 585–593

Furbetta M, Tuveri T, Rosatacelli C et al 1983 Molecular mechanism accounting for milder types of thalassaemia major. Journal of Paediatrics 103: 35–39

Gianni A M, Bregni M, Cappellini M D et al 1983 A gene controlling fetal hemoglobin expression in adults is not linked to the non-α globin cluster. EMBO Journal 2: 921–926

Goldsmith M E, Humphries R K, Ley T, Cline A, Kantor J A, Nienhuis A W 1983 'Silent' nucleotide substitution in a β^+-thalassaemia globin gene activates splice site in coding sequence RNA. Proceedings of the National Academy of Sciences of the United States of America 80: 2318–2322

Goodbourn S E Y, Higgs D R, Clegg J B, Weatherall D J 1983 Molecular basis of length polymorphism in the human α-globin gene complex. Proceedings of the National Academy of Sciences of the United States of America 80: 5022–5026

Goossens M, Dozy A M, Embury S H et al 1980 Triplicated α-globin loci in humans. Proceedings of the National Academy of Sciences of the United States of America 77: 518–521

Goossens M, Lee K Y, Leibhaber S A, Kan Y W 1982 Globin structural mutant $\alpha^{\text{Leu–Pro}}$ is a novel cause of α-thalassaemia. Nature 296: 864–865

Harrison J J, Anisowicz A, Gadi I K, Raffeld M, Sanger R 1983 Azacytidine-induced tumorigenesis of CHEF/18 cells: correlated DNA methylation and chromosome changes. Proceedings of the National Academy of Sciences of the United States of America 80: 6606–6610

Higgs D R, Clegg J B, Weatherall D J, Serjeant B E, Serjeant G R 1984 Interaction of the $\alpha\alpha\alpha$ globin gene haplotype and sickle haemoglobin. British Journal of Haematology 58: 671–678

Higgs D R, Aldridge B E, Lamb J et al 1982 The interaction of alpha-thalassemia and homozygous sickle-cell disease. New England Journal of Medicine 306: 1411–1446

Higgs D R, Goodbourn S E Y, Wainscoat J S, Clegg J B, Weatherall D J 1981a Highly variable regions of DNA flank the human α globin genes. Nucleic Acids Research 9: 4213–4223

Higgs D R, Goodbourn S E Y, Proudfoot N J, Lamb J, Clegg J B, Weatherall D J 1983 The functional significance of a poly(A) signal mutation. Nature 306: 398–400

Higgs D R, Old J M, Pressley L, Clegg J B, Weatherall D J 1980a A novel α-globin gene arrangement in man. Nature 284: 632–635

Higgs D R, Pressley L, Aldridge B et al 1981b Genetic and molecular diversity in nondeletion Hb H disease. Proceedings of the National Academy of Sciences of the United States of America 78: 5833–5837

Higgs D R, Pressley L, Clegg J B et al 1980b Detection of alpha thalassaemia in Negro infants. British Journal of Haematology 46: 39–46

Higgs D R, Weatherall D J 1983 Alpha thalassaemia. In: Piomelli S, Yachnin S (eds) Current topics in hematology, 4. Alan R Liss Inc, New York, p 37–97

Hunt D M, Higgs D R, Winichagoon P, Clegg J B, Weatherall D J 1982 Haemoglobin Constant Spring has an unstable α chain messenger RNA. British Journal of Haematology 51: 405–413

Jagadeeswaran P, Tuan D, Forget B G, Weissman S M 1982 A gene deletion ending at the midpoint of a repetitive DNA sequence in one form of hereditary persistence of fetal haemoglobin. Nature 296: 469–470

Jeffreys A J 1979 DNA sequence variants in the $^{G}\gamma$-, $^{A}\gamma$-, δ- and β-globin genes of man. Cell 18: 1–10

Jones R W, Old J M, Trent R J, Clegg J B, Weatherall D J 1980 Major rearrangement in the human β-globin gene cluster. Nature 291: 39–44

Jones R W, Old J M, Trent R J, Clegg J B, Weatherall D J 1981 Restriction mapping of a new deletion responsible for $^{G}\gamma(\delta\beta)^0$ thalassaemia. Nucleic Acids Research 9: 6813–6825

Kan Y W, Dozy A M 1978 Polymorphisms of DNA sequence adjacent to human β-globin structural gene: relation to sickle mutation. Proceedings of the National Academy of Sciences of the United States of America 75: 5631–5635

Kan Y W, Lee K Y, Furbetta M, Angius A, Cao A 1980 Polymorphism of DNA sequences in the beta globin gene region. Application to prenatal diagnosis of β^0 thalassaemia in Sardinia. New England Journal of Medicine 302: 185–188

Kanavakis E, Metaxatou-Mavromati A, Kattamis C, Wainscoat J S Wood W G 1983 The triplicated α gene locus and β thalassaemia. British Journal of Haematology 54: 201–207

Kanavakis E, Wainscoat J S, Wood W G et al 1982 The interaction of α thalassaemia with heterozygous β thalassaemia. British Journal of Haematology 52: 465–473

Kazazian H H, Phillips J A, Boehm C D, Vik T A, Mahoney M J, Ritchey A K 1980 Prenatal diagnosis of β-thalassemias by amniocentesis: Linkage analysis using polymorphic restriction endonuclease. Blood 56: 926–930

Kinniburgh A J, Maquat L E, Schedt T, Rachmilewitz E, Ross J 1982 mRNA-deficient β^0-thalassaemia results from a single nucleotide deletion. Nucleic Acids Research 10: 5421–5427

Kioussis D, Vanin E, deLange T, Flavell R A, Grosveld F G 1983 β-globin gene inactivation by DNA translocation in $\gamma\beta$-thalassaemia. Nature 306: 662–666

Lang K M, Spritz R A 1983 RNA splice site selection: evidence for a $5' > 3'$ scanning model. Science 222: 1351–1355

Lauer J, Shen C-K J, Maniatis T 1980 The chromosomal arrangement of human α-like globin genes: sequence homology and α-globin gene deletions. Cell 20: 119–130

Letvin N L, Linch D C, Beardsley G P, McIntyre K W, Nathan D G 1984 Hydroxyurea augments fetal hemoglobin production in anemic monkeys. New England Journal of Medicine 310: 869–873

Ley T J, de Simone J, Anagnou N P et al 1982 5-azacytidine selectively increased γ-globin synthesis in a patient with β^+ thalassemia. New England Journal of Medicine 307: 1469–1475

Ley T J, deSimone J, Noguchi C T et al 1983 5-Azacytidine increased γ-globin synthesis and reduces the proportion of dense cells in patients with sickle cell anemia. Blood 62: 370–380

Liebhaber S A, Goossens M J, Kan Y W 1980 Cloning and complete nucleotide sequence of human $5'$-α-globin gene. Proceedings of the National Academy of Sciences of the United States of America 77: 7054–7058

Liebhaber S A, Goossens M, Kan Y W 1981b Homology and concerted evolution at the $\alpha 1$ and $\alpha 2$ loci of human α-globin. Nature 290: 24–29

Liebhaber S A, Kan Y W 1981 Differentiation of the mRNA transcripts originating from the $\alpha 1$- and $\alpha 2$-globin loci in normals and α-thalassemics. Journal of Clinical Investigation 68: 439–446

Maniatis T, Fritsch E F, Lauer J, Lawn R M 1980 The molecular genetics of human hemoglobins. Annual Review of Genetics 14: 145–178

Melis M A, Piratsu M, Galanello R, Furbetta A, Tuveri T, Cao A 1983 Phenotypic effect of heterozygous α and β^0-thalassemia interaction. Blood 62: 226–229

Michelson A M, Orkin S H 1980 The $3'$ untranslated regions of the duplicated human α-globin genes are unexpectedly divergent. Cell 22: 371–377

Moschonas N, DeBoer E, Grosveld F G et al 1981 Structure and expression of a cloned β^0 thalassemic globin gene. Nucleic Acids Research 9, 4391–4401

Mount S, Steitz J 1983 Lessons from mutant globins. Nature 303: 380–381

Nicholls R D, Higgs D R, Clegg J B, Weatherall D J 1985 α^0-Thalassaemia due to recombination between the $\alpha 1$-globin gene and an Alu-I repeat. Blood (in press)

Old J M, Ayyub H, Wood W G, Clegg J B, Weatherall D J 1982a Linkage analysis of nondeletion hereditary persistence of fetal hemoglobin. Science 215: 981–982

Old J M, Petrou M, Modell B, Weatherall D J 1984 Feasibility of antenatal diagnosis of β thalassaemia by DNA polymorphisms in Asian Indian and Cypriot populations. British Journal of Haematology 57: 255–263

Old J M, Ward R H T, Petrou M, Karagozlu F, Modell B, Weatherall D J 1982b First trimester diagnosis for haemoglobinopathies: a report of 3 cases. Lancet ii: 1413–1416

Orkin S H 1978 The duplicated human α-globin genes lie close together in cellular DNA. Proceedings of the National Academy of Sciences of the United States of America 75: 5950–5954

Orkin S H, Antonarakis S E, Kazazian H H 1984 Polymorphism and molecular pathology of the human beta-globin gene. Progress in Hematology 13: 49–74

Orkin S H, Goff S C 1981a The duplicated human α-globin genes: Their relative expression as measured by RNA analysis. Cell 24: 345–351

Orkin S H, Goff S C 1981b Nonsense and frameshift mutations in β^0-thalassemia detected in cloned β-globin genes. Journal of Biological Chemistry 256: 9782–9784

Orkin S H, Goff S C, Hechtman R L 1981a Mutation in an intervening sequence splice junction in man. Proceedings of the National Academy of Sciences of the United States of America 78: 5041–5045

Orkin S H, Goff S C, Nathan D G 1981b Heterogeneity of DNA deletion in $\gamma\delta\beta$-thalassemia. Journal of Clinical Investigation 67: 878–884

Orkin S H, Kazazian H H, Antonarakis S E et al 1982a Linkage of β-thalassaemia mutations and β-globin gene polymorphisms with DNA polymorphisms in human β-globin gene cluster. Nature 296: 627–631

Orkin S H, Kazazian H H, Antonarakis S E, Ostrer H, Goff S C, Sexton I B 1982b Abnormal RNA processing due to the exon mutation of the β^E globin. Nature 300: 768–769

Orkin S H, Markham A F, Kazazian H H 1983 Direct detection of the common Mediterranean β thalassemis gene with synthetic DNA probes. An alternative approach for prenatal diagnosis. Journal of Clinical Investigation 71: 775–779

Orkin S H, Michelson A 1980 Partial deletion of the α-globin structural gene in human α-thalassaemia. Nature 286: 538–540

Orkin S H, Old J, Lazarus H et al 1979a The molecular basis of α thalassemia: Frequent occurrence of dysfunctional alpha loci detected by restriction endonuclease mapping. Cell 17: 33–42

Orkin S H, Old J M, Weatherall D J, Nathan D G 1979b Partial deletion of β-globin gene DNA in certain patients with β^0-thalassemia. Proceedings of the National Academy of Sciences of the United States of America 76: 2400–2404

Ottolenghi S, Giglioni B, Comi P et al 1979 Globin gene deletion in HPFH $\delta^0\beta^0$ thalassemia and Hb Lepore disease. Nature 278: 654–657

Ottolenghi S, Giglioni B, Taramelli R et al 1982 Molecular comparison of $\delta\beta$ thalassemia and hereditary persistence of fetal hemoglobin DNAs: Evidence of a regulatory area? Proceedings of the National Academy of Sciences of the United States of America 79: 2347–2351

Piratsu M, Kan Y W, Cao A, Conner B J, Teplitz R L, Wallace R B 1983a Prenatal diagnosis of β-thalassemia. Detection of a single nucleotide mutation in DNA. New England Journal of Medicine 309: 284–287

Piratsu M, Kan Y W, Lin C C, Baine R M, Holbrook C T 1983b Hemolytic disease of the newborn caused by a new deletion of the entire β-globin cluster. Journal of Clinical Investigation 72: 602–609

Poncz M, Ballantine M, Solowiejczyk D, Barak I, Schwartz E, Surrey S 1982 β-thalassemia in a Kurdish Jew. Journal of Biological Chemistry 257: 5994–5996

Pressley L, Higgs D R, Aldridge B, Metaxatou-Mavromati A, Clegg J B, Weatherall D J 1980a Characterisation of a new α thalassemia 1 defect due to a partial deletion of the α globin gene complex. Nucleic Acids Research 8: 4889–4898

Pressley L, Higgs D R, Clegg J B, Perrine R P, Pembrey M E, Weatherall D J 1980b A new genetic basis for hemoglobin-H disease. New England Journal of Medicine 303: 1383–1388

Pressley L, Higgs D R, Clegg J D, Weatherall D J 1980c Gene deletions in α thalassemia prove that the 5' ς locus is functional. Proceedings of the National Academy of Sciences of the United States of America 77: 3586–3589

Proudfoot N J, Gil A, Maniatis T 1982 The structure of the human zeta-globin gene and a closely linked, nearly identical pseudogene. Cell 31: 553–563

Proudfoot N J, Maniatis T 1980 The structure of a human α-globin pseudogene and its relationship to α globin gene. Cell 21: 537–544

Slightom J L, Blechl A E, Smithies O 1980 Human fetal $^G\gamma$- and $^A\gamma$-globin genes: Complete nucleotide sequences suggest that DNA can be exchanged between those duplicated genes. Cell 21: 627–638

Spence S E, Pergolizzi R G, Donovan-Peluso M, Kosche K A, Dobkin C S, Bank A 1982 Five nucleotide changes in the large intervening sequence of a β globin gene in a β^+ thalassaemia patient. Nucleic Acids Research 10: 1283–1294

Spritz R A, DeRiel J K, Forget B G, Weissman S M 1980 Complete nucleotide sequence of the human δ-globin gene. Cell 21: 639–646

Spritz R A, Forget B G 1984 The thalassemias: molecular mechanisms of human genetic disease. American Journal of Human Genetics (in press)

Spritz R A, Jagadeeswaran P, Choudhary P V et al 1981 Base substitution in an intervening sequence of a β^+-thalassemic human globin gene. Proceedings of the National Academy of Sciences of the United States of America 78: 2455–2459

Tamagnini G P, Lopes M C, Castanheira M E, Wainscoat J S, Wood W G 1983 β^+ thalassaemia — Portuguese type: clinical, haematological and molecular studies of a newly defined form of β thalassaemia. British Journal of Haematology 54: 189–200

Thein S L, Old J M, Wainscoat J S, Petrou M, Modell B, Weatherall D J 1984a Population and genetic studies suggest a single origin for the Indian deletion β^0 thalassaemia. British Journal of Haematology 57: 271–278

Thein S L, Al-Hakim I, Hoffbrand A V 1984b Thalassaemia intermedia: a new molecular basis. British Journal of Haematology 56: 333–337

Trecartin R F, Leibhaber S A, Chang J C et al 1981 β^0 thalassaemia in Sardinia is caused by a nonsense mutation. Journal of Clinical Investigation 68: 1012–1016

Treisman R, Orkin S H, Maniatis T 1983 Specific transcription and RNA splicing defects in five cloned β-thalassaemia genes. Nature 302: 591–596

Treisman R, Proudfoot N J, Shander M, Maniatis T 1982 A single-base change at a splice site in a β^0-thalassemic gene causes abnormal RNA splicing. Cell 29: 903–911

Trent R J, Higgs D R, Clegg J B, Weatherall D J 1981 A new triplicated α-globin gene arrangement in man. British Journal of Haematology 49: 149–152

Trent R J, Jones R W, Clegg J B, Weatherall D J, Davidson R, Clegg J B 1984 $(^A\gamma\delta\beta)^0$ thalassaemia: similarity of phenotype in four different molecular defects, including one newly described. British Journal of Haematology 57: 279–290

Tuan D, Feingold E, Newman M, Weissman S M, Forget B G 1983 Different 3' end point deletions causing $\delta\beta$-thalassemia and hereditary persistence of fetal hemoglobin: implications for the control of γ-globin gene expression in man. Proceedings of the National Academy of Sciences of the United States of America 80: 6937–6941

Tuan D, Murnane M J, deRiel J K, Forget B G 1980 Heterogeneity in the molecular basis of hereditary persistence of foetal haemoglobin. Nature 285: 335–337

Van der Ploeg L H T, Donings A, Oort M, Roos D, Bernini L, Flavell R A 1980 γ-β-thalassemia studies showing that deletion of the γ- and δ-genes influences β-globin gene expression in man. Nature 283: 637–642

Wainscoat J S, Bell J I, Old J M 1983a Globin gene mapping studies in Sardinian patients homozygous for β^0 thalassaemia. Molecular Biology and Clinical Medicine 1: 1–10

Wainscoat J S, Higgs D R, Kanavakis E et al 1983b Association of two DNA polymorphisms in the α-globin gene cluster; implications for genetic analysis. American Journal of Human Genetics 35: 1086–1089

Wainscoat J S, Kanavakis E, Wood W G et al 1983c Thalassaemia intermedia — the interaction of α and β thalassaemia. British Journal of Haematology 53: 411–416

Wainscoat J S, Old J M, Weatherall D J, Orkin S H 1983d The molecular basis for the clinical diversity of β thalassaemia in Cypriots. Lancet i: 1235–1237

Wainscoat J S, Old J M, Wood W G, Rent R J, Weatherall D J 1984 Characterisation of an Indian $(\delta\beta)^0$ thalassaemia 58: 353–360

Weatherall D J, Clegg J B 1975 The α-chain termination mutants and their relationship to the α-thalassaemias. Philosophical Transactions of the Royal Society, London (Biol) 271: 411–455

Weatherall D J, Clegg J B 1981 The thalassaemia syndromes, 3rd edn. Blackwell Scientific Publications, Oxford

Weatherall D J, Clegg J B 1982 Thalassemia revisited. Cell 29: 7–9

Weatherall D J, Old J M 1983 Antenatal diagnosis of the haemoglobin disorders by analysis of fetal DNA. Molecular Biology and Medicine 1: 151–155

Weatherall D J, Pressley L, Wood W G, Higgs D R, Clegg J B 1981 Molecular basis for mild forms of homozygous beta-thalassaemia. Lancet i: 527–529

Weller P, Jeffreys A J, Wilson V, Blanchetot A 1984 Organization of the myoglobin gene. EMBO Journal 3: 439–446

Westaway D, Williamson R 1981 An intron nucleotide sequence variant in a cloned β^+-thalassaemia gene. Nucleic Acids Research 9: 1777–1788

Williamson R, Eskdale J, Coleman D V, Niazi M, Loeffler F E, Modell B 1981 Direct gene analysis of chorionic villi; a possible technique for first trimester diagnosis of haemoglobinopathies. Lancet ii: 1127

Winichagoon P, Higgs D R, Goodbourn S E Y, Clegg J B, Weatherall D J 1982 Multiple arrangement of the human embryonic human zeta globin genes. Nucleic Acids Research 10: 5853–5868

Winichagoon P, Higgs D R, Goodbourn S E Y, Clegg J B, Weatherall D J, Wasi P 1984 The molecular basis of α-thalassaemia in Thailand. The EMBO Journal 3: 1813–1818

Wood W G, Weatherall D J 1983 Developmental genetics of the human haemoglobins. Biochemical Journal 215: 1–10

Note added to press proofs

Since this review went to press several other mutations of the α or β globin gene clusters have been reported which are of considerable importance in relating structural abnormalities to abnormal function of these gene clusters. Two varieties of β^0 thalassaemia have been reported which appear to be associated with unusually high levels of haemoglobin F production in heterozygotes (Gilman et al, British Journal of Haematology 56: 339, 1984; Padanilam et al, Blood 64: 941, 1984). Single base mutations have been described upstream of the γ globin genes in the $^G\gamma\,\beta^+$ and Greek forms of HPFH which may be regions which are involved in the neonatal suppression of γ globin gene synthesis (Collins et al, Proceedings of the National Academy of Sciences USA 81: 4894, 1984; Giglioni et al, EMBO Journal 3: 2641, 1984). It has been found that the so-called 'silent' form of β thalassaemia is due to a mutation which is not linked to the β globin gene cluster; the β globin gene is structurally normal and functions normally in an in vitro transcription system (Semenza et al, Cell 39: 123, 1984). A new mutation which causes β^+ thalassaemia, a C$\rightarrow$T change at position 654 of IVS-2, has been found in a Chinese individual (Takihara et al, Biochemical and Biophysical Research Communications 121: 324, 1984). A form of α^0 thalassaemia has been observed in Black populations which is due to a long deletion which involves both the ζ and α globin genes (Felice et al, Blood, 63: 1253, 1984). Finally, a new Ava II polymorphism has been found in strong linkage disequilibrium with the common form of β thalassaemia in Mediterranean populations. This new polymorphism greatly increases the feasibility of prenatal diagnosis in these populations (Wainscoat et al, Lancet ii: 1299, 1984).

4. Sickle cell disease

G. R. Serjeant

Advances in clinical medicine are often linked to the development or application of new techology. The rapid development and sophistication of recombinant DNA technology has contributed both to diagnostic procedures and also to elucidating some of the genetic factors responsible for the remarkable variability of homozygous sickle cell (SS) disease. The application of nuclear magnetic resonance has increased the understanding of intracellular polymer formation and consequently the pathophysiology of sickle cell disease. X-ray crystallographic studies have suggested new models for the structure of the HbS polymer and a variety of physical techniques have been used to investigate the delay time in aggregation of HbS molecules which is critically important to the sickling process.

However, not all advances have depended on the application of new or sophisticated technology. Much knowledge is also being acquired by studies of the natural history of the disease. In Jamaica and in the United States, the monitoring of large patient populations over long periods of time is providing important new information on the natural history of the disease, and the determinants of severity. These patient populations are also allowing the application of statistical and epidemiological techniques not previously possible in sickle cell disease. Some of the areas of new knowledge will be highlighted in this brief review.

DIAGNOSIS

Genotypes

There are four principle genotypes of sickle cell disease. Homozygous sickle cell (SS) disease in which the sickle cell gene is inherited from both parents, sickle cell-haemoglobin C (SC) disease in which the Hb S gene is inherited from one parent and the Hb C gene from the other, and two forms of sickle cell-β thalassaemia. These forms result from the inheritance of the sickle cell gene and one of two different β thalassaemia genes, the β^0 thalassaemia gene in which there is an absence of β chain synthesis, and the β^+ thalassaemia gene with only a partial suppression of β chain synthesis. The production of normal β chains results in the synthesis of 20–30% Hb $A(\alpha_2\,\beta_2)$ in sickle cell-β^+ thalassaemia in Black populations. This markedly inhibits sickling and sickle cell-β^+ thalassaemia is a mild condition with clinical similarities to SC disease whereas sickle cell-β^0 thalassaemia is generally a severe condition similar to SS disease. It is vital to differentiate the two forms of sickle cell-β thalassaemia since they have different clinical and haematological features and a different prognosis. The electrophoretic patterns in these conditions are shown in Figure 4.1.

Differentiation of the major genotypes depends upon alkaline and acid haemoglobin electrophoresis, Hb A_2 quantitation, and family studies and presents little problem in

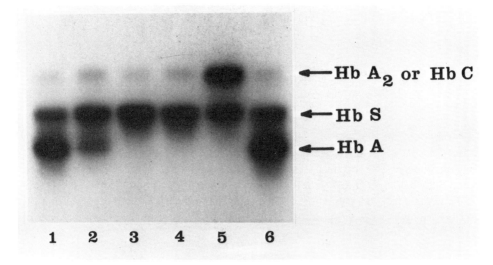

Fig. 4.1   Electrophoretic patterns of the four major genotypes of sickle cell disease. 1 Sickle cell trait control. 2 Sickle cell–β^+ thalassaemia. 3 Homozygous sickle cell disease. 4 Sickle cell–β^0 thalassaemia. 5 Sickle cell–haemoglobin C disease. 6 Sickle cell trait control (courtesy of Dr P. Milner).

the postnatal period. In the neonatal period the differentiation of SS disease, $S\beta^0$ thalassaemia, and $S\beta^+$ thalassaemia may be difficult in the absence of family studies.

Prenatal diagnosis
Prenatal diagnosis is more complex and has, in the past, required fetal blood sampling and sophisticated techniques to detect small amounts of β chain. The application of recombinant DNA technology has revolutionised prenatal diagnosis which may now be made by direct examination of DNA from amniotic fluid cells.

The first such approach used the restriction endonuclease Hpa I which recognised a remote restriction site linked to the Hb S gene (Kan & Dozy, 1978a). This linkage occurred in over 80% of individuals and the diagnosis of SS disease could be made in approximately 70% of offspring but preliminary testing of both parents was necessary to confirm the presence of linkage (Kan & Dozy, 1978b). The restriction enzyme Dde I directly identifies the site of the sickle mutation (Chang & Kan, 1981; Geever et al, 1981), by recognising the sequence CTNAG (where N is any nucleotide). In Hb S there is a substitution of thymidine for adenine (CCT–GAG–GAG to CCT–GTG–GAG) and so this recognition site is lost. However the multitude of Dde I cleavage sites produces many small DNA fragments which are difficult to analyse and the large amounts of DNA required necessitates culture with a 5-week delay in reaching the diagnosis. The restriction enzyme Mst II is also specific for the sickle mutation cleaving DNA at the sequence CCTNAGG and therefore giving greater specificity than Dde I (Chang & Kan, 1982; Orkin et al, 1982). This method has the advantage of dealing with larger DNA fragments, increased sensitivity and the ability to make the diagnosis in only 2 weeks. These procedures utilise DNA obtained by amniocentesis but DNA may be obtained directly from chorionic villi (Williamson et al, 1981) allowing the diagnosis to be made as early as 7 weeks of gestation (Goosens et al, 1983).

Role of prenatal diagnosis

The technology available for prenatal diagnosis may have advanced dramatically but the role of this procedure is only poorly defined. Apart from cultural, religious, and logistic considerations, the scientific basis for abortion of SS children is highly questionable. In transfusion-dependent homozygous β^0 thalassaemia, a severe clinical course may be predicted but in SS disease, the determinants of severity in adults are poorly understood and impossible to predict in the prenatal period. In carefully selected families with only SS children, in which the parents desire further children but wish to ensure that they are normal, prenatal diagnosis may offer a welcome option.

PATHOPHYSIOLOGY

Oxygen tension, pH, and hypertonicity are recognised as determinants of in vitro sickling, but are difficult to quantitate in the in vivo situation. Irreversibly sickled cell (ISC) counts have been used as an indicator of in vivo sickling although these correlate only poorly with most clinical events. Furthermore studies of cell deformability during deoxygenation indicate that resistance to filtration increases before sickling occurs (Messer & Harris, 1970), suggesting that subtle cellular changes precede the morphological changes of sickling.

Polymer formation

The sickle deformity is presumed to result from the organisation of deoxygenated Hb S molecules into polymers, although secondary membrane changes may occur later. Controversy continues on the structure of the Hb S polymer although there is general agreement that molecules of deoxy Hb S are stacked in a gradual helix around a vertical axis and that such structures measure 20–22 nm in diameter (Crepeau et al, 1978). Proposed models however have included tubular or solid structures with 6, 8, 14, or 16 molecules in each layer.

Analysis of the physical factors influencing molecular aggregation has also contributed to understanding the sickling process. Using a variety of physical techniques capable of detecting polymer, Hofrichter et al (1974, 1976) were able to show a considerable delay before the sudden increase in haemoglobin aggregation. They invoked a model incoporating processes of nucleation, growth and alignment (Fig. 4.2) which is potentially of great importance because of the physical characteristics determining this delay time. The rate-limiting step in polymerisation was calculated to be proportional to the 10th or 15th power of deoxy Hb S activity implying that a decrease of haemoglobin concentration from 35 to 34 g/dl would be associated with a doubling of the delay time before the onset of polymer formation.

Nuclear magnetic resonance, by measuring the amount of freely rotating haemoglobin molecules or the amount immobilised in polymer, has the potential of quantitating intracellular polymerised Hb S. As expected, the fraction of polymer increased with falling oxygen saturation but it was possible to demonstrate polymer in cells from SS disease at oxygen saturations greater that 95% (Noguchi et al, 1980). Part of the explanation results from the non-ideal behaviour of proteins at very high concentrations (Noguchi & Schechter, 1981), haemoglobin within the red cell at a

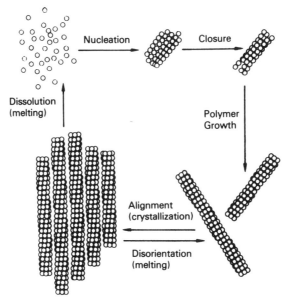

Fig. 4.2   Mechanism of deoxyhaemoglobin S aggregation as proposed by Hofrichter et al (1976).

concentration of 34 g/dl behaving chemically as if it were almost 100 times more concentrated than it actually is.

Red cell heterogeneity
Red cells vary in size, shape, density, and haemoglobin composition, both within individuals and within populations with SS disease. This red cell heterogeneity has long been recognised morphologically but may be quantitated by stractan or phthalate gradients to separate subpopulations of red cells with different characteristics. Using this technique it has been possible to show that ISCs become consistently more dense upon deoxygenation and that similar changes occur with reversibly sickled cells (Fabry & Nagel, 1982). It will be of interest to see whether such dense cell populations are relevant to the pathophysiology of sickle cell disease.

Endothelial adherence
Oxygenated Hb S containing red cells adhere abnormally to cultured human or bovine endothelium (Hoover et al, 1979; Hebbel et al, 1980a) which may be a further factor in the pathophysiology of sickle cell disease. The degree of adherence varies between individuals and has been claimed to correlate with indices of vaso-occlusion in SS disease (Hebbel et al, 1980b). However this adherence is markedly influenced by fibrinogen and other acute phase reactants and it is unclear to what extent this adherence is simply reflecting such factors.

CLINICAL ASPECTS

Acute splenic sequestration
This is one of the most important determinants of morbidity and mortality in young children with SS disease, and was the commonest single cause of death in the first year

of life in the Jamaican cohort study (Rogers et al, 1978a). Attacks occur as early as 10 weeks and become increasingly uncommon after the age of 5 years. The spleen suddenly enlarges trapping the circulating red cell mass with an acute fall in circulating haemoglobin level and peripheral circulatory failure. Attacks may be extremely rapid progressing to death within 4–5 hours. They are frequently recurrent with continuing mortality during second and third episodes (Topley et al, 1981). Treatment of the acute event is by transfusion to maintain peripheral oxygen delivery. Following transfusion the red cells trapped in the spleen are usually released with a marked increase in circulating haemoglobin level, and decrease in the size of the spleen. Recurrent attacks may be prevented by prophylactic splenectomy (Emond et al, 1984) but it is vital that such children be given protection against pneumococcal infection. The aetiology of these attacks is unknown, so it is impossible to prevent first attacks of acute splenic sequestration. In the Jamaican cohort study, parents have been taught to detect splenomegaly and hence allow earlier diagnosis.

Pneumococcal disease
Pneumococcal septicaemia and meningitis are also major causes of morbidity and mortality in early childhood in SS disease. Occurring most commonly before the age of 2 years (Lobel & Bove, 1982; Rogers et al, 1978b), the increased risk of developing pneumococcal meningitis has been calculated to be between 20 and 600 times that in the general population (Kabins & Lerner, 1970; Barrett-Connor, 1971).

Septicaemia is frequently fulminant with high fever (104–106°F), disordered neurological functions (coma, convulsions, ataxia), petechiae with evidence of disseminated intravascular coagulation, shock and the Waterhouse–Friderichsen syndrome associated with adrenal haemorrhage. The clinical course is usually short with a mean interval between presentation and death of 24 hours and reported mortality rates of the order of 50%. There is some evidence of a recent decrease in this mortality rate (Powars et al, 1981) perhaps because of increased awareness, earlier diagnosis and more prompt therapy.

The fulminant nature of septicaemic episodes is also illustrated by the lack of the typical inflammatory cerebrospinal fluid changes in white cells, protein, and glucose in the presence of positive c.s.f. cultures (Seeler et al, 1972; Lobel & Bove, 1982), observations of pneumococci in the leptomeninges without signs of an inflammatory reaction (Kabins & Lerner, 1970), the demonstration of diplococci within vacuolated neutrophils on a blood film (McDonald & Eichner, 1978), and the lack of elevated white cell count in peripheral blood in fatal cases (Lobel & Bove, 1982).

Treatment consists of parenteral penicillin, corticosteroids in the presence of shock, and heparin if there is evidence of disseminated intravascular coagulation.

Detection of children at risk
Children at the greatest risk of developing septicaemia may be identified by the early appearance of splenomegaly (Rogers et al, 1978b). Splenomegaly in children with SS disease appears to be temporally related to the onset of functional asplenia. In a prospective study, 12 out of 13 pneumococcal isolations occurred in children in which the spleen became palpable in the first 6 months of life although such children represented only 37% of the total group (Fig. 4.3). Thus, in children diagnosed at birth, the simple clinical observation of splenomegaly in the first 6 months allows

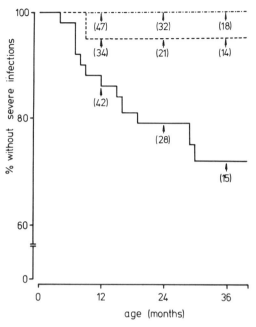

Fig. 4.3 Occurrence of severe infections according to age at first appearance of splenomegaly. Spleen first felt at 6 months or earlier, n = 50 (———), between 7–12 months, n = 38 (– – –), after 12 months or not at all, n = 47 (–·–·–·–). Figures in parentheses are numbers still at risk at yearly intervals. (From Rogers et al, 1978b and *The Lancet*.)

detection of the group at greatest risk from subsequent overwhelming infection, and if necessary prophylactic measures may be concentrated in this group.

Prevention of pneumococcal disease
Prevention of pneumococcal infection has been based on prophylactic penicillin or on pneumococcal vaccines. Potential disadvantages of prophylactic penicillin include problems of compliance, delay in acquired immunity to the pneumococcus, and the emergence of penicillin resistant strains. Failure to take oral penicillin regularly has been well documented in rheumatic fever prophylaxis, less than half the children taking oral penicillin regularly after 3 months. The use of slow-release intramuscular preparations requires only monthly attendance but injections are painful. Blood levels of pencillin may be unrecordable at the end of the four-week period although no data are available on tissue levels. Preliminary experience in a Jamaican study which ensured 100% compliance by delivering long-acting penicillin in a home visiting programme, indicated that no pneumococcal infections occurred during the duration of the programme (ages 6–36 months) although there were four septicaemias clustered in the 12-month period following termination of penicillin (Fig. 4.4) (John et al, 1984). It seems highly likely that such clustering reflects the exposure to pneumococci of a hypersusceptible group which had had little opportunity to acquire immunity during effective prophylaxis, but this hypothesis requires confirmation. Preliminary data suggest that if problems of compliance can be overcome, penicillin offers

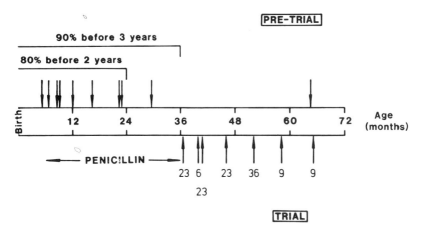

Fig. 4.4   Patterns of pneumococcal isolations from the blood or cerebrospinal fluid in the cohort study before and during the use of prophylactic penicillin (6–36 months).

effective prophylaxis for the duration of the regimen, but a seriously increased risk attends termination of penicillin prophylaxis at the age of 3 years.

PNEUMOCOCCAL VACCINE

Potential disadvantages of the pneumococcal vaccine include the problems of serotypes not represented within the vaccine, the poor antigenicity of some serotypes, and the age-dependence of antibody response which is frequently poor before the age of 2 years when the risk of pneumococcal disease is highest. Preliminary experience in a non-randomised, non-controlled trial of octavalent vaccine in patients with SS disease suggested that the incidence of pneumococcal septicaemia was significantly lower than in a comparison group (Ammann et al, 1977). Experience with the 14 valent vaccine has indicated that vaccine break-throughs are not uncommon especially with types 6, 19, and 23 (Overturf et al, 1979, 1982; Ahonkhai et al, 1979; Broome et al, 1980; John et al, 1984). In the Jamaican study, 13 pneumococcal septicaemias occurred among vaccinated children and although breakthroughs appeared more common in those vaccinated between 6–11 months, infections also occurred in children vaccinated in their second and third years. The response to vaccination may be improved by adjuvants or revaccination but little data are available on this at present.

With the available information, pneumococcal prophylaxis must commence at the age of 6 months and can only be based on penicillin. Jamaican experience suggests that termination of prophylactic penicillin at 3 years of age is premature. Pneumococcal vaccination could be delayed under penicillin cover until 2 years of age with possibly revaccination at 4 years before termination of penicillin prophylaxis. Any febrile event occurring after termination of penicillin prophylaxis should be vigorously treated as a possible pneumococcal infection.

The aplastic crisis

The aplastic crisis is an acute self-limited total erythroid aplasia lasting 5–10 days. Attacks are frequently preceded by an upper respiratory tract type of infection, occur in epidemics, and frequently affect siblings with SS disease. These observations suggest an infective aetiology, but bacteriological and viral studies have previously failed to incriminate a common causal organism. Six cases of aplastic crisis in SS disease in London had evidence of recent parvovirus infection (Pattison et al, 1981) and subsequent analysis of stored sera from a Jamaican epidemic in 1979–1981 revealed evidence of recent parvovirus infection in 24 out of 28 (86%) cases (Serjeant et al, 1981a). Subsequently a similar agent has been incriminated in aplastic crises associated with hereditary spherocytosis, homozygous β thalassaemia and pyruvate kinase deficiency, and has been shown to inhibit erythroid burst forming and colony forming units in bone marrow culture (Mortimer et al, 1983; Duncan et al, 1983).

This is the first time parvovirus infection has been incriminated in human disease. The fact that the aplastic crisis is rarely if ever recurrent, suggests that it may be caused by a single organism or an immunologically related group of organisms. This raises the possibility of protecting children from the aplastic crisis by specific vaccines.

Iron deficiency

Traditional teaching states that iron released by haemolysis is available for reutilisation and that iron deficiency is uncommon in haemolytic conditions. This was supported by the ample tissue iron present in early autopsies in patients with sickle cell disease. It now seems that much of this iron was acquired from oral iron therapy or multiple transfusions. With the decreasing use of transfusion in the management of sickle cell disease, evidence of iron deficiency is not uncommon in pregnant women (Anderson, 1972; Roopnarinesingh, 1976; Oluboyede, 1980) and other groups (Vichinsky et al, 1981; Rao & Sur, 1983).

Whether iron deficiency in SS disease should be treated is controversial. Lowering the intracellular haemoglobin concentration reduces the sickling tendency and a low MCV may be associated with more mild haematological features (Serjeant et al, 1981b). The milder clinical courses of S β° thalassaemia (Serjeant et al, 1979) and of SS disease with homozygous α thalassaemia 2 (Higgs et al, 1982) compared to control groups with SS disease are probably attributable to a low MCHC, low MCV, or both. Treatment of iron deficiency may increase the number of irreversibly sickled cells (Rao & Sur, 1983) and it has been suggested that iron deficiency may be beneficial in SS disease (Lincoln et al, 1973). However iron deficiency may have deleterious effects on growth and performance (Oski & Honig, 1978) and its effects on blood flow and cell deformability are not necessarily beneficial (Hutton, 1979; Yip et al, 1983). Controlled clinical trials are needed to assess the potential advantages and disadvantages of iron deficiency in SS disease.

Folate deficiency

Haemolysis increases the folate requirements in sickle cell disease. In some areas this haemolytic load may be increased further by malaria and when associated with low dietary folate may cause frank megaloblastic change. This complication is recognised in the USA and the Caribbean but appears to be particularly common in West Africa and has led to routine folate supplementation.

Folic acid is cheap and harmless and this supplementation has been the mainstay of therapy without any recent attempts to assess its relevance. The occurrence of psychological dependence on folic acid in some patients in Jamaica prompted a double-blind randomised study of folate supplementation in children aged 6 months to 4 years (Rabb et al, 1983). Following one year's supplementation, no differences between the supplemented and placebo treated groups were apparent in total haemoglobin or in height and weight velocity. No cases of megaloblastic anaemia occurred in the placebo treated group. The MCV was, on average, 4 fl less in the folate supplemented children aged 2–4 years but the evidence suggests that this difference represented the unveiling of iron deficiency in the folate-replete group.

Folate supplementation is logical when the increased demands of accelerated haemolysis are further increased by the demands of rapid growth in infancy, adolescence, or pregnancy. In other situations the need for supplementation should be carefully assessed to avoid psychological dependence.

Painful crisis

Most painful crises result from a limited form of bone marrow necrosis in the juxta-articular areas of long bones. The necrosis presumably results when the consumption of oxygen by rapidly dividing erythropoietic tissue exceeds the supply. The juxta-articular areas of bone are most commonly affected because they occur at a 'watershed' between the two vascular systems supplying bone, the main nutrient artery, and the perforating synovial branches. Precipitating factors are most commonly environmental cold, infections, and pregnancy especially the last trimester and postpartum period, and occasionally dehydration, and emotional or physical stress. The mechanisms whereby these factors cause marrow necrosis is unknown but reduction in oxygen supply is more likely than increased oxygen consumption.

The painful crisis is treated by alleviating any precipitating factor, relief of pain, rehydration, and reassurance. With adequate reassurance, analgesic requirements may be dramatically decreased, and addictive preparations should be avoided if at all possible. It is customary to rehydrate orally or if necessary intravenously because fluid loss from pyrexia and from hyposthenuria may not be replaced by increased drinking during the painful crisis.

There is no good evidence supporting more specific measures. Urea given intravenously in the treatment of the painful crisis (Opio & Barnes, 1972; Co-operative Urea Trials Group, 1974a,b) or orally in their prevention (Lipp et al, 1972; Lubin & Oski, 1973; Gail et al, 1982) showed no benefit in controlled trials. Cyanate therapy inhibits polymerisation of Hb S decreasing haemolysis and increasing the haemoglobin level, but a double-blind, controlled, cross-over study failed to show a decrease in painful crises despite haematological improvement (Harkness & Roth, 1975). Toxic effects included weight loss, peripheral neuropathies, and cataracts, and trials with parenteral cyanate therapy were therefore terminated. Studies continue with extracorporeal carbamylation but the nature of the therapy and sophistication of equipment limit the clinical application of this approach.

Rendering cells less likely to sickling by decreasing the mean cell haemoglobin concentration has also been attempted. Using the synthetic vasopressin analogue, DDAVP, in combination with a high fluid intake and dietary sodium restriction, Rosa et al (1980) were able to reduce the frequency of painful crises during 100–190 day observation periods and considered that acute hyponatraemia reduced the duration of established painful crises. However, these results could not be confirmed by Charache & Walker (1981) and the discipline required to maintain hyponatraemia make it unlikely that this would be a realistic out-patient therapy.

Trials with a drug cetiedil which inhibits sickling by a presumed membrane effect (Benjamin et al, 1980) are currently in progress.

Proliferative retinopathy

Proliferative sickle retinopathy (PSR) is an important complication of vaso-occlusion in the peripheral retina. Avascular areas develop, and at the border of these avascular areas, abnormal arteriovenous communication give rise to proliferation of new vessels (Fig. 4.5). These new vessel systems are important because they bleed giving rise to vitreous haemorrhage with transient visual impairment and may cause retinal detachment with permanent blindness.

An unexpected observation in PSR is its greater frequency in the more benign conditions, sickle cell-haemoglobin C disease and sickle cell-β^+ thalassaemia (Condon & Serjeant, 1972a,b,c). Analysis of haematological indices in patients with and without PSR in a search for prognostic factors indicated that in SS disease, PSR was more common in patients with high total haemoglobin and low fetal haemoglobin (Hb F) levels (Hayes et al, 1981a). Similar analyses in patients with SC disease indicated only a relationship with low Hb F levels (Hayes et al, 1981b). An apparently highly significant relationship with total haemoglobin in males with SC disease was found to be entirely secondary to a strong age-related trend in haemoglobin levels. From these analyses haematological differences did not appear to account for the striking differences between genotypes. Studies of whole blood and plasma viscosity, and of red cell deformability in patients with SC disease also failed to reveal differences in patients with and without PSR (Serjeant et al, 1984).

Studies of the natural history of sickle cell eye disease indicate a high incidence of auto-infarction of PSR lesions in SS disease (Condon & Serjeant, 1980). Vaso-occlusion of new vessels as they formed might prevent the development of PSR. It is then possible to envisage a model which would reconcile the high incidence of PSR in SC disease with its relative clinical and haematological mildness. Patients with the lowest vaso-occlusive indices would be unlikely to develop retinal infarction in the first place. Those with moderate vaso-occlusive indices would be more likely to develop retinal infarction and the sequence of vessel changes proceedings to PSR. Patients with the highest vaso-occlusive indices would frequently manifest retinal infarction but the vaso-occlusion would also affect new vessels inhibiting the development of PSR. This model should be testable in patients with SS disease. Patients with SC disease would represent a group with moderate vaso-occlusive indices.

Until the factors leading to the development of PSR are better understood, prevention of this complication is not possible. The optimum therapy for established PSR is currently the subject of clinical trials. Photocoagulation of the feeder vessels to PSR lesions reduces the incidence of vitreous haemorrhage but a high incidence of retinal tears occurred with the argon laser and a high incidence of choroidal neovascularisation occurred with the xenon arc (Jampol et al, 1983). Ablation of ischaemic retina by scatter photocoagulation with the argon laser has been followed by spontaneous closure of PSR lesions whether applied to the entire circumference

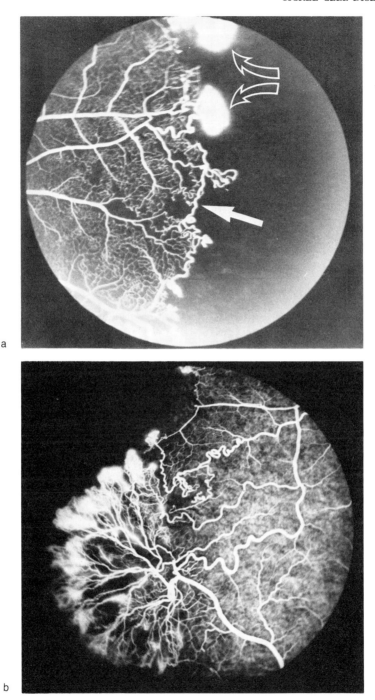

Fig. 4.5   Fluorescein angiograms in proliferative sickle retinopathy **a** Left temporal periphery in a 31-year-old patient with SS disease. Dark area in right half of field is avascular retina. Abnormal arteriovenous communications (solid arrow) at junction of vascular and avascular zones give rise to proliferative lesions which leak fluorescein (curved arrows). **b** Right temporal periphery in a 26-year-old patient with SC disease demonstrating larger proliferative lesion.

(Cruess et al, 1983) or to the sector adjacent to PSR lesions (Rednam et al, 1982). These therapies are currently being assessed in a controlled trial.

Priapism

Priapism is an important manifestation in older boys and men with SS disease, and occurred in 42% patients aged over 15 years in a Jamaican survey (Emond et al, 1980). Two basic clinical patterns occur, short stuttering episodes of 1–6 hours duration, usually at night, and associated with normal intervening sexual function and major attacks lasting more than 24 hours which are usually followed by impotence. Stuttering episodes have prognostic significance, one-quarter of affected Jamaican patients proceeding to a major attack, and over half of the major attacks being preceded by a history of stuttering episodes.

Treatment of the acute attack must be directed to drainage of the corpora cavernosa with consequent relief of pain. In the past, the drainage has been effected by aspiration, or the creation of corporasaphenous shunts. A much simpler procedure is creation of a shunt between the corpora cavernosa and the corpus spongiosum (Winter, 1979) which has been successful in some cases (Baron & Leiter, 1978; Noe et al, 1981) but requires proper assessment.

Therapy of the stuttering episode is important because of the risk of progression to major attacks. In preliminary Jamaican studies, stilboestrol 5 mg daily has been effective in stopping attacks. Impotence following major attacks appears to be due to permanent damage of the vessel system involved in the process of erection. Ejaculation is normal and the ability to have intercourse may be restored by the insertion of a penile prosthesis. Preliminary experience with the Small–Carrion prosthesis indicates that surgical insertion of the prosthesis may be difficult because of fibrosis in the corpora cavernosa, but successful sexual function has been obtained in five out of seven patients (Lawson-Douglas, personal communication).

Pregnancy

Pregnancy in SS disease is associated with an increased rate of abortions, still-births and low birth weight babies and in the mother may precipitate painful crises, the acute chest syndrome, and occasionally death.

Regular antenatal care is essential and intrauterine growth should be monitored clinically, and if possible, by ultrasound. Folic acid and iron supplementation may be given regularly for the duration of the pregnancy. Deliveries should be by the normal vaginal route unless there are obstetric indications otherwise.

Prophylactic heparin may prevent pulmonary embolism in pregnancy (Hendrickse et al, 1972) but has not been subjected to controlled clinical trial. The role of transfusion in the management of pregnancy is also controversial. A marked improvement in maternal and fetal morbidity has undoubtedly occurred at the same time as the increasing use of partial exchange transfusion (Morrison & Wiser, 1976a,b). However, this improvement has also been apparent in series not using exchange transfusion (Charache et al, 1980; Miller et al, 1981), and is attributable, at least in part, to improving medical and obstetric management. The contribution of partial exchange transfusion will remain unclear until it is assessed in controlled clinical trials.

Synonymous with the management of pregnancy is the need for contraceptive advice. If no further pregnancies are required, tubal ligation offers a safe, permanent method of contraception. For short-term reversible contraception, it is frequently assumed that oral contraceptives, depot preparations of progesterone, and intrauterine devices are contraindicated in women with sickle cell disease who are therefore recommended to use the less secure barrier methods. Such a policy is totally unjustified. The risks of pregnancy although small, are real, and far exceed the theoretical risks of any of these forms of contraception.

Intrauterine devices have been considered contraindicated because of the increased susceptibility to infections in sickle cell disease, but there are no data to indicate that such patients are more liable to uterine infections.

Oral contraceptives have been considered inadvisable because of the risks of cerebral and pulmonary thrombosis in a condition already prone to these complications. However, cerebrovascular complications in sickle cell disease occur most frequently before the age of 12 years and after the age of 40 years, whereas contraceptive advice is most commonly requested between the ages of 18–35 years. These different age patterns do not exclude a cumulative effect although there are no well documented reports of cerebrovascular complications in women with SS disease while on oral contraceptives, despite the probably large numbers that must be at risk.

A depot preparation of medroxyprogesterone acetate requiring 3-monthly administration appears to be an effective contraceptive and is in widespread use in many countries. A 2-year crossover study in Jamaica indicated that medroxyprogesterone acetate was associated with significant increases in haemoglobin, Hb F, red cell mass, and red cell survival and significant decrease in irreversibly sickled cells, reticulocytes, and bilirubin levels (De Ceulaer et al, 1982). There was also a significant reduction in the number of days of bone pain while on treatment. These observations are consistent with an inhibition of in vivo sickling and since most of the haematological changes were in a direction likely to be beneficial, medroxyprogesterone acetate might have the dual advantages of providing effective contraception and clinical and haematological improvement.

In the Jamaican clinic, intrauterine devices, medroxyprogesterone acetate, and oral contraceptives are recommended in that order to patients requesting advice on reversible methods. Experience in recent years has given no reason to change that advice.

UNDERSTANDING THE NATURAL HISTORY

Some of the most important recent advances in sickle cell disease have been in understanding the natural history of the disease. Studies of the natural history based both on neonatal screening (O'Brien et al, 1976; Serjeant et al, 1974) and on ascertainment at later ages are increasing awareness of the marked variability of SS disease. Both the Jamaican sickle cell clinics and the Co-operative Study of Sickle Cell Disease co-ordinated by the Sickle Cell Disease Branch of the National Institutes of Health are committed to following large groups of patients over long periods of time. These studies are serving to reduce the gross symptomatic bias inherent in hospital based patients by the long-term follow up of a broad spectrum of cases. This variable clinical course in SS disease is illustrated at one extreme by children who, in the first year of life, have repeated vaso-occlusive episodes, acute splenic sequestration, and death from pneumococcal septicaemia, and at the other extreme by patients who at the age of 50–60 years do not even recognise that they have a disease. Since both extremes of this clinical spectrum fulfil the criteria for the diagnosis of homozygous sickle cell disease, it is clear that other genetic or environmental factors must contribute to this variability in clinical and haematological expression.

α Thalassaemia

Part of this variability is now recognised to result from the inheritance of α thalassaemia (Embury et al, 1982; Higgs et al, 1982). α Thalassaemia 2, which results from the deletion of one of a pair of tightly linked α globin genes, is common among Black populations, reaching a prevalence of approximately 35% in Jamaicans. The homozygous form would therefore be expected to occur in approximately 3%.

The association of SS disease with homozygous α thalassaemia results in an elevated proportional Hb A_2 and a reduced MCV, most cases being predictable from these features (Fig. 4.6). Comparison of age/sex matched groups of SS patients with homozygous α thalassaemia 2 (2 genes), heterozygous α thalassaemia 2 (3 genes), and a normal α globin gene complement (4 genes) indicated that the 2-gene group had a higher haemoglobin, lower MCV, reticulocyte, and irreversibly sickled cell counts (Table 4.1), and a greater persistence of splenomegaly, less acute chest syndrome, and less chronic leg ulceration compared to 4-gene controls whereas the 3 gene group had intermediate features (Higgs et al, 1982). Red cell survival was prolonged in the 2-gene group (De Ceulaer et al, 1983). Viscosity studies also indicated that cells from the 2-gene group were more deformable on passage through a 5 micron polycarbonate

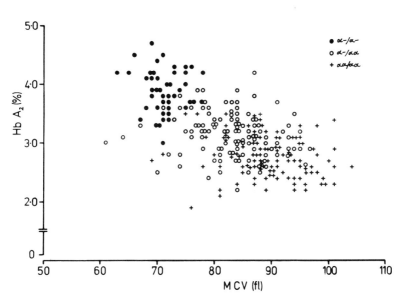

Fig. 4.6 Relationship between proportional Hb A_2 and mean cell volume in patients with SS disease and homozygous α thalassaemia 2 (●), heterozygous α thalassaemia 2 (○), and a normal α globin gene complement (+). (From Higgs et al, 1982, reproduced with permission of the *New England Journal of Medicine*.)

Table 4.1 Comparison of haematological features in the three subgroups of SS disease according to number of α globin genes

Variable	4 Gene			3 Gene			2 Gene		
	n	mean	s.d.	n	mean	s.d.	n	mean	s.d.
HbA$_2$ (%)	88	2.78	0.36	44	3.11	0.34	44	3.87	0.38
[1]HbF (%)	88	1.84 (5.3)	0.61	44	1.76 (4.8)	0.51	44	1.58 (3.8)	6.61
Hb (g/dl)	88	7.80	1.09	44	8.12	1.00	44	8.84	1.29
MCHC (g/dl)	88	34.8	1.7	44	34.3	1.6	44	32.8	1.3
RBC ($\times 10^{12}$/1)	88	2.56	0.39	44	2.90	0.47	44	3.86	0.59
MCV (fl)	88	90.1	6.1	44	84.4	7.8	44	71.2	3.2
MCH (pg)	88	31.4	2.6	44	29.0	3.0	44	23.6	1.4
[2]Reticulocytes (%)	88	2.55 (11.9)	0.34	44	2.33 (9.3)	0.27	44	2.00 (6.4)	0.27
[3]ISC (%)	55	2.88 (7.7)	0.32	24	2.91 (8.3)	0.28	29	2.60 3.5)	0.21
[4]Total bilirubin (mg/dl)	88	1.34 (2.8)	0.33	44	1.23 (2.4)	0.36	44	0.93 (1.5)	0.27

[1-4]Means and s.ds calculated after logarithmic transformation (see text).
[1]$\log_{10}$ (HbF + 1), [2]$\log_{10}$ (rectics + 1), [3]$\log_{10}$ (ISC + 10), [4]$\log_{10}$ (tot bil + 1).
Figures in parentheses represent means re-expressed in original units.

filter than their 4-gene controls (Serjeant et al, 1983). However not all patients with SS disease and homozygous α thalassaemia 2 were mildly affected and painful crises were not demonstrably less frequent in this group. It is possible that the beneficial effects of the reduction in vivo sickling are offset by the rheological disadvantages of the higher haemoglobin level since a high haemoglobin renders patients more prone to proliferative sickle retinopathy (Hayes et al, 1981a) and to avascular necrosis of the femoral head (Hawker et al, 1982). These studies indicated that the highest risk group were those with high haemoglobin levels and low Hb F levels, characteristic of patients patients with homozygous α thalassaemia 2.

Heterocellular persistence of fetal haemoglobin
Expression of the disease is also influenced by Hb F, high levels being associated with less haemolysis, less vaso-occlusion and generally more mild clinical and haematological features. Sickle cell disease in Saudi Arabia is generally associated with high levels of Hb F and a benign course, but such benign courses also occur in Black populations. Factors influencing the production of Hb F are only poorly understood, but it is clear that genetic factors are important. The decline of Hb F in young children is influenced by parental Hb F levels (Mason et al, 1982). A raised level in an AS parent is always associated with a high Hb F in their SS offspring, but a high Hb F in an SS patient is not always associated with an elevated Hb F in an AS parent. Preliminary genetic data appear to be compatible with the hypothesis of 2 alleles at an F-cell producing locus, an H allele determining high levels and an L allele determining low levels giving the possibility of LL, HL, and HH phenotypes (Boyer et al, 1984). The H allele would always result in elevated Hb F production in SS disease and could be inherited from either and HL or HH parent compatible with the parental observations above.

Environmental factors
The effect of environmental factors is less well documented but the disease tends to be more mild in patients with better socioeconomic circumstances. The mechanism of this effect is likely to be multi-factorial with better nutrition, better immunisation, better clothing, better public health measures, more aware and attentive parents, and easier access to medical care. These environmental effects require closer study since this offers the most immediate opportunities for influencing the clinical severity of the disease.

The spectrum of SS disease
As the genetic and environmental factors become better understood, it will be possible to define a group of syndromes within the genotype of homozygous sickle cell disease. The number of functional α globin genes and the phenotype for heterocellular Hb F production each interact with SS disease changing the haematological and clinical characteristics. There are certain to be further genetic factors as yet undefined. In the future it will be possible to be more precise about these genetic subdivisions, explaining the variability of the disease, but also in predicting the prognosis in individual patients.

REFERENCES

Ahonkhai V I, Landesman S H, Fikrig S M, Schmalzer E A, Brown A K, Cherubim C E et al, 1979 Failure of pneumococcal vaccine in children with sickle-cell disease. New England Journal of Medicine 301: 26–27

Ammann A J, Addiego J, Wara D W, Lubin B, Smith W B, Mentzer W C 1977 Polyvalent pneumococcal-polysaccharide immunization of patients with sickle-cell anemia and patients with splenectomy. New England Journal of Medicine 297: 897–900

Anderson M F 1972 The iron status of pregnant women with hemoglobinopathies. American Journal of Obstetrics and Gynecology 113: 895–900

Baron M, Leiter E 1978 The management of priapism in sickle cell anemia. Journal of Urology 119: 610–611

Barrett-Connor E 1971 Bacterial infection and sickle cell anemia. Medicine 50: 97–112

Benjamin L J, Kokkini G, Peterson C M 1980 Cetiedil: Its potential usefulness in sickle cell disease. Blood 55: 265–70

Boyer S H, Dover G J, Serjeant G R, Antonarakis S E, Embury S H, Smith K D et al, 1984 Production of F cells in sickle cell anemia: regulation by a polymorphic genetic locus separate from the beta-globin gene cluster. Blood, in press

Broome C V, Facklam R R, Fraser D W 1980 Pneumococcal disease after pneumococcal vaccination: An alternative method to estimate the efficacy of pneumococcal vaccine. New England Journal of Medicine 303: 549–552

Chang J C, Kan Y W 1981 Antenatal diagnosis of sickle cell anaemia by direct analysis of the sickle mutation. Lancet ii: 1127–1129

Chang J C, Kan Y W 1982 A sensitive new prenatal test for sickle-cell anemia. New England Journal of Medicine 307: 30–32

Charache S, Walker W G 1981 Failure of desmopressin to lower serum sodium or prevent crisis in patients with sickle cell anemia. Blood 58: 891–896

Charache S, Scott J, Niebyl J, Bonds D 1980 Management of sickle cell disease in pregnant patients. Obstetrics and Gynecology 55: 407–410

Condon P I, Serjeant G R 1972a Ocular findings in homozygous sickle cell anemia in Jamaica. American Journal of Ophthalmology 73: 533–543

Condon P I, Serjeant G R 1972b Ocular findings in hemoglobin SC disease in Jamaica. American Journal of Ophthalmology 74: 921–931

Condon P I, Serjeant G R 1972c Ocular findings in sickle cell thalassemia in Jamaica. American Journal of Ophthalmology 74: 1105–1109

Condon P I, Serjeant G R 1980 Behaviour of untreated proliferative sickle retinopathy. British Journal of Ophthalmology 64: 404–411

Cooperative Urea Trials Group 1974a Clinical trials of therapy for sickle cell vaso-occlusive crises. Journal of the American Medical Association 228: 1120–1124

Cooperative Urea Trials Group 1974b Treatment of sickle cell crisis with urea in invert sugar. Journal of the American Medical Association 228: 1125–1128

Crepeau R H, Dykes G, Garrell R, Edelstein S J 1978 Diameter of haemoglobin S in fibres in sickled cells. Nature 274: 616–617

Cruess A F, Stephens R F, Magargal L E, Brown G C 1983 Peripheral circumferential retinal scatter photocoagulation for treatment of proliferative sickle retinopathy. Ophthalmology 90: 272–277

De Ceulaer K, Hayes R J, Gruber C, Serjeant G R 1982 Medroxyprogesterone acetate in homozygous sickle cell disease. Lancet ii: 229–231

De Ceulaer K, Higgs D R, Weatherall D J, Hayes R J, Serjeant B E, Serjeant G R 1983 Alpha-thalassemia reduces the hemolytic rate in homozygous sickle-cell disease. New England Journal of Medicine 309: 189–90

Duncan J R, Potter C G, Cappelini M D, Kurtz J B, Anderson M J, Weatherall D J 1983 Aplastic crisis due to parvovirus infection in pyruvate kinase deficiency. Lancet ii: 14–16

Embury S H, Dozy A M, Miller J, Davis J R, Kleman K M, Preisler H et al, 1982 Concurrent sickle-cell anemia and alpha-thalassemia. New England Journal of Medicine 306: 270–274

Emond A M, Holman R, Hayes R J, Serjeant G R 1980 Priapism and impotence in homozygous sickle cell disease. Archives of Internal Medicine 140: 1434–1437

Emond A M, Morais P, Venugopal S, Carpenter R C, Serjeant G R 1984 The role of splenectomy in homozygous sickle cell disease in childhood. Lancet, in press

Fabry M E, Nagel R L 1982 The effect of deoxygenation on red cell density: significance for the pathophysiology of sickle cell anemia. Blood 60: 1370–1377

Gail M, Beach J, Dark A, Lewis R, Morrow H 1982 A double-blind randomized trial of low-dose oral urea to prevent sickle cell crises. Journal of Chronic Diseases 35: 151–161

Geever R F, Wilson L B, Nallaseth F S, Milner P F, Bittner M, Wilson J T 1981 Direct identification of sickle cell anemia by blot hybridisation. Proceedings of the National Academy of Science of the United States of America 78: 5081–5085

Goosens M, Dumez Y, Kaplan L, Lupker M, Chabert C, Henrion R et al, 1983 Prenatal diagnosis of sickle-cell anemia in the first trimester of pregnancy. New England Journal of Medicine 309: 831–833

Harkness D R, Roth S 1975 Clinical evaluation of cyanate in sickle cell anemia. Progress in Hematology 9: 157–184

Hayes R J, Condon P I, Serjeant G R 1981a Haematological factors associated with proliferative retinopathy in homozygous sickle cell disease. British Journal of Ophthalmology 65: 29–35

Hayes R J, Condon P I, Serjeant G R 1981b Haematological factors associated with proliferative retinopathy in sickle cell-haemoglobin C disease. British Journal of Ophthalmology 65: 712–717

Hawker H, Neilson H, Hayes R J, Serjeant G R 1982 Haematological factors associated with avascular necrosis of the femoral head in homozygous sickle cell disease. British Journal of Haematology 50: 29–34

Hebbel R P, Yamada O, Moldow C F, Jacob H S, White J G, Eaton J W 1980a Abnormal adherence of sickle erythrocytes to cultured vascular endothelium: possible mechanism for microvascular occlusion in sickle cell disease. Journal of Clinical Investigation 65: 154–160

Hebbel R P, Boogaerts M A B, Eaton J W, Steinberg M H 1980b Erythrocyte adherence to endothelium in sickle-cell anemia: a possible determinant of disease severity. New England Journal of Medicine 302: 992–995

Hendrickse J P de V, Harrison K A, Watson-Williams E J, Luzzatto L, Ajabor L N 1972 Pregnancy in homozygous sickle-cell anaemia. Journal of Obstetrics and Gynaecology of the British Commonwealth 79: 396–409

Higgs D R, Aldridge B E, Lamb J, Clegg J B, Weatherall D J, Hayes R J et al, 1982 The interaction of alpha-thalassemia and homozygous sickle-cell disease. New England Journal of Medicine 306: 1441–1446

Hofrichter J, Ross P D, Eaton W A 1974 Kinetics and mechanism of deoxyhemoglobin S gelation: A new approach to understanding sickle cell disease. Proceedings of the National Academy of Sciences of the United States of America 71: 4864–4868

Hofrichter J, Ross P D, Eaton W A 1976 A physical description of hemoglobin S gelation. In: Hercules J I, Cottam G L, Waterman M R, Schecter A N (eds) Proceedings of the symposium of molecular and cellular aspects of sickle cell disease. National Institutes of Health, Bethseda, Maryland, p 185–223

Hoover R, Rubin R, Wise G, Warren R 1979 Adhesion of normal and sickle erythrocytes to endothelial monolayer cultures. Blood 54: 872–876

Hutton R D 1979 The effect of iron deficiency on whole blood viscosity in polycythaemic patients. British Journal of Haematology 43: 191–199

Jampol L M, Condon P, Farber M, Rabb M, Ford S, Serjeant G R 1983 A randomised clinical trial of feeder vessel photocoagulation of proliferative sickle cell retinopathy 1. Preliminary results. Ophthalmology 90: 540–545

John A B, Ramlal A, Jackson H, Maude G H, Waight Sharma A, Serjeant G R 1984 Prevention of pneumococcal infection in children with homozygous sickle cell disease. British Medical Journal, in press

Kabins S A, Lerner C 1970 Fulminant pneumococcemia and sickle cell anemia. Journal of the American Medical Association 211: 467–471

Kan Y W, Dozy A M 1978a Polymorphism of DNA sequence adjacent to human beta-globin structural gene: relationship to sickle mutation. Proceedings of the National Academy of Sciences of the United States of America 75: 5631–5635

Kan Y W, Dozy A M 1978b Antenatal diagnosis of sickle-cell anaemia by DNA analysis of amniotic-fluid cells. Lancet ii: 910–912

Lincoln T L, Aroesty J, Morrison P 1973 Iron-deficiency anaemia and sickle-cell disease: a hypothesis. Lancet ii: 260

Lipp E C, Rudders R A, Pisciotta A V 1972 Oral urea therapy in sickle-cell anemia. Annals of Internal Medicine 76: 765–768

Lobel J S, Bove K E 1982 Clinicopathologic characteristics of septicemia in sickle cell disease. American Journal of Diseases of Children 136: 543–547

Lubin B H, Oski F A 1973 Oral urea therapy in children with sickle cell anemia. Journal of Pediatrics 82: 311–313

Mason K P, Grandison Y, Hayes R J, Serjeant B E, Serjeant G R, Vaidya S et al, 1982 Post-natal decline of fetal haemoglobin in homozygous sickle cell disease: relationship to parenteral Hb F levels. British Journal of Haematology 52: 455–463

McDonald C R, Eichner E R 1978 Concurrent primary pneumococcemia, disseminated intravascular coagulation, and sickle cell anemia. Southern Medical Journal 71: 858–859

Messer M J, Harris J W 1970 Filtration chararacteristics of sickle cells: rates of alteration of filterability after deoxygenation and reoxygenation, and correlations with sickling and unsickling. Journal of Laboratory and Clinical Medicine 76: 537–547

Miller J M, Horger E O, Key T C, Walker E M 1981 Management of sickle hemoglobinopathies in pregnant patients. American Journal of Obstetrics and Gynecology 141: 237–241

Morrison J C, Wiser W L 1976a The use of prophylactic partial exchange transfusion in pregnancies associated with sickle cell hemoglobinopathies. Obstetrics and Gynecology 48: 516–520

Morrison J C, Wiser W L 1976b The effect of maternal partial exchange transfusion in the infants of patients with sickle cell anemia. Journal of Pediatrics 89: 286–289

Mortimer P P, Humphries R K, Moore J G, Purcell R H, Young N S 1983 A human parvovirus-like virus inhibits haematopoietic colony formation in vitro. Nature 302: 426–429

Noe H N, Wilimas J, Jerkins G R 1981 Surgical management of priapism in children with sickle cell anemia. Journal of Urology 126: 770–771

Noguchi C T, Torchia D A, Schechter A N 1980 Determination of deoxyhemoglobin S polymer in sickle erythrocytes upon deoxygenation. Proceedings of the National Academy of Science of the United States of America 77: 5487–5491

Noguchi C T, Schechter A N 1981 The intracellular polymerization of sickle hemoglobin and its relevance to sickle cell disease. Blood 58: 1057–1068

O'Brien R T, McIntosh S, Aspnes G T, Pearson H A 1976 Prospective study of sickle cell anemia in infancy. Journal of Pediatrics 89: 205–210

Oluboyede O A 1980 Iron studies in pregnant and non-pregnant women with haemoglobin SS or SC disease. British Journal of Obstetrics and Gynecology 87: 989–96

Opio E, Barnes P M 1972 Intravenous urea in treatment of bone-pain crises of sickle-cell disease. Lancet ii: 160–162

Orkin S H, Little P F R, Kazazian H H, Boehm C D 1982 Improved detection of the sickle mutation by DNA analysis. Application to prenatal diagnosis. New England Journal of Medicine 307: 32–36

Oski F A, Honig A S 1978 The effects of therapy on the developmental scores of iron deficient infants. Journal of Pediatrics 92: 21–25

Overturf G D, Field R, Edwards R 1979 Death from type 6 pneumococcal septicemia in a vaccinated child with sickle cell disease. New England Journal of Medicine 300: 143

Overturf G D, Rigau-Perez J G, Honig G, Selzer J, Powars D, Steele R et al, 1982 Pneumococcal polysaccharide immunization of children with sickle cell disease. II Serologic response and pneumococcal disease following immunization. American Journal of Pediatric Hematology and Oncology 4: 25–35

Pattison J R, Jones S E, Hodgson J, Davis L R, White J M, Stroud C E 1981 Parvovirus infections and hypoplastic crises in sickle cell anaemia. Lancet i: 664–665

Powars D, Overturf G, Weiss J, Lee S, Chan L 1981 Pneumococcal septicemia in children with sickle cell anemia. Changing trend of survival. Journal of the American Medical Association 245: 1839–1842

Rabb L M, Grandison Y, Mason K, Hayes R J, Serjeant B E, Serjeant G R 1983 A trial of folate supplementation in children with homozygous sickle cell disease. British Journal of Haematology 54: 589–94

Rao J N, Sur A M 1980 Iron deficiency in sickle cell disease. Acta Paediatrica Scandinavica 69: 337–40

Rednam K R V, Jampol L M, Goldberg M F 1982 Scatter retinal photocoagulation for proliferative sickle cell retinopathy. American Journal of Ophthalmology 93: 594–599

Rogers D W, Clarke J M, Cupidore L, Ramlal A M, Sparke B R, Serjeant G R 1978a Early deaths in Jamaican children with sickle cell disease. British Medical Journal 1: 1515–1516

Rogers D W, Vaidya S, Serjeant G R 1978b Early splenomegaly in homozygous sickle cell disease: an indicator of susceptibility to infection. Lancet ii: 963–965

Roopnarinesingh S 1974 Iron stores in pregnant women with hemoglobinopathies. American Journal of Obstetrics and Gynecology 118: 29–33

Rosa R M, Bierer B E, Thomas R, Stoff J S, Kruskall M, Robinson et al, 1980 A study of induced hyponatremia in the prevention and treatment of sickle-cell crisis. New England Journal of Medicine 303: 1138–42

Seeler R A, Metzger W, Mufson M A 1972 Diplococcus pneumoniae infections in children with sickle cell anemia. American Journal of Diseases of Children 123: 8–10

Serjeant B E, Forbes M, Williams L L, Serjeant G R 1974 Screening cord bloods for detection of sickle cell disease in Jamaica. Clinical Chemistry 20: 666–669

Serjeant G R, Sommereux A M, Stevenson M, Mason K, Serjeant B E 1979 Comparison of sickle cell-β^0 thalassaemia with homozygous sickle cell disease. British Journal of Haematology 41: 83–93

Serjeant G R, Topley J M, Mason K, Serjeant B E, Pattison J R, Jones S E, Mohammed R 1981a Outbreak of aplastic crisis in sickle cell anaemia associated with parvovirus-like agent. Lancet ii: 595–597

Serjeant G R, Foster K, Serjeant B E 1981b Red cell size and the clinical and haematological features of homozygous sickle cell disease. British Journal of Haematology 48: 445–449

Serjeant B E, Mason K P, Kenny M W, Stuart J, Hiiggs D R, Weatherall D J et al, 1983 Effects of alpha thalassaemia on the rheology of homozygous sickle cell disease. British Journal of Haematology 55: 479–486

Serjeant B E, Mason K P, Condon P I, Hayes R J, Kenny M W, Stuart J, Serjeant G R 1984 Blood rheology and proliferative retinopathy in sickle cell-haemoglobin C disease. British Journal of Ophthalmology, in press

Topley J M, Rogers D W, Stevens M C G, Serjeant G R 1981 Acute splenic sequestration and hypersplensim in the first five years in homozygous sickle cell disease. Archives of Diseases in Childhood 56: 765–769

Vichinsky E, Kleman K, Embury S, Lubin B 1981 The diagnosis of iron deficiency anemia in sickle cell disease. Blood 58: 963–968

Williamson R, Eskdale J, Coleman D V, Niazi M, Loeffler F E, Modell B M 1981 Direct gene analysis of chorionic villi: a possible technique for first-trimester antenatal diagnosis of haemoglobinopathies. Lancet ii: 1125–1127

Winter C C 1979 Priapism treated by modification of creation of fistulas between glans penis and corpora cavernosa. Journal of Urology 121: 743–744

Yip R, Clark M R, Jain S, Shohet S B, Dallman P R 1983 Red cell membrane stiffness in iron deficiency. Blood 62: 99–106

5. Malaria and the red cell

L. Luzzatto

Intracellular parasitism entails always, by definition, a most intimate association between two entirely different organisms, but the modalities of the association vary a great deal. For instance, the naked genome of certain animal viruses is able to utilise to its own advantage all the apparatus for macromolecule synthesis existing in the host cells. Intracellular rickettsiae have their own organelles and enzymes for nucleic acid and protein synthesis, but they exploit energy provided by the metabolism of the host cells. In the case of mammalian malaria a complete eukaryotic cell, the *Plasmodium*, carries out its own autonomous reproductive cycle inside a non-replicating non-nucleated host cell, while literally digesting the latter's cytoplasm. This situation is unique, in that the host erythrocyte is biologically largely disabled, by virtue of having given up, in the course of its own maturation, not only its nucleus but also mitochondria, ribosomes, and their respective metabolic machinery; whereas the parasite is endowed with these and other organelles, and with the capacity to replicate them. Thus, at the cellular level we would expect that the parasite will have the upper hand, and the host cell will normally be destroyed. However, because the host has the advantage of being not just a cell, but a very complex multicellular organism, it can respond to the infection in other ways. Thus, although this type of parasitism is indeed unique, we can perhaps dissect it in the conventional way: that is, by analysing how the fate of the parasite is affected by the host, and how the host as a whole is affected by the parasite.

Accordingly, the haematological aspects of malaria will be discussed here in these terms. No attempt will be made to review classical malariology. Rather, we shall concentrate on recent progress relating to three major topics: 1) the invasion of erythrocytes and the intraerythrocytic schizogonic cycle of the parasite; 2) malarial anaemia; and 3) genetic red cell factors that affect the parasite. Given the size of this chapter, the discussion will be almost entirely confined to the parasite which has the greatest clinical and public health importance, i.e. *Plasmodium falciparum*. For much more extensive coverage the reader is referred to the three-volume monograph edited by J. P. Kreier (1980), and to two recent multiauthor volumes; one on malaria in general (British Medical Bulletin, 1982), and one specifically on malaria and the red cell (Ciba Foundation Symposium, 1983). Haematological aspects have been covered in reviews (Esan, 1975; Fleming, 1981). A concise coverage of clinical and immunological aspects is given by Miller (1984), and an extensive one by Bruce-Chwatt (1985).

BIOLOGY OF THE SCHIZOGONIC CYCLE

The parasite cycle in red blood cells is characterised by two sharply marked discrete events, namely invasion of the cell and cell burst with release of new parasites (*merozoites*). The intervening period of intracellular development is a continuum, within which it is convenient to distinguish the early *ring* form (with one or two nuclei), the mature *trophozoite* (with one or two nuclei), and the *schizont* (with three to 24 nuclei) (Fig. 5.1). From the classical pattern of tertian fever it had been correctly inferred at the beginning of the century that the duration of the cycle is of 48 hours. However, details of the time sequence remained elusive, because only rings are regularly seen in the peripheral blood of patients with *P. falciparum* malaria. It seemed that more mature forms had a tendency to hide in internal organs, and indeed they can be found in very large numbers in the placenta of women who have malaria at the time of delivery (Edington & Gilles, 1975); and, postmortem, in the spleen and in the brain of patients who have died with 'cerebral' malaria. The mechanism of this peculiar behaviour remained obscure, until very recently it has been shown that

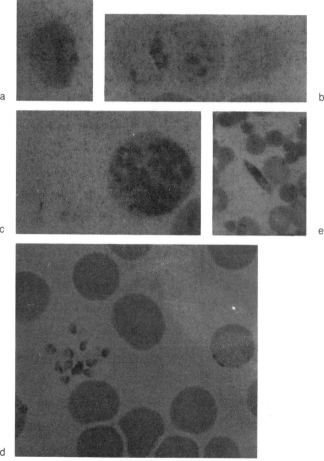

Fig. 5.1   The schizogonic (asexual) intraerythrocytic cycle of *Plasmodium falciparum*. a) Early ring form; b) mature trophozoite; c) segmented (multinuclear) schizont; d) merozoites released from red cell, ready to reinvade. At a stage between a) and b) the parasite has an option to continue the above cycle or to differentiate into a sexual form, or gametocyte e). The gametocyte may persist in peripheral blood for up to 14 days, but it cannot further develop, unless ingested by a mosquito vector during a 'blood meal'. From the point of view of the human host it is a dead-end.

schizonts cause changes in the erythrocyte membrane that make cells containing this form of the parasite adhere to the vascular endothelium (David et al, 1983).

The introduction of an in vitro culture of *P. falciparum* by Trager & Jensen (1976) has been probably the single major advance in the biology of this organism since it was discovered at the turn of the century. In vitro growth of *P. falciparum* had been obtained before (reviewed by Trager, 1978), but this was largely confined to development of parasites which had already invaded red cells in vivo, with little or no reinvasion of new red cells in vitro. By contrast, Trager's system (Trager & Jensen, 1976) has achieved indefinite, continuous, cyclic propagation of the parasite, provided fresh cells are added at regular intervals. With hindsight, it is noteworthy that the improvements on previous attempts which produced success were relatively simple: namely, a better control of pH obtained by supplementing a conventional tissue culture medium with HEPES buffer; and, perhaps most important, a lowering of the oxygen concentration in the gas phase from 21 to 13%. The culture mimics precisely the in vivo intraerythrocytic cycle, and it makes all its developmental forms easily and directly accessible to investigation and experimentation. The 48-hour periodicity is faithfully preserved, and we can assign reasonably accurate times to the various stages of the cycle (see Fig. 5.2), which can be now individually analysed.

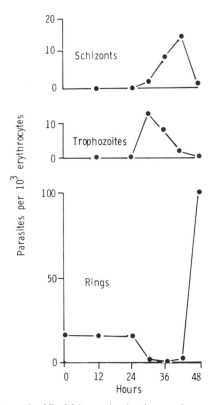

Fig. 5.2 Development and growth of *P. falciparum* in vitro in a synchronous culture. It is seen from the time-course that ring forms mature into trophozoites which mature into schizonts, until the next generation of rings is produced by the schizonts. (Courtesy of Mr E A Usanga.)

Invasion

The merozoite is the only asexual form of *Plasmodium* that exists as a free-floating organism in the blood plasma of an infected host. It is extremely vulnerable in its nakedness (Fig. 5.1d), and its lifespan is probably measured in minutes. Thus, for a merozoite the invasion of a new red cell is literally an urgent matter of life or death. It appears that contact between a merozoite and an erythrocyte takes place initially by random motion. The two cells may then bounce back, or contact may be followed up by firm adhesion (Aikawa et al, 1978). We do not yet know the statistical ratio between the probabilities of either one or the other event taking place. However, we can identify an encounter as successful (from the point of view of the parasite) by an incipient invagination of the red cell membrane. This is associated with formation of a tight annular junction between the two cell membranes. The nature of these phenomena at the molecular level is far from clear, but we have two important pieces of information. On the side of the red cell, one of the major membrane glycoproteins, glycophorin, is involved in the process in an important way. The initial suggestion for this came from the observation by Miller et al (1977) that $En^a(-)$ red cells had a 50% reduction in susceptibility to invasion. Since then, Pasvol and his associates have tested systematically red cells with numerous genetic variants of glycophorin, the protein carrying the antigenic specificities of the MNSs system. Highly significant correlations were found, and in particular $Wr^b(-)$ red cells had a dramatically reduced susceptibility to invasion to less than 10% of normal (Pasvol & Jungery, 1983). In the meantime, Perkins (1981) found that soluble glycophorin in the culture medium inhibited invasion of normal cells, and this approach was subsequently extended to the use of individual sugars, which were interpreted as blocking invasion by competition with membrane glycophorin (Jungery et al, 1983). (The plasma syalo-glycoprotein, orosomucoid, already known to behave as an acute-phase protein, has also been found very recently to inhibit red cell invasion by *P. falciparum* in vitro: Friedman, 1983.) A direct toxic effect on the parasite cannot be ruled out by these experiments, but they were corroborated by the finding that antiglycophorin mono-clonal antibodies also block invasion. On the parasite side, we do not yet know which specific component is involved in junction formation. However, electron microscopy has revealed that orientation of the parasite is non-random, in that a special structure, first referred to as 'paired organelles' and then as rhoptry is regularly found directly underneath the parasite–host cell interface (Aikawa, 1983). It is possible that this structure is involved in an active process that brings about movement of the annular junction and penetration into the red cell.

A very promising new approach to a more detailed understanding of the invasion process is opened up by the observation that haemoglobin-depleted erythrocytes ('resealed ghosts') are competent in vitro for parasitisation by *P. falciparum* (Olson & Kilejian, 1982). This system makes it possible to analyse what cell factors, other than the membrane itself, are required for penetration by the parasite. It is already clear that the ATP concentration is one of them, and Dluzewski et al (1983) have suggested that this may be related to its role in spectrin phosphorylation, but they have shown by dilution experiments that some other cytoplasmic substance is also important. This may be related to the preference of the parasite for young red cells and reticulocytes compared to older cells (Luzzatto et al, 1969; Pasvol et al, 1980).

Intraerythrocytic development

Just as a red cell appears hollow at the centre when flattened and fixed on a slide, but is in fact only very thin in that area, so the *P. falciparum* 'ring' (Fig. 5.1a) is actually a disc, so thin at the centre that only the outer contour is visualised by standard stains. Until recently, the sequence of morphological changes associated with parasite development had to be reconstructed by arranging images seen in blood by a process of reasonable interpolation aided by some guesswork. The first most conspicuous change is an increase in size of the cytoplasm, leading to the form referred to as mature trophozoite (Fig. 5.1b); this is followed by 'segmentation', i.e. the appearance of numerous nuclei, each of them surrounded by a very small amount of cytoplasm (Fig. 5.1c). In vitro cultures have confirmed this sequence, which can be analysed in detail on statistically significant sample sizes by synchronising the parasite population. This can be achieved in two ways. Either the mature schizonts can be isolated by flotation in gelatin solution (Pasvol et al, 1978b) or by centrifugation (Saul et al, 1982) and then used to infect new red cells; or a culture can be treated with sorbitol (Lambros & Vanderberg, 1979), which is toxic to mature forms of the parasite (probably because of permeability changes in the host cell induced by the parasite at this stage): only rings will survive and these can be allowed to develop after removal of sorbitol. By either technique a cohort of parasites of approximately the same developmental age is obtained. By this approach it has been possible to further define morphogenesis: for instance, it is clear that nuclear division precedes cytoplasmic segmentation, thus producing what looks like a multinucleated syncythium before individual merozoites are seen. In addition, it has been possible to chart the time-course of macromolecule synthesis (Sodeinde & Luzzatto, 1982). DNA synthesis takes place at the late trophozoite stage, meaning that it precedes immediately nuclear division, as though there is hardly any G2 phase in the parasite cycle. The bulk of RNA synthesis, i.e. mainly ribosomal RNA synthesis, peaks just before DNA synthesis. By contrast, protein synthesis takes place throughout the cycle, although at a rate which is far from uniform. Not surprisingly, different proteins are made at different times, and a number of protein species resolved by polyacrylamide gel electrophoresis can be regarded as 'stage-specific', in that they are synthesised by rings, by trophozoites, and by schizonts respectively (Kilejian, 1980; Sodeinde & Luzzatto, 1982; Brown et al, 1983).

It is clear that in the course of intraerythrocytic development the parasite makes use of various genes according to a very definite and complex programme. This is reminiscent of what happens in other parasite–host cell systems, such as bacteriophage in a bacterial cell, or an animal virus in a eukaryotic cell, where some genes are referred to as 'early' and others as 'late', depending on the time when they are activated. In the case of bacteriophage many host–cell functions are characteristically shut off upon infection, as the cell's metabolic machinery is taken over for the purpose of viral functions and viral reproduction. In the case of *Plasmodia* there is little to shut off in the host red cell, and the metabolic machinery is the parasite's own. In the bacteriophage system some but not all of the morphogenetic events that take place within the host cell are now understood at the molecular level (Luria et al, 1978), whereas we are very far from this goal in the case of malaria. Among the many questions that are still open, we shall mention just two.

1. We do not know the mechanism of gametocytogenesis. From the morphological point of view, it appears that at an early trophozoite stage the parasite has the option of either continuing in the asexual schizogonic cycle which we have briefly outlined, or becoming a gametocyte, which entails giving up nuclear division and ending up in a cell with a single nucleus and a relatively abundant cytoplasm. It is not clear, however, whether the choice can be made by each individual parasite, or whether some of them are predetermined one way or the other. In this context, it is of interest that the rodent parasite *Plasmodium berhei*, extensively used as an experimental model for human malaria, has been known for a long time to lose the capacity to produce gametocytes when propagated through serial blood passages from mouse to mouse rather than via mosquito (see Bishop, 1955). The mechanism of this phenomenon is unknown, but it has been reported that its time-course parallels that of a decrease in a certain fraction of repetitive DNA from *P. berghei*'s genome. The human parasite *P. falciparum*, when serially passaged in culture, also loses competence for gametocytogenesis. This highlights the fact that certain changes probably do take place as a *P. falciparum* culture becomes an 'established strain'. We have observed more than once that parasites from a patient's infected blood may undergo several rounds of replication in vitro only to die out eventually. This suggests that either adaptive or selective processes may be taking place, and therefore it is not impossible that established strains are indeed expanded colonies of mutants specially fit for our culture conditions. Sexual versus asexual development can certainly be regarded as a true differentiation process, and therefore as another expression of how sophisticated the parasite's control of genomic expression must be. A certain balance between the two options has clearly important biological implications for the parasite. Indeed, gametocytes are an absolute requirement for continuous transmission through the mosquito vector, and it is noteworthy in this respect that gametocytes last several days in circulation. On the other hand, if a high proportion of intraerythrocytic parasites became gametocytes early in the course of the infection, that absolute number would be very small. Thus, it would seem expedient, from the *Plasmodium*'s point of view, to allow a substantial pool of asexual parasites to build up, and then have a finite proportion enter the gametocyte path. This is exactly what seems to take place in the natural infection, and it has been claimed that the presence of antibodies or of other 'adverse' conditions favours gametocytogenesis. Certainly, from the patient's point of view, if all parasites became gametocytes this would terminate their proliferation. It is intriguing to think of therapeutic measures which would induce the parasites to take this option.

2. Although it is obvious that physical and chemical changes in the host cell become more pronounced as the parasite matures, it is not yet clear how precisely they are produced. For instance, it has been shown that permeability to certain anions and the membrane potential increase (Mikkelsen et al, 1982), but the anion transport membrane protein (band 3) appears to be unaffected (Kutner et al, 1982). Several studies have indicated that parasite-coded proteins become associated with the red cell membrane at the schizont stage (Perkins, 1982; Hommel et al, 1983). Some of these may be involved in the electron-microscopically visible 'knobs' which are found on the surface of red cells infected with certain strains of *P. falciparum* but not with others (Kilejian, 1983; Aikawa & Rabbage, 1983). However, Gruenberg & Sherman (1983) did not detect any difference in the protein pattern of purified erythrocyte

membranes from erythrocytes infected with 'knobby' and 'knobless' strains. However, insertion of a specific parasite protein into the host cell plasma membrane has been clearly demonstrated in at least one other system (*Bdellovibrio bacteriovorus* in *Escherichia coli*: Guerrini et al, 1982). Even though the amounts involved may be small, this phenomenon is attracting much attention because it has helped already to identify antigenic proteins that may be crucial to the development of protective immunity (Perrin et al, 1980).

Incidentally, I find it attractive to think that one of the reasons why *P. falciparum* is so successful a parasite is because it can manage to produce so little external changes in the red cell for probably at least half of its asexual cycle (*i.e.*, until the late trophozoite stage). In the laboratory, erythrocytes containing rings are practically impossible to separate from uninfected erythrocytes: by analogy, in vivo they can probably escape the surveillance systems of the body because they are not recognized as abnormal. With other species of human *Plasmodia* red cells are characteristically altered at a much earlier stage in the cycle, and indeed parasitaemias are never as high as with *P. falciparum*.

The outcome of schizogony

We know very little about how the red cell is finally lysed, but it is not surprising that the almost complete consumption of its cytoplasm would have drastically altered its mechanical and osmotic properties (as suggested, for instance, by the aforementioned susceptibility to sorbitol). On slides prepared from cultures rich in schizonts clusters of merozoites are frequently observed (Fig. 5.1d). These probably arise by mechanical damage during spreading of red cells which were ready to burst, indicating that the individual merozoites were already formed. It is possible that some similar mechanical trauma in the capillaries releases merozoites in vivo. One wonders whether invasion of red cells by more than one parasite — a classical feature of *P. falciparum* infection — arises from sib merozoites soon after their emergence. This will be tested eventually by using genetically marked strains and analysing whether doubly or trebly infected cells contain always the same kind of parasites or otherwise.

A question of considerable importance with respect to the natural course of a malaria attack is the overall efficiency of the schizogonic cycle. In other words, how many new red cells are invaded from the offspring of one schizont? In cultures, it is difficult to obtain a multiplication factor greater than five in a single cycle, even though the average number of nuclei per schizont is nearer 16. In operational terms, merozoite viability can only be defined by their competence for reinvasion. Thus, whether only one schizont in four produces viable parasites, or whether each schizont produces only one viable merozoite out of four is a moot point. However, it is possible that in vivo the reinvasion efficiency is higher. The actual figure will have a dramatic effect on the course of the infection, since it will be the base of the parasite's exponential growth (e.g. a reinvasion efficiency of 12 would mean that parasites grow in successive cycles by the powers of 12).

MALARIA AND ANAEMIA

Anaemia is, of course, the most prominent haematological manifestation of malaria. Although there is evidence for a variety of pathogenetic mechanisms, which will be mentioned below, there is no need to elude the simple-minded idea that the baseline pathophysiological process is direct destruction of parasitised red cells. Thus, malaria is in the first place a haemolytic disorder. Indeed, in the absence of any interference with the exponential growth of the parasite population, total destruction of circulating red cells would eventually be the outcome, even if maximal regenerative response by the bone marrow did take place. In practice, the infection can never develop in quite this way, because either host defence mechanisms and therapeutic intervention will prevent such an outcome, or some form of organ damage will fatally curtail the infection before global red cell destruction can take place. Nevertheless, the enormous capacity for erythrocyte invasion by *Plasmodium falciparum* is well illustrated by experimental models in the few non-human primates that can be infected by this organism: the splenectomised chimpanzee (*Pan satytus:* see Hickman et al, 1966), the owl monkey (*Aotus trivigatus:* Geiman et al, 1969) and the squirrel monkey (*Saimiri scireus:* Gysin & Fandeur, 1983). In these animals very high levels of parasitaemia, up to 90%, have been seen.

At any rate, it is now quite clear that in *P. falciparum* malaria haemolysis is not only mechanical and anaemia is not only haemolytic. That destruction of non-parasitised red cells can take place has been known since reports of 'blackwater fever' appeared early in this century (Marchiafava & Bignami, 1931). This phrase aptly describes the fortunately rare occurrence of haemoglobinuria associated with intravascular haemolysis. The precise mechanism of this is unknown, but the abrupt onset and massive destruction of red cells is reminiscent of what happens with incompatible blood transfusion or with an attack of paroxysmal nocturnal haemoglobinuria, i.e. sudden activation of the complement cascade. In keeping with this, the Coombs test has been found positive in acute malaria (Facer et al, 1979; Facer, 1980; Abdalla & Weatherall, 1982), but it has been characteristically erratic (see Kueh & Yeo, 1982), probably for two reasons. Firstly, in some cases only complement is present on the red cell surface, and therefore good 'broad spectrum' reagents (i.e. sera containing anticomplement) are needed. Secondly, the time during which complement and/or IgG are on red cells tends to be quite short, presumably because complement-coated red cells are rapidly destroyed. Thus, the positive Coombs test may be quite transient, and in individual instances it has been found to become negative within 1–3 days (personal observation). Whereas complement activation can undoubtedly lead to intravascular haemolysis (see above), it is probably more common that removal of cells takes place through erythrophagocytosis by macrophages, and this can be seen sometimes dramatically even in the peripheral blood, mostly by monocytes (Fig. 5.3; Luzzatto, 1981; Vernes, 1980), but sometimes by neutrophils and even by eosinophils. Such obvious morphological observations in peripheral blood are again rather rare, because they are transient. However, much more frequent, and diagnostically useful is the finding in monocytes of malarial pigment, the only undigested remnant of the parasite after phagocytosis of parasitised cells. On the basis of work with *P. berghei* in mice, it has been claimed that substances released from macrophages may be responsible for some of the pathological processes associated with malaria (Clark et al, 1981).

A malaria attack is an acute condition, but malaria attacks can be recurrent in endemic areas, especially in children. Thus, we might expect to find also 'anaemia of chronic infection'. Although this phrase is accepted as part of established haematolo-

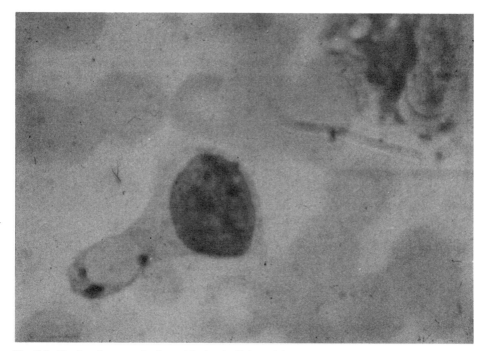

Fig. 5.3 Erythrophagocytosis of parasitised red cells in peripheral blood from a patient with acute *P. falciparum* malaria.

gical parlance, it does not actually stipulate a specific pathogenetic mechanism. Recently, by serial reticulocyte counts and by examining the bone marrow of patients with malaria, evidence has been obtained for defective red cell production (Weatherall et al, 1983), and for derangements of events associated with erythroid cell maturation (Wickramasinghe et al, 1982).

It is not within the scope of this chapter to even summarise the very complex topic of immune processes in malaria (see Playfair, 1982). It is only too obvious that the immune, semi-immune or non-immune status of the host will affect, among other things, the severity of anaemia. In addition, special physiological situations such as pregnancy may affect the immune status, and malaria has been shown to be a major factor in the prevalence and pattern of anaemia in pregnancy in malaria-endemic areas (Fleming, 1981). Nutritional factors also play a role, whether indirect or direct. For instance, malaria-related haemolysis will increase folic acid requirement, and megaloblastic anaemia will develop if this vitamin is limited in the diet. The general nutritional status may be important in another way. For instance, Murray et al (1975) have reported a dramatically high incidence of acute malaria attacks in people restored to adequate diet after having been subjected to famine conditions. They noted that this was associated with a sudden increase in serum iron levels. This is in agreement with flaring-up of malaria after treatment of iron deficiency (Masawe et al, 1974). One might now see these findings as related to the in vitro result that desferrioxamine inhibits the growth of *P. falciparum* (Raventos et al, 1982), suggesting that availability of iron in the medium is essential for the parasite.

Whereas the concept of 'acute malaria' does not require any more rigorous definition than this phrase already states, 'chronic malaria' is an ill-defined concept. In endemic areas recurrent attacks of *P. falciparum* malaria may be simply the result of repeated infections, without any need to postulate persistence of the parasite (which is well documented with *P. malariae*). However, asymptomatic parasitaemia in adults in endemic areas is quite common, and it is possible that this reflects a synbiotic relationship which may be broken by unknown intercurrent events. Finally, it is worth mentioning that in endemic areas the concept of 'controls' (unless deliberately protected by chemoprophylaxis) is rather loose: a child who does not have malaria today may have had it 1 month ago and may have it again tomorrow.

In summary, there are at least three ways in which malaria causes anaemia: 1) mechanical destruction of parasitised red cells; 2) 'immune' destruction of non-parasitised red cells; 3) ineffective erythropoiesis. 1) and 2) are haemolytic processes in the strict sense, whereas 3) is a form of decreased production of viable red cells. 1) operates in all cases, whereas 2) and 3), for reasons which we do not yet fully understand, are more erratic. This probably accounts for the lack of a uniform correlation between the parasite rate and the degree of anaemia in patients with malaria.

GENETIC FACTORS IN HOST RED CELLS

That host genes are important in determining or shaping the course of infectious disease has been suspected for decades from clinical observation, and has now been proven in a number of cases (see Luzzatto, 1984). Not surprisingly, genes involved in the immune response are often implicated, and this is probably true for malaria as well (Piazza et al, 1972). However, the situation for intracellular parasites is bound to be a special one. Indeed, susceptibility of mice to experimental leishmaniasis is a function of genes expressed in macrophages (Bradley & Blackwell, 1981), and in human malaria it was only to be expected that genes expressed in red cells should play a major role. The evidence has been amply reviewed elsewhere (Miller & Carter, 1976; Luzzatto, 1979; Wyler, 1982; Luzzatto & Battistuzzi, 1984). Here I shall summarise only recent data pertaining to a number of genetic systems. Clearly a major booster to these studies has been the availability of in vitro cultures as a tool; not only because they enable us to analyse and manipulate the system in ways which are inconceivable in vivo, but also because it is much easier to carry out experiments in a laboratory than to gather significant clinical data on large numbers of patients in hospitals or in the field. However, such studies have been successful in the past, and they have given the necessary leads. It may be worth emphasising that, while in vitro studies may and almost certainly will enable us to elucidate fully mechanisms of protection against malaria afforded by individual genes, the ultimate proof of their biological significance must be based on clinical evidence of protection, whether already existing or forthcoming.

Haemoglobin S

Previous evidence showed that AS cells sickle more readily when they are parasitised than when they are not (Fig. 5.4a: Luzzatto et al, 1970). This has been confirmed in cultures (Roth et al, 1978). One likely mechanism is that the parasite's metabolism lowers introerythrocytic pH, which favours sickling. The remaining question is whether sickling *per se* damages the parasite irremediably (Friedman, 1978; Pasvol et al, 1978), or whether it interrupts the cycle by causing the parasitised sickled cells to be an easy prey for macrophages. We have found recently that AS cells infected in vitro with *P. falciparum* are indeed phagocytosed preferentially by autologous peripheral blood monocytes (A. Pinching, E. Dudman, L. Luzzatto, unpublished observations). Although it is even possible that both mechanisms actually operate in vivo, the well-known fact that malaria can be extremely severe and sometimes lethal in SS homozygotes is, in this writer's opinion, one argument in favour of parasite removal being mediated by phagocytosis, rather than caused directly by sickling. Indeed, if sickling per se was sufficient, killing of the parasites ought to be more effective in homozygous red cells, which certainly sickle more readily. On the other hand, if killing requires macrophage activity we can easily visualise that this may be inadequate in SS homozygotes, where removal of parasitised cells will compete with that of ordinary irreversibly sickled cells, and the spleen is often functionally impaired. The fact that patients with sickle cell disease — as opposed to AS heterozygotes — are not malaria-resistant (Fig. 5.4b) must always be remembered as an important point in clinical practice, quite apart from its implications in terms of protective mechanisms.

Other abnormal haemoglobins

Protection against malaria by haemoglobin C has been suggested on grounds of epidemiological data (see Ringelhann et al, 1976). In vitro, there is reduced growth of *P. falciparum* in red cells from CC homozygotes but not from AC heterozygotes (Pasvol & Wilson, 1982). For red cells with haemoglobin E in vitro culture findings have been conflicting (Santiyanont & Wilairat, 1981; Nagel et al, 1981; Pasvol & Wilson, 1982). Since it is now clear, from the pathophysiological and molecular point of view, that Hb E is a form of β^+-thalassaemia (Orkin, 1982), see in this respect the following paragraph.

Thalassaemia genes

Although thalassaemia is the genetic disorder for which the notion of a malaria-related genetic polymorphism was first proposed (Haldane, 1949), studies of in vitro cultures have so far been of limited value in explaining the mechanism (Friedman, 1979; Pasvol & Wilson, 1982). However, the case for malaria selection has been greatly strengthened, in this writer's opinion, by the impressive extent of heterogeneity of the polymorphic thalassaemia genes that has become apparent in the last 20 years (see Weatherall & Clegg, 1981). It seems inconceivable that so many independently arisen mutant genes, each one causing severe or total loss of reproductive fitness in the homozygous state, could have increased in frequency in many populations in the absence of a selective agent, and from geographical considerations malaria remains the one and only obvious candidate (see also recent data on the extremely high frequency of α-thalassaemia genes in Papua New Guinea: Oppenheimer et al, 1984.

Ovalocytosis

Red cells with this characteristic morphology have been reported to be common in populations from Papua New Guinea (see Nurse, 1981), and they have been found to

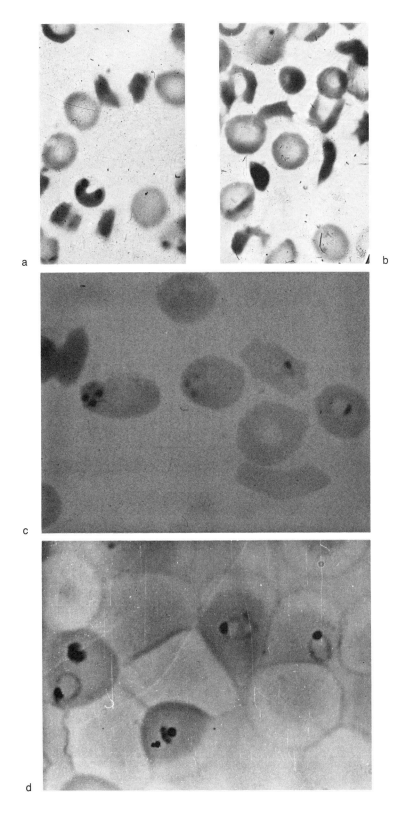

a

b

c

d

be relatively resistant to *P. falciparum* infection in vitro (Kidson et al, 1981). While the authors favour the view that this phenomenon is due to a general alteration of the cytoskeleton, it is noteworthy that ovalocytic cells also exhibit abnormal expression of certain antigens, including some that belong to the MN system (Booth et al, 1977), i.e. glycophorins. On the other hand, it is difficult to assess the significance of the in vitro observation in terms of biological selection at the population level, because the genetics of this form of ovalocytosis has not yet been worked out. Moreover the protection is certainly not absolute (Fig. 5.4c).

Glucose 6-phosphate dehydrogenase (G6PD) deficiency

This is the single genetic abnormality of red cells which has the highest prevalence on a world-wide scale. The evidence for malaria selection of the underlying polymorphic allelic genes, first proposed by Allison (1960) and Motulsky (1960) has been fully reviewed elsewhere (Luzzatto & Testa, 1978; Luzzatto, 1979; Luzzatto & Battistuzzi, 1984). Briefly, it is based on geographical and micro-geographical evidence; on field-studies of clinical malaria; on the distribution of parasites in normal and G6PD-deficient red cells of heterozygous females who are genetic mosaics as a result of X-chromosome inactivation (Fig. 5.4d); and on the results of in vitro culture studies. With respect to the last item, Friedman (1979) first showed that G6PD-deficient red cells, under various conditions of oxidative stress, supported growth of *P. falciparum* at a reduced rate, when compared to control cells. Subsequently it was found, by using synchronised cultures, that this was true even under standard culture conditions, and that it was based on impaired intracellular development rather than failure of invasion (Luzzatto, 1981b; Roth et al, 1983). The mechanism whereby the G6PD-deficient cell environment affects adversely the parasite might be related to gluathione metabolism (Eckman & Eaton, 1979; Roth et al, 1982), such as impaired breakdown of reactive oxygen intermediates toxic for the parasite (Clark & Hunt, 1983). (A further element of complication in the network that includes the malaria parasite, the genetics of the host and the rest of the environmental factors, has been introduced by the finding that isouramil, a substance contained in glycosylated form in fava beans, inhibits *P. falciparum* growth under certain experimental conditions (Golenser et al, 1983).) However, two important points deserve attention. Firstly, it is necessary to rule out possible artefacts consequent on storage lesions of G6PD-deficient red cells in vivo. Secondly, poor development of *P. falciparum* in G6PD-deficient red cells cannot per se explain balanced polymorphism, since in vivo protection is a prerogative of G6PD-deficient heterozygous females and not of G6PD-deficient hemizygous males (Bienzle et al, 1972; Bienzle et al, 1981). In this respect, it was shown recently that, compared to normal red cells, G6PD-deficient red cells become just as competent to support growth of the parasite if the latter has already carried out several schizogonic cycles in them (Luzzatto et al, 1983). This finding eliminates the question of a storage lesion. At the same time, it demonstrates

Fig. 5.4   Red cells of any genotype can be infected by malaria parasites. a) From AS individual; b) from a patient with a sickle cell anaemia; c) from hereditary elliptocytosis; d) from a patient heterozygous for G6PD deficiency. G6PD(+) cells are stained and G6PD(−) cells are unstained by this method and parasites are seen to be present preferentially in the former.

an adaptive phenomenon taking place in the parasite, which suggests a possible explanation of the paradox whereby in vivo heterozygotes are relatively resistant against *P. falciparum* malaria whereas hemizygotes are not. Indeed, in a hemizygous male (or in a homozygous female) with only G6PD-deficient red cells, adaptation will rapidly take place and parasitaemia may reach dangerous levels just as in a normal person, i.e. there is no protection. On the other hand, in a heterozygous female in whom normal and G6PD-deficient red cells coexist, a parasite finds itself having, at each new invasion event, an approximately even chance to enter a normal or a deficient cell, thus decreasing the chance for adaptation. We do not yet know what the adaptation phenomenon consists in, i.e. what metabolic features of the parasite are actually modified. However, an obvious possibility is that G6PD itself is actually involved. Specifically, we now have evidence that development of *P. falciparum* in G6PD-deficient cells actually induces the parasite to synthesise its own G6PD (E. A. Usanga & L. Luzzatto, *Nature*, in the press), i.e. to turn on a gene that was previously expressed less (see Heimpelmann & Wilson, 1981) or not at all.

In summary, G6PD-deficiency heterozygotes have been shown to have a measure of protection against life-threatening levels of *P. falciparum* parasitaemia. The impairment of growth in G6PD-deficient erythrocytes must be related to the metabolic characteristics of these cells. However, the mechanism of resistance must include some other factor, which is a prerogative of heterozygotes. This factor is likely to be their unique red cell mosaicism, which interferes with adaptation of the parasite to the G6PD-deficient intraerythrocytic environment.

It is clear from the data summarised in this section that malaria, through its tremendous selective force, has contributed a great deal to shape the genetic structure of many human populations. On the other hand, it is equally important to remember that no single gene or combination of genes has yet been found to confer absolute resistance to *P. falciparum*. (By contrast, Duffy-negative red cells do have total resistance to *Plasmodium vivax*: Miller et al, 1975.) Any individual patient with clinical malaria must be treated as such, and any non-immune individual must be protected by correct chemoprophylaxis when exposed to infection in an endemic area.

CURRENT PROSPECTS

As students of biology, we have learnt to see malaria as a model system of a unicellular organism with a unique life cycle. As students of medicine, we came to know malaria as a potentially formidable killer, whose threat had to do more with missed diagnosis than with shortage of therapeutic measures. The present revival of interest in malaria — certainly a major credit to the WHO/UNDP/World Bank Special Programme for Tropical Diseases — regards both medicine and biology. On the public health front, one was hoping that malaria eradication, successfully carried out in a number of islands after World War II, would continue also in continental areas, while clinical cases could be treated with available drugs. We are now witnessing a situation in which resistance to chloroquine, and even to sulphadoxine–pyrimethamine combinations, is gradually spreading (Wernsdorfer, 1983), *before* substantial progress towards eradication in major continental areas has been achieved. It is obvious that the hope of a vaccine (Cohen, 1982) now stands out as an imperative priority.

Advances in the last three years have been drawing from the available recombinant

DNA technology. A genomic library of *P. falciparum* in lambda phage was first constructed (Goman et al, 1982), and can be used for searching for any plasmodial gene. Ellis et al (1983) then reported cloning and expression in *E. coli* of a portion of *P. knowlesi* protein, identified as a sporozoite antigen which was already known to induce protective immunity. A *P. falciparum* cDNA library from parasites grown in vitro was constructed in the expression vector λgt11 (Kemp et al, 1983). Several of the polypeptides expressed were characterised and were found to react with sera from people living in endemic areas, proving that they are antigens, at least some of which may be capable of inducing protective immunity in humans. Now the successive steps in the development from sporozoites to exo-erythrocytic merozoites have been described for *P. berghei* in the rat (the only remaining missing link in the life cycle of the plasmodial parasites: Meis et al, 1983); and the liver forms of *P. vivax* have been successfully cultured in human hepatocytes (Mazier et al, 1984). These strides will now further help towards an understanding of what portions of its genome are expressed in its different forms, and how the switch in activity from one set of genes to another actually operates.

Note added to press proofs
Progress in the molecular biology of malaria has become so explosive since this chapter was written that it is impossible even to list all the relevant literature. From the point of view of a possible vaccine against *P. falciparum* the most important advances have been the cloning from this organism and partial sequencing of both the major sporozoite surface protein (Enea et al 1984 Science 225: 628–630) and of two major immunogenic proteins found on the surface of merozoites (Coppel et al 1983 Nature 306: 751–756; Hall et al 1984 Nature 311: 379–380; Coppel et al 1984 Nature 310: 789–792). From the structural point of view a most remarkable finding is that portions of each one of these proteins consist of numerous tandem repeats of short stretches of aminoacids (4–12). A minor protein expressed in blood forms has also been cloned in a genomic expression library (Koenen et al 1984 Nature 311: 382–384) and again it contains a repeat (of 9 aminoacids). The significance of these repeats is not yet understood, but their presence in several proteins and the fact that certain aminoacids tend to recur in them suggest that they may play an important role in the biology of the parasite.

REFERENCES

Abdalla S, Weatherall D J 1982 The direct antiglobulin test in *P. falciparum* malaria. British Journal of Haematology 51: 415–425

Aikawa M 1983 Host–parasite interaction: electron microscopic study. In: Guardiola J, Luzzatto L, Trager W (ed) Molecular biology of parasites. Raven Press, New York, p 1–31

Aikawa M, Miller L H, Johnson J, Rabbege J R 1978 Erythrocyte entry by malarial parasites: a moving junction between erythrocyte and parasite. Journal of Cell Biology 77: 72–82

Aikawa M, Rabbege J R 1983 Electron microscopy of knobs in *Plasmodium falciparum*-infected erythrocytes. Journal of Parasitology 69(2): 435–437

Allison A C 1960 Glucose 6-phosphate dehydrogenase deficiency in red blood cells of East Africans. Nature 186: 531

Baserga B 1937 Sull'infestazione dei reticoliciti da parte dei plasmodi della malaria. Rivista di Malariologia 1: 38–41

Bienzle U, Ayeni O, Lucas A O, Luzzatto L 1972 Glucose-6-phosphate dehydrogenase and malaria. Greater resistance of females heterozygous for enzyme deficiency and of males with non-deficient variant. Lancet i: 107–110

Bienzle U, Guggenmoos-Holzmann I, Luzzatto L 1981 Plasmodium falciparum malaria and human red cells. I. A genetic and clinical study in children. International Journal of Epidemiology 10: 9–15

Bishop A 1955 Problems concerned with gametogenesis in haemosporidiidea, with particular reference to the genus *Plasmodia*. Parasitology 45: 163–185

Booth P B, Serjeantson S, Woodfield D G, Amato D 1977 Selective depression of blood group antigens associated with hereditary ovalocytosis among Melanesions. Vox Sanguinis 32: 99–110

Bradley, D J, Blackwell J M 1981 Genetics of susceptibility to infection. In: Michal F (ed) Modern genetic concepts and techniques in the study of parasites. Schwabe, Basel

Brown K N, Boyle D B, Newbold C I 1983 Maturation of the intracellular parasite and antigenicity. In: Malaria and the red cell. Ciba Foundation Symposium 94, Pitman, London, p 24–36

Ciba Foundation Symposium 94 1983 Malaria and the red cell. Pitman, London

Bruce-Chuvatt L J 1985 Essential malanology, 2nd edn. Heinemann, London

Clark I A, Virelizier J-L, Carswell E A, Wood P R 1981 Possible importance of macrophage-derived mediators in acute malaria. Infection and Immunity 31: 1058–1066

Clark I A, Hunt N H 1983 Evidence for reactive oxygen intermediates causing hemolysis and parasite death in malaria. Infection and Immunity 39: 1–6

Cohen S 1982 Progress in malaria vaccine development. British Medical Bulletin 38: 161–165

Cohen S (ed) 1982 Malaria. British Medical Bulletin 38

David P H, Hommel H, Miller L H, Udeinya U J, Oligino L D 1983 Parasite sequestration in *Plasmodium falciparum* malaria: spleen and antibody modulation of cytoadherence of infected erythrocytes. Proceedings of the National Academy of Sciences of the USA 80: 5075–5079

Dluzewski A R, Rangachari K, Wilson R J M, Gratzer W B 1983 A cytoplasmic requirement of red cells for invasion by malarial parasites. Molecular and Biochemical Parasitology 9: 145–160

Eckman J R, Eaton J W 1979 Dependence of plasmodial glutathione metabolism on the host cell. Nature 278: 754–756

Edington G M, Gilles H M 1975 Pathology in the tropics. Arnold, London

Ellis J, Ozaki L S, Gwadz R W, Cochrane A H, Nussenzweig V, Nussenzweig R S, Godson G N 1983 Cloning and expression of *E. coli* of the malarial sporozoite surface antigen gene from *Plasmodium knowlesi*. Nature 302: 536–538

Esan G J F 1975 Haematological aspects of malaria. Clinical Haematology 4: 247–256

Facer C A 1980 Direct Coombs antiglobulin reactions in Gambian children with *Plasmodium falciparum* malaria. Clinical and Experimental Immunology 39: 279–288

Facer C A, Bray R S, Brown J 1979 Direct Coombs antiglobulin reactions in Gambian children with *Plasmodium falciparum* malaria. I. Incidence and class specificity. Clinical and Experimental Immunology 35: 119–127

Fleming A F 1981 Haematological manifestations of malaria and other parasitic diseases. Clinical Haematology 10: 983–1011

Friedman M J 1978 Erythrocytic mechanism of sickle cell resistance to malaria. Proceedings of the National Academy of Sciences of the USA 75: 1994–1997

Friedman M J 1979 Oxidant damage mediates variant red cell resistance to malaria. Nature 280: 245–249

Friedman M J 1983 Control of malaria virulence by $_1$-acid glycoprotein (Orosomucoid), an acute-phase (inflammatory) reactant. Proceedings of the National Academy of Sciences of the USA 80: 5421–5424

Geiman Q M, Siddiqui W A, Schnell J V 1969 Biological basis for susceptibility of *Aotus trivigatus* to species of *Plasmodia* from man. Military Medicine 134: 780–786

Golenser J, Miller J, Spira D T, Navok T, Chevion M 1983 Inhibitory effect of a fava bean component on the in vitro development of *Plasmodium falciparum* in normal and glucose-6-phosphate dehydrogenase deficient erythrocytes. Blood 61: 507–510

Goman M, Langley G, Hyde J E, Yankovsky N K, Zolg J W, Scaife J G 1982 The establishment of genomic DNA libraries for the human malaria parasite *Plasmodium falciparum*; identification of individual clones by hybridisation. Molecular and Biochemical Parasitology 5: 391–400

Gruenberg J, Sherman I W 1983 Isolation and characterization of the plasma membrane of human erythrocytes infected with the malarial parasite *Plasmodium falciparum*. Proceedings of the National Academy of Sciences of the USA 80: 1087–1091

Guerrini F, Romano V, Valenzi M, Di Giulio M, Mupo M R, Sacco M 1982 Molecular parasitism in the *Escherichia coli–Bdellovibrio bacteriovorus* system: translocation of the matrix protein from the host to the parasite outer membrane. EMBO Journal 1: 1439–1444

Gysin J, Fandeur T 1983 *Saimiri Sciureus* (Karyotype 14-7): an alternative experimental model of *Plasmodium falciparum* infection. American Journal of Tropical Medicine and Hygiene 32: 461–467

Haldane J B S Disease and evolution. Ricerca Scientifica 19 (Suppl 1): 3–13

Hempelmann E, Wilson R J M 1981 Detection of glucose-6-phosphate dehydrogenase in malarial parasites. Molecular and Biochemical Parasitology 2: 197–204

Hickman R L, Gochenour W S, Marshall J D, Guilloud N B 1966 Drug resistant *Plasmodium falciparum* in the chimpanzee. Military Medicine 131: 935–943

Hommel M, David P H, Oligino L D 1983 Surface alterations of erythrocytes in *Plasmodium falciparum* malaria. Journal of Experimental Medicine 157: 1137–1148

Jungery M, Pasvol G, Newbold C I, Weatherall D J 1983 A lectin-like receptor is involved in invasion of erythrocytes by *Plasmodium falciparum*. Proceedings of the National National Academy of Sciences of the USA 80: 1018–1022

Kemp D J, Coppel R L, Cowman A F, Saint R B, Brown G V, Anders R F 1983 Expression of *Plasmodium falciparum* blood-stage antigens in *Escherichia coli*: detection with antibodies from immune humans. Proceedings of the National Academy of Sciences of the USA 80: 3787–3791

Kidson C, Lamont G, Saul A, Nurse G T 1981 Ovalocytic erythrocytes from Melanesions are resistant to invasion by malaria parasites in culture. Proceedings of the National Academy of Sciences of the USA 78: 5829–5832

Kilejian A 1980 Stage-specific proteins and glycoproteins of *Plasmodium falciparum*: identification of antigens unique to schizonts and merozoites. Proceedings of the National Academy of Sciences of the USA 77: 3695–3699

Kilejian A 1983 Immunological cross-reactivity of the histidine-rich protein of *Plasmodium lophurae* and the knob protein of *Plasmodium falciparum*. Journal of Parasitology 69: 257–261

Kreier J P (ed) 1980 Malaria, vols 1–3. Academic Press, New York

Kueh Y K, Yeo K L 1982 Haematological alterations in acute malaria. Scandinavian Journal of Haematology 29: 147–152

Kutner S, Baruch D, Ginsburg H, Cabantchik Z I 1982 Alterations in membrane permeability of malaria-infected human erythrocytes are related to the growth stage of the parasite. Biochimica et Biophysica Acta 687: 113–117

Lambros C, Vanderberg J 1979 Synchronization of *Plasmodium falciparum* erythrocytic stages in culture. Journal of Parasitology 65: 418–420

Luria S E, Darnell J E, Baltimore D, Campbell A 1978 General virology, 3rd edn. Wiley, New York

Luzzatto L 1979 Genetics of red cells and susceptibility to malaria. Blood 54: 961–976

Luzzatto L 1981a Talassemia e selezione malarica. Minerva Medica 72: 603–612

Luzzatto L 1981b Genetics of human red cells and susceptibility to malaria. In: Michal F (ed) Modern genetic concepts and techniques in the study of parasites. Tropical Diseases Research Series No 4. Schwabe, Basel, p 257–274

Luzzatto L 1984 Genetic factors modifying tropical disorders. In: Warren K S, Mahmoud A A F (ed) Tropical and geographical medicine, McGraw Hill, New York, p 77–87

Luzzatto L, Usanga E A, Reddy S 1969 Glucose 6-phosphate dehydrogenase deficient red cells: resistance to infection by malarial parasites. Science 164: 939

Luzzatto L, Nwachuku-Jarrett E S, Reddy S 1970 Increased sickling of parasitised erythrocytes as mechanism of resistance against malaria in the sickle-cell trait. Lancet i: 319–321

Luzzatto L, Testa U 1978 Human erythrocyte glucose 6-phosphate dehydrogenase: structure and function in normal and mutany subjects. Current Topics in Hematology 1: 1–70

Luzzatto L, Sodeinde O, Martini G 1983 Genetic variation in the host and adaptive phenomena in *Plasmodium falciparum* infection. In: Malaria and the red cell, Ciba Foundation Symposium No 94. Pitman, London, p 159–173

Luzzatto L, Battistuzzi G 1984 Glucose 6-phosphate dehydrogenase. In: Harris H, Hirschhorn K (ed) Advances in Human genetics, vol 14, pp 217–329

Marchiafava A, Bignami C 1931 La infezione malarica, 2nd edn Vallardi, Milano

Masawa A E J, Muindi J M, Sway G B R 1974 Infections in iron deficiency and other types of anaemia in the tropics. Lancet ii: 314–317

Mazier D, Landau I, Druilhe P, Mitgen F, Guguen-Guillouzo C, Baccam D, Baxter J, Chigot J-P, Gentilini M 1984 Cultivation of the liver forms of *Plasmodium vivax* in human hepatocytes. Nature 307: 367–369

Meis J F G M, Verhave J P, Jap P H K, Sinden R E, Meuwissen J H E T 1983 Malaria parasites — discovery of the early liver form. Nature 302: 424–426

Mikkelsen R B, Tanabe K, Wallach D F H 1982 Membrane potential of *Plasmodium*-infected erythrocytes. Journal of Cell Biology 93: 685–689

Miller L H 1984 Malaria. In: Warren K, Mahmoud A (ed) Tropical and geographical medicine. McGraw-Hill, New York, p 223–239

Miller L H, Mason S J, Dvorak J A, McGinniss M H, Rothman I K 1975 Erythrocyte receptors for (*Plasmodium knowlesi*) malaria: Duffy blood group determinants. Science 189: 561

Miller L H, Carter R 1976 Innate resistance in malaria. Experimental Parasitology 40: 132–146

Miller L H, Haynes J D, McAuliffe F M, Shiroishi T, Durocher J R, McGinniss M H 1977 Evidence for differences in erythrocyte surface receptors for the malarial parasites, *Plasmodium falciparum* and *Plasmodium knowlesi*. Journal of Experimental Medicine 146: 277

Motulsky A G 1960 Metabolic polymorphisms and the role of infectious diseases in human evolution. Human Biology 32: 28

Murray M J, Murray A B, Murray N J, Murray M B 1975 Refeeding-malaria and hyperferraemia. Lancet i: 653

Nagel R L, Raventos-Suarez C, Fabry M E, Tanowitz H, Sicard D, Labie D 1981 Impairment of the growth of *Plasmodium falciparum* in Hb EE erythrocytes. Journal of Clinical Investigation 68: 303–305

Nurse G T 1981 Haematological genetics: Oceania. Clinical Haematology 10: 1051–1067

Olson J A, Kilejian A 1982 Involvement of spectrin and ATP in infection of resealed erythrocyte ghosts by the human malarial parasite, *Plasmodium falciparum*. Journal of Cell Biol Biology 95: 757–762

Oppenheimer S J, Higgs D R, Weatherall D J, Barker J, Sparkev R A 1984 Alpha-thalassaemia in Papua New Guinea. Lancet i: 424

Orkin S 1982 Abnormal RNA processing due to exon mutation of β^E-globin gene. Nature 300: 768–769

Pasvol G, Jungery M 1983 Glycophorins and red cell invasion by *Plasmodium falciparum*. In: Evered D, Whelan J (ed) Malaria and the red cell, Ciba Symposium No 94, Pitman, London, p 174–195

Pasvol G, Weatherall D J, Wilson R J M 1978a Cellular mechanism for the protective effect of haemoglobin S against *P. falciparum* malaria. Nature 274: 701–703

Pasvol G, Wilson R J M, Smalley M E, Brown J 1978b Separation of viable schizont-infected red cells of *Plasmodium falciparum* from human blood. Annals of Tropical Medicine and Parasitology 72: 93–94

Pasvol G, Weatherall D J, Wilson R J M 1980 The increased susceptibility of young red cells to invasion by the malarial parasite *Plasmodium falciparum*. British Journal of Haematology 45: 285–295

Pasvol G, Wilson R J M 1982 The interaction of malaria parasites with red blood cells. British Medical Bulletin 38: 133–140

Perkins M 1981 The inhibitory effect of erythrocyte membrane proteins on the in vitro invasion of the human malarial parasite (*Plasmodium falciparum*) into its host cell. Journal of Cell Biology 90: 563–567

Perkins M 1982 Surface proteins of schizont-infected erythrocytes and merozoites of *Plasmodium falciparum*. Molecular and Biochemical Parasitology 5: 55–64

Perrin L H, Ramirez E, Lambert P H, Miescher P A 1980 Inhibition of *Plasmodium falciparum* growth in human erythrocytes by monoclonal antibodies. Nature 289: 301–303

Piazza A, Belvedere M C, Bernoco D, Conighi C, Contu I, Curtoni E S, Mattiuz P L, Mayr W, Richiardi P, Scudeller G, Ceppellini R 1972 HL-A variation in four Sardinian villages under differential selective pressure by malaria. In: Histocompatibility testing. Munksgaard, Copenhagen, p 73–84

Playfair J H L 1982 Immunity to malaria. British Medical Bulletin 38: 153–159

Raventos-Suarez C, Pollack S, Nagel R L 1982 *Plasmodium falciparum:* Inhibition of in vitro growth by desferrioxamine. American Journal of Tropical Medicine and Hygiene 31: 919–922

Ringelhann B, Hathorn M K S, Jilly P, Grant F, Parniczky G 1976 A new look at the protection of hemoglobin *AS* and *AC* genotypes against Plasmodium falciparum infection: a census tract approach. American Journal of Human Genetics 28: 270–279

Roth E F Jr, Friedman M, Ueda Y, Tellez I, Trager W, Nagel R L 1978 Sickling rates of human AS red cells infected in vitro with *Plasmodium falciparum* malaria. Science 202: 650–652

Roth E F, Raventos-Suarez, C, Perkins M, Nagel R L 1982 Glutathione stability and oxidative stress in *P. falciparum* infection in vitro: responses of normal and G6PD deficient cells. Biochemical and Biophysical Research Communications 109: 355–362

Roth E F, Raventos-Suarez C, Rinaldi A, Nagel R L 1983 Glucose-6-phosphate dehydrogenase deficiency inhibits in vitro growth of *Plasmodium falciparum*. Proceedings of the National Academy of Sciences of the USA 80: 298–299

Santiyanout R, Wilairat P 1981 Red cells containing hemoglobin E do not inhibit malaria parasite development in vitro. American Journal of Tropical Medicine and Hygiene 30: 541–543

Saul A, Myler P, Elliott T, Kidson C 1982 Purification of mature schizonts of *Plasmodium falciparum* on colloidal silica gradients. Bulletin of the World Health Organisation 60: 755–759

Sodeinde O, Luzzatto L 1982 Erythrocyte cycle of *Plasmodium falciparum*: synthesis of nucleic acids and proteins. In: Nuclear techniques in the study of parasitic infections. IAEA, Vienna, p 447–461

Trager W 1982 Cultivation of malaria parasites. British Medical Bulletin 38: 129–131

Trager W, Jensen J B 1976 Human malaria parasites in continuous culture. Science 193: 673

Vernes A 1980 Phagocytosis of *P. falciparum* parasitised erythrocytes by peripheral monocytes. Lancet ii: 1297–1298

Weatherall D J, Clegg J (ed) The thalassaemia syndromes, 3rd edn. Blackwell, Oxford

Weatherall D J, Abdalla S, Pippard M J 1983 The anaemia of *Plasmodium falciparum* malaria. In: Malaria and the red cell. Ciba Foundation Symposium No 94, Pitman, London, p 74–88

Wernsdorfer W H 1983 Paludisme pharmacorésistant: situation d'urgence Chronique OMS 37: 12–15

Wickramasinghe S N, Abdalla S, Weatherall D J 1982 Cell cycle distribution of erythroblasts in *P. falciparum* malaria. Scandinavian Journal of Haematology 29: 83–88

Wyler D J 1982 Malaria: host–pathogen biology. Reviews of Infectious Diseases 4: 785–797

6. Immunological analysis of tissue sections in diagnosis of lymphoma

H. Stein   D. Y. Mason

INTRODUCTION

Classification of lymphoma

For many years lymphoid neoplasms were a relatively neglected subject among histopathologists. Although Robb-Smith in 1938 proposed a scheme whereby the complex range of histological appearances seen in these disorders could be classified, it was not until the 1960s, after a simple scheme had been introduced by Rappaport (1966), that an interest in lymphoma diagnosis began to spread. Within a few years two major alternative classification systems were proposed, one from Lennert's group in Kiel (Lennert et al, 1975), and the other from Lukes & Collins (1975) in the United States. Both of these latter schemes represented improvements upon Rappaport's system since they correctly identified many lymphoid neoplasms as arising from germinal centre (follicular) lymphoid cells. Both systems recognised that tumours termed 'histiocytic' by Rappaport were in reality neoplasms of large lymphoid cells.

The appearance of these histological classification schemes coincided with advances in the clinical management of lymphoma patients (notably the introduction of effective radiotherapy and chemotherapy regimes), which gave them clinical relevance. This factor led to the appearance in the early 1970s of additional classification schemes, including ones from the British Lymphoma Group (Bennett et al, 1974), a WHO sponsored system (Mathé et al, 1976) and the classification proposed by Dorfman (1974). However, the existence of these multiple classifications caused confusion among clinicians and prompted one haematologist to make the satirical proposal that the time had arrived for a 'classification of lymphoma classifications' (Kay, 1974). This proposal was not entirely facetious since it reflected frustration among clinicians at the absence of a single classification scheme on which there was common agreement among histopathologists. This frustration finally led to the initiation of a multicentre comparison of lymphoma classifications, aimed at producing a single concensus scheme which could be used in the practical clinical management of lymphoma patients.

This project involved the review of a large number of lymphoma biopsies by pathologists who had been selected as either having been responsible for a classification system or because of their wide experience in lymphoma pathology. Its culmination was the appearance in 1982 of a 'Working Formulation' for the classification of lymphomas (National Cancer Institute sponsored study, 1982). However, some of the pathologists involved in this project felt that the material provided for them to review (consisting of single haematoxylin and eosin stained sections from each biopsy) was inadequate and certainly the publication of the final scheme did not herald the end to the divergence between different lymphoma pathologists over the classification of lymphoid neoplasms. One of the major participants in the 'Working Formulation' project has detailed in print the errors which he believes it to contain (Rilke & Lennert, 1981).

The outsider might therefore question whether the 'Working Formulation' has been more valuable than the 'classification of classifications' proposed by Kay in his jeu d'esprit of 1974. However, if nothing else, the exercise made it clear that attempts to establish a perfect lymphoma classification are weakened by the fact that their basis (the assessment of tissue morphology in paraffin sections) is an imperfect and subjective process.

The appearance in the late 1970s of monoclonal antibodies which could define antigens on lymphoid cells with great precision thus offered a new and very welcome means of resolving this impasse. In the present chapter a review is given of the recent results obtained using these reagents for analysing different types of lymphoid neoplasm. Since the methods used for this purpose are still restricted in their use, this chapter begins with a consideration of technical aspects of lymphoma immuno-cytochemistry.

Monoclonal antibodies used for lymphoma classification

The number of white cell associated antigens defined by monoclonal antibodies has lengthened steadily since the first reagents of this type were produced, and there is little evidence that the end of this list is in sight. Realisation of the potential confusions generated by the existence of numerous different monoclonal antibodies of overlapping specificities prompted the organisation in 1982 and 1984 of two International Workshops on Leukocyte Differentiation Antigens defined by monoclonal antibodies. Of crucial importance in these Workshops has been the use of techniques (e.g. immunoprecipitation of radiolabelled cellular constituents) which enable the molecules recognised by individual monoclonal antibodies to be biochemically characterised. As a result, a number of generally recognised constituents on lymphoid cells are beginning to be defined. Table 6.1 lists antibodies which are of relevance in the context of the classification of lymphoproliferative disorders.

In addition to these biochemically defined markers, a number of lymphoid cellular antigens have been identified using monoclonal antibodies which are less extensively characterised (since it has not been possible to identify their target molecules).

Table 6.1 Monoclonal antibodies of value for the immunohistological analysis of lymphoid tissue and bone marrow biopsies

Antibody	Source	Specificity
Anti-epithelial intermediate filaments and others		
LE61	Dr E. B. Lane (1)	Cytokeratin
LP34	Dr E. B. Lane (2)	Cytokeratin
NR4	Dr M. Osborn (3)	Neurofilament
DE.R.11	Dr M. Osborn (4)	Desmin
E29	Author's laboratory (5)	Mil-fat-globule membrane
S1–61	Dr J. Vanstapel (6)	S-100 protein
Anti-leucocyte		
PD7/26⎱ 2B11⎰	Author's laboratory (7)	leucocyte common antigen
2D1	Dr P. Beverley (8)	

Antibody	Source	Specificity
Anti-B cell		
Anti-IgM	BRL[+]	IgM
Anti-IgD	DAKO	IgD
Anti-IgG	BRL	IgG
Anti-IgA	BRL	IgA
Anti-kappa	BRL	Kappa chains
Anti-lambda	DAKO	Lambda chains
To15	Author's laboratory (9)	B cell associated antigen gp140
Tül	Dr A. Ziegler (10)	Follicle mantle lymphocytes
Anti-T cell		
T1	DAKO	T cell associated antigen gp 65–69 000
Leu-1	Becton Dickinson	
OKT11/Lyt3	ORTHO/NEN (12)	Sheep erythrocyte receptors gp 50 000
UCHT1	Dr P. Beverley (13)	T cell receptor associated antigen gp 19 000
OKT3	ORTHO (14)	
Tül4	Dr A. Ziegler (15)	T cell associated antigen gp 40 000. Similar to WT1 Tax et al (1981)
T2	DAKO	
Tü33	Dr A. Ziegler (16)	T cell associated antigen gp 120 000
Leu-3a	Becton Dickinson (17)	T helper/inducer cell
OKT4	ORTHO	
OKT8	ORTHO (18)	T suppressor/cytotoxic cells
T8	DAKO	
Antibodies to accessory cells		
NA1/34	Dr A. McMichael (19)	Cortical thymocytes, Langerhans cells, Interdigitating cells
R4/23	Author's laboratory (20)	follicular dendritic cells
Anti-macrophage		
Antimonocyte 1	BRL (21)	monocytes/macrophages
Antimonocyte 2	BRL (22)	monocytes/macrophages
OKM 1	ORTHO (23)	C3bi-receptor
Mo2	Dr S. Schlossman (24)	monocytes/macrophages
S-HCL3	Dr R. Schwarting (25)	monocytes/macrophages plus hairy cell leukaemia
UCHMI	Dr P. Beverley (26)	monocytes/macrophages
Anti-activated T cell		
Anti-TAC	Dr Waldman (27)	interleukin 2 receptor
Tü69	Dr A Ziegler (28)	activated T cells, but not resting T cells
Ki-24	Author's laboratory (29)	subset of activated T cells and B cells
Miscellaneous		
VIL-A1	Dr W. Knapp (30)	CALLA gp 100 000
J5	Dr J. Ritz (31)	CALLA gp 100 000
C3RT05	Author's laboratory (32)	C3b receptor
Tü35	Dr A. Fiegler (33)	HLA-DR plus DC
Ki-1	Author's laboratory (34)	Hodgkin and Sternberg–Reed cells gp 116/126 000
Ki-67	Author's laboratory (35)	proliferation-associated nuclear antigen

+BRL = Besethda Research Laboratory
(1, 2) Lane (1982, 1984): (3, 4) Debus et al (1983a, b): (5) Cordell et al (1984): (6) Vanstapel et al (1984), (submitted): (7) Warnke et al (1984): (8) Beverley (1981): (9) Stein et al (1982); Mason et al (1984): (10) Ziegler et al (1981): (11) Engleman et al (1981): (12) Verbi et al (1982): Kamoun et al (1981): (13) Beverley & Callard (1981): (14) Reinherz et al (1980): (15, 16) Ziegler et al (unpublished): (17) Evans et al (1978): (18) Reinherz et al (1980): (19) McMichael et al (1979): (20) Naiem et al (1983): (21) Ugolini et al (1980) (22) Kennett (1980): (23) Breard et al (1980): (24) Todd et al (1984): (25) Schwarting et al (1984): (26) Hogg et al (1984) (submitted), (1984): (27) Uchiyama et al (1981): (28) Ziegler et al (unpublished): (29) Stein et al (1983): (30) Knapp et al (1982): (31) Ritz et al (1981): (32) Gerdes et al (1982): (33) Ziegler et al (1982): (34) Schwab et al (1982): (35) Gerdes et al (1984)

Nevertheless a number of these antibodies are of value for the classification of lymphoproliferative disorders and they are included in Table 6.1.

Tissue sections versus cell suspensions

Initial studies aimed at classifying lymphoproliferative disorders by immunocyto-chemical techniques (even before the advent of monoclonal antibodies) involved the preparation of cell suspensions from samples of neoplastic lymphoid tissue. These investigations established that immunological typing could differentiate between B and T cell lymphomas but it was not fully appreciated that the preparation of cell suspensions from neoplastic lymphoid tissue introduces a number of major problems, e.g. neoplastic cells and normal cells become mixed, tissue architecture can no longer be visualised, fragile neoplastic cells may be lost, etc. In consequence the phenotyping data obtained may be difficult to interpret.

For these reasons increasing use has been made in recent years of tissue sections for immunological phenotyping of lymphoproliferative disorders. The first studies of this sort, dating from the early 1970s, were inevitably restricted in their scope since they involved the use of polyclonal antisera and paraffin embedded tissues. In conse-quence, the results obtained were limited to the demonstration of intracytoplasmic immunoglobulin of monotypic type in lymphomas and in cases of Hodgkin's disease, and subsequently of lysozyme and α-1 antitrypsin (as markers of histiocytic cells).

In the late 1970s the first indication was given of the value of applying immuno-cytochemical techniques to frozen sections of human lymphoma. These studies, performed by Warnke & Levy (1978), indicated that surface membrane immuno-globulin of monoclonal type could be demonstrated on neoplastic lymphoid cells by immunofluorescent staining of cryostat sections. Immunofluorescent labelling, however, is not optimal for this type of work, since it prevents the visualisation of tissue morphology and does not provide permanent preparations. Consequently, the description in 1980 by Stein and co-workers of immunoperoxidase methods for detecting surface membrane immunoglobulin on neoplastic lymphoid cells in cryostat sections represented a major advance. Shortly afterwards, this technique was used in conjunction with monoclonal antibodies for labelling lymphoma samples, and the wide range of specificities detectable with these reagents meant that the scope of this technique was greatly enhanced.

Technical aspects of frozen section immunohistology

This topic may be considered under the following headings: preparation of tissue for sectioning, preparation of frozen sections, immunohistological labelling procedures.

PREPARATION OF TISSUE FOR SECTIONING

If tissues are exposed to conventional histological fixatives, the antigenic determinants on most membrane molecules are very rapidly denatured. It is hence essential, if immunohistological studies are to be performed, that tissue is obtained fresh. However, it is important to appreciate that tissue antigens are relatively stable in unfixed tissue and studies can thus be performed on tissue which has been kept in an unfixed state for many hours, or even days, and also on postmortem material. If tissue needs to be kept for a period before freezing (e.g. during transport from one hospital to another) it should be placed in physiological saline or tissue culture medium to prevent drying.

Tissue for immunohistological examination should be cut into small segments before cryostat sectioning. The tissue may then be handled in the same way as a frozen biopsy in a routine histological laboratory, i.e. by direct freezing on a cryostat chuck. However, it may be necessary, when examining lymphoid tissue, to perform further studies after the initial immunohistological screen, and it is advisable to store portions of the tissue for possible subsequent sectioning. For this purpose tissue may be wrapped in aluminium foil, frozen by immersion in liquid nitrogen and then stored in liquid nitrogen or at $-70°C$. A more satisfactory system, however, involves immersing tissue fragments in saline in soft plastic tubes, freezing this sample in liquid nitrogen and then storing the sample at $-70°C$. To recover the tissue for sectioning, the plastic tube is cut away and the frozen plug of tissue and saline removed.

Although lymphoid tissue biopsies are most widely used in immunohistological studies of lymphoproliferative disorders, it may be noted that cryostat sections may also be prepared from bone marrow trephine cases, and then labelled with monoclonal antibodies. The technique for sectioning is in essence identical to that used for lymphoid tissue biopsies, although care is needed to ensure sectioning in the correct axis. Details are given in the recent publication by Falini et al (1984a).

PREPARATION OF FROZEN SECTIONS

Sections are prepared in a cryostat in the conventional manner and picked up on uncoated glass slides. They are then dried thoroughly at room temperature. In initial studies from the authors' laboratories sections were dried by placing them in the chamber of a freeze-drying apparatus. However, it is apparent that this step is not essential and drying on the bench for any period between a few hours to overnight gives fully adequate results.

Once slides have been dried they should be fixed by immersion in acetone for 10 minutes at room temperature and then air-dried. They are then either used immediately for immunohistological labelling (see below) or stored for future use. This is best performed by wrapping the slides in aluminium foil and then keeping them at $-20°C$. Slides stored in this way will give satisfactory results for several weeks. After longer periods of storage there may be some morphological deterioration, although antigenic reactivity is usually unaffected.

IMMUNOHISTOLOGICAL LABELLING PROCEDURES

Initially immunohistological labelling of cryostat sections with monoclonal antibodies was performed in the author's laboratories by immunoperoxidase techniques. The first procedure to be employed was a simple two-stage indirect technique in which incubation with monoclonal antibody (for 30–60 minutes) was followed by a brief wash in buffered saline and incubation for a further 30 minutes with peroxidase-conjugated rabbit anti-mouse Ig. The slides were then washed and the peroxidase reaction developed using diaminobenzidine/H_2O_2. This method is of adequate sensitivity for the analysis of many antigens and samples. However, considerable increase in sensitivity can be obtained by carrying out a further incubation with peroxidase-conjugated anti-rabbit Ig after incubation with peroxidase-conjugated

Table 6.2 Differential diagnosis of problem cases by immunohistological staining (and esterase reactivity)

	Leucocyte common [1]	Cytokeratins [2]	EMA [3]	S-100 [4]	B or T [5] cell markers	Chloro-acetate esterase	Neurofilament [6]	Desmin [7]
Large cell 'undifferentiated' tumours								
Malignant large cell lymphomas	+	−	−	−	+	−	−	−
Anaplastic carcinomas	−	+	+	−/+	−	−	−	−
Malignant melanomas	−	−	−	+	−	−	−	−
Non-lymphoid sarcomas	−	−	−	n.d.	−	−	−	−
Small round cell tumours of childhood								
Acute lymphoblastic lymphoma/leukaemia	+	−	−	−	+	−	−	−
Acute myeloid leukaemia/myelosarcoma	+	−	−	−	−	+	−	−
Neuroblastoma	−	−	−	n.d.	−	−	+	−
Rhabdomyosarcoma	−	−	−	n.d.	−	−	−	+
Ewing sarcoma	−	−	−	n.d.	−	−	−	−

n.d. = no data
[1] detected with PD7/26; [2] detected with LE61 or LP34; [3] detected with E29; [4] detected with S1–61; [5] detected with the anti-B cell and anti-T cell antibodies listed in Table 1; [6] detected with NR4; [7] detected with DE.R. 11

anti-mouse Ig (and before the development of the peroxidase reaction) (Stein et al, 1982b).

More recently increasing use has been made in the authors' laboratories (Cordell et al, 1984) of an immunoalkaline phosphatase technique, the APAAP technique, which is more sensitive than currently available immunoperoxidase methods, and yields a vivid red reaction product more readily seen than that of the peroxidase reaction (Falini et al, 1984a).

Distinction of malignant lymphomas from non-lymphoid neoplasms

Since the treatment of malignant lymphomas is very different from that of non-lymphoid tumours, it is important to distinguish with certainty between the two types of neoplasms. Although this is usually an easy matter, there is a significant minority of biopsies in which the differential diagnosis between malignant lymphoma and non-lymphoid tumours is difficult or impossible on histological grounds.

These problem cases fall into two main groups (Table 6.2): large cell tumours predominantly occurring in adults; and small cell tumours of childhood. Until now the histopathologist's decision has been based solely on morphological criteria, supplemented occasionally by special stains (e.g. PAS). However, it is now possible, using a panel of monoclonal antibodies against a variety of antigens and also the enzyme chloracetate esterase reaction, to classify nearly all problem cases according to the cell or tissue of origin (for details see Table 6.2).

One obstacle to the widespread use of these lineage specific antibodies for routine diagnosis of problem biopsies lies in the fact that the antigens they detect are destroyed by formalin fixation. However, monoclonal antibodies have recently been reported which recognise formalin resistant determinants on leucocyte common antigen (Warnke et al, 1983), cytokeratins, milk fat globule, carcino-embryonic antigens and desmin. Recently Gatter et al (1984) reported on 37 paraffin embedded tumour biopsies which had been referred for immunohistological typing because of difficulty in deciding on morphological grounds whether the tumour was a primitive carcinoma or a malignant lymphoma. In all but one case, the diagnosis could be established from the staining reactions of two antibodies (anti-leucocyte common and anti-epithelial membrane antigen, Table 6.3).

Hence haematologists should in the future be able to make increasing use of immunostaining for the diagnosis of neoplasms of questionable origin, even when only routinely processed paraffin embedded tissue is available. It is of interest that the study summarised in Table 6.3 contained a surprisingly high percentage of lympho-

Table 6.3 Immunohistological typing of routinely processed malignant tumour biopsies with monoclonal antibodies against leucocyte common antigen (Anti-LC) and epithelial membrane (milk fat globule) antigen (anti-EMA)

Number of cases	Anti-LC	Anti-EMA	Conclusion
30	+	−	Lymphoma
7	−	+	Carcinoma
1	−	−	Further antibodies needed

Cases were included in this series (Gatter et al, 1984) on the basis of having been undiagnosable on routine histological examination. Many biopsies were of poorly differentiated morphology, although in some cases the diagnostic difficulty was related to poor tissue preservation

mas (in relation to the overall incidence of this type of neoplasm). This suggests that many routine pathologists are unfamiliar with the full range of morphological appearances seen in lymphoma and indeed that the mistaken diagnosis of a lymphoma as a carcinoma may be an unsuspectedly common occurrence.

Subdivision of malignant lymphomas

Hodgkin's disease had already been separated from lymphosarcoma by the end of the last century. When it was found, in the first two decades of this century, that the cells of lymphoid tissue are composed of two major types, i.e. lymphoid cells and histiocytes, the concept emerged that the neoplasms arising in lymphoid tissue are derived from one or other of these two cell categories. This concept was generally accepted and also adopted by Rappaport (see Fig. 6.1).

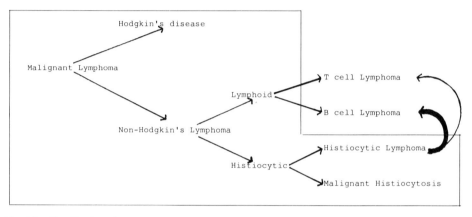

Fig. 6.1   Classification of malignant lymphomas before and after the introduction of immunological labelling techniques. The terms within the enclosed area represent Rappaport's classification scheme. Subsequently lymphoid neoplasms were recognised as being of B or T cell type. Immunological methods also showed that most neoplasms in the histiocytic category are also B cell (most frequently) or T cell derived. However, there is still disagreement between different authorities on the magnitude of the residual categories of true histiocytic neoplasms ('malignant histiocytosis').

Immunological studies in the late 1960s revealed that lymphoid cells are also not homogenous, but rather are composed of two major populations, i.e. thymus-derived cells (T cells) and bone marrow-derived cells (B cells) (Fig. 6.2). In the early 1970s, it was shown that lymphoid cell-derived lymphomas show the same dichotomy as normal lymphoid cells, so that both B and T cell type lymphomas can be identified (Preud'homme & Seligmann, 1972). These immunological studies also revealed that most lymphomas of histiocytic type (usually referred to in the literature as 'reticulum cell sarcoma') are B cell derived (Stein et al, 1972, 1974), with a smaller number being of T cell origin (see Fig. 6.1). However, the majority of pathologists continued to believe in the existence of a third category of lymphoma, representing neoplasms derived from true histiocytes.

The Kiel and the Lukes and Collins classification systems were the first schemes in which the heterogeneity of lymphoid cells was taken into account. In this article we have, with few exceptions, applied the terminology of the Kiel classification. In this scheme different lymphoma categories are listed in an order which is intended to reflect an increasing degree of malignancy. However, as Wright & Isaacson (1983) and one of us (Stein et al, 1981) have pointed out, this is an unsound basis for tumour classification since new treatments, which may change prognosis, are constantly being introduced. It appears to us more relevant to base lymphoma classification primarily on the cell of origin, and to group those entities together which are derived from related cells. This also has the advantage that the classification is easy to learn when

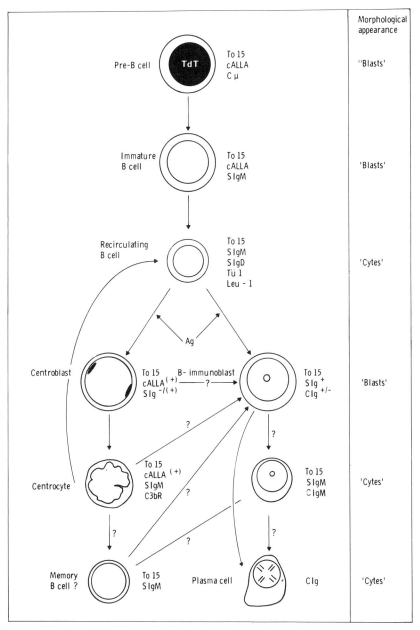

Fig. 6.2   Scheme of B cell differentiation showing markers expressed at different maturation stages.

one is familiar with the maturation sequence of the normal lymphoid cells. For these reasons some adaptations to the Kiel classification were inevitable. These consist of inclusion of diseases not recognised in the classification (such as endemic and non-endemic pleomorphic T cell lymphoma, and polymorphic large cell lymphomas morphologically resembling histiocytic neoplasms) and a change of order to facilitate discussion. Table 6.4 shows the order in which we will discuss the malignant lymphomas.

Table 6.4

Lymphomas of B cell type
Lymphoblastic lymphomas/leukaemias (LB)
   pre-B-cell type
   B-non-Burkitt type
   Burkitt type
Chronic lymphocytic leukaemia of B cell type (B-CLL)
Prolymphocytic leukaemia of B cell type (B-PLL)
Hairy cell leukaemia (HCL)
Centroblastic-centrocytic lymphoma (CB-CC)
Centrocytic lymphoma (CC)
Centroblastic lymphoma (CB)
Immunoblastic lymphoma of B cell type (B-IB)
Lymphoplasmacytic/cytoid lymphoma (LPL)
Plasmacytoma (Ploma)

Lymphomas of T cell type
Lymphoblastic lymphoma/leukaemia (T-LB/T-ALL)
Chronic lymphocytic leukaemia of T cell type (T-CLL)
Prolymphocytic leukaemias of T cell type (T-PLL)
Cutaneous T cell lymphomas (CTCL)
Pleomorphic T cell lymphomas (PMT)
   endemic, HTLVI-positive type (ATLL)
   non-endemic, HTLV-negative type
Immunoblastic lymphoma of T cell type (T-IB)
Lymphoma of plasmacytoid T cells

Hodgkin's disease
Polymorphic large cell lymphomas resembling true histiocytic neoplasms

---

B CELL LYMPHOMAS

In order to gauge how closely immunological types identified by monoclonal antibodies correlate with morphological categories of the Kiel system, we have classified 162 B cell lymphomas on immunological grounds into homogenous groups and then reviewed their histological features (Stein et al, 1984b). This approach (Table 6.5) yielded seven major categories. A total of 128 cases fitted clearly into one of these seven immunological types. The correlation with morphology (last column of Table 6.5) shows that two immunological categories (types 2 and 3) were consistently associated with a specific morphological type of lymphoma (i.e. hairy cell leukaemia, follicular centroblastic centrocytic lymphoma). Type 5 (Burkitt-like immunophenotype) and type 6 (pre-B cell phenotype) cases all categorised morphologically as lymphoblastic lymphoma. There was also a good (although less than absolute) correlation between types 1 and 4 and their morphological features. Type 1 covered all B chronic lymphocytic leukaemia cases but was not specific for this disease entity

Table 6.5 Immunological categorisation of B cell non-Hodgkin's lymphoma. Relationship to histological classification (Kiel)

Immuno- logical type	B cell antigen To15	IgM	IgD	IgG	CALLA	Tü1	Leu-1	S-HCL3	Presence of DRC**	Histological type
I	+	+	+	−	−	+	+	−	none or few	16/18 B-CLL; 3/11 LPL
II	+	+/−	+/−	+/−	−/+	−	−	+	none	12/12 HCL
III	+	+/−	−/+	+/−	+	+/−	−	−	spherical meshwork	22/22 follicular CB-CC
IV	+	+	+/−	−	−	−	+	−	diffuse or nodular meshwork	17/18 CC
V	+	+	−/+	−	+	−	−	−	none or few	9/9 LB (Bu); 1/1 LB (BnonBu); 1/1 LB(U)
VI	+	−	−	−	++	−	−	−	none	3/10 LB (U); 4/5 LB (B non-Bu); 1/10 LB (U)
VII	+/−	+/−	−/+	−/+	−	−	−	−	some cases show meshwork pattern	9/23 CB; 11/18 IB; 1/18 CC; 4/11 LPL;

B-CLL = chronic lymphocytic leukaemia
LPL = lymphoplasmacytic/cytoid lymphoma
HCL = hairy cell leukaemia
follicular CB-CC = follicular centroblastic-centrocytic lymphoma

CC = centrocytic leukaemia
LB (Bu) = lymphoblastic lymphoma, Burkitt type
LB (BnonBu) = lymphoblastic lymphoma, B non-Burkitt-type
LB (U) = lymphoblastic lymphoma, unclassified
IB = immunoblastic lymphoma

* Immunological data was based on an analysis of 162 cases. The majority of cases were also classified according to the Kiel scheme (see last column) although cases in which the morphological category was not clear cut have been excluded.
** DRC = dendritic reticulum cells.

since it also contained three of 11 lymphoplasmocytic/cytoid lymphomas. Nearly all cases of centrocytic lymphomas and one case of immunoblastic lymphoma were found in type 4. The last type (7) included approximately half of the large cell lymphomas and two centrocytic lymphomas and four LP immunocytomas, indicating that the type 7 marker profile was most characteristic of large cell lymphomas.

Taken together, these results indicated that immunohistological typing identifies no new lymphoma categories, but only entities corresponding to groups already disting-uished in the Kiel classification. This substantiates the view that most, if not all, B cell lymphoma types described in the Kiel classification represent true biological entities rather than arbitrary subjective groupings.

Tables 6.6 and 6.7 show the result of performing the reverse exercise, i.e. classifying lymphomas morphologically and then examining their immunological features. The results indicate that all B cell lymphomas in which 'cytes' rather than 'blasts' proliferate consistently express HLA-DR, the B cell-associated antigen To15 and surface immunoglobulin; whereas among the lymphomas of 'blast' type, HLA-DR, B cell antigens or surface immunoglobulins are missing in a substantial number of cases.

The main immunological characteristics of each lymphoma category will be discussed separately.

Lymphomas of early B cells (Fig. 6.3)

All lymphomas with an 'early B cell' phenotype (TdT-positive-Braziel et al, 1983, and/or CALLA strongly positive-Greaves et al, 1983) fall into the morphological category of lymphoblastic lymphoma, as do all lymphomas of early T cells, showing that the neoplasms of early lymphoid cells irrespective of their origin have similar morphological appearances.

The first clear evidence that lymphoblastic lymphoma is not a homogeneous entity emerged when Burkitt lymphomas were separated as a distinct subtype (Berard et al, 1969). Immunological studies in the late 1970s revealed an even greater heterogeneity among lymphoblastic lymphomas. Three types of lymphoblastic lymphomas were distinguished on the basis of surface Ig and T cell antigen expression (T type, B type and non-T-non-B type), the latter being the most frequent. The detection of cytoplasmic mu-chains in 20–40% of the non-B, non-T lymphoblastic lymphoma cases indicates a relationship of these cases to pre-B cells (Vogler et al, 1978; Brouet et al, 1979; Greaves et al, 1979). In a recent immunohistological study (Stein et al, 1984), we could demonstrate that use of the monoclonal antibody To15 directed against a B cell-associated antigen (gp140 000), in conjunction with the antibody Tü14, reactive with a T cell-associated antigen (gp40 000), allowed all 14 cases of non-T-non-B lymphoblastic lymphoma to be identified as either T or B cell-derived (Table 6.8). Since normal pre-B cells express To15 on their surface and/or within the cytoplasm (Campara et al, 1985) we regard the To15-positive Ig-negative and CALLA-positive lymphoblastic lymphoma cases as arising from pre-B cells.

It is of interest to note that the two categories defined by immunological typing (i.e. pre-B cell type and immature B cell type) do not completely correlate with morphological varieties, e.g. lymphoblastic lymphoma of B cell type includes cases which fall into different immunological groups (Table 6.8). Since these histological

Table 6.6 Immunohistological labelling reactions of B cell lymphoma (156 cases)

Antigens/ Antibodies	BLASTS			CYTES			BLASTS		CYTES		
	early B cells			recirculating B cells			germinal centre cells			secreting Ig-producing cells	
	LB pre-B n=7	LB B-nonBU n=2	LB-BU n=11	B-CLL n=18	B-PLL n=5	HCL n=16	CB-CC n=22	CC n=18	CB* n=23	B-IB* n=18	LPL n=11	Ploma n=5
HLA-DR	7[a]	2	11	18	5	16	22	18	19	16	11	0
Pan-B To15	7	2	11	18	5	16	22	18	21	16	11	0
S IgM	0	1	8	17	5	11	10	16	12	10	10	0
S IgD	0	0	3	16	3	6	7	15	4	5	7	0
S IgG	0	1	0	0	1	3	11	1	4	3	3	0
S IgA	0	0	0	0	0	1	1	0	1	1	0	4
κ	0	2	6	10	4	7	11	5	9	7	7	4
λ	0	0	3	7	0	9	8	12	6	5	3	1
κ & λ	0	0	0	0	0	0	3	0	0	1	1	0
κ:λ ratio		0:2	2:1	1.4:1	0:4	1:1.3	1.3:1	1:2.4	1.6:1	1.4:1	2:1	4:1
S Ig negative	7	0	0	0	0	0	0	0	7	4	0	0
Cytoplasmic Ig	n.a.	n.a.	n.a.	0	n.a.	n.a.	n.a.	n.a.	n.a.	n.a.	n.a.	5
CALLA	7	2	11	0	0	2	22	16	9	4	0	1
Tü1	0	1	0	18	n.a.	0	16	0	5	1	7	0
C3b receptor	1	0	0	6	4	0	22	17	2	3	4	0
Leu-1/T1	0	0	0	18	2	0	0	17	1	1	6	0
Tü33	0	0	0	9	0	0	0	13	0	0	0	0
T11/Lyt3	0	0	0	2	0	0	0	0	0	0	0	0
UCHT1/T3	0	0	0	0	0	0	0	0	0	0	0	0
Leu3a/T4	0	0	0	0	0	0	0	0	0	0	0	0
T8	0	0	0	0	0	0	0	0	0	0	0	0
NA1/34	0	0	0	0	0	0	0	0	0	0	0	0
Anti-monocyte 1	0	0	0	0	0	0	0	0	0	0	0	0
Anti-monocyte 2	0	0	0	0	0	0	0	0	0	0	0	0
OKM1	0	0	0	0	0	0	0	0	0	0	0	0
S-HCL3	0	0	0	0	0	16	0	0	0	0	0	0

[a] number of cases

LB pre-B = lymphoblastic lymphomas of pre-B cell type; LB B-non-BU = lymphoblastic lymphomas of B non-Burkitt type; LB BU = lymphoblastic lymphomas of Burkitt type; B-CLL = chronic lymphocytic leukaemia of B cell type; B-PLL = prolymphocytic leukaemia of B cell type; HCL = hairy cell leukaemia; CB-CC = follicular centroblastic-centrocytic lymphoma; CC = centrocytic lymphoma; CB = centroblastic lymphoma; B-IB = immunoblastic lymphoma of B cell type; LPL = lymphoplasmcytic/cytoid lymphoma; Ploma = plasmacytoma.

* In view of the frequently subjective nature of the morphological distinction between centroblastic and immunoblastic neoplasms, the cases included in this study were restricted to samples showing histologically typical features of one or other category.

Table 6.7 Associated cells and growth pattern in B cell lymphoma (156 cases)

	LB pre-B n=7	LB B-non BU n=2	LB BU n=11	B-CLL n=25	PLL n=1	HCL n=16	CB-CC n=22	CC n=18	CB n=23	IB n=18	LPL n=11	Plasma-cytoma n=5
Meshwork of follicular dendritic cells[1]	0	0	2²	2²	0	0	22	16	8	0	0	0
Interdigitating cells[3]	0	0	0	0	0	0	8	0	0	0	0	0
T zones	0	0	0	0	0	0	22	2	5	0	0	0
Follicular growth pattern	0	0	0	0	0	0	22	2	5	0	0	0

[1] Detected with R4/23.
² The meshwork of the follicular dendritic cells was confined to small foci.
[3] Detected with NA1/34.

Table 6.8 Classification of lymphoblastic lymphoma/leukaemia

	Categories identified by phycloncal antibodies				*Categories identified by monoclonal antibodies*				
Pre-monoclonal type	T cell antigen[1]	SIg	CALLA	Number of cases	gp40 T-Ag[2]	T3[4] antigen	SRBC receptor	Pan B To15	New Classification
T	+	–	–/+	15	+	+/–	–/+	–	Common or late thymic
				14 ⟨ 3 / 11	+	–/+	–/+	–	Pre- or early thymic
Non-T-non-B	–	–	+/–		+	–	–	+	Pre-B
B	–	+	+	12	–	–	–	+	Immature B

[1] In the premonoclonal era a variety of polyclonal anti-thymocyte antisera were used to identify T cell neoplasms.
[2] This antigen is detected with monoclonal antibody Tü14 (similar to antibody WT-1 (Tax et al, 1981 and 3AA; Haynes, 1981)
[3] Detected with antibodies OKT11, Leu5, etc.
[4] Detected with antibody OKT3. Antibody UCHT1 (Beverley et al, 1981) detects the same molecule (a glycoprotein of 19 000 mol wt) and gives positive reactions in a higher proportion of cases.

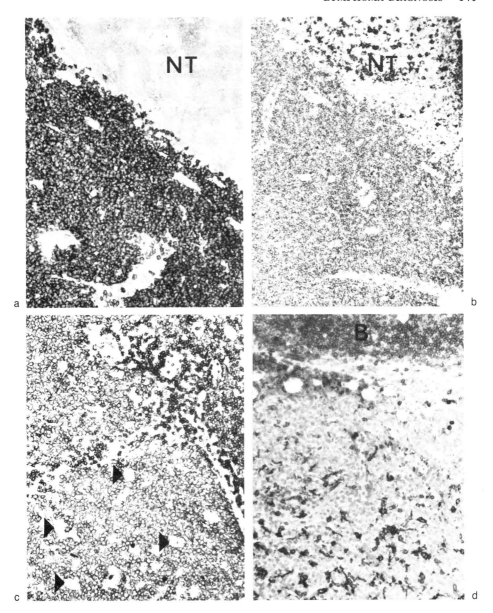

Fig. 6.3   Lymphoblastic lymphoma belonging to the B cell lineage.
a — Lymphoblastic lymphoma of pre-B cell type stained for CALLA (antibody VIL-A1). Tumour cells are strongly positive, whereas uninvolved normal tissue (NT) is unstained. Staining with the pan-B cell antibody To15 produced a similar labelling pattern.
b — Adjacent section stained for HLA-DR, showing strongly stained tumour cells. T cells in the area of uninvolved normal tissue (NT) are negative, but are intermingled with strongly positive interdigitating reticulum cells.
c — Lymphoblastic lymphoma of Burkitt type stained with the pan-B cell antibody To15. The great majority of tumour cells and the residual B cells (upper right) are stained whereas the starry sky macrophages (arrowed) are unstained.
d — Same case as in **c**, stained for C3b receptor. The tumour cells are negative whereas the residual B cells (B) and the starry sky macrophages lying between the tumour cells are positive.

groups are known from previous studies to differ in their prognosis, it will be of interest to see whether these cases will behave clinically according to their morphological or their immunological type.

Chronic lymphocytic leukaemia of B cell type (B-CLL)

The immunophenotype in our series of 18 cases of B-CLL (Table 6.6) proved to be highly constant, and was characterised by the expression of HLA-DR, B cell antigen To15, Tü1 and T1/Leu-1; by the frequent expression of surface IgM and surface IgD; and by the absence of easily detectable cytoplasmic immunoglobulins, CALLA and S-HCL3.

Comparison of the morphological and immunological phenotype of B-CLL cells with that of normal B cells shows that B-CLL cells most closely resemble follicular mantle lymphocytes, a subpopulation of recirculating B cells (Howard et al, 1972). Both B-CLL cells and follicular mantle lymphocytes express surface IgM (Fig. 6.4a), surface IgD and Tü1, and lack easily detectable amounts of cytoplasmic immunoglobulin and CALLA. However, the similarity does not hold true for other antigens. C3b receptors are always present on follicular mantle lymphocytes, but are expressed in only 30% of B-CLL samples. T1/Leu-1 antigen also appears to be abundantly expressed on CLL cells, whereas B cells (including follicular mantle lymphocytes reviewed by Martin et al, 1981) are believed to be devoid of this antigen. However, recently, by maximising the sensitivity of immunoenzymatic staining, we have found weak expression of T1/Leu-1 on normal follicular mantle lymphocytes (Fig. 6.4b). Hence the apparent differences between B-CLL cells and follicular mantle lymphocytes may be quantitative rather than qualitative. This is supported by a recent finding of Janossy's group (Bofill et al, 1985) showing that fetal primary B cell follicle cells express T1/Leu-1 with the same intensity as B-CLL cells. Taken together, these data suggest that the B-CLL cell is derived from an immature primary B cell follicle cell.

It may be added that lymph nodes infiltrated by CLL cells contain very few follicular dendritic cells (Fig. 6.4c), providing further indirect evidence for the derivation of this neoplasm from follicular mantle zone cells.

Prolymphocytic leukaemia of B cell type (B-PLL)

Only five cases have been immunophenotyped, four cases using suspended cells and one case by immunostaining sections of splenic tissue. All our five cases of B-PLL differed from B-CLL in the absence of Tü1, an antigen consistently expressed on typical B-CLL cases (Table 6.6). Gobbi et al (1983) reported that the T1/Leu-1 antigen is absent from B-PLL. However, our own results are not in agreement since two of the five cases expressed this antigen.

Hairy cell leukaemia (HCL)

Since the morphology of HCL cells is unique, it is tempting to assume that these cells must bear antigens specific for this cell type. This assumption has prompted several groups to raise monoclonal antibodies against HCL cells. However, none of the antibodies reported (HC1, HC2, S-HCL1 and S-HCL3) has been specific for hairy cells (Posnet et al, 1982; Schwarting et al, 1984; Falini et al, 1974b). Nevertheless, these reagents may be of diagnostic value in differentiating HCL from B and T cell

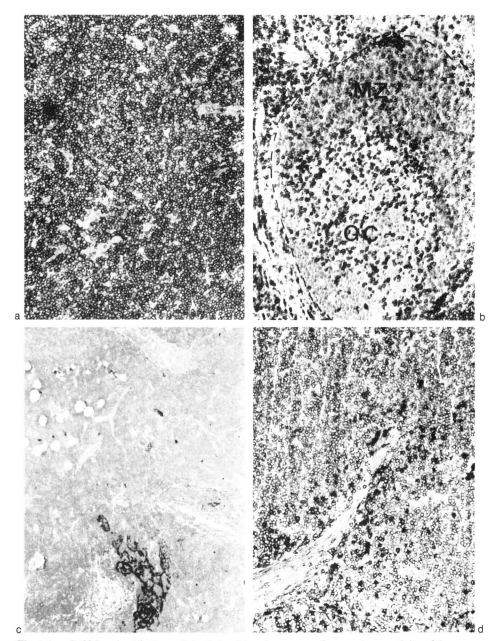

Fig. 6.4a — B-CLL stained for kappa light chains. Note the strong surface membrane staining of the majority of the neoplastic cells.

b — Tonsil stained for T1/Leu-1 antigen using a sensitive multilayer immunoalkaline phosphatase method. In addition to strong staining of T cells, follicular mantle zone (MZ) B lymphocytes are weakly labelled. Expression of this antigen on mantle zone cells is not detectable by conventional immunocytochemical methods. B cells in the germinal centre (GC) are negative, although numerous antigen-positive T cells are present in this region. A dotted line shows the periphery of the lymphoid follicle.

c — Lymph node from a case of B-CLL stained for follicular dendritic cells (FDC) showing a small residual focus of these cells.

d — Lymphoplasmacytic lymphoma stained for kappa light chains. In addition to the ring-like surface labelling on many neoplastic cells, stronger staining of a minority of tumour cells is seen, representing more differentiated cells producing cytoplasmic Ig.

lymphomas (see Table 6.6). Antibody S-HCL3 is particularly valuable in this context (although it also reacts with macrophages) since it has given strong staining of all neoplastic cells in every case of HCL tested (16 samples) and shows no labelling of neoplastic cells in other types of NHL (88 cases tested). In keeping with the proven B cell nature of HCL, all cases have shown strong staining with the B cell specific antibody To15. Thus, although HCL cannot at present be positively identified by a single monoclonal antibody, it may be diagnosed by the use of two antibodies in combination, i.e. the B cell specific antibody To15 (or other B cell specific antibodies, such as S-HCL1) and S-HCL3 (Schwarting et al, 1984; Falini et al, 1984b). It should be noted that HCL is the only type of lymphoid neoplasm which we have found to react with both To15 and S-HCL3 simultaneously.

Apart from these positive immunological features, HCL differs from other NHL in that it consistently lacks C3b receptors (recognised by C3RTo5), Tü1, T1/Leu-1 and B2 (Stein et al, 1981b; Falini et al, 1984b; Pallesen et al, 1984 and this study). These data thus indicate that HCL possesses a distinctive antigenic profile. Since the antigens recognised by To15 and S-HCL3 appear to be expressed by all the neoplastic cells in any individual case, the diagnostic value of these antibodies for identifying HCL cells is clearly greater than that of tartrate-resistant acid phosphatase.

The fact that antibody S-HCL3 also reacts strongly with macrophages, raises again the question of the relationship of hairy cells to cells of the mononuclear phagocyte system. However, the expression of surface Ig of one light chain type, the reactions with monoclonal anti-B cell antibodies, the demonstration of Ig synthesis in vitro (Cohen et al, 1979) and the detection of Ig gene rearrangement (Korsmeyer et al, 1983) provided overwhelming evidence for the B cell nature of HCL.

Centroblastic/centrocytic lymphoma (CB-CC)

This type of lymphoma imitates the reactive germinal centre both in its follicular growth pattern and in its cellular composition, i.e. the presence of both centroblasts and centrocytes. Our immunohistological studies of 22 cases of follicular CB-CC (presented in Table 6.6) show that this tumour consists of follicular-like structures filled with neoplastic B cells (Fig. 6.5a), as demonstrated by staining for the B cell antigen To15 and by the restriction of surface Ig to one light chain type (with three exceptions discussed below). The neoplastic B cells present in the follicles differed in their antigenic profile from all other lymphoma types (see Table 6.6). They constantly expressed C3b receptors (in varying density and on varying percentage of the cells) and lacked T1/Leu-1 (with one exception). The T1/Leu-1-positive case was morphologically on the borderline between follicular CB-CC and centrocytic lymphoma. All cases expressed CALLA, staining usually being sharply limited to the cells of the neoplastic follicles (Fig. 6.5) (Ritz et al, 1981a; et al, 1982a, Habeshaw et al, 1983). It should be noted that normal germinal centre cells also express CALLA with the same density and distribution (Fig. 6.6a) (Stein et al, 1982a).

In line with previous studies (Warnke & Levy, 1978) the neoplastic B cells expressed surface Ig. Follicular CB-CC proved to be the only B cell lymphoma in which the surface Ig was as frequently IgG as IgM.

The immunohistological demonstration of normal 'bystander cells' in follicular CB-CC further underlined the striking similarity between the architecture of follicular CB-CC and follicular hyperplasia. A sharply defined meshwork of follicular dendritic

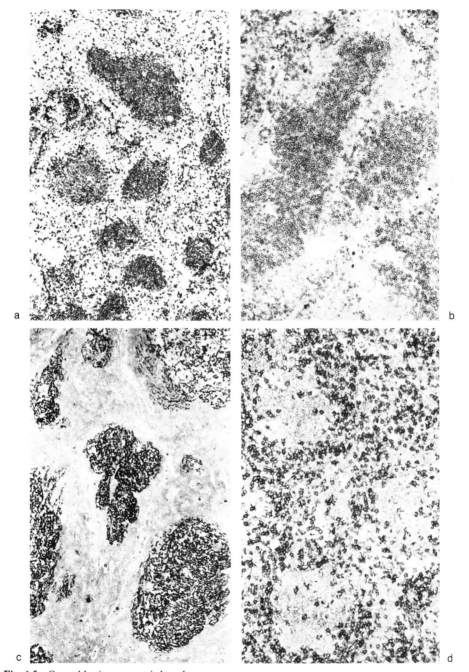

Fig. 6.5   Centroblastic-centrocytic lymphoma.

a — Staining for IgM. All the cells in the neoplastic follicles and scattered cells in the interfollicular region are positive.

b — Staining for CALLA with the antibody VIL-A1. Staining is confined to cells present in the neoplastic follicles.

c — Staining for follicular dendritic cells (FDC). The neoplastic follicles contain a well demarcated FDC meshwork.

d — Staining with OKT11 (reactive with SRBC receptor present on most T cells). Neoplastic B cells in the follicles are negative, but many cells surrounding the follicles are positive.

cells was demonstrated (with antibody R4/23 (Fig. 6.5c) and anti-C3b receptor) within the neoplastic follicles in each of 22 cases of follicular CB-CC, closely resembling that present in reactive germinal centres (Fig. 6.6b) (Stein et al, 1982a). This pattern of cellular arrangement is thus pathognomonic for follicular CB-CC. A second feature constantly associated with follicular CB-CC is the presence around neoplastic follicles of a more or less well-developed T cell zone (Fig. 6.5d). The distribution of T cells of helper and supressor phenotype and of Leu-7-positive cells (natural killer cells) was very similar to that found in follicular hyperplasia, with the exception that suppressor T cells were present more frequently within neoplastic follicles than within normal follicles.

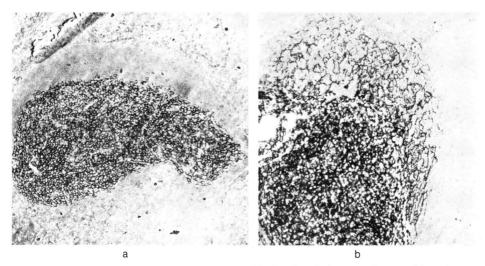

a   b

Fig. 6.6   Tonsil. **a** — Staining for CALLA (antibody VIL-A1). Germinal centre cells are positive, whereas all other cells (including follicular mantle lymphocytes) are negative.
b — Staining for follicular dendritic cells (FDC) with antibody R4/23. A meshwork of FDC within the germinal centre and in the inner part of the follicular mantle zone is visualised.

In three of our 22 cases of follicular CB-CC the individual B cells of the neoplastic follicles stained for both kappa and lambda chains. The same unexpected finding has also been observed by other investigators (e.g. Habeshaw et al, 1979, personal communication), but remains unexplained at present.

These findings provide strong evidence that follicular CB-CC, as defined in the Kiel classification, is indeed a single entity and argues against the subdivision of this histological category into subtypes (as occurs in the Working Formulation).

Centrocytic lymphoma (CC)
This type of lymphoid neoplasm is defined as a lymphoma consisting solely of germinal centre cells of centrocytic type. In classifications other than the Kiel scheme this type of lymphoma is not treated as a separate entity, e.g. in the Lukes–Collins classification, it is included with follicular centre cell lymphoma, small and large cleaved (roughly equivalent to CB-CC in the Kiel classification). This alternative view of the classification of CC reflects the fact that the neoplastic cells in CC show a morphological resemblance to those of CB-CC. Indeed there is a further similarity

between the two entities, i.e. the presence of the meshwork of follicular dendritic cells (Stein et al, 1982a, 1984b) in 16 of our 18 CC cases (Table 6.7 and Fig. 6.7). However, analysis of antigenic profile confirms our previous studies (Stein et al, 1982a) showing that there are many differences between CC and follicular CB-CC (see Table 6.6).

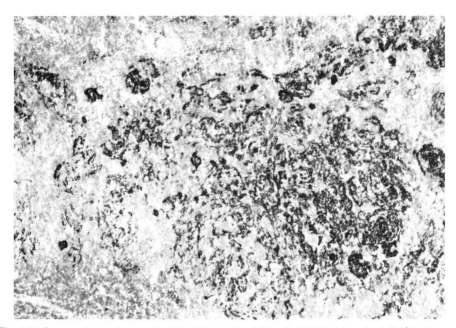

Fig. 6.7 Centrocytic lymphoma stained for follicular dendritic cells (FDC) with antibody R4/23. A vaguely nodular, poorly demarcated meshwork of FDC is seen.

As Table 6.7 shows, two cases of CC exhibited a follicular growth pattern associated with the presence of well-defined follicular dendritic cell meshworks surrounded by T cell zones. These two cases were morphologically on the borderline between centrocytic lymphoma and follicular CB-CC; however, the antigen profile of these two cases corresponded fully with that of typical CC (Table 6.6). These two cases prompted us to compare the relationship between the distribution of follicular dendritic cells and the growth pattern in our cases of CC. As expected it was noted that the more nodular the DRC meshwork pattern the more nodular the morphological growth pattern. This study also clearly showed that a follicular growth pattern is only seen if the nodular meshwork of follicular dendritic cells is surrounded by T cell zones.

Two cases of centrocytic lymphoma deviated from the immunohistological pattern described above in that they were negative for T1/Leu-1 and for Tü33 and lacked follicular dendritic cells. Whether these two cases represent a different lymphoma type or only a variant of typical CC remains to be seen.

In conclusion our immunological data supports the view that centrocytic lymphoma is a separate entity, clearly distinguishable in most cases from other lymphoma categories.

Cell of origin of centrocytic lymphoma
It has been argued that centrocytic lymphoma cells derive from germinal centre cells because of the morphological similarity between the two cell types and the presence of follicular dendritic cells among the centrocytic lymphoma cells. However centrocytic lymphoma cells constantly express T1/Leu-1, and in a majority of cases Tü33, whereas these antigens are expressed in reactive tissue by T cells but only few if any centrocytes. Furthermore centrocytic lymphoma cells are devoid of CALLA (present on normal centroblasts and centrocytes) but express delta chains (absent from reactive centrocytes).

It has also been suggested that centrocytic lymphoma cells derive from follicular mantle zone cells. However, the differences in morphology and the constant absence of Tül from centrocytic lymphoma cells argues against such a relationship (the Tül antigen being constantly expressed on follicular mantle lymphocytes).

The differences in phenotype between centrocytic lymphoma cells and any normal B cell may be explained either by changes in antigenic expression associated with malignant transformation or by derivation from an as yet unidentified B cell subset. We favour the latter alternative (Stein et al, 1982a), and suggest, for reasons set out in Table 6.9, that there are two types of centrocytes, and that centrocytic lymphoma derives from type II.

Table 6.9   Evidence for two types of centrocytes

	Centrocyte type I	Centrocyte type II
Occurring as a major population in normal germinal centres	+	−
Present in follicular CB-CC	+	−
Present in centrocytic lymphoma	−	+
B cell antigen To15	+	+
SIgM or SIgG	+	−
Heavy chain class restricted to SIgM (or SIgM and IgD)	−	+
CALLA	+	−
Tül	+/−	−
C3b receptor (C3RT05)	+	+/−
Leu-1	−	+
Tü33	−	+/−

Centroblastic lymphoma (CB) and immunoblastic lymphoma (B-IB)
These two morphological categories will be discussed together. The 'classical' morphological features of these two types are clear-cut and easily distinguishable (Lennert et al, 1978). However, in individual cases it is often impossible to distinguish between them on histological grounds, due to the fact that a mixed population of cells is present, some resembling centroblasts, and others immunoblasts. The difficulty in morphologically differentiating CB from B-IB has caused a great deal of confusion, leading a number of lymphoma experts to suggest that the two categories should be included in a single group of 'large cell lymphomas'. However, there is evidence from follow-up studies that these two lymphoma types differ in survival times and response to treatment (Meusers et al, 1979; Strauchen et al, 1978).

The introduction of procedures for phenotyping with monoclonal antibodies on tissue sections has thus raised the possibility of investigating whether the two entities are truely distinct. The results of our studies (given in Tables 6.6 and 6.7) revealed only minor differences between CB and B-IB. The former type of neoplasm was more often surface Ig-negative and more frequently expressed CALLA and Tü1, and it was associated in some cases with a more or less well developed follicular dendritic cell meshwork (not found in any of the IB cases). The presence of the follicular dendritic cell meshwork in CB was associated in five cases with T zones, resulting in a follicular architecture. Apart from these minor differences the antigenic profiles of CB and IB had much in common. In both types there are cases which lacked HLA-DR, the B cell antigen To15 or surface Ig, although there were no biopsies in which both B cell antigen and surface Ig were both absent.

The case to case variation in phenotype among the CB and IB makes it difficult to interpret the data obtained. One possibility is that CB and B-IB are not fundamentally distinct entities. The alternative view is that the minor differences seen are indeed a reflection of true differences in cellular origin but that currently available monoclonal antibodies are not adequate to establish this distinction.

Multilobated lymphomas of B cell type, a variant of centroblastic lymphoma?

Among our series of non-Hodgkin's lymphomas there were two cases in which the tumour cells contained multilobated nuclei very similar to the cases described by Pinkus et al (1979) and Weinberg and Pinkus (1981) as a variant of T cell lymphoma. However both our cases were of B cell nature (B cell antigen To15-positive and surface Ig-positive), indicating that multilobated nuclei are not restricted to T cell lymphomas. Since the morphological and antigen phenotype of these two cases most resembled that of normal and neoplastic centroblasts these two cases appear to be a multilobated variant of CB.

Lymphoplasmacytic/cytoid lymphoma (LP-immunocytoma)

This lymphoma type is characterised by the presence of numerous surface Ig-positive/cytoplasmic Ig-negative neoplastic B cells accompanied by small numbers of cytoplasmic Ig-positive cells (Fig. 6.4d) (Lennert et al, 1975). The cytoplasmic Ig is of the same single light chain type as the surface Ig. Two of the cases in our series of 11 LP-immunocytomas showed a phenotype identical to B-CLL, and may represent an atypical B-CLL variant possessing the capacity to differentiate towards plasma cells. All other LP-immunocytoma cases differed clearly from B-CLL in that they lacked Leu-1 and Tü33 antigens. Four cases of LP-immunocytoma also lacked Tü1, providing a further indication of its difference from B-CLL. The immunophenotype of the T1/Leu-1-negative cases was not found in any of the other lymphoma types studied, and these cases hence appear to represent a distinct entity.

T CELL LYMPHOMAS

Table 6.10 shows the results of an attempt to correlate morphological features in T cell lymphomas with antigen profile and the presence of HTLVI. The results indicate that among the many markers investigated there is none that is restricted to a single morphological T cell lymphoma category. Furthermore, it is evident from Table 6.11 that the immunological phenotypes of most T cell lymphomas show considerable variability and overlap. However, there is one additional marker, although not T cell

Table 6.10 Labelling reactions of neoplastic cells and associated cells in T cell lymphomas/leukaemias

	T-ALL T-LB a)	T-CLL a)	b)	T-PLL b)	Cutaneous T cell L — Sezary S. a)	Cutaneous T cell L — M.F. a)	Pleomorphic T cell Lymphoma — ATLL c)	b)	Non-endemic cases — small a)	medium a)	large a)	T-IB a)	L. of plasmacytoid cells a)
Neoplastic cells													
Tü14 (3A1, WT1)	26/26	2/2	0/15	5/5	3/7	0/11	0/20	0/5	4/7	4/7	2/4	3/5	
UCHT1, T3	23/26	2/2	15/15	13/13		10/11	13/15		7/7	7/7	4/4		0/1
T11/Lyt3	16/26	2/2	15/15	17/17	6/7	10/11	30/31	5/5	7/7	7/7	4/4	4/5	0/1
Leu-1/T1	22/26	2/2			7/7	10/11	27/31		7/7	7/7	4/4	5/5	1/1
Tü33	12/26	2/2				10/11			6/7	6/7	3/4	5/5	
NA1/34, T6	15/26	0/3	0/15	0/13	0/8	0/11			0/7	0/7	0/4	0/5	0/1
T4/Leu-3a	11/26	2/2	0/15	8/13	7/8	11/11	30/31	5/5	7/7	6/7	2/4	2/5	1/1
T8	10/26	0/2	15/15	5/13	0/8	0/1	0/31	0/5	0/7	1/7	0/4	1/5	0/1
TdT	5/5		0/15	0/17				0/5					0/1
CALLA (VIL-A1)	14/16	0/2		0/13	0/8	2/11	4/31		0/7	0/7	0/4	1/5	1/1
HLA-DR (Tü35)	2/26	0/2		0/13	0/8	2/11[d]	0/11		1/7	2/7	1/4	1/5	1/1
B cell antigen To15	0/26	0/2			0/8	0/11	0/11		0/7	0/7	0/4	0/5	0/1
S Ig	0/26	0/2	0/15	0/13	0/8	0/11	0/31	0/5	0/7	0/7	0/4	0/5	0/1
Associated cells													
Follicular dendritic cells (R4/23 positive)	0/20	2/2	e	e	e	0/11	e	e	3/7	4/6	2/4	3/5	0/1
Interdigitating cells (NA1/34 positive)	0/20	2/2	e	e	e	11/11[f]	e	e	4/7	3/7	2/4	1/4	0/1

a) Stein et al (1984); Feller et al (1984); b) Catovsky et al (1983); c) Takatsuki et al (1982); Yamada (1983)
d) Large number of Langerhans cells were present in these cases and the possibility could not be excluded that HLA-DR was present on these cells rather than on the tumour cells
e) No data available
f) Skin biopsies were investigated in all 11 cases, and many of the NA1/34 positive dendritic cells were hence probably Langerhans cells and not interdigitating reticulum cells.

Abbreviations: T-ALL = acute lymphoblastic leukaemia of T type; T-LB = lymphoblastic lymphoma of T-type; T-CLL = chronic lymphocytic leukaemia of T-type; T-PLL = prolymphocytic leukaemia of T type; M.F. = mycosis fungoides; ATLL = adult T cell lymphocyte lymphoma/leukaemia; T-IB = immunoblastic lymphoma of T-type.

Table 6.11 Immunophenotypes of T-lymphoblastic lymphomas/leukaemias arranged in a putative differentiation sequence

| | No. of cases | HLA-DR | Tü14 | UCHT1[a] | Leu-1 | NA1/3 | CALLA | T11 | T4 | T8 | Tü33 | Clinical diagnosis | | | Mediastinal mass |
												ALL	LB	ALL/LB	
Prethymic															
I	2	+	+									1[b]	1	0	1
II	1		+									1			
Early thymic															
III	2		+	+	+							1	1	0	0
IV	5		+	+	+	+/−	+/−					0/4	2/4	2/4	0/4
V	4		+	+	+	+/−	+/−	+				1/2	0/2	1/2	2/2
VI	2		+	+	+	+	+/−	+	+/−	+/−		1	1	0	1
Common thymic															
VII	6		+	+	+	+	+	+	+	+	+	1/5	3/5	0/5	5/5
Late thymic															
VIII	4		+	+	+	+/−	+/−	+	+/−	+/−	+	1/4	3/4	0/4	2/2

[a] Detects the same molecule as OKT3 but gives positive reactions in a higher proportion of cases
[b] number of cases

specific, which correlates well with morphology: i.e. the presence of deoxynucleotidyl transferase (TdT), an enzyme selectively associated with lymphoblastic morphology (Braziel et al, 1983). In normal cells of the T lineage TdT is restricted in its occurrence to cortical thymocytes and to neoplasms of early T cells, i.e. thymic derived and prethymic 'lymphoblasts' (reviewed by Bollum, 1979; Janossy et al, 1980; Habeshaw et al, 1979). In consequence, there is general agreement that T cell lymphomas can be divided into two main groups:

1. *TdT-positive* cases, representing thymic and prethymic T cell lymphoblastic lymphoma/leukaemia, e.g. a proliferation of 'medium sized blasts (lymphoblasts)', the phenotype of which resembles that of thymocytes and their precursors. Such neoplasms have an aggressive clinical course and affect mainly children and young adults.

2. *TdT-negative* peripheral (post-thymic) T cell lymphomas/leukaemia, e.g. proliferations of morphologically more mature T cells. These conditions are seen mainly in adults.

Prethymic and thymic (TdT-positive) lymphoblastic lymphomas/leukaemias (T-LB/T-ALL)

Using the classical immunological and enzyme markers (sheep red cell rosetting, complement mediated (EAC) rosetting, polyclonal anti-T cell sera and polyclonal anti-common ALL antisera) and localised acid phosphatase reactivity, considerable heterogeneity in the phenotype of lymphoblastic leukaemia has been demonstrated. More recently the availability of an extensive panel of T cell reactive monoclonal antibodies has provided the opportunity for more detailed analysis of T-LB/T-ALL in relation to normal T cell differentiation (Fig. 6.8). These studies (Reinherz et al, 1980; Bernard et al, 1981; Greaves et al, 1981) have indicated an even greater heterogeneity of T-LB/T-ALL than was evident in earlier studies. The results of our own studies (Feller et al, 1984; Stein et al, 1984b) are presented in Tables 6.10 and 6.11. A major finding was the detection of an antibody (Tü14) that reacts with all cases of T-LB/T-ALL, but is unreactive with B cell neoplasms and with a proportion of mature T cell lymphomas. Similar findings had been obtained with the monoclonal antibody WT1 (Tax et al, 1981) and 3A1 (Catovsky et al, 1983), both of which identified the same 40 000 molecular weight protein as Tü14. These findings are important because there is no other T cell associated antigen which shows this constant expression in early T cells.

The immunophenotyping reactions were used as the basis of an attempt to correlate our cases of T-LB/T-ALL with different differentiation stages (Feller et al, 1984; Stein et al, 1984b). This led to a slightly different and extended scheme (Table 6.11) compared to that proposed by Greaves et al (1981), eight major subsets of prethymic and thymic T cells being identified. Category 7 (the common cortical thymic phenotype) possesses an antigen profile identical to that of nearly all normal cortical thymocytes. Categories 1–6 are defined by decreasing incompleteness of this composite antigen profile and probably represents earlier (and possibly prethymic) phenotypes. Surprisingly two of the cases expressing only Tü14 were HLA-DR-positive. HLA-DR-positive T-LB/T-ALL has not been described and normal cortical lymphocytest are also reported to be HLA-DR-negative. However, we have shown that weak HLA-DR expression on a varying percentage of normal cortical thymocytes can be demonstrated by staining frozen sections and touch imprints of thymus (Stein et al, 1984b). This finding emphasises that HLA-DR expression may potentially occur earlier in T cell differentiation than has previously been thought.

Greaves et al (1981) interpreted all cases of T cell ALL in their study which expressed either T8 or T4 alone as being more immature than those carrying both of these antigens (corresponding to our category 7). However, the demonstration of the late cortical thymocyte marker Tu33 on some of these cases suggests that a proportion of T8+/T4− or T8−/T4+ cases represent a differentiation stage later and not earlier than that of common cortical thymocytes.

On the whole our immunophenotyping studies confirm the work of others (Greaves et al, 1981; Catovsky et al, 1983) showing that T-ALL and T-LB are overlapping diseases but that the two diseases tend to show arrest at a different maturation stage, e.g. most T-ALL have a prethymic or immature thymic phenotype whereas T-LB tends to be associated with a more mature cortical phenotype.

The assessment of T cell lymphomas for the expression of CALLA revealed — in agreement with other studies (e.g. Greaves et al, 1981) — that this antigen was largely restricted to T-ALL/T-LB, with only four exceptions in our series of 65 cases of peripheral (post-thymic) T cell lymphomas (see Table 6.10).

Thiel et al (1980) have previously suggested that cases of lymphoma or leukaemia in which the neoplastic cells simultaneously express T antigens and CALLA represents a hybrid form of neoplasm, lying between common ALL and T-ALL, (so-called CT form of ALL). The results in our series of cases are hence surprising, in that CALLA expression was not associated with an early differentiation stage but rather with a more mature thymic phenotype (Table 6.11). This suggests that pre-T cells are, in contrast to pre-B cells, CALLA-negative and that T cells acquire CALLA during intrathymic differentiation (Fig. 6.8).

Peripheral T cell lymphomas/leukaemias

In the following section five categories of peripheral T cell leukaemia/lymphoma will be described. A number of rare or minor categories (e.g. T cell prolymphocytic lymphoma) are excluded, for reasons of space.

Chronic lymphocytic leukaemia of T type

As Table 6.10 shows, two types may be distinguished: one of helper/inducer T cell phenotype (T4+, T8−), the other exhibiting a suppressor/cytotoxic T cell phenotype (T4−, T8+). This latter immunophenotype is characterised morphologically by the presence of azurophilic granules in the cytoplasm. We are only aware of functional assays of this latter T-CLL type. These assays revealed that the neoplastic cells from most cases did not suppress B cell differentiation in vitro (Hoffman et al, 1982; Thien et al, 1982) but functioned instead in most instances as killer cells (Rumke et al, 1982).

Many of the T4−, T8+ T-CLL cases have only a modest lymphocytosis at presentation, and may be clinically stable for many years. Hence the truly malignant nature of this disorder has sometimes been questioned. However, the observation that spontaneous regressions never occur and that in some patients a clear progression to a more aggressive neoplasm takes place (Catovsky et al, 1982; Hoffman et al, 1982), suggests that these disorders represent a truly neoplastic proliferation. This view is further substantiated by the finding that the surface marker profile of the cells in this disorder differs from that of normal T suppressor cells, i.e. the T cell associated 40 000 molecular weight glycoprotein recognised by antibodies Tü14, 3A1 and WT1 is absent from the neoplastic cells, while being present on 85% of normal peripheral T cells, including all T8+ cells (Haynes, 1981; Catovsky et al, 1983).

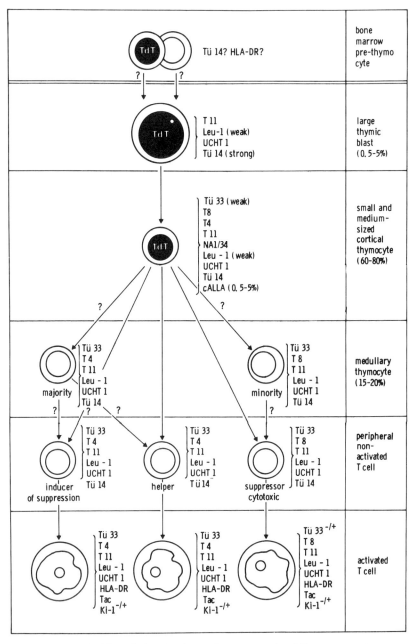

Fig. 6.8　Scheme of T cell differentiation showing markers expressed at different maturation stages.

Cutaneous T cell lymphoma Sezary syndrome (SS) and mycosis fungoides (MF)
Immunologically SS and MF have been described as peripheral T cell lymphomas with a surface antigen profile (Kung et al, 1981; Boumsell et al, 1981) and in vitro function of helper T cells (Broder et al, 1976; Berger et al, 1979), with the exception of rare cases in which the tumour cells have shown a T suppressor phenotype and/or acted in vitro as T suppressor cells (Hopper & Haren, 1980; Haynes et al, 1982). The results of our immunohistological analysis are given in Table 6.10. They show that SS and MF are very similar to each other in immunophenotype, all cases being of T-helper/inducer cell type.

A new finding is that all cases of MF showed a negative reaction for the T cell associated antigen gp40 000 recognised by Tü14, while this antigen was expressed on the cells of three out of seven cases of SS. This finding points to a possible difference in the neoplastic cell type involved in SS and MF.

Pleomorphic T cell lymphoma

This group of T cell lymphomas is characterised by a proliferation of T cells of varying sizes, with very irregular nuclei. On the basis of virological testing for the presence of human (or adult) T cell leukaemia virus (HTLVI) at least two types or groups of pleomorphic T cell lymphomas can be distinguished: (a) endemic (e.g. South Western Japan) HTLV-positive cases usually called adult T cell lymphoma leukaemia (ATLL); and (b) non-endemic HTLV-negative cases.

Endemic HTLV positive cases
Although all immunological studies have shown that the tumour cells in ATLL are of T helper cell type (i.e. are T4+ — see Table 6.10), most functional studies have shown that they suppress rather than induce B cell differentiation in vitro (Yamada, 1983; Hattori et al, 1981). This finding became understandable when it was shown that T4 cells contained two subsets: one promotes B cell differentiation while the other is normally inert but acquires potent suppressor activity following pokeweed mitogen stimulation (Thomas et al, 1981, 1982). Hence ATLL probably derives from this second T4 subset, and thus contrasts with classical Sezary syndrome and mycosis fungoides, both of which arise from the first subset (Fig. 6.8).

Immunohistological labelling has furthermore revealed that ATLL cases are consistently negative for the T cell associated antigen gp40 detected by the monoclonal antibodies 3A1 (Catovsky et al, 1983) and Tü14 (Feller et al, 1984). The absence of this antigen may therefore enable HTLV-positive lymphomas to be distinguished from the majority of non-endemic pleomorphic T cell lymphomas.

Non-endemic cases of pleomorphic T cell lymphomas
These vary greatly in their immunophenotype and there are no specific differences in the antigenic profile between the three morphological variants distinguished (for further details see Table 6.10).

Immunohistological staining with the anti-follicular dendritic cell antibody R4/23 produced an unexpected finding. In more than one-third of the cases the neoplastic areas contained an ill-defined meshwork of follicular dendritic cells without associated

B cells (Fig. 6.9). These follicular dendritic cell meshworks were not visible in conventionally stained sections. These findings suggest that follicular dendritic cells may have a functional relationship not only with B cells but also with T helper/inducer cells.

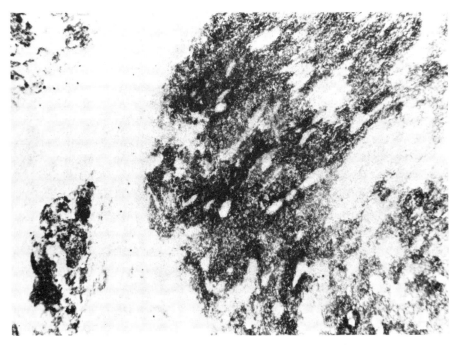

Fig. 6.9   Pleomorphic T cell lymphoma (T4+, T8−) stained with antibody R4/23. The tumour contains large areas of FDC meshwork.

T-immunoblastic lymphoma
Only five of the 71 cases of T cell lymphoma neoplasms were of this type. The results of the immunohistological investigations (Table 6.10) showed that three cases were of T helper and one of T suppressor phenotype, and one lacked both of these markers. It is noteworthy that three of the five T immunoblastic lymphomas contained ill-defined meshworks of follicular dendritic cells.

Lymphoma of plasmacytoid T cells
Although this lymphoma type is very rare it deserves a short comment because of its unusual plasmacytoid morphology. It appears to derive from a normal T cell (found in small numbers in reactive lymphoid tissue), which contains abundant ergastoplasm (although the secreted product is unknown) and shows a distinctive immunophenotype (see Table 6.10). Its plasmacytoid appearance is easily recognisable following Giemsa staining. Although this cell has been recognised for at least 10 years, it is only recently that its neoplastic counterpart has been reported (Müller-Hermelink et al, 1984).

HODGKIN'S DISEASE

Many theories have been propounded concerning the origin and identity of the tumour cells (Hodgkin (H) and Sternberg–Reed (SR) cells) in Hodgkin's disease. The most recent hypotheses have variously suggested a derivation from B cells, macrophages, follicular dendritic cells, interdigitating reticulum cells, myelomonocytic precursor cells and dendritic cells of Steinman type.

A recently performed comparison (Stein et al, 1982b, 1983) (for details see Table 6.12) of the antigen and enzyme profile of Hodgkin and Sternberg–Reed cells with that of other cell types of the haemolymphoid system revealed that H and SR cells are different from all known cell populations. They may hence represent a previously unidentified cell population, or, alternatively, an as yet unrecognised differentiation stage of a known cell type. This latter conclusion was supported by studies with the monoclonal antibody Ki-1, raised against the Hodgkin's disease derived cell line L428 (Schwab et al, 1982). This antibody stained H and SR cells selectively in tissue affected by Hodgkin's disease (Fig. 6.10a); while in normal tissue it showed a unique staining pattern, reacting with the small population of large cells preferentially localised around B cell follicles (Fig. 6.10b). In this context it is of interest that in Hodgkin's disease the H & SR cells are also preferentially localised around B cell follicles and that the perifollicular region tends to be the site of earliest involvement in Hodgkin's disease. These findings suggested that perifollicular large cells detected with the Ki-1 antibody are the normal equivalent of H and SR cells.

Table 6.12 Comparison of the antigenic and enzymatic profile of the major cell types of the lymphoid system

Markers	H and SR cells	Macro-phages	IDC	FDC	Myeloid cells	B cells	Resting T cells
Lysozyme	−	+	−	−	+	−	−
α_1-Antitrypsin	−/+	+	−	−	+	−	−
Anti-monocyte 1	−	+	−	+	−/+	−	−
Anti-monocyte 2	−	+	−	(+)	−/+	−	−
S-HCL3	−	+	−	−	−/+	−	−
OKM-1	−	+	−	+	+	−	−
Mo2	−	+	−	+	−/+	−	−
UCHM1	−	+	−	+	−/+	−	−
R4/23	−	−	−	+	−	−	−
CR3/To5	−	+	−	+	+	+	−
NA1/34	−	−/(+)	+	−	−	−	−
3C4	+/−	−	−	−/+	+	−	−
Peroxidase	−	−	−	−	+	−	−
Chloroacetate esterase	−	−	−	−	+	−	−
Anti-Ig	−	−	−	+	−	+	−
To15 (anti-B cell)	−	−	−	−/(+)	−	+	−
OKT11, Lyt3	−	−	−	−	−	−	+
UCHT1, T3	−	−	−	−	−	−	+
Ki-1	+	−	−	−	−	−	−
Ki-24	+/−	−	−	−	−	−	−

+ = all cells positive; (+) = all cells positive, but weakly; +/− = more positive than negative; −/+ = more negative than positive; −/(+) = only few cells positive.
For further details of the antibodies used see Table 6.1. IDC = interdigitating reticulum cells; FDC = follicular dendritic cells

The finding (Diehl et al, 1983; Stein et al, 1984a) that two newly established Hodgkin's disease-derived cell lines (L540, L591) express (in addition to Ki-1) the T cell associated antigens T11 and/or T3, and one of them (in addition to Ki-1 and the T cell antigens) the B cell antigen To15, prompted us to reinvestigate cases of

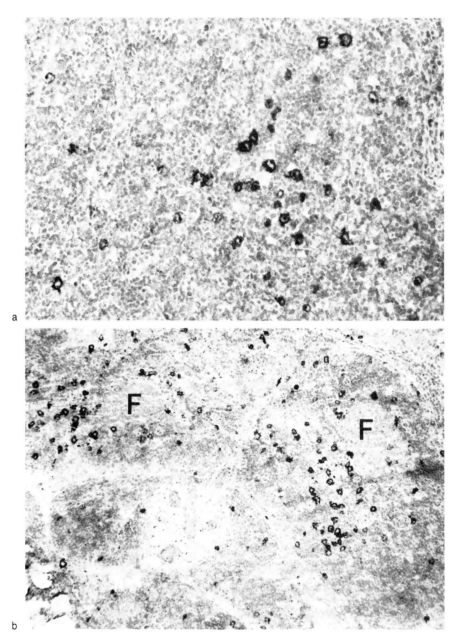

Fig. 6.10a — Hodgkin's disease stained with antibody Ki-1. The Hodgkin and Sternberg–Reed cells are positive, whereas all other cells are unstained.
b — Reactive lymph node stained with the antibody Ki-1. A small population of large cells preferentially localised around the B cell follicles (F) are visualised.

Hodgkin's disease which contained clusters of Hodgkin and Sternberg–Reed cells using the recently developed highly sensitive multilayer APAAP immunoalkaline phosphatase labelling technique (Cordell et al, 1984). The result of this investigation, shown in Table 6.13, revealed, in contrast to earlier studies (Poppema et al, 1982; Stein et al, 1982b), that H and SR cells of many cases of Hodgkin's disease show clear-cut staining with anti-T cell antibodies (relatively frequent) and/or with anti-B cell antibodies (less frequent).

Table 6.13   Antigenic reactivity of Hodgkin and Sternberg–Reed cells and activated T cells

Markers	H + SR cells	Activated T cells
To15	−/+[a]	?
OKT11, Ly3	+/−[a]	+
UCHT1, OKT3	+/−[a]	+
Ki-1	+	few to many +[b]
Ki-24	+/−	few to many +[b]
HLA-DR	+	+
Tü69	+/(−)	+
Tac	+/(−)	+

[a] As revealed by sensitive immunohistological methods in Hodgkin's biopsies containing aggregates of H and SR cells.
[b] The percentage of Ki-1-positive and K-24-positive cells varies with the activating agent used, e.g. PHA, pokeweed mitogen, IL2, etc. The positive cells are usually much larger than the negative ones.

Comparing the revised immunophenotype of Hodgkin and Sternberg–Reed cells with that of other cells it is evident that the phenotype of H and SR cells resemble most closely activated T cells (Fig. 6.8). A number of cases of Hodgkin's disease were therefore stained with two antibodies (anti-Tac and Tü69) which react with activated T cells but not with resting T cells (anti-Tac and Tü69 being directed against the interleukin 2 receptor: Leonard et al, 1982 unpublished data). Both antibodies produced strong staining of Hodgkin and Sternberg–Reed cells in the majority of the cases investigated. Immunolabelling of T cells stimulated with mitogens (and in addition, in some experiments, with interleukin 2) revealed that approximately 3–20% of the T cells had become Ki-1-positive. Further double labelling experiments of normal tonsil cells revealed that approximately 20% of the Ki-1-positive cell population expressed the T11 antigen (SRBC receptor).

Taken together these recent data suggest that Hodgkin and Sternberg–Reed cells and the Ki-1-positive cell population localised around normal B cell follicles may represent a subset or a differentiation stage of activated T cells.

LARGE CELL LYMPHOMAS RESEMBLING TRUE HISTIOCYTIC NEOPLASMS

There is much controversy about the frequency of true histiocytic lymphoma and malignant histiocytosis. Lukes et al (1978) categorised only one neoplasm as being of true histiocytic origin amongst 245 cases of non-Hodgkin's lymphoma studied, whereas Van der Valk et al (1982) reported a histiocytic origin for approximately 10–15% of all non-Hodgkin's lymphomas. Isaacson & Wright (1978) and Isaacson et al (1983) have also reported a high frequency of histiocyte derived lymphomas; however their findings were based on a study of gastrointestinal lymphomas,

[1] Recent studies (Stein et al, 1985) revealed that the tumour cells in nodular lymphocyte predominant Hodgkin's disease contain j chains and are thus B cell derived.

particularly those arising in coeliac disease patients. Both laboratories used lysozyme and α-1 antitrypsin as macrophage markers, but stressed that lysozyme was positive in only a minority of cases, whereas α-1 antitrypsin was detectable in most cases.

To clarify these results we have investigated 32 cases of polymorphic large cell lymphoma (all fulfilling the morphological criteria, reviewed by Wright & Isaacson, 1983, of true histiocytic malignancies: Fig. 6.11a) for the presence of lysozyme, α-1 antitrypsin, for histiocyte associated antigens and for markers of B cells, T cells and Hodgkin and Sternberg–Reed cells. The results of this study are presented in Table 6.14. Staining for lysozyme and macrophage antigens identified a small group (only two cases) in which the tumour cells were positive for lysozyme and all six macrophage associated antigens; and hence appeared to be truly histiocytic in origin. In nine of the remaining 30 cases the tumour cells lacked these markers but were positive for Ki-1 (Fig. 6.11b) and for α-1-antitrypsin, often positive for T cell antigens and sometimes positive for the pan-B cell antigen To15. A further 18 cases expressed Ki-1 but were negative for α-1-antitrypsin (and lysozyme). These cases thus showed a similar antigen profile to the nine lysozyme-negative, α-1-antitrypsin-positive cases (suggesting that both α-1-antitrypsin-positive and -negative cases belong to the same category). Comparing the immunophenotype of this category with that of normal cells and other tumours of lymphoid tissue, it is evident that the antigen profile of all the lysozyme-negative cases resembles that of H and SR cells (Table 6.14) rather than histiocytes. Surprisingly three of the cases fulfilling the morphological criteria of histiocytic malignancies were surface Ig-positive, showing how widely the morphology of neoplastic B cells can vary.

Our conclusions from these findings are:

1. Lysozyme is a reliable marker of histiocytes since it proved to be consistently associated with other histiocytic markers.

2. α-1-antitrypsin is not specific for malignant histiocytes, since it may occur in polymorphic large cell lymphomas which lack lysozyme (and other histiocytic markers) and which express antigens associated with H and SR cells.

3. Most cases of morphologically defined histiocytic neoplasms are lymphocytic in origin, and the tumours cells either show a close antigenic resemblance to H and SR cells (and highly activated T cells: Fig. 6.8) or (less commonly) are of B cell origin (Ig-positive).

IMMUNOHISTOLOGICAL IDENTIFICATION OF PROLIFERATING CELLS IN NON-HODGKIN'S LYMPHOMAS WITH THE MONOCLONAL ANTIBODY Ki-67

It is suggested that measurement of the number of cells in proliferation in a lymphoma may provide an indication of response to therapy and survival. In particular this approach might allow the prognosis of individual patients within a single histological category to be predicted. The recent production of monoclonal antibody Ki-67 that recognises a nuclear antigen present in all proliferating cells (G1, S and G2 cells) but not in resting cells (G null cells) (Gerdes et al, 1983; Gerdes et al, 1984b) now makes it possible to assess rapidly the growth fraction of an individual tumour by immunostaining.

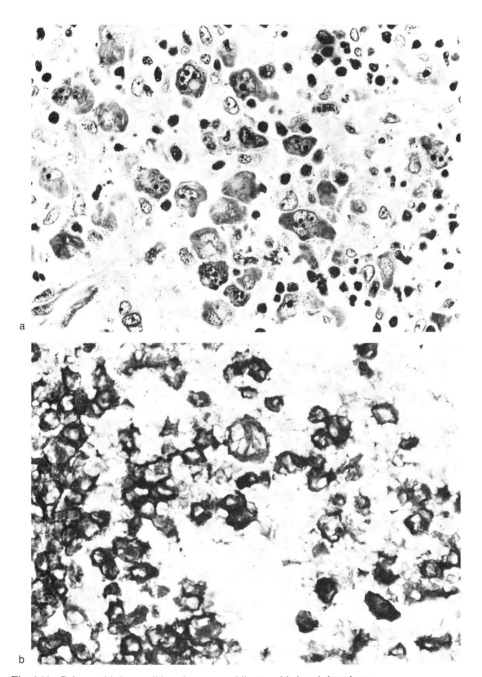

Fig. 6.11 Polymorphic large cell lymphoma resembling true histiocytic lymphoma.
a — Histologic appearance (plastic embedding, Giemsa stain).
b — Staining with the antibody Ki-1. The tumour cells are strongly positive whereas the residual normal cells are unstained.

Table 6.14 Comparison of the immunolabelling reactions of 32 polymorphic larger cell lymphomas (morphologically resembling histiocytic neoplasms) with those of Hodgkins (H) and Sternberg–Reed (SR) cells of 20 cases of Hodgkins disease

Morphological type of tumour cells	No. of cases	Lysozyme	α_1AT[a]	Macrophage[b] antigens	HLA-DR	S Ig	Pan B To15	T3, T11	Ki-1
Polymorphic large cell lymphomas	2 ⎫ 9 ⎪ 32 18 ⎬ 3 ⎭	+ − − −	+ + − −	+ − − −	+ + + +	− − − +	−/+ −/+ −/+ +/−	− +/− +/− −	− + + −
H + SR cells	20	−	−/+	−	+	−	−/+	+/−	+

[a] α_1-Antitrypsin; [b] Antigens detected by OKM1, Mo 2, S-HCL3, anti-monocyte 2, UCHM1.
+ = all cases positive; +/− = more cases positive than negative; −/+ = more cases negative than positive; − = all cases negative.
The 32 cases in this series were selected using Wright & Isaacson's (1983) criteria for the morphological identification of true histiocytic neoplasms.

In initial studies (Gerdes et al, 1984a) the proliferation rate, in terms of the number of Ki-67-positive cells, has been related to histological type and grade of malignancy in a series of 142 cases of non-Hodgkin's lymphomas.

The results (Table 6.15 and Figs 6.12, 6.13a, 6.13b) show a highly significant

Table 6.15 Ki-67-positive cells in low and high grade non-Hodgkin's lymphoma

| | Percentage of Ki-67-positive neoplastic cells | |
Morphological degree of malignancy	less than 26%	more than 26%
Low grade	54[a]	7
High grade	5	76

[a] Number of cases

correlation between the proportion of Ki-67-positive cells and the morphologically defined grade of malignancy. However, comparison of the Ki-67 values in different histologically defined lymphoma types indicates that the division of non-Hodgkin's lymphomas into high and low grade represents an oversimplification. Some morphologically defined lymphoma types show relatively little variation around the mean in the number of proliferating cells. However, within other lymphoma categories there is considerable scatter in the number of proliferating cells, so that the proliferation rates

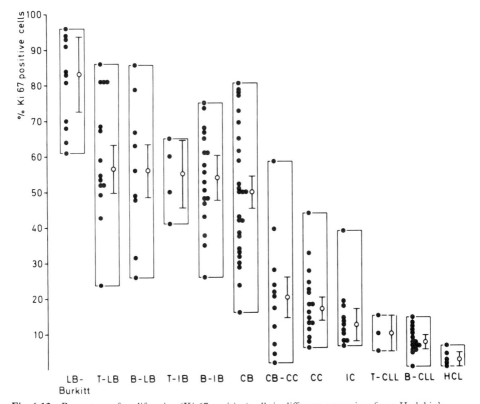

Fig. 6.12 Percentage of proliferating (Ki-67-positive) cells in different categories of non-Hodgkin's lymphomas. The mean value in each category is indicated; one s.d.

of low grade lymphomas overlap with those of high grade malignancies. Follow-up studies are needed to establish which of the two parameters (i.e. morphological degree of malignancy or the proportion of Ki-67-positive cells) correlates better with response to therapy and with survival in individual cases.

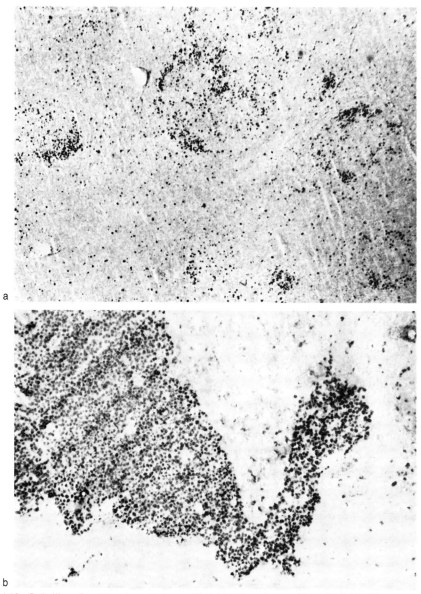

Fig. 6.13   Labelling of proliferating cells in non-Hodgkin's lymphoma with antibody Ki-67.
a—Centroblastic-centrocytic lymphoma. Only a minority of the cells are labelled, most of them associated with the follicles.
b—Lymphoblastic lymphoma of Burkitt type. Nearly all tumour cells are labelled, whereas only a few stained cells are seen in the uninvolved tissue.

Acknowledgement
This work was supported by the Deutsche Forschungsgemeinschaft, Deutsche Krebshilfe and the Leukaemia Research Fund.

REFERENCES

Bennett M H, Farrer-Brown G, Henry K, Jelliffe A M 1974 Classification of non-Hodgkin's lymphomas (letter to the editor). Lancet ii: 405
Berard C, O'Conor G T, Thomas L B, Torloni H 1969 Histopathological definition of Burkitt's tumor. Bulletin of the World Health Organisation 40: 601
Berger C L, Warburton D, Raefat J et al 1979 Cutaneous T cell lymphoma: neoplasm of T cells with helper activity. Blood 53: 642
Bernard A, Boumsell L, Reinherz E L et al 1981 Cell surface characterization of malignant T cells from lymphoblastic lymphoma using monclonal antibodies: evidence for phenotypic differences between malignant T cells from patients with acute lymphoblastic leukaemia and lymphoblastic lymphoma. Blood 57: 1105
Beverley P 1981 Production and use of monoclonal antibodies in transplant immunology. Proceedings XIth International Course on Transplant and Clinical Immunology, Excerpta Medica 87, Amsterdam
Beverley P C L, Callard R E 1981 Distinctive functional characteristics of human 'T' lymphocytes defined by E rosetting as a monoclonal anti-T cell antibody. European Journal of Immunology 11: 329
Bofill M, Janossy, G, Janossa M, Burford G D, Seymour G J, Wernet P, Kelsman E 1985 Human B cell development II. Subpopulations in the human fetus. Journal of Immunology 134: in press
Bollum F J 1979 Terminal deoxynucleotidyl transferase as a hematopoietic cell marker. Blood 54: 1203
Boumsell L, Bernard A, Reinherz E et al 1981 Surface antigens of malignant Sezary and T-CLL cells correspond to those of mature cells. Blood 57: 526
Braziel R M, Keneklis T, Donlon J A, Hsu S-M, Cossman J, Bollum F J et al 1983 Terminal deoxynucleotidyl transferase in non-Hodgkin's lymphoma. American Journal of Clinical Pathology 80: 655
Breard J M, Reinherz E L, Kung P C, Goldstein G, Schlossman S F 1980 A monoclonal antibody reactive with human peripheral blood monocytes. Journal of Immunology 124: 1943
Broder S, Edelson R L, Lutzner M A et al 1976 The Sezary syndrome: a malignant proliferation of helper T cells. Journal of Clinical Investigation 58: 1297
Brouet J-C, Preud'homme J-L, Penit G et al 1979 Acute lymphoblastic leukemia with pre B cell characteristics. Blood 54: 269
Campana D, Janossy G, Bofill M, Trejdosiewicz K, Ma D Hoffbrand A V, Mason D Y et al 1985 Human B cell development I. Phenotypic differences of B lymphocytes in the bone marrow and peripheral lymphoid tissue. Journal of Immunology 134: in press
Catovsky D, Linch D C, Beverley P C L 1982 T-cell disorders in haematological diseases. Clinics in Haematology 11: 661
Catovsky D, San Miguel J F, Soler J, Matutes E, Melo J V, Bourikas G et al 1983 T-cell leukaemias — immunologic and clinical aspects. Journal of Experimental and Clinical Cancer Research 2: 229
Cohen H J, George E R, Kremer W B 1979 Hairy cell leukemia: Cellular characteristics including surface immunoglobulin dynamics and biosynthesis. Blood 53: 764
Cordell J L, Falini B, Erber W, Ghosh A, Abdulaziz Z, MacDonald S et al 1984 Immunoenzymatic labeling of monoclonal antibodies using immune complexes of alkaline phosphatase and monoclonal anti-alkaline phosphatase (APAAP complexes). The Journal of Histochemistry and Cytochemistry 32: 219
Debus E, Weber K, Osborn M 1983a Monoclonal antibodies specific for glial fibrillary acidic (GFA) protein and for each of the neurofilament triplet polypeptides. Differentiation 25: 193
Debus E, Weber K, Osborn M 1983b Monoclonal antibodies to desmin, the muscle-specific intermediate filament protein. EMBO J 2: 2305
Diehl V, Burrichter H, Schaadt M, Kirchner H H, Fonatsch C, Stein H et al 1983 Modern trends in human leukemia V. In: Neth, Gallo, Graves, Moore, Winkler (eds) Haematology and Blood Transfusion. Springer-Verlag, Berlin and Heidelberg 28, p 411
Dorfman R F 1974 Classification of non-Hodgkin's lymphomas (letter to the editor). Lancet i: 1295
Engleman E G, Warnke R, Fox R I, Dilley J, Benike C J, Levy R 1981 Studies of human T lymphocytic antigens recognized by a monoclonal antibody. Proceedings of the National Academy of Sciences 78: 1791
Evans R L, Lazarus H, Penta A C, Schlossman S F 1978 Two functionally distinct subpopulations of human T cells that collaborate in the generation of cytotoxic cells responsible for cell-mediated lympholysis. Journal of Immunology 120: 1423

Falini B, Martelli M F, Tarallo F, Moir D J, Cordell J L, Gatter K C et al 1984a Immunohistological analysis of human bone marrow trephine biopsies using monoclonal antibodies. British Journal of Haematology 56: 365

Falini B, Schwarting R, Erber W, Posnett D N, Martelli M F, Grignani F et al 1984b The differential diagnosis of hairy cell leukaemia with a panel of monoclonal antibodies. American Journal of Clinical Pathology (in press)

Feller 1984 unpublished data

Gatter K C, Alcock C, Heryet A, Pulford K A, Taylor-Papadimitriou J, Stein H, Mason D Y 1984 The differential diagnosis of routinely processed anaplastic tumours using monoclonal antibodies. American Journal of Clinical Pathology (in press)

Gerdes J, Dallenbach F, Lennert K, Lemke H, Stein H 1984a Proliferation rates in malignant non-Hodgkin's lymphomas as determined in situ with the monoclonal antibody Ki-67 (submitted)

Gerdes J, Lemke H, Baisch H, Wacker H-H, Schwab U, Stein H 1985b Cell cycle analysis of a cell proliferation associated human nuclear antigen defined by the monoclonal antibody Ki-67 (submitted)

Gerdes J, Naiem M, Mason D Y, Stein H 1982 Human complement (C3b) receptors defined by a mouse monoclonal antibody. Immunology 45: 645

Gerdes J, Schwab U, Lemke H, Stein H 1983 Production of a mouse monoclonal antibody reactive with a human antigen associated with cell proliferation. International Journal of Cancer 31: 13

Gobbi M, Caligaris-Cappio F, Janossy G 1983 Normal equivalent cells of B cell malignancies: analysis with monoclonal antibodies. British Journal of Haematology 54: 393

Greaves M F, Hariri G, Newman R A, Sutherland D R, Ritter M A, Ritz J 1983 Selective expression of the common acute lymphoblastic leukemia (gp100) antigen on immature lymphoid cells and their malignant counterparts. Blood 61: 628

Greaves M F, Rao J, Hariri G, Verbi W, Catovsky D, Kung P 1981 Phenotypic heterogeneity and cellular origins of T cell malignancies. Leukemia Research 5: 281

Greaves M F, Verbi W, Vogler L B et al 1979 Antigenic and enzymatic phenotypes of pre-B subclass of acute lymphoblastic leukaemia. Leukemia Research 3: 353

Habeshaw J A, Bailey D, Stanfeld A G, Greaves M F 1983 The cellular content of non Hodgkin lymphomas: A comprehensive analysis using monoclonal antibodies and other surface marker techniques. British Journal of Cancer 47: 327

Habeshaw J A, Catley P F, Stanfeld A G et al 1979 Terminal deoxynucleotidyl transferase activity in lymphoma. British Journal of Cancer 39: 566

Hattori T, Uchiyama T, Toibana T, Takatsuki K, Uchino T 1981 Surface phenotype of Japanese adult T-cell leukemia cells characterized by monoclonal antibodies. Blood 58: 645

Haynes B F 1981 Human T lymphocyte antigens as defined by monoclonal antibodies. Immunological Review 57: 127

Haynes B F, Hensley L L, Jegasothy B V 1982 Phenotypic characterization of skin-infiltrating T cells in cutaneous T-cell lymphoma: comparison with benign cutaneous T-cell infiltrates. Blood 60: 463

Hoffman F M, Smith D, Hocking A 1982 T cell chronic lymphocytic leukaemia with suppressor phenotype. Clinical and Experimental Immunology 49: 401

Hogg N, MacDonald S, Slusarenko M, Beverley P C L 1984 Monoclonal antibodies specific for human monocyte, granulocytes and endothelium (in press)

Hopper J E, Haren J M 1980 Studies on a Sezary lymphocyte population with T-suppressor activity: Suppression of Ig synthesis of normal peripheral blood lymphocytes. Clinical Immunology and Immunopathology 17: 43

Howard J C, Hunt S V, Gowans J L 1972 Identification of marrow-derived and thymus-derived small lymphocytes in the lymphoid tissue and thoracic duct lymph of normal rats. Journal of Experimental Medicine 135: 200

Isaacson P, Wright D H 1978 Malignant histiocytosis of the intestine: its relationship to malabsorption and ulcerative jejunitis. Human Pathology 9: 661

Isaacson P, Wright D H, Jones D B 1983 Malignant lymphoma of true histiocytic (monocyte/macrophage) origin. Cancer 51: 80

Janossy G, Bollum F J, Bradstock K F, Ashley J 1980 Cellular phenotypes of normal and leukaemic haemopoietic cells determined by selected antibody combinations. Blood 56: 430

Kamoun M, Martin P J, Hansen J A, Brown M A, Siadak A W, Nowinski R C 1981 Identification of a human T lymphocyte surface protein associated with the E-rosette receptor. Journal of Experimental Medicine 153: 207

Kay H E M 1974 Classification of non-Hodgkin's lymphoma. Lancet ii: 586

Kennett R H 1980 In: Monoclonal antibodies Kennett R H, McKearn T J, Bechtol K B (eds) Plenum Press, New York, p 365

Knapp W, Majdic O, Betelheim P, Liszka K 1982 VIL-A1, a monoclonal antibody reactive with common acute lymphatic leukemia cells. Leukemia Research 6: 137

Korsmeyer S J, Greene W C, Cossman J, Hsu S-M, Jensen J P, Neckers L M et al 1983 Rearrangement and expression of immunoglobulin genes and expression of Tac antigen in hairy cell leukemia. Proceedings of the National Academy of Science USA 80: 4522

Kung P C, Berger C L, Goldstein G et al 1981 Cutaneous T cell lymphoma characterization by monoclonal antibodies. Blood 57: 261

Lane E B 1982 Monoclonal antibodies provide specific intramolecular markers for study of epithelial tonofilament organisation. Journal of Cell Biology 92: 180

Lane E B et al 1985 (manuscript in preparation)

Lennert K, in collaboration with Mohri N, Stein H, Kaiserling E, Müller-Hermelink H K 1978 Malignant lymphomas other than Hodgkin's disease. Handbuch der speziellen pathologischen Anatomie und Histologie 1/3B. Springer-Verlag, Berlin, Heidelberg, New York

Lennert K, Stein H, Kaiserling E 1975 Cytological and functional criteria for the classification of malignant lymphomata. British Journal of Cancer 31: 29

Leonard W J, Depper J M, Uchiyama T, Smith K A, Waldmann T A, Greene W C 1982 A monoclonal antibody that appears to recognize the receptor for human T-cell growth factor; partial characterization of the receptor. Nature 300: 267

Lukes R J, Collins R D 1975 New approaches to the classification of the lymphomata. British Journal of Cancer 31: 1

Lukes R J, Parker J W, Taylor C R et al 1978 Immunological approach to non-Hodgkin's lymphomas and related leukemias. Analysis of the results of multiparameter studies of 425 cases. Seminars in Hematology 15: 322

Martin P J, Hansen J A, Siadak A N, Nowinski R C 1981 Monoclonal antibodies recognizing human T lymphocytes and malignant human lymphocytes: a comparative study. Journal of Immunology 127: 1920

Mason D Y, Stein H, Gerdes J, Falini B, Erber W N, MacDonald S, Gatter K C et al 1984 To15: A monoclonal antibody of value for the immunocytochemical detection of normal and neoplastic B lymphoid cells (submitted)

Mathé G, Rappaport H, O'Connor G T, Torloni H 1976 Histological and cytological typing of neoplastic diseases of haematopoietic and lymphoid tissues. World Health Organization, Geneva (International Histological Classification of Tumors, No. 14)

McMichael A J, Pilsh J K, Galfre G, Mason D Y, Fabre J W, Milstein C 1979 A human thymocytic antigen defined by a hybrid myeloma monoclonal antibody. European Journal of Immunology 9: 205

Meusers P, Bartels H, Brittinger G, Common H, Duehmke E, Fuelle H H et al 1979 Heterogeneity of diffuse 'histiocytic' lymphoma according to the Kiel classification (letter to the editor). New England Journal of Medicine 301: 384

Müller-Hermelink H K, Stein H, Steinmann G, Lennert K 1984 Malignant lymphoma of plasmacytoid T cells. Morphologic and immunologic studies characterizing a special type of T cell. American Journal of Surgical Pathology 7: 849

Naiem M, Gerdes J, Abdulaziz Z, Stein H, Mason D Y 1983 Production of a monoclonal antibody reactive with human dendritic reticulum cells and its use in the immunohistological analysis of lymphoid tissue. Journal of Clinical Pathology 36: 167

National Cancer Institute Sponsored Study 1982 National Cancer Institute sponsored study of classification of non-Hodgkin's lymphomas: Summary and description of a working formulation for clinical usage. Cancer 49: 2112

Pallesen G, Kerndrup G, Ellegaard J 1984 Further evidence for the B-cell nature of hairy cells. A study using immunostaining of splenic tissue with a wide panel of monoclonal antibodies. Blut (in press)

Pinkus G S, Said J W, Hargreaves H 1979 Malignant lymphoma, T cell types: A distinct morphologic variant with large multilobated nuclei, with a report of four cases. American Journal of Clinical Pathology 72: 540

Poppema S, Bhan A K, Reinherz E L, Posner M R, Schlossman S F 1982 In situ immunologic characterization of cellular constituents in lymph nodes and spleen involved by Hodgkin's disease. Blood 59: 226

Posnett D N, Chiorazzi N, Kunkel H G 1982 Monoclonal antibodies with specificity for hairy cell leukemia cells. Journal of Clinical Investigation 70: 254

Preud'homme J L, Seligmann M 1972 Surface bound immunoglobulins as a cell marker in human lymphoproliferative diseases. Blood 40: 777

Rappaport H 1966 Tumors of the hematopoietic system. Atlas of Tumor Pathology, Sect. 3, Fasc. 8. Armed Forces Institute of Pathology, Washington, DC

Reinherz E L, Kung P C, Goldstein G, Levy R H, Schlossman S F 1980 Discrete stages of human introthymic differentiation: Analysis of normal thymocytes and leukemic lymphoblasts of T lineage. Proceedings of the National Academy of Science USA 77: 1588

Rilke F, Lennert K 1981 A perspective of the Kiel classification in relation to other recent classifications of non-Hodgkin's lymphoma, with special reference to the working formulation. In: Histopathology of non-Hodgkin's lymphomas (based on the Kiel classification). Springer-Verlag, Berlin, Heidelberg, New York, p 112

Ritz J, Nadler L M, Bhan A K, Notis-McConarty J, Pesando J M, Schlossman S F 1981a Expression of common acute lymphoblastic leukemia antigen (CALLA) by lymphomas of B-cell and T-cell lineage. Blood 58: 648

Ritz J, Pesando J M, Sallau S E, Clavel L A, Notis-McConarty J, Rosenthal P et al 1981b A monoclonal antibody to human acute lymphoblastic leukemia antigen. Nature 283: 583

Robb-Smith A H T 1938 Reticulosis and reticulosarcoma: a histological classification. Journal of Pathology and Bacteriology 47: 457

Rumke H C, Miedema F, ten Berge I J M et al 1982 Functional properties of T cells in patients with chronic T lymphocytosis and chronic T cell neoplasia. Journal of Immunology 129: 419

Schwab U, Stein H, Gerdes J, Lemke H, Kirchner H, Schaadt M, Diehl V 1982 Production of a monoclonal antibody specific for Hodgkin and Sternberg–Reed cells of Hodgkin's disease and a subset of normal lymphoid cells. Nature 299: 65

Schwarting R, Stein H, Wang C Y 1984 The monoclonal antibodies S-HCL 1 and S-HCL 3 allow the diagnosis of hairy cell leukaemia. Blood (in press)

Stein H, Bonk A, Gerdes J, Lennert K 1981 Zytologische ableitung der malignen non-Hodgkin-lymphome. Verhandlungen der deutschen Gesellschaft fur Dermatologie 32: 188

Stein H, Bonk A, Tolksdorf G, Lennert K, Rodt H, Gerdes J 1980 Immunohistologic analysis of the organization of normal lymphoid tissue and non-Hodgkin's lymphomas. Journal of Histochemistry and Cytochemistry 28: 746

Stein H, Gerdes J, Lemke H, Burrichter H, Diehl V, Gatter K, Mason D Y 1984a Hodgkin's disease and so-called malignant histiocytosis: neoplasms of a new cell type? Oncology 12 (in press)

Stein H, Gerdes J, Mason D Y 1982a The normal and malignant germinal centre. Clinics in Haematology 11: 531

Stein H, Gerdes J, Schwab U, Lemke H, Diehl V, Mason D Y et al 1983 Evidence for the detection of the normal counterpart of Hodgkin and Sternberg–Reed cells. Hematological Oncology 1: 21

Stein H, Gerdes J, Schwab U, Lemke H, Mason D Y, Ziegler A et al 1982b Identification of Hodgkin and Sternberg–Reed cells as a unique cell type derived from a newly-detected small-cell population. International Journal of Cancer 30: 445

Stein H, Kaiserling E, Lennert K 1974 Evidence for B-cell origin of reticulum cell sarcoma. Virchows Archives A. 364: 51

Stein H, Lennert K, Feller A, Mason D Y 1984b Immunohistological analysis of human lymphoma: Correlation of histological and immunological categories. Advances in Cancer Research 42: 67

Stein H, Lennert K, Parwaresch M R 1972 Malignant lymphomas of B-cell type. Lancet ii: 855

Stein H, Mason D Y, Gerdes J, Ziegler A, Naiem M, Wernet P, Lennert K 1981 Immunohistology of B-cell lymphomas. Knapp W (ed) Leukemia Markers p 99

Strauchen J A, Young R C, De Vita V T, Anderson T, Fantone J C, Berard C W 1978 Clinical relevance of the histopathological subclassification of diffuse 'histiocytic' lymphoma. New England Journal of Medicine 299: 1382

Takatsuki K, Uchiyama T, Ueshima Y, Hattori T, Toibana T, Tsudo M et al 1982 Adult T cell leukemia: Proposal as a new disease and cytogenetic, phenotypic, and functional studies of leukemic cells. In: Hanaoka M, Takatsuki K, Shimoyama M (eds) Gann monograph on cancer research no. 28 Adult T cell leukemia and related diseases. Japan Scientific Societies Press, Tokyo and Plenum Press, New York and London, p 13

Tax W J M, Willems H W, Kibbelaar M D A et al 1981 Monoclonal antibodies against human thymocytes and T-lymphocytes. Protides of Biological Fluids 29: 701

Thiel E, Rodt H, Huhn D, Netzel B, Grosse-Wilde H, Gane Shaguru K et al 1980 Multimarker classification of acute lymphoblastic leukemia: Evidence for further T subgroups and evaluation of their clinical significance. Blood 56: 759

Thien S L, Catovsky D, Oscier D et al 1982 T-chronic lymphocytic leukaemia presenting as primary hypogammaglobulinaemia — evidence of a proliferation of T-suppressor cells. Clinical and Experimental Immunology 47: 670

Thomas Y, Rogozinski L, Irigoyen O H et al 1981 Functional analysis of human T cell subsets defined by monoclonal antibodies. IV Induction of suppressor cells within the OKT4+ population. Journal of Experimental Medicine 154: 459

Thomas Y, Rogozinski L, Irigoyen O H et al 1982 Functional analysis of human T cell subsets defined by monoclonal antibodies. V Suppressor cells within the activated OKT4+ population belong to a distinct subset. Journal of Immunology 128: 1386

Todd R F, Nadler L M, Schlossman S F 1981 Antigens on human monocytes identified by monoclonal antibodies. Journal of Immunology 126: 1435

Uchiyama T, Broder S, Waldmann T A 1981 A monoclonal antibody (Tac) reactive with activated and functionally mature T cells. 1 Production of anti-Tac monoclonal antibody and distribution of Tac(+) cells. Journal of Immunology 126: 1393

Ugolini V, Nunez G, Smith G R, Stastny P, Capra J D 1980 Initial characterization of monoclonal antibodies against human monocytes. Proceedings of the National Academy of Science USA 77: 6764

Van der Valk P, Meijer C J L M, Willemze R, van Oosterom A T, Spaander P J, te Velde J 1982 Histiocytic sarcoma (true histiocytic lymphoma): A clinicopathological study of 20 cases. In: Histiocytic sarcoma, thesis, University of Leiden

Vanstapel J, Peteers B, Cordell J L, Heyns W, de Wolf-Peeters C, Desmet V J, Mason D Y 1984 Production of monoclonal antibodies directed against antigenic determinants common to the alpha and beta chain of bovine brain S-100 (submitted).

Verbi W, Greaves M F, Schneider C, Koubek K, Janossy G, Stein H et al 1982 Monoclonal antibodies OKT 11 and OKT 11A have pan-T reactivity and block sheep erythrocyte 'receptors'. European Journal of Immunology 12: 81

Vogler L B, Christ W M, Bockmann D E et al 1978 Pre-B cell leukemia: a new phenotype of childhood lymphoblastic leukemia. New England Journal of Medicine 298: 872

Warnke R A, Gatter K C, Falini B, Hildreth P, Woolston R-E, Pulford K et al 1983 Diagnosis of human lymphoma with monoclonal antileukocyte antibodies. New England Journal of Medicine 309: 1275

Warnke R, Levy R 1978 Immunopathology of follicular lymphomas: A model of B-lymphocyte homing. New England Journal of Medicine 298: 481

Weinberg D S, Pinkus G S 1981 Non-Hodgkin's lymphoma of large multilobated cell type: A clinicopathologic study of ten cases. American Journal of Clinical Pathology 76: 190

Wright P G, Isaacson P G 1983 Malignant lymphomas of the monocyte/macrophage system (histiocytic lymphomas) In: Gottlieb L S, Neville A M, Walker F (eds) Biopsy pathology of the lymphoreticular system. Chapman & Hall, London, ch 11, p 244

Yamada Y 1983 Phenotypic and functional analysis of leukemic cells from 16 patients with adult T-cell leukemia/lymphoma. Blood 61: 192

Ziegler A, Stein H, Muller C, Wernet P 1981 Tu1: A monoclonal antibody defining a B cell subpopulation — usefulness for the classification of non-Hodgkin's lymphomas. In: Knapp W (ed) Leukemia markers.

Ziegler A, Uchanska-Ziegler B, Zenthen J, Wernet P 1982 HLA-antigen expression at the single cell level on a K562 and B cell hybrid: an analysis with monoclonal antibodies using bacterial binding assays. Somatic Cell Genetics 8: 775

7. Allogeneic and autologous bone marrow transplantation

P. B. McGlave   N. K. C. Ramsay   J. H. Kersey

INTRODUCTION

Human bone marrow contains the progenitors of all lymphoid and myeloid cells. It has been demonstrated satisfactorily in clinical trials that transplanted marrow from normal syngeneic or allogeneic donors can replace defective lymphoid systems in children with immunodeficiencies, can provide a new haematopoietic system in individuals with severe aplastic anaemia and can allow lymphohaematopoietic reconstitution following high-dose cytoreductive therapy for malignancies. Bone marrow transplantation has been used to replace abnormal cell lines in enzyme deficiency states such as the mucopolysaccharidoses, and in the haemoglobinopathies. Attempts to prolong survival substantially in patients with malignancy who receive intensive cytoreduction followed by infusion of autologous marrow have not been rewarding; however, methods to 'purge' malignant cells from autologous marrow prior to reinfusion are being investigated.

The most important obstacles to the development of BMT have been infection and graft versus host disease (GVHD). Progress has been made in the prevention and treatment of infection in this uniquely immunocompromised population, and in the understanding of the pathophysiology and clinical course of GVHD. Innovative approaches to the prevention of GVHD including in vivo or ex vivo removal or inactivation of donor T-lymphocytes with biological or chemical agents are being investigated.

At present, allogeneic BMT is confined to patients with siblings matched at the major histocompatibility loci (MHC). Efforts are underway to use selectively mismatched, related donors after manipulation of donor marrow. Programmes are also being designed to find unrelated, MHC-matched donors from the general population.

CLINICAL APPLICATION OF BONE MARROW TRANSPLANTATION

The clinical application of bone marrow transplant (BMT) has been preceded by the development of practical methods to assay the major histocompatibility complex (MHC) both through serotyping of HLA-A, B, C and DR determinants (Dupont et al, 1977) and through D-typing with the mixed leukocyte culture system (MLC) (Bach & van Rood, 1976). Techniques for circumventing major ABO differences between donor and recipient have been developed (Bensinger et al, 1981; Blacklock et al, 1982; Lasky et al, 1983). Marrow harvesting techniques have been standardised (Thomas & Storb, 1970). Marrow harvesting does not pose a major hazard or inconvenience to the donor (Bortin & Buckner, 1983). Wide experience with supportive care, particularly parenteral nutrition has been obtained (Weisdorf et al,

1984). As described subsequently, methods have been developed to ablate malignancy, to immunosuppress recipients, to prevent and treat most infections, and to prevent and treat graft versus host disease. Despite early concerns, only rare cases of second malignancy have been recognised in matched BMT patients (Schubach et al, 1982).

MARROW TRANSPLANTATION FOR IMMUNODEFICIENCY DISORDERS

Primary immunodeficiency disorders lend themselves to the study of clinical BMT because the recipient's immunodeficiency makes it unlikely that donor marrow will be rejected immunologically. The first successful human marrow transplants were performed in patients with primary immunodeficiency disorders (Gatti et al, 1968). The early cases demonstrated that patients who received marrow from an HLA-matched, MLC unreactive sibling show immunologic reconstitution with evidence of repopulation by donor lymphocytes, erythrocytes, megakaryocytes and myeloid cells.

Bone marrow transplant for severe combined immunodeficiency disease (SCID)
The largest experience in the use of marrow transplantation for immunodeficiency disorders is with SCID. These patients require no pretransplant conditioning when allogeneic transplant is performed between MHC-matched siblings. As of 1981 a total of 57 patients with SCID were transplanted using matched sibling donors (Good et al, 1981). Fifty-six per cent of patients were alive with long-term remissions, and the incidence of GVHD was 30%. The majority of SCID patients lack a matached sibling donor, and attempts have been made to use other stem cell sources. These attempts will be discussed in the section of this chapter devoted to mismatched BMT.

Bone marrow transplantation for Wiskott–Aldrich syndrome (WAS)
Wiskott–Aldrich syndrome is an X-linked, generally fatal disorder with major dysfunction of lymphocytes and haematopoietic cells. Since patients with this disease have partial immune function, immunosuppressive therapy (Bach et al, 1968) and more recently immunosuppression combined with myeloblative therapy such as high-dose busulfan, or total body irradiation have been used to treat patients prior to marrow transplantation. Limited experience with the use of HLA non-identical donor marrow for treatment of WAS suggests that engraftment will be a problem until improved conditioning regimens are developed (Filipovich et al, 1983).

BMT for other immunodeficiency syndromes
A great potential exists for the use of BMT in treatment of other immunodeficiency syndromes. Common variable immunodeficiency can be a life-threatening disorder which develops late in childhood and in adults and leads to a progressive diminution of immunological function. One such patient has undergone successful transplantation in Minnesota (Filipovich et al, 1983). Other disorders associated with immunodeficiency which have been successfully treated with bone marrow transplantation include congenital neutrophil dysfunction (Camitta et al, 1977), Kostmann's syndrome (Rappaport et al, 1980) and Chediak–Higashi syndrome.

MARROW TRANSPLANTATION FOR SEVERE APLASTIC ANAEMIA (SAA)

Allogeneic bone marrow transplant

Since the first report of a successful bone marrow transplant in severe aplastic anaemia (Thomas et al, 1972), bone marrow transplantation has evolved as the therapy of choice for patients with severe aplastic anaemia who have matched donors. A prospective study performed between 1974 and 1977 compared androgen therapy for patients who did not have matched donors with bone marrow transplantation for patients who had matched sibling donors (Camitta et al, 1979). Of the patients who received androgens, 30% lived 1 year; over half of the patients died of infection or haemorrhage within 6 months of diagnosis. Long-term survival for the transplant patients was significantly improved (57%).

The initial studies of bone marrow transplantation for severe aplastic anaemia demonstrated improvement in outcome over the natural history of the disease; however, with the use of the standard immunosuppressive preparation (cyclophosphamide, 50 mg/kg/d × 4 days), rejection occurred in 30–60% of the patients (Kersey et al, 1980; Storb et al, 1982). Retransplantation was attempted in most cases, but the mortality was high.

The main reason for failure in transplanted patients was rejection of the donor marrow. Transfusion of patients prior to transplantation causes sensitisation to minor donor antigens, thus emphasising the need for early marrow transplant following the diagnosis of severe aplastic anaemia. In a series of 30 untransfused patients reported by the Seattle group, allogeneic transplantation had a high success rate using cyclophosphamide alone (Storb et al, 1980). Twenty-five of the 30 patients are surviving from 9–84 months with a median follow-up of 19.5 months.

Several conditioning regimens have been developed in an attempt to decrease rejection rates and to improve survival in transfused aplastics undergoing bone marrow transplant. The addition of radiation therapy to cyclophosphamide as preparation for BMT was a logical step. In a series of 23 transfused patients receiving cyclophosphamide and low dose (300 cGy) total body irradiation (TBI), only one patient rejected the graft. The actuarial survival was 61% at 1 year and 49% at 2 years. Age was a significant factor in this study, patients less than 25 years of age had a 2-year survival of 82% compared to 31% for older patients (Gale et al, 1981).

At the University of Minnesota, single-dose total-lymphoid irradiation (TLI) (750 cGy) was used in combination with cyclophosphamide. This preparative regimen was based in part on studies in animals suggesting that TLI could successfully condition bone marrow transplant recipients (Kersey et al, 1980). In a series of 40 patients, rejection occurred in only one patient. Seventy-two per cent of the patients are surviving from 1.5–59 months with a median follow-up of 2 years. Contrary to the experience of other BMT groups, recipient age was not a significant factor in outcome. Two-year survival for patients less than 18 years of age was 77% compared to 62% for those greater than or equal to 18 years (Ramsay et al, 1983a).

In a report from Paris, thoraco-abdominal irradiation with lung shielding combined with cyclophosphamide also reduced the rejection rate. Long-term survival, however, was not markedly improved (Devergie & Gluckman, 1982).

Biological and chemical immunosuppressants have also been added to the preparative regimen prior to transplant. The group in Boston has added procarbazine and anti-thymocyte globulin to cyclophosphamide in 14 patients before grafting (Parkman et al, 1978a). Rejection was decreased, and 64% of the patients in this small series are surviving. Investigators at Hammersmith have used cyclophosphamide as a preparation for BMT, and have used Cyclosporin A as a postgrafting immunosuppressive. In a series of 23 patients the graft failure rate was low (3/23) with 70% of the patients surviving (Hows et al, 1982).

The Seattle team has used donor peripheral blood as a source of additional stem cells in combination with cyclophosphamide as the single conditioning agent (Storb et al, 1978). In a series of 65 transfused patients who received additional donor buffy coat, 13% rejected their marrow grafts. The long-term survival of these patients is 71%; however, an increased incidence of chronic GVHD approaching 50% has been observed with this approach (Storb et al, 1982). Several factors predicting rejection have been identified (Storb et al, 1983).

Syngeneic bone marrow transplantation

Bone marrow transplantation using an identical twin donor for the treatment of severe aplastic anaemia is usually followed by engraftment of the marrow cells without the use of any immunosuppression. In certain cases, however, this has not occurred, suggesting that factors in the microenvironment may affect sustained engraftment. In a review of syngeneic transplants for severe aplastic anaemia, only 11 of 22 patients had sustained complete haematologic recovery following the initial infusion of bone marrow without any immunosuppression (Lu, 1981). Seven additional patients, however, had complete recovery following the use of cyclophosphamide or low-dose total-body irradiation and marrow infusion from the same donor. The fact that these patients required immunosuppression to achieve sustained engraftment suggests that either immunologic factors or a defective microenvironment play a role in the aetiology of their aplasia (Appelbaum et al, 1980).

Treatment of severe aplastic anaemia with immunosuppressive therapy

Speck et al (1977) observed recovery of marrow in a substantial number of patients with severe aplastic anaemia followed therapy with antilymphocyte globulin (ALG) alone or combined with the infusion of haploidentical bone marrow. A recent article confirms Speck's initial observations (Camitta et al, 1983). In this prospective, randomised trial, patients received either androgens and supportive care or ALG, androgens and haploidentical bone marrow. The survival was 76% at 2 years for the patients who received ALG versus 31% for the control group. Another immunosuppressive agent, methylprednisolone has also shown promise for the treatment of aplastic anaemia as reported by Bacigalupo et al (1981).

Over the next decade, the role of bone marrow transplantation versus immunosuppressive therapy for severe aplastic anaemia will need to be clarified. One of the disadvantages of immunosuppressive therapy is the fact that the haematologic recovery is often not complete and recurrence of aplasia occurs. On the other hand, GVHD remains a major obstacle to bone marrow transplantation, especially in older patients. These factors make it imperative that these therapies be analysed in prospective randomised studies which evaluate not only survival, but also duration and completeness of response.

TREATMENT OF MALIGNANCY WITH BONE MARROW TRANSPLANTATION

Treatment of acute non-lymphocytic leukaemia (ANLL) with allogeneic bone marrow transplantation

The Seattle Bone Marrow Transplantation Group first tested the concept that high-dose chemotherapy and total body irradiation (TBI) followed by transplantation of marrow from an identical twin or HLA-matched siblings could ablate refractory leukaemia and establish normal haematopoiesis (Thomas et al, 1977). Patients were parpared for transplantation with a regimen which has been standardised to include cyclophosphamide (60 mg/kg/d × 2 days) followed by TBI (1000 cGy administered as a single dose at 5–7 cGy/min). A majority of patients died within 3 months from acute GVHD or from opportunistic infection. Other patients survived the acute period to die of chronic GVHD or of relapse. Six to 11 years after BMT, 13 of 110 of these 'end stage' patients survive (Thomas, 1982). This preliminary study demonstrated that allogeneic BMT following preparation with high doses of cyclophosphamide and TBI could provide long-term complete remissions in some cases of refractory disease. Analysis of actuarial disease-free survival curves suggested that patients treated with BMT for acute leukaemia who survived disease-free for 2 years would probably never relapse. Additional preparative therapy did not improve outcome of BMT for patients with advanced disease (UCLA Bone Marrow Transplantation Group, 1977).

Transplant performed during first remission has been more successful (Thomas et al, 1979a). Of 87 patients transplanted for ANLL in first remission in Seattle, more than 50% are alive and in remission. Only five of 87 have relapsed after BMT, and fewer than 10% are expected to relapse (Thomas, 1982). Isolated relapses, however, have been reported as late as $5\frac{1}{2}$ years after transplant for remission ANLL (Oliff et al, 1978) and can occur in extramedullary sites (To et al, 1983). Relapses, with few exceptions (Elfenbein et al, 1978), have occurred in recipient-type marrow cells (Newburger et al, 1981).

Follow-up of 33 patients (median age = 28 years) transplanted in first remission at City of Hope using a slightly different preparation confirm the Seattle findings. Actuarial disease-free survival was 60% with a median disease-free survival of 18 months and an actuarial relapse rate of 21% (Forman et al, 1983).

In an attempt to reduce the toxicity of irradiation, the University of Minnesota BMT group modified the preparative regimen to include 750 cGy TBI given at the faster dose rate of 26 cGy/min (Kersey et al, 1982). Actuarial survival for this young group of 17 patients (median age = 14 years) was 65% at 2 years with a relapse rate of 12%. Only 6% of patients developed interstitial pneumonia.

Several theoretical advantages exist for the use of fractionated irradiation in treatment of malignancy (Shank et al, 1981). Recently, Thomas et al (1982a) have compared the use of single dose (1000 cGy) and fractionated (200 cGy × 6 in 6 days) TBI in the treatment of ANLL in remission. There was no difference in the degree of toxicity or in the incidence of interstitial pneumonia between the two groups. A survival advantage existed for patients given the fractionated regimen ($p = 0.05$). Deaths resulting from causes other than leukaemia accounted for the significant difference in survival between the two groups.

Dinsmore et al (1983a) have speculated that intervals between irradiation doses of

24 hours or greater may permit cycling changes that would be expected to reduce the net leukaemic cell kill when compared to shorter intervals. Studies testing the effectiveness of shortened intervals between fractionated radiation doses are underway at the Memorial Sloan–Kettering bone marrow transplant unit.

Santos et al (1983) have recently studied the use of high-dose busulphan and cyclophosphamide as preparation for BMT in a group of 51 patients with ANLL. Time to engraftment averaged 20 days. Major side-effects included oral mucositis, skin hyperpigmentation and haemorrhagic cystitis. Approximately 30% of the patients developed interstitial pneumonitis, usually attributed to CMV and usually fatal. Recurrent or persistent leukaemia occurred in only three patients. Actuarial disease-free survival was 44% in the first remission patients. Ten patients survive disease-free at greater than 2 years. Comparative studies must be performed to determine if the novel preparation of busulphan and cyclophosphamide has advantages over preparative regimens requiring irradiation.

A retrospective study analysing data pooled from a variety of BMT centres confirms the effectiveness of BMT as treatment for ANLL suggested by single institution studies (Gale et al, 1982). Seventy-six first remission patients achieved an actuarial 2-year disease-free survival of 48%; however, actuarially predicted relapse rate was 32%.

Treatment of acute non-lymphocytic leukaemia in second or greater remission with bone marrow transplantation

O'Reilly (1983) recently reported that seven of 11 patients transplanted during second remission of ANLL survived in complete remission 6–37 months after grafting with no relapse. Three-year survival for this group is 64%, which does not differ from that obtained in patients transplanted in first remission (Dinsmore et al, 1982). Excellent results were attributed, in part, to fractionated irradiation.

Results from other single institution studies (Blume et al, 1980; Buckner et al, 1982; Applebaum et al, 1983a; Santos et al, 1983) and retrospective analysis of group data (Bortin et al, 1983) found 2-year survival rates of 25–45%, with relapse rates as high as 50%. Although transplant in second remission may be more effective than conventional therapy, a high relapse rate can be expected.

Comparison of conventional chemotherapy and bone marrow transplantation for treatment of acute non-lymphocytic leukaemia in remission

Some investigators have speculated that BMT represents no more than a very intensive consolidation administered to patients who, by virtue of age, successful induction of remission, absence of early relapse and other less tangible factors are already selected for good prognosis. This concept is supported by recent excellent results reported by Weinstein et al (1980) and updated by Mayer et al (1982) in which patients treated with the 'VAPA' protocol have a remission induction rate of 70%. Thirty-three of 67 patients induced (49%) are disease-free survivors at 19 months. These results may be biased by the 55% disease-free survival of children. The reported relapse rate of 50% of complete remission patients is also of concern. Other investigators using an identical approach have not been able to obtain the excellent results reported. Comparison of conventional therapy and BMT as treatment for remission ANLL are in order.

The efficacy of BMT and conventional therapy have recently been compared (Lumley et al, 1982). Of 53 patients transplanted in first complete remission, 33 (62%) are alive and 32 (60%) are in remission. In the conventional arm, 26 of 51 (51%) are alive and 18 (34%) of 53 in remission. Eighteen per cent of BMT patients have relapsed, while 64% of those in the conventional arm have relapsed.

In a comparative study reported by Appelbaum et al (1982a), 14 of 45 patients (31%) without matched siblings who obtained complete remission from ANLL remain in complete remission while 30 have relapsed. Of 32 patients receiving BMT after similar induction therapy, 18 (50%) are alive in complete remission, 4 relapsed, and 10 died of non-leukaemic causes. Projected 5-year disease-free survival of 47% in the BMT group and 20% in the conventional therapy group was predicted.

Comparison of BMT and conventional therapy for ANLL are difficult to carry out (Begg et al, 1984). Selection biases and comparability of care must be considered. Early analysis of survival curves must be avoided. The quality of survival may be difficult to assess. Although GVHD complicates the majority of allogeneic transplants, it poses significant long-term problems in only 10–15% of transplanted individuals (Sullivan et al, 1981). Quality of life may be impaired in patients receiving conventional therapy when successive courses of high-dose maintenance therapy are employed.

The importance of age on outcome in transplant for acute non-lymphocytic leukaemia

Thomas (1982) analysed the importance of age on outcome of BMT for 75 patients with ANLL transplanted in first remission. Actuarial 2-year survival for 23 patients less than 20 years of age was 70%; actuarial survival for 30 patients 20–29 years of age was 44% and for 22 patients between the ages of 30 and 50 years, actuarial survival was 26%. Survival for patients less than 30 years of age was better ($p = 0.03$) than for older patients. Thomas attributed better survival to a decreased incidence of GVHD. As discussed by O'Reilly (1983), older patients may be more susceptible to GVHD or may be more susceptible to reactivation of latent viruses such as CMV, herpes simplex, and herpes zoster (Neiman et al, 1977).

Allogeneic bone marrow transplantation for acute lymphoblastic leukaemia (ALL)

Chemotherapy is the treatment of choice for patients with 'good risk' childhood type ALL (Chessells, 1982). A subset of children with ALL have so-called 'high risk' features and fare less well. These features include a high white blood cell count, B lymphocyte phenotype, specific chromosome abnormalities or central nervous system involvement at the time of diagnosis (Greaves, 1981). Similarly, individuals over 16 years of age may have a less favourable prognosis (Willenze et al, 1980), although this point is arguable (Clarkson et al, 1981). Original pilot studies tested the efficacy of BMT in treatment of second remission ALL, more recent studies included 'high risk' first complete remission patients.

Of 22 patients reported in the first published series (Thomas et al, 1979b), 27% are reported to be in unmaintained remission at $3\frac{1}{2}$–5 years after BMT (Storb, 1982). Subsequent reports from Seattle (Johnson et al, 1981), from City of Hope (Scott et al, 1983), from the Westminster Bone Marrow Transplantation Team (Barrett et al, 1983) and from the Minnesota BMT group (Woods et al, 1983) suggest that preparation with cyclophosphamide and single-dose TBI is effective in providing long-term disease-free survival after transplant for ALL in remission. Of note, the major cause of failure was relapse which ranged from 30–40% in most series. Isolated extramedullary relapses have been reported (Cairo et al, 1982; Ashford et al, 1983).

Recently, Dinsmore et al (1983a) have prepared remission ALL patients for transplant with a novel regimen including 11 doses of fractionated TBI followed by cyclophosphamide. Most males also received irradiation to the testes. At a median of 24 months, 14 of 22 patients transplanted in second remission are disease-free survivors. The importance of the fractionated schedule in decreasing relapse has not been fully evaluated.

A recent study from the International Bone Marrow Transplant Registry retrospectively analysed the effect of disease status at transplant on outcome of bone marrow transplant (Gale et al, 1983). Patients with ALL transplanted in first or second complete remission had an actuarial survival of 43% and an actuarial relapse rate of 32% at 4 years, which compared favourably ($p < 0.01$) with transplant in patients with more advanced disease. The authors concluded that transplant at first or second complete remission was superior to transplant later in the course of disease; however, a clear-cut advantage of transplant in first remission for high-risk patients over BMT in second remission was not discernible.

Bone marrow transplantation for chronic myelogenous leukaemia (CML)

Fefer et al (1982) first demonstrated that cytogenetic and clinical complete remission from CML could be obtained using BMT technique and syngeneic donor–recipient pairs. Allogeneic BMT performed during blast crisis can provide complete remission from CML; however, disease-free survival is shortened by toxicity and infection when debilitated patients are treated (Doney et al, 1981; McGlave et al, 1981).

Although BMT performed during accelerated phase of disease can ablate the abnormal clone in most cases (McGlave et al, 1982a, 1984), this approach is associated with relapse and with high mortality. Recently, Goldman et al (1983) have updated their experience of BMT performed during chronic phase. Twenty-three of 29 matched patients remain disease-free survivors at 3–120 weeks. Several other reports have recently been published which support the concept that BMT can be used in chronic phase or in early accelerated phase to provide complete remission from CML (Messner et al, 1981; Champlin et al, 1982; Clift et al, 1982; Speck et al, 1982). Retrospective reviews of pooled data and prospective trials are under way to determine the most efficacious timing of BMT in CML, and to determine the relative risk of transplant at various ages in patients with CML. Myelofibrosis and osteosclerosis complicating CML can be cured with BMT and should not disqualify patients from such therapy (McGlave et al, 1982; Oblon et al, 1983).

Bone marrow transplantation for other haematologic malignancies

Appelbaum et al (1983b) have recently reported on BMT as treatment for 10 patients with myelodysplastic syndromes. Three patients prepared for transplantation with cyclophosphamide alone relapsed; however, six of seven patients prepared with cyclophosphamide plus TBI are disease-free survivors. Other groups have reported transplant for preleukaemic syndromes (Stuart et al, 1983), and for preleukaemia following therapy of Hodgkin's disease (Tricot et al, 1982; Gyger et al, 1983).

Recent reports have also suggested that multiple myeloma may respond to allogeneic BMT (Ozer et al, 1983), although relapses have occurred after transplant. Bone marrow transplantation has also been used to treat lymphoma (O'Leary et al, 1983) and acute myelosclerosis (Wolf et al, 1982).

Autologous bone marrow transplantation

Reinfusion of stored, autologous haematopoietic stem cells after cytoreductive therapy for malignancy permits the use of very high doses of antineoplastic agents without concern for myelotoxicity. A matched donor is not required, and the detrimental effects of GVHD and GVHD prophylaxis are not experienced.

A potential drawback to therapy of leukaemia with autologous BMT is loss of the putative graft vs. leukaemia effect. Weiden et al (1981) have suggested that the occurrence of GVHD could be associated with protection from recurrent leukaemia. Recipients of syngeneic BMT had a 54% incidence of leukaemic relapse at 1 year while recipients of allogeneic BMT who did not develop GVHD had a 1-year relapse incidence of 37% and patients who developed acute or chronic GVHD had a relapse incidence of 27%.

John Goldman and his colleagues at the Hammersmith Hospital investigated the application of autologous BMT to the treatment of chronic myelogenous leukaemia (Goldman et al, 1981; Goldman & Lu, 1982). Patients with Ph'-positive CML in chronic phase underwent leukapharesis so that peripheral blood haematopoietic stem cells could be harvested. Untreated, autologous stem cells were frozen in liquid nitrogen, then reinfused (Lowenthal et al, 1976) after patients received high dose cytoreductive therapy for blast crisis. Only rare patients reverted to a partial Ph'-negative state. The majority of patients reported in several studies have succumbed to either persistent or to relapsing CML.

Phillips et al (1983) have noted that treatment of relapse lymphoma patients with 1500 to 2000 cGy of localised irradiation, high-dose cyclophosphamide, fractionated total body irradiation, and infusion of unadulterated autologous marrow cells led to a high rate of engraftment and complete remission. Five of 14 patients survived disease-free at a median of 1 year.

Ex vivo manipulation of the marrow with chemical or biological agents which selectively remove malignant cells without disturbing haematopoietic stem cells is an appealing approach. The Johns Hopkins group has used the marrow 'purging' agent 4-hydroperoxycyclophosphamide (4HC) to prepare marrow for reinfusion (Sharkis et al, 1980). Four of 30 patients with advanced ANLL remain in complete remission from 449 to 881 days after 4HC treatment of marrow and autologous BMT (Kaiser et al, 1983).

The development of specific monoclonal antibodies that bind to antigen sites on leukaemic cells (Greaves et al, 1981) without affecting normal haematopoietic stem cells (Ash et al, 1982) has made it possible to remove leukaemia cells selectively from the marrows of remission patients. Ritz et al (1982) reported on four patients with advanced ALL who received an infusion of autologous marrow subjected to three cycles of treatment with complement and the monoclonal antibody J5. This monoclonal antibody identifies the common ALL antigen (CALLA) found on leukaemia cells in most cases of ALL. In this preliminary report, two of three patients are in remission over 1 year after transplantation and a third relapsed with leukaemia cells bearing the common ALL antigen.

Therapy employing a single monoclonal antibody may not affect all leukaemic stem cells. The group at Minnesota has incubated remission ALL marrow with a 'cocktail' of three monoclonal antibodies and complement (Jansen et al, 1982; LeBien et al, 1983). Early results of a clinical trial reported by Ramsay et al (1983b) demonstrate that six of 12 patients with advanced ALL treated in remission and transplanted with autologous marrow exposed to the monoclonal antibody plus complement 'cocktail' are in complete remission at a median of 6 months. Five patients have relapsed. Engraftment occurred in all patients. Further, studies are under way at Minnesota to refine the technique of marrow incubation with monoclonal antibodies plus complement (LeBien & Stepan, 1983).

BONE MARROW TRANSPLANTATION FOR INHERITED DISORDERS

The marrow stem cell can be used to replace cells which are defective because of an inborn error which provides either a missing or an abnormal gene product. Bone marrow transplantation has been used to treat both sickle cell anaemia (Johnson et al, 1983) and thalassaemia (Thomas et al, 1982b). The abnormal macrophage-derived osteoclast found in osteopetrosis has been replaced first in the animal model (Walker, 1975) and in at least three human patients (Coccia et al, 1980; Sorell et al, 1981; Sieff et al, 1982). The enzyme deficiency and clinical features of the mucopolysaccharidoses have been treated successfully with allogeneic BMT (Hobbs et al, 1982). Early reports of successful BMT for Sanfilippo B disease (Hugh-Jones et al, 1982) and for Maroteaux–Lamy disease (Krivit et al, 1982) have also been published. A problem of overriding concern in the treatment of the polysaccharidoses with BMT is whether neurological deficits seen in these diseases will also be corrected.

GRAFT VERSUS HOST DISEASE

Graft versus host disease (GVHD) is a pathological process in which engrafted donor T-lymphocytes respond to alloantigens expressed on recipient lymphocytes of the lymphopoietic and haematopoietic system. Activated T-lymphocytes then produce damage to recipient target organs by either direct or indirect effects (Billingham, 1968; Beschorner et al, 1980; Vallera et al, 1981). Certain factors have been associated with increased risk of GVHD including older recipient age (Gluckman et al, 1981), female donor (Storb et al, 1977; Bortin et al, 1981), infusion of non-irradiated buffy coat cells during the early transplant course (Storb et al, 1982), and HLA B-18 phenotype (Storb et al, 1983).

Clinical presentation of acute graft vs. host disease

Graft versus host disease can be divided into an acute and a chronic form. Acute GVHD occurs in 30–70% of patients receiving MHC-identical allogeneic transplants and may be an indirect cause of death in 20–40% of affected patients (Bortin et al, 1981). Acute GVHD is most commonly manifested by disruption of the epithelial surfaces of the skin, liver and GI tract leading to rash, cholestatic hepatitis, and diarrhoea; and by delayed reconstitution of the lymphohaematopoietic system (Gale et al, 1978; Noel et al, O'Reilly, 1983; Neudorf et al, 1984).

The rash of acute GVHD initially consists of a faint, maculopapular eruption which may be evanescent or may spread rapidly to a confluent, erythematous, scaly, pruritic rash involving most of the body surface (Hood et al, 1977). Histological findings include a sparse lymphocyte infiltrate with disruption of the normal architecture by basilar vacuolisation, necrosis of individual epidermal cells ('single-cell necrosis') and occasionally separation of the dermal–epidermal junction (Sale et al, 1977; Parkman et al, 1980).

Evidence of liver involvement includes elevated cholestatic and hepatocellular enzymes and hyperbilirubinaemia. Histological findings include extensive bile duct damage ranging from single-cell necrosis to complete obliteration of bile ducts with minimal inflammatory changes and relative sparing of parenchymal tissue (Beschorner et al, 1980; Sloane et al, 1980; Farthing, 1982). Portal or central vein endotheliolitis has also been described (Snover et al, 1984). Hepatic GVHD must be distinguished from other forms of liver damage associated with BMT (Shulman et al, 1980a).

Gastrointestinal involvement is reflected by diarrhoea often associated with abdominal cramping. Stool loss of 2–3 litres per day may occur. Rectal biopsy is helpful in distinguishing acute GVHD from infection; however, rectal pathology found within three weeks of radiation therapy may be secondary to irradiation rather than to GVHD (Epstein et al, 1980). Histological lesions include single cell necrosis of the crypts, crypt drop-out and loss of mucosal surfaces in a patchy to diffuse distribution (Sale et al, 1979). Radiographic evaluation of the bowel reveals rapid transit, excess luminal fluid, thickened, flattened folds and thickened bowel wall (Fisk et al, 1981). Histological evidence of gastrointestinal involvement can also be found in the duodenum, stomach, and oesophagus and can occur independent of GI symptoms (Snover et al, 1984).

Clinical presentation and histopathology of chronic graft versus host disease
Chronic GVHD is sometimes characterised as GVHD persisting or occurring at greater than 100 days after BMT. Between 15–40% of patients develop chronic GVHD, a process pathologically distinct from acute GVHD (Simes et al, 1977; Shulman et al, 1980b; Sullivan et al, 1981).

Skin involvement occurs in about 75% of cases of chronic GVHD (Neudorf et al, 1983) and may present as a localised lesion with dyspigmented or indurated nodules showing a scanty infiltrate of lymphocytes, eosinophils and focal fibrosis. Alternatively, generalised chronic GVHD of skin can occur, presenting as an erythematous rash, which, when untreated, progresses to poikiloderma, hyperpigmentation, sclerosis, atrophy, contractures, or periungal changes. Histological changes include architectural alterations with hyperkeratosis, acanthosis, rete cell necrosis, and hyalinisation. Solar and radiation exposure may exacerbate chronic GVHD of the skin (Zwaan et al, 1980; Sullivan et al, 1981) as may viral infections (Fenyk et al, 1978).

Xerophthalmia, photophobia, and eye discomfort occur in chronic GVHD. Corneal erosions can occur. Xerostomia, and mucosal placques may be found, and oral mucosal biopsies may distinguish oral GVHD from superficial fungal infections or from CMV infection. Biopsy of the labial mucosa often shows mucosal atrophy, and necrosis of squamous cells.

The liver is also commonly involved in chronic GVHD. Cholestatic changes predominate. In progressive cases the histology includes damage to or loss of small- and medium-sized bile ducts, occasional single-cell necrosis of duct epithelium, scant inflammatory infiltrates, peri-portal fibrosis, and changes of chronic active hepatitis (Berman et al, 1980). Hepatic GVHD can resemble primary biliary cirrhosis or liver transplant rejection (Fennell, 1981).

Chronic GVHD can cause oesophageal disease resembling scleroderma with abnormal manometry, small intestinal disease with malabsorption syndrome, crampy pain, diarrhoea and inanition. Roentgenograms can be dramatic with mucosal nodularity, segmentation of diseased bowel, bowel wall oedema (Fisk et al, 1981). Histological changes include submucosal fibrosis, loss of smooth muscle and hyalinisation.

The immune system in acute and chronic graft versus host disease

The lymphoid system is a major target organ for both acute and chronic GVHD. Under normal circumstances immunoglobulin levels and B-cell numbers return to normal levels within 3–6 months after BMT (Korsmeyer et al, 1982; Tsoi, 1982; Witherspoon et al, 1982). Absolute lymphocyte count and T-lymphocyte number become normal in the first 3 months after BMT, and immune function is normal within 1 year (Forman et al, 1981). T-lymphocyte function as tested by MLC responsiveness returns early irrespective of GVHD status; however, T-lymphocyte response to lectins is delayed in patients with acute GVHD. In acute GVHD, normalisation of the helper/suppressor ratio may take greater than 2 years (Noel et al, 1978; Friederich et al, 1982).

In chronic GVHD prolonged deficiency of humoral immunity occurs (Pahwa et al, 1982). Abnormalities include in vitro production of IgG antibodies against host epithelial cells (Witherspoon et al, 1981), circulating immune complexes and complement activation (Graze & Gale, 1979), immune complex deposition, and enhanced susceptibility to infection with encapsulated organisms (Atkinson et al, 1979).

Cellular immune defects in chronic GVHD include increased populations of suppressors T-lymphocytes, slow return of helper T-cell number (Reinherz et al, 1979; Friederich et al, 1982), presence of monocytes capable of non-specific suppression of T-lymphocyte transformation (Tsoi et al, 1980), and abnormal B-cell antibody production. T-lymphocyte response to lectins is delayed in patients with chronic GVHD (Atkinson et al, 1982; Quinones et al, 1983).

In vivo T-lymphocyte modification as prophylaxis of GVHD

Prophylaxis of GVHD is based on the concept that removal or destruction of donor T-lymphocytes can prevent GVHD (Tyan, 1973; Rodt et al, 1974; Vallera et al, 1981). A variety of chemical or biological agents have been administered to allogeneic BMT recipients in an attempt to modify or destroy post-thymic T-lymphocytes.

The post-grafting GVHD prevention regimen most commonly used consists of intravenous methotrexate given to 100 days. This regimen is based on dog studies (Storb et al, 1970) and serves as a standard for comparison of other regimens. Recently a modification of this regimen in which methotrexate is given for only four doses after transplant has been used successfully (Smith et al, 1983). Complications associated with the use of prophylactic methotrexate include severe oral mucositis and delayed engraftment.

Although early attempts at in vivo modification or removal of post-thymic donor T-lymphocytes with antithymocyte globulin (ATG) or antilymphocyte globulin (ALG) were not successful, Ramsay et al (1982) have demonstrated a significantly decreased incidence of acute GVHD (21%) in young patients treated with the combination of methotrexate, prednisone and ATG when compared with a group receiving methotrexate alone (48%). No significant difference in survival could be demonstrated between the methotrexate prophylaxis group (48%) and the metho- trexate, prednisone and ATG prophylaxis group (52%).

One pilot study has been completed recently at the University of Minnesota in which the T-lymphocyte specific monoclonal antibody OKT_3 was infused intra- venously with corticosteroids in an attempt to prevent GVHD. Preliminary results suggest no advantage over the combination of methotrexate, prednisone and ATG currently used to prevent GVHD (Filipovich, 1984).

Cyclosporin A (CSA) is one of a family of fungal metabolites which has proven to be a potent immunosuppressive (Borel et al, 1976; Hess et al, 1982). Cyclosporin A has a selective action against post-thymic T-lymphocytes (Morris, 1981) and is not myelotoxic in the human (Gordon & Singer, 1979).

Cyclosporin has been ineffective in the treatment of established acute GVHD in humans undergoing allogeneic BMT (Powles et al, 1978). Powles et al (1980a), reporting on the Royal Marsden experience, describe the prophylactic use of CSA in 23 patients undergoing allogeneic BMT. Four of 23 patients developed fatal GVHD and another 1 patient developed grade 3 skin GVHD. A majority of patients required CSA therapy for 4–6 months. Three patients have experienced relapse of leukaemia and two developed renal failure. No secondary malignancies were seen.

After preliminary work (Tutschka et al, 1981) the group at Johns Hopkins undertook a pilot study to determine the effectiveness of CSA in preventing GVHD and in preventing interstitial pneumonitis in allogeneic BMT patients (Tutschka et al, 1983). Twenty-one of 22 patients engrafted at a median of 14 days. The incidence of clinically relevant GVHD was 36% which compared favourably with historical controls. No untoward incidence of relapse or second malignancy was seen. The authors felt that CSA alone did not provide adequate prophylactic therapy for acute GVHD.

Deeg et al (1983) have compared the properties of CSA with those of methotrexate in the prevention of acute GVHD following allogeneic BMT for acute leukaemia or for chronic myelogenous leukaemia. Although CSA treatment shortened time to engraftment, decreased transfusion needs and shortened hospital stay, the authors concluded that there was no overall improvement with regard to GVHD prevention, survival or prevention of interstitial pneumonitis.

In a retrospective analysis of data from the MultiCenter European Bone Marrow Transplantation Group, Zwaan & Hermans (1983) compared methotrexate and CSA prophylaxis for acute GVHD. Although a borderline ($p = 0.05$) significant difference in severity of GVHD in favour of the CSA group could be demonstrated, no significant difference in the actuarial survival, GVHD-free survival, or interstitial pneumonitis-free survival could be demonstrated between groups treated with either CSA or methotrexate.

In addition to its potential benefits as an immunosuppressive agent, CSA used in the setting of allogeneic BMT may have several advantages over alternative forms of GVHD prophylaxis. Atkinson et al (1983) demonstrated that patients treated with CSA experienced an earlier rise in absolute neutrophil count, received fewer platelets and granulocyte transfusions and experienced fewer febrile days than retrospectively controlled groups receiving methotrexate. The presence and severity of oral mucositis was marked decreased in the CSA group.

Virtually all clinical studies suggest the potential for severe nephrotoxicity when CSA is used in the setting of allogeneic BMT. In an early study Powles et al (1980a) noted a reversible rise in BUN and serum creatinine associated with the administration of CSA. In a coded histological review, Shulman et al (1981), described a characteristic pattern of arteriolar and glomerular capillary thrombosis, mesangial sclerosis, and severe tubulointerstitial disease in patients receiving CSA. The author noted that the combination of CSA and Amphotericin B may be nephrotoxic.

In the previously cited pilot study from Johns Hopkins (Tutschka et al, 1983), nine patients developed moderate renal failure, and three of these nine required dialysis. Histopathological examination of the kidneys in patients with severe renal dysfunction revealed vacuolisation of the tubules with finely granular casts suggesting tubular necrosis.

Hows et al (1983) characterised two distinct patterns of nephrotoxicity in patients treated with CSA. Early nephrotoxicity occurred in the majority of patients during the first 4 weeks of CSA therapy and was often associated only with a reversible rise in BUN and creatinine. The authors demonstrated a correlation between trough CSA levels and plasma urea and creatinine levels. Even when aminoglycoside levels were carefully kept within therapeutic levels, the concomitant use of these drugs and CSA predisposed to nephrotoxicity. The authors, however, were unable to confirm the synergistic effect of CSA and Amphotericin B found to be instrumental in provoking nephrotoxicity by both Shulman et al (1981) and Tutschka et al (1983). A more serious form of nephrotoxicity occurred at greater than 4 weeks after transplant associated with rising CSA levels, hypertension, thrombocytopenia and red cell fragmentation.

Because CSA is metabolised by liver and excreted in bile (Beveridge, 1982) several authors have speculated that the insults inflicted on the liver during allogeneic BMT including venocclusive disease, GVHD, infection, and damage by hepatotoxic drugs might interfere with the metabolism of CSA. Post-mortem examination of liver specimens, reported by Tutschka et al (1983), revealed large patches of sharply demarcated coagulative necrosis located in the midzone, periportal and centrilobular regions with intensive immunoperoxidase staining for CSA at the periphery of the necrotic regions.

Other side effects of CSA administration include grand mal seizures when CSA is given concurrently with methylprednisolone (Durrant et al, 1982; Hows et al, 1983); gastric intolerance, tremor, hirsutism (Tutschka et al, 1983), abnormal nail growth, anorexia and flat affect (Hows et al, 1983).

Ex vivo removal of T-lymphocytes from donor marrow as prophylaxis for GVHD

In addition to the use of biological and chemical agents for the in vivo prophylaxis of GVHD, a novel strategy has recently been pioneered in which post-thymic donor

T-lymphocytes are removed with specific biological agents ex vivo before infusion of donor marrow.

Reisner et al (1980) have demonstrated that mature T-lymphocytes, but not haematopoietic stem cells possessed the receptor for the plant lectin soybean agglutinin (SBA). Soybean agglutinin in high concentration causes agglutination of T-lymphocytes. Marrow mononuclear cells depleted of T-lymphocytes by soybean agglutination can be further purified by sequential sheep RBC rosetting. This technique has been tested in two separate studies involving haploidentical donor-recipient combinations transplanted for a variety of immunodeficiencies (Filipovich et al, 1983) and in one group of mismatched donor recipient combinations receiving transplant for acute leukaemia (O'Reilly, 1983). GVHD has not been a major problem in any of these pilot studies. Engraftment, however, has not been reliable.

One of the first monoclonal antibodies to be tested in human allogeneic BMT was OKT$_3$, a commercially produced monoclonal which blocks the T-lymphocyte proliferative response to lectins and inhibits cytotoxic T-lymphocyte function. In a pilot study, Filipovich et al (1982), incubated matched donor marrow cells in vitro with 1 mg of purified OKT$_3$ for 30 minutes without exogenous complement. The patients tolerated infusion of marrow well and the time to engraftment was normal. Unfortunately, no decrease in the incidence of acute GVHD was seen. The failure of OKT$_3$ to eliminate GVHD was supported in a study by Prentice et al (1982), in which 17 matched patients received marrow incubated in vitro with OKT$_3$ minus complement. These patients had a similar incidence of acute GVHD, although the severity was believed to be reduced.

Recently, Prentice et al (1984), have reported excellent results in prevention of graft versus host disease by ex vivo removal of mature T-lymphocytes with a 'cocktail' consisting of the anti-T-monoclonal antibodies MBG6 and RFT8 plus rabbit complement. More than 99% of mature T-cells were removed from the marrow using this technique. Only two of 13 evaluable matched patients (median age 19 years, range 7–36 years) developed mild acute skin GVHD, and no cases of moderate or severe GVHD occurred. Median day of white cell engraftment was day +26, slightly later than the historical control of day +22 at this centre.

Another method used to deplete marrow of T-lymphocytes in vitro depends on the cell killing ability of immunotoxins: plant toxins linked covalently to monoclonal antibody with specific affinity for post-thymic T-lymphocytes. At Minnesota, extensive work has been done with the toxin ricin derived from the castor bean and made up of an A chain and a B chain. The B chain binds to galactose receptors on the cell surface. Once the ricin molecule has penetrated the cell, the A chain enzymatically causes irreversible inhibition of protein synthesis by binding to ribosomes. If the reaction is carried out in the presence of sufficient quantities of lactose, cell killing can be confined to those cells displaying the specific antigen attacked by the monoclonal antibody linked with ricin (Olsnes & Pihl, 1973).

Vallera et al (1982, 1983) demonstrated successful ex vivo removal of T-lymphocytes from mouse marrow using the ricin + anti-T-lymphocyte monoclonal system. Filipovich et al (1984) have recently reported successful use of in vitro ricin + monoclonal T-lymphocyte depletion in matched human patients receiving allogeneic BMT. Two patients received donor marrow incubated with equal quantities of 3 anti-T-lymphocyte monoclonal antibodies: TA-1, T101, and UCHT-1, which were covalently linked to whole ricin. Both patients (ages 5 and 6½ years) engrafted early. No graft versus host disease occurred. Further clinical trials testing the efficacy of immuno-toxins are underway at the University of Minnesota.

Therapy of graft versus host disease
The use of adrenal corticosteroid therapy in the treatment of GVHD is widely accepted, but has not been evaluated rigorously. Tutschka et al (1981) recently demonstrated that 2.5 mg/kg/d methylprednisolone was as effective as higher doses in the treatment of GVHD, although individual patients not responding to this low dose did respond to higher doses. Other investigators have reported encouraging results with high-dose bolus methylprednisolone therapy for GVHD (Bacigalupo et al, 1983), including one report of 70% response rate.

Sullivan et al (1981) have recently reviewed the therapy of chronic GVHD. In 52 patients studied, the combination of prednisone with Azathioprine was best tolerated and most useful in treatment. In the prolonged treatment of chronic GVHD, supportive care is essential. Prophylaxis against Pneumocystis carinii with trimethoprim/sulphamethoxazole combinations and against encapsulated organisms with penicillin is important. Reduction of fungal superinfection of the GI tract prevents systemic fungal infections in this setting. Protection of skin with sun screen may prevent exacerbation of dermatitis and artificial moistening of mucosal surfaces may prevent ulceration and dryness.

INFECTION IN BONE MARROW TRANSPLANTATION

Following cytoreductive preparation for BMT, defence against infection is markedly compromised for variable periods of time. Absolute granulocyte number may be low before BMT and remains virtually zero or at least 2–3 weeks after transplant (Thomas et al, 1977). Profound defects in immunoglobulin production are seen in the first year after allogeneic BMT (Korsmeyer et al, 1982; Witherspoon et al, 1982) which may persist or worsen if GVHD occurs. Onset of chronic GVHD may affect immunoglo-bulin production and cell mediated immunity.

Meyers & Thomas (1981) have divided the post-BMT course into three periods characterised by a high incidence of various infections. The early granulocyto-penic period lasts 20–30 days and is characterised by susceptibility to bacterial and fungal infections (Winston et al, 1979). Infection with enteric pathogens, with Gram-positive or with diphtheroid bacteria can be seen, as can fatal infections with uncommon fungal pathogens such as aspergillus (Peterson et al, 1982). Aggressive use of prophylactic and empiric antibiotics, and empiric amphotericin B have lessened these problems. The use of prophylactic and empiric granulocyte therapy has been reported to be helpful in reducing infection immediately after BMT (Clift et al, 1978); however, granulocyte infusions may increase susceptibility to CMV infection (Hersman et al, 1982). Laminar air flow (LAF) protective isolation may be helpful in the support of granulocytopenic patients after transplant (Buckner et al, 1978a).

In the second and third months after BMT, the risk of viral and protozoan infections is high. Cytomegalovirus (CMV) is the most common and most important infection occurring during this period (Meyers et al, 1983) with an incidence ranging from 33–50% in most series (Winston, 1979). As many as 20% of patients receiving allogeneic BMT for acute leukaemia die from CMV disease (Meyers & Thomas, 1981). Interstitial pneumonitis is the most common clinical presentation of disseminated CMV infection with an incidence of 20% and a mortality rate as high as 80% (Meyers & Thomas, 1981). After severe immunosuppression CMV can affect virtually any epithelial surface, including bile duct epithelium, gastric mucosa, colonic epithelium, oropharyngeal surfaces, oesophagus and skin.

Cytomegalovirus infections may result from reactivation of latent endogenous virus or from exogenous infection, most commonly borne by blood products (Winston et al, 1980; Yeager et al, 1981; Hersman et al, 1982). Prophylactic administration of hyperimmune globulin may be effective in preventing disseminated CMV infection (Winston, 1982; Meyers et al, 1983; O'Reilly et al, 1983b). No antiviral agent has been demonstrated to be effective in preventing or treating CMV (Balfour, 1983). Trials using blood products taken from antibody-negative donors to support BMT recipients are underway at our institution and elsewhere, based on excellent results with similar trials to prevent CMV infection in the newborn (Yeager et al, 1981).

During the second and third months following BMT, infections with other viruses are common. O'Reilly et al (1982) have reported latent papovavirus activation which may produce hepatitis or encephalitis, and the Johns Hopkins group has implicated several enteric viruses as a cause of gastroenteritis (Yolken et al, 1982). Disseminated infections with Herpes simplex virus or Herpes varicella virus are seen (Neiman et al, 1977). Prophylaxis and treatment of herpes infection with Acyclovir have made an impact on the mortality from herpes-related virus infection after marrow transplant (Selby et al, 1979; Mitchell et al, 1981; Saral et al, 1981).

Pneumocystis carinii infection can now be prevented or treated with trimethoprim-sulphamethoxazole therapy (Hughes et al, 1977). This drug must be used with caution since its use has been associated with delayed engraftment (Kobrinsky & Ramsay, 1980). Trimethoprim-sulphamethoxazole may have the additional benefit of decreasing Gram-negative sepsis when used prophylactically in granulocytopenic patients (Peterson et al, 1982).

Interstitial pneumonitis represents another complication in the second and third months after BMT which can often be ascribed to infection. An incidence of 20–40% has been reported (O'Reilly, 1983). Cytomegalovirus is the most common pathogen, being found in 44% of histologically proven cases in one series (Meyers et al, 1982). Other pathogens causing interstitial pneumonitis include Herpes virus, adenovirus and Pneumocystis carinii (Neiman et al, 1977; Yolken et al, 1982). In O'Reilly's review (1983), however, 56% of interstitial pneumonitides were idiopathic. The Johns Hopkins group has reported a 'lymphocytic bronchitis' perhaps secondary to GVHD and histologically resembling respiratory syncitial virus infection (Beschorner et al, 1981). Although some cases of pneumonitis may be ascribed to radiation therapy (Peters et al, 1979), other causes must be implicated since preparation for syngeneic transplantation of patients with leukaemia requires TBI and these patients seldom develop interstitial pneumonia (Meyers et al, 1975; Appelbaum et al, 1982b).

Patients who survive the first 3 months following allogeneic BMT are still at risk of infection. Herpes zoster infections can occur late in the course (Atkinson et al, 1979). The risk of infection seems to be greater if chronic GVHD occurs. In a recent review of the Seattle experience (Sullivan et al, 1983), 105 of 198 patients developed Varicella zoster at a median of 201 days. Interstitial pneumonitis developed in 28 of 198 patients. Pneumonia and bacteraemia secondary to *S. pneumonia*, *H. influenza* and *E. coli* were also serious problems. Forty-two of 198 patients died of infection. We and others have taken the precaution of treating chronic GVHD patients with prophylactic antibiotics for as long as GVHD or immunosuppressive therapy continues.

ALLOGENIC BMT FOR PATIENTS WHO DO NOT HAVE A MATCHED, SIBLING DONOR

The use of mismatched, related donors in allogenic bone marrow transplantation
Application of allogeneic BMT techniques has largely been limited to patients with a sibling donor matched at the major histocompatibility loci. The use of mismatched, related donors for the treatment of SCID with allogeneic BMT was a logical first area to study since host immune function could be expected to be diminished. O'Reilly (1983), summarising current experience, notes that seven of 16 patients with genotypically haploidentical donors receiving allogeneic BMT for SCID are long-term survivors. GVHD and failure to establish immune reconstitution were major problems (Good et al, 1981).

Results with BMT for severe aplastic anaemia in the mismatched, related donor settings had been very disappointing. Filipovich et al (1983), reviewing the Minnesota experience found that three of six patients transplanted without TBI preparation rejected donor marrow, and that only one of six patients is a long-term survivor. Hansen et al (1981), reviewing the Seattle experience, found that only one of nine severe aplastic anaemia patients prepared with cyclophosphomide alone and receiving marrow from related donors other than genotypically HLA-identical siblings survived. Three patients died of GVHD, five of rejection.

Experience with mismatched, related allogeneic BMT as treatment for acute leukaemia is more promising. In Hansen's report, seven of 17 patients receiving marrow from haploidentical donors survived. In the Minnesota experience Filipovich et al, 1983), four of eight patients receiving cyclophosphomide plus TBI and mismatched, related donor marrow for malignancy or for osteopetrosis are alive; however, 9/11 of evaluable patients developed moderate or severe GVHD, and 50% of patients developed interstitial pneumonitis.

Another approach to the use of mismatched, related marrow is selective removal of donor post-thymic T-lymphocytes, which have been shown to be important in the pathogenesis of GVHD. The strategy of avoiding post-thymic donor lymphocytes by using fetal haematopoietic stem cells in the treatment of SCID with bone marrow transplant has been attempted (O'Reilly et al, 1980), but overall success has been poor. Application of fetal liver allogeneic BMT in aplastic anaemia or leukaemia has been unrewarding (Lucarelli et al, 1980).

Techniques for ex vivo removal of mature T-lymphocytes from donor marrow by monoclonal antibody plus complement, lectin soybean agglutination, or monoclonal antibody plus ricin conjugates in the matched, related donor recipient situation are discussed in the section on GVHD in this chapter. These techniques have been used to attempt successful mismatched, related allogeneic BMT as well.

O'Reilly et al (1983a) have recently described results from the Memorial Sloan–Kettering Cancer Center experience of transplant of histoincompatible, related donor marrow for treatment of SCID using reisner's technique (Reisner et al, 1980) of T-lymphocyte depletion with soybean agglutination and E-rosette depletion. Eleven of 12 patients were durably engrafted, with full T-lymphocyte reconstitution in eight patients. Two patients required further immunosuppression and a second graft. GVHD was a minor problem. Filipovich et al (1983) have reviewed the Minnesota experience in which seven patients with SCID received mismatched, related donor marrow after a similar T-lymphocyte depletion. Six of seven patients have shown immunologic reconstitution and no patient developed GVHD or interstitial pneumonitis. Two of seven patients are full chimeras, while five of seven are partial chimeras.

Experience with T-lymphocyte depleted mismatched, related donor marrow in the treatment of malignant conditions is less rewarding. Of 12 'poor risk' leukaemia patients receiving transplant preparation with cyclophosphomide and TBI, only six were durably engrafted on the first attempt, while five required further immunosuppression (O'Reilly, 1983).

An equally disturbing problem has recently been reported by Bozdech et al (1983). Of 25 patients receiving mismatched, related allogeneic BMT for malignancy after T-lymphocyte depletion of donor marrow with CT-2 monoclonal antibody to sheep red blood cell receptors + complement, four patients have developed a widespread immunoblastic lymphoproliferative disorder within four months of transplant.

The use of unrelated donors in allogeneic BMT

Storb's experience with allogeneic BMT in the unrelated, DLA identical dog suggest that such transplants are feasible; however, sustained engraftment and GVHD are problems (Storb et al, 1977). Although the chance of two unrelated individuals being HLA phenotypically identical, the recognition of common HLA A, B, D haplotypes, and the development of large banks containing the HLA identities of many individuals does make it feasible to perform computer-aided searches for HLA matched, non-sibling allogeneic BMT donors. Several such large search mechanisms have been set up in the United Kingdom and in the USA (McCullough et al, 1983). Successful non-sibling MHC-matched allogeneic bone marrow transplants have been reported for SCID (O'Reilly et al, 1977), severe aplastic anaemia (Gordon-Smith et al, 1982; Duquesnoy et al, 1983) and acute leukaemia (Hansen et al, 1980).

REFERENCES

Appelbaum F R, Fefer A, Cheever M A et al 1980 Treatment of aplastic anemia by bone marrow transplantation in identical twins. Blood 55(6): 1033–1039

Appelbaum F R, Cheever M A, Fefer A et al 1982a A prospective study of the value of maintenance therapy or bone marrow transplantation in adult acute nonlymphoblastic leukemia. Blood 60 (Suppl 1): 163a

Appelbaum F R, Meyers J D, Fefer A et al 1982b Nonbacterial nonfungal pneumonia following marrow transplantation in 100 identical twins. Transplantation 33: 265–268

Appelbaum F R, Clift R A, Buckner C D et al 1983a Allogeneic marrow transplantation for acute nonlymphocytic leukemia after first relapse. Blood 61(5): 949–953

Appelbaum F R, Storb R, Ramberg R E et al 1983b Treatment of preleukemia with allogeneic marrow transplantation. Blood 62(Suppl 1): 217a

Ash R, Jansen J, Kersey J, LeBien T, Zanjani E 1982 Normal human pluripotential committed hematopoietic progenitors do not express the p24 antigen detected by monoclonal antibody B A-2: Implications for immunotherapy of lymphocytic leukemia. Blood 60: 13010–1316

Ashford R F U, Cassoni A M, Bowcock S et al 1983 Isolated testicular relapse after bone marrow transplantation for acute lymphoblastic leukaemia. Lancet ii: 228

Atkinson K, Storb R, Prentice R L et al 1979 Analysis of late infections in 89 long-term survivors of bone marrow transplantation. Blood 53: 720

Atkinson K, Biggs J C, Ting A, Concannon A J, Dodds A J, Pun A 1983 Cyclosporin A is associated with faster engraftment and less mucositis than methotrexate after allogeneic bone marrow transplantation. British Journal of Haematology 53: 265–270

Bach F H, van Rood J J 1976 The major histocompatibility complex. New England Journal of Medicine 295: 806

Bacigalupo A, Podesta M, Van Lint M T et al 1981 Severe aplastic anaemia: Correlation of in vitro tests with clinical response to immunosuppression in 20 patients. British Journal of Haematology 47: 423–433

Bacigalupo A, van Lint M T, Frassoni F et al 1983 High dose bolus methylprednisolone for the treatment of acute graft versus host disease. Blut 46: 125–132

Balfour H H 1983 Cytomegalovirus disease: Can it be prevented? Annals of Internal Medicine 98: 544–546

Barrett A J, Kendra J R, Lucas C F et al 1983 Bone marrow transplantation for acute lymphoblastic leukaemia. British Journal of Haematology 52: 181–188

Begg C B, McGlave P B, Bennett J M, Cassileth P A, Oken M M 1984 A critical comparison of allogeneic bone marrow transplantation and conventional chemotherapy as treatment for allogeneic non-lymphocytic leukemia. Journal of Clinical Oncology 2: 369–378

Bensinger W I, Buckner C D, Thomas E D, Clift R A 1981 ABO-incompatible marrow transplants. Transplantation 33(4): 427

Berman M, Rabin M, O'Donnell et al 1980 The liver in long-term survivors of marrow transplant–chronic graft-versus-host disease. Journal of Clinical Gastroenterology 2: 53–63

Beschorner W E, Saral R, Hutchins G M, Tutschka P J, Santos G W 1978 Lymphocytic bronchitis associated with graft versus host disease in recipients of bone marrow transplants. New England Journal of Medicine 299: 1030–1036

Beschorner W, Pino J, Boitnott J, Tutschka P, Santos G 1980 Pathology of the liver with bone marrow transplantation. American Journal of Pathology 99: 369–381

Beveridge T 1982 Combined European experience with cyclosporin A in bone marrow transplantation. Experimental Hematology 10(11): 88

Billingham R E 1968 The biology of graft-versus-host reactions. In: The Harvey Lecture Series 62, 1966–1967. New York, Academic Press, p 21–78

Blacklock H A, Gilmore M J M L, Prentice H G et al 1982 ABO incompatible bone marrow transplantation: removal of red blood cells for donor marrow avoiding recipient antibody depletion. Lancet i: 1061–1064

Borel J F, Feurer C 1976 Biological effects of Cyclosporin A: A new antilymphocytic agent. Agents Actions 4/6: 468

Bortin M, Rimm A 1981 Treatment of 144 patients with severe aplastic anemia using immunosuppression and allogeneic marrow transplantation. A report from the International Bone Marrow Transplantation Registry. Transplant Proceedings 13: 227–229

Bortin M, Buckner C 1983 Major complications of marrow harvesting for transplantation. Experimental Hematology 11: 916–921

Bortin M, Gale R P, Kay H E M, Rimm A A 1983 Bone marrow transplantation for acute myelogenous leukemia: Factors associated with early mortality. Journal of the American Medical Association 249: 1166–1175

Bozdech M J, Finlay J L, Trigg M E et al 1983 Monoclonal B-cell lymphoproliferative disorder following monoclonal antibody (CT2) T cell-depleted allogeneic bone marrow transplantation. Blood 62(5 Suppl 1): 218a

Buckner C D, Clift R A, Sanders J E et al 1978a protective environment for marrow transplant recipients: A prospective study. Annals of Internal Medicine 89: 893

Buckner C D, Clift, R A, Thomas E D et al 1982 Allogeneic marrow transplantation for patients with acute nonlymphoblastic leukemia in second remission. Leukemia Research 6: 395–399

Cairo M, Weetman R M, Baehner R L 1982 Isolated testicular leukemia following bone marrow transplant for acute lymphocytic leukemia. American Journal of Pediatric Hematology/Oncology 4: 41–44

Camitta B M, Quesenbury P J, Parkman R 1977 Bone marrow transplantation from infant with neutrophil dysfunction. Experimental Hematology 5: 109–116

Camitta B M, Thomas E D, Nathan D G, Gale R P, Kopecky K J, Rappeport J M, Santos G, Gordon-Smith E C, Storb R 1979 A prospective study of androgens and bone marrow transplantations for treatment of severe aplastic anemia. Blood 53: 504–514

Camitta B, O'Reilly R J, Sensenbrenner L et al 1983 Antithoracic duct lymphocyte globulin therapy. Blood 62(4): 883–888

Champlin R, Ho W, Arensen E, Gale R P 1982 Allogeneic bone marrow transplantation for chronic myelogenous leukemia in chronic or accelerated phase. Blood 60: 1038

Chessells J M 1982 Acute lymphoblastic leukemia. Seminars in Hematology 19: 155–171

Clarkson B, Schauer P, Mertelsmann R et al 1981 Results of intensive treatment of acute lymphoblastic leukemia in adults. In: Burchenal J, Oettgen H F (eds) Cancer, achievements, challenges and prospects for the 1980s. New York, Grune & Stratton, p 301–317

Clift R A, Sanders J E, Thomas E D, William B, Buckner C D 1978 Granulocyte transfusions for the prevention of infection in patients receiving bone marrow transplants. New England Journal of Medicine 298: 1052

Clift R A, Buckner C D, Thomas E D et al 1982 Treatment of chronic granulocytic leukaemia in chronic phase by allogeneic bone marrow transplantation. Lancet 8299ii: 621–622

Coccia P, Krivit W, Cervenka J et al 1980 Successful bone marrow transplantation for infantile malignant osteopetrosis. New England Journal of Medicine 302: 701–708

Deeg H J, Storb R, Buckner C D, Clift R, Thomas E D 1983 Acute non-lymphoblastic leukemia in first remission (ANL) and chronic myelogenous leukemia in chronic phase (CML) treated by allogeneic marrow transplantation: A randomized study of methotrexate (MTX) versus cyclosporine (CSP) for the prevention of graft-vs-host disease (GVHD). Blood 62(Suppl 1): 220a

Devergie A, Gluckman E 1982 Bone marrow transplantation in severe aplastic anemia following cytoxan and thoracoabdominal irradiation. Experimental Hematology 10(Suppl 10): 14–16

Dinsmore R, Kirkpatrick D, Flomenberg N, Gulati S, Shank, S, O'Reilly R J 1982 Allogeneic bone marrow transplantation for acute nonlymphocytic leukemia. Blood 60(Suppl 1): 595a

Dinsmore R, Kirkpatrick D, Flomenberg N et al 1983a Allogeneic bone marrow transplantation for patients with acute lymphoblastic leukemia. Blood 62: 381–388

Dinsmore R, Reich L, Kapoor N, Kirkpatrick D, O'Reilly R J 1983b ABO-incompatible bone marrow transplantation: Removal of erythrocytes by starch sedimentation. British Journal of Haematology 54: 441

Doney K C, Buckner C D, Thomas E D et al 1981 Allogeneic bone marrow transplantation for chronic granulocytic leukemia. Experimental Hematology 9(10): 966–971

Dupont B, Hansen J A, Good R A, O'Reilly R J 1977 Histocompatibility testing for clinical bone marrow transplantation. In: Ferrara G B (ed) HLA system — new aspects. Elsevier–North Holland Biomedical, New York, p 153

Duquesnoy R J, Zeevi A, Marrari M, Hackbarth S, Camitta B 1983 Bone marrow transplantation for severe aplastic anemia using a phenotypically HLA-identical, S B compatible unrelated donor. Transplantation 35: 566

Durrant S, Chipping P M, Palmer S, Gordon-Smith E C 1982 Cyclosporin A methylprednisolone and convulsions. Lancet ii: 829–830

Elfenbein G J, Brogaonkar D S, Bias W B et al 1978 Cytogenetic evidence for recurrence of acute myelogenous leukemia after allogeneic bone marrow transplantation in donor hematopoietic cells. Blood 52: 627–635

Epstein R J, McDonald G V, Sale G E, Shulman H M, Thomas E D 1980 The diagnostic accuracy of the rectal biopsy in acute graft-versus-host disease: a prospective study of thirteen patients. Gastroenterology 78: 764–771

Farthing M J, Clark M L, Sloane J P et al 1982 Liver disease after bone marrow transplantation. Blood 23: 465–475

Fefer A, Cheever M A, Greenberg P D et al 1982 Treatment of chronic granulocytic leukemia with chemoradiotherapy and transplantation of marrow from identical twins. New England Journal of Medicine 306: 63–68

Fenyk J R Jr, Smith C M, Warkentin P I et al 1978 Sclerodermatous graft-versus-host disease limited to an area of measles exanthem. Lancet i: 472–473

Filipovich A 1984 Personal communication

Filipovich A H, Ramsay N K C, Warkentin P et al 1982 Pretreatment of donor bone marrow with monoclonal antibody OKT$_3$ for prevention of acute graft-versus-host disease in allogeneic histocompatible bone marrow transplantation. Lancet i: 1266–1269

Filipovich A H, Ramsay N K C, McGlave P et al 1983 Mismatched bone marrow transplantation at the University of Minnesota; use of related donors other than HLA MLC identical siblings and T cell depletion. In: Recent Advances in BMT. Alan R Liss Inc, New York, p 769–783

Filipovich A H, Vallera D A, Youle R J, Quinones R R, Neville D M Jr, Kersey J H 1984 Ex-vivo treatment of donor bone marrow with anti-T-cell immunotoxins for prevention of graft-versus-host disease. Lancet i: 469–472

Fisk J, Schulman H, Greening R, McDonald G V, Sale G, Thomas E D 1981 Gastrointestinal radiographic features of human graft-versus-host disease. American Journal of Roentgenology 136: 329–336

Forman S J, Spruce W E, Farbenstein M J et al 1983 Bone marrow ablation followed by allogeneic marrow grafting during first complete remission of acute nonlymphocytic leukemia. Blood 61: 439–442

Friederich W, O'Reilly R J, Koziner B, Gebhard D F Jr, Good R A, Evans R L 1982 T lymphocyte reconstitution in recipients of bone marrow transplants with and without graft-versus-host disease:

imbalances of T cell subpopulations having unique regulatory and cognitive functions. Blood 59: 696–700

Gale R P, Opelz G, Mickey M R, Graze P R, Saxon A 1978 Immunodeficiency following allogeneic bone marrow transplantation. Transplant Proceedings 10: 233

Gale R P, Ho W, Feig S et al 1981 Prevention of graft rejection following bone marrow transplantation. Blood 57: 9–12

Gale R P, Kay H E M, Rimm A A, Bortin M M 1982 Bone marrow transplantation for acute myelogenous leukaemia in first remission. (Report of the 15th International Bone Marrow Transplant Registry). Lancet 2: 1006–1009

Gale R P, Kersey J H, Bortin M M et al 1983 Bone marrow transplantation for acute lymphoblastic leukemia. Lancet 2: 663–667

Gatti R A, Meuwissen, Allen H D et al 1968 Immunological reconstitution of sex-linked lymphopenic immunological deficiency. Lancet ii: 1366

Goldman J M, Johnson S A, Catovsky D, Wareham N J, Galton D A G 1981 Autografting for chronic granulocytic leukemia. New England Journal of Medicine 304: 700

Goldman J M, Lu D-P 1982 New approaches in chronic granulocytic leukemia: origin, prognosis and treatment. Seminars in Hematology 19: 241–256

Goldman J M, Baughn A S J, Cranfield T et al 1983 Allogeneic bone marrow transplantation for patients with chronic granulocytic leukemia. Blood 62(Suppl 1): 216a

Good R A, Kapoor N, Pahwa R N et al 1981 Current approaches to the primary immunodeficiencies. In: Fourgerean M, Dausset J (eds) Immunology 80. Academic Press, New York, p 907–929

Gordon M Y, Singer J W 1979 The effects of cyclosporin A and colony formation by human lymphoid and myeloid cells. Nature 279: 433

Gordon-Smith E C, Fairhead S M, Chipping P M et al 1982 Bone marrow transplantation for severe aplastic anaemia using histocompatible unrelated volunteer donors. British Medical Journal 285: 835

Greaves M F 1981 Analysis of the clinical and biological significance of lymphoid phenotypes in acute leukemia. Cancer Research 41: 4752–4766

Greaves M F, Janossy G, Peto J et al 1981 Immunologically defined subclasses of acute leukoblastic leukaemia in children: their relationship to presentation features and prognosis. British Journal of Haematology 48: 179–197

Gyger M, Pereault C, Boileau J et al 1983 Restoration of normal hematopoiesis by bone marrow ablation in allogeneic marrow transplantation in the case of Hodgkin's disease therapy-related preleukemia. Blood 61: 1279–1281

Hansen J A, Clift R A, Thomas E D, Buckner D C, Storb R, Giblett E R 1980 Transplantation of marrow from an unrelated donor to a patient with acute leukemia. New England Journal of Medicine 303: 565–567

Hansen J, Clift R, Mickelson E, Nisperos B, Thomas E D 1981 Marrow transplantation from donors other than HLA identical siblings. Human Immunology 1: 31–40

Herberman R B 1981 Natural killer cells and their possible roles in resistance against disease. Clinical Immunology 1: 1–65

Hersman J, Meyers J D, Thomas E D, Buckner C D, Clift R 1982 The effect of granulocyte transfusions on the incidence of cytomegalovirus infection after allogeneic marrow transplantation. Annals of Internal Medicine 96: 149–152

Hess A D, Tutschka P J, Zhang P, Santos G W 1982 Effect of cyclosporin A on human lymphocyte responses in vitro IV. Production of T cell stimulatory growth factors and development of responsiveness to these growth factors in CsA-treated primary MLR cultures. Journal of Immunology 128: 360–367

Hobbs J R, Hugh-Jones K, Jones D C Q et al 1982 Bone marrow transplantation has corrected the systemic disease of 3 patients with Hurler's mucopolysaccharidosis. Experimental Hematology 10: 48–49

Hood A F, Soter N A, Rappeport J, Gigli I 1977 Graft-versus-host reactions. Cutaneous manifestations following bone marrow transplantation. Archives of Dermatology 113: 1087

Hows J, Palmer S, Gordon-Smith E 1982 Use of cyclosporin A in allogeneic bone marrow transplantation for severe aplastic anemia. Transplant 33: 382–386

Hows J N, Chipping P M, Fairhead S, Smith J, Baughan A, Gordon-Smith E C 1983 Nephrotoxicity in bone marrow transplant recipients treated with cyclosporin A. British Journal of Haematology 54: 69–78

Hugh-Jones K, Kendra J, Jones D C Q et al 1982 Treatment of Sanfilippo B disease (MP111B) by bone marrow transplant. Experimental Hematology 10: 50–51

Hughes W T, Kuhn S, Chaudhary S et al 1977 Successful chemoprophylaxis for Pneumocystis carinii pneumonitis. New England Journal of Medicine 297: 1419

Jansen J, Ash R, Zanjani E, LeBien T, Kersey J H 1982 Monoclonal antibody B A-1 does not bind to hematopoietic precursor cells. Blood 59: 1029–1035

Johnson F L, Thomas E D, Clark B S, Chard R L, Hartmann J R, Storb R 1981 A comparison of marrow transplantation with chemotherapy for children with acute lymphoblastic leukemia in second or subsequent remission. New England Journal of Medicine 305: 846–851

Johnson F L, Look A T, Gockerman J, Ruggiero M, Dallapozza L, Billings F T 1983 Marrow transplantation for sickle cell anemia. Blood 62(5 Suppl 1): 223a

Kaizer H, Stuart R K, Brookmeyer R, Colvin N, Santos G W 1983 Autologous bone marrow transplantation in acute leukemia: a Phase 1 study of in vitro treatment of marrow with 4-Hydroperoxy-cyclophosphamide (4HC) to purge tumor cells. Blood 62(5 Suppl 1): 224a

Kersey J H, Kruger J, Song C, Kloster B 1980 Prolonged bone marrow and skin allograft survival after pretransplant conditioning with cyclophosphamide and total lymphoid irradiation. Transplantation 29: 388–391

Kersey J H, Ramsay N K C, Kim T et al 1982 Allogeneic bone marrow transplantation in acute non-lymphocytic leukemia, a pilot study. Blood 60: 400–403

Kobrinsky N L, Ramsay N K C 1980 Acute megaloblastic anemia induced by high dose trimethoprim-sulfamethoxazole. Annals of Internal Medicine 94: 780–781

Korsmeyer S, Elfenbein G, Goldman C et al 1982 B cell, helper T cell, and suppressor T cell abnormalities contribute to disordered immunoglobulin synthesis in patients following bone marrow transplantation. Transplantation 33: 184–189

Krivit W, Kersey J, Pierpont M E et al 1982 Bone marrow transplantation as treatment for Marateaux Lamy syndrome (Type VI mucopolysaccharidosis). Blood 60(Suppl 1): 606

Lasky L C, Warkentin P I, Kersey J H, Ramsay N K C, McGlave P B, McCullough J 1983 Hemotherapy in patients undergoing blood group incompatible bone marrow transplantation. Transfusion 23: 277–285

LeBien T, Ash R, Zanjani E, Kersey J 1983 In vitro cytodestruction of leukemia cells in human bone marrow using a 'cocktail' of monoclonal antibodies. In: Neth R (ed) Hematology and blood transfusion, vol 28. Springer-Verlag, New York, p 112–116

LeBien T W, Stepan D E 1983 Use of a leukemic cell clonogenic assay to define conditions for autologous marrow treatment with BA-1, BA-2 and BA-3 and rabbit complement. Blood 62(5 Suppl 1): 224a

Lowenthal R M, Park D S, Goldman J M, Th'ng H K, Hill R S, Whyte D 1976 The cryo-preservation of leukaemia cells: morphological and functional changes. British Journal of Haematology 34: 105–117

Lu D 1981 Syngeneic bone marrow transplantation for treatment of aplastic anemia: Report of a case and review of the literature. Experimental Hematology 9: 257–263

Lucarelli G, Porcellini A, Delfini C et al 1980 Fetal liver transplantation in aplastic anemia and acute leukemia in fetal liver transplantation. Excerpta Medica 514: 284

Lumley H S, Powles R L, Morgenstern G R, Clink H M 1982 Matched allogeneic sibling BMT for acute myeloid leukaemia in first remission. Experimental Hematology 10(Suppl 10): 70–71

Mayer R J, Weinstein H J, Coral F S, Rosenthal D S, Frei E 1982 The role of intensive post-induction chemotherapy in the management of patients with acute myelogenous leukemia. Cancer Treatment Review 66: 1455

McCullough J, Rogers G, Dahl R et al 1985 Development and operation of a program to recruit unrelated volunteers for bone marrow donation. New England Journal of Medicine (Submitted)

McGlave P B, Miller W J, Hurd D D, Arthur D C, Kim T 1981 For the University of Minnesota Bone Marrow Transplantation Team: Cytogenetic conversion following allogenic bone marrow transplantation for advanced chronic myelogenous leukemia. Blood 58(5): 1050–1052

McGlave P B, Arthur D C, Kim T H, Ramsay N K C, Hurd D D, Kersey J H 1982a Successful allogeneic bone marrow transplantation for patients in the accelerated phase of chronic granulocytic leukaemia. Lancet 8299ii: 625–627

McGlave P B, Brunning R D, Hurd D D, Kim T H 1982b Reversal of severe myelofibrosis and osteosclerosis following allogeneic bone marrow transplantation for chronic myelogenous leukaemia. British Journal of Haematology 52: 189–194

McGlave P B, Arthur D C, Weisdorf D et al 1984 Allogeneic bone marrow transplantation as treatment for accelerating chronic myelogenous leukemia. Blood 63: 219–222

Messner H A, Curtis J E, Norman C 1981 Allogeneic bone marrow transplantation in patients with CML prior to blastic crisis. Blood 58(5): 175a (Suppl 1)

Meyers J D, Spencer H C, Watts J C et al 1975 Cytomegalovirus pneumonia after human marrow transplantation. Annals of Internal Medicine 82: 181

Meyers J D, Thomas E D 1981 Infection complicating bone marrow transplantation. In: Rubin R H, Young L S (eds) The clinical approach to infection in the immunocompromised host. Plenum Inc, New York

Meyers J D, Leszczynski J, Zaia J A et al 1983 Prevention of cytomegalovirus infection by cytomegalovirus immune globulin after marrow transplantation. Annals of Internal Medicine 98: 442–446

Mitchell D C, Bean B, Gentry S R, Groth K E, Boen J R, Balfour H H 1981 Acyclovir therapy for mucocutaneous herpes simplex infections in immunocompromised patients. Lancet i: 389

Morris P J 1981 Cyclosporin A — overview. Transplant 32: 349–354

Neiman P E, Reeves W, Ray G et al 1977 A prospective analysis of interstitial pneumonia and opportunistic viral infection among recipients of allogeneic bone marrow grafts. Journal of Infectious Diseases 136: 754

Neudorf S M, Filipovich A H, Kersey J 1983 Recent advances in bone marrow transplantation, a technical workshop. American Association of Blood Banks 147–160

Neudorf S, Filipovich A, Ramsay N, Kersey J 1984 Prevention and treatment of acute graft versus host disease. Seminars in Hematology 21(2): 91–100

Newburger P E, Latt S A, Pesando J M et al 1981 Leukemia relapse in donor cells after allogeneic bone marrow transplantation. New England Journal of Medicine 304: 712–714

Noel D R, Witherspoon R P,.Storb R et al 1978 Does graft-versus-host disease influence the tempo of immunologic recovery after allogeneic human marrow transplantation? An observation on 56 long-term survivors. Blood 51: 1087

Oblon D J, Elfenbein G J, Braylin R C, Jones J, Weiner R S 1983 Reversal of myelofibrosis associated with chronic myelogenous leukemia after allogeneic bone marrow transplantation. Experimental Hematology 11: 681–685

O'Leary R, Ramsay N K C, Nesbit M E et al 1983 Bone marrow transplantation for non-Hodgkin's lymphoma in childhood and young adults: a pilot study. American Journal of Medicine 74: 497

Oliff A, Ramu N-P, Poplack D 1978 Leukemic relapse five and a half years after allogeneic bone marrow transplantation. Blood 52: 281–284

Olsnes S, Pihl A 1973 Different biological properties of the two constituent peptide chains of ricin. Biochemistry 12: 3121–3126

O'Reilly R J, Dupont B, Pahwa S et al 1977 Reconstitution in severe combined immunodeficiency by transplantation of marrow from an unrelated donor. New England Journal of Medicine 297: 1311

O'Reilly R J, Kapoor N, Kirkpatrick D 1980 Fetal tissue transplants for severe combined immunodeficiency — their limitations and functional potential. In: Seligmann M, Hitzig W H (eds) Primary immunodeficiencies. New York, Elsevier/North Holland, p 419

O'Reilly R J, Lee F K, Grossbard E et al 1981 Papovavirus excretion following marrow transplantation: incidence and association with hepatic dysfunction. Transplant Proceedings 13: 262

O'Reilly R J 1983 Allogeneic bone marrow transplantation: current status and future directions. Blood 62: 941–964

O'Reilly R J, Brochstein J, Kirkpatrick D 1983a Transplantation of histoincompatible, soybean lectin (SBA) separated, E-rosette depleted marrow for severe combined immunodeficiency (SCID) and leukemia: MHC-related graft resistance in leukemic transplant recipients. Blood 62(5 Suppl 1): 227a

O'Reilly R J, Reich L, Gold J et al 1983b A randomised trial of intravenous hyperimmune globulin for the prevention of cytomegalovirus (CMV) infections following marrow transplantation. Preliminary results. Transplant Proceedings 15: 1405

Ozer H, Han T, Nussbaum-Blumenson A, Henderson E S, Fitzpatrick J, Higby D J 1983 Allogeneic bone marrow transplantation and idiotype monitoring in multiple myeloma. Blood 62(5 Suppl 1): 228a

Pahwa R N, Friedrich W, O'Reilly R J, Good R A 1982 Abnormal humoral immune responses in peripheral blood lymphocyte cultures of bone marrow transplant recipients. Proceedings of the National Academy of Sciences of the USA 79: 2663

Parkman R, Rappeport J, Camitta B, Levey R H, Nathan D G 1978a Successful use of multiagent immunosuppression for bone marrow transplantation of sensitized patients. Blood 52: 1163–1169

Parkman R, Rappeport J, Rosen F 1980 Human graft-versus-host disease. Journal of Investigative Dermatology 74: 276

Peterson P, McGlave P, Ramsay N et al 1982 Infectious diseases following bone marrow transplantation — emergence of aspergillus as a major cause of mortality. Infection Control 4: 81

Phillips G, Wolf F, Herzig G et al 1983 Localized radio therapy followed by cyclophosphamide, fractionated total body irradiation and autologous marrow transplantation for refractory malignant lymphoma. Blood 61(5 Suppl 1): 228a

Powles R L, Barrett A J, Clink H, Kay H E M, Sloane J, McElwain T J 1978 Cyclosporin A for the treatment of graft-versus-host-disease in man. Lancet ii: 1327

Prentice H G, Bateman S M, Bradstock K F, Hoffbrand A V 1980 High dose methylprednisolone therapy in established acute graft versus host disease. Blut 41: 175–177

Prentice H, Janossy G, Skeggs D et al 1982 Use of anti-T-cell monoclonal antibody OKT3 to prevent graft-versus-host disease in allogeneic bone marrow transplantation for acute leukaemia. Lancet i: 700–703

Prentice H G, Blacklock H A, Janossy G et al 1984 Depletion of T-lymphocytes in donor marrow prevents significant graft-versus-host disease in matched allogeneic leukaemic marrow transplant recipients. Lancet i: 472–476

Quinones R, McGlave P B, Ramsay N K C, Kersey J H 1984 Human bone marrow transplantation. In: Fairbanks V F (ed) Current hematology III. Biology of BMT. John Conley, New York, pp 317–351

Ramsay N K C, Kersey J, Robinson L et al 1982 A randomized study of prevention of acute graft-versus-host disease. New England Journal of Medicine 306: 392–397

Ramsay N K C, Kim T H, McGlave P et al 1983a Total lymphoid irradiation and cyclophosphamide conditioning prior to bone marrow transplantation for patients with severe aplastic anemia. Blood 62: 622–626

Ramsay N, LeBien T, Nesbit M et al 1983b Autologous bone marrow transplantation for acute lymphoblastic leukemia following marrow treatment with BA-1, BA-2, BA-3 and rabbit complement. Blood 62(5 Suppl 1): 228a

Rappaport J M, Parkman R, Newburger P 1980 Correction of infantile agranulocytosis (Kostmann's syndrome) and allogeneic bone marrow transplantation. American Journal of Medicine 68: 605–609

Reisner Y, O'Reilly R, Kapoor N, Good R A 1980 Allogeneic bone marrow transplantation using stem cells fractionated by lectins: VI. In vitro analysis of human and monkey bone marrow cells fractionated by sheep red blood cells and soybean agglutinin. Lancet ii: 1320–1324

Ritz J, Sallan S E, Bast R C, Lipton J M, Nathan D G, Schlossman S F 1982 Autologous bone marrow transplantation in CALLA positive ALL following in vitro treatment with J5 monoclonal antibody and complement. Blood 58(5): 175a(Suppl 1)

Rodt H, Theirfelder S, Eulitz M 1974 Anti-lymphocyte antibodies and marrow transplantation III. Effect of heterologous anti-brain antibodies on acute secondary disease in mice. European Journal of Immunology 4: 15–19

Sale G E, Lerner K G, Barker E A et al 1977 The skin biopsy in the diagnosis of acute graft versus host disease in man. American Journal of Pathology 89: 621–636

Sale G E, Shulman H M, McDonald G V, Thomas E D 1979 Gastrointestinal graft-versus-host disease in man. A clinicopathologic study of the rectal biopsy. American Journal of Surgery and Pathology 3: 291–299

Santos G W, Kaizer H 1982 Bone marrow transplantation in acute leukemia. Seminars in Hematology 19(3): 227–239

Santos G W, Tutschka R J, Brookmeyer R et al 1983 Marrow transplantation for acute nonlymphocytic leukemia after treatment with busulfan and cyclophosphamide. New England Journal of Medicine 309: 1347–1353

Saral R, Burns W H, Laskin O L, Santos G W, Lietman P S 1981 Acyclovir prophylaxis of herpes-simplex-virus infections. A randomized double-blind controlled trial in bone marrow transplantation recipients. New England Journal of Medicine 305: 63

Schubach W H, Hackman R, Neiman P E, Miller G, Thomas E D 1982 A monoclonal immunoblastic sarcoma in donor cells bearing Epstein–Barr virus genomes following allogeneic marrow grafting for acute lymphoblastic leukemia. Blood 60: 180

Scott E, Forman S J, Spruce W E et al 1983 Bone marrow ablation followed by allogeneic bone marrow transplantation for patients with high risk acute lymphoblastic leukemia during complete remission. Transplantation Proceedings 15: 1395–1396

Selby P J, Powles R L, Jameson B et al 1979 Parenteral acyclovir therapy for herpes virus infections in man. Lancet ii: 1267

Shank B, Hopfan S, Kim J et al 1981 Hyperfractionated total body irradiation for bone marrow transplantation. International Journal of Radiation Oncology, Biology and Physiology 7: 1109

Sharkis S J, Santos G W, Colvin M 1980 Elimination of acute myelogenous leukemic cells from marrow and tumor suspensions in the rat with 4-Hydroperoxycyclophosphamide. Blood 55: 521–523

Shulman H, McDonald G, Matthews D et al 1980a An analysis of hepatic venoocclusive disease and centrolobular hepatic degeneration following bone marrow transplantation. Gastroenterology 79: 1178–1191

Shulman H M, Sullivan K M, Weiden P L et al 1980b Chronic graft-versus-host syndrome in man: a clinicopathological study of 20 long-term Seattle patients. American Journal of Medicine 69: 204–217

Shulman H, Striker G 1981 Nephrotoxicity of cyclosporin A after allogeneic marrow transplantation: Glomerular thromboses and tubular injury. New England Journal of Medicine 305: 1392

Sieff C, Chessell S J, Levinsky R et al 1982 Allogeneic bone marrow transplantation in infantile malignant osteopetrosis. Lancet i: 437–441

Simes M A, Hohansson E, Rapola J 1977 Scleroderma-like graft-versus-host disease as late consequence of bone marrow transplantation. Lancet ii: 831

Sloane J, Farthing M, Powles R 1980 Histopathological changes in the liver after allogeneic bone marrow transplantation. Journal of Clinical Pathology 33: 344–350

Smith B R, Parkman R P, Lipton J M, Nathan D G, Rappaport J M 1983 Efficacy of short course (four dose) methotrexate following bone marrow transplantation for prevention of graft-vs-host disease. Blood 62(Suppl 1): 230a

Snover D C, Weisdorf S A, Ramsay N K C, McGlave P, Kersey J 1984 Hepatic graft versus host disease: a study of the predictive value of liver biopsy in diagnosis. Hepatology 4(1): 123–130

Sorell M, Kapoor N, Kirkpatrick D et al 1981 Marrow transplantation for juvenile osteopetrosis. American Journal of Medicine 70: 1280–1287

Speck B, Gluckman E, Haak H L, van Rood J 1977 Treatment of aplastic anemia by antilymphocytic globulin with and without bone marrow infusion. Lancet ii: 1145–1148

Speck B, Gratwohl A, Nissen C, Osterwalder B, Muller M, Bannert B 1982 Allogeneic bone marrow transplantation for chronic granulocytic leukemia. Experimental Hematology 10: 48

Storb R, Epstein R B, Graham T C, Thomas E D 1970 Methotrexate regimens for control of graft-versus-host disease in dogs with allogeneic marrow grafts. Transplantation 9: 240–246

Storb R, Weiden P L, Graham T C, Lerner K G, Thomas E D 1977 Marrow grafts between DLA-identical and homozygous unrelated donors. Transplantation 24: 165

Storb R, Thomas E D, Weiden P L et al 1978 One-hundred-ten patients with aplastic anemia treated by marrow transplantation in Seattle. Transplant Proceedings 10: 135

Storb R, Thomas E D 1979 Human marrow transplantation. Transplantation 28: 1–3

Storb R, Thomas E D, Buckner C D et al 1980 Marrow transplantation in thirty 'untransfused' patients with severe aplastic anemia. Annals of Internal Medicine 92: 30–36

Storb R 1982 Bone marrow transplantation in cancer. Clinical Trials 5: 146

Storb R, Doney K C, Thomas E D et al 1982 Marrow transplantation with or without donor buffy coat cells for 65 transfused aplastic anemia patients. Blood 59: 236–246

Storb R, Prentice R L, Thomas E D et al 1983 Factors associated with graft rejection after HLA identical marrow transplantation for aplastic anemia. 55: 573–585

Stuart R K, Mangan A F 1983 Apparent cure of the 50-refractory anemia by syngeneic bone marrow transplantation. Blood 62(5 Suppl 1): 230a

Sullivan K M, Shulman H M, Storb et al 1981 Chronic graft-versus-host disease in fifty-two patients: adverse natural course and successful treatment with combination immunosuppression. Blood 57: 267–276

Sullivan K M, Dahlbert S, Storb R et al 1983 Infection acquisition and prophylaxis in chronic graft-versus-host disease (GVHD). Blood (5 Suppl 1): 230a

Sullivan K M, Weiden P, Storb R, Buckner C D, Thomas E D 1983 preparative regimens and results of second marrow transplant (MT) after graft rejection or leukemic recurrence. Blood 62(Suppl 1): 231a

Thomas E D 1982 The role of marrow transplantation in the eradication of malignant disease. Cancer 49(10): 1963

Thomas E D, Storb R 1970 Technique for human marrow grafting. Blood 36: 507

Thomas E D, Buckner C D, Storb R et al 1972 Aplastic anaemia treated by marrow transplantation. Lancet i: 284–289

Thomas E D, Buckner C D, Banaji M et al 1977 One hundred patients with acute leukemia treated by chemotherapy, total body irradiation, and allogeneic marrow transplantation. Blood 49: 511

Thomas E D, Buckner C D, Clift R A et al 1979a Marrow transplantation for acute nonlymphoblastic leukemia in first remission. New England Journal of Medicine 301: 597–599

Thomas E D, Sanders J E, Fluornoy N et al 1979b Marrow transplantation for patients with acute lymphoblastic leukemia in remission. Blood 54: 468–476

Thomas E D, Buckner C D, Clift R A et al 1982a Marrow B M T for ANLL in first remission using fractionated or single-dose irradiation. International Journal of Radiation Oncology 8: 817–821

Thomas E D, Buckner C D, Sanders J E et al 1982b Marrow transplantation for thalassaemia. Lancet ii: 227

Tricot G, Van Hoof A, Boogaerts M A, Thomas S 1982 Bone marrow transplantation in a patient with secondary leukemia. Experimental Hematology 10(Suppl 10): 83

Tsoi M-S, Storb R, Dobbs S, Medill L, Thomas E D 1980 Cell-mediated immunity to non-HLA antigens of the host by donor lymphocytes in patients with chronic graft-versus-host disease. Journal of Immunology 125: 2258–2262

Tsoi M-S, Storb R, Dobbs S, Thomas E D 1981 Specific suppressor cells in graft-host tolerance of HLA-identical marrow transplantation. Nature 292: 355–357

Tsoi M 1982 Immunological mechanisms of graft-versus-host disease in man. Transplantation 33: 459–464

Tutschka P J, Hess A D 1981 Cyclosporin A in bone marrow transplantation — Baltimore experience in preclinical studies. In: Baum S J, Ledney G D (eds) Experimental hematology today. Springer Verlag, New York, p 99

Tutschka P J, Farmer E, Beschorner W E et al 1981 Therapy of acute graft versus host disease. Experimental Hematology 9: 126

Tutschka P J, Beschorner W E, Hess A D, Santos G W 1983 Cyclosporin A to prevent graft versus host disease: A pilot study in 22 patients receiving allogeneic marrow transplants. Blood 61: 318–325

Tyan M L 1973 Modification of severe graft versus host disease with antisera to the theta antigen or to whole serum. Transplantation 15: 601–604

UCLA Bone Marrow Transplantation Group 1977 Bone marrow transplantation with intensive combination chemotherapy/radiation therapy (SCARI) in acute leukemia. Annals of Internal Medicine. 86: 155–161

Vallera D, Soderling C, Carlson G, Kersey J 1981 Bone marrow transplantation across major histocompatibility barriers in mice. Effects of elimination of T cells from donor grafts by pre-treatment with monoclonal Thy 1.2 plus complement antibody alone. Transplantation 31: 218–222

Vallera D, Youle R, Neville D, Kersey J 1982 Bone marrow transplantation across MHC barriers: V protection of mice from lethal graft-versus-host disease by pretreatment of donor cells with monoclonal anti-thy-1.2 coupled to toxic ricin. Journal of Experimental Medicine 155: 949–954

Vallera D, Youl R, Neville D, Soderling C, Kersey J 1983 Anti T-cell monoclonal antibody-toxin conjugates as reagents for experimental GVHD prophylaxis are not selectively reactive with murine stem cells. Transplantation 36: 73–80

Walker D G 1975 Bone resorption restored in osteopetrotic mice by transplant of normal bone marrow and spleen cells. Science 190: 784–785

Weiden P L, Sullivan K, Flournoy N, Storb R, Thomas E D and the Seattle Marrow Transplant Team 1981 Antileukemic effect of graft-versus-host disease: Contribution to improved survival after allogeneic marrow transplantation. New England Journal of Medicine 304: 1529–1533

Weinstein H J, Mayer R J, Rosenthal D S et al 1980 Treatment of acute myelogenous leukemia in children and adults. New England Journal of Medicine 303: 473

Weisdorf S, Hofland C, Sharp H et al 1984 Total parenteral nutrition in bone marrow transplantation: a clinical evaluation. Pediatric Gastroenterology 3: 95–100

Willemze E R, Drenthe-Schonk A M, Rossum J et al 1980 Treatment of acute lymphoblastic leukaemia in adolescents and adults. Scandinavian Journal of Hematology 24: 421–428

Winston D J, Gale R P, Meyer D V, Young L S and the UCLA Transplantation Group 1979 Infectious complications of human bone marrow transplantation. Medicine 58: 1

Winston D J, Pollard R B, Ho W G et al 1982 Cytomegalovirus immune plasma in bone marrow transplant recipients. Annals of Internal Medicine 97: 11–18

Witherspoon R P, Lum L G, Storb R, Thomas E D 1982 In vitro regulation of immunoglobulin synthesis after human marrow transplantation. II. Deficient T and non-T lymphocyte function within 3–4 months of allogeneic, syngeneic, or autologous marrow grafting for hematologic malignancy. Blood 59: 844–850

Wolf J L, Spruce W E, Bearman R M et al 1982 Reversal of acute malignant myelosclerosis by allogeneic bone marrow transplantation. Blood 59: 191–193

Woods W G, Nesbit M E, Ramsay N K C et al 1983 Intensive therapy followed by bone marrow transplantation for patients with acute lymphocytic leukemia in second or subsequent remission: Determination of prognostic factors. Blood 61: 1182–1189

Yeager A S, Grumet F C, Hafleigh E B, Arvin A M, Bradley J S, Prober C G 1981 Prevention of transfusion-acquired cytomegalovirus infections in newborn infants. Journal of Pediatrics 98: 281–287

Yolken R H, Bishop C A, Townsend T R et al 1982 Infectious gastroenteritis in bone marrow transplant recipients. New England Journal of Medicine 306: 1009

Zwaan F E, Jansen J, Noordijk E M 1980 Graft versus host disease limited to areas of irradiated skin. Lancet 1: 1081–82

Zwaan F E, Hermans J 1983 Report of the European Bone Marrow Transplant — Leukemia Working Party. Experimental Hematology 11(Suppl 13): 3–6

8. The prophylaxis and treatment of infections in patients with bone marrow failure

H. G. Prentice   I. M. Hann

INTRODUCTION

Arguably the success of our treatment of malignant disease has resulted in the opening of a Pandora's box of challenges for the clinician involved in the management of infection in the compromised host. The patient with bone marrow failure, be it idiopathic or iatrogenically induced, is subject to all the microbial risks of the normal host and many more besides: the so-called opportunistic infections. This chapter will deal with some selected aspects of infection in these patients and will not attempt to cover the specific problems of congenital deficiency states.

It would appear timely to review the topic of infection in the immunocompromised patient in view of the increasing toxicity, to the bone marrow, of modern chemo/radiotherapy and the rising use of 'supralethal' therapy followed by bone marrow transplantation for both haematological malignancies and other disorders. With these approaches to therapy the underlying disease is not always the determinant of patient survival, but as often as not, it is the risk of fatal infection.

Some problems of infection prophylaxis or treatment in the compromised host are solved. Within the herpes group viruses there exists an interesting contrast. Herpes simplex and zoster infections are almost totally preventable, but at the other end of the spectrum cytomegalovirus (CMV) remains refractory to therapeutic intervention and is now considered the single most sinister pathogen in the bone marrow transplant (BMT) recipient.

Some of the controversial areas we will explore include the use (and dangers!) of white cell transfusion; the use of empirical antibiotic combinations in the febrile neutropenic patient and the length of treatment in the responding patient; gastrointestinal decontamination selective or total and the use of protective environments.

We must emphasise the pivotal role we ascribe to the place of a multidisciplinary team in the management of these 'at risk' patients. Advances detailed in this chapter have involved the collaboration of the clinical haematologist and microbiologist. They have never been achieved outwith the context of carefully controlled clinical trials which, for the most part, require multi-institutional co-operation. Since prevention of infection is paramount, the first section of this review deals with the factors predisposing these patients to infection. The types of infection occurring in these patients are shown in Table 8.1.

FACTORS PREDISPOSING TO INFECTION

It should be emphasised that establishment of opportunistic infection is a multifactorial process, i.e. the loss of a protective barrier plus the absence of a cellular or

199

Table 8.1   Major pathogens and their clinical correlates in marrow failure.

Class Bacteria		
Gram negative:	*Pseudomonas* species	Septicaemia Skin (ecthyma gangrenosum), lung, perianal
	Klebsiella	Septicaemia, pneumonia, perianal
	Escherichia coli	Septicaemia, perianal
	Serratia species	Septicaemia
	Enterobacteriaciae	Septicaemia
	Legionella	Pneumonia, Encephalopathy, Renal failure
Gram positive:	*Staphylococcus aureus*	Pneumonia, skin
	Staphylococcus epidermidis	Septicaemia, catheter related
	Corynbacteria	Septicaemia/catheter related
	Bacillus cereus	Septicaemia, skin inflamation/necrosis
	Strep. pneumoniae	Lung, septicaemia
Anaerobes	*Chlostridium difficile*	Pseudomembranous colitis
	Bacteroides sp.	Brain abscess, Septicaemia, fistulation
Acid-fast bacilli	*Mycobacteria*	Pneumonia, meningitis
	Pittsburgh pneumonia agent	Pneumonia
Fungi	*Candida* species *Torulopsis*	Oropharyngeal, gastrointestinal tract, pneumonia
	Aspergillus sp.	Pneumonia, sinuses
	Zygomycoses	Sinuses
	Cryptococcus	Skin, C.N.S. Septicaemia, pneumonia
Viruses	Herpes simplex type I	Oropharyngeal ulceration, dissemination (pneumonia, encephalitis)
	Herpes zoster	Shingles, chickenpox, pneumonia
	Cytomegalovirus	Pneumonia/hepatitis chorioretinitis
	Measles	Pneumonia/encephalitis SSPE
Protozoan sp.	*Pneumocystis carinii*	Pneumonia
	Toxoplasma gondii	'Glandular fever like syndrome' Pneumonia Hepatitis Necrotising encephalitis
Parasites	*Stronglyoides*	Skin rash (serpiginous) Pneumonia

humoral response to penetration by pathogens. The individual facets are analysed in this section.

Cell mediated immunity

Granulocytopenia
A temporal relationship exists between the onset of neutropenia and infection and between the risk of infection and the absolute neutrophil count (Bodey et al, 1966). Whether or not this is a direct association, related to concurrent damage to protective barriers or to coincidental factors is not proven. The infections associated with neutropenia or impaired neutrophil function are most commonly due to the Gram negative bacteria such as *Escherishia coli*, *Klebsiella* and *Pseudomonas* and Gram positive bacteria such as *Staphylococcus aureus* (Levine et al, 1974). The sites commonly are local invasion, e.g. oral and perianal sepsis and/or bacteraemia. In the upper respiratory tract Gram positive and Gram negative organisms colonise and produce local infection and sometimes pneumonia.

Lymphopenia and lymphocyte dysfunction
Cellular immune dysfunction is frequent in patients with lymphoid malignancy and those receiving chemo/radiotherapy and steroid therapy. These defects are associated with infection by intracellular parasites such as protozoa and mycobacteria, which are believed to derive from reactivation of latent organisms as is also the case in herpes simplex, zoster and cytomegalovirus infections. Protozoal infection with *Pneumocystis carinii* is unusual in any other setting; toxoplasmosis is also seen as reactivation or new infection.

Defects in humoral immunity

Patients with chronic lymphoid malignancies such as chronic lymphocytic leukaemia (CLL) and multiple myeloma (MM) have impaired production of antibody and suffer repeated infection by encapsulated Gram positive organisms such as *Streptococcus pneumoniae*, with recurrent upper and lower respiratory tract infections.

Breakdown of physical barriers

Loss of mucosal integrity
Chemo/radiotherapy—induced mucosal damage is a major cause of compromise leading to direct access to the circulation (Mackowak et al, 1981) of otherwise non-pathogenic flora and known pathogens with potentially fatal consequences. We (Hann et al, 1983) have also suggested that mucosal damage due to reactivation of herpes simplex in the oropharyngeal mucosa represents an important portal of entry for other infecting organisms in the compromised host.

Intravenous catheters
Direct venous catheter access in peripheral veins is associated with a high incidence of local morbidity but fewer episodes of serious bacteraemia than has become commonplace with the recent increased use of long term indwelling central venous catheters. Despite access via subcutaneous tunnels, the frequently used right atrial

catheter (Hickman et al, 1979) *has* been associated with a high incidence of bacteraemia due to *Staphylococcus epidermidis*, corynebacteria, anaerobic spore-bearing rods etc. (Winston & Hewitt, 1979), and yeasts.

Other indwelling foreign bodies or obstructions such as urinary catheters or even calculi can lead to local and subsequently disseminated infection. Even minor procedures such as marrow aspiration are more dangerous in patients with other immune deficiencies and demand scrupulous attention to aseptic techniques.

Malnutrition

Hughes et al (1974) showed that protein malnutrition alone could lead in rats to an increased risk of *Pneumocystis carnii* which has also been observed in epidemic form in malnourished human populations in times of civil strife. Malnutrition has also been shown by Law et al (1974) to be associated with anergy in the surgical patient. Preoperative hyperalimentation can improve these parameters but is not totally without risk as a source of infection due to contaminating fungi and coagulase negative staphylococci in particular. The patient with bone marrow failure due to chemotherapy or marrow transplantation is likely to be at risk although with several other competing factors this might not be easy to dissect.

Splenectomy

Absence of the spleen due to infarction (sickle cell disease) or surgical removal for malignant disease, or other reasons, is well recognised as a risk factor for subsequent overwhelming infection due to encapsulated Gram positive organisms such as *Strep pneumoniae*

Loss of colonisation resistance

Alterations in the normal microbial flora of the GI tract, especially following exposure to broad spectrum antibiotics, will lead frequently to the overgrowth of potential pathogens such as yeasts and Gram negative bacteria. The immunocompromised host fails to suppress these organisms which leads to dissemination in a significant minority of patients.

SOURCES OF INFECTION AND SURVEILLANCE CULTURES

Even in the context of modest patient protection, such as handwashing, half the infections in the compromised host are not exogenously acquired but are due to invasion by or reactivation of organisms which are part of the endogenous flora (in the gastrointestinal tract etc.) or are previously latent such as herpes viruses, and mycobacteria. More than 80% of infections are attributable to organisms which are present at or adjacent to the site of infection, as shown by Schimpff et al (1979), e.g. stool colonisation and perianal sepsis.

In the absence of a protected environment, exogenously acquired infection could be expected to account for approximately 50% of episodes of sepsis in the compromised host (Schimpff et al, 1972). Simple isolation measures may drastically reduce the risk of these infections but, in the absence of effective decontamination, the benefit will be masked.

Surveillance cultures have been of value in defining the percentage of patients who become infected with endogenous organisms. In clinical practice they can occasionally predict the onset of infection with a particular organism and may give invaluable early information about sensitivity patterns when a patient develops a fever. Studies at the Baltimore Cancer Research Centre by Schimpff et al (1972) showed that 55% of patients colonised with *Pseudomonas aeroginosa* subsequently developed bacteraemia, whereas the incidence was only 15% with *Klebsiella* spp., 7% of *E. coli* and 8% of *Staph. aureus*. In addition, 31% of patients colonised with other *Pseudomonas* species became bacteraemic with the same organism, indicating that colonisation with this group of organisms is tantamount to infection. It is also the case that most *Staph. aureus* infections follow nasal colonisation. These factors show the importance of surveillance cultures and suggest the feasibility of some 'prophylactic' therapeutic options. In a similar way, herpes simplex culture positivity from mucosae is occasionally a prodromal finding to ulcerative lesions. The interpretation of fungal (particularly *Candida* species) positive culture is much more problematical. However, in practical terms, *Aspergillus* lung infection and sinus infection are frequently preceded by upper airway colonisation (Schwartz et al, 1984). Also, the presence of *Candida pseudohyphae* in smears from mucosal plaques and a heavy culture result from the oropharynx (Kostiala et al, 1982) are highly suggestive of infection, which may thereafter disseminate.

PROPHYLAXIS OF INFECTION (Table 8.2)

Most exogenously acquired infections in the compromised host originate from clearly identifiable sources such as airborn transmission (e.g. *Aspergillus* spp. and *Legionella*), food (e.g. *Pseudomonas* species on salads), fingers (Gram positive and Gram negative bacteria), fomites (e.g. bedclothes etc.) and via iv catheters (e.g. coagulase negative

Table 8.2 Recommended antimicrobial prophylaxis in allogeneic marrow transplant recipients (as an example of an immunocompromised host)

Purpose	Drug	Route	Duration
GI fungal supression[1]	1. Ketoconazole	p.o.	6 months
	2. Amphotericin B[2] or Nystatin } Syrup	p.o.	6 months
'Total' GI Bacterial decontamination	3. Colistin plus	p.o.	During period of neutropenia + with sterile diet
	4. Neomycin	p.o.	
Pneumocystis carinii prophylaxis	5. Co-trimoxazole	p.o.	6 months
Herpes simplex or zoster prophylaxis[3]	6. Acyclovir	i.v./p.o.	6 weeks ? 6 months
CMV prophylaxis	7. CMV hyperimmune globulin	i.m. or i.v.[4]	? 3–4 months

[1] Start at least one day before and finish at least one day after antibiotics.
[2] Not available in USA as yet.
[3] Seropositive patients
[4] If i.v. preparation.

staphylococci). In addition many infections are attributable to invasion by, or reactivation of, endogenous organisms, such as *Candida* species, Gram negative bacteria, *Herpesvirus* and *Mycobacteria*. The aim of prophylaxis must be to decontaminate the patient with suppressive antimicrobial chemotherapy (e.g. non-absorable antibiotics, antifungal and antiviral drugs) and to provide a 'sterile' environment, in which the patient is also protected from attendants and family by hand washing and physical barriers (e.g. masks and gloves).

Decontamination of the patient

Prior to isolation of the compromised host in a sterile environment (vide infra) attempts should be made at decontamination of the patient otherwise the sterile environment will, itself, become a reservoir for reinfection. Skin and hair should be washed in a solution containing an antiseptic such as chlorhexidine and creams of the same antiseptic should be applied to the nose and vagina. Mouthwashes of chlorhexidine or iodine-containing solutions should be used at least 6-hourly.

A topic of some controversy is the use of GI decontamination. 'Total' decontamination has been shown to be of benefit in regimens utilising non-absorbable antibiotics such as the GVN regimen (gentamicin, vancomycin and nystatin) (Schimpff et al, 1975) or FRACON (framycetin, colistin and nystatin) developed by Storring and colleagues (1977) or, more recently NEOCON (neomycin, colistin and nystatin) a more palatable modification of FRACON by the same group (Watson & Jameson, 1979).

The risk of invasive fungal infection has been underestimated antemortem by clinicians although colonisation of the gastrointestinal tract is well recognised. The risk increases with the length of the period of neutropenia and the accompanying damage to the integument, and is therefore more common in patients with aplasia but also during remission induction therapy for acute leukaemia. Up to 37% of such patients coming to autopsy will be found to have such an infection and this is often the cause of death (Estey et al, 1982). Antifungal prophylaxis with nystatin is ineffective (DeGregorio, 1982) even when combined with amphotericin B as shown by Hann et al (1982b). In both studies the antifungal prophylaxis might well be considered suboptimal today, but were 'standard' in the USA and the UK at the time. In the latter study ketoconazole 400 mg daily (adult dose) was statistically superior to nystatin/amphotericin in all but the recipients of total body irradiation, probably because of the poor absorption of the drug in the latter group (Hann et al, 1982b). It should be noted that ketoconazole should not be used concurrently with cyclosporin A since displacement from protein binding of the latter may lead to increased toxicity (Gluckman, 1983). Our current recommendation is that a combination of ketoconazole with either nystatin or amphotericin B suspension be used.

The major drawbacks of these antibacterial/antifungal combinations is poor patient compliance but, nevertheless, up to 60% of patients will achieve useful GI decontamination.

An alternative to 'total' decontamination has been the use of selective (or partial) decontamination with co-trimoxazole or nalidixic acid with or without polymyxin B and combined with nystatin. These combinations are used in the anticipation of preservation of colonisation resistance to aerobic and fungal pathogens (Buck & Cooke, 1969; Van der Waaij et al, 1972). Initial overwhelming enthusiasm for the co-trimoxazole/nystatin approach produced a number of encouraging papers documenting significant reduction in bacterial infection rates (e.g. Watson et al, 1982; Pizzo et al, 1983) followed by a very large multi-institution study which showed no efficacy except in a small minority of patients receiving high dosage chemotherapy (Zinner et al, 1982). Of more concern is the evidence for the emergence of infection due to co-trimoxazole resistant organisms. The concurrent use of non-absorbable antibiotics reduced infections due to enterobacteriaceae (cf. co-trimoxazole alone) and also the number of infections attributable to co-trimoxazole resistant organisms in a study by Rozenberg-Arska et al, 1983.

In a comparative study between co-trimoxazole plus nystatin and nalidixic acid plus nystatin, Wade & colleagues (1983) showed, in leukaemia patients undergoing remission induction therapy, that the period of granulocytopenia was longer in the co-trimoxazole arm confirming a suggestion of a similar problem in marrow transplant recipients (Watson, 1982). Wade also showed that whilst fewer Gram negative infections were seen in the co-trimoxazole arm there was a higher isolation of filamentous fungi. The time to acquisition of first infection was impressively longer in the co-trimoxazole arm (17 versus 8 days). Selective antimicrobial modulation (SAM) to eliminate aerobic and facultative anaerobic gram negative rods from the G I tract was reported by Guiot & colleagues (1983) to reduce the risk of infection during remission induction therapy compared to placebo (3/16 vs 8/12). The protocol included neomycin, nalidixic acid, polymyxin B and amphotericin B. Minimal other precautions were taken (e.g. sterile food was *not* used). No survival benefit was apparent but the reduction in morbidity was impressive. Some caution must be expressed about the use of nalidixic acid following the report of additive GI toxicity during high dose melphalan therapy (Voute et al, 1983).

There is an urgent need for a large single institution study of total versus selective decontamination which might well incorporate some of the newer antipseudomonal derivatives of nalidixic acid such as norfloxacin or ciprofloxacin.

Environmental studies and diet
Several studies have compared the antimicrobial effectiveness of reverse barrier isolation such as laminar air flow (LAF) or isolation rooms with filtered air.

Bodey and colleagues have demonstrated the dramtically reduced pathogen count in the air of LAF rooms which when combined with non-absorbable antibiotics compared favourably with neither method of prophylaxis (reviewed in Pizzo & Levine, 1977; Schimpff, 1980). An important and consistent observation has been the elimination of *Aspergillus* infections which have accounted for 4% mortality in our own marrow transplant programme lacking these facilities (Prentice et al, unpublished observation). Relatively cheap air filtration can be equally effective and should be considered essential for particularly high risk patient categories (i.e. BMT recipients). Less impressive has been the evidence of a survival advantage, although for patients transplanted for aplastic anaemia in Seattle there was evidence of both a reduced incidence of graft versus host disease and of increased survival (Storb, 1983).

As has already been pointed out there is not likely to be any advantage in 'isolating' a patient who has not first undergone decontamination. Similarly it is illogical to give other than sterile food and drinks to a patient in whom gastrointestinal decontamination is being attempted. It is *essential* that patients in whom reverse-barrier isolation is contemplated are nursed in isolation from the outset to prevent acquisition of hospital infection whilst undergoing endogenous decontamination, and on completion are transferred to the sterile environment. It would also appear logical to discharge the patient home direct from isolation, especially when subsequent readmission is anticipated.

MANOEUVRES DESIGNED TO ENHANCE HOST DEFENCES

Mucus membranes and skin
Any loss of integrity of either the skin or mucus membranes adds a further dimension to the immunocompromised state. Many drugs and radiation are associated with loss of the gastrointestinal mucosal barrier. This is sometimes unavoidable but many patients experience mucosal (oropharyngeal) ulceration which is avoidable, probably in the case of fungal overgrowth and almost always where it is attributable to reactivation of herpes simplex infection (vide infra).

The patient with bone marrow failure including that due to modern intensive therapy for haematological malignancy requires long-term venous access. In a short number of years the use of right atrial indwelling catheters has become routine. Coincidentally we have witnessed the widespread adoption of partially effective gastrointestinal decontamination. Thus bacteraemia attributable to life-threatening enterobacteriaceae has declined to be replaced by an apparent epidemic of Gram positive infections — regularly described as being 'catheter related'. This may not have been entirely fair, but there is some evidence that rigorous catheter care can prevent this problem (Rogers, 1984).

Prophylactic granulocytes
Logic suggests that total replacement therapy in granulocytopenia would reduce the mortality from sepsis to that seen in the normal population. That we might ever achieve total replacement seems unlikely, but surprisingly encouraging results for therapy and prophylaxis with granulocytes have been reported, even with what must be considered inadequate numbers (reviewed by Buckner & Clift, 1984).

The cost and cost effectiveness as well as procurement logistics have overwhelmed the early enthusiasm of most clinicians and the reports of pulmonary toxicity and, of more concern, the transfer of cytomegalovirus (CMV) infection in marrow transplant recipients, have discouraged widespread use.

Active immunisation
The vast majority of patients with haematological disease would not be expected to mount a normal humoral response to vaccination and this is best documented in Hodgkin's disease (Siber, 1978). A *Pseudomonas* vaccine which was effective in normal volunteers showed no protection in controlled trials in patients with malignant disease and children with acute leukaemia (Young et al, 1973; Hagbin et al, 1973). On the other hand, patients undergoing planned splenectomy for benign haematological disease such as hereditary spherocytosis, should receive multivalent pneumococcal vaccination *prior* to splenectomy. This group should *also* receive lifelong penicillin since some of the serotypes are not sufficiently immunogenic. All patients with

functional hyposplenism, including patients with chronic graft versus host disease (Winston et al, 1979) should take penicillin, since immunisation will be suboptimal in this setting, including patients splenectomised as part of the treatment for chronic granulocytic leukaemia (Brown et al, 1983).

Studies of the place of hepatitis B and pneumococcal vaccination in marrow transplant recipients and their donors are currently underway. Several vaccines against viral infections are under evaluation. We hold out little hope for efficacy in patients with impaired immunity.

Passive immunisation
Two recent studies have provided evidence that the passive adminstration of CMV hyperimmune gamma globulin (Myers et al, 1983) or plasma (Winston et al, 1982) provide significant protection against CMV pneumonitis following bone marrow transplantation. This protective effect was only demonstrable in patients who were seronegative and did not receive granulocyte transfusion during the study period. Passive immunisation has been used in the prevention of other viral infections most notably herpes zoster (Brunel et al, 1969) and measles. In both examples prophylaxis is usually given following contact but preliminary results suggest that this is not effective in measles.

Perhaps the most ambitious studies in passive immunisation are those of Ziegler and colleagues (1982) who have been working (for many years) with antibody raised against the core polysaccharide common to most Gram negative organisms. Antibody raised against the mutant *E. coli* J5 is protective against the endotoxaemic consequences of Gram negative bacteraemia. Initial animal studies showed protection against the local and generalised Schwartzman reactions (Braude et al, 1972; 1973; Ziegler et al 1973). Further animal studies lead eventually to studies in man. In subjects thought to have Gram negative bacteraemia, control or J5 plasma was given along with 'optimal' antibiotic therapy. Deaths were reduced to 22% (23 of 103) from 39% in the control group (Ziegler, 1982). A subsequent prophylactic study in leukaemia demonstrated no benefit in infection rate, febrile days or mortality possibly due to inadequate dosing or rapid catabolism or absorption (McCutchan, 1983). A subsequent study in high risk surgical patients receiving repeated infusions of J5 serum in Switzerland is showing a significant benefit in sepsis, shock and death. Further studies using 'adequate' prophylaxis in neutropenic patients are underway.

Neutralisation of endotoxaemia
In a brief review of the literature Bannatyne & Cheng (1983) have made the tantalising proposal that the proven anti-endotoxic effects of polymyxin B might be exploited clinically.

Acceleration of myeloid regeneration following chemotherapy
Ample preclinical evidence (Joyce & Chervenik, 1980) exists which suggests that the granulocyte elevation seen in patients receiving lithium carbonate (for depressive illness) might be exploitable in man to accelerate recovery of granulocytes following chemotherapy or marrow transplantation. Data suggests that the stem cell fraction is also expanded. A reduction in the 'period of risk' could cause dramatic benefits in prevention of infection.

Protection of patients against reactivation of latent micro-organisms

Although *Pneumocystis carnii* may be acquired it seems likely that many cases are due to reactivation of latent infection. *Pneumocystis* prophylaxis has been shown by Hughes et al (1977) to be readily achievable with co-trimoxazole. The patients at most risk are children with lymphoblastic leukaemia on maintenance therapy, patients following marrow transplantation for any disorder and patients with the acquired immune deficiency syndrome (AIDS), but the latter have shown a disconcertingly high sensitivity to this drug (see Ch. 14).

Herpes simplex reactivation can be prevented even in marrow transplant recipients by acyclovir (Saral, 1982; Hann, 1983) and it seems likely that this will also be the case for herpes zoster. On the other hand we are unconvinced of any protective effect of acyclovir against cytomegalovirus (see passive immunisation) although antiviral agents with in vitro activity against CMV are soon to enter clinical trials. Prophylaxis with acyclovir analogues with good absorption from the gastrointestinal tract are under study (HGP unpublished) and these may well make long-term prophylaxis practicable.

Reactivation of tuberculosis is not uncommon following intensive immunosuppression and it is now our common practice to give 'prophylactic' isoniazid to any patient with either radiological or PPD evidence of infection.

Immunomodulation

The role of levamisole (and other agents) in the enhancement of immunity in the immunocompromised host awaits investigation.

EMPIRICAL AND SPECIFIC THERAPY FOR INFECTIONS IN NEUTROPENIC PATIENTS

One of the greatest challenges in managing patients with malignancy is what to do with an unexplained fever. Even in retrospect it is usually only possible to make a specific microbiological diagnosis in half the patients (EORTC, 1978; Pizzo et al, 1982a) and half of these episodes are bacteraemias. In our own series of patients over the last 3 years the rate has been higher at 66% of microbiologically documented infections (Sage et al, 1983). Thus, accurate early diagnosis is very difficult and the infections often follow a fulminant and fatal course if untreated. This has led to the early institution of empirical therapy, the consequence of which has been an overall reduction in mortality from 50% to around 5% in the last 10 years. This remarkable success achieved despite intensification of anticancer therapy and a consequent higher incidence of infection, was made possible because of accurate definition of the spectrum of infection in these patients. The EORTC series of trials and others have documented that the Gram negative bacilli, particularly *Pseudomonas aeruginosa*, *Klebsiella* spp. and *E. coli* were the major risk. However, there has recently been a definite increase in the incidence of gram positive infections (Wade et al, 1982; Sage et al, 1983) which are occasionally fatal and frequently resistant to a wide range of antibiotics. The EORTC trials have shown a surprisingly good activity of β-lactam/aminoglycoside combinations against *Staph. aureus* but consideration should be given to the use of vancomycin as a first or second line agent where resistant Gram positive organisms are prevalent. In view of the possible association of these organisms with the widespread use of co-trimoxazole prophylaxis and indwelling silastic catheters, consideration must be given to the discontinuation of the former and strict asepsis in the use of the latter.

The best proven combination of antibiotics for empirical use is an aminoglycoside and ureidopenicillin (EORTC, 1978; Gurwith et al, 1978) There is no evidence that one aminoglycoside is better than another except where there is a local high incidence of gentamicin resistance. Ureidopenicillins (azlocillin or piperacillin) have a lower sodium content than the older carboxypenicillins (carbenicillin and ticarcillin) and are associated with a lower level of bacterial resistance (Gaya, 1983).

The second important principle of therapy is antibiotic synergism which has been proven to have vital clinical significance (Klastersky & Zinner, 1982). These authors showed clinical response rates to synergistic combinations of 79% compared to 45% with non-synergistic ones. In addition, adequate serum bactericidal titres are necessary for a good respnse in Gram negative bacteraemia; a titre of >1:8 producing superior results (Klastersky et al, 1974; Platt et al, 1981). In this respect we seem to be moving towards the type of approach used in subacute bacterial endocarditis. Appreciation of these facts brings in to perspective the recent rush towards use of monotherapy with third-generation cephalosporins. These antibiotics have a spectrum of activity which may include the major Gram negative pathogens but with subsequent loss of some of the anti-Gram positive activity exhibited by their maligned predecessors. The tortuous nosology of this rapidly-expanding group of antibiotics have made their understanding very difficult for clinicians and attempts have been made to clarify this (Table 8.3) and we will point out some of the difficulties associated with their use. The five groups described divide the drugs into categories which are

Table 8.3 The cephalosporins

'Category'	Name	Gram +ve	Enterobacteria + haemophilic*	Pseudomonas	Bacteroides
			MIC mg/l		
Oral Group	Cephalexin ⎫ Cephradine ⎬	1–4	4–8	>128	>128
	Cefaclor	1–4	1	>128	>128
'Gram positive' group	a) Cephaloridine Cefazolin b) Cephalothin Cephacetrile	0.03	1–2	>128	32–64
'Gram negative' group	a) Cefamandole Cefuroxime b) Cefotaxime	0.5–2	0.06–1	32–>128	8–764
Pseudomonas group	a) Ceftazidime	4–32	0.25–0.5	1–2	16
	Ceftriaxone	4–32	0.25–1	4–8	2–32
	b) Cefoperazone	1–8	0.25–2	4–8	4–8
	Cefsulodin	2–8	>128	2–4	>128
Anaerobe group (Cephamycins)	Cefoxitin	2	2–4	>128	4–8
	Moxalactam	4–16	0.25–0.5	8–16	0.5
	Cefotetan	–	0.06	128	4–32

* Includes *Haemophilus, Bordetella, Legionella, Campylobacter*.
This table is based on Williams D J 1983.

clinically applicable. The oral group has low antibacterial activity relative to the parenteral cephalosporins. Their main activity is against Gram positive organisms and some enterobacteria. The so-called Gram positive group has the highest activity against these organisms and consists of those antibiotics: (a) which are metabolically stable and others (b) which are unstable. The Gram negative group has a good activity against many aerobic Gram negative rods, with the best potency against *Haemophilus influenzae*. Cefotaxime is metabolically unstable. The *Pseudomonas* group has high activity against this organism and Enterobacteria with the (a) subgroup being more stable to plasmid-mediated β-lactamases. The cephamycins have high stability to β-lactamases of aerobic and anaerobic bacteria (Williams, 1983).

The excellent in vitro activity of the modern cephalosporins has led to their use both in combination and alone. There is no evidence that polypharmacy such as the use of an aminoglycoside combined with two or more β-lactam agents confers any clinical advantage (Gaya, 1983). However, there is a need for efficacious β-lactam combinations to overcome the toxicity problems of the aminoglycoside/β-lactam combinations. Monotherapy would seem to be a rather faint hope at present because of the limited spectrum of the third generation cephalosporins and the sacrifice of synergistic activity. Unfortunately, many of the double β-lactam combinations are antagonistic (Zinner et al, 1981; Forbes et al, 1981). This occurs when cefoxitin is combined with many of the other cephalosporins and penicillins, and with cefazolin plus ureidopenicillins, cefotaxime with azlocillin; cephalothin with piperacillin and moxalactam with carbenicillin. In contrast, piperacillin with either cefotaxime or ceftazidime performs well in vitro and deserves further study in clinical trials.

It cannot be assumed from in vitro results or the multiple small studies with cephalosporins in compromised patients that these agents will be efficacious and safe. The third EORTC trial has shown a very disappointing efficacy for an amikacin/cefotaxime combination (Gaya, 1983). The response to both this regimen and to amikacin/ticarcillin were inferior in the therapy of Gram negative bacteraemias. There is additionally a real problem with enterocolitis caused by *Clostridium difficile* where the cephalsporin is mainly excreted in the bile, as with cefoperazone (Sage et al, 1983; Carlberg et al, 1982). The assumption that the cephalosporins are non-toxic has been further dented by the realisation that there may be adverse effects on platelet function and hypoprothrombinaemia (Smith & Lipsky, 1983). This has now led to the routine concurrent use of moxalactam and vitamin K to prevent serious bleeding problems.

THE MANAGEMENT OF THE PATIENT WITH A PERSISTENT PYREXIA (Table 8.4)

However effective the empirical combination of antibiotics is and even with the broadest spectrum of antibacterial cover which is obtained, approximately one-third of patients will remain pyrexial at 72–96 hours (Klastersky, 1983). Clearly, if a likely pathogen has been isolated then the initial drug combination should be adjusted with regard to the invitro sensitivity pattern. Synergistic combinations should be chosen and ideally bactericidal activity in the serum should be optimal. Granulocyte transfusion therapy has its major supportive role in persistent profoundly granulocytopenic patients whose defined bacterial infection does not respond to 'appropriate'

Table 8.4   A rational approach to the management of granulocytopenic febrile patients

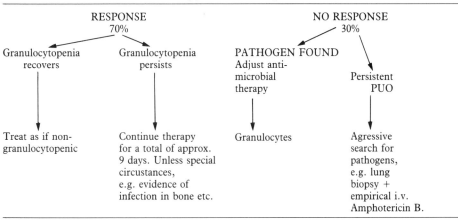

| EMPIRICAL ANTIBIOTICS |
| Synergistic + Bactericidal |
| Aminoglycoside + Ureidopencillin |

RESPONSE 70% — NO RESPONSE 30%

Granulocytopenia recovers → Treat as if non-granulocytopenic

Granulocytopenia persists → Continue therapy for a total of approx. 9 days. Unless special circustances, e.g. evidence of infection in bone etc.

PATHOGEN FOUND — Adjust anti-microbial therapy → Granulocytes

Persistent PUO → Agressive search for pathogens, e.g. lung biopsy + empirical i.v. Amphotericin B.

Based on Klastersky J 1983 and EORTC Trial III Gaya 1983.

therapy (Highby et al, 1975; Vogler & Winston, 1977). The underlying fault with this modality of treatment is the great difficulty in giving adequate numbers. If what is usually regarded to be a good dose of 2.5×10^{10} granulocytes is given to an adult, this represents only 5% of the body's daily production and a tiny percentage of the total pool. A normal person would also be able to mount a 10- to 20-fold increase in granulocyte production when infected. Attempts to improve the response to granulocytes by selecting a group of patients at high risk of gram negative bacteraemia (with high fever, profound granulocytopenia ± shock) and giving transfusions empirically as soon as possible after inception of fever has not shown an advantage over conventional antibiotic therapy (EORTC, 1983). There is no defined role for the use of granulocyte therapy in patients with fungal infections although it is known that polymorphs can damage hyphal forms of *Aspergillus* and *Mucor* (Schimpff, 1983). There is a need for clinical studies in these situations although caution will continue to be needed with concurrent use of parenteral amphotericin B. It has been suggested that there is an interaction leading to severe pulmonary reactions (Wright et al, 1981) although it seems more likely that this represents new infection rather than some unexplained toxicity (Dana et al, 1981, 1983).

There remains the 'hard core' of profoundly granulocytopenic patients with PUO after 3 or 4 days of antibiotic therapy. In clinical terms this is the most challenging problem which is faced day in and day out and very few attempts have been made to address it adequately. A proportion may have non-infectious diseases and consideration should be given at this stage to phenomena such as graft versus host disease. A number will have viral, protozoal and other defined infections for which a vigorous search needs to be mounted. However, there is ample evidence that a high proportion of these patients have fungal infections which carry a high mortality (De Gregorio et al, 1982). These authors and many others have also documented an increasing incidence of fungal infection in both leukaemic chemotherapy and transplant patients.

There is also evidence from one study that the control of fungal infections is better when specific therapy is instituted early (Pizzo et al, 1982b). Certainly the response of well-established fungal infections to treatment is disappointing. Rapid diagnosis eludes the present microbiological methods. Therefore, the approach of the third EORTC trial whereby patients were randomised to receive or not to receive parenteral amphotericin B at this stage has a strong basis in logic (Klastersky, 1983). This interim report showed that 7 of 31 (22%) patients who did not receive amphotericin B eventually died of fungal infection, including three with proven disseminated fungal infection at postmortem. The patients receiving amphotericin B had a 16% mortality with no proven cases of disseminated fungal infections. This trial is continuing but shows an initial trend towards a benefit for this approach.

HOW LONG SHOULD THE ANTIBIOTICS BE CONTINUED?

The length of an antibiotic course in a patient who responds to this therapy is another critical problem. There has been a tendency to continue until the granulocyte count recovers but there is good evidence that this predisposes the patient to subsequent fungal infection (EORTC, 1978) and a greater chance of ototoxicity, nephrotoxicity and hypokalaemia. This has to be weighed in the balance against the possibility of recrudesence of infection which in some series has been very high with short course of antibiotics (Pizzo et al, 1979). In the third EORTC Trial (Klastersky, 1983) 'improving' patients were randomised to receive a 9-day course or to carry on until the granulocytes exceeded $0.5 \times 10^9/l$. 118 patients had the shorter course and there was a 10% mortality compared with 9% in the patients receiving the longer course.

SPECIFIC THERAPY FOR SOME MAJOR PATHOGENS IN THE COMPROMISED HOST

It would be impossible in a review of this nature to do more than scratch the surface of the problem of specific therapy. We will thus confine ourselves to those major pathogens which present to the clinician looking after patients with bone marrow failure and which are not obviously 'covered' by the initial empirical antibiotic regimen.

Troublesome bacteria

As previously stated, the widespread use of indwelling venous catheters has revolutionised the management of patients with bone marrow failure. This has brought with it a difficult problem with the acquisition of catheter-related organisms, particularly *Staphylococcus epidermidis*, *corynebacteria* species, *Bacillus* species, anaerobic spore-bearing rods and *Candida* species. The latter will be dealt with separately. The catheter-related organisms are unfortunately very adaptable beasts and are frequently only sensitive to rifampicin and/or vancomycin, both of which drugs are associated with considerable hepatic, renal and other toxicities. Earlier studies with the empirical use of antistaphylococcal drugs such as methicillin or cephalothin in addition to the usual broad spectrum Gram negative 'cover', did not show any real benefit (Gurwith et al, 1978; EORTC, 1978). A more logical approach nowadays would be to add vancomycin where these bacteria are a problem (Bodey, 1983). However, as has been previously stated, the rate of infection with these organisms can be reduced greatly by meticulous aseptic techniques in the management of catheters.

In the last few years clues have at last come to light as to the cause of some of the febrile pneumonia syndromes which had previously been such a mystery. There is no doubt that some of these incidents are due to drugs particularly bleomycin. However, we now know that *Legionella pneumophilia* (Fraser et al, 1977), Pittsburgh pneumonia agent (Rogers et al, 1979) and 'atypical legionella-like organisms' (Thomason et al, 1979) are responsible for some of these episodes.

Legionella pneumonia is now known to have occurred since 1947, using retrospective serological and culture diagnosis (McDade et al, 1979). Sporadic cases occur as well as clusters related to defective air-conditioning units, shower heads and potable water. Hyperchlorination of water and adjustment of water temperatures have been shown to be of value as control measures (Fisher-Hoch et al, 1981). The clinical features are a valuable diagnostic clue and include: a temperature of >38.9°C, bradycardia, changes in mental status (similar to a toxic confusional state), pleural effusions, chills, diarrhoea, renal and heptic dysfunction. Chest X-ray usually shows patchy alveolar infiltrates followed by consolidation of the affected lobe, followed by spread to other areas (Meyer, 1981). The best approach to diagnosis is clinical suspicion along with direct fluorescence assay on sputum, sputum culture and serial immunofluorescent antibody tests. Therapy should be initially with intravenous erythromycin (4–6 g/day in adults) with the addition of rifampicin (600 mg b.d) in non-responsive cases. An alternative would be to use tetracycline. Similar therapy has been shown to be of value in the therapy of Pittsburgh pneumonia agent and legionella-like organisms, although co-trimoxazole has also been shown to be effective.

Protozoan and parasitic infections

Although babesiosis, toxoplasmosis, malaria, Leishmaniasis and stronglylodosis have all been described in the immunocompromised host, the only member of the group regularly seen is *Pneumocycstis carinii*, although its incidence has been reduced with the adoption of co-trimoxazole prophylaxis. *Pneumocystis* infection is a common occurrence among young children (Meuwissen et al, 1977; Stagno et al, 1979) in whom person-to-person spread is unusual.

The clinical features of *Pneumocystis* pneumonia have been clearly defined (Walzer et al, 1976). Non-productive cough, dyspnoea, tachypnoea, hypoxia, fever and confusion along with an absence of chest rales are the usual findings. Chest X-ray shows diffuse bilateral alveolar infiltrates in most cases although atypical patterns do occur and cause diagnostic difficulty. Whether or not to perform invasive investigations in patients with atypical pneumonia or those not responding to antibiotics is a very thorny question (Rossiter et al, 1979) and a dogmatic approach does not work in clinical practice. Non-specific polypharmacy of undiagnosed pneumonias is clearly a potentially dangerous approach because the drugs probably interact in antagonistic and potentially toxic ways. Also, if one is confident of a specific diagnosis then dosage and potentially synergistic combinations can be pursued with vigour. In the context of *Pneumocystis carinii* pneumonia it has also to be appreciated that this organism tends to coexist with other pathogens, particularly CMV, in patients with pneumonia and

40% of pneumocystis pneumonias do not initially respond to specific therapy (Hughes et al, 1978). Thus, in an ideal world it would be best always to make a specific diagnosis using the technique which provides the greatest chance of finding the causative organism(s), i.e. open lung biopsy. However, it is our practise and that of others to give a trial of co-trimoxazole therapy for a period of 48–72 hours following which, in the absence of improvement or any defined pathogen, an open lung biopsy is performed. Other procedures such as percutaneous thoracic closed needle aspirations under fluoroscopic guidance, transtracheal aspiration and fibreoptic brush bronchoscopy all have problems associated with them and are giving way to large volume broncheo-alveolar lavage.

High-dose co-trimoxazole is as effective as pentamidine in treatment of this disorder and is less toxic (Hughes et al, 1978). Clinical improvement may be slow, taking up to a week, and thus the usual policy is to give 72–96 hours of therapy with pentamidine being added if there is an inadequate response. There is no conclusive evidence of antagonism between these agents in man. Recurrence is well documented (Hughes & Johnson, 1971) and thus co-trimoxazole prophylaxis is indicated in the face of continuing immunosuppression.

Fungal infections

Amphotericin B remains the cornerstone of antifungal therapy and the toxophobia which exists in many clinicians' minds is not justified. Certainly, there is a great need for more effective and less toxic compounds, but it is possible to give therapeutic courses of this drug without unacceptable irreversible side-effects. The rigors and bone pain associated with its use can be controlled with pethidine, with or without chlorpheniramine or corticosteroids. The nephrotoxicity is usually reversible and only very high doses cause permanent renal damage but caution must be exercised where other nephrotoxic agents (e.g. aminoglycosides) are used concurrently. Another myth which needs to be dispelled is that one needs to build up the dosage over a prolonged period of time. In order to be effective, amphotericin B should be given in full dosage over the first 48 hours, i.e. $0.5–1.0 \, mg/kg/day$. When a response has been achieved then it can be given in a $1.2 \, mg/kg$ alternate day regimen, which is better tolerated (Meunier-Carpentier, 1983a). The duration of therapy is more controversial although recovery is often associated with bone marrow regeneration. Disseminated candidiasis, invasive pulmonary aspergillosis or mucormycosis (which often involves the sinuses) may require a high total dose of amphotericin in the order of 1–2 g in adults. The fact remains that many patients do not respond and other therapeutic combinations along with procedures such as removal of infected catheters and surgical debridement of sinus infections are often required.

The combination of amphotericin B and 5-flourocytosine has been shown to be effective in culture and animal models (Bennett et al, 1979). However, its use in patients with bone marrow failure has not been established and there is a real problem of further bone marrow suppression when using the latter drug, particularly following bone marrow transplantation. In a similar way, rifampicin shows promise in vitro as an agent which may be used in combination with amphotericin B, with the proviso that hepatic toxicity may be enhanced, and further clinical studies are needed (Meunier-Carpentier, 1983b). The imidazoles, miconazole and ketoconazole, have little role to play in this situation and may be antagonistic to amphotericin B.

Antiviral therapy

Interest in antiviral therapy has been resurrected recently, both because of the problem of recurrent viral disease associated with bone marrow transplantation and the availability of a non-toxic drug which is effective against herpes simplex (HSV) and varicella/zoster (VZV), that is acycloguanosine [acyclovir 9-(2-hydroxyethoxy-methyl)guanine]. This agent depends for its activity on a much higher affinity for viral than for human cellular thymidine kinase (Elion, 1982). The incidence of herpes zoster in transplant patients is about 40% (Watson, 1983) and 20–40% of these disseminate, with a mortality rate of 5%. HSV develops in 50–60% of seropositive patients (Saral et al, 1981; Hann et al, 1983). Acyclovir has proved effective therapeutically against both classes of viruses and is now the treatment of choice (Selby et al, 1979; Balfour et al, 1983). Resistance or reduced sensitivity of HSV to acyclovir has been reported and is usually due to strains lacking thymidine kinase (Burns et al, 1982). This is a situation which requires constant monitoring now that acyclovir is being used prophylactically, but initial evidence suggests that these strains are *less* virulent and less frequently establish latency.

The reported incidence of CMV infection in bone marrow transplant patients varies with the degree of effort and expertise applied to its diagnosis. Figures vary from 10–50% with between a quarter to two-thirds of these episodes involving pneumonitis (Watson, 1983). There are, however, factors which predispose to CMV pneumonitis, i.e. recipient seropositivity, age >12 yr, lung radiation >6 Gy, recipient seronegativity with donor seropositivity, mismatches and the use of granulocyte therapy (Meyers et al, 1983). Whatever the incidence, there is no doubt that the majority of CMV pneumonitis episodes are fatal, being in excess of 90% in some series (Meyers & Thomas, 1981). Neither adenine arabinoside nor acyclovir appear to affect the clinical course of CMV pneumonitis (Young, 1983). Also, initial experience with the newer agents bromovinyl deoxyuridine (BVDU) or interferon from various sources has not been encouraging (Watson, 1983). Experimental drugs that have some promise include phosphonoformic acid, 5-trifluorothymidine (TFT), 8-(1, 3-dihydroxy-2-propoxymethyl) guanine (DHPG) and 2′fluoro-5-iodo arabinosyl cytosine (FIAC). All of these appear to have useful in vitro activity and are being actively studied in clinical trials (Martin et al, 1983; Lopez et al, 1980; Young, 1983). This promises to be an exciting era in the development of effective antiviral treatment.

CONCLUSIONS

Despite the use of progressively more intensive therapy in haematological (and other) malignancy the rate of death due to infection has not increased. With the recent introduction of promising new antimicrobial agents, especially in the area of prophylaxis and the acquisition of powerful new antibiotics for empirical therapy, we may reasonably look forward to a decline in this problem in the near future.

Areas in which there is an urgent need for new developments include the rapid diagnosis of bacterial, viral (Griffiths et al, 1984) and particularly invasive fungal infection and the introduction of better therapy (higher therapeutic index) for invasive fungal infection and new antiviral drugs.

We are confident that man's ingenuity continues to outflank the adaptability of micro-organisms — but only just!

Acknowledgements

We wish to thank the Leukaemia Research Fund for their continued support, Drs Paul Noone, Roger Sage and Paul Griffiths for their helpful comments and their major roles in the supportive care of our patients and Mrs Megan Evans for typing this manuscript.

REFERENCES

Balfour H H, Bean B, Laskin O L et al 1983 Acyclovir halts progression of herpes zoster in immunocompromised patients. New England Journal of Medicine 308: 1448–1454

Bannatyne R M, Cheung R 1983 Polymyxin — an endotoxin inactivator. In: Easmon C S F, Gaya H (eds) Second International Symposium on infections in the immunocompromised host. Academic Press, London, pp 279–280

Bennett J E, Disnuikes W E, Duma R J et al, 1979 A comparison of amphotericin B alone and combined with flucytosine in the treatment of cryptococcal meningitis. New England Journal of Medicine 301: 126–131

Bodey G P, Buckley M, Sathe Y S et al, 1966 Quantitative relationships between circulating leukocytes and infection in patients with acute leukaemia. Annals of Internal Medicine 64: 328–344

Bodey G P 1983 Factors predisposing cancer patients to infection. Presented to the International Society of Chemotherapy Abstr. 3: 3–8

Braude A I, Douglas H 1972 Passive immunization against the local Schwartzman reaction. Journal of Immunology 108: 505–512

Braude A I, Douglas H, Davis C E 1973 Treatment and prevention of intravascular coagulation with antiserum to endotoxin. Journal of Infectious Diseases 128: S157–164

Brunel P A, Ross A, Miller L H, Kuo B 1969 Prevention of varicella by zoster immune globulin. New England Journal of Medicine 280: 1191–1194

Buck A C, Cooke E M 1969 The fate of ingested pseudomonas aeruginosa in normal persons. Journal of Medical Microbiology 2: 581–585

Buckner C D, Clift R A 1984 Prophylaxis and treatment of infections in the immunocompromised host by granulocyte transfusions. In: Prentice H G (ed) Infections in haematology, Clinics in Haematology 13: 3

Burns W H, Saral R, Santos G W et al 1982 Isolation and characterisation of resistant herpes simplex virus after acyclovir therapy. Lancet ii: 421–423

Carlberg H, Alestig K, Nord C E, Trollfors B 1981 Intestinal side effects of cefoperazone. Journal of Antimicrobial Chemotherapy 10: 483–487

Dana B W, Durie B G M, White R F, Huestis D W 1981 Concomitant adminstration of granulocyte transfusions and amphotericin B in neutropenic patients: absence of significant pulmonary toxicity. Blood 57: 90–94

Dana B W, Durie B G M, White R F et al 1983 The significance of pulmonary infiltrates developing in patients receiving granulocyte transfusions. British Journal of Haematology 53: 437–443

De Gregorio M W, Lee W M F, Linker C A, Jacobs R A, Ries C A 1982 Fungal infections in patients with acute leukaemia. American Journal of Medicine 73: 543–548

De Gregorio M W, Lee W M F, Ries C A 1982 Candida infections in patients with acute leukaemia. Ineffectiveness of nystatin prophylaxis and relationship between oropharyngeal and systemic candida. Cancer 50: 2780–2784

Dresser R K, Ultman J E 1972 Risk of severe infection in patients with Hodgkin's disease or lymphoma after diagnostic laparotomy and splenectomy. Annals of Internal Medicine 77: 143–146

Elion G B 1982 Mechanism of action and selectivity of acyclovir. American Journal of Medicine 73: 7–13

EORTC International Antimicrobial Therapy Group 1978 Three antibiotic regimens in the treatment of infection of febrile granulocytopenic patients with cancer. Journal of Infectious Diseases 137: 14–29

EORTC International Antimicrobial Therapy Project Group 1983 Early granulocyte tranfusions in high risk febrile neutropenic patients. Schweiz Medizinische Wochenschrift Supplement. 14: 46–48

Estey E H, Keating M J, McCredie K B et al 1982 Causes of initial remission induction failure in acute myelogenous leukemia. Blood 60: 309–315

Fisher-Hoch S P, Bartlett C L R, Tobin J O H et al 1981 Investigation and control of an outbreak of Legionnaires disease in a district general hospital. Lancet ii: 118–121

Forbes M, Kuck N A, Testa R T 1981 Combinations of beta-lactram antibiotics: Antibacterial effects in vitro and in vivo 1981. Current Chemotherapy and Immunotherapy Proceedings 12th International Congress of Chemotherapy, Florence 1: 50–51

Fraser D W, Tsai T R, Orenstein W et al 1977 Legionnaires disease: Description of an epidemic. New England Journal of Medicine 297: 1189–1197

Gaya H 1983 Rational basis for the choice of regimens for empirical therapy of sepsis in granulocytopenic patients: A review of the experience 1973–1983 of the EORTC Antimicrobial Therapy Project Group. Presented to The International Chemotherapy Congress, Vienna, Abstr. 3: 22–28

Gaya H 1983 Synergism and antagonism of atibiotic combinations. Presented to the International Chemotherapy Congress, Vienna. Abstr. 44: 3–42

Griffiths P D, Panjwani D D, Stirk P R et al 1984 Rapid diagnosis of cytomegalovirus infection in immunocompromised patients by detection of early antigen fluorescent foci. Lancet ii: 1242–1245

Guiot H F L, Van den Brock P J, Van der Meer J W M, Van Furth R 1983 Selective antimicrobial decontamination of the intestinal flora of patients with acute non-lymphocytic leukaemia: A double-blind, placebo-controlled study. Journal of Infectious Diseases 147: 615–623

Gurwith M, Brunton J L, Lank B, Ronald A R, Harding G K M, McCullough D W 1978 Granulocytopenia in hospitalised patients. A prospective comparison of two antibiotic regimens in the empiric therapy of febrile patients. American Journal of Medicine 64: 127–132

Haghbin M, Armstrong D, Murphy M L 1973 Controlled prospective trial of Pseudomonas aeruginosa vaccine in children with acute leukemia. Cancer 32: 761–766.

Hann I M, Prentice H G, Keaney M et al 1982a The pharmacokinetics of ketoconazole in severely immunocompromised patients. Journal of Antimicrobial Chemistry 10: 489–496

Hann I M, Prentice H G, Corringham R et al 1982b Ketoconazole versus nystatin plus amphotericin B for fungal prophylaxis in severely immunocompromised patients. Lancet i: 826–829

Hann I M, Prentice H G, Blacklock H A et al 1982 Acyclovir prophylaxis of herpes virus infections in severely immunocompromised patients. Experimental Hematology 10: 2–4

Hann I M, Prentice H G, Blacklock H A et al 1983 Acyclovir prophylaxis against herpes virus infections in severely immunocompromised patients: randomised double-blind trial. British Medical Journal 287: 375–442

Hickman R O, Buckner C D, Clift R A et al 1979 A modified right atrial catheter for access to the venous system in marrow transplant recipients. Surgery, Gynecology and Obstetrics 148: 871–875

Higby D J, Yates J W, Henderson E S, Holland J F 1975 Filtration leukapheresis for granulocyte transfusion therapy: Clinical and laboratory studies. New England Journal of Medicine 292: 761–766

Hughes W T, Johnson W W 1971 Recurrent pneumocystis carinii pneumonia following apparent recovery. Journal of Pediatrics 79: 755–759

Hughes W T, Price R A, Sisko F, Haron W S, Kafatos A G, Schouland M, Smythe P M 1974 Protein-calorie malnutrition: A host determinant for P. carinii infection. American Journal of Diseases of Children 128: 44–52

Hughes W T, Kuhn S, Chaudhary S et al 1977 Successful chemoprophylaxis for Pneumocystis carinii pneumonia. New England Journal of Medicine 197: 1419–1427

Hughes W T, Feldman S, Chaudhary S C et al 1978 Comparison of pentamidine isethionate and trimetehoprim-sulphamethoxazole in the treatment of pneymocystis carinii pneumonia. Journal of Pediatrics 92: 285–291

Klastersky J, Daneau D, Swings G, Weerts D 1974 Antibacterial activity in serum and urine as a therapeutic guide in bacterial infections. Journal of Infections Diseases 129: 187–193

Klastersky J, Zinner S H 1982 Synergistic combinations of antibiotics in Gram-negative infections. Review of Infectious Diseases 4: 294–301

Klastersky J 1983 A co-operative trial of empirical treatment in febrile neutropenic patients. The Third EORTC Trial. Presented at the International Chemotherapy Congress. Abstr. 71: 33–35

Klastersky J 1983 Management of infection in granulocytopenic patients. Journal of Antimicrobial Chemotherapy 12: 102–104

Kostiala I, Kostiala A, Kahapää A 1982 Acute fungal stomatitis in patients with hematologic malignancies: quantity and species of fungi. Journal of Infectious Diseases 146: 101

Law D K, Dudnick S J, Abdon N I 1974 The effects of protein-calorie malnutrition on immune competence of the surgical patient. Surgery Gynecology and Obstetrics 139: 257–266

Levine A S, Schimpff S C, Graw R G Jr et al 1974 Haematologic malignancies and other marrow failure states. Progress in the management of complicating infections. Seminars in Haematology 11: 141–202

Lopez C, Watanabe K, Fox J J 1980 2'-fluoro-5-iodo-aracytosine; a potent and selective anti-herpes virus agent. Antimicrobial Agents and Chemotherapy 17: 803–806

Mackowak P et al 1981 quoted by Hann et al 1983

Martin J C, Dvorak C A, Suree D F, Matthews T R, Verheyden J P H 1983 9-(1, 3-dihydroxy-2-propoxymethyl) guanine: a new potent and selective anti-herpes agent. Journal of Medical Chemistry, in press 26(5): 759–761

McCutchan J A, Wolf J L, Zeigler E J, Braude A I 1983 Ineffectiveness of single dose human antiserum to core glycolipid (E. Coli JS) for prophylaxis of bacteremic, gram negative infections in patients with prolonged neutropenia. Schweizerische Medizinische Wochenschrift S1440–45

McDade J E, Brenner D J, Bozeman F M 1979 Legionnaires disease bacterium isolated in 1949. Annals of Internal Medicine 90: 659–661

Meunier-Carpentier F, 1983a How to prevent and treat fungal infections. Presented to the International Chemotherapy Congress, Vienna. Abstr. 3: 29–35

Meunier-Carpentier F 1983b Treatment of mycoses in cancer patients. American Journal of Medicine Suppl Jan. 74–79

Meuwissen J H E T, Tauber I, Leeuwenberg A D E M et al 1977 Parasitologic and serologic observations of infection with pneumocystis in human. Journal of Infectious Diseases 136: 43–49

Meyer R D 1981 Legionnaires disease in the compromised host. In: Rubin R H, Young L S (eds) Clinical approach to infection in the compromised host. Plenum, New York p 269–334

Meyers J D, Thomas E D 1981 Infections complicating bone marrow transplantation. In: Rubin R H, Young L S (eds) Clinical approach to infection in the compromised host. Plenum, New York, p 507–552

Meyers J D, Flournoy N D, Thomas E D 1982 Non-bacterial pneumonia after allogenic marrow transplantation. Review of ten years experience. Review of Infectious Diseases 4(6): 1119–1132

Meyers J D, Leszczynski J, Zaia J A, Flournoy N, Newton B, Snydman R, Wright G G, Levin M J, Thomas E D 1983 Prevention of cytomegalovirus infection by cytomegalovirus immune globulin after marrow transplantation. Annals of Internal Medicine 98: 442–446

Pizzo P A, Levine A S 1977 The utility of protected environment regimens for the compromised host. In: Brown E B (ed) Progress in haematology. Grune & Stratton, New York, p 311–332

Pizzo P A, Robichaud J K, Gill F A, Witelsky F G, Levinse A S, Deisseroth A B et al 1979 Duration of empiric antibiotic therapy in granulocytopenic patients with cancer. American Journal of Medicine 67: 194–200

Pizzo P A, Robichaud K J, Edwards B K, Schumaker C, Kramer B S, Johnson A 1983 Oral antibiotic prophylaxis in patients with cancer: A double-blind randomised placebo controlled trial. Journal of Pediatrics 102: 125–133

Pizzo P A, Robichaud K J, Wesley R, Commers J R 1982a Fever in the paediatric and young adult patient with cancer. A prospective study of 1001 episodes. Medicine 61: 153–165

Pizzo P A, Robichaud K J, Gill F A, Witelsky F G 1982b Empiric antibiotic and antifungal therapy for cancer patients with prolonged fever and granulocytopenia. American Journal of Medicine 72: 101–111

Platt R, Ehrlich S L, Afarian J, O'Brien T F, Pennington J E, Kass E H 1981 Moxalactam therapy of infections caused by cephalothin-resistant bacteria. Antimicrobial Agents and Chemotherapy 20: 351–355

Rogers T R et al 1985 Prevention of infection in neutropenic bone marrow transplant patients. In: Schonfeld H (ed) Antibiotics & chemotherapy, vol 33. Karger, Basle, pp 90–1131

Rogers B H, Donowitz G R, Walker G K et al 1979 Opportunistic pneumonia: A clinicopathogenic study of five cases caused by an unidentified acid-fast bacterium. New England Journal of Medicine 301: 959–961

Rossiter S J, Miller D C, Chung A M et al 1979 Lung biopsy in immunocompromised hosts. American Journal of Medicine 59: 488–496

Rubin R H, Young S L 1981 Clinical approach to infection in the compromised host. Plenum Medical Book Co, New York

Sage R, Hann I, Stirling L, Prentice H G, Corringham R T, Gray R et al 1983 Netilmicin and cefoperazone versus netilmicin and piperacillin versus netilmicin and ticarcillin versus netilmicin and mezlocillin in the empirical treatment of febrile neutropenic patients. Presented to the International Chemotherapy Congress. Abstr. 84: 51054

Saral R, Burns W H, Laskim O L, Santos G W, Lietman P W 1981 Acyclovir prophylaxis of herpes simplex virus infections. A randomised double-blind controlled trial in bone marrow transplant recipients. New England Journal of Medicine 305: 63–67

Schimpff S C, Young V M, Greene W H et al 1972 Origin of infections in acute non-lymphocytic leukaemia. Significance of hospital acquisition of potential pathogens. Annals of Internal Medicine 77: 707–714

Schimpff S C, Greene W H, Young V M et al 1975 Infection prevention in acute nonlymphocytic leukaemia. Annals of Internal Medicine 82: 351–358

Schimpff S C, Aisner J, Wiernik P M, 1979 Infection in acute non-lymphocytic leukaemia. The alimentary canal as a major source of pathogens. In: Van der Waaij D, Verhoen J (eds) New criteria for antimicrobial therapy. Amsterdam, Excerpta Medica, p 12–29

Schimpff S C 1980 Infection prevention during granulocytopenia. In: Remington J S, Swatz M N (eds) Current clinical topics in infectious diseases. McGraw Hill, New York, p 85–106

Schwartz R S, Mackintosh F R, Scurier S L, Greenberg P L 1984 Multivariate analysis of factors associated with invasive fungal disease during remission induction therapy for acute myelogenous leukemia. Cancer 53: 411–419

Selby P J, Powles R L, Jameson B et al 1979 Parenteral acyclovir therapy for herpes virus infections in man. Lancet ii: 1267–1270

Siber G R, Weitzman S A, Aisenberg A C, Weinstein H J, Schiffman G 1978 Impaired antibody response to pneumococcal vaccine after treatment for Hodgkin's disease. New England Journal of Medicine 299: 442–448

Smith C R, Lipsky J J 1983 Hypoprothrombinaemia and platelet dysfunction caused by cephalosporin and oxalactam antibiotics. Journal of Antimicrobial Chemotherapy 11: 496–498

Stagno S, Pifer L L, Hughes W T et al 1979 Pneumocystis carnii, a cause of pneumonitis in young immunocompetent infants. In: Interscience Conference on Antimicrobial Agents and Chemotherapy. Boston, American Society for Microbiology

Storb, R, Prentice R L, Buckner C D et al 1983 Graft-versus-host disease and survival in patients with aplastic anemia treated by marrow grafts from HLA-identical siblings. New England Journal of Medicine 308: 302–307

Storring R A, Jameson B, McElwain T J et al 1977 Oral non-absorbable antibiotics prevent infection in acute non-lymphoblastic leukaemia. Lancet ii: 837–840

Thomason B W, Harris P P, Hicklin M D et al 1979 A legionella-like organism related to WIGA in a fatal case of pneumonia. Annals of Internal Medicine 91: 673–676

Van der Waaij D, Berghuis J M, Lekkerkerk J E C 1972 Colonization resistance of the digestive tract of mice during systemic antibiotic treatment. Journal of Hygiene 70: 605–610

Vander Waaij D 1978 The colonisation resistance of the digestive tract in man and animals. Presented at VI International Symposium for Gnotobiology. Ulm, Germany

Vogler W R, Winston E F 1977 A controlled study of the efficacy of granulocyte transfusions in patients with neutropenia. American Journal of Medicine 63: 548–555

Wade J C, Schimpff S C, Newman K A, Wiernick P J 1982 Staphylococcus epidermidis: An increasing cause of infection in patients with granulocytopenia. Annals of Internal Medicine 97: 503–508

Wade J C, de Longhck, Newman K A, Crowley J, Wiernik P H, Schimpff S C 1983 Selective antimicrobial modulation as prophylaxis against infection during granulocytopenia: Trimethoprim — sulfamethoxazole vs. nalidixic acid. Journal of Infectious Diseases 147: 4, 624–634

Walzer P D, Perl D P, Krogstad D J et al 1976 Pneumocystis carinii pneumonia in the United States: Epidemiological diagnostic and clinical features, In: Robbins J B, De Vita V T Jr, Dutz W. (eds) NCI Monograph #43, Washington, p 55–63

Watson J G, Jameson B 1979 Antibiotic prophylaxis for patients in protective isolation. Lancet i: 1183

Watson J G, Jameson B, Powles R L, McElwain, T J, Lawson D N, Judson I et al 1982 Co-trimoxazole versus non-absorbable antibiotics in acute leukaemia. Lancet i: 6–9

Watson J G 1983 Problems of infection after bone marrow transplantation. Journal of Clinical Pathology 36: 683–692

Williams D J 1983 Antimicrobial activity of new beta-lactams. Presented to the International Chemotherapy Congress 1983. Abstr. 13: 1–6

Winston D, Howitt W L 1979 Micro-organisms causing infection in the compromised host with special references to infection with unusual micro-organisms. In: Bodey G P, Rodriguez V (eds) Hospital associated infections in the compromised host. Marcel Dekker, New York, p 61 155

Winston D J, Schiffman G, Wang D C et al 1979 Pneumococcal infections after human bone-marrow transplantation. Annals of Internal Medicine 91: 835–841

Winston D J, Pollard R B, Ho W G et al 1982 Cytomegalovirus immune plasma in bone marrow tranplant recipients. Annals of Internal Medicine 97: 11–18

Wright D G, Robichaud K J, Pizzo P A, Deisseroth A B 1981 Lethal pulmonary reactions associated with the combined use of amphotericin B and leucocyte tranfusions. New England Journal of Medicine 304: 1186–1189

Young L S, Meyer R D, Armstrong D 1973 Pseudomonas aeruginosa vaccine in cancer patients. Annals of Internal Medicine 79: 518–527

Young L S 1983 Therapy and prevention of viral and parasitic infections in the cancer patient. Presented to the International Chemotherapy Congress, Vienna. Abstr. 3: 36–42

Young R C, Corder M P, Hayes H A et al 1972 Delayed hypersensitivity in Hodgkin's disease. A study of 103 untreated patients. American Journal of Medicine 52: 63–72

Zeigler E J, Douglas H, Sherman J E et al 1973 Treatment of E. Coli and Klebsiella bacteremia in agranulocytic animals with antiserum to UDP-GAL epimerase-deficient mutant. Journal of Immunology 111: 433–438

Zeigler E J, McCutchan J A, Frierer J et al 1982 Treatment of gram-negative bacteremia and shock with human antiserum to mutant Escherichia coli. New England Journal of Medicine 307: 1225–1230

Zinner S H, Lastersky J, Gaya H, Bernard C, Ruff J C 1981 In vitro and in vivo studies of three antibiotic combinations against Gram-negative bacteria and Staph. aureus. Antimicrobial Agents and Chemotherapy 20: 463–469

Zinner S, Gaya H, Glauser M, Hann I, Klastersky J, Schimpff S 1982 Co-trimoxazole and reduction of risk of infection in neutropenic patients. Second International Symposium on Infection in the Immunocompromised Host. Academic Press, New York, p 262–264

9. Viruses, *onc* genes and leukaemia

G. Franchini   R. C. Gallo

INTRODUCTION

Study of retroviruses and retroviral transforming genes, v-*onc*s, and their cellular homologue c-*onc*s, and the isolation of transforming genes by DNA transfection, have provided new insights into the understanding of the mechanisms of animal tumor-igenesis. Our laboratory has been interested in studying retroviruses and retroviral related sequences in human haematopoietic malignancies. We will briefly summarise some information on the only known class of human retroviruses, the family of related T-lymphotropic retroviruses called human T-cell leukaemia/lymphoma virus (HTLV) and the link of some of these viruses to the cause of adult T-cell malignancies. We will also describe data on the structure, expression, and chromo-somal localisation of some known human *onc* genes and their relationship to specific chromosomal rearrangement or amplification in haematopoietic malignancies with particular emphasis on work performed in our laboratory. Finally, we will discuss the relationship of the transforming genes isolated by DNA transfection techniques with the known viral *onc* genes and the mechanism of *onc* gene co-operation in vitro that could be the basis of neoplastic transformation.

THE HUMAN T-CELL LEUKAEMIA/LYMPHOMA VIRUS (HTLV) AND ADULT T-CELL LEUKAEMIA/LYMPHOMA (ATLL)

The HTLV genome

The HTLV genome has been molecularly cloned and sequenced (Manzari et al, 1983; Seiki et al, 1983). The HTLV structural genes *gag*, *pol*, and *env* are included within the 5' and 3' long terminal repeats (LTR). An interesting feature of HTLV is the presence of a region of 2000 nucleotides between the end of the *env* gene and the 3' LTR, termed the pX region. DNA sequence analysis of the pX region has revealed the presence of four open reading frames that have the potential to encode small polypeptides. However, nothing is known to date about the possible function of the protein product of the pX region. Molecular hybridisation of fragments of the HTLV genome, representing *gag*, *pol*, *env*, and pX region, with human and other vertebrate species DNA revealed the presence in human DNA of sequences distantly related to the HTLV *pol* and *env* gene (Franchini et al, 1984). No other sequences were detected in vertebrate DNAs, indicating that HTLV does not contain a cell-derived *onc* gene.

HTLV epidemiology

The study of HTLV epidemiology has been approached by screening the patients' sera for the presence of anti-HTLV antibodies against the major core proteins p24 and p19 (Kalynaraman et al, 1982a; Posner et al, 1981; Robert-Guroff et al, 1981, 1982, 1983) and by hybridising the leukaemic cell DNAs with molecular cloned HTLV DNA (Wong-Staal et al, 1983). These two methods allow the discrimination between cases that are antibody-negative and provirus-positive and vice versa and give a more complete picture of HTLV epidemiology.

Serological survey

The presence of natural antibodies in the sera of normal people as well as sera of patients with T-cell malignancies and their healthy relatives was detected by radioimmunoprecipitation (RIP) and by solid-phase radioimmunoassay (RIA). The results indicated the existence of endemic areas for HTLV infection in Japan and the Caribbean basin (Kalynaraman et al, 1982a; Catovsky et al, 1982). A very high association was found between the presence of serum antibodies and a T-cell malignancy designated ATLL (Takatzuki et al, 1977) in Japan and T-LCL in the Caribbean. Typically but not always the two diseases share such clinical features as aggressive course (more than 80%), disseminated skin lesions (50%), hepatospleno-megaly (50%), hypercalcaemia (50–75%), and presence of circulating pleomorphic multinucleated lymphocytes. ATLL and T-LCL clearly are the same disease. Several other cases of HTLV-positive ATLL have been described worldwide. Very interestingly, a high percentage of the healthy relatives of ATLL patients are seropositive as compared with the random healthy donor, indicating that close contact seems to be required for viral transmission. In addition, sera of patients from the endemic areas with other kinds of haematopoietic malignancies were also positive for HTLV antibodies (Gallo et al, 1983; N. Gibbs et al, personal communication). The percentage of HTLV-positive patients with ATLL-unrelated neoplasms is statistically very significant when compared with the random population. It is not clear yet if this correlation reflects a secondary disease association or whether it might represent a fortuitous infection of individuals in an endemic area. Interestingly enough, in one seropositive Jamaican patients with B-cell chronic lymphocytic leukaemia, the neoplastic B cell did not carry HTLV sequences in the genomic DNA whereas the normal T lymphocytes of the same patient did. It is possible that, in contrast to a direct role in T-cell malignancies, infection with HTLV in the T cells of these B-cell neoplasias leads to an increased risk of neoplastic transformation either because of the production of B-cell growth factor and expansion of a B-cell proliferative pool (Salahuddin et al, 1984) or to decreasing T-cell immune surveillance by altering T-cell immunity.

Molecular survey

A screening of fresh samples of human haematopoietic malignancies was performed using cloned HTLV probes (Wong-Staal et al, 1983). Out of 111 samples that we analysed for the presence of HTLV sequences integrated in the neoplastic cell DNA, 18 were positive for the HTLV provirus. All the 18 patients displayed the clinical manifestation of adult T-cell leukaemia/lymphoma. The neoplastic cells seem to be derived from the clonal expansion of a single infected cell and the leukaemic DNAs contain from one to three proviral copies. Table 9.1 summarises only the fresh cases that we analysed with molecular hybridisation and excludes the studies on several cell lines established from patients with ATLL. Many more fresh cases of ATLL from Japan, the USA, and other parts of the world have been analysed by other criteria only (i.e. virus isolation, serum antibodies, or viral antigens in cultured cells).

The other 93 haematopoietic malignancies have been studied with hybridisation conditions that allow the uncovering of viruses distantly related to HTLV. Related sequences were found in one case of chronic myeloid leukaemia and in the DNA of

Table 9.1   HTLV-I and HTLV-II proviruses in human haematopoietic neoplastic fresh-cell DNAs

Disease	Number of cases	HTLV positive	Average copy number
ATLL (USA)*	3	3	1.5
ATLL (Japan)*	8	8	1.5
ATLL (Caribbean)*	2	2	3.0 or more
ATLL (Brazil)*	1	1	3.0
AML	31	0	—
AMML	3	0	—
CML	9	1†	?
ALL	8	0	—
CTCL	8	0	—
Others	25	0	—
HCL	5	0	—

ATLL, adult T-cell leukaemia–lymphoma; AML, acute myeloid leukaemia; AMML, acute myelomonocytic leukaemia; CML, chronic myeloid leukaemia; CTCL, cutaneous T-cell lymphoma; HCL, hairy-cell leukaemia.
* Many more cases of ATLL have been found positive for the presence of HTLV by various criteria: virus isolation, immunofluorescence, etc., but the proviral DNA has not been studied in such cases, usually because of lack of sufficient amount of fresh cells.
† This case contains sequences distantly related to HTLV-I (Wong-Staal et al, 1983).

the T-cell line established from a patient with a T-cell variant of hairy-cell leukaemia (HCL), from which a new virus, denominated HTLV-II, has been isolated (Popovic et al, submitted) and cloned (Gelmann et al, 1984; Chen et al, 1983). Comparative analysis between the HTLV-I and HLTV-II genomes indicates that the two viruses have less than 10% homology in the nucleic acid sequences. All the other cases of haematopoietic malignancies tested were negative for both HTLV-I and HTLV-II. These data together indicate a tight association between HTLV-I and ATLL but such a correlation has not been found between HTLV-II and HCL, possibly because HTLV-II has only been isolated from a rare T-cell variant of HCL.

HTLV properties

As we discussed earlier, the HTLV genome does not carry a cell-derived *onc* gene. However, HTLV is able to immortalise normal human cord blood T cells (Popovic et al, 1983) and bone marrow T-cells in vitro (Markham et al, 1983; Salahuddin et al, 1983). The transformed cells display features of the primary leukaemic cells of patients with ATLL: (1) decreased requirement for the in vitro growth of exogenous T-cell growth factor (TCGF or interleukin 2) and in some cases complete TCGF independence; (2) increased number of TCGF receptors and transferrin receptors; (3) morphological changes of some cells to cells having lobulated nuclei or multinucleated giant cells, resembling the phenotype of the leukaemic cells of patients with ATLL.

MECHANISMS OF LEUKAEMOGENESIS BY RETROVIRUSES

The retroviruses are grouped into two major classes according to their pathogenicity. The acute leukaemia viruses, rare in nature, induce polyclonal neoplasms in a few weeks when inoculated in animals. The oncogenic potential of these viruses resides in a set of sequences of cellular origin designated *onc* genes. The *onc* genes seem to be acquired through a recombination process of a given virus with the DNA of the host origin. The acute leukaemia viruses have the capability to transform the appropriate target cell in vitro. In contrast, the chronic leukaemia viruses do not transform cells in vitro, and cause monoclonal disease after a relatively long latency period. In most of the naturally occurring leukaemias in which a chronic leukaemia virus has been identified as the aetiological agent, the leukaemogenic mechanism is not known. In the avian leukaemia-virus-induced B-cell lymphoma and erythroblastosis, one of the steps in the oncogenic process seems to be the integration of viral sequences in the vicinity of a cellular *onc* gene, c-*myc* or c-*erb* B respectively (Hayward et al, 1981; Fung et al, 1983). The insertion of viral sequences in those DNA loci induces the transcriptional activation of the contiguous cellular *onc* genes. In the rat thymoma induced by the Moloney strain of murine leukaemia virus, a similar mechanism has been described in which the viral genome integrates preferentially in two common domains of the host DNA (Tsichlis et al, 1983). In some cases the transcription of contiguous genes is activated and such genes do not seem to be related to the known viral *onc* genes. Therefore, one of the mechanisms for leukaemogenesis by some chronic leukaemia viruses appears to be mediated by the activation of cellular genes. However, this mechanism does not appear to be operative in all systems.

How does HTLV transform T cells?

HTLV seems to belong to the class of the chronic leukaemia viruses because it lacks a cell-derived *onc* gene and it is associated with a monoclonal disease that occurs after a long latency period. There is no evidence for a common region of human DNA where HTLV integrates. We have attempted to investigate the possible mechanism of transformation by HTLV in vitro and in vivo, asking whether the expression of viral genes is necessary for the initiation and/or maintenance of transformation and/or whether cellular genes are transcriptionally activated by HTLV infection. In the primary cell lines established from patients with ATLL and in the vitro transformed cell the HTLV genome is always expressed in several species of messenger RNA (our unpublished results): a 9 kb mRNA which represents the genomic read-through RNA and a 4 kb mRNA which contains sequences homologous to the envelope gene and the pX region, and might encode for the envelope protein. Several other subgenomic mRNAs can be detected in most of the RNAs analysed, including a specific mRNA for the pX region. We analysed also the RNAs of fresh incultured neoplastic cells. The RNA of one patient, S.D., contained several mRNA species, whereas the neoplastic cells of four other patients did not express any viral mRNAs. These data would suggest that viral gene product(s) might not be necessary for the maintenance of the late neoplastic state in vivo. The fact that the HTLV infected, immortalised, cord blood or bone marrow T cells always express viral mRNA suggests that in vitro proliferation of T cells may be mediated by some viral protein product, the most likely candidate being the pX protein(s). By extrapolation, it is conceivable that the expression of viral gene(s) might be important also in the early phase of transformation in vivo. A second event should induce the clonal selection of the leukaemic population in vivo, possibly through the activation of specific cellular genes. Following this rationale, the RNAs of cultured and fresh leukaemic cells obtained from several patients were studied in search of transcriptional activation of cellular genes. Since both the primary leukaemic T-cell lines established from patients and the infected cord blood T cells often grow independently of exogenous TCGF, we analysed whether HTLV infection can induce increased expression of TCGF in the fresh and cultured leukaemic cells. To study the expression of the TCGF gene, we utilised a recombinant clone containing the 1000 nucleotides of cDNA obtained from the human TCGF mRNA (Clark et al, 1984). Only the primary cell line (HUT 102 and MO) of two patients infected with HTLV-I and HTLV-II, respectively, expressed detectable levels of TCGF mRNA (Arya et al, 1984) (see Table 9.2). Both the fresh cells analysed were negative for TCGF expression. We, therefore, conclude that although usually both the fresh and the cultured cells do express high levels of TCGF receptor we can rule out a simple autostimulation mechanism that would explain the immortal growth of the neoplastic T cells. Lastly, we studied the expression of several human homologues of viral *onc* genes in fresh and cultured leukaemic cells. The c-*erb*, c-*sis*, c-*fes*, c-*myc*, c-*abl*, c-*Ha-ras*, c-*Ki-ras*, and c-*myb* were used as labelled probes against the RNAs of HTLV-infected cells, fresh and cultured. No transcriptional activation of the above-mentioned *onc* genes was found, with the exception of the c-*sis* gene, which was expressed at high levels in two of the cell lines examined (MO and HUT 102) (our unpublished results). Our data suggests that HTLV infection in vitro and in some cases in vivo does not correlate with transcriptional activation of the cellular *onc* genes that we have tested. However, it is possible that another c-*onc* gene not examined is specifically activated by HTLV infection.

CELLULAR *ONC* GENES

The cellular *onc* genes have been identified through two independent lines of work: (1) the study of the transforming genes of the acutely transforming retroviruses (v-*onc*) and their cellular homologues (c-*onc*s); (2) the development of DNA-mediated gene transfer techniques and the isolation of genes able to induce morphological transformation of mouse fibroblasts in vitro. A large proportion of the genes isolated with the latter approach are related to a small family of retroviral *onc* genes. We will review some data on retroviral-related *onc* genes; in particular, we will discuss their genetic structure, RNA expression, chromosomal localisation, and the relationship of oncogenes rearrangement and/or amplification with specific human neoplasias. Finally, we will briefly summarise some data on the cellular *onc* genes isolated by the DNA transformation assay on mouse fibroblasts.

Retroviral-related cellular response

To date, about 20 cellular *onc* genes (c-*onc*s) have been identified using molecularly cloned viral *onc* genes (v-*onc*s). Their genomic organisation is similar to other cellular genes. Most of them are interrupted by large intervening sequences, and are

Table 9.2 Viral and cellular genes expression in HTLV-infected cells

RNA source	Viral genes	TCGF (IL-2)	c-sis	c-fes	c-myc	c-abl	c-Ha-ras/ c-Ki-ras	c-erb
Cell lines								
MI	+	−	−	−	+	−	+	−
MJ	+	−	−	−	+	−	+	−
HUT 102	+	±	+	−	+	−	+	−
UK	+	ND	−	−	ND	−	+	−
MO*	+*	±	±	−	ND	−	+	−
Fresh neoplastic cells								
SD	+	−	−	−	+	−	ND	ND
GS	−	−	−	−	+	−	ND	ND

* The MO cell line is infected with HTLV-II. MO RNA was hybridised with HTLV-II probe.

transcribed in RNA that is spliced to a smaller mRNA. The cellular *onc* genes have been evolutionarily conserved from avians to humans and vestigial sequences related to some of them are present in the *Drosophila* genome (Shilo et al, 1982). Table 9.3 shows a summary of the genes of cellular origin transduced by retrovirus in different species. The transformation potential of this class of retroviruses, the acute leukaemia viruses, is due to the protein product of their *onc* genes. The plasma membrane is a frequent localisation of the virus *onc* genes protein. Few protein products have been localised in the nucleus. For the majority of the viral *onc* genes, the activity of the protein product is not known with the exception of the *src*, *yes*, *fes* (*fps*), *abl*, and *ros* that have tyrosine kinase activity. Inoculation of the acute leukaemia viruses leads to various types of leukaemias–lymphomas in animals. In order to investigate if the cellular homologues of the viral *onc* genes play a role in human haematopoietic malignancies, we and others have cloned several human *onc* genes and studied their genetic organisation, their expression, and their chromosomal localisation in human neoplasms.

Onc gene expression in human lymphomas and leukaemias

The human cellular homologues of the avian myeloblastosis virus, c-*myb* (Franchini et al, 1983), avian myelocytomatosis virus, c-*myc* (Dalla-Favera et al, 1982b), simian sarcoma virus, c-*sis* (Dalla-Favera et al, 1981), and feline sarcoma virus, c-*fes* Franchini et al, 1982), have been cloned in our laboratory (see Wong-Staal & Gallo, 1982 for an earlier review). In addition to the above-mentioned genes, we also used the v-*abl onc* gene in a survey of fresh and cultured haematopoietic leukaemias (Westin et al, 1982b). Table 9.4 summarises the data. The *myc* gene was expressed at moderate levels in all the cells analysed and a high level of the 2.4 Kb mRNA transcript was detected (Westin et al, 1982a) in the human promyelocytic cell line HL60 (Collins et al, 1977). Such high levels of expression decrease when HL60 undergoes in vitro differentiation after induction with retinoic acid or dimethyl sulphoxide. High expression of the c-*myc* gene has also been reported in some human Burkitt cell lines (Nishikura et al, 1983). A single mRNA species of 4.5 kb related to the *myb* gene is also detected in HL60 and the *myb* RNA is markedly reduced in the differentiated HL60 cells (Westin et al, 1982b). In contrast to c-*myc*, c-*myb* expression is restricted to immature T cells and to myeloid and erythroid precursor cell lines. Very interestingly the *myb* gene is expressed at high levels in the fresh cells and in the cell lines established from patients with T-cell acute lymphoblastic leukaemia. The c-*cis* gene or platelet-derived growth factor gene (Doolittle et al, 1983; Waterfield et al, 1983) encodes for a single 4.5 kb mRNA. The c-*sis* gene appears to be expressed in the mature T-cell line HUT 102 infected with the human T-cell leukaemia/lymphoma virus (HTLV-I). As described previously in this chapter, another neoplastic T-cell line producing HTLV-II expresses the *sis* mRNAs. The biological meaning of the c-*sis* activation in the HTLV-positive mature T cell is not well understood yet. However, it is interesting that c-*sis* is often expressed in a variety of human glioblastoma and sarcoma cell lines (Eva et al, 1981), but not in normal fibroblasts or other solid tumour types. The strict correlation between the expression of the *sis* gene in these specific tumours in association with the known function of the *sis* gene (promoting growth of fibroblasts, glial cells, and smooth muscle cells) stimulates the hypothesis that the activation of the c-*sis* expression in glioblastoma and sarcoma may be an important

Table 9.3　Some properties of viral *onc* genes

v-*onc*	Retrovirus	Species of isolation	Activity of the transforming protein	Cellular localisation
src	Rous sarcoma virus	Chicken	Tyrosine kinase	Plasma membrane
yes	Y73 sarcoma virus	Chicken	Tyrosine kinase	
fes(fps)	ST feline (Fujinami) sarcoma virus	Cat (chicken)	Tyrosine kinase	Cytoplasm
abl	Abelson murine leukaemia virus	Mouse	Tyrosine kinase	Plasma membrane
ros	UR II avian sarcoma virus	Chicken	Tyrosine kinase	Plasma membrane
erb B	Avian erythroblastic virus	Chicken	Tyrosine kinase	Plasma membrane
fms	McDonough feline sarcoma virus	Cat		Cytoplasm
mos	Moloney murine sarcoma virus	Mouse		Cytoplasm
raf	3611 Murine sarcoma virus	Mouse		
Ha-ras-1	Harvey murine sarcoma virus	Rat	Guanosine diphosphate or triphosphate binding	Plasma membrane
Ki-ras-2	Kirstein murine sarcoma virus	Rat		Plasma membrane
myb	Avian myeloblastosis virus	Chicken		Nuclear matrix
myc	Avian MC24 myelocytomatosis virus	Chicken		Nuclear matrix
fos	FBJ osteosarcoma virus	Mouse		Nucleus
sis	Simian sarcoma virus	Woolly Monkey	Platelet-derived growth factor	Nucleus
rel	Reticuloendothelosis virus	Turkey		Cytoplasm
ski	Avian SKV770 virus	Chicken		

Table 9.4 Expression of *onc* genes in human haematopoietic cells

Cell type	Source	mRNA species detected with					
		v-abl Kb 7.2, 6.4, 3.8, 2.0	*v-myc* Kb 2.7	*v-myb* Kb 4.5	*v-Ha-ras* Kb 6.5, 5.8, 1.5	*v-sis* Kb 4.3	*v-fes* unknown
Myeloid	KG-1	+ +	+ +	+ +	+	–	–
	HL60	+ +	+ + + +	+ +	+	–	–
	HL60 + DMSO, RA	+ +	±	–	+	–	–
	Fresh AML cells (4 patients)						
Erythroid	K562	+ +	+ +	+ +	+	–	–
Lymphoid T cells	CEM	+ +	+ +	+ + +	+	–	–
	MOLT4	+ +	+ +	+ + +	+	–	–
	HUT78	+ +	+ +	–	+	+	–
	HUT102	+ +	+ +	–	+	–	–
B cells	Raji	+ +	+ +	–	+	–	–
	Daudi	+ +	+ +	–	+	–	–
	NC37	+ +	+ +	–	+	–	–
Normal peripheral lymphocytes		NT	+ +	–	NT	NT	NT
Normal peripheral lymphocytes + PHA		NT	+ +	–	NT	NT	NT

NT, not tested.

step in the pathogenesis of these tumours. However, it is clear that not all sarcomas express detectable c-*sis* mRNA.

Multiple transcripts of the c-*abl* and c-*Ha-ras* gene were found in all samples examined, whereas the c-*fes* transcript was not found in RNA from any cell line or fresh cell examined. In summary: (1) some onc genes are universally expressed (*abl*, *Ha-ras*, *myc*) and they may play a role in very basic cellular functions, (2) some (c-*myb*, c-*sis*) are expressed in specific cell types and at specific stages of differentiation and might be important in tissue differentation, and (3) some of them may have a very transient expression in development (c-*fes*, c-*fos*, c-*fms*: Muller et al, 1983a,b).

Onc gene amplification in human leukaemias and lymphomas

As we reported previously, an unusually high expression of the c-*myc* RNA is present in the HL60 cell line. Therefore, we investigated the genetic organisation of the c-*myc* gene in the DNAs of cultured neoplastic promyelocytes of the HL60 cell line as well as in the fresh primary cells from which the cell line was established. In both DNAs, the c-*myc* gene was amplified several times (Dalla-Favera et al, 1982d) as compared with other normal human DNAs. Chromosomal studies on drug-resistant cell lines indicated that gene amplification correlates with the presence of double minute (DMs) chromosome, homogeneously staining regions (HSRs), or abnormally banded regions (ABRs). The first two structures are interchangeable. In fact, a recent report describes the amplified *myc* gene on an ABR of an abnormal chromosome $8q^+$ in a passage of HL60 in which the DM cannot be detected any more. Several other cases of human promyelocytic leukaemia have been analysed, but c-*myc* amplification seems to be a rare event in this disease. Nevertheless, we cannot rule out that it might have played an important role in the pathogenesis of some cases of promyelocytic leukaemia. Another example of *onc* gene amplification has been reported (Collins & Groudine, 1983) in the cell line K562 originally established from a patient with chronic myeloid leukaemia. The c-*abl* is amplified and rearranged in this cell line. In this case also increased transcription of the c-*abl* gene has been observed. Several human leukaemias and lymphomas have been analysed in our laboratory for amplification of the *onc* genes c-*myc*, c-*abl*, c-*myb*, c-*fes*, and c-*sis*. We did not detect other cases out of 200 analysed. We concluded, therefore, that while gene amplification could be a more rare mechanism of *onc* gene activation, it is not a basic pathogenetic step in human leukaemia and lymphoma.

Onc genes and chromosomes

Several pieces of evidence indicate that non-random chromosomal aberrations correlate with some human malignancies. In 96% of the cases of chronic myeloid leukaemia (CML), the neoplastic cells carry a chromosomal marker (Philadelphia [Ph']) originated by a reciprocal translocation of part of the long arm of chromosome 9 and 22 (Rowley, 1983). In Burkitt's lymphoma the chromosomal aberration of the neoplastic clone involves chromosome 8 in a reciprocal translocation with chromosome 14 (90% of the cases), 2 (5%), and 22 (5%). Two cellular *onc* genes, c-*myc* and c-*abl*, have been localised at the breakpoint in the chromosome marker of some cases of Burkitt's lymphoma and CML, respectively. The c-*myc* gene is at band q24 of chromosome 8 (Dalla-Favera et al, 1982a; Taub et al, 1982). In Burkitt's lymphoma a fragment of the long arm of chromosome 8 translocates to the chromosomes 14, 2, and

22. The recipient chromosomes contain the genes encoding for the μ heavy chains, κ light chains, and λ light chains of immunoglobulin, respectively. In one-third of the Burkitt cell lines analysed carrying the (8:14) translocation, the c-*myc* gene and the μ gene are in the same DNA restriction fragment (Dalla-Favera et al, 1983) indicating that the *myc* gene in these cases translocates to a point immediately adjacent to the immunoglobulin heavy chain locus. Surprisingly, the two genes are arranged in this translocation in opposite directions of transcription. Several years ago, it had been proposed (Klein, 1981) that the relocation of cellular genes in a different region of the chromosomal DNA could lead to the activation of their transcription and possibly have a primary role in neoplastic transformation. Does the relocation of c-*myc* lead to the persistent activation of this gene and this in turn to continued B-cell proliferation (Nishikura et al, 1983; Maguire et al, 1983)? This point is not completely clarified but the c-*myc* gene on the normal chromosome 8 in a Burkitt's lymphoma cell line is transcriptionally silent. However, the c-*myc* gene translocated on chromosome 14 is actively transcribed (Nishikura et al, 1983). Inappropriate expression, rather than simply increased expression of the c-*myc* gene in its new location, may play a key role in B-cell transformation. Similar chromosomal alteration involving the *myc* gene and the immunoglobulin genes are present in the plasmocytomas of mice and rats. In the avian species, the mechanism of c-*myc* activation in B-cell lymphoma does not occur through chromosomal translocation. In a very high percentage of cases of B-cell lymphoma induced by the avian leukosis virus (ALV) in chickens, the insertion of the viral promoter in the vicinity of the c-*myc* gene correlates with its transcriptional activation (Hayward et al, 1981). *myc* activation, detected in four different species, supports a role for the cellular *myc* protein product in B-cell malignancies, although it is still possible that this is an effect of the development of the B-cell lymphoma rather than a key factor in the pathogenesis of the disease.

The human c-*abl* maps at the q34 band of chromosome 9 (de Klein et al, 1982). Analysis of several cases of chronic myeloid leukaemia with translocation (9:22) showed that c-*abl* is translocated to the Philadelphia (Ph') chromosome (22q⁻) (Bartram et al, 1983). The break point on chromosome 9 maps within 14000 nucleotides of the human c-*abl* gene in one of three cases of Ph'-positive CML patients (Heisterkamp et al, 1983). Enhanced expression of the *abl* gene in the Ph'-positive neoplastic cells, however, has not yet been fully documented. The association of the c-*abl* with the chromosomal alteration that is pathognomic for chronic myeloid leukaemia (96% of cases) suggests the c-*abl* may be involved in the pathogenesis of this human malignancy. A second possible candidate gene in the pathogenesis of CML could be the c-*sis* gene (or platelet-derived growth factor [PDGF]). This *sis* gene is on chromosome 22 (q13) (Dalla-Favera et al, 1982c). The break point of chromosome 22 in the (Ph) formation is thought to be at the level of band q11; therefore, the *sis* gene translocates to chromosome 9 (Groffen et al, 1983). To date there is no evidence that elevation or alteration of the c-*cis* gene expression is present in the neoplastic cells of patients with CML.

The c-*myb* gene is on chromosome 6 (q22–24) (Harper et al, 1983). The 6q⁻-chromosomal marker with the break point localised at band q22 has been described in several cases of lymphoma and leukaemia. The c-*fes* gene maps on chromosomes 15 (Harper et al, 1983). In acute promyelocytic leukaemias (APL), a reciprocal translocation involving chromosomes 15 and 17 is frequently described.

The c-*fes* gene translocates to chromosome 17q⁻. Because discordant data are available on the break point on chromosome 15; because it is not known whether the critical chromosome marker in APL is the 15q$^+$ or the 17q$^-$ (Sheer et al, 1983) and because c-*fes* does not appear to be expressed in APL, the relevance of the c-*fes* translocation in APL is still very uncertain. Several other *onc* genes have been mapped on human chromosomes (for a recent review see Yunis, 1983), but their association with specific chromosomal markers in human tumours is still uncertain.

Transforming genes isolated by DNA-mediated transfer

The development of DNA-mediated gene transfer techniques provided a novel approach for the isolation of transforming genes. DNA from fresh and cultured human tumours can confer a stable transformed phenotype to adequate recipient cells. The NIH 3T3 cells, an aneuploid murine fibroblast permanently growing cell line, has been used in most of the transforming assay. The NIH 3T3 cells are immortalised in culture, but they still maintain contact inhibition. DNAs containing activated transforming genes can induce foci formation in the mouse fibroblast. Isolated foci can be selected and grown and the cellular DNA can be tested for the presence of foreign DNAs. Dominant transforming genes have been isolated through the transfection assay and molecularly cloned from a variety of human tumours. The DNAs of lung, colon, bladder, skin, and breast carcinomas, neuroblastomas, rhabdomyosarcomas, and glioblastomas scored positive on NIH 3T3, as well as several DNAs from human myeloid and lymphoid malignancies.

The *ras onc* gene family and the B-lym genes

Each *onc* gene isolated by DNA-mediated transfer is closely related to a counterpart present in the DNA of normal cells. As we discussed earlier, the normal human genome contains another group of genes that have been transduced by retroviruses (retroviral related *onc* genes). It became evident that such distinction between the two different groups is artifactual. Almost all the *onc* genes identified by DNA transfection belong to the *ras onc* gene family. The only exceptions are the B-lym genes isolated by Goubin et al (1983) and Diamond et al (1983). These then are the only new genes discovered by this technique.

The *ras onc* gene family represents a group of genes related to the v-*onc* genes of Harvey murine sarcoma virus (HaSV) and Kirsten murine sarcoma virus (KiSV). Four members of each family can be distinguished in the human genome (Chang et al, 1982). The c-*Ki-ras*-1 and the c-*Ki-ras*-2 are located on chromosomes 6 and 12, respectively (O'Brien et al, 1983). The two genes isolated from normal human DNA do not induce foci formation when transfected unmodified in the NIH 3T3 mouse fibroblast cells. On the contrary, the c-*Ki-ras*-2 genes isolated from about 15% of human colon and lung carcinoma cell lines do transform NIH 3T3 mouse fibroblasts (McCoy et al, 1983; Shimizu et al, 1983). Similarly, the two mouse cellular homologues of the HaSV *onc* gene, the c-*Ha-ras*-1 and c-*Ha-ras*-2, mapped on chromosomes 11 and X, respectively (O'Brien et al, 1983), do not score on the NIH 3T3 transfection assay. An activated form of the c-*Ha-ras*-1 has been isolated from the DNA of the bladder carcinoma cell line EJ/T24 (Parada et al, 1982; Pulciani et al, 1982; Shih et al, 1982).

DNA sequencing of the activated form of H-*ras* and Ki-*ras* indicates that these genes acquire malignant properties by single point mutation in position 12 or 61 of their respective p21 protein products (Reddy et al, 1982; Tabin et al, 1982; Taparowsky et al, 1982). Very importantly, Feig et al (1984) and Santos et al (1984) have recently shown that the activated form of Ki-*ras* in the DNAs of an ovarian carcinoma and lung carcinoma is the result of a somatic mutation. The two groups showed that the DNAs of tumoral tissue from both patients did not carry the activated form of K-*ras*. These data suggest that the Ki-ras activation may contribute to the development of neoplasia in a certain number of human tumours.

Another member of the c-*ras* family (N-*ras*) has been isolated by transfection of DNA from the neuroblastoma cell line SK-N-SM, the HL60 promyelocytic cell line, and fibrosarcoma and rhabdomyosarcoma cell lines (Hall et al, 1983; Murray et al, 1983; Shimizu et al, 1983) and it has been assigned to the human chromosome 1 (Hall et al, 1983). The activated form of the N-*ras* gene carries a single point mutation leading to the substitution of glutamine by lysine in position 61.

The detection of activated *onc* genes of the *ras* family appears to be independent of the tumour phenotype (the same gene has been isolated from transformed fibroblasts and promyelocytes) and only 10–15% of the fresh tumour and tumour cell lines have yielded active *onc* genes in the transfection assay in mouse fibroblasts. It is possible that in the remaining 90% of cases, the activated genes may act as recessive genes and therefore escape the assay systems or that other activated genes are involved and require different recipient cells to induce the phenotypical change of transformation. An exception to the above-mentioned genes is the B-*lym*-1 gene isolated from the chicken avian leukosis virus-induced B-cell lymphoma (Goubin et al, 1983). In contrast to the *ras* family gene, the B-*lym*-1 genes are activated in most (80–100%) of the cases of the specific tumour type. A homologue gene has also been isolated from human Burkitt's lymphoma cell lines and localised to the human chromosome 1 (Diamond et al, 1983). The B-*lym* genes of chicken and man are not related to the *ras* family. The chicken B-*lym*-1 protein product is a small 65-amino-acid protein. The amino terminal region of the transferrin family of protein shows homology to both the chicken and human B-*lym*-1 protein products. It is therefore possible that the B-*lym* and Hu-B-*lym*-1 proteins may act as growth factors.

Onc gene co-operation as a basic mechanism in neoplastic transformation

Several lines of evidence suggest that more than one *onc* gene could be involved in specific tumours. One example is the bursal lymphoma induced by ALV in chicken. As we discussed previously, the insertion of ALV induces the transcriptional activation of the c-*myc* gene. Yet another *onc* gene, the B-*lym*-1, is activated in this tumour. Similarly, both the c-*myc* and the Hu-B-*lym*-1 are activated in Burkitt's lymphoma. In two neoplasias of the same cellular lineage (B lymphocytes) the same genes are activated in different species. In the HL60 cell line *myc* activation occurs through gene amplification and HL60 DNA also contains an activated N-*ras* gene. Yet, on the other hand, as noted earlier, such amplifications are usually not found, and DNA from 90% of tumours do not score in the transfection assay.

The human *ras* gene does not transform embryo fibroblast unless they are already immortalised prior to transfection. However, the embryo fibroblast can be immortalised if the *ras* gene is cotransfected with the polyoma large T antigen or the viral or cellular *myc* gene (Land et al, 1983). Similarly, the EJ/T24 gene lacks complete transforming activity when transfected in hamster immortalised by carcinogens (Newbold & Overell, 1983). Cotransfection of the T24 and the polyoma middle T with the adenovirus early region 1A is also required to obtain transformation of primary baby rat kidney cells (Ruley, 1983). These data indicate that in vitro transformation requires more than one gene function and, by extrapolation, that more genes could be involved in in vivo tumorigenesis.

REFERENCES

Arya S K, Wong-Staal F, Gallo R C 1984 Expression of T-cell growth factor gene in human T-cell leukemia–lymphoma virus infected cells. Science 223: 1086–1088

Bartram C R, de Klien A, Hagemeijer A, van Agthoven T, van Kessel A G, Bootsma R et al 1983 Translocation of c-abl oncogene correlates with the presence of a Philadelphia chromosome in chronic myelocytic leukaemia. Nature 306: 277–280

Catovsky D, Greaves M F, Rose M, Galton D A G, Goopden A W G, McCluskey D R et al 1982 Adult T-cell lymphoma–leukemias in blacks from the West Indies. Lancet i: 639–643

Chang E H, Gonda M A, Ellis R W, Scolnick E M, Lowy D R 1982 Human genome contains four genes homologous to transforming genes of Harvey and Kirsten murine sarcoma viruses. Proceedings of the National Academy of Sciences, USA 79: 4848–4852

Chen I S Y, McLaughlin J, Gasson J C, Clark S C, Golde D W 1983 Molecular characterization of genome of a novel human T-cell leukemia virus. Nature 305: 502–504

Clark S C, Arya S K, Wong-Staal F, Matsumoto-Kobayashi M, Kay R M, Kaufman R J et al 1984 Human T-cell growth factor: partial amino acid sequence of the proteins expressed by normal and leukemic cells, molecular cloning of the mRNA from normal cells, analysis of gene structure, and expression in different human cell types. Proceedings of the National Academy of Sciences 81: 2543–2547

Collins S J, Gallo R C, Gallagher R E 1977 Continuous growth and differentiation of human myeloid leukemic cells in suspension culture. Nature 270: 347–349

Collins S J, Groudine M T 1983 Rearrangement and amplification of c-abl sequences in the human chronic myelogenous leukemia cell line K-562. Proceedings of the National Academy of Sciences USA 80: 4813–4817

Dalla-Favera R, Gelmann E P, Gallo R C, Wong-Staal F 1981 A human onc gene homologous to the transforming gene (v-sis) of simian sarcoma virus. Nature 292: 31–35

Dalla-Favera R, Bregni R, Erikson J, Patterson D, Gallo R C, Croce C M 1982a Human c-myc onc gene is located on the region of chromosome 8 that is translocated in Burkitt's lymphoma cells. Proceedings of the National Academy of Sciences USA 79: 7824–7827

Dalla-Favera R, Gelmann E P, Martinotti S, Franchini G, Papas T, Gallo R C, Wong-Staal F 1982b Cloning and characterization of different human sequences related to the onc gene (v-myc) of different human sequences related to the onc gene (v-myc) of avian myelocytomatosis virus (MC29). Proceedings of the National Academy of Sciences USA 79: 6497–6501

Dalla-Favera R, Gallo R C, Giallongo A, Croce C M 1982c Chromosomal localization of the human homologue (c-sis) of the simian sarcoma virus *onc* gene. Science 218: 686–688

Dalla-Favera R, Wong-Staal F, Gallo R C 1982d *Onc* gene amplification in promyelocytic leukemia cell line HL60 and primary leukemic cells of the same patient. Nature 299: 61–63

Dalla-Favera R, Martinotti S, Gallo R C, Erikson J, Croce C M 1983 Translocation and rearrangements of the c-myc oncogene locus in human undifferentiated B-cell lymphomas. Science 219: 963–967

de Klein A, van Kessel A G, Grosveld G, Bartram C R, Hagemeijer A, Bootsma D et al 1982 A cellular oncogene is translocated to the Philadelphia chromosome in chronic myelocytic leukaemia. Nature 300: 765–767

Diamond A, Cooper G M, Ritz J, Lane M A 1983 Identification and molecular cloning of the human Blym transforming gene activated in Burkitt's lymphoma. Nature 305: 112–116

Doolittle R F, Hunkapillar M W, Hodd L E, Devare S G, Robbins K C, Aaronson S A, Antoniades H N 1983 Simian sarcoma virus onc gene, v-sis, is derived from the gene (or genes) encoding a platelet-derived growth factor. Science 221: 275–277

Eva A, Robbins K C, Andersen P R, Srinvasan A, Tronick S R, Reddy E P et al 1981 Cellular genes analogous to retroviral onc genes are transcribed in human tumor cells. Nature 95: 116–119

Feig L A, Bast R C Jr, Knapp R C, Cooper M C 1984 Somatic activation of ras^K gene in a human ovarian carcinoma. Science 223: 698–680

Franchini G, Gelmann E P, Dalla-Favera R, Gallo R C, Wong-Staal F 1982 Human gene (c-fes) related to the *onc* sequences of Snyder–Theilen feline sarcoma virus. Molecular and Cellular Biology 2: 1014–1019

Franchini G, Wong-Staal F, Baluda M A, Lengel C, Tronick S R 1983 Structural organization and expression of human DNA sequences related to the transforming gene of avian myeloblastosis virus. Proceedings of the National Academy of Science, USA 24: 7385–7389

Franchini G, Wong-Staal F, Gallo R C 1984 Molecular studies on human T-cell leukemia virus and adult T-cell leukemia. Journal of Investigative Dermatology 83: 063S–066S

Fung Y K, Lewis W G, Crittenden L B, Kung M J 1983 Activation of the cellular oncogene c-*erb* B by LTR insertion: Molecular basis for induction of erythroblastosis by avian leukosis virus. Cell 33: 357–368

Gallo R C, Kalyanaraman V S, Sarngadharan M G, Sliski A, Vonderheid E C, Maeda M et al 1983 Association of the human type C retrovirus with a subset of adult T-cell cancers. Cancer Research 43: 3892–3899

Gelmann E P, Franchini G, Manzari V, Wong-Staal F, Gallo R C 1984 Molecular cloning of a new unique human T-cell leukemia virus (HTLV-II). Proceedings of the National Academy of Sciences, USA 81: 993–997

Goubin G, Goldman D S, Luce J, Neiman P E, Cooper G M 1983 Molecular cloning and nucleotide sequence of a transforming gene detected by transfection of chicken B-cell lymphoma DNA. Nature 302: 114–119

Groffen J, Heisterkamp N, Stephenson J R, van Kessel A G, de Klein A, Grosveld G, Bootsma D 1983 c-sis is translocated from chromosome 22 to chromosome 9 in chronic myelocytic leukemia. Journal of Experimental Medicine 158: 9–15

Hall A, Marshall C J, Spurr N K, Weiss R A 1983 Identification of transforming gene in two human sarcoma cell lines as a new member of the ras gene family located on chromosome 1. Nature 303: 396–400

Harper M E, Franchini G, Love J, Simon M F, Gallo R C, Wong-Staal F 1983 Chromosomal sublocalization of human c-*myb* and c-*fes* cellular *onc* genes. Nature 304: 169–171

Hayward W S, Neel B G, Astrin S M 1981 Induction of lymphoid leukosis by avian leukosis virus: Activation of a cellular *onc* gene by promoter insertion. Nature 240: 475–480

Heisterkamp N, Stephenson J R, Groffen J, Hansen P F, de Klein A, Bartram C R, Grosveld G 1983 Localization of the c-abl oncogene adjacent to a translocation breakpoint in chronic myelocytic leukaemia. Nature 306: 239–242

Kalynaraman V S, Sarngadharan M G, Nakao Y, Ito Y, Gallo R C 1982a Natural antibodies to the structural core protein (p24) of the human T-cell leukemia (lymphoma) retrovirus (HTLV) found in sera of leukemia patients in Japan. Proceedings of the National Academy of Sciences, USA 79: 1653–1657

Kalynaraman V S, Sarngadharan M G, Robert-Guroff M, Miyoshi I, Blayney D, Golde D, Gallo R C 1982b A new subtype of human T-cell leukemia virus (HTLV-II) associated with a T-cell variant of hairy cell leukemia. Science 218: 571–573

Klein G 1981 The role of gene dosage and genetic transpositions in carcinogenesis. Nature (London) 294: 313–315

Land H, Paradi L F, Weinberg R A 1983 Tumorigenic conversion of primary embryo fibroblast requires at least two cooperating oncogenes. Nature 304: 596–602

Maguire R T, Robins T S, Thorgiersson S S, Heilman C A 1983 Expression of cellular myc and mos genes in undifferentiated B cell lymphomas of Burkitt and non-Burkitt types. Proceedings of the National Academy of Sciences, USA 80: 1947–1950

Manzari V, Wong-Staal F, Franchini G, Colombini S, Gelmann E P, Oroszlan S et al 1983 Human T-cell leukemia–lymphoma virus (HTLV): cloning of an integrated defective provirus and flanking cellular sequences. Proceedings of the National Academy of Sciences, USA 80: 1574–1578

Markham P D, Salahuddin S Z, Kalyanaraman V S, Popovic M, Sarin P S, Gallo R C 1983 Infection and transformation of fresh human umbilical cord blood cells by multiple sources of human T-cell leukemia–lymphoma virus (HTLV). Internal Journal of Cancer 31: 413–420

McCoy M S, Toole J J, Cunningham J M, Chang E H, Lowy D R, Weinberg R A 1983 Characterization of human colon/lung carcinoma oncogene. Nature 302: 79–81

Muller R, Slamon D J, Adamson E D, Tremblay J M, Muller D, Cline M J, Verma I M 1983a Transcription of c-onc genes, c-ras-Ki and c-fms during mouse development. Molecular and Cellular Biology 3: 1062–1064

Muller R, Tremblay J M, Adamson E D, Verma I M 1983b Tissue and cell type-specific expression of two human c-onc genes. Nature 304: 454–456

Murray M J, Cunningham J M, Parada L F, Dautry F, Lebowitz P, Weinberg R A 1983 The HL-60 transforming sequence: A ras oncogene coexisting with altered myc genes in hematopoietic tumors. Cell 33: 749–757

Newbold R F, Overell R W 1983 Fibroblast immortality is a prerequisite for transformation by EJ c-Ha-ras oncogene. Nature 304: 648–651

Nishikura K, Ar-Rushdi, Erikson J, Watt R, Rovers G, Croce C M 1983 Differential expression of the normal and of the translocated human c-myc oncogenes in B cell. Proceedings of the National Academy of Sciences USA 80: 4822–4826

O'Brien S J, Nash W G, Goodwin J L, Lowy D R, Chang E H 1983 Dispersion of the ras family of transforming genes to 4 different chromosomes in man. Nature 302: 839–843

Parada L F, Tabin C J, Shih C, Weinberg R A 1982 Human E J Bladder carcinoma oncogene is a homologue of the Harvey sarcoma virus ras gene. Nature 297: 474–478

Popovic M, Sarin P S, Robert-Guroff M, Kalyanaraman V S, Mann D, Minowada J, Gallo R C 1983 Isolation and transmission of human retrovirus (human T-cell leukemia virus). Science 219: 856–859

Posner L E, Robert-Guroff M, Kalyanaraman V S, Poiesz B J, Ruscetti F W, Bunn P A et al 1981 Natural antibodies to the retrovirus HTLV in patients with cutaneous T-cell lymphomas. Journal of Experimental Medicine 154: 333–346

Pulciani S, Santos E, Lauver A V, Long L K, Robbins K C, Barbacid M 1982 Oncogenes in human tumor cell lines: Molecular cloning of a transforming gene from human bladder cells. Proceedings of the National Academy of Sciences, USA 79: 2845–2849

Reddy E P, Reynolds R K, Santos E, Barbacid M 1982 A point mutation is responsible for the acquisition of transforming properties by the T24 human bladder carcinoma oncogene. Nature 300: 149–152

Robert-Guroff M, Ruscetti F W, Posner L E, Poiesz B J, Gallo R C 1981 Detection of the human T-cell lymphoma virus p19 in cells of some patients with cutaneous T-cell lymphoma and leukemia using a monoclonal antibody. Journal of Experimental Medicine 154: 1957–1964

Robert-Guroff M, Nakao Y, Notaki K, Ito Y, Sliski A, Gallo R C 1982 Natural antibodies to the human retrovirus, HTLV, in a cluster of Japanese patients with adult T-cell leukemia. Science 215: 975–978

Robert-Guroff M, Kalyanaraman V S, Blattner W A, Popovic M, Sarngadharan M G, Maeda M et al 1983 Evidence for human T-cell lymphoma–leukemia virus infection of family members of human T-cell lymphoma–leukemia virus positive T-cell leukemia–lymphoma patients. Journal of Experimental Medicine 157: 248–258

Rowley J D 1983 Human oncogene locations and chromosome aberrations (news). Nature 301: 290–291

Ruley H E 1983 Adenovirus early region 1A enables viral and cellular transforming genes to transform primary cells in culture. Nature 304: 602–606

Salahuddin S Z, Markham P D, Wong-Staal F, Franchini G, Kalyanaraman V S, Gallo R C 1983 Restricted expression of human T-cell leukemia–lymphoma virus (HTLV) in transformed human umbilical cord blood lymphocytes. Virology 129: 51–64

Salahuddin S Z, Markham P D, Lindner S G, Gootenberg J, Popovic M, Hemmi H et al 1984 Lymphokine production by cultured human T cells transformed by human T cell leukemia lymphoma virus I. Science 223: 703–706

Santos E, Martin-Zanis D, Reddy E P, Pierotti M A, Della Porta G, Barbacid M 1984 Malignant activation of u-K-ras oncogene in lung carcinoma but not in normal tissue of the same patient. Science 223: 661–664

Seiki M, Hattori S, Hirayama Y, Yoshida M 1983 Human adult T-cell leukemia virus: Complete nucleotide sequence of the provirus genome integrated in leukemia cell DNA. Proceedings of the National Academy of Sciences, USA 80: 3618–3622

Sheer D, Hiorns L R, Stanley K F, Goodfellow P N, Swallow D M 1983 Genetic analysis of the 15 : 17 chromosome translocation associated with acute promyelocytic leukemia. Proceedings of the National Academy of Sciences USA 80: 5007–5011

Shih C, Weinberg R A 1982 Isolation of transforming sequence from a human bladder carcinoma cell line. Cell 29: 161–169

Shilo B Z, Weinberg R A 1982 DNA sequence homologous to vertebrate oncogenes are conserved in Drosophila melanocytosis. Proceedings of the National Academy of Sciences, USA 78: 6789–6792

Shimizu K, Goldfarb M, Suard Y, Perucho M, Li Y, Kamata T et al 1983 Three human transforming genes are related to the viral ras oncogenes. Proceedings of the National Academy of Sciences, USA 80: 2112–2116

Tabin C J, Bradley S M, Bargmann C I, Weinberg R A, Papageorge A G, Scolnick E M et al 1982 Mechanism of activation of a human oncogene. Nature 300: 143–149

Takatzuki K, Uchinyama J, Sagawa K, Yodos J 1977 Adult T-cell leukemia in Japan. In: Seno S, Takaku F, Irino S (eds) Topics in hematology. Excerpta Medica, Amsterdam, Oxford, p 73–77

Taparowsky E, Suard Y, Fasano O, Shimizu K, Goldfarb M, Wigler M 1982 Activation of the T24 bladder carcinoma transforming gene is linked to a single amino acid change. Nature 300: 762–765

Taub R, Kirsch I, Morron C, Lenoir G, Swan D, Tronick S et al 1982 Translocation of the c-myc gene into immunoglobulin heavy chain locus in human Burkitt lymphoma and murine plasmacytoma cells. Proceedings of the National Academy of Sciences, USA 79: 7837–7841

Tsichlis P N, Strauss P G, Hu L F 1983 A common region for proviral DNA integration in Mo-MuLV-induced rat thymic lymphomas. Nature 302: 445–448

Waterfield M D, Scrace G T, Whittle N, Strobant P, Johnsson A, Wasteson A et al 1983 Platelet-derived growth factor is structurally related to the putative transforming protein p28sis of simian sarcoma virus. Nature 304: 35–39

Westin E H, Gallo R C, Arya S K, Eva A, Souza L M, Baluda M A et al 1982a Differential expression of the *amv* gene in human hematopoietic cells. Proceedings of the National Academy of Sciences, USA 79: 2194–2198

Westin E H, Wong-Staal F, Gelmann E P, Dalla-Favera R, Papas T S, Lautenberg J A et al 1982b Expression of cellular homologues of retroviral onc genes in human hematopoietic cells. Proceedings of the National Academy of Sciences, USA 79: 2490–2494

Wong-Staal F, Gallo R C 1982 The transforming genes of primates and other retroviruses and their human homologs. In: Klein G (ed) Advances in Viral Oncology, Vol I, Raven Press, New York, p 153–171

Wong-Staal F, Hahn B, Manzari V, Colombini S, Franchini G, Gelmann E P, Gallo R C 1983 A survey of human leukemias for sequences of a human retrovirus HTLV. Nature 302: 626–628

Yunis J J 1983 The chromosomal basis of human neoplasia. Science 221: 227–236

10. The myelodysplastic syndromes and preleukaemia

G. E. Francis   A. V. Hoffbrand

INTRODUCTION

Historical perspective

The observation that acute myeloid leukaemia (AML) can be preceded by a refractory cytopenic state accompanied by dysplasia of one or more haemopoietic cell lineages was made at the turn of the century (von Leube, 1900; Parkes-Weber, 1904). Although this early observation was confirmed by a number of groups, it was not until 1953, when Block and co-workers published their paper 'Preleukaemic Acute Human Leukaemia', that the concept of a preleukaemic state was established. In 1956 Bjorkman described patients with preleukaemic sideroblastic leukaemia and in 1965 Dameshek suggested that idiopathic acquired sideroblastic anaemia (IASA) is an early phase of erythremic myelosis or the Di Guglielmo syndrome. Dacie et al (1959) and Vilter et al (1967) described patients, including some who were preleukaemic, with refractory anaemia (RA) (also called aregenerative anaemia). The classification refractory anaemia with excess of myeloblasts (RAEB) was introduced by Dreyfus et al in 1970 and Zittoun (1976) described subacute and chronic myelomonocytic leukaemia (CMML) as a distinct haematological entity.

In a series of papers from 1970 onwards (Linman, 1970; Saarni & Linman, 1973; Linman & Bagby, 1978), Linman and co-workers established a set of diagnostic criteria for the 'preleukaemic syndrome' PLS (or haemopoietic dysplasia), which were sufficiently discriminating to identify prospectively those patients with a very high likelihood of developing AML. Table 10.1 shows the set of diagnostic criteria proposed by Linman & Bagby in 1978. These papers were important in that they focused attention on patients within the broad categories RA and IASA with the

Table 10.1   Diagnostic criteria for PLS proposed by Linman & Bagby 1978

PREREQUISITES

Peripheral blood
a) Anaemia
b) Oval macrocytes
Marrow
a) Megaloblastic erythropoiesis and/or ringed sideroblasts
b) Abnormal megakaryocytes and/or disorderly granulopoiesis
c) Absence of overt leukaemia (<5% blasts: no Auer bodies)
Other
a) Absence of vitamin B_{12} or folate deficiency
b) No cytotoxic therapy in past 6 months

Corroborative findings included: blood — nucleated RBCs, immature granulocytes, hypochromia without iron deficiency, bizarre platelets, thrombocytopenia, monocytosis or atypical monocytoid cells, pseudo-Pelger anomaly; marrow — erythrocytic hyperplasia, megakaryocytic hyperplasia.

highest frequency of leukaemic transformation (by excluding patients without dyspoiesis in an additional lineage as well as dyserythropoiesis). Because transformation rates to AML in this group are high (nearly 75% in Linman & Bagby's, 1976 study) and because they do not already have accumulation of primitive cells as in RAEB and CMML, these patients are ideal candidates for prospective study of the evolution of leukaemia.

In 1982 the FAB group (Bennett et al, 1982) introduced proposals for the classification of the myelodysplastic syndromes (MDS) and defined five groups: (1) refractory anaemia (RA), (2) RA with ring sideroblasts (RAS equivalent to IASA), (3) RA with excess of blasts (RAEB), (4) RAEB in transformation, (5) chronic myelomonocytic leukaemia (CMML). This is the most widely accepted current scheme (Bennett et al, 1984; Galton, 1984) and we will use it as a basis for the discussion of others.

Other syndromes with an increased risk of transformation into AML, such as Down's syndrome, chromosomal breakage syndrome, paroxysmal nocturnal haemoglobinuria and aplastic anaemia, although termed as 'preleukaemic' by some workers, are not included in the MDS, since they do not share the qualitative haemopoietic cell changes found in myelodysplastic syndromes. These syndromes will not be described in this chapter.

Terminology and classification schemes

One of the major problems in evaluating the early literature on any aspect of the myelodysplastic syndromes has been the lack of consistent schemes of definition and classification. This renders comparison of results of any sort (e.g. rates of leukaemic transformation, karyotypic abnormalities, in vitro studies) from different groups extremely difficult. Table 10.2 compares the FAB scheme (Bennett et al, 1982) to those of others and lists terms that tend to be used synonymously. Even where the terms used are the same, different authors may have slightly different definitions with important consequence. For example, in some studies refractory anaemia includes patients with both hyper- and hypocellular bone marrow, in others those with hypocellular marrows are excluded (Reizenstein & Lagerlöf, 1972). In this example, one would anticipate different leukaemic transformation rates with the different definitions since, in the latter scheme, exclusion of patients with aregenerative anaemia and hypocellular marrow excludes patients with aplastic anaemia, a group which only occasionally undergoes leukaemic transformation (Mohler & Levell, 1958).

Are the MDS one or more states?

The range of clinical features and haematological findings consistent with a diagnosis of MDS is very wide, but there are also many features in common. Most patients suffer from a bi- or tri-lineage dyspoiesis (Bennett et al, 1982; Linman & Bagby, 1978). This, and the results of chromosome and in vitro studies, suggests a defect in the multipotent haemopoietic stem cell. A possible exception is CMML, where minimal dysplastic changes in erythroid and megakaryocyte series cells are seen in some cases. The FAB group, however, came to the conclusion that CMML is closer to MDS than to other chronic myeloproliferative disorders. Within the RA and RAS groups there is considerable heterogeneity, particularly with respect to the tendency to leukaemic transformation. The FAB group (Bennett et al, 1982) stated that in

Table 10.2 Classification schemes and nomenclature of MDS

FAB (1982)	Linman & Bagby (1978)	Other schemes		Synonyms**
RA	RA*	Vilter (1967) RA types: I, II, III		Aregenerative anaemia; Refractory cytopenia (RC)
RA with sideroblasts	PLS — — — IASA*			Sideroachrestic anaemia; Idiopathic refractory sideroblastic anaemia (IRSA)
RAEB	Patients with more than 5% myeloblasts in the marrow were excluded from PLS	RAEM Dreyfus (1970)	SL, SML, OL (Izrael et al, 1975; Rheingold et al, 1963; Nelson, 1976)	Refractory cytopenia with excess of myeloblasts (RCEM); Refractory anaemia with excess of myeloblasts (RAEM)
RAEB in transformation				Smouldering leukaemia (SL); Subacute myeloid leukaemia (SML)
CMML			CMML (Miecher & Farquet, 1974; Goldstone et al, 1976; Skinnider et al, 1977)	Oligoblastic leukaemia (OL)

The dashed lines indicate definitions not comparable to a single FAB category.
* Patients with RA or IASA without dyspoiesis of either granulocyte or megakaryocyte lineages were excluded from PLS.
** Caution is required because strict definitions of these terms can vary.

RA 'the granulocyte and megakaryocyte series almost always appear normal', but from Linman & Bagby's work (1976 and 1978) it is clear that patients within the RA group with defects in granulocyte and/or megakaryocyte series have a much higher leukaemic transformation rate than RA as a whole. Patients with refractory anaemia with no morphological, cytogenetic or in vitro evidence of involvement of the granulocyte and megakaryocyte lineages may well be a separate group. Only when this group is clearly defined and adequately studied will it be possible to determine whether these patients do indeed have a preleukaemic state, since patients with bi- or trilineage defects might be entirely responsible for leukaemic transformations seen in this group.

Similarly patients with IASA (RAS) with and without defects of other lineages seem to be two distinct groups. Cheng et al (1979) reviewed 268 cases of IASA and found only 27 who underwent leukaemic transformation. Linman & Bagby (1978) included patients with sideroblastic anaemia in the preleukaemic category (patients with a 50–75% incidence of leukaemic transformation) only if they had defects in other lineages. Cheng et al (1979) in their 268 cases, also found that thrombocytopenia and subnormal LAP scores were associated with patients who suffered leukaemic transformation. The spectrum of karyotypic abnormalities also seems to be different in IASA compared to PLS. Whereas the latter have karyotypic abnormalities which largely overlap with those of AML, the $20q^-$ syndrome appears to be a form of IASA not usually associated with transformation to AML (Sokal et al, 1980).

On the other hand, RA and RAS without dyspoiesis of another lineages might represent not a different disorder, but an earlier stage in the same disorder. The lower transformation rate might not be observed if follow-up of these patients was for decades rather than years.

The relationship to acute leukaemia

The relationship of the myelodysplastic states to acute leukaemia is not fully understood. There are a variety of different hypothetical schemes depicted in Figure 10.1. Some believe that where a chromosomal abnormality exists, patients already have the leukaemic defect and that the spectrum of clinical findings (from MDS to AML) depends on the response of the host to the neoplastic clone (Sandberg, 1980). This view of a myelodysplastic phase as an 'aleukaemic leukaemia' or leukaemia presenting in 'spontaneous remission' has been widely discussed (Killman, 1976; Baserga, 1976; Pierre, 1974; Maldonado et al, 1976). Linman & Bagby's (1976) view was that preleukaemia (as they defined it) represented a stage or stages in the evolution of AML. Multiple genetic changes are thought to be involved in the formation of many solid tumours and in leukaemia (Burch, 1960). If myelodysplasia represents a stage in a multi-step process, karyotypic abnormalities common to AML and MDS should represent the preliminary changes and an occult or overt additional genetic change should precede leukaemic transformation. Although additional karyotypic abnormalities have been observed coincident with leukaemic transformation (Sandberg, 1980; Pierre, 1975), there appear to be few karyotypic abnormalities confined to AML and not occasionally observed in MDS. We therefore consider it more likely that leukaemia is a multi-step process in which the order of acquisition or even the combination of changes required can vary and that the myelodysplastic states represent patients whose cells have undergone only a proportion of the changes required for acquisition of the leukaemic phenotype(s). This latter scheme also seems more plausible since, with different orders of changes, there could be very heterogeneous clinico-pathological pictures corresponding to various combinations of defects and this is consistent with the wide range of features in the MDS.

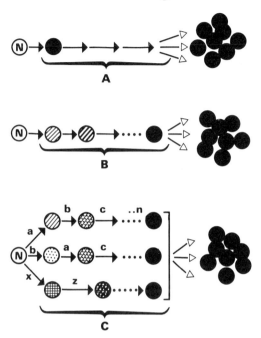

Fig. 10.1   Three hypothetical schemes of the relationship between the normal (N), preleukaemic (shaded) and leukaemic (filled) states. (A) A clone of leukaemic cells already exists in preleukaemia, but is restrained from rapid expansion, in some way, by the host (e.g. Killman, 1976). (B) The cells become progressively more abnormal, acquiring additional defects. The different MDS represent different stages (e.g. Linman & Bagby, 1976). (C) Leukaemogenesis is a multistep process in which either the order or spectrum of genetic changes is different. In the top two routes, changes (a) (stripes) and (b) (dots) occur in either order. In the third route, entirely different changes, x and y (hatching) also lead to leukaemia.

The relationship between MDS and AML implies that, in most cases, the primary defect has its origin in a multipotent haemopoietic progenitor cell. In both AML and MDS the karyotypic and in vitro evidence (see below) strongly suggests defects in granulocytic, erythrocytic and megakaryocytic lineages and thus implicates the common progenitor of these lineages. A recent report (Hehlmann et al, 1983) of a patient with sideroblastic anaemia progressing to a mixed acute lymphoblastic-myelomonoblastic leukaemia is most intriguing and suggests that the lesion in some cases may be in the common lymphoid-myeloid progenitor.

HAEMATOLOGICAL AND CLINICAL FEATURES

General clinical features

Typically the patients are over 50 years old, of either sex but with a male predominance in most series. Presenting features are those of anaemia or infection or easy bruising or haemorrhage. Some cases are detected on routine blood testing. A proportion occur after previous radiotherapy or chemotherapy. Apart from features due to bone marrow failure, clinical examination reveals splenomegaly in about a third of cases.

Incidence

With the widespread problems of definition, it is difficult to get a reliable estimate of incidence of the various categories of MDS. Incidences related to the FAB scheme from five recent reports are given in Table 10.3.

Table 10.3 Myelodysplastic syndromes. Incidence of the different types, no. (%)

	Tricot et al (1984a)	Mufti et al (1984a)	Weisdorf et al (1983)	Todd & Pierre (1983)	Coiffer et al (1983)
Type					
RA	25 (29)	53 (38)	30 (43)	149 (56)**	60
RAS	12 (14)	21 (15)	23 (33)	56 (21)	20
CMML	11 (13)	31 (22)	1 (1)	29 (11)	15*
RAEB	14 (17)	25 (18)	9 (13)	27 (10)	97
RAEB-T	23 (27)	11 (8)	6 (9)	3 (1)	—
	85	141	69	264	192

*Classified as subacute myelomonocytic leukaemia. **Includes 23 refractory cytopenias.

General haematological features

In most cases there are abnormalities in all three myeloid lines (Fig. 10.2). The peripheral red cells usually show oval macrocytes and may show tear drops, hypochromasia and punctate basophilia. There may be circulating normoblasts. The MCV is usually raised and the reticulocyte count is low for the degree of anaemia. The red cells may show decreased levels of some enzymes (e.g. pyruvate kinase, 2,3-diphosphoglyceromutase), changes in expression of antigens (e.g. A, B, H, I) and, rarely, a positive acidified lysis test. The bone marrow, which is of increased or normal and only occasionally reduced cellularity, may show megaloblastic changes with multinuclearity, gigantism, cytoplasmic vacuolation, nuclear budding, karyor-rhexis and, on iron staining, increased siderotic granules with partial or complete ring sideroblasts. Despite the megaloblastic changes, the deoxyuridine suppression test is normal, showing the defect in DNA synthesis is not at thymidylate synthetase, and serum vitamin B_{12} and folate levels are normal.

The granulocytes typically are agranular or show abnormal granulation, pseudo-Pelger forms and cells resembling both myelocytes and monocytes (para-myeloid cells); circulating monocytes may be increased. Agranular (type I) or granular (type II) blasts may be present. Abnormal promyelocytes with a bluish-grey cytoplasm, fine nuclear chromatin and pale nucleoli are frequent. Neutrophil functional defects are commonly present with reduced bactericidal, phagocytic and chemotactic activity (Martin et al, 1983). Cytochemical abnormalities were reviewed by Schmalzl et al (1978). Giant or hypogranular platelets may be circulating and the marrow shows micromegakaryocytes, giant hypolobulated forms, or megakaryocytes with frag-mented nuclei and dysmegakaryocytopoiesis. Platelets may show reduced adhesion and aggregation so that the bleeding time is inappropriately prolonged for the degree of thrombocytopenia.

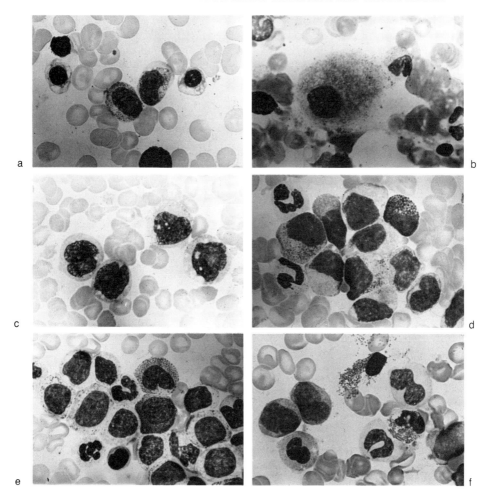

Fig. 10.2   Morphological appearances in the myelodysplastic syndrome.
a Vacuolated normoblasts and abnormal myelocytes.
b A micro megakaryocyte.
c Monocytes in peripheral blood.
d Abnormal and agranular promyelocytes, myelocytes and polymorphs.
e Abnormal monocytes and myelocytes and cells with features of both series ('paramyeloid' cells).
f Agranular and pelger-like polymorphs and increased myeloblasts.

Specific features

Refractory anaemia (RA)

This group includes, but is not synonymous with, the preleukaemic syndrome (PLS) as defined by Linman & Bagby (1978) (see Table 10.2). As mentioned above, the FAB group considered only a minority of patients in this group to have the additional abnormalities of granulocyte or megakaryocyte lineages necessary for inclusion in PLS. Anaemia was a prerequisite for the diagnosis of PLS (Linman & Bagby, 1978) but the FAB group suggested that rarely, patients with neutropenia and/or thrombocytopenia but no anaemia could be included in this category. Milner et al (1977) reported occasional patients with the other features of PLS but no anaemia. It was felt, however, that the term refractory anaemia was preferable to refractory cytopenia, since the use of the latter might encourage inclusion of patients with neutropenias and thrombocytopenias of unknown aetiology and most have little in common with the MDS.

The peripheral blood in RA shows reticulocytopenia, variable dyserythropoiesis and infrequently (in the FAB group's experience) dysgranulopoiesis. There are not more than 1% blasts in the blood and fewer than 5% in the marrow. There are no Auer rods. The marrow is hyper- or normocellular and dyserythropoietic features may include coarse siderotic granulation distinct from true ring sideroblasts (Hast et al, 1978) although the latter may also be present (up to 15%).

The incidence of acute leukaemia in RA is difficult to assess, since different groups have followed patients with different degrees of involvement of the other lineages. This heterogeneity of subjects presumably accounts for the divergent transformation rates observed.

RA with ring sideroblasts (RAS, IASA)

This corresponds most closely to the primary or idiopathic acquired sideroblastic anaemia used by earlier authors (Dacie & Mollin, 1966). The FAB group include a minority of cases with defects of granulocytes and/or megakaryocytes who would therefore be included in the PLS, but who were excluded from IASA by earlier workers (Mollin & Hoffbrand, 1968).

A dimorphic anaemia with a raised or normal MCV is typical. Ring sideroblasts comprise >15% of nucleated red cells in the marrow and morphological changes are mainly confined to the red cell series. It seems likely that a defect in haem synthesis underlies the ring sideroblast formation and this is secondary to a major disturbance of erythropoiesis, with other abnormalities in the erythroid series present, e.g. megaloblastic features in at least half the cases. Ring sideroblasts are also common in the other MDS. In a recent study of 133 cases, 40 could be classified as RAS (Juneja et al, 1983a), with 21–86% of marrow erythroblasts typed as ring sideroblasts. Thirtysix of the remaining 93 MDS cases also showed ring sideroblasts.

The incidence of leukaemia after long-term follow-up of RAS varies widely from 4–24% from series to series, again probably mainly reflecting the variable proportion of patients with bi- or tri-lineage dysplasia and also partly the variable length of follow-up (Table 10.4). In some, but not all studies, thrombocytopenia or severe anaemia at presentation was associated with a higher incidence of acute leukaemia.

Table 10.4 Incidence of AML after follow-up of primary acquired sideroblastic anaemia

	Number	Number of acute leukaemias (%)
Kushner et al (1971)	61	3 (5)
Streeter et al (1977)	80	9 (11)
Cheng et al (1979) (survey of literature)	268	27 (10)
Levy et al (1979)	25	6 (24)
Beris et al (1983)	45	8 (18)
Todd & Pierre (1983)	54	9 (17)
Weisdorf et al (1983)	23	1 (4)

Refractory anaemia with excess of blasts (RAEB)
The morphological features of the blood and bone marrow cells in RAEB are similar to those of the other MDS. The peripheral blood shows less than 5% blasts but the marrow shows between 5% and 20% blasts. Auer rods are typically absent, but cases otherwise identical have been described with such inclusions (Weisdorf et al, 1981; Seigneurin & Audhuy, 1983). Some RAEB cases may be difficult to discriminate from FAB-AML M6. It has recently been proposed by the FAB group that when the marrow erythroblast count is equal to or more than 50%, cases with >30% myeloblasts among the non-erythroid cells in the marrow should be classified as AML M6 and those with 20–30% as RAEB.

RAEB in transformation (RAEB-T)
The FAB group recognise a category of cases between RAEB and definite AML which they classify as RAEB-T, showing 5% or more blasts in the peripheral blood and 20–30% blasts in the bone marrow. These cases carry a poor prognosis. RAEB and RAEB-T closely resemble 'subacute' or 'smouldering' myeloblastic leukaemia (SML) described by other groups (Table 10.2).

Chronic myelonomonocytic leukaemia (CMML)
This condition has been classified in the MDS by some groups and with the chronic or subacute leukaemias by others. It shares many of the quantitative and qualitative haemopoietic changes of the other MDS but is characterised by frequent splenomegaly, the presence in the peripheral blood of a monocytosis of $>1.0 \times 10^9/l$ and a raised serum and urine lysosyme and polyclonal hyperimmunoglobulinaemia in two-thirds of the patients (Solal-Celigny et al, 1984). Occasionally, these patients show gum hypertrophy and serous effusions. The total leucocyte count is usually raised and the marrow shows a normal or moderately increased proportion of blasts, e.g. 2–28% (mean 11%) in 35 cases reported by Solal-Celigny et al (1984). When blasts are more frequent the condition is classified as subacute myelomonocytic leukaemia (Zittoun, 1976) or as RAEB or RAEB-T.

Secondary MDS
AML is now recognised as a relatively common consequence of cytotoxic therapy or radiotherapy for solid tumours or for non-neoplastic diseases. There is a particularly high incidence (10% or more) in Hodgkin's disease patients who have received combined modality therapy, in myeloma (17%) and in cancer, e.g. ovarian (2%). In about 75% of these patients developing AML, there is a prodromal myelodysplastic phase with features similar to those in the primary MDS (Pederson-Bjergaard et al, 1981). Marrow fibrosis, cytogenetic abnormalities (Rowley et al, 1981), a shorter transition time into overt acute leukaemia and a poorer response to chemotherapy are more common in the secondary than primary cases of MDS. MDS may also present de novo with another malignant disease, most commonly meyloma, lymphoma or carcinoma. The increased risk of myelodysplasia in each of these conditions in the absence of chemotherapy or radiotherapy or with similar doses of different drugs or radiation remains to be evaluated. It is clear, however, that features of myelodysplasia must be carefully sought, particularly in patients with otherwise inappropriate degrees of anaemia, leucopenia or thrombocytopenia.

Prognosis

The decision whether or not to treat and the sort of treatment to use depends partly on the age of the patient, the types of clinical problem suffered and an assessment of the patient's overall prognosis. A number of scoring systems have been devised to predict the outcome based on the degree of anaemia, leucopenia, thrombocytopenia and proportion of blasts in the peripheral blood and bone marrow. A simple scheme of Mufti et al (1984a) allocates a score of one each to (a) blasts $\geq$ 5% in the marrow, (b) platelets $<100 \times 10^9/l$, (c) neutropenia $<2.5 \times 10^9/l$ and (d) haemoglobin $<10\,g/dl$. Of 141 patients, 12 scored four and showed a median survival of only 8.5 months, most frequently dying of acute leukaemia, 62 patients scored two or three, showing a median survival of 22 months, most frequently dying of infections or bleeding. Sixty-seven patients scored zero or one and survived for a median of 62 months. Within each subtype of the MDS, this scoring system separated patients with a better or worse prognosis. In another series (Weisdorf et al, 1983), poor prognosis was predicted by clinical and haematological manifestation of a severe cytopenia and by myeloid immaturity in the marrow. Failure of more than one line predicted a median survival of only 8 months. Todd & Pierre (1983) found the prognosis worse in RAEB and CMML than in RA or RC. In their series, the presence of an abnormal karyotype carried an unfavourable prognosis but this has not been an entirely consistent finding although confirmed by a number of different groups (see below). Tricot et al (1984a) in a study of 85 patients found an abnormal localisation of immature myeloid precursors in the trephine biopsy, circulating myeloblasts, age, FAB classification and granulocyte count to have prognostic value (in the order given).

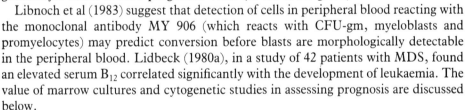
Libnoch et al (1983) suggest that detection of cells in peripheral blood reacting with the monoclonal antibody MY 906 (which reacts with CFU-gm, myeloblasts and promyelocytes) may predict conversion before blasts are morphologically detectable in the peripheral blood. Lidbeck (1980a), in a study of 42 patients with MDS, found an elevated serum B_{12} correlated significantly with the development of leukaemia. The value of marrow cultures and cytogenetic studies in assessing prognosis are discussed below.

Treatment

This ranges from that used for de novo cases of AML with multiple cycles of intensive chemotherapy or bone marrow transplantation on the one hand to simple observation with, where needed, supportive care on the other. In between, some cases are treated with gentle chemotherapy or with drugs aimed at inducing differentiation of the haemopoietic cells.

Supportive therapy

The decision to start red cell transfusions depends on clinical symptoms as well as on haemoglobin level. In RAS, iron overload may become a problem after 50–100 units have been transfused and subcutaneous desferrioxamine should be used. Prophylactic platelet transfusions are not used routinely in patients with thrombocytopenia unless substantial spontaneous bruising or haemorrhage occurs. Epsilon-amino-caproic acid may be used to assist haemostasis and low-dose corticosteroid therapy is often used to reduce haemorrhage, although this is not completely proven to be effective and may predispose to infection by reducing neutrophil function. Recurring infections, most frequently bacterial, present the major life-threatening problem and urgent treatment of these with broad spectrum intravenous antibiotics is often necessary.

Conventional AML therapy

1. CHEMOTHERAPY

Some workers have found poor responses to chemotherapy as used in de novo AML. Armitage et al (1981) treated 20 patients with AML following MDS by intensive therapy and only three went into full remission (in two cases prolonged). However, only eight of the patients received an anthracycline and none continuous infusions of cytosine arabinoside. The three patients who responded were relatively young and had not received previous chemotherapy. More recently, Murray et al (1983) obtained complete remission in three patients (aged 62, 72 and 69) with AML following MDS, using continuous cytosine arabinoside, doxorubicin and 6-thioguanine. Mufti et al (1983) obtained complete remission in a further three. More recently Capizzi et al (1984) have had promising results using a combination of high dose cytosine arabinoside and asparaginase. However, the overall response rate in these conditions is substantially lower than in de novo AML (Cohen et al, 1979; Joseph et al, 1982) and this is particularly so in the secondary MDS (Pedersen-Bjergaard et al, 1981; Anderson et al, 1981; Rowley et al, 1981).

2. BONE MARROW TRANSPLANTATION

Appelbaum et al (1984) treated 10 patients with MDS and life-threatening pancytopenia (age 4–54, median 13 years) by allogeneic transplantation. All 10 grafted but in the three receiving cyclophosphamide conditioning alone, the abnormal clone persisted or returned. Among the seven patients treated with cyclophosphamide and total body irradiation, six were alive and well, without evidence of the disease at 3–20 months. Bhaduri et al (1979) and Gyger et al (1983) also describe single cases of secondary MDS successfully transplanted.

Single agents

1. CORTICOSTEROIDS

Most cases do not respond. However, a minority do improve with large doses and Bagby et al (1980) reported that it was possible to use in vitro culture techniques to predict this (see below).

2. LOW-DOSE CYTOSINE ARABINOSIDE (ara-C)

Reports that differentiation could be induced in vitro in AML at low concentrations of ara-C (Griffin et al, 1982) and may be able to do this in vivo in AML (Housset et al, 1982) have led to renewed interest in this therapy for the MDS. However, the mechanism of action is not yet established and cytogenetic analyses suggest that low-dose ara-C acts not as a differentiation inducer but principally as a cytotoxic agent, since the abnormal clone disappears in remission. Baccarani & Tura (1979) reported improvement in a case of MDS given low-dose ara-C. Griffin et al (1983) treated 14 patients, all with excess blasts, and eight responded for 2–14 months, multiple responses occurring with multiple courses of therapy in some patients. Baccarani et al (1983) treated seven patients with RAEB, four with RAEB-T and one with CMML. One showed a partial remission, one an isolated increase in haemoglobin level and one an isolated increase in granulocyte count. Solal-Celigny et al (1984) obtained complete remissions in four of six patients with CMML. Castaigne et al (1983), Winter et al (1983) and Roberts et al (1983) all report partial remission in a few cases of MDS. Mufti et al (1984b) obtained an improvement in eight of 18 cases treated including four complete remissions. On the other hand, Najean & Pecking (1979) observed no remissions among 20 patients. Tricot et al (1984b) treated 26 patients with MDS and obtained complete remission in three and 12 showed good and seven partial responses but not full remission. Major complications were observed in 14/38 courses of therapy with five deaths attributable to therapy while of the 18 patients of Mufti et al (1984b), 15 required hospital admission for intensive support care and two died during the cytopenic phase, even with their comparatively low dose of 10 mg b.d. subcutaneously for 3 weeks, most workers using a slightly higher dose, e.g. 10 mg/m^2 b.d. Thus, this treatment is not necessarily benign, and often causes prolonged pancytopenia with marrow hypocellularity.

3. OTHER CYTOTOXIC DRUGS

Various studies have used single agents including 6-mercaptopurine, 6-thioguanine, oral VP16 and razoxane with a wide spectrum of responses, almost invariably partial.

Differentiation inducing agents

That such agents might be of benefit in AML and some cases of MDS is implicit in the current view of normal haemopoiesis (Fig. 10.3). The amplification of the system and the proportion of mature cells depends in both normal and disease states on the balance between proliferation (cell division) and differentiation rates. Agents are described as differentiation inducers on the basis of in vivo or in vitro experiments in which they increase the proportion of mature cells produced, but in the context of MDS it may be important to discriminate between two fundamentally different modes of action. Figure 10.3 illustrates these. First, true differentiation inducers, i.e. agents which force differentiation, which in turn limits proliferative capacity by hastening terminal maturation to non-dividing cells. Secondly, agents which slow the proliferation rate but not the differentiation rate (such agents may hasten the differentiation rate by lengthening the specific phase of the cell cycle when the cell is receptive to differentiation induction (Boyd & Metcalf, 1984)). Agents like dimethyl sulphoxide (DMSO), vitamin D_3, retinoic acid, phorbol esters and dimethylformamide appear to belong to the first group. Dimethyl sulphoxide (DMSO) and retinoic acid induce granulocytic differentiation and vitamin D_3 and phorbol esters induce predominantly monocytic differentiation. Inhibitors of DNA synthetic enzymes fall into the second group: these include many agents reported to induce differentiation in leukaemic cells, cytosine-arabinoside, 6-mercaptopurine, 6-thioguanine, aphidicolin (an inhibitor of DNA polymerase).

Although both types of agent reduce the amplification of the system and increase the proportion of mature cells, there is an important difference, particularly relevant in MDS patients in whom cytopenia is pronounced. If proliferation is inhibited via differentiation the reduced amplification of the system might be compensated for by an increased stem cell proliferation rate. Where inhibitors of DNA synthesis are used, these are non-selective and may also inhibit stem cell division and thus reduce the efficiency of compensation.

Clinical trials of both types of agent in MDS have been somewhat limited to date.*
Besa et al (1983) obtained a temporary remission with retinoic acid in one case also
given high-dose corticosteroids. Waxman & Schreiber (1983) treated three patients
with retinoic acid, hydroxyurea and DMSO and obtained remissions in two, while
Gold et al (1983a) treated 17 patients with MDS with 13-cis-retinoic acid and of 15

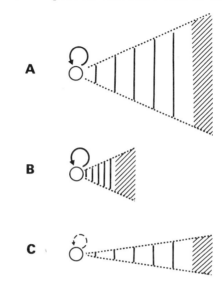

Fig. 10.3   The proliferation/differentiation balance and differentiation inducers.
There are two ways in which the proportion of mature cells (hatched area) can be increased (B + C).
(A) Shows a schematic of the normal proliferation/differentiation balance. The number of progeny a stem
cell produces depends on the number of cell divisions before terminal division (this is the amplification of
the system, depicted here as the size of the triangle). The rate at which terminal maturation is achieved
depends upon the rate at which cells undergo a series of differentiation/maturation steps (depicted as
vertical lines).
(B) True differentiation inducers, speed up the rate of differentiation (closer vertical lines) and increase the
proportion of mature cells, but reduce the amplification of the system. This reduction in amplification can,
however, be compensated for by increasing stem cell renewal (arrow) and thus the size of the stem cell pool.
(C) Agents which slow proliferation (narrow triangle) but do not slow the differentiation/maturation rate
(vertical lines) also reduce the amplification of the system and have been shown to increase the proportion of
mature cells formed in vitro. However, since these agents slow the proliferation rate, the ability to
compensate for reduced amplification by expanding the stem cell pool may also be compromised (broken
arrow).

evaluable patients, five showed some (usually minor) improvement in haematological
status after 3 weeks of therapy had been given. Reversible hepatotoxicity occurred at
the highest dose level (125 mg/m²/day). Flynn et al (1983) report the successful use of
retinoic acid in vivo in a case of refractory acute promyelocytic leukaemia.

IN VITRO STUDIES

General features

There are several caveats to be borne in mind when interpreting the literature on this
subject. First, the problems of definition of the MDS greatly affect results, because
the different types of MDS have different culture appearances and therefore inclusion

*See note added in proof.

or exclusion of any category affects the overall result (cf. CMML and RAEB, Sultan et al, 1974).

The second problem lies in the lack of uniformity of culture methods. There are several methods for the culture of most haemopoietic progenitors, and with each method, culture conditions, particularly culture time, scoring criteria and culture stimuli used, can have a profound effect on results.

Granulocyte-macrophage colonies (CFUgm)

This technique (introduced by Pike & Robinson, 1970), and variants of it, have been the culture techniques most widely applied to the study of the MDS. Numerous studies have shown that growth of leukaemic cells in these cultures is abnormal. Most cases show growth of only small clusters of cells and no clones large enough to be scored as colonies (usually defined as clones of 40 or more cells). Where colonies are present, the colony to cluster ratio is, almost without exception, low. The different culture patterns in AML partly reflect the differentiation stage of clonogenic cells accumulating in different patients (Francis et al, 1981a,b). Naturally most workers studying MDS have been interested in determining at what stage the leukaemic culture pattern emerges. Results vary for the different classes of MDS and are best considered separately.

In patients with the diagnostic criteria for PLS, consistently over two-thirds show reduced or absent colony formation, e.g. 23/27 (85%) of patients studied by us (including 21 patients previously reported: Francis et al, 1983). Five groups using similar culture techniques and criteria for the definition of a colony found similar results to ours (Greenberg et al, 1976; Milner et al, 1977; Beran & Hast, 1978; Verma et al, 1979; Linman & Bagby, 1976) but Senn et al (1980) using methylcellulose rather than semi-solid agar, a longer culture duration (12–14 days) and a smaller colony size definition, found only 15% (5/33) patients with reduced colonies. Day 14 CFU-gm are earlier cells than day 7 CFU-gm and clone size potential also relates to progenitor stage (Francis et al, 1981a), so it is difficult to relate Senn et al's results to those of other groups. Only 9/27 (33%) of our patients, when first tested, had the typically leukaemic pattern of reduced/absent colonies accompanied by greatly increased clusters (clones of 2–39 cells). Most had either normal (10/27; 37%) or reduced (8/27; 30%) clusters (often associated with absent colonies), a picture more like that seen in aplasia than in leukaemia, although a proportion of AML cases show no growth in this system. Again the cluster definition influences the results and the proportion of patients with increased clusters was lower in two studies where the cluster definition excluded clones of 2–5 and 2–8 cells respectively (Milner et al, 1977; Beran & Hast, 1978).

In IASA, it has been suggested that the culture pattern is more normal (Sultan et al, 1974) and this fits with the observation of the FAB group (Bennet et al, 1982) that IASA is infrequently accompanied by dysgranulopoiesis and perhaps with the lower leukaemic transformation rate in this group than in PLS or RAEB (Table 10.4).

RAEB may be discriminated from CMML on the basis of culture findings (Sultan et al, 1974). The latter is associated with the prolific growth of both colonies and clusters and characteristic background of solitary cells, whereas in the former the picture is like that in the PLS. This is not, however, observed in all types of cultures and was not found when the source of CSA for the cultures was conditioned medium from a tumour cell line (GCT-CM) (Gold et al, 1983b). GCT-CM has a different biological activity from leucocyte derived CSA (Francis et al, 1982d).

Secondary PLS shows a similar culture pattern to that seen in primary PLS. Pedersen-Bjergaard et al (1981) showed that colony formation was reduced in 14/16 patients whereas cluster formation was varied being, either raised, normal or lowered.

Several reviews of the early literature suggest that there is a progressive decline in colonies in PLS and that colony numbers might be a useful prognostic index for leukaemic transformation, but this has not been borne out by subsequent studies. Greenberg et al (1971) noted progressive decline in colonies in a patient prior to leukaemic transformation and Linman & Bagby (1976) found that markedly reduced or absent colony formation was associated with 3/5 cases of transformation whereas 0/5 patients with only moderately reduced colony growth underwent transformation. A later study by Greenberg et al (1976) and one of our own (Francis et al, 1983) showed neither differences in transformation rate in patients whose cells did and did not form colonies, nor a difference in marrow colony forming capacities between patients who did and did not undergo leukaemic transformation.

Culture pattern does seem to have a correlation to transformation rate. Both Verma et al (1979) and our own group (Francis et al, 1983) found that patients with low total clones (reduced colonies and clusters) show a rather stable course. This is not, however, a particularly useful prognostic test since the behaviour of patients who do not have this pattern is very varied. Kinetic studies of CFU-gm may also be helpful since change in kinetic parameters may precede transformation by 10 months (Karsdorf et al, 1983).

Erythroid bursts and colonies (BFUe and CFUe)

Fewer studies have been performed using erythroid culture techniques. Two types of erythroid precursor can be grown. Both are dependent on erythropoietin. The earlier of the two, the so-called BFUe (burst forming unit erythroid) also requires an additional stimulus, usually supplied as phytohaemagglutinin-stimulated leucocyte conditioned medium (PHA-LCM). Koeffler et al (1978a) found erythroid colonies (CFU-e; day 7 or 8) to be normal or increased in PLS, showing that despite the anaemia, the erythroid colony-forming cell pool is normal or expanded. This suggests that the defect in erythropoiesis is either not present in vitro, or occurs at a later stage than those corresponding to in vitro erythroid colony formation. However, Chui & Clark (1982) found reduced or absent BFUe and variable CFUe in the blood PLS pateints and Ruutu (1984) found reduced marrow CFUe and/or BFUe in all (32) MDS patients tested.

Mixed-lineage colonies (CFU-gemm)

This is a comparatively recent culture technique and has not therefore been widely used yet in MDS. Senn et al (1982) have found that marrow samples in 13/14 patients with PLS showed no detectable formation of granulocytic, erythrocytic, macrophage, megakaryocyte colonies. This could indicate reduced CFU-gemm levels or abnormal function with failure to form colonies in vitro.

Blast cell colonies

This type of culture was introduced for the growth of leukaemic blasts. The method uses stimuli and culture conditions which favour the growth of T-lymphocytes, so these must be removed before bone marrow samples are cultured (Buick, 1977). With this technique, AML samples characteristically grow colonies of blasts, but normal marrow and blood cells fail to produce colonies. Senn et al (1982) found that 11/15 PLS patients and 5/7 IASA patients intermittently had low numbers of blast-CFU circulating in the blood. In RAEB, 2/3 patients had a 'leukaemic' pattern with high numbers of blast-CFU.

Long term marrow cultures

There are comparatively few studies as yet using this technique (Gartner & Kaplan, 1980) which was an adaptation of the method of Dexter et al (1974, 1977) for the culture of murine bone marrow. Our preliminary studies of MDS patients (Francis et al, unpublished) show that marrow from these patients will proliferate in this system, but retains the maturation defects in the CFU-gm produced in vitro that were observed when direct cultures were examined. In a proportion of cultures the maturation defect appears to progress and the significance of this remains to be elucidated.

Defective maturation in vitro

Evidence of defective maturation has been found not only in the clonal assays mentioned above but also by using suspension culture techniques. Koeffler & Golde (1978) examined bone marrow cells from three preleukaemic patients in suspension culture. They chose patients with prominent karyotypic abnormalities so that it could be established that it was the growth of the abnormal clone that was being studied and not out-growth of residual normal cells. Maturation did occur in the abnormal cells, but was delayed relative to normal controls. Defective maturation was also observed in diffusion chamber studies by Elstner et al (1983).

Results of studies of differentiation and maturation in granulocyte-macrophage colonies have been varied. Verma et al (1979) found 3/19 patients with PLS had predominantly blasts in either colonies or clusters and the remaining 16 had normal differentiation in their colonies (by this they meant that they had observed neutrophils in the colonies). Lidbeck (1980b) studying a mixed group of patients with MDS (excluding CMML) found that patients with defective colony formation had a reduced percentage of mature neutrophils in clones, whereas patients with normal colony growth did not. However, only neutrophil and not neutrophil-macrophage colonies were examined and the staining technique used did not permit accurate separation of immature cells (myeloblasts, promyelocytes and myelocytes) from one another. In contrast to these two groups, Senn et al (1980) found that colonies from 33 patients could not be distinguished from those of patients without haematological malignancy.

Recent improvements made to both Romanowsky and dual esterase (non-specific and chloracetate esterase) techniques for staining colonies in agar gels (Francis et al, 1982b), permit much more accurate identification of maturation stages of cells in granulocyte-macrophage colonies. We have examined clone cell maturity from patients both with and without defective colony formation and have found evidence of maturation delay. Only a very low percentage of normal day 7 clones contain blasts and over 70% usually contain mature neutrophils and/or macrophages. Cultures from patients with PLS show a delay in the normal decline of clones containing blasts and a delay in the increase in the proportion of clones containing mature granulocytes and macrophages (Fig. 10.4). This clone cell immaturity can be quite subtle and difficult to detect using inadequate staining techniques. It is best detected by calculating a clone maturity index defined as the percentage of total clones (colonies and clusters) containing mature neutrophils plus percentage of clones containing mature macrophages, divided by the percentage clones containing blasts. Figure 10.4 shows results

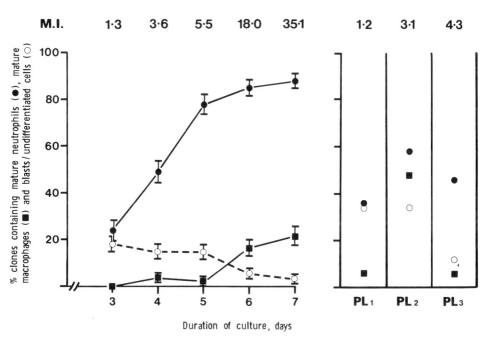

CELLULAR MATURATION IN PRELEUKAEMIA

Fig. 10.4 The left panel shows changes in clone cell maturity with time in a representative culture of marrow from a healthy donor. A clone maturity index (M.I.) gives a sensitive measure of this change. M.I. = % clones containing mature neutrophils + % clones containing mature macrophages ÷ % clones containing blasts. The panels on the right show three representative results for day 7 cultures on preleukaemia. M.I. in each case was calculated from differential counts on 200 clones. Gels stained with Wright–Giemsa and for non-specific and chloracetate esterase gave comparable results.

for three patients with PLS (one with normal colony numbers) and the change of clone maturity index with time for a normal marrow sample. Maturity indices at day 7 in PLS were equivalent to those of normal marrow between approximately days 3–5 of culture. These techniques have a potential use in the examination of the balance between proliferation and differentiation and its disturbance in MDS. Differentiation inducing agents are currently being evaluated using these and related techniques.

gm-CSA and other regulators
Granulocyte-macrophage colony stimulating activity (gm-CSA) and the related glycoproteins g-CSA and m-CSA are thought to be regulators of granulo- and monopoiesis in animals and man. Although a small amount of gm-CSA circulates in

the blood, the gm-CSA produced within the bone marrow correlates with granulo-poietic activity in man (Francis et al, 1981c) and seems to act as the principal granulopoietic regulator. The marrow production of gm-CSA is modulated by two factors: positively, by a circulating factor (responsible for the adherent-cell-dependent CSA in human serum (Francis et al, 1977b, 1980) and, negatively, by inhibition of marrow cell CSA production by neutrophils, possibly by their lactoferrin (Broxmeyer et al, 1978; Francis et al, 1981c).

The most striking abnormalities of gm-CSA in PLS occur within the bone marrow (Francis et al, 1983) but changes in leucocyte derived CSA have also been observed (Greenberg et al, 1971; Senn et al, 1976). Current evidence suggests that decreased CSA production is characteristic of the stable preleukaemic phase and that leukaemic transformation is preceded by overproduction of bone marrow CSA (Francis et al, 1983). AML is not uniformly accompanied by elevated bone marrow endogenous CSA (Francis et al, 1982c) so this change does not merely represent acquisition of a leukaemic property. The measurement of the bone marrow endogenous CSA provides a good predictive test for leukaemic transformation (Francis et al, 1983). This assay (Francis et al, 1981c), detects the level of granulopoietic stimulator present in the patients bone marrow sample (endogenous CSA). In a study of 21 patients, we found a significantly more rapid rate of transformation and a higher proportion of patients undergoing transformation, in patients with raised endogenous CSA. 5/7 patients in the high CSA group underwent transformation within 4 months of the marrow assay, whereas this was observed in only 2/14 of the remaining patients, at 27 and 35 months after the assay. Serial studies in one of these two patients detected a change from low to elevated endogenous CSA 6 weeks prior to transformation.

The significance of the raised endogenous CSA is not clear. Although CSA is a potent proliferation stimulus, circumstantial evidence suggests that it is not causally related to the change in behaviour of the leukaemic clone which characterises leukaemic transformation. Steroids of the androstane group increase endogenous CSA in vitro and probably also in vivo (Francis et al, 1977a) and yet androgen therapy does not appear to accelerate leukaemic evolution (Najean et al, 1979).

Studies of other haemopoietic regulators have been limited. Koeffler et al (1978a) demonstrated that erythroid progenitors have a normal responsiveness to erythro-poietin. The importance of feedback inhibition of granulopoiesis by prostaglandin E, acidic isoferritin and lactoferrin has not been fully established in normal haemo-poiesis, but inhibition is reported to be reduced in leukaemia (Broxmeyer et al, 1981; Pelus et al, 1979). Recently, Gold et al (1983) showed loss of prostaglandin E inhibition of CFU-gm in 9/12 MDS patients.

The role of lymphocytes

T lymphocytes have been implicated in a number of different ways in the production of cytopenias. They have also been shown to have a role in the regulation of the proliferation/differentiation balance of CFU-gm, at least in vitro (Francis et al, 1982b), so their presence and function in MDS is worth examining.

Bagby (1980), suggested that cortisol sensitive T-lymphocytes were suppressing granulopoiesis in a small proportion of PLS patients. Glucocorticoid therapy is beneficial in only a small proportion of PLS patients but is hazardous in others. In an attempt to determine a means of predicting response, Bagby et al (1980) found that bone marrow cultures from 5/34 patients showed an increase in colonies with the addition of cortisol in vitro. Three of these patients responded to prednisone clinically, whereas none of the 29 remaining patients did so. Two mechanisms appear to operate. Some patients have cortisol sensitive T-lymphocytes suppressing granulopoiesis, but in others the stimulatory effect in vitro seems due to a direct action on CFUgm (Bagby, 1980).

Impaired T-cell and NK-cell function, including depressed mitogenic response, seems to be a common feature of PLS and MDS (Porzsolt & Heimpel, 1982; Knox et al, 1983). In view of the possible involvement of the common lymphoid-myeloid stem cell in MDS (see above) it would be interesting to determine whether the defective cells are part of the abnormal clone.

T lymphocytes influence the proliferation/differentiation balance in vitro and if normal marrow cells are grown in CFU-gm cultures on feeder layers depleted of T-lymphocytes (T3+, MBG6+) the differentiation rate slows so that the resulting granulocyte-macrophage colonies contain relatively immature cells (Francis et al, 1982a,b). Replacement of T8+ lymphocytes in the system reverses this effect. In MDS, colonies show varying degrees of maturation defect (see above). It may therefore be relevant that Bynoe et al (1983) found an absolute decrease in T8+ peripheral blood lymphocytes in MDS patients (although relative deficiency of T4+ cells was even more prominent). Four out of six T8+ lymphocyte deficient MDS patients were also observed by Knox et al (1983).

General implications

There are several general implications to be gleaned from the results of the in vitro studies. First, at least in patients in the PLS category, the culture studies confirm abnormalities of the committed progenitors of more than one lineage, suggesting a stem cell defect in these patients. Culture studies performed in combination with cytogenetic studies confirm first, that it is the abnormal clone which we observe in vitro and not merely residual normal cells which grow in culture and secondly, that CFUgm and CFUe share the same genetic defect, where there is one.

The culture studies also provides a possible explanation for the growth advantage of these abnormal cells, for although they do not apparently divide faster than normal cells they do have delayed differentiation. Delayed differentiation prolongs the time spent in the proliferative pool and increases the amplification of the dysplastic clone.

KARYOTYPIC ABNORMALITIES

There has been an upsurge in the interest in karyotypic abnormalities in AML and MDS following recent developments in research into the role of oncogenes in carcinogenesis. These genes, probably involved in growth regulation in their normal state, may become aberrantly expressed if transported to a new site on the genome by a chromosomal translocation (cellular oncogenes) or by a virus (viral oncogenes) or if they undergo mutation or amplification. The recognition of the existence of non-random karyotypic abnormalities in any particular malignancy is important because it focuses attention on known oncogenes in the chromosomes involved. We have therefore mentioned the known chromosomal locations of oncogenes wherever relevant, see also chapter 9.

Incidence

As with the culture studies above, methodological considerations are important. Only a low proportion of the abnormal cells are in cell cycle in vivo and analysis after short term (1–4 day) culture may therefore reveal cells with chromosomal abnormalities more efficiently than the classical direct method (1–2 h incubation) (Knuutila et al, 1981). The detection of some abnormalities is particularly dependent on the method (cf. t(15; 17) in acute promyelocytic leukaemia). Laboratories performing short term cultures for karyotype analysis rarely control the level of specific growth stimuli gm-CSA and multi-CSF on which the growth of both leukaemic and normal progenitors depends. It seems likely, since many MDS and AML marrow samples are deficient in gm-CSA (Francis et al, 1983, 1982c) and are relatively insensitive to gm-CSA (Francis et al, 1979) that the proportion of abnormal cells detected might be improved if gm-CSA and multi-CSA were added to short term cultures.

At the second international workshop on chromosomes in leukaemia (1980a) 51% of the 244 patients studied with 'preleukaemia' had chromosomal abnormalities. Although the details of diagnostic criteria were not given, it was recorded that the group contained patients with secondary PLS (see below) and this may influence the incidence. Linman & Bagby (1976) estimated the incidence for karyotypic abnormalities in patients fulfilling their criteria to be 50–60% and individual studies confirm this estimate (e.g. 6/11–54.5% — of PLS patients studied by Kanatakis et al, 1983). Other studies using somewhat different criteria for preleukaemia have different estimates (e.g. Pierre, 1974 observed approximately 35% abnormal karyotypes).

RAS (IASA) appears to have a lower incidence of chromosomal abnormality. Of 25 reported IASA patients, five (20%) had abnormal chromosomes (Ayraud et al, 1983; Mende et al, 1980; Nowell, 1981). The incidence in RA is more difficult to assess, but appears higher if the group includes more patients with the PLS criteria. In some reports, the incidence is much lower than in the PLS (e.g. 3/22 — 13.6% of patients studied by Ayraud et al, 1983). RAEB and PLS appear approximately comparable in their incidence of abnormalities, although comparisons on large well-defined groups have not been made. In all categories, leukaemic transformation rates are generally highest in patients with chromosomally abnormal clones (Ayraud et al, 1983; Greenberg, 1983, Gold et al, 1983) and the incidence of abnormalities in the different classes of MDS broadly correlates with transformation rates. Patients with a mixture of normal and abnormal clones have longer median survival times than patients with only abnormal clones (Panani et al, 1980).

Common abnormalities

The abnormalities observed are non-random and the most frequently observed types of abnormalities are very similar to those observed in AML. A comparison of the incidences of the most frequently observed abnormalities in AML, MDS and PLS is shown in Table 10.5.

Monosomy 7 (-7) was the most frequent specific aberration found in preleukaemia at the 2nd International Workshop (1980a) and is high in MDS and AML (though exceeded by trisomy 8 in these groups). There has been great interest in this condition and it has been suggested that the acquisition of monosomy 7 represents part of a specific pathogenic pathway of AML (Pasquali et al, 1982). AML patients with monosomy 7 have a somewhat different clinical and haematological picture from other patients (Borgstrom et al, 1980). Monosomy 7 is associated with a specific myeloproliferative disorder in childhood which has a high risk of progression to AML (Sieff et al, 1981). The 7q$^-$ abnormality is also comparatively common, possibly more so in AML than in MDS. Chromosome 7 is the location of the cellular homologue of the erb-B oncogene. This gene may code for the EGF (epidermal growth factor) receptor (Downward et al, 1984).

Table 10.5 Incidence of specific chromosomal abnormalities (%)

Specific aberrations	AML[+]	MDS[++]	PLS[++]
+8	21.0	21.2	16.9
−7	14.5	16.5	17.6
t(8; 21)	10.1 (M2)	NR	0*
5q$^-$	8.1	15.8	13.6
t(15; 17)	7.1 (M3)	NR	0
+21	6.0	NR	1.6
−5	5.2	4.7	2.4
7q$^-$	4.8	0.7	1.7
−21	4.7	NR	NR
t(9; 22)	3.6	NR	0**
iso(17q)	1.6	NR	1.6
20q$^-$	1.1	NR	6.4
+19	NR (<1.0)	NR	4.0
45-X	NR (<1.0)	NR	1.6
45-Y	NR (<1.0)	NR	5.6
Total cases	496	278	244

[+] AML patients from Mitelman & Levan survey (1979).
[++] MDS patients from the same survey, the group includes some patients with myelosclerosis, Ph[l] negative CML, thrombocytosis and pancytopenias in addition to MDS as defined by FAB criteria.
[+++] PLS patients from second international workshop on chromosomes in leukaemia (1980a). The diagnostic criteria used were not strictly comparable with the Linman & Bagby criteria.
* One case has been observed in RAEB (Gold et al, 1983).
** One case was reported by Bonati et al (1982).
NR Frequency of specific abnormality not recorded.

Trisomy 8 (+8) is also common to PLS, MDS and AML. In contrast the t(8; 21) translocation appears to be virtually confined to AML and not to occur at high frequency in PLS and MDS. This abnormality is associated with the morphological category AML FAB-M2 (Second International Workshop, 1980b) although not completely confined to their category (Swirsty et al, 1984). Cellular homologues of two different oncogenes are located on the long arm of chromosome 8, c-myc and c-mos. The region of the chromosome to which c-mos maps is at or near the breakpoint in the t(8; 21) (Neel et al, 1982).

The 5q$^-$ abnormality (usually an interstitial deletion) is the third most frequent in PLS and MDS, but appears somewhat less frequent in AML (Table 10.5). Where this is the sole abnormality, the clinical picture is usually that of a refractory anaemia with a slight increase in blasts (Van den Berghe et al, 1974) but sporadic cases have presented as polycythaemia vera (Westin & Weinfeld, 1977) or thrombocytosis (Nowell & Finnan, 1977).

The 20q$^-$ deletion is also common in PLS and somewhat less common in AML (Table 10.5). Mitelman & Levan (1981) reviewed 25 cases with PLS and five cases with AML. In the same review 24.1% of 83 patients with polycythaemia vera had this defect.

Other relatively common abnormalities in the PLS group (Table 10.5) include: trisomy 19, 45-X and 45-Y (although the significance of the incidence of the latter is difficult to assess in a group of patients containing so many elderly males). A family with X-linked familial PLS and AML has also been described (Li et al, 1979).

Relation to findings in AML

Chromosomal abnormalities are found in approximately 50% of AML cases (First International Workshop on Chromosomes in Leukaemia, 1978). The chromosomes most frequently involved either alone or in combination in aberrations are: nos 8 (37.1%), 21 (33.4%), 7 (22.4%), 17 (19.6%) and 5 (17.1%). At least one of these chromosomes is involved in 77.4% of cases with an abnormal karyotype (Mitelman & Levan, 1981). The appearance of 'fuzzy' and ill-defined chromatids occurs both in AML and in MDS patients. The significance of this abnormality is not fully understood (Sandberg, 1980). The two most commonly observed translocations were t(8;21), associated with AML FAB group M2 and t(15;17) associated with acute promyelocytic leukaemia (FAB M3) (10.1% and 7.1% of all karyotypic abnormalities respectively). Table 10.5 shows the differences in the incidence of the specific abnormalities in AML and MDS. Since the 2nd International Workshop additional non-random abnormalities have been identified (Yunis, 1983). There is an association between pericentric inversion of 16 or 16q⁻ and AML-M4 with eosinophilia. Abnormalities involving the long arm of chromosome 11 (11q23) either deletions (11q⁻) or translocations t(9;11), t(11;19), are associated with AML, M5 and M4. The translocation t(6;9) occurs in myeloproliferative disorders and AML. The incidence of all of the above has not yet been fully evaluated in MDS. Oncogenes c-ras^H, c-ets, c-abl, c-myb are located on chromosomes 11, 11, 9 and 6 respectively.

Secondary MDS and AML

In secondary MDS and in AML in patients with previously treated malignant disease, the karyotypic abnormalities are more frequent and have rather consistent features (Rowley et al, 1981). Of 25 such patients with an abnormal karyotype, 23 showed loss of part or all of no. 5 and/or no. 7. Loss of chromosome 5 was noted only in patients who previously had malignant lymphoma, whereas loss of 7 was seen both after lymphoma and after other malignancies. Chromosome changes similar to these are seen in 25% of aneuploid patients with AML (Rowley et al, 1981) and a proportion of MDS patients with no history of chemo- or radiotherapy. Mitelman et al (1978) had similar findings when they studied two groups of patients with AML, 23 patients with, and 33 without, occupational exposure to mutagenic/carcinogenic agents. Karyotypic abnormalities were present in 82.6% of the exposed group and only 24.2% of the non-exposed group. Over 80% of the patients with abnormalities in the exposed group had at least one of four particular changes, monosomy 5 or 7 or trisomy 8 or 21. In the non-exposed group, none had monosomy 5 and one monosomy 7, none had trisomy 8 and one trisomy 21. The remaining aberrations in the non-exposed group were not found in the exposed group.

Implications

The broadly overlapping patterns of karyotypic abnormalities in the MDS and AML are consistent with the view of the MDS as either a stage in leukaemogenesis or a leukaemia that is 'aleukaemic'. There are, however, differences between the frequencies of the specific abnormalities. AML has a higher incidence of t(8; 21) and t(15; 17) and a lower incidence of 5q$^-$ and 20q$^-$. This kind of difference could be explained if the AML group contains patients with abnormalities which are associated with a very short, or no preleukaemic phase. The broad spectrum of abnormalities is consistent with there being different 'routes' of leukaemogenesis (hypothesis C in Fig. 10.1). Such heterogeneity need not reflect different routes of leukaemogenesis at the metabolic level, since several genetic defects can lead to the same biological outcome. For example, interference with growth-factor-mediated cell proliferation could occur with either inappropriate production of the factor, or of its receptor, or with activation of any of the intracellular signals (phosphorylation, cyclic nucleotides, ion fluxes, cytoskeletal changes) which link binding of growth factor to the proliferative response (Rosengurt, 1983). Multiple factors regulate the proliferation and differentiation of haemopoietic cells so there are many possible alternatives.

In addition to implications relating to the relationship between MDS and AML, it is worth noting that many of the specific chromosomal changes seen in MDS are also seen in the classic myeloproliferative disorders (e.g. polycythaemia vera, meylofibrosis, essential thrombocythaemia) albeit with different incidences. Monosomy 7 and trisomy 8 have both been observed in MPD. Trisomy 9 which is relatively infrequent in PLS (0.8% in the PLS survey of Table 10.5) has been reported primarily in MPD and AML (Sandberg, 1980) and may thus represent a route of development of AML which involves MPD and which is not commonly associated with the features of PLS.

CONCLUSIONS

The MDS have some common features, but are heterogeneous with respect to 1) haematological features, 2) incidence of leukaemic transformation and 3) incidence of karyotypic abnormalities. This heterogeneity could represent different stages in the same process, or different routes of leukaemic evolution (accompanied by different rates or probabilities of further change to AML). On balance we favour the latter hypothesis.

Concerning classification, patients with RAEB, RAEB-T and CMML already have some degree of accumulation of primitive cells which characterises the leukaemic process and it seems useful to discriminate between these patients and patients with less than 5% blasts (RA and RAS). Within the RA + RAS (IASA) group, the diagnostic criteria of Linman & Bagby (1978) appear to perform the important service of discriminating between patients with high and low probabilities of leukaemic transformation, if rigorously applied. The difference in transformation rates between PLS and the broader RA + RAS category is so striking that one wonders if those patients with involvement of only the erythroid lineage may not have a different defect (say, one confined to erythroid stem cells) which is not significantly associated with leukaemic evolution. To test this, much more stringent tests for abnormalities of the other lineages in RA + RAS will be required.

The integrated study of MDS, at the clinical, cellular, chromosomal and genetic level, offers exciting prospects for unravelling the mysteries of leukaemogenesis.

Acknowledgements

G. E. F. is a Wellcome Senior Research Fellow in Clinical Science. Funding is also received from Cancer Research Campaign and the Leukaemia Research Fund. We would like to thank Mrs Megan Evans for typing the manuscript.

REFERENCES

Anderson R L, Bagby G C Jnr, Richert-Boe K, Magenis R E, Koler R D 1981 Therapy-related preluekemic syndrome. Cancer 47: 1867–1871

Appelbaum F R, Storb R, Ramberg R E, Shulman H M, Buckner C D, Clift R A, Deeg H J, Fefer A, Sanders J, Stewart P, Sullivan K, Witherspoon R P, Thomas E D 1984 Allogeneic marrow transplantation. In the treatment of preleukemia Anals of Internal Medicine 100: 689–693

Armitage J O, Dick F R, Needleman S W, Burns C P 1981 Effect of chemotherapy for the dysmyelopoietic syndrome. Cancer Treatment Reports 65: 601–605

Ayraud N, Donzeau M, Raynaud S, Lambert J-C 1983 Cytogenic study of 88 cases of refractory anemia. Cancer Genetics and Cytogenetics 8: 243–248

Baccarani M, Tura S 1979 Differentiation of myeloid leukaemic cells: new possibilities for therapy. British Journal of Haematology 42: 485–490

Baccarani M, Zaccaria A, Bandini G, Cavazzini G, Fanin R, Tura S 1983 Low dose arabinosyl cytosine for treatment of myelodysplastic syndromes and subacute myeloid leukemia. Leukemia Research 7: 539–545

Bagby G C Jr, Gabourel J D, Linman J W 1980 Glucocorticoid therapy in the preleukemic syndrome (hemopoietic dysplasia). Identification of responsive patients using in vitro techniques. Annals of Internal Medicine 92: 55–58

Bagby G C Jr 1980 Mechansisms of glucocorticoid activity in patients with the preleukemic syndrome (hemopoietic dysplasia). Leukemia Research 4: 571–580

Baserga A 1976 Preleukemic states in the light of the leukemia cytogenetics. Blood Cells 2: 285–289

Bennett J M, Catovsky D, Daniel M-T, Flandarin G, Galton D A G, Gralnick H R, Sultan C The French-American-British (FAB) Co-operative Group 1982 Proposals for the classification of the myelodysplastic syndromes. British Journal of Haematology 51: 189–199

Bennett J M, Catovsky D, Daniel M-T, Flandrin G, Galton D A G, Gralnick H R, Sultan C 1984 Myelodysplastic syndromes: is another classification necessary? British Journal of Haematology 56: 515–517

Beran M, Hast R 1978 Studies on preleukemia. II. In vitro colony forming capacity in aregenerative anaemia with hypercellular bone marrow. Scandinavian Journal of Haematology 21: 139–149

Beris Ph, Graf J, Miescher P A 1983 Primary acquired sideroblastic and primary acquired refractory anemia. Seminars in Hematology 20: 101–113

Besa E C, Granick J, Itri L, Nowell P C 1983 Complete hematologic and cytogenic remission in a patient with dysmyelopoietic syndrome treated with 13-cis retinoic acid. Blood 62: (Suppl 1) 199a

Bhaduri S, Kubanek B, Heit W, Pfleiger H, Kurrle E, Fliedner T M, Heimpel H 1979 A case of preleukemia — reconstitution of normal marrow function after bone marrow transplantation (BMT) from identical twin. Blut 38: 145–149

Bjorkman S E 1956 Chronic refractory anemia with sideroblastic bone marrow. A study of four cases. Blood 11: 250–259

Block M, Jacobson L O, Bethard W F 1953 Preleukaemic acute human leukemia. Journal of the American Medical Association 152: 1018–1028

Bonati A, Talamazzi T, Valenti P L, Manini M 1982 Ph¹-positive preleukemic syndrome with early evolution in acute myeloid leukemia. Haematologica 67: 418–423

Borgstrom G H, Teerenhovi L, Vuopio P, De la Chapelle A, Van den Berghe H, Brandt L, Golomb H M, Louwagie A, Mitelman F, Rowley J D, Sandberg A A 1980 Clinical implications of monosomy 7 in acute nonlymphocytic leukemia. Cancer Genetics and Cytogenetics 2: 115–126

Boyd A W, Metcalf D 1984 Induction of differentiation in HL60 leukaemic cells: a cell cycle dependent all-or-none event. Leukemia Research 8: 27–43

Broxmeyer H E, Smithyman A, Eger R R, Meyers P A, DeSousa M 1978 Identification of lactoferrin as the granulocyte derived inhibitor of CSA production. Journal of Experimental Medicine 148: 1052–1067

Broxmeyer H E, Bognacki J, Dorner M H, DeSousa M 1981 The identification of leukemia-associated inhibitory activity (LIA) as acidic isoferritins. A regulatory role for acidic isoferritins in the production of granulocytes and macrophages. Journal of Experimental Medicine 153: 1426–1444

Buick R N, Till J E, McCulloch E A 1977 Colony assay for proliferative blast cells circulating in myeloblastic leukemia. Lancet i: 862–863

Burch P R J 1960 Radiation carcinogenesis. A new hypothesis. Nature 185: 135–142

Bynoe A G, Scott C S, Ford P, Roberts B E 1983 Decreased T helper cells in the myelodysplastic syndromes. British Journal of Haematology 54: 97–102

Capizzi R L, Poole M, Cooper M R, Richards II F, Stuart J J, Jackson D V Jnr, White D R, Spurr C L, Hopkins J O, Muss H B, Rudnick S A, Wells R, Gabriel D, Ross D 1984. Treatment of poor risk acute leukemia with sequential high-dose Ara-c and asparaginase. Blood 63: 694–700

Castaigne S, Daniel M-T, Tilly H, Herait P, Degos L 1983 Does treatment with Ara-C in low dosage cause differentiation of leukemic cells? Blood 62: 85–86

Cheng D S, Kushner J P, Wintrobe M M 1979 Idiopathic refractory sideroblastic anaemia: incidence and risk factors for leukaemic transformation. Cancer 44: 724–731

Chui D H K, Clarke B J 1982 Abnormal erythroid progenitor cells in human preleukemia. Blood 60: 362–367

Cohen J R, Creger W P, Greenberg P L, Schrier S L 1979 Subacute myeloid leukemia — A clinical review. American Journal of Medicine 66: 959–966

Coiffier B, Adeleine P, Viela J J, Bryon M, Fiere D, Gentilhomme O, Vuvan H 1983 Dysmyelopoietic syndromes: a search for prognostic factors in 193 patients. Cancer 52: 83–90

Dacie J V, Mollin D L 1966 Siderocytes, sideroblasts and sideroblastic anaemia. Acta Medica Scandinavica 445: (Suppl) 237–248

Dacie J V, Smith M D, White J C, Mollin D L 1959 Refractory normoblastic anaemia: a clinical and haematological study of seven cases. British Journal of Haematology 5: 56–82

Dameshek W 1965 Sideroblastic anaemia: is this a malignancy? British Journal of Haematology 11: 52–58

Dexter T M, Lajtha L G 1974 Proliferation of haemopoietic stem cells in vitro. British Journal of Haematology 28: 525–530

Dexter T M, Allen T D, Lajtha L G 1977 Conditions controlling the proliferation of haemopoietic stem cells in vitro. Journal of Cell Physiology 91: 335–344

Downward J, Yarden Y, Mayes E, Scrace G, Totty N, Stockwell P, Ullrich A, Schlessinger J, Waterfield M D 1984 Close similarity of epidermal growth factor receptor and v-erb-B oncogene protein sequences. Nature 307: 521–527

Dreyfus B, Rochant H, Sultan C, Clauvel G P, Yvart G, Chesneau A M 1970 Les anemies refractaire avec exces de myeloblastes dans la moelle. Etude de 11 observations. Nouvelle Presse Medicine 78: 359–364

Elstner E, Schultze E, Ihle R, Schutt M, Stobe H 1983 Proliferation and maturation of haemopoietic cells from patients with preleukaemia and aplastic anaemia in agar and diffusion chamber cultures. In: Neth, Gallo, Greaves, Moore & Winkler (eds) Haematology and blood transfusion, vol 28: modern trends in human leukaemia V. Springer-Verlag, Berlin

First International Workshop on Chromosomes in Leukemia (1977) 1978 British Journal of Haematology 39: 311–316

Flynn P J, Miller W J, Weisdorf D J, Arthur D C, Brunning R, Branda R F 1983 Retinoic acid treatment of acute promyelocytic leukemia: in vitro and in vivo observations. Blood 62: 1211–1217

Francis G E, Berney J J, Bateman S M, Hoffbrand A V 1977a The effect of androstanes on granulopoiesis in vitro and in vivo. British Journal of Haematology 36: 501–510

Francis G E, Berney J J, Hoffbrand A V 1977b Stimulation of human haemopoietic cells by colony stimulating factors: Adherent cell dependent colony stimulating activity in human serum. British Journal of Haematology 35: 625–638

Francis G E, Berney J J, Chipping P M, Hoffbrand A V 1979 Stimulation of human haemopoietic cells by colony stimulating factors: sensitivity of leukaemic cells. British Journal of Haematology 41: 545–562

Francis G E 1980 A bioassay system for two types of colony stimulating factor in human serum. Experimental Hematology 8: 749–762

Francis G E, Berney J J, Tuma G A, Wing M A, Hoffbrand A V 1980 Divergent sensitivities of leukemic cells to human placental conditioned medium and leucocyte feeder layers. Leukemia Research 4: 531–536

Francis G E, Bol S J, Berney J J 1981a Proliferative capacity, sensitivity to colony stimulating activity and buoyant density: linked properties of granulocyte-macrophage progenitors from normal human bone marrow. Leukemia Research 5: 243–250

Francis G E, Berney J J, Bodger M P, Bol S J L, Wing M A, Hoffbrand A V 1981b Clone size potential and sensitivity to colony stimulating activity: differentiation linked properties of granulocyte-macrophage progenitor cells. Stem Cells 1: 124–139

Francis G E, Rhodes E G H, Berney J J, Wing M A, Hoffbrand A V 1981c Bone marrow endogenous colony stimulating factor(s): relation to granulopoiesis in vivo. Experimental Hematology 9: 332–345

Francis G E, Tuma G A, Berney J J, Hoffbrand A V 1981d Sensitivity of acute myeloid leukaemia cells to colony stimulating activity: relation to response to chemotherapy. British Journal of Haematology 49: 259–267

Francis G E, Guimaraes J E, Granger S, Tidman N, Berney J J, Wing M A, Janossy G, Hoffbrand A V
1982a Distinct T-lymphocyte subsets affect granulo-monocytic differentiation and proliferation. Stem
Cells 2: 76–87

Francis G E, Guimaraes J E, Berney J J, Granger S, Wood E A, Wing M A, Hoffbrand A V 1982b
T-lymphocyte subsets and partial uncoupling of granulocyte-macrophage progenitor cell differentiation
and proliferation in normal cells. Experimental Hematology Review (Suppl 12) 179–193

Francis G E, Berney J J, Wing M A, Tuma G A, Hoffbrand A V 1982c Relative and absolute deficiency of
bone marrow endogenous CSA in acute myeloid leukemia: relation to response to chemotherapy.
Leukemia Research 6: 165–173

Francis G E, Wing M A, Berney J J 1982d Brief Report: Qualitative differences in the biological activity of
two sources of colony-stimulating factor: GCT conditioned medium and leucocyte feeder layers.
Experimental Hematology 10: 493–498

Francis G E, Wing M A, Miller E J, Berney J J, Wonke B, Hoffbrand A V 1983 Use of bone marrow
culture in prediction of acute leukaemic transformation in preleukaemia. Lancet i: 1409–1412

Galton D A G 1984 The myelodysplastic syndromes. Clinical and Laboratory Haematology 6: 99–112

Gartner S, Kaplan H S 1980 Long term culture of human bone marrow cells. Proceedings of the National
Academy of Science USA 77: 4756–4759

Gold E J, Mertelsmann R H, Loretta M I, Gee T, Arlin Z, Kempin S, Clarkson B, Moore M A S 1983a
Phase I clinical trial of 13-cis-retinoic acid in myelodysplastic syndromes. Cancer Treatment Reports 67:
981–986

Gold E J, Conjalka M, Pelus L M, Jhanwar S C, Broxmeyer H, Middleton A B, Clarkson B D, Moore
M A S 1983b Marrow cytogenetic and cell-culture analyses of the myelodysplastic syndromes: insights
into pathophysiology and prognosis. Journal of Clinical Oncology 1: 627–633

Goldstone A H, Cawley J C, Hayhoe F G 1976 Leukemias, lymphomas and allied disorders. Saunders,
London

Greenberg P L, Nichols B A, Schrier S L 1971 Granulopoiesis in acute myeloid leukemia and preleukemia.
New England Journal of Medicine 284: 1225–1232

Greenberg P L, Mara B, Bax J, Brossel R, Schrier S L 1976 The myeloproliferative disorders. Correlation
between clinical evolution and alterations of granulopoiesis. American Journal of Medicine 61: 878–891

Greenberg P L 1983 The smouldering myeloid leukemic states: clinical and biologic features. Blood 61:
1035–1044

Griffin J, Munro D, Major P, Kufe D 1982 Induction of differentiation of human myeloid leukemia cells by
inhibitors of DNA synthesis. Experimental Hematology 10: 774–781

Griffin J D, Wisch J W, Kufe D W 1983 Therapy of preleukemic syndromes with low dose continuous
infusion cytosine arabinoside. Blood 62: (Suppl 1) 203a

Gyger M, Perreault C, Boileau J, Aymard J-P, Bonny Y, Lacombe M, Lavallee R, d'Angelo G, Tawil E
1983 Restoration of normal hematopoiesis by bone marrow ablation and allogenic marrow
transplantation in a case of Hodgkin's disease therapy-related preleukemia. Blood 61: 1279–1281

Hast R 1978 Studies on human preleukemia IV. Clinical and prognostic significance of sideroblasts in
aregenerative anaemia with hypercellular bone marrow. Scandinavian Journal of Haematology 21:
396–402

Hehlmann R, Zonnchen B, Thiel E, Walther B 1983 Idiopathic refractory sideroachrestic anemia (IRSA)
progressing to acute mixed lymphoblastic-myelomonoblastic leukemia. Blut 46: 11–21

Housset M, Daniel M T, Degos L 1982 Small doses of Ara-C in the treatment of acute myeloid leukaemia:
differentiation of myeloid leukaemia cells? British Journal of Haematology 51: 125–129

Izrael V, Jacuillat C, Chastaing G, Weil M, De Heaulme M, Boiron M, Bernard J 1975 Donnees nouvelles
sur les leucemies oligoblastiques. A propos d'une analyse de 120 cas. Nouvelle Presse Medicale 4:
947–952

Joseph A S, Cinkotal K I, Hunt L, Geary C G 1982 Natural history of smouldering leukemia. British
Journal of Cancer 46: 160–166

Juneja S K, Imbert M, Sigaux F, Jouault H, Sultan C 1983a Prevalence and distribution of ringed
sideroblasts in primary myelodysplastic syndromes. Journal of Clinical Pathology 36: 566–569

Juneja S K, Imbert M, Jouault H, Scoazek J-Y, Sigaux F, Sultan C 1983b Haematological features of
primary myelodysplastic syndromes (PMDS) at initial presentation: a study of 118 cases. Journal of
Clinical Pathology 36: 1129–1135

Kanatakis S, Chalevalakis G, Economopoulos Th, Panani A, Ferti A, Vamvasakis E, Arapakis G 1983
Correlation of haematological, electron microscopic and cytogenetic findings in 20 patients with
preleukaemia. Scandinavian Journal of Haematology 30: 89–94

Karsdorf A, Dresch C, Metral J, Najean Y 1983 Prognostic value of the combined suicide level of
granulocyte progenitors and the labelling index of precursors in preleukemic states and oligoblastic
leukemias. Leukemia Research 7: 279–286

Killman S A 1976 Preleukemia: does it exist? Blood Cells 2: 81–105

Knox J S, Greenberg B R, Anderson R W, Rosenblatt L S 1983 Studies of T-lymphocytes in preleukaemic disorders and acute nonlymphocytic leukemia: In vitro radiosensitivity, mitogenic responsiveness, colony formation, and enumeration of lymphocyte subpopulations. Blood 61: 449–455

Knuutila S, Vuopio P, Elonan E, Siimes M, Kovanen R, Borgstrom G H, De la Chapelle A 1981 Culture of bone marrow reveals more cells with chromosomal abnormalities than the direct method in patients with hematologic disorders. Blood 58: 369–375

Koeffler H P, Cline M J, Golde D W 1978a Erythropoiesis in preleukemia. Blood 51: 1013–1019

Koeffler H P, Golde D W 1978b Cellular maturation in human preleukemia. Blood 52: 355–361

Kushner J P, Lee G R, Wintrobe M M, Cartwright G E 1971 Idiopathic refractory sideroblastic anemia. Clinical and laboratory investigation of 17 patients and reviews of the literature. Medicine 50: 139–159

Lewy R I, Kansu E, Gabuzda T 1979 Leukemia in patients with acquired sideroblastic anemia: an evaluation of prognostic indicators. American Journal of Hematology 6: 323–331

Li F P, Marchetto D J, Vawter G F 1979 Acute leukaemia and preleukaemia in eight males in a family: an x-linked disorder? American Journal of Hematology 6: 61–69

Libnoch J A, Patrick C W, Griffin J, Keller R H 1983 Flow cytometric cell surface marker analysis as a predictor of leukemic transformation in the myelodysplastic syndrome. Blood 62: (Suppl 1) 176a

Lidbeck J 1980a Studies on hemopoietic dysplasia (the preleukemic syndrome). Acta Medica Scandinavica 208: 459–462

Lidbeck J 1980b In vitro colony and cluster growth in haemopoietic dysplasia (the preleukaemic syndrome). II. Identification of a maturation defect in agar cultures. Scandinavian Journal of Haematology 25: 113–123

Linman J W 1970 Myelomonocytic leukemia and its preleukemic phase. Journal of Chronic Disorders 22: 713–716

Linman J W, Bagby G C 1978 The preleukemic syndrome (hemopoietic dysplasia) Cancer 42: 854–864

Linman J W, Bagby G C Jr 1976 The preleukemic syndrome: clinical and laboratory features, natural course and management. Blood Cells 2: 11–31

Maldonado J E, Maigne J, Lecoq D 1976 Comparative electron-microscopic study of the erythrocytic line in refractory anemia (pre-leukemia) and myelomonocytic leukemia. Blood Cells 2: 167–185

Martin S, Baldock S C, Ghoneim A T M, Child J A 1983 Defective neutrophil function and microbicidal mechanisms in the myelodysplastic disorders. Journal of Clinical Pathology 36: 1120–1128

Mende S, Weissenfels I, Pribilla W 1980 Zytogenetische und hamatologische verlaufsbeobachtungen bei idiopathischer refraktarer sideroblastischer anamie (IRSA). Blut 41: 367–376

Miescher P A, Farquet J J 1974 Chronic myelomonocytic leukemia in adults. Seminars in Hematology 11: 129–139

Milner G R, Testa N G, Geary C G, Dexter T M, Muldal S, MacIver J E, Lajtha L G 1977 Bone marrow culture studies in refractory cytopenia and 'smouldering leukaemia'. British Journal of Haematology 35: 251–261

Mitelman F, Brandt L, Nilsson P G 1978 Relation among occupational exposure to potential mutagenic/carcinogenic agents, clinical findings, and bone marrow chromosomes in acute nonlymphocytic leukemia. Blood 52: 1229–1237

Mitelman F, Levan G 1981 Clustering of aberrations to specific chromosomes in human neoplasms. IV. A survey of 1871 cases. Hereditas 95: 79–139

Mohler D N, Leavell B S 1958 Aplastic anemia: an analysis of 50 cases. Annals of Internal Medicine 49: 326–362

Mollin D L, Hoffbrand A V 1968 Sideroblastic anaemia. In: Dyke S C (ed) Recent advances in clinical pathology. Churchill, London, p 273–298

Mufti G J, Oscier D G, Hamblin T J, Bell A J 1983 Low doses of cytarabine in the treatment of myelodysplastic syndrome and acute myeloid leukemia. New England Journal of Medicine 309: 1653–1654

Mufti G J, Stevens J R, Oscier D G, Hamblin T J, Machin D 1984a Myelodysplastic syndromes: a scoring system with prognostic significance. British Journal of Haematology (in press)

Mufti G J, Oscier D G, Hamblin T J, Copplestone A, Abidis M N 1984b Cytarabine in pre-leukaemia Lancet i; 1187

Murray C, Cooper B, Kitchens L W Jnr 1983 Remission of acute myelogenous leukemia in elderly patients with prior refractory dysmyelopoietic anemia. Cancer 52: 967–970

Najean Y, Pecking A, Co-operative Group for the Study of Aplastic and Refractory Anaemias 1979 Refractory anemia with excess of blast cells: prognostic factors and effect of treatment with androgens or cytosine arabinoside — results of a trial in 58 patients. Cancer 44: 1976–1982

Neel B J, Jhanwar S C, Chaganti R S K, Hayward W S 1982 Two human c-onc genes are located on the long arm of chromosome 8. Proceedings of the National Academy of Sciences USA 79: 7842–7846

Nelson D A 1976 Cytomorphological diagnosis of the acute leukemias. Seminars in Oncology 3: 201–208

Nowell P C, Finnan J B 1977 Isochromosome 17 in atypical myeloproliferative and lymphoproliferative disorders. Journal of the National Cancer Institute 59: 329–334

Nowell P C 1981 Preleukemias. Human Pathology 12: 522–530

Panani A, Papayannis A G, Sioula E 1980 Chromosome aberrations and prognosis in preleukaemia. Scandinavian Journal of Haematology 24: 97–100

Parkes-Weber F 1904 A case of leukanaemia. Transactions of the Pathological Society of London 55: 288–296

Pasquali F, Bernasconi P, Casalone R, Fraccaro M, Bernasconi C, Lazzarino M, Morra E, Alessandrino E P, Marchi M A, Sanger R 1982 Pathogenetic significance of 'pure' monosomy 7 in myeloproliferative disorders. Analysis of 14 cases. Human Genetics 62: 40–51

Pedersen-Bjergaard J, Philip P, Mortensen B T, Ersboll J, Jensen G, Panduro J, Thomsen M 1981 Acute non lymphocytic leukemia, preleukemia and acute myeloproliferative syndrome secondary to treatment of other malignant diseases. Clinical and cytogenetic characteristics and result of in vitro culture of bone marrow and HLA typing. Blood 57: 712–723

Pelus L M, Broxmeyer H E, Kurland J I, Moore M A S 1979 Regulation of macrophage and granulocyte production. Journal of Experimental Medicine 150: 277–292

Pierre R V 1974 Preleukemic states. Seminars in Hematology 11: 73–92

Pierre R V 1975 Cytogenetic studies in preleukemia: studies before and after transition to acute leukemia in 17 subjects. Blood Cells 1: 163–172

Pike B L, Robinson W A 1970 Human bone marrow colony growth in agar gel. Journal of Cell Physiology 76: 77–84

Porzsolt F, Heimpel H 1982 Impaired T-cell and NK-cell function in patients with preleukaemia. Blut 45: 243–248

Reizenstein P, Lagerlof B 1972 Aregenerative anemia with hypercellular sideroblastic marrow. A preleukemic condition. Acta Haematologia 47: 1–12

Rheingold J J, Kaufman R, Adelson E, Lear A 1963 Smouldering acute leukemia. New England Journal of Medicine 268: 812–815

Roberts J D, Ershler W B, Tindle B H, Stewart J A 1983 Low dose cytosine arabinoside in smouldering myeloid leukaemic states. Blood 62: (Suppl 1) 207a

Rowley J D, Golomb H M, Vardiman J W 1981 Nonrandom chromosome abnormalities in acute leukemia and dysmyelopoietic syndromes in patients with previously treated malignant disease. Blood 58: 759–767

Rozengurt E 1983 Growth factors, cell proliferation and cancer: an overview. Molecular Biological Medicine 1: 169–181

Ruutu T, Partanen S, Lintula R, Teerenhovi L, Knuutila S 1984 Erythroid and granulocyte-macrophage colony formation in myelodysplastic syndromes. Scandinavian Journal of Haematology 32: 395–402

Saarni M J, Linman J W 1973 The hematologic syndrome preceding acute myeloid leukemia. American Journal of Medicine 55: 38–48

Sandberg A A 1980 The chromosomes in human cancer and leukemia. Elsevier, North Holland

Schmalzl F, Konwalinka G, Michelmayr G, Abbrederis K, Braunsteiner H 1978 Detection of cytochemical and morphological anomalies in 'preleukaemia'. Acta Haematologica 59: 1–18

Second International Workshop on Chromosomes in Leukemia (1979) 1980a Chromosomes in preleukemia. Cancer Genetics and Cytogenetics 2: 108–113

Second International Workshop on Chromosomes in Leukemia (1979) 1980b Morphological analysis of acute promyelocytic leukemia (M3) and t(8; 21) cases. Cancer Genetics and Cytogenetics 2: 97–98

Second International Workshop on Chromosomes in Leukaemia (1979) 1980c Chromosomes in acute promyelocytic leukemia. Cancer Genetics and Cytogenetics 2: 103–107

Seigneurin D, Audhuy B 1983 Auer rods in refractory anemia with excess of blasts: presence and significance. American Journal of Clinical Pathology 80: 359–362

Senn J S, Pinkerton P H, Price G B, Mak T W, McCulloch E A 1976 Human preleukaemia cell culture studies in sideroblastic anaemia. British Journal of Cancer 33: 299–306

Senn J S, Curtis J E, Pinkerton P H, Till J E, McCulloch E A and The Toronto Area Preleukemia Group 1980 The distribution of marrow granulopoietic progenitors among patients with preleukemia. Leukemia Research 4: 409–413

Senn J S, Messner, H A, Pinkerton P H, Chang L, Nitsch, B, McCulloch E A and The Toronto Area Preleukemia Study Group 1982 Peripheral blood blast cell progenitors in human preleukemia. Blood 59: 106–109

Sieff C A, Chessells J M, Harvey B A M, Pickthall V J, Lawler S 1981 Monosomy 7 in childhood: a myeloproliferative disorder. British Journal of Haematology 49: 235–249

Siftier B, Adeleine P, Viala J, Bryon P A, Fiere D, Gentilhomme O, Vuvan H 1983 Dysmyelopoietic syndromes: a search for prognostic factors in 193 patients. Cancer 52: 83–90

Skinnider L F, Card R T, Padmanabh S 1977 Chronic myelomonocytic leukaemia. American Journal of Clinical Pathology 67: 339–346

Sokal G, Michaux J L, Van den Berghe H 1980 The karyotype in refractory anaemia and preleukaemia. Clinics in Haematology 9: 129–139

Solal-Celigny P, Desaint B, Herrera A, Chastang C, Armar M, Vroclans M, Brousse N, Mancilla F, Renoux M, Bernard J-F, Biovia P 1984 Chronic myelomonocytic leukaemia according to FAB classification: analysis of 35 cases. Blood 63: 634–638

Streeter R F, Presant C A, Reinhard E 1977 Prognostic significance of thrombocytosis in idiopathic sideroblastic anemia. Blood 50: 427–432

Sultan C, Marquet M, Joffroy Y 1974 Etude de certaines dysmyelopoieses acquises idiopathiques et secondaires par culture de moelle in vitro. Annales de Medicine Interne 125: 599–602

Swirsky D M, Li Y S, Matthews J G, Flemans R J, Rees J K H, Hayhoe F G J 1984. 8; 21 translocation in acute granulocytic leukaemia: cytological, cytochemical and clinical features. British Journal of Haematology 56: 199–213

Todd W M, Pierre R V 1983 Preleukemia: a long term prospective study of 326 patients. Blood 62: (Suppl 1) 184a

Tricot G, De Wolf-Pesters C, Vlietinck R, Verwilghen R L 1984a Bone marrow histology in myelodysplastic syndromes II prognostic value of ALIP. British Journal of Haematology 58: 217–226

Tricot G, De Bock R, Dekker A W, Boogaerts M A, Peetermans M, Punk K, Verwilghen R L 1984b Low dose Cytosine Arabinoside (ARA-C) in myelodysplastic syndromes. British Journal of Haematology 58: 231–240

Van den Berghe H, Cassiman J J, David G, Fryns J-P, Michaux J-L, Sokal G 1974 Distinct haematological disorder with deletion of long arm of No. 5 chromosome. Nature 251: 437–438

Verma D S, Spitzer G, Dicke K A, McCredie K B 1979 In vitro agar culture patterns in preleukemia and their clinical significance. Leukemia Research 3: 41–49

Vilter R W, Will J J, Jarrold T 1967 Refractory anemia with hyperplastic bone marrow (aregenerative anemia) Seminars in Hematology 4: 175–193

von Leube W 1900 Rapid verlaufende schwere anamie mit gleichzeitiger leukamischer veranderung des blutbildes. Berlin Klinische Wochenschrifte 37: 85–97

Waxman S, Schreiber C 1983 In vitro induction of differentiation of bone marrow by chemotherapeutic agents in myeloproliferative disorders. Blood 62: (Suppl 1) 156a

Weisdorf D J, Oken M M, Johnson G J, Rydell R E 1981 Auer rod positive dysmyelopoietic syndrome. American Journal of Hematology 11: 397–402

Weisdorf D J, Oken M M, Johnson G J, Rydell R E 1983 Chronic myelodysplastic syndrome: short survival with or without evolution to acute leukaemia. British Journal of Haematology 55: 691–700

Westin J, Weinfeld A 1977 The development of chromosome abnormalities in polycythaemia vera (PV). Results from a follow-up study. Helsinki Chromosome Conference, Aug 29–31, 1977 Abstract 219

Winter J N, Weil S C, Variakojis D, Kwaan H, LeBeau M, Rowley J, Marder R J 1983 Chronic myelomonocytic leukemia: a clinicopathologic cytogenetic and phenotypic analysis. Blood 62: (Suppl 1) 186a

Yunis J J 1983 The chromosomal basis of human neoplasia Science 221: 227–286

Zittoun R 1976 Subacute and chronic myelomonocytic leukaemia: a distinct haematological entity. British Journal of Haematology 32: 1–7

Note added to press proofs
A new approach to therapy of MDS and refractory AML has emerged from recent in vitro experiments (Francis et al, 1985). These studies demonstrated that DNA synthesis inhibitors and 'true differentiation inducers' such as retinoic acid, dimethylsulphoxide and N-methylformamide, act via different mechanisms. Very low doses of DNA synthesis inhibitors (ara-C, 6-thioguanine, 6-mercaptopurine) which prolong S-phase without killing the cells, greatly potentiate the action of differentiation inducers, so much so, that we undertook a pilot clinical trial using suitable combinations of agents. Only one, that of 13-cis-retinoic acid $(50–100\,mg/m^2/24h)$ and 6-thioguanine $(10–20\,mg/m^2/24h)$ is evaluable to date (Francis G E, Mufti G J, Guimaraes J E T, Hamblin T J, unpublished observations). Seven patients with either MDS or AML have received 9 courses and 6/9 courses were associated with haematological responses (as defined by Tricot et al 1984b). Since responses were observed after lack of response to retinoic acid as a single agent (2 cases) or to ara-C (3 cases), the results suggest that the drug combination may be superior to single agents of either type (the prediction of our in vitro results).

Reference
Francis G E, Guimaraes J E T, Berney J J, Wing M A 1985 Synergistic interaction between differentiation inducers and DNA synthesis inhibitors: a new approach to differentiation induction in myelodysplasia and acute myeloid leukaemia. Leukaemia Research (in press).

11. Protein C and the regulation of thrombosis and haemostasis

J. E. Gardiner   J. H. Griffin

INTRODUCTION

In 1960 Seegers laboratory showed that digestion of crude bovine prothrombin preparations with purified thrombin led to the development of potent anticoagulant activity. This anticoagulant protein was named autoprothrombin IIa since it was considered to be derived from prothrombin (Seegers et al, 1972). A decade later it was shown that this protein is a separate protein which is not derived from prothrombin (Marciniak et al, 1967, 1970).

From studies carried out on purified bovine vitamin K-dependent proteins, a 'new' protein was described by Stenflo (1976) which he termed protein C. This protein was subsequently shown to be a zymogen precursor of autoprothrombin IIa (Seegers et al, 1976). Protein C was purified from barium citrate pellets of bovine plasma (Stenflo, 1976) and is a member of the vitamin K-dependent serine protease zymogens present in blood plasma (Stenflo, 1976; Esmon et al, 1976; Kisiel et al, 1976, 1977).

The conversion of protein C to a serine protease, activated protein C, is accompanied by the release of a tetradecapeptide with a molecular weight of 2000 daltons from the heavy chain (Kisiel et al, 1976). This reaction can be brought about by trypsin (Kisiel et al, 1976), thrombin (Kisiel et al, 1977), and the purified factor X activator from Russell's viper venom (Kisiel et al, 1976). Activated protein C is a powerful anticoagulant enzyme which prolongs the clotting time of plasma in various clotting assays (Kisiel et al, 1977; Marlar et al, 1982).

Activated protein C is also profibrinolytic following its intravenous infusion into dogs (Seegers et al, 1972; Zolton & Seegers, 1973; Comp & Esmon, 1981). Thus, the antithrombotic activities of activated protein C are potentially multiple, including both anticoagulant and profibrinolytic activities.

In this chapter we will attempt to give a comprehensive, though not exhaustive, review of the evidence which suggests that protein C is a major regulatory protein of thrombosis and haemostasis.

BIOCHEMISTRY AND FUNCTIONING OF PROTEIN C

Protein C is a vitamin K-dependent protein and has been purified and well characterised from bovine plasma (Stenflo, 1976; Seegers et al, 1976; Esmon et al, 1976; Kisiel et al, 1977; Esmon et al, 1980). Purification of the human protein by Kisiel (1979) as well as our own laboratory has shown that is is similar to the bovine molecule. The apparent molecular weight of bovine protein C is 54 300 and it consists of two polypeptide chains, mol. wt = 43 800 and 23 500, linked by disulphide bonds (Kisiel & Davie, 1981). From an analysis of polyacrylamide gels in the presence of sodium dodecyl sulphate (SDS), the molecular weight of unreduced human protein C is estimated as 62 000 (Kisiel, 1979). Following reduction of the native molecule, a heavy chain of mol. wt = 41 000 and a light chain of mol. wt = 21 000 are seen. Both human and bovine protein C are glycoproteins, the bovine form containing about 18% carbohydrate distributed on the heavy and light chains (Kisiel et al, 1976) while the human protein contains about 23% carbohydrate (Kisiel, 1979).

The complete amino acid sequence of bovine protein C has been determined (Stenflo & Fernlund, 1982; Fernlund & Stenflo, 1982). The heavy chain is homologous to the other serine proteases and contains the components of the 'charge relay system' typical of the serine proteases: histidine-56, aspartic acid-102, and serine-201 (Stenflo & Fernlund, 1982). The heavy chain has three carbohydrate side chains at asparagine residues 93, 154, and 170. The sequence of the light chain has a very high degree of homology to the other vitamin K-dependent plasma proteins up to position 44 (Bucher et al, 1976; Fernlund & Stenflo, 1982) which is beyond the eight γ-carboxyglutamic acid residues. In other regions of the molecule, there is somewhat less homology to factors IX and X. When the amino acid sequence of the light chain of bovine protein C was determined, an assignment could not be made at position 71 (Fernlund & Stenflo, 1982). However, recently Drakenberg et al (1983) identified that residue as erythro-β-hydroxyaspartic acid, an unusual amino acid carrying one negative charge. Although β-hydroxyaspartic acid has been found in the urine of man and some animals (Ikegani, 1975), it had not been found in a plasma protein before. The function of this modified amino acid residue in protein C is unknown and there is as yet no evidence to suggest that its biosynthesis is dependent upon vitamin K.

Activation of protein C

In order for protein C to function as an enzyme, the molecule must be activated by limited proteolysis. This activation can be effected in vitro by using α-thrombin (Kisiel et al, 1977) but the slow rate of activation was taken to imply that it might not be physiologically significant. However, Esmon, Owen, and coworkers showed that a thrombin receptor exists on the surface of endothelial cells and that this receptor, named thrombomodulin, functions as a cofactor in the activation of protein C (Esmon & Owen, 1981; Esmon et al, 1982a,b). Esmon et al (1982a) isolated thrombomodulin from perfused rabbit lungs by extraction with Triton X–100 followed by affinity chromatography on two columns of diisopropyl phosphoryl-(DIP)-thrombin-agarose. The latter procedure takes advantage of the fact that thrombin binds very tightly to thrombomodulin and DIP-thrombin acts as a competitive inhibitor of thrombin. Polyacrylamide gel electrophoresis of purified thrombomodulin under non-reducing conditions in the presence of SDS reveals a protein molecule with an apparent molecular weight of 74 000. Thrombomodulin binds thrombin with high affinity, $K_d = 0.48$ nM, to form a $1:1$ molar complex and this complex activates protein C at least 1000 times faster than free thrombin (Esmon & Owen, 1981). Figure 11.1 depicts a model which has been suggested by Esmon et al (1982c) for the activation of protein C. The cofactor, thrombomodulin, remains bound to the endothelial cells during the activation of protein C by thrombin (Esmon & Owen, 1981). A stable complex is initially formed between thrombin and thrombomodulin, and this complex then binds and activates protein C which is subsequently released into solution as activated protein C.

Thrombomodulin appears to be an extrinsic membrane protein since it can be released by EDTA, high salt or non-ionic detergents (Esmon & Owen, 1981; Esmon et al, 1982a). An unusual feature of this protein is that it functions equally as well as a cofactor in solutions of non-ionic detergents in the presence or absence of phospholipid bilayers (Esmon et al, 1982a,b; Esmon & Owen, 1981; Owen & Esmon, 1981). This finding suggests that unlike the other vitamin K-dependent zymogens which are activated by the binding of the enzyme and substrate to negative charged phospholipid surfaces through their component γ-carboxyglutamic acid (gla) residues in the

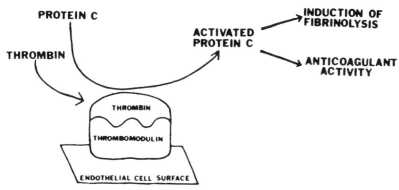

Fig. 11.1 Proposed schematic model for in vivo protein C activation. (Reprinted with permission from Comp P C, Jacocks R M, Ferrell G L, Esmon C T 1982 Activation of protein C in vivo. Journal of Clinical Investigation 70: 127–134.)

presence of calcium (Esmon et al, 1982a), protein C activation is not strictly dependent on phospholipids. Esmon et al (1983) investigated the potential function of the gla residues in the calcium-dependent activation of protein C by removing the amino terminus containing these residues through selective proteolysis with chymotrypsin and comparing the activation of this gla-domainless protein C to that of the intact protein. Their results showed the amino terminal region containing gla is not required for normal activation by thrombin: thrombomodulin but that the gla residues are essential for the expression of potent anticoagulant activity (Esmon et al, 1983). Moreover, they found that protein C possesses a gla-independent high affinity calcium-binding site which is required for recognition by the thrombin: thrombomodulin complex.

Activation of protein C is thought to occur normally on thrombomodulin at the surface of the vascular endothelium, not in solution. Esmon et al (1983a) compared the requirements for protein C activation over the endothelial cell surface to those of the soluble system in order to determine the contribution of the cell surface to the activation of protein C. They showed that both native protein C and gla-domainless protein C were activated at the same rate by purified thrombomodulin:thrombin whilst protein C was activated at least 50-fold faster by thrombin on the surface of the endothelial cells. The difference in rates of protein C activation is reflected in the markedly different K_m values for protein C and gla-domainless protein C (Esmon et al, 1983a). When thrombin is complexed to thrombomodulin it is no longer able either to clot fibrinogen or to activate factor V (Esmon et al, 1982b). It has recently been demonstrated that thrombomodulin may also act to inhibit and/or reverse platelet activation by thrombin (Esmon et al, 1983b).

Thrombomodulin therefore provides a mechanism by which the multiple well established procoagulant functions of thrombin can be rapidly altered to anticoagulant functions. This may be of high significance with regard to the regulation of haemostasis.

Recently it was suggested that human coagulant factor Va is a cofactor for the activation of protein C during blood clotting in vitro (Salem et al, 1983a). Further studies showed that the light chain of factor Va of mol. wt = 78 000 is the component of factor Va which accelerates protein C activation (Salem et al, 1983b).

Salem et al (1983c) investigated protein C activation in solution using isolated thrombomodulin and the light chain of factor Va. They found that the light chain was less potent in the activation process than thrombomodulin, and that, unlike thrombo-modulin in solution, factor Va-enhanced activation by thrombin required the presence of the gla-domain of protein C. In addition, the light chain of factor Va could inhibit thrombomodulin but not the converse. Since thrombomodulin has been identified as a cofactor for protein C activation located on the surface of endothelial cells, a study was carried out on the effects of cultured cells on protein C activation stimulated by factor Va (Maruyama et al, 1983) under conditions where protein C activation is undetectable in the presence of thrombin alone. It was suggested from the results of this study that factor Va can stimulate protein C activation on cells containing thrombomodulin (Maruyama et al, 1983).

Inhibition of activated protein C

Activated protein C has been reported to lose activity following exposure to serum (Marciniak, 1970) and Marlar & Griffin (1980) have shown that normal plasma inhibits the amidolytic activity of the enzyme. This protein C inhibitor has been purified from plasma (Suzuki et al, 1983a) and has an apparent molecular weight of 57 000 and a plasma concentration of approximately 5 μg/ml. The inhibitor blocks the anticoagulant and the amidolytic activities of activated protein C. Suzuki et al (1983a) showed that preincubation of the isolated inhibitor with diisopropylfluorophosphate, EDTA, or parachloromercuribenzoate does not affect its ability to inhibit activated protein C which suggests that it does not act as an enzyme. Since stoichiometric amounts of the inhibitor are required to neutralise activated protein C, it is likely that the inhibitor forms a 1 : 1 complex with the enzyme (Suzuki et al, 1983a).

Since activated protein C destroys factors V and VIII: C in plasma (Marlar et al, 1981), Marlar & Griffin (1980) proposed that a deficiency of protein C inhibitor in plasma from patients with combined factor V/VIII deficiency could be the molecular basis for this disease, due to chronic consumption of factors and VIII:C by activated protein C. These workers showed that plasmas from four unrelated patients with combined factor V/VIII deficiency disease failed to inhibit human activated protein C in an amidolytic assay (Marlar & Griffin, 1980). Similar experiments were carried out by Giddings et al (1982) on stored plasma samples from 21 patients with the combined factor V/VIII deficiency and the results, though variable, tended to confirm those of Marlar & Griffin (1980). However, the original hypothesis was recently questioned by reports that plasmas from factor V/VIII deficient patients were able to inhibit normally activated protein C (Kisiel & Canfield, 1982; Canfield & Kisiel, 1982; Suzuki et al, 1983b; Bertina et al, 1983). In light of these conflicting observations, the factor V/VIII deficient plasmas originally studied by Marlar & Griffin (1980) were reinvestigated using a modified assay for activated protein C (Gardiner & Griffin, 1984). The results demonstrated the presence of protein C inhibitory activity in the patient plasmas and showed that the activity was readily lost when the plasmas were frozen and thawed.

The reported absence of protein C inhibitory activity in those patient plasmas (Marlar & Griffin, 1980) may thus have been caused by freezing and thawing of the plasmas. It seems, therefore, that a simple deficiency of protein C inhibitor is not at this time demonstrably responsible for combined factor V/VIII deficiency disease.

Anticoagulant properties of activated protein C

Inactivation of factor Va by activated protein C
Factor V is an essential non-enzymatic component of the prothrombinase complex which also comprises phospholipid, calcium ions, and the serine protease, factor Xa. This complex accelerates factor Xa—catalysed prothrombin activation (Milstone, 1964; Nesheim et al, 1979; Rosing et al, 1980). Platelets can substitute for factor Va and phospholipid in the prothrombinase complex (Milstone, 1964) and stimulation of platelets causes the appearance of a receptor for factor Xa on the platelet surface, this receptor being at least partially composed of factor Va and phospholipid (Miletich et al, 1978; Tracy et al, 1979). The activation of prothrombin is brought about by its simultaneous interaction with the factor Va and phospholipid which leads to the exposure of peptide bonds susceptible to factor Xa (Dahlback & Stenflo, 1980).

Bovine as well as human factor V consists of a single-chain polypeptide of mol. wt = 330 000 (Nesheim et al, 1979; Esmon, 1979) which is relatively inactive until cleaved by thrombin to form factor Va (Dahlback, 1980; Esmon, 1979). Human factor Va consists of two subunits, a heavy chain mol. wt = 105 000 and a light chain mol. wt = 71 000 to 74 000 (Suzuki et al, 1982). The subunits can be dissociated in EDTA with loss of biological activity and reassociated in the presence of Ca^{2+} ions, a process which is accompanied by the restoration of biological activity (Esmon, 1979).

Plasma factor Va can be inactivated by activated protein C in the presence of phospholipid and Ca^{2+} (Tracy et al, 1979). Several groups have shown that bovine activated protein C can also block the platelet prothrombin-converting activity (Comp & Esmon, 1979; Dahlback & Stenflo, 1980). It was demonstrated that this effect was due to proteolysis of the platelet factor Va which partially constitutes the factor Xa receptor. Factor Xa is able to protect factor Va on platelets from activated protein C (Dahlback & Stenflo, 1980; Comp & Esmon, 1979), and since the platelet receptor for factor Xa is partly composed of factor Va (Tracy et al, 1981; Kane et al, 1980), the ability of factor Xa to protect factor Va may be important for the regulation of the activation of prothrombin.

The proteolytic destruction of factor Va by activated protein C has been studied by a number of laboratories. Walker et al (1979) showed that the inactivation of factor Va by activated protein C was accompanied by a cleavage in the heavy chain. Canfield et al (1978) as well as Suzuki et al (1983c) also observed inactivation associated with cleavage in the heavy chain of factor Va following treatment with activated protein C. It has, however, been reported that activated protein C brought about a cleavage in the light chain (mol. wt = 82 000) of factor Va leading to the appearance of two polypeptides mol. wt = 54 000 and 34 000 (Canfield et al, 1982).

Recently Walker (1979, 1980) reported that protein S, another vitamin K-dependent plasma protein whose function has not yet been firmly established, can stimulate the rate of the inactivation of factor Va by activated protein C by enhancing the binding of the enzyme to phospholipid vesicles. Walker proposed that the equimolar binding of protein S to activated protein C on the surface of phospholipids is required to form a factor Va inactivation complex. Bovine protein S possesses a peptide bond at Arg-54 which is very susceptible to proteolysis by thrombin (Dahlback, 1983). Suzuki et al (1983d) investigated the effect of thrombin-modified protein S on factor Va inactivation by activated protein C. They showed that intact protein S stimulated the factor Va inactivation by activated protein C whereas thrombin-modified protein S apparently suppressed the inactivation. Protein-phospholipid binding experiments showed that although intact protein S enhanced the binding of activated protein C to phospholipid stoichiometrically, thrombin-modified protein S seemed to not only suppress the complex formation, but also to dissociate the complex. This suggests that thrombin-modified protein S regulates the action of activated protein C towards factor Va on phospholipid (Suzuki et al, 1983d).

Inactivation of factor VIII : C by activated protein C
Vehar & Davie (1980) showed that in the presence of phospholipid Ca^{2+}, activated bovine protein C blocked the coagulant activity of purified bovine factor VIII:C and thrombin-activated bovine VIII:C. The inactivation of the thrombin-activated factor VIII:C was accompanied by a cleavage in the VIII:C molecule which led to the proposal that the loss of coagulant activity caused by activated protein C was associated with the disappearance of an 83 000 molecular weight species.

Marlar et al (1981, 1982) showed that activated protein C inactivated factor VIII:C as well as factor V coagulant activity of human plasma. Moreover, partially purified thrombin-activated factor VIII:C is inactivated forty times faster than factor VIII:C.

Recently a study was carried out on the effect of activated protein C on thrombin-activated purified human factor VIII:C (Fulcher et al, 1984). The results showed that proteolysis of factor VIII:C by activated protein C was accompanied by a reduction in the size of all the polypeptides except for a major doublet at mol. wt = 79 000 to 80 000. A new polypeptide band was generated at mol. wt = 45 000. The inactivation or porcine VIII:C by activated porcine protein C has also been studied (Lollar et al, 1983) using a fluorimetric assay in conjunction with SDS-polyacrylamide gel electrophoresis of ^{125}I-labelled factor VIII:C. The loss of activity of factor VIII:C in the presence of activated protein C was parallelled by proteolysis of the ^{125}I-factor VIII:C heavy chain. The light chain was relatively resistant to proteolysis.

The results of the studies carried out with human (Fulcher et al, 1984) and porcine (Lollar et al, 1983) factor VIII:C are similar to those obtained by Vehar & Davie (1980) with the bovine molecules and are also analogous to results obtained by other groups from studies carried out on the proteolytic cleavage of factor Va by activated protein C (Walker et al, 1979; Canfield et al, 1978, Suzuki et al, 1983c).

Fibrinolytic properties of activated protein C
In addition to its function as an anticoagulant, activated protein C has been shown by Seegers and coworkers (1972), (Zolton & Seegers, 1973) to enhance fibrinolysis.

Comp & Esmon (1980) confirmed that fibrinolytic activity can be generated both in vivo and in vitro in response to activated protein C. They reported that infusion of bovine activated protein C into anaesthetised dogs resulted in rapid blood clot lysis in blood withdrawn from treated animals. The administration of activated protein C caused an increase in the plasma levels of plasminogen activator activity that is adsorbable to lysine-sepharose (Comp & Esmon, 1981). Neither protein C zymogen nor DFP-treated activated protein C were able to enhance clot lysis, suggesting that the observed response requires the active site of activated protein C (Comp & Esmon, 1981). Since activated protein C does not directly activate plasminogen, Esmon et al (1982) suggested that the enhancement of fibrinolysis is brought about by the release of plasminogen activator from the endothelium covering the luminal surface of the vascular system. In addition, Comp & Esmon (1981) showed that although the addition of activated protein C to plasma alone is sufficient to generate some slightly enhanced fibrinolytic activity, the effect is more marked when activated protein C is added to a mixture of plasma and blood cells. From a consideration of these results, it was proposed that activated protein C generates a secondary messenger, or family of messengers, which in turn causes the elevation of circulating plasminogen activator activity (Comp & Esmon, 1981).

CLINICAL RELEVANCE OF PROTEIN C

Deficiency of protein C in hereditary thrombotic disease

Reports that activated protein C is a potent in vitro anticoagulant and an in vivo profibrinolytic agent led to the proposal that an inherited deficiency of this protein might also be involved in thromboembolic disease. Until recently, clinical research on human protein C has been limited due to the absence of satisfactory functional assays, only immunologic assays being available. The immunologic assays for protein C have been based on Laurell rocket techniques. Using such an assay, our laboratory analysed 40 normal plasmas and showed that the plasma level of protein C antigen was $4 \mu g/ml$. This assay was also used in the detection of the first family with an inherited deficiency of protein C and associated venous thromboembolic disease (Griffin et al, 1981). In this family the propositus had 41% of protein C and the father and paternal uncle had 35% and 45% of normal protein C levels respectively (Fig. 11.2). From these results Griffin et al (1981) proposed that an inherited deficiency of protein C in heterozygote patients who exhibit approximately half normal plasma levels of protein C antigen, can be associated with a tendency to venous thrombotic disease. Since those initial findings were made, over 24 families have been found with inherited protein C deficiency associated with thromboembolic disease (Bertina et al, 1982, 1983; Pabinger-Fasching et al, 1983; Broekmans et al, 1983a,b; Horellou et al, 1983; Marlar & Endres-Brooks, 1983). The clinical manifestations of protein C deficiency often involve thrombophlebitis or pulmonary emboli in late adolescence or young adulthood following significant trauma. Histories of recurring venous thrombosis as well as pulmonary emboli are typical but not necessary findings. A small minority of patients with half normal levels of protein C may remain asymptomatic. Broekmans et al (1983a,b) examined 35 patients in 12 families deficient in protein C and reported that there there was a 60% incidence of pulmonary emboli and deep venous thrombosis. More than 50% of the patients presented with thrombotic disease by the age of 30 years and, by the age of 40 years, over three-quarters of the patients were affected.

Protein C deficiency is inherited as an autosomal recessive trait (Griffin et al, 1981, 1983; Broekmans et al, 1983a). Hereditary venous thromboembolic disease has also been associated with inherited deficiencies of plasminogen (Aoki et al, 1978; Wohl et al, 1979), fibronogen (Beck et al, 1965; Al-Mondhiry et al, 1975; Egeberg, 1967) and

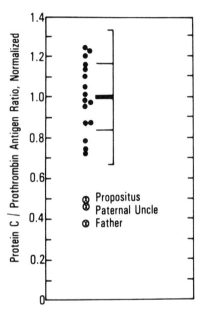

Fig. 11.2   Determination of protein C antigen levels in plasmas from three affected members of a family with recurrent thrombotic disease. The protein C to prothrombin antigen ratio for 16 patients (controls) and three family members undergoing coumarin anticoagulant therapy was determined. Brackets represent normalised mean (1.0) and one or two standard deviations. (Reprinted with permission from Griffin J H et al, 1981.)

antithrombin III (Egeberg, 1967; Marciniak et al, 1974). In patients with antithrombin III or protein C deficiency, a half normal plasma level of either protein is sufficient for a predisposition to venous thrombotic disease. Nevertheless, until recently there was no assay available for measuring the activity of protein C in plasma and therefore it was not clear whether the reduced levels of protein C present in the deficient patients were functionally abnormal. However, Comp & Esmon (1984) have developed a functional assay and this has been used to supplement immunologic assays of protein C in patients from four families with inherited protein C deficiency since control studies showed a good correlation between protein C antigen and protein C functional activity in 40 normal plasmas (Griffin et al, 1983). In four families containing 14 patients with half normal or lower protein C antigen, the level of functional protein C was generally correlated with antigenic levels. Among these patients, eight presented with venous thrombotic disease. The six asymptomatic patients in these families included three young adults and three children. Protein C deficiency exhibited autosomal inheritance (Griffin et al, 1983).

Bertina et al (1983), Sala et al (1983), and Francis & Patch (1983) have also developed functional assays for plasma protein C. Bertina et al (1983) reported a good correlation between protein C activity and antigen in the plasma of 20 patients not treated with oral anticoagulants who had previously been found to be heterozygotes for protein C deficiency. Two related patients were detected where the protein C antigen was normal while the protein C activity was significantly below the lower limits of the normal range. These patients suffered from thrombotic disease and Bertina et al (1983) suggested that those patients were heterozygotes for an abnormal protein C molecule. Our laboratory has also identified four patients with normal protein C antigen but half-normal activity, presumably reflecting the presence of abnormal protein C molecules (Griffin et al, 1983).

Protein C deficiency and purpura fulminans
A neonate has been described with a severe protein C deficiency who presented with relapsing purpura fulminans syndrome 11 hours after birth (Branson et al, 1983). Using the immunologic Laurell rocket technique, no protein C antigen could be detected in the patient's plasma. The mother and two brothers had between 25% and 40% of normal plasma protein C antigen suggesting that the patient may have been homozygous for protein C deficiency. The possible link between a deficiency of protein C and the expression of purpura fulminans initially suggested by this study has since been confirmed by Marciniak et al (1983) from an investigation of an inbred family from a rural Appalachian area. Similarly, two other infants with striking thrombotic problems associated with a homozygous protein C deficiency have been recently described (Seligsohn et al, 1984; Marlar et al, 1983).

Treatment of patients with oral anticoagulants causes a fall in the level of vitamin K-dependent plasma proteins, including protein C (Vigano et al, 1983; Epstein et al, 1983). Vigano et al (1983) showed that the rate of decrease of protein C antigen is closer to that factor VII than of factors IX, X and prothrombin. Epstein et al (1983) reported that in patients on coumarin, protein C antigen declined much faster than factor X antigen and activity, or factor IX activity and that protein C fell at the same rate as factor VII. A half-life for protein C of 6 to 8 hours was inferred in these studies (Vigano et al, 1983; Epstein et al, 1983). Infusion of commercial factor IX concentrate containing protein C into an infant with homozygous protein C deficiency suggested a half-life of approximately 8 hours for protein C (Sills et al, 1983). The short half-life of protein C may moderate anticoagulant effects during initiation of anticoagulant therapy. The development of thrombotic complications or of skin necrosis (vide infra) at the onset of oral anticoagulation may reflect the rapid drop in protein C while prothrombin and factors IX and X transiently remain near normal levels. This emphasises the widely recognised value of initiating oral anticoagulant therapy under the cover of heparin therapy until a stable state of anticoagulation is reached in order to reduce the risk of thrombosis.

Protein C deficiency and skin necrosis
Oral anticoagulant therapy has been used to treat protein C deficiency (Griffin et al, 1981; Bertina et al, 1982). Broekmans et al (1983c) reported an isolated protein C deficiency in two patients with coumarin-induced skin necrosis and suggested that protein C deficiency is one of the components in the pathogenic mechanism for the

development of skin necrosis during rapidly developing vitamin K deficiency (Broekmans et al, 1983c). McGehee et al (1983) reported the onset of haemorrhagic necrosis with familial protein C deficiency in a patient hospitalised for recurrent thrombophlebitis, following administration of coumarin.

Protein C deficiency in disseminated intravascular coagulation and other diseases

In view of the fact that in many cases of intravascular coagulation proteins participating in the pathways of clotting and fibrinolysis are activated and consumed

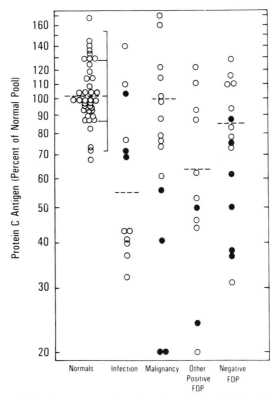

Fig. 11.3 Plasma protein C antigen concentrations in various groups of patients. Each point represents a value from a single patient or a normal donor. Solid circles indicate the presence of liver disease, whereas open circles indicate the absence of liver disease. Protein C concentrations are shown in relation to the normal plasma pool (n = 15), which was found to have 4.0 µg/ml protein C. Brackets around the mean of the normals indicate the limits of 1 and 2 standard deviations. The dashed line for each patient group indicates the mean of the log-transformed data points. FDP indicates fibrin degradation products. (Reprinted with permission from Griffin J H et al 1982.)

(Rapaport, 1977), it was suggested that the level of protein C could be altered in these cases if indeed protein C plays a role in the regulation of coagulation and the prevention of thrombosis in vivo (Griffin et al, 1982). Using immunological techniques, the level of protein C antigen was measured in plasmas of patients with suspected intravascular coagulation who all had elevated levels of fibrin degradation products. This study showed that in the 53 patients suspected of intravascular coagulation, 24 presented with significantly decreased levels of protein C antigen (Fig.

11.3). In addition, 75% of patients with liver disease had decreased protein C levels, consistent with the assumption that protein C is synthesised in the liver like the other vitamin K-dependent coagulation factors. In the absence of liver disease, intravascular coagulation was associated with low levels of protein C antigen. In the three cases of acute defibrination in the absence of liver disease, all the patients had low levels of protein C. From a consideration of this data, Griffin et al (1982) suggested that since extensive activation of the coagulation system in vivo during intravascular coagulation is associated with a marked reduction of plasma protein C, this protein is a physiologic participant in the pathways of coagulation reactions.

Mannucci et al (1982) also found protein C antigen levels reduced in patients with the disseminated intravascular coagulation syndrome and in patients with chronic liver disease. Acquired defects of protein C also developed after surgery in patients operated on for major or minor procedures.

Oral anticoagulants have been shown to cause a decrease in the level of protein C, together with other vitamin K-dependent proteins.

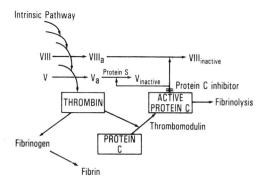

Fig. 11.4   The role of activated protein C in the regulation of haemostasis. Thrombin converts factors V and VIII to active cofactors, Va and VIIIa. Thrombin also activates protein C in a reaction greatly accelerated by the endothelial surface cofactor, thrombomodulin. Activated protein C inactivates factors Va and VIIIa very potently by limited proteolysis. Protein S may be a cofactor for activated protein C in regulating factor Va. Protein C inhibitor, a plasma protein, neutralises activated protein C by forming a stoichiometric inhibitor: enzyme complex. (Reprinted with permission from Gardiner J E, Griffin J H 1983 Human protein C and thromboembolic disease. In: Brown E B (ed) Progress in hematology XIII. Grune & Stratton Inc, London, p 265–278.)

SUMMARY

Figure 11.4 illustrates the mode of action of activated protein C as an anticoagulant and as a profibrinolytic agent. Protein C is activated by a complex composed of thrombin and the endothelial cell cofactor, thrombomodulin. Activated protein C then inactivates factors Va and VIIIa. A more detailed description of this scheme appears in the figure caption.

The recently established association between congenital deficiency of protein C and thrombotic disease has demonstrated the clinical importance of this protein. However, it is clear that much remains to be done in biochemical and clinical studies of both protein C and its inhibitor.

REFERENCES

Al-Mondhiry H A B, Bilezikian S B, Nossel H L 1965 Fibrinogen 'New York' — an abnormal fibrinogen associated with thromboembolism: functional evaluation. Blood 45: 607–619

Aoki N, Moroi M, Sakata Y, Yoshida N, Matsuda M 1978 Abnormal plasminogen, A hereditary molecular abnormality found in a patient with recurrent thrombosis. Journal of Clinical Investigation 61: 1186–1195

Beck E A, Chararche P, Jackson D P 1965 A new inherited coagulation disorder caused by an abnormal fibrinogen ('fibrinogen Baltimore'). Nature 208: 143–145

Bertina R M, Broekmans A W, van der Linden I K, Mertens K 1982 Protein C deficiency in a Dutch family with thrombotic disease. Thrombosis and Haemostasis 48: 1–5

Bertina R M, van Wijngaarden A, Schlegel N, Marotte R, Alexandre P A 1983 Functional assay for the inhibitor of activated protein C in plasma. Thrombosis and Haemostasis (Abst) 50: 342

Bertina R M, Broekmans A W, van Es-Krommenhoek T, van Wijngaarden A 1983 The use of a functional assay for plasma protein C in the diagnosis of protein C deficiency. Thrombosis and Haemostasis (Abst) 50: 350

Bick R L 1978 Disseminated intravascular coagulation and related syndromes: Etiology, pathophysiology, diagnosis and management. American Journal of Hematology 5: 265–282

Branson H, Katz J, Marble R, Griffin J H 1983 Inherited protein C deficiency and a coumarin-reponsive chronic relapsing purpura fulminans syndrome in a neonate. Lancet 1983: 1165–1168

Broekmans A W, van der Linden I K, Veltkamp J J, Bertina R M 1983a Prevalence of isolated protein C deficiency in patients with venous thrombotic disease and in the population. Thrombosis and Haemostasis (Abst) 50: 350

Broekmans A W, Veltkamp J J, Bertina R 1983b Congenital protein C deficiency and venous thromboembolism. New England Journal of Medicine 309: 340–344

Broekmans A W, Bertina M R, Loelinger E A, Hofmann V, Klingemann H G 1983c Protein C and the development of skin necrosis during anticoagulant therapy. Letter to Thrombosis and Haemostasis 49(3): 255

Bucher D, Nebelin E, Thomsen J, Stenflo J 1976 Identification of γ-carboxyglutamic acid residues in bovine Factors IX and X and in a new vitamin K-dependent protein. FEBS Letters 68: 293–296

Canfield W K, Nesheim M, Kisiel W, Mann K G 1978 Proteolytic inactivation of bovine Factor Va by bovine activated protein C. Circulation (Abst) 57, 58: Supp II, 210

Canfield W K, Kisiel W 1982a Evidence of normal functional levels of activated protein C inhibitor in combined Factor V/VIII deficiency disease. Journal of Clinical Investigation 70: 1260–1272

Canfield W, McMullen B, Kisiel W 1982b Amino terminal sequence studies of bovine factor Va. Federation Proceedings 41: 655

Comp P C, Esmon C T 1979 Activated protein C inhibits platelet prothrombin-converting activity. Blood 54: 1272–1281

Comp P C, Esmon C T 1980 Evidence for multiple roles for activated protein C in fibrinolysis. In: Mann K G, Taylor F (eds) The regulation of coagulation. Elsevier North Holland, Inc, New York, p 583–588

Comp P C, Esmon C T 1981 Generation of fibrinolytic activity by infusion of activated protein C into dogs. Journal of Clinical Investigation 68: 1221–1228

Comp P C, Nixon R, Esmon C T 1984 Determination of functional levels of protein C, an antithrombotic protein, using thrombin/thrombomodulin complex. Blood 63: 15–21

Dahlback B 1980 Human coagulation Factor V purification and thrombin-catalyzed activation. Journal of Clinical Investigation 66: 583–591

Dahlback B, Stenflo J 1980 Inhibitory effect of activated protein C on activation of prothrombin by platelet-bound Factor Xa. European Journal of Biochemistry 107: 331–335

Dahlback B 1983 Purification of human vitamin K-dependent protein S and its limited proteolysis by thrombin. Journal of Biological Chemistry 209: 837–846

Drakenberg T, Fernlund P, Roepstorff P, Stenflo J 1983 β-hydroxyaspartic acid in vitamin K dependent proteins. Proceedings of the National Sciences of the USA 80: 1802–1806

Egeberg O 1965 Inherited antithrombin deficiency causing thrombophilia. Thrombosis et Diathesis Haemorrhagica 13: 516–530

Egeberg O 1967 Inherited fibrinogen abnormality causing thrombophilia. Thrombosis et Diathesis Haemorrhagica 17: 176–187

Epstein D J, Bergum P W, Raport S I 1983 Kinetics of protein C depression after coumadin adminstration. Circulation (Abstr) 68: Supp III, 316

Esmon C T, Stenflo J, Suttie J W, Jackson C M 1976 A new vitamin K-dependent protein (a phospholipid-binding zymogen of a serine esterase). Journal of Biological Chemistry 251: 3052–3056

Esmon C T 1979 The subunit structure of thrombin-activated Factor V. Isolation of activated Factor V, separation of subunits and reconstruction of biological activity. Journal of Biological Chemistry 254: 964–973

Esmon C T, Comp P C, Walker F S 1980 Functions for protein C. In: Suttie J W (ed) Vitamin K metabolism and vitamin K-dependent proteins. University Park Press, Baltimore, p 72–83

Esmon C T, Owen W G 1981 Identification of an endothelial cell cofactor for thrombin-catalyzed activation of protein C. Proceedings of the National Academy of Sciences of the USA 78: 2249–2252

Esmon N L, Owen W G, Esmon C T 1982a Isolation of membrane-bound cofactor for thrombin-catalyzed activation of protein C. Journal of Biological Chemistry 257: 859–864

Esmon C T, Esmon N L, Harris K W 1982b Complex formation between thrombin and thrombomodulin inhibits both thrombin-catalyzed fibrin formation and Factor V activation. Journal of Biological Chemistry 257: 7944–7947

Esmon C T, Esmon N L, Saugstad J, Owen W G 1982c Activation of protein C by a complex between thrombin and endothelial cell surface protein. In: Nossel H L, Vogel J H (eds) Pathobiology of the endothelial cell. Academic Press Inc, New York, p 121–136

Esmon N L, DeBault L E, Esmon C T 1983a Proteolytic formation and properties of γ-carboxyglutamic acid domainless protein C. Journal of Biological Chemistry 258: 5548–5553

Esmon N L, Carroll R C, Esmon C T 1983b Thrombomodulin blocks the ability of thrombin to activate platelets. Journal of Biological Chemistry 258: 12238–12242

Fernlund P, Stenflo J 1982 Amino acid sequence of the light chain of bovine protein C. Journal of Biological Chemistry 257: 12170–12179

Francis R B, Patch M J 1983 A functional assay for protein C in human plasma. Thrombosis Research 32: 605–613

Fulcher C, Gardiner J, Griffin J, Zimmerman T 1984 Proteolysis of human Factor VIII procoagulant protein with thrombin and activated protein C. Blood 63: 486–489

Gardiner J, Griffin J 1983 Studies of human protein C inhibition in normal and Factor V/VIII deficient plasmas. Thrombosis Research 36: 197–203

Giddings J C, Sugrue A, Bloom A L 1982 Quantitation of coagulant antigens and inhibition of activated protein C in combined V/VIII deficiency. British Journal of Haematology 52: 496–502

Griffin J H, Evatt B, Zimmerman T S, Kleiss A J, Wideman C 1981 Deficiency of protein C in congenital thrombotic disease. Journal of Clinical Investigation 68: 1370–1373

Griffin J H, Mosher D F, Zimmerman T S, Kleiss A J 1982 Protein C, an antithrombotic protein, is reduced in hospitalized patients with intravascular coagulation. Blood 60: 261–264

Griffin J H, Bezeaud A, Evatt B, Mosher D 1983 Functional and immunologic studies of protein C in thromboembolic disease. Blood (Abst) 62: 301a

Horellou M H, Samama M, Concard J, Bertina R M 1983 Protein C deficiency in three unrelated French patients with venous thrombosis. Thrombosis Haemostasis (Abst) 50: 351

Ikegami T 1975 Studies on the mechanism of β-hydroxyaspartic acid. Acta Medica Okayana 29: 241–247

Kane W H, Lidhout M J, Jackson C M, Majerus P W 1980 Factor Va-dependent binding of Factor Xa to human platelets. Journal of Biological Chemistry 255: 1170–1174

Kisiel W, Ericsson L H, Davie E W 1976 Proteolytic activation of protein C from bovine plasma. Biochemistry 15: 4893–4900

Kisiel W, Canfield W M, Ericsson L H, Davie E W 1977 Anticoagulant properties of bovine plasma protein C following activation by thrombin. Biochemistry 16: 5824–5831

Kisiel W 1979 Human plasma protein C. Isolation, characterization and mechanism of activation by α-thrombin. Journal of Clinical Investigation 64: 761–769

Kisiel W, Davie E W 1981 Protein C (a review). Methods in Enzymology 80: 320–332

Kisiel W, Canfield W M 1982 Evidence of normal functional levels of activated protein C inhibitor in Factor V/VIII combined deficiency disease. Federation Proceedings 41: 655

Lollar P, Knutson G J, Fass D N 1983 Inactivation of porcine Factor VIII : C by activated protein C. Blood (Abst) 62: 288a

Mammen E F, Thomas W R, Seegers W H 1960 Activation of purified prothrombin to autoprothrombin I or autoprothrombin II (platelet cofactor II or autoprothrombin II-A). Thrombosis et Diathesis Haemorrhagica 5: 218

Mannucci P M 1982 Deficiencies of protein C, an inhibitor of blood coagulation. Lancet, ii: 463–467

Marciniak E, Murano G, Seegers W H 1967 Inhibitor of blood clotting derived from prothrombin. Thrombosis et Diathesis Haemorrhagica Stuttgart 18: 161

Marciniak E 1970 Coagulation inhibitor elicited by thrombin. Science 170: 452–453

Marciniak E, Farley C H, DeSimone P A 1974 Familial thrombosis due to antithrombin III deficiency. Blood 43: 219–231

Marciniak E, Wilson H D, Marlar R A 1983 Neonatal purpura fulminans as expression of homozygosity for protein C deficiency. Blood (Abst) 62: 303a

Marlar R A, Griffin J H 1980 Deficiency of protein C inhibitor in combined Factor V/VIII deficiency disease. Journal of Clinical Investigation 66: 1186–1189

Marlar R A, Kleiss A J, Griffin J H 1981 Human protein C: Inactivation of Factors V and VIII in plasma by the activated molecule. Annals of the New York Academy of Sciences 370: 303–310

Marlar R A, Kleiss A J, Griffin J H 1982 Mechanism of action of human activated protein C, a thrombin-dependent anticoagulant enzyme. Blood 59: 1064–1072

Marlar R A, Endres-Brooks J 1983 Recurrent thromboembolic disease due to heterozygous protein C deficiency. Thrombosis and Haemostasis (Abst) 50: 351

Marlar R A, Sills R H, Montgomery R R 1983 Protein C in commercial Factor IX (F IX) concentrations (CONC) and its use in the treatment of 'homozygous' protein C deficiency. Blood (Abst) 62: 303a

Maruyama I, Salem H, Majerus P W 1983 Coagulation Factor Va binds to human umbilical vein endothelial cells (HUVE) and accelerates protein C activation. Blood (Abst) 62: 303a

McGehee W G, Klotz T A, Epstein D J, Rapaport S I 1983 Coumarin-induced necrosis in a patient with familial protein C deficiency. Blood (Abst) 62: 304a

Miletich J P, Jackson C M, Majerus P W 1978 Properties of the Factor Xa binding site on human platelets. Journal of Biological Chemistry 253: 6908–6916

Milstone J H 1964 Thrombokinase as prime activator of prothrombin: Historical perspectives and present status. Federation Proceedings 23: 742–748

Morita T, Mizuguchi J, Iwanga S 1982 The Fifth Congress of the Japanese Society on Thrombosis and Haemostasis (Abst) p 83

Nesheim M E, Taswell J B, Mann K G 1979 The contribution of bovine Factor V and Va to the activity of prothrombinase. Journal of Biological Chemistry 254: 10952–10962

Nesheim M E, Myrmel K H, Hibbard L, Mann K G 1979 Isolation and characterization of single chain bovine Factor V. Journal of Biological Chemistry 254: 508–517

Owen W G, Esmon C T 1981 Functional properties of an endothelial cell cofactor for thrombin-catalyzed activation of protein C. Journal of Biological Chemistry 256: 5532–5535

Pabinger-Fasching I, Bertina R M, Lechner K, Niessner H, Korninger C 1983 Hereditary protein C deficiency in two Austrian families. Thrombosis and Haemostasis (Abst) 50: 343

Rapaport S I 1977 Defibrination syndromes. In: Williams W J, Beutler E, Erslev A J, Rundles R W (eds) Hematology, 2nd edn. McGraw Hill, New York, p 1454–1480

Rosing J, Tans G, Govers-Riemslag J W P, Zwaal R F A, Hemker H C 1980 The role of phospholipids and Factor Va in the prothrombinase complex. Journal of Biological Chemistry 255: 274–283

Sala N, Owen W G, Collen D 1983 Functional assay of protein C in human plasma. Thrombosis and Haemostasis (Abst) 50: 352

Salem H H, Broze G J, Miletich J P, Majerus P W 1983a Human coagulation Factor Va is a cofactor for the activation of protein C. Proceedings of the National Academy of Sciences of the USA 80: 1584–1588

Salem H H, Broze G J, Miletich J P, Majerus P W 1983b The light chain of Factor Va contains the activity of Factor Va that accelerates protein C activation by thrombin. Journal of Biological Chemistry (communication) 258: 8531–8534

Salem H H, Esmon N L, Esmon C T, Majerus P W 1983c Protein C activation in the presence of coagulation Factor Va and thrombomodulin. Blood (Abst) 62: 309a

Seegers W H, McCoy L E, Groben H D, Sakuragawa N, Agrawal B B L 1972 Purification and some properties of autoprothrombin II-A: An anticoagulant perhaps also related to fibrinolysis. Thrombosis Research 1: 443–460

Seegers W H, Novoa E, Henry R L, Hassouna H I 1976 Relationship of 'New' vitamin K-dependent protein C and 'Old' autoprothrombin II-A Thrombosis Research 11: 633–642

Seligsohn U, Berger A, Abend M, Rubin L, Attias D, Zivelin A, Rapaport S I 1984 Homozygous protein C deficiency manifested by massive venous thrombosis in the newborn. New England Journal of Medicine, 310: 559–562

Sills R H, Humbert J R, Montgomery R R, Marlar R A 1983 Clinical Course and therapy of an infant with severe 'homozygous' protein C deficiency. Blood (Abst) 62: 310a

Stenflo J 1976 A new vitamin K-dependent protein: Purification from bovine plasma and preliminary characterization. Journal of Biological Chemistry 251: 355–363

Stenflo J, Fernlund P 1982 Amino acid sequence of the heavy chain of bovine protein C. Journal of Biological Chemistry 257: 12180–12190

Suzuki K, Nishioka J, Hashimoto S 1983a Protein C inhibitor: Purification from human plasma and characterization. Journal of Biological Chemistry 258: 163–168

Suzuki K, Nishioka J, Hashimoto S 1983b Characterization of protein C inhibitor purified from human plasma. Thrombosis and Haemostasis (Abst) 50: 342

Suzuki K, Nishioka J, Hashimoto S 1983d Regulation of activated protein C by thrombin-modified protein S. Journal of Biological Chemistry 94: 699–705

Suzuki K, Dahlback B, Stenflo J 1982 Thrombin-catalyzed activation of human coagulation Factor V. Journal of Biological Chemistry 257: 6556–6564

Suzuki K, Stenflo J, Dahlback B, Teodorsson B 1983c Inactivation of human coagulation Factor V by activated protein C. Journal of Biological Chemistry 258: 1914–1920

Tracy P B, Peterson J M, Nesheim M E, McDuffie F C, Mann K G 1979 Interaction of coagulation Factor V and Factor Va with platelets. Journal of Biological Chemistry 254: 10354–10361

Tracy P B, Nesheim M E, Mann K G 1981 Coordinate binding of Factor Va and Factor Xa to the unstimulated platelet. Journal of Biological Chemistry 256: 743–751

Vehar G A, Davie E W 1980 Preparation and properties of bovine Factor VIII. Biochemistry 19: 401–410

Vigano S, Mannucci P M, Solinas S, Bottasso B, D'Angelo A, Marani G 1983 Early fall of protein C during short-term anticoagulant therapy. Thrombosis and Haemostasis (Abst) 50: 310

Walker F J, Sexton P W, Esmon C T 1979 The inhibition of blood coagulation by activated protein C through the selective inactivation of activated Factor V. Biochimica et Biophysica Acta 571: 333–342

Walker F J 1980 Regulation of activated protein C by a new protein. A possible function for bovine protein S. Journal of Biological Chemistry 255: 5521–5524

Walker F J 1981 Regulation of activated protein C by protein S. The role of phospholipid in Factor Va inactivation. Journal of Biological Chemistry 256: 11128–11131

Wohl R C, Summaria L, Robbins K C 1979 Physiological activation of human fibrinolytic system. Journal of Biological Chemistry 254: 9063–9069

Zolton, R P, Seegers W H 1973 Autoprothrombin II-A: Thrombin removal and mechanism of induction of fibrinolysis. Thrombosis Research 3: 23–33

12. Monoclonal antibodies and coagulation

E. G. D. Tuddenham   A. Goodall

INTRODUCTION

Haemostasis

The complex cascade of protein interactions and cellular responses that occur following injury to a blood vessel wall and that rapidly lead to formation of a fibrin-platelet plug, has been studied intensively over many years. However, the large number of interactions, coupled with the instability and minute quantities of many of the proteins involved have long delayed a completely mechanistic understanding of haemostasis. A detailed account of these phenomena cannot be the subject of this chapter and the reader is referred to recent texts (Bloom & Thomas, 1981; Colman et al, 1982). Our purpose is to show the extent to which monoclonal antibodies are being used to illuminate the intricacies of the haemostatic process and to provide tools for purifying and defining the proteins involved.

Monoclonal antibodies

The original demonstration by Kohler and Milstein in 1975 of the production of monoclonal antibodies to sheep red cell membrane antigens heralded the beginnings

Table 12.1

Factor	McAb
Prekallikrein	−
HMW kininogen	−
XII	−
XI	−
IX	+
VIII:C	+
VIII:vWF	+
X	−
VII	−
V	+
II	+
Fibrinogen	+
Protein C	−
Plasminogen	+
XIII	−
Antithrombin III	−

+ McAb reported

of a technology that has amply lived up to their modest suggestion that hybridoma-derived antibodies 'could be valuable for medical and industrial use' (Kohler & Milstein, 1975).

The technology was rapidly applied, with great success, to the elucidation of complex cell membrane antigens. In particular, a much greater understanding of human lymphocyte diversity has been made possible (Janossy, 1982). Monoclonal antibodies to soluble proteins, however, only started to be described in any number, several years later.

Among the plasma proteins, the group of enzymes and cofactors involved in coagulation had been well studied by immunochemical techniques using both hetero e.g. (Zimmerman et al, 1971) and alloantibodies (Shapiro & Hultin, 1975). It is perhaps a little surprising, therefore, to note that the first monoclonal antibody to a coagulation factor appeared in the literature as late as 1981 (Katzmann et al, 1981a). This antibody was directed against bovine factor V and was used in the purification of this protein. Following that report, descriptions of monoclonal antibodies to seven of the 16 plasma proteins involved in haemostasis or its inhibition have appeared (Table 12.1). In addition to plasma factors, monoclonal antibodies have been raised to the membrane antigens of the platelet.

Production of monoclonal antibodies to coagulation factors

For the basic methodology of production of monoclonal antibodies the reader is referred to the review by Galfre & Milstein (1981) and to McMichael & Fabre (1982). There are, however, aspects of their production that are worth considering here.

The nature of the immunogen appears to be critical. In theory, it is quite possible to raise monoclonal antibodies to very impure antigens since the technology allows for controlled dissection of the immune response. An impressive example of this theory in practise was seen in the work of Secker et al (1980) who succeeded in raising a monoclonal antibody to α interferon from a mouse that had been injected with antigen that was only 1% pure. A survey of the literature on monoclonal antibodies raised to coagulation factors, however, demonstrates that the greatest successes have been achieved when high-purity immunogen was used. This has been the case for factors V (Katzmann et al, 1981a), IX (Goodall et al, 1982a) and in particular for factor VIII:C (Muller et al, 1981; Rotblat et al, 1983a) where immunisation with isolated VIII:C has proved much more effective than the use of the whole factor VIII complex (see below).

The primary screening methods employed for the detection of the monoclonal antibodies when first formed are also critical (see Fig. 12.1). Early work with soluble antigens, including coagulation factors used direct binding immunoradiometric assays in which the target antigen was immobilised on a solid-phase support and bound monoclonal antibodies were detected with a species-specific anti-immunoglobulin. Such assays are highly sensitive but where the target antigen is relatively impure and where the same preparation of antigen is used both for the immunisation and as the target in the detection system, antibodies that occur against the impurities will appear positive in the screening assay. An example of this phenomenon was reported by Sola et al (1982) who raised a series of antibodies to factor VIII related antigen (VIIIR:Ag) and in addition found one that was directed against fibrinogen which was presumed to be present as an impurity in their factor VIII preparation. The screening technique first described by Katzmannet et al (1981b) overcomes the specificity problem. Monoclonal antibody is first captured by a species-specific anti-immunoglobulin reagent immobilised on the solid-phase then incubated with the antigen which, if bound, is then detected with a highly specific, labelled, polyclonal antiserum. This method has been successfully employed in identifying monoclonal antibodies to porcine VIIIR: Ag (Katzmann et al, 1981b) human VIII: CAg (Rotblat et al, 1983a) and human VIIIR: Ag (Goodall et al, 1983b, 1984). In addition to the advantage of specificity afforded by this technique, it overcomes the potential problem described by Katzmann and colleagues (1981b) for VIIIR: Ag. They described a group of monoclonal antibodies that bound to porcine VIIIR: Ag when it was in the fluid phase but several of these failed to react with the antigen if it was immobilised on a solid phase. Their explanation of this phenomenon was that the epitopes on the molecule that were recognised by these monoclonal antibodies were preferentially hidden when the antigen bound to the solid-phase.

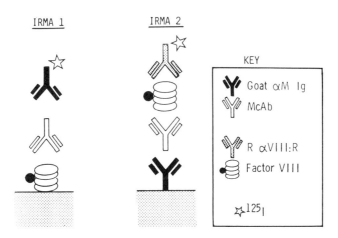

Fig. 12.1   Diagrams representing two binding assays that can be used to screen hybridomas. In these examples the antigen is factor VIII, but the systems are applicable to any soluble protein. IRMA 1 has antigen coated onto plastic (tubes or beads) to which culture supernatant is added. Monoclonals will bind to any antigen(s) present, therefore the assay is only as specific as the purity of the antigen. Adsorbed monoclonal is detected with radiolabelled (or enzyme linked) goat antimouse Ig. In IRMA 2 the solid phase bears the goat anti-mouse Ig which will capture any monoclonal from culture supernatant. Antigen is then added and allowed to react with immobilised monoclonal. Finally a specific radiolabelled antibody (allo or hetero) is added as tracer. The specificity of this system is determined by the final antibody layer.

Monoclonal antibodies that recognise functionally important epitopes on the target antigen can be detected at initial screening if their effect on the antigenic function is examined. Monoclonal antibodies that inhibit factor IX activation (Goodall et al, 1982) and human factor VIII:C function (Rotblat et al, 1983a) are examples of the power of this technique. Clearly a combination of screening techniques that incorporates both binding and funconal assays maximises the chance of detecting the full range of monoclonal antibodies raised in each fusion. It is sometimes found that monoclonal antibodies which are detected in an inhibitor assay can be negative in a specific binding assay (Rotblat et al, 1983a). Immunohistological screening can also be considered as valuable for the detection of monoclonal antibodies to factor VIIIR: Ag since the pattern of expression of this antigen in vascular endothelial cells is so characteristic. The specificity of antiplatelet antibodies can also be confirmed by this technique. A discussion of the advantages of immunohistological screening is given by Naiem et al (1982).

Applications of monoclonal antibodies to coagulation factors

The uses to which these antibodies have been put are various and are summarised in Table 12.2. Specific examples relating to the individual factors will be considered in following sections of this chapter but it is relevant at this juncture to outline some general principles of their use and to discuss the desired properties of monoclonal antibodies for such applications.

Table 12.2 Applications of monoclonal antibodies to coagulation factors

---

Immunochemistry
Topological mapping of epitopes, correlation with function
Study of activation neoantigens

Immunopurification
High-purity proteins obtained for biochemical and functional studies

Immunodepletion
Specific removal of individual factors from normal plasma allows the preparation of 'artificial substrates' for specific coagulation assays

Immunoassay
Specificity of McAbs for distinct antigenic epitopes allows the precise and sensitive detection of trace coagulant proteins

Immunodiagnosis
The presence or absence of specific, functional antigenic epitopes can be probed in pathological variant proteins

Immunolocalisation
Detection of the presence of coagulation factors in tissue

Functional/biochemical studies

One of the primary applications of monoclonal antibodies in coagulation research is to further the investigation of the structure of individual coagulation factors and to study their interactions. Since monoclonal antibodies are, by definition, biochemically homogeneous and specific for single antigenic epitopes they can be used as probes for unique antigenic sites. The multiple epitope reactivity present in even the most specific of polyclonal antisera limits the dissection of the antigenic molecule. Where monoclonal antibodies exert an effect on the function of the antigenic molecule, very precise information can be forthcoming as will be discussed later in this chapter. In addition, linking functional effects to electroblotting techniques (Burnette, 1981) (the so-called 'Western blot') antigenic epitopes could be mapped by localising the binding of the monoclonals to the subunits of complex macromolecular coagulation proteins.

Immunoaffinity purification/immunodepletion

Many coagulation factors such as factor VIII:C and factor IX are trace proteins and are thus difficult to isolate as homogeneous preparations by conventional separation methods (Jackson & Nemerson, 1980; Miletich et al, 1980). The study of the functional and biochemical properties of such proteins has therefore been somewhat restricted.

The combined advantages of specificity and unlimited quantity, offered by monoclonal reagents, has made feasible the immunoaffinity purification of coagulation factors in sufficient quantities for analysis. Homogeneous preparations of factor V (Katzmann et al, 1981a) and of human factor VIII:C (Fulcher & Zimmerman, 1982; Rotblat et al, 1983b) have been produced in this way.

Monoclonal antibodies can be selected for this purpose, not only on the basis of their specificity but also for their affinity/avidity for the particular antigenic epitope. The correct antibody affinity for such a purpose would be one that is not so great as to render the antigen irremovable from the immunoabsorbant under non-denaturing conditions, but not so weak as to give low antigen yields.

Antibodies with high affinities for their target antigens can, however, prove most useful as immunoabsorbants for the removal of individual coagulation factors from plasma. This can yield artificially produced 'deficient plasma' for use in one-stage diagnostic coagulation assays, as has been demonstrated for factor IX (Goodall et al, 1982a). Such plasmas which are essential for the diagnosis and clinical monitoring of various bleeding disorders are normally only obtainable from severely affected patients. This source is becoming increasingly limited, due to the successful maintenance therapy given to these individuals.

Immunoassays

Several examples of immunoassays have been described that substitute monoclonal antibodies for polyclonal antisera (Muller et al, 1981; Brown et al, 1983; Kessel & Langford, 1983; Ogata et al, 1983; Rotblat et al, 1983a; Stel et al, 1983a; Goodall et al, 1983, 1984). The advantages of using monoclonal reagents are that they offer a greater degree of specificity and reproducibility. However, the antigenic variability seen in many of the coagulation disorders implies that the selection of reagents will be critical.

Antibodies that recognise functionally important antigenic epitopes could lead to assays that detect functionally active antigens in patient's plasma but there is evidence as will be discussed below, that often several discrete antigenic epitopes can be involved in a functional site. This could be overcome by the judicious selection of individual antibodies, or the compilation of controlled 'cocktails' of two or more antibodies. Monoclonal-based assays can highlight antigenic variants as has been seen with a semimonoclonal antibody assay for VIII:CAg (Rotblat et al, 1983a) in which plasma that was partially deficient in VIII:CAg (as detected in a one-site IRMA using an alloantiserum) proved totally deficient when tested with the monoclonal antibody. Whilst the selection of the correct antigenic specificity is critical, the antibody affinity/avidity and the biochemical constitution of the individual monoclonal antibodies are also important.

For many reasons, which are outlined in Table 12.3, monoclonal antibodies are suited for use in immunoradiometric assays (i.e. labelled antibody assays). The problems associated with the routine purification and labelling of antigen as required for radioimmunoassays are then overcome. However, the affinity of the monoclonal antibody needs to be high to allow sufficient 'signal' binding since individual monoclonals do not have the advantages of multiple epitope recognition, present in polyclonal antisera. In addition, some monoclonal antibodies prove unsuitable for labelling in that the addition of a radio or enzyme tracer inactivates antibody function due to individual biochemical composition. Technical modifications can overcome this problem in most but not all cases. In general, monoclonal reagents are ineffective in immunoprecipitation systems, either in fluid-phase or in gel-based immuno-diffusion assays, such as the Laurell-rocket immunoelectrophoresis technique, common in coagulation laboratories. This is due to the monospecificity of the antibodies which prevents the formation of the large immune complexes needed to obtain a precipitate. Precipitation reactions can be obtained when for example, an IgM class antibody is used or if the antibody recognises a repeated epitope on the antigenic molecule. However, IgM antibodies tend to be relatively unstable and of low affinity and immunoprecipitation with monoclonal antibodies is invariably weak.

Table 12.3   The use of monoclonal antibodies in immunoassays

Assay design	Advantages of McAbs	Disadvantages of McAbs
Fluid-phase RIA	Specificity Unlimited quantity	Small immune complexes
Solid-phase RIA	Specificity Unlimited quantity	
Fluid-phase IRMA	Specificity Unlimited quantity	Small immune complexes thus separation of Ag-Ab complexes can only be achieved with large molecular weight antigens
Solid-phase IRMA	Specificity Unlimited quantity	Restricted epitope recognition can lead to low tracer binding
	Non-competing McAbs can be used on each site allowing assay to be performed more rapidly in a single step	

In general the most suitable immunoassay system for use with monoclonal antibodies is the two-site, solid-phase IRMA. An advantage of using monoclonal antibodies in such an assay, over the use of comparable polyclonal antisera, is that non-competing monoclonal antibodies can be selected that recognise different antigenic epitopes. A complementary use of two or more such antibodies on either the solid-phase or as 'tracer' means that the assay can be performed in a single incubation in which antigen, tracer antibody and solid-phase antibody are mixed (Goodall et al, 1982b). In addition to the simplification of the assay by the removal of one washing and incubation step, this one-step method can also lead to a more rapid assay with the same degree of antigen sensitivity as is obtained in a lengthier two-step process (Goodall, 1983).

Immunohistology
High-affinity, specific monoclonal reagents can be applied to the immunolocalisation of hitherto elusive proteins. This technique using polyclonal antibodies to VIII: Ag has demonstrated this protein in the vascular endothelium (Bloom et al, 1973; Hoyer et al, 1973; Jaffe, 1977) in megakaryocytes (Nachman et al, 1977; Rabellino et al, 1981) and the storage of this protein in platelets (Howard et al, 1974; Nachman & Jaffe, 1975). Lack of specific antisera has, however, hindered the detection of any of the other coagulation proteins in tissue. An interesting report has appeared of the use of a monoclonal antibody for the detection of VIII: CAg in the sinusoidal endothelial cells of normal human liver (Stel et al, 1983b). The site of synthesis of this protein has been a mystery for many years and studies on the products from isolated or perfused organs have been inconclusive in pinpointing the exact site or sites of production of VIII: C (Bloom, 1979). It is, however, noteworthy that although high affinity antibodies exist to many of the coagulation factors that we know from animal studies

to be synthesised in the liver (e.g. factors IX and V) no report has appeared of the immunolocalisation of these proteins in any tissue. Whether this is due to low concentration or to sequestration of the nascent proteins in the hepatocyte in a form that is unavailable to the antibodies, is unresolved at present.

Therapeutic applications of monoclonal antibodies
No reports of the direct or indirect use of monoclonal antibodies in the therapy of haemostatic disorders has appeared but it is worthwhile speculating on the potential for these reagents in this context. Clearly immunopurification of specific coagulation factors, for use in deficient patients could offer an advantage over currently used fractionation methods which give, at best a purity of 1%. Affinity purification would also help to eliminate the viral and other risk factors that can occur in clinical concentrate and cryoprecipitate.

Conceivably anti-idiotype monoclonals might be used to remove circulating antibodies to factor VIII:C that arise spontaneously (autoantibody) or in some treated haemophiliacs (alloantibody).

Fibrinogen

The first monoclonal antibody specific to human fibrinogen (Fg) was reported by Kennel and colleagues in 1981. These workers immunised rats with fragment D (Fg-D) hoping to obtain antibody specific to neoantigens unique to this plasmin degradation product. Hybridomas were obtained by fusion with mouse myeloma and cultures screened for binding to plastic adsorbed fragment D. Some monoclonal antibodies were obtained that reacted equally with native Fg and Fg-D, and others that reacted preferentially with Fg-D. Unfortunately the latter were not absolutely specific to Fg-D and so could not be used to assay Fg degradation products in plasma, but the direction of future work was clearly signposted.

The following year Wilner and co-workers (1982) described three monoclonals to human fibrinogen (1 IgM and 2 IgG$_1$) derived from mouse–mouse hybridomas. Two of these (both IgG) were shown to bind to the D fragment produced by plasmin cleavage of fibrinogen or fibrin but one of them failed to bind to fragment D derived from cross-linked fibrin, although they were evidently directed at closely linked epitopes. It appeared that the combining sites were lost upon reduction of disulphide bridges, suggesting conformational specificity of these antibodies. The IgM antibody bound only to fibrinogen and not to cleavage products.

Another monoclonal antibody to human fibrinogen was produced as a by-product in a fusion from a mouse immunised with factor VIII by Sola, Avner and colleagues (1982, 1983). This monoclonal antibody resembled the IgM antibody produced by Wilner in its binding characteristics and was presumed to be specific for a secondary or tertiary structural conformation since it showed no affinity for fibrinogen-derived fragments or isolated chains (Aα, Bβ or γ). Kennel and Lankford reported in the same year (1983) a solid-phase radioimmunoassay of fragment D based on two monoclonals. The solid-phase antibody was the one first described by these authors in 1981 (see above) which although of low affinity, selectively bound fragment D. The fluid phase antibody was a high-affinity monoclonal that reacted equally well with fibrinogen and fragments. Although sensitive and specific, this assay as described, could not be applied to clinical plasma samples since non-specific adsorption gave 50%

apparent cross-reactivity between Fg and FgD at 2 mg fibrinogen/ml (normal plasma range 2–4 mg/ml). Presumably the assay could be used on serum samples but no results of clinical assays were given.

The first practical clinical application of monoclonals to fibrin derivatives was demonstrated by Elms, Bunce and colleagues (1983). In a very interesting paper they described an assay virtually specific for plasminolytic products of cross-linked fibrin and particularly the D dimer. This assay was based on a non-selective monoclonal to fibrin and degradation products as solid phase with a tracer antibody specific to D dimer and larger complexes containing cross-linked gamma chains.

With this assay 30 out of 30 serum samples from patients with disseminated intravascular coagulation were found to contain excessive amounts of D dimer, as did the majority of samples from patients with venous thrombosis and/or embolism. The assay was more specific diagnostically than a conventional FDP assay in these groups of patients, and was found helpful in distinguishing fibrinolysis from fibrinogenolysis.

Monoclonal antibodies to a α chain regions of human fibrinogen were elegantly characterised by Ehrlich and colleagues (1983). The immunogen used was a CNBr cleavage fragment of cross-linked α chain polymers. The epitopic binding sites of two monoclonals were localised to within Aα 540–544 and Aα 259–276 respectively, sites involved in polymerisation of fibrin. Both epitopes were evidently sequence determined in contrast to the conformational binding sites of all previously described monoclonals to fibrinogen. These and similar well-defined monoclonals should prove useful as probes of structure function relationships. In their exhaustive review of surface markers of fibrinogen and derivatives revealed by antibody probes, Plow & Edgington (1982) made the following prediction. 'The use of hybridoma antibodies will greatly facilitate interpretation of data for the basic molecular studies and should also facilitate the development of reagents for clinical use.' Clearly, this is already coming to pass.

Prothrombin

A large number of mouse hybridomas secreting antibody-specific for human prothrombin were produced in fusions performed by Lewis and the Furies (1983). Eight of these were selected for cloning and all proved to produce antibody-specific for prothrombin fragment 1 — known to be the most immunogenic portion of the molecule. One of the antibodies proved to be directed at a conformation specifically stabilised by calcium ions. Thus it bound no prothrombin in the absence of calcium, and binding reached saturation at 0.2 mM Ca^{++}. Prothrombin bound to immobilised monoclonal with this characteristic could be totally eluted with EDTA. The remaining seven monoclonals showed no calcium dependence of binding but all showed no or greatly reduced binding of descarboxy prothrombin, indicating that the digamma carboxy glutamate residues found in the N terminal region of the protein were involved in all the binding epitopes. Calcium-dependent conformations of the vitamin K-dependent coagulation factors are of great interest, since they are involved in phospholipid binding essential for normal function. Antibodies to such sites should prove useful for functional studies and also offer a convenient method of purification since immunoaffinity adsorbed protein can be eluted by EDTA without denaturation and consequent loss of enzymatic function.

Another group of monoclonals to prothrombin were raised by Lee et al (1983).

Factor V

An antibody specific for coagulation factor V was one of the first reported monoclonals specific for a coagulation factor and was described by Katzmann and colleagues in 1981 (Katzmann et al, 1981a). The antibody was used as an immunoaffinity reagent to complete the purification of the human protein that hitherto had only been partially purified. Fully activatable factor V could be eluted from Sepharose-bound monoclonal under mild conditions (1.2 M NaCl) in 50% yield with over 1000-fold enhancement of purity in a single step. The few remaining contaminants were removed by subsequent affinity chromatography on phyl sepharose.

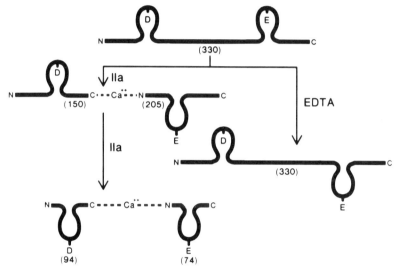

Fig. 12.2 Scheme to show interaction of monoclonal antibodies α_2D and α_2E with their respective epitopes D and E, located on the D chain and E chain regions of bovine factor V. Prior to modification by thrombin (IIa) or EDTA the epitopes are concealed. Apparent molecular weights ($\times 10^{-3}$) are indicated. Upon proteolytic activation by IIa first E then D are exposed and can bind α_2E and α_2D. Calcium chelation by EDTA exposed only epitope E. (Reproduced with permission from Foster et al, 1983a.)

The same group at the Mayo (Foster et al, 1982) next reported on studies in which 13 monoclonal antibodies to bovine factor V and/or factor Va were raised. One of these monoclonals bound only V and not thrombin-activated V (Va). The others reacted either equally well or in varying degrees with V and Va. Inhibition of biological activity likewise varied from none to total in antibody from different clones. Studies with antibody from four of these clones were reported on in two further papers from this group (Tucker et al, 1983; Foster et al, 1983a). Clone IB6 produced an antibody designated α_1 D binding to the 94K subunit (D chain) and clone IIC3 an antibody called α_1E binding to the 74K subunit (E chain). Using these antibodies and dansylated factor Xa, it was shown that the E chain of factor Va contains the binding site for factor Xa, since this interaction was perturbed by the E-chain specific monoclonal α_1E and not by α_1D. Both of these antibodies bound equally well to procofactor V and to the thrombin-activated derivative Va. Two other antibodies were described in the second paper, α_2D and α_2E, that reacted only with thrombin-modified factor V (see Fig. 12.2). Since the epitope for α_2D was localised to the NH$_2$

terminal region of the D chain and α_2E to the CO OH terminal of the E chain it could be concluded that these two regions were conformationally modified by the action of thrombin. Calcium chelation with EDTA also exposed the α_2E but not the α_2D combining site. Also during 1983 (Foster et al, 1983b) the Mayo group reported on 10 new monoclonals to human factor V and further observations using their original monoclonal αHV1 (op. cit.) that enabled the protein to be purified. The specificities ranged from exclusive binding to factor V to preferential binding to Va. The epitope for αHV1 was shown to be located on the lighter of the two thrombin-derived chains of Va (70K as compared to 93K) which could be dissociated with EDTA leaving the 70K chain bound to immobilised antibody. Thus a relatively simple experiment with this monoclonal provided considerable insight into the structure of thrombin activated human factor V. The authors concluded that these monoclonal antibodies would be '. . . of further use as biospecific immunochemical probes of the structure and function of human factor V and tools for the assessment of the role of factor V under normal and pathologic conditions'.

Factor VIII:C
Extensive efforts have been directed towards raising monoclonals to the procoagulant part of the factor VIII complex (VIII:C). The reasons for this are not far to seek. VIII:C is deficient in the two commonest types of inherited bleeding disorder — haemophilia A and von Willebrand's disease. Although antibodies to VIII related antigen (VIIIR:Ag) can be readily raised in rabbits or emus (heteroantibody), the only potent specific antibodies to VIII:C available were those occurring in a proportion of haemophiliacs (isoantibody) and rarely in previously normal individuals (autoantibody). Furthermore, the iso- and autoantibodies were seldom of high enough titre to be used in radiometric assays for VIII:C antigen. Muller and colleagues (1981) succeeded in isolating a clone-making antibody IB3 that potently inhibited VIII:C by coagulation assay. The mice had been immunised with immunoaffinity purified VIII:C contaminated by only traces of VIIIR:Ag. The antibody was of mixed heavy chain subtype — IgG$_1$ and IgG$_2$b and only partially destroyed VIII:C activity even at low titre. A kinetic experiment to test the effect of IB3 on Xa generation by purified IXa and whole factor VIII complex showed an increased lag phase suggesting an effect of the antibody on the activation of VIII:C. IB3 could also be used as the first-phase antibody in a two-site IRMA technique where the tracer was a radiolabelled human anti VIII:C. The assay gave similar results to those obtained with a standard two-site VIII:CAg assay except that no VIII:CAg binding was found in serum. This supports the idea that the monoclonal was directed against a thrombin-sensitive epitope.

The following year Sola and colleagues (1982) immunised with whole factor VIII and obtained three clones making antibody to VIIIR.Ag, three against VIII:C and one against fibrinogen. Specificity of the anti-VIII:C monoclonals was proved by 100% inhibition of VIII:C activity. No specific application of these particular monoclonals has been described to date. Also in 1982, Fass and colleagues obtained three monoclonal antibodies to porcine VIII:C which they used to further purify VIII:C to a final specific activity of $6\,u/\mu g$ or 3×10^5-fold over plasma. The immunogen used was whole porcine factor VIII but the booster dose prefusion was VIII:C deficient in von Willebrand factor. Two of these antibodies partly inhibited VIII:C activity, and two (not the same pair) absorbed VIII:C when immobilised from partly purified VIII:C in 0.25 M CaCl$_2$. Furthermore, active VIII:C could be eluted from the non-inhibitor monoclonal-linked to Sepharose with 50% ethylene glycol. The material so eluted had the specific activity mentioned above and on SDS polyacrylamide gel electrophoresis consisted of three bands mol. wt. 166 000, 130 000 and 76 000. The two higher molecular weight bands were thrombin sensitive. Elution of bound VIII:C from the monoclonal antibody–Sepharose column with EDTA yielded the two higher molecular weight protein bands. Subsequent elution with ethylene glycol recover the 76 000 mol. wt. band alone. These experiments showed for the first time the constitution of pure porcine VIII:C and that the three chains were held together by calcium-dependent interactions. The precise stoichiometry of these interactions could not be stated with certainty due to doubts about partial proteolysis during purification.

Fulcher & Zimmerman (1983) immunised mice with VIII:C of high purity and obtained a monoclonal antibody (IgG$_1$) with weak inhibitory activity but which bound most of the protein from their highly purified VIII:C preparation (2000 u/mg). This was used as a criterion to distinguish VIII:C protein bands on SDS PAGE from those due to contaminants. The binding epitope involved was thrombin sensitive. Since proteins could only be eluted from immobilised monoclonal at 3 M Na SCN the evidence for binding was necessarily subtractive, no biological activity being present in the eluate. By this logic they deduced that the protein corresponding to VIII:C activity consisted of multiple molecular weight forms ranging from a doublet at 79–80 000 up to a band at 188 000 with at least 6 bands of intermediate molecular weight.

Brown and colleagues (1983) immunised mice with whole factor VIII and obtained only one clone out of 1400 that inhibited VIII:C. This had an apparent Bethesda inhibitor titre of 1410 units/mg IgG and was of subclass IgG$_1$K. Like previously described monoclonals to VIII:C (except Sola et al, 1982) it did not completely neutralise VIII:C activity at any titre. It was very slow-acting and gave 10-fold greater inhibition after 18 hours incubation at 37°C than after the standard 2 hours in the Bethesda assay. Fab fragments were prepared and radiolabelled for competitive binding studies which showed no displacement of the monoclonal by either a haemophilic or an acquired antibody to VIII:C. The labelled Fab could be used after affinity purification in a one-site IRMA for VIII:CAg. A two-site IRMA using haemophilic antibody as first phase was also set up and used to assay VIII:CAg in haemophilic and normal plasma. Results showed close correlation between VIII:C and VIII:CAg in 10 haemophilic plasmas. In both one- and two-site assays serum gave higher binding than plasma. Thrombin pretreatment of purified VIII increased the rate of binding of labelled monoclonal. These results suggest that this monoclonal binds preferentially to a neoantigen exposed to thrombin similar to some of the monoclonals to bovine and human factor V referred to above. A very interesting application of the monoclonal was to use the binding data to derive an independent estimate of the molecular weights of VIII:C in plasma at 345 000.

In marked contrast to the very large-scale screening needed to detect a single clone in the paper just discussed, was the report of nine monoclonals from a single fusion from Rotblat et al (1983a). The mouse had been immunised with highly purified VIII:C (specific activity 1598 units/mg) and cultures were screened by both an inhibitor and a binding type assay. All positive clones were specific for VIII:C and some were very potent inhibitors of the biological activity, e.g. 7151 Bethesda units/mg IgG. Several of these antibodies could be used as the first phase in a two-site IRMA where the second phase labelled antibody was derived from a haemophilic inhibitor. VIII:CAg in 19 haemophilic plasmas was measured both by epitope specific two-site assay and by fluid-phase assay using the haemophilic antibody alone. VIII:CAg values correlated well in these assays in all except two haemophilic samples which were CRM^+ by one-site but CRM^- by two-site assay indicating epitope deletion or alteration at the site defined by the first-phase monoclonal. Blocking studies indicated little or no cross-reactivity between these monoclonals. In subsequent work (Rotblat et al, in press) one of the monoclonals (C8) has been used to purify VIII:C to homogeneity, and five have been used in protein blotting studies to define epitope localisation within protein subunits.

Finally, in 1983, Stel and co-workers (Stel et al, 1983a) described sensitive VIII:CAg assays based solely on six monoclonals to VIII:C. One system adopted was to immobilise three different monoclonals on Sepharose beads as the immunoadsorbent and use a fourth labelled monoclonal as the radiotracer. A lower limit of sensitivity of 0.0005 u/ml plasma is claimed for this assay, i.e. comparable to the best sensitivity previously reported with haemophilic antibody. Only two out of 13 severe haemophilic plasmas (VIII:C < 0.01 u/ml) appeared truly CRM negative by this assay.

Stel et al (1983b) have also used one of these monoclonals to study immunohistological localisation of VIII:CAg and claim that the sinusoidal lining endothelial cells of the liver are positive in normal but negative in haemophilic liver sections. This exciting observation remains to be confirmed by other workers or with different monoclonals.

Monoclonal antibodies to factor VIII:C proved to be extremely useful and probably indispensable during the recently announced successful production of factor VIII by 'genetic engineering'[1]. Thus, they were used to purify the protein from blood, to identify the subunits of the natural product by 'Western blotting', to identify the protein produced in bacteria from a partial clone and to prove the identity of biosynthetic factor VIII made in mammalian tissue culture.

Factor IX

Human factor IX was purified to homogeneity and used to raise a series of monoclonals, the first report of which appeared in 1982 (Goodall et al, 1982a). A monoclonal-designated RFF-IX/1 was shown to potently inhibit factor IX alone and when immobilised to efficiently remove factor IX from whole plasma. This observation was utilised in the practical demonstration of a method of making factor IX deficient plasma from normal plasma, that could be used as substrate in the one-stage factor IX activity assay. Subsequent work (Goodall et al, 1983) has shown the use of this antibody in purification of factor IX and also in monoclonal-based assays for factor IX antigen (Mikami et al, in preparation).

Bertina and van der Linden (1982) reported briefly without details that they had isolated a monoclonal to factor IX which bound to all 26 factor IX variants tested but to two of these with much-reduced affinity compared to the other 24. Thompson

[1] A joint project of Genentech Inc., San Francisco, Speywood Laboratories, Wrexham and the Haemophilia Centre, Department of Haematology, Royal Free Hospital School of Medicine, London.

(1983) described a monoclonal directed to an epitope on the heavy chain of factor IXa. The monoclonal was used as the solid-phase absorbent in a two-site IRMA with ^{125}I goat antifactor IX as tracer. Three variant factor IX molecules were identified in plasma of Christmas disease patients that contained 100 to 500 times as much IX:Ag detected by polyclonal as by monoclonal IRMA. It was proposed that these variants have an amino acid substitution affecting epitope recognition between residues 188 and 359 (the heavy chain region of factor IX).

Platelets

The attention of those raising monoclonal antibodies to platelets has centred around the membrane glycoproteins I, II and III (McGregor et al, 1983). Several groups have described monoclonal antibodies that exert effects on platelet function via their binding to one or other of these glycoprotein complexes. Such data has reinforced the theory of platelet function that had been previously deduced from observation of platelet disorders and biochemical and immunochemical studies using polyclonal antisera (Berndt & Phillips, 1981). Much of this work has been well reviewed by Tobelem et al (1982). A summary of the reactivities of published monoclonal antibodies against platelet membrane antigens is given in Table 12.4.

Findings from studies with these antibodies are, in accord with the concept that platelet membrane glycoprotein Ib (GP Ib) which is lacking in Bernard–Soulier syndrome, is the receptor for VIII:vWF following ristocetin activation. The GP IIb/IIIa complex which is lacking from the platelet membrane in Glanzmann's thrombasthenia, forms the fibrinogen binding site following thrombin activation. VIII:vWF also binds to this antigen complex following thrombin treatment but this binding is blocked by fibrinogen.

The first description of a monoclonal antibody to platelet membrane glycoproteins was the AN 51 antibody produced in Oxford which was shown to bind to GP I (McMichael et al, 1981). This antibody failed to bind to platelets from patients with Bernard–Soulier syndrome but reacted normally with thrombasthenic platelets. Studies of its effects on platelet function showed that it blocked ristocetin-induced platelet aggregation and inhibited ristocetin-induced VIII:vWF binding (Ruan et al, 1981). It was also seen to inhibit platelet subendothelium binding. AN 51 had no effect, however, on platelet aggregation induced by ADP, thrombin or collagen.

This antibody, plus a second monoclonal that reacted with the GP IIb/IIIa complex have been of use in studying the megakaryocyte/platelet lineage. In brief, the GP IIb/IIIa complex is seen to appear early in megakaryocyte maturation whilst the GP I protein is only seen on mature megakaryocytes and platelets (Vainchenker et al, 1982). The presence of the IIb/IIIa complex on megakaryocytes has been used by Damiani et al (1983) to immunopurify megakaryocytes from bone marrow.

Montgomery et al (1983) have used two monoclonal antibodies; one directed against GP Ib, which is potent inhibitor of both ristocetin-induced platelet aggregation and VIII:vWF binding, and one directed against the GP IIa/IIIb complex, to diagnose, respectively, Bernard–Soulier syndrome and Glanzmann's thrombasthenia.

Thiagarajan et al (1983) have described various monoclonal antibodies, two of which are directed against the same epitope on the IIb/IIIa complex. Both totally blocked aggregation induced by collagen. They also inhibited the second wave of ADP-induced aggregation, and gave partial inhibition of epinephrine-induced

Table 12.4

McAb	Ag	Inhibition of aggregation by:					Inhibition of binding of:		Binding to platelets from patients with:		References
		Ris	Thr	Col	ADP	Epi	VIII:vWF	Fib	BSS	GT	
AN 51	GPI	+	−	−	−		+		−	+	Ruan et al, 1981; McMichael et al, 1981
AP1	GPIb	+					+		−	+	Montgomery et al, 1983
AP2	GPIIb/IIIa								+	−	
B2.12	GPIIb/IIIa	−		+	+	+		+	+	−	Thiagarajan et al, 1983;
B59.2	GPIIb/IIIa	−									
B37.3	GPIIb/IIIa	−		−	−	−		−	+		di Minnoet et al, 1983
A₂A₉	GPIIb/IIIa	−	+	+	+	+		+			Bennet et al 1983
6DI	GPIb	+					+	−	−		Coller et al, 1983a
10E5	GPIIb/IIIa	−	+	±	+	+		+			Coller et al, 1983b
Tab	GPIIb/IIIa	−		−	−			−			McEver et al, 1983
T10	GPIIb/IIIa	−	−	+	+			+			

Ris = ristocetin, Thr = thrombin, Col = collagen, Epi = epinephrine, Fib = fibrinogen.
BSS = Bernard–Soulier syndrome, GT = Glanzmann's thrombasthenia.

aggregation. Both antibodies were negative on platelets from patients with Glanzmann's thrombasthenia. One of these antibodies was shown by di Minno et al (1983) to block ADP, collagen and arachidonic acid-induced binding of fibrinogen as well as blocking secretion caused by these agents. No effect was seen, however, on thromboxane-B_2 synthesis.

A third antibody, described by Thiagarajan et al (1983), which also did not react with thrombasthenic platelets, had no effect on function. Antibody B1.12 which is an IgG_1-class monoclonal that binds to platelets and 20% of peripheral blood lymphocytes produced marked platelet aggregation in a calcium-dependent reaction. This aggregation could be blocked with the inhibitory anti-GP IIb/IIIa antibodies.

The role of the GP IIb/IIIa complex in fibrinogen binding as an important step in platelet aggregation has also been confirmed by Bennett et al (1983). They describe a monoclonal antibody that blocks fibrinogen binding to ADP-stimulated platelets. This antibody inhibited platelet aggregation induced by ADP, epinephrine and thrombin. On immunoprecipitation it was seen to bind a complex of proteins with molecular weights attributable to the IIb/IIIa complex. Interestingly, however, this antibody, though blocking fibrinogen binding, had no effect on secretion, unlike the reagents described previously. Multiple fibrinogen binding sites must exist on the GP IIb/IIIa complex that play different roles in platelet function.

Two studies on the platelet membrane glycoproteins are described by Coller et al. In their first study (Coller et al, 1983a) they reported a monoclonal antibody that blocked ristocetin- and bovine von Willebrand factor-induced platelet aggregation and prevented the binding of VIII : vWF to ristocetin-treated platelets. This antibody also decreased platelet retention. Immunoprecipitation showed it to react with a membrane antigen whose size approximated to that of GP Ib. Platelets from two patients with Bernard–Soulier syndrome did not bind this antibody.

In the complementary study Coller et al (1983b) described a monoclonal that blocked ADP, thrombin and epinephrine-induced aggregation. It inhibited fibrinogen binding to ADP-stimulated platelets, blocked secretion, and reacted very poorly with thrombasthenic platelets. It also markedly inhibited platelet–glass interactions. By contrast to their first antibody, this monoclonal was without effect on ristocetin-induced aggregation. Immunoprecipitation and immunopurification studies indicated the antigen recognised by this antibody was the GP IIb/IIIa complex.

Two interesting monoclonal reagents are described by McEver and co-workers (1983). Both of these antibodies bound to the IIb/IIIa complex as demonstrated in immunoprecipitation studies. One (T10) was capable of totally inhibiting ADP-induced platelet aggregation whilst the other (Tab) had no effect on this function. Analysis of the epitope binding characteristics of these two antibodies by crossed-immunoelectrophoresis indicated that the non-inhibitory antibody, Tab, bound to glycoprotein IIb whilst the inhibitory antibody, T10 failed to bind to the dissociated complex, suggesting that this functional epitope was conformationally determined, that is expressed only when the glycoprotein complex was intact.

Factor VIII-von Willebrand factor/factor VIII-related antigen

Several groups have reported monoclonal antibodies to human or porcine VIII: vWF. The group at the Mayo Clinic (Katzmann et al, 1981b), described 20 monoclonals to porcine VIIIR: Ag half of which cross-reacted with human factor VIIIR: Ag. Of these cross-reacting monoclonal antibodies, two were capable of inhibiting platelet aggregating factor (PAF) and ristocetin-induced porcine platelet aggregation though they were clearly directed against different antigenic epitopes. However, neither had any effect on ristocetin-induced human platelet aggregation. Thus, at least part of this functionally-important domain is antigenically dissimilar in porcine and human VIIIR:Ag. These antibodies did not produce in vivo effects to correlate with the in vitro inhibition (Bowie et al, 1983). The reason for this poor correlation could be because different sites on the porcine VIII:vWF molecule may be involved in ristocetin cofactor activity and its mediation of the in vitro bleeding time. It is thought that a monoclonal antibody directed against a protein can recognise a sequence of approximately six amino acids. Such an epitope could therefore comprise only a minute portion of the functional site or sites on the very large VIIIR:Ag molecule.

The first published report of monoclonal antibodies raised against human VIII:vWF was from Sola and her colleagues (Sola et al, 1982). Seven antibodies were described that bound to VIII:vWF which had been immobilised on a solid-phase. Of these, three had a partial and additive effect on ristocetin-induced platelet aggregation. However, complete inhibition was not seen and it can be concluded that these interesting reagents are directed against epitopes on the VIIIR:Ag molecule only weakly associated with its platelet binding activity.

Ogata and others (Ogata et al, 1983) described one antihuman VIII:vWF monoclonal antibody that blocks ristocetin-induced platelet aggregation. This antibody has a partial inhibitory effect on platelet retention by glass beads and clearly recognises an important functional epitope on the molecule. Antibodies with similar reactivities have been obtained in the author's laboratory (Goodall et al, 1983, 1984). However, the application of these reagents to the immunoradiometric detection of VIIIR:Ag in either a two-site (Ogata et al, 1983) or one-site assay (Goodall et al, 1983) gave slightly different findings. Both antibodies yielded values for VIIIR:Ag in normal subjects that correlated well with functionally-active VIII:vWF. However, Ogata's antibodies showed some discrepancy between VIIIR:Ag and VIII:vWF activity levels in the plasma from patients with von Willebrand's disease, in contrast to our own findings (Fig. 12.3).

A preliminary report from Sultan's group indicates that their recently produced monoclonal antibodies, which inhibit ristocetin-induced platelet aggregation, when used to detect VIIIR:Ag gave values that did not correlate with the ristocetin cofactor assay (Sultan et al, 1983).

From these data, it is probable that several antigenic epitopes are involved in the binding of VIII:vWF to ristocetin-activated platelets.

Platelet retention by glass beads is an indicator of adhesion (albeit to a non-physiological surface) and thus there appears to be a correlation between the VIII:vWF sites involved in both ristocetin-induced platelet aggregation and platelet adhesion since one monoclonal can inhibit both (Ogata et al, 1983; Goodall et al,

Fig. 12.3
A = VIII:vWF vs VIIIR:Ag measured in the one-site IRMA using RFF-VIII:R/2 for normals (●) and patients with vWD (○) (all types).
B = VIII:vWF vs VIIIR:Ag measured in the two-site IRMA using a monoclonal antibody reported by Ogata et al (1983): for normals (●) and patients with vWD (○). Data redrawn from op. cit.
r = correlation coefficient for von Willebrand's disease plasma data.

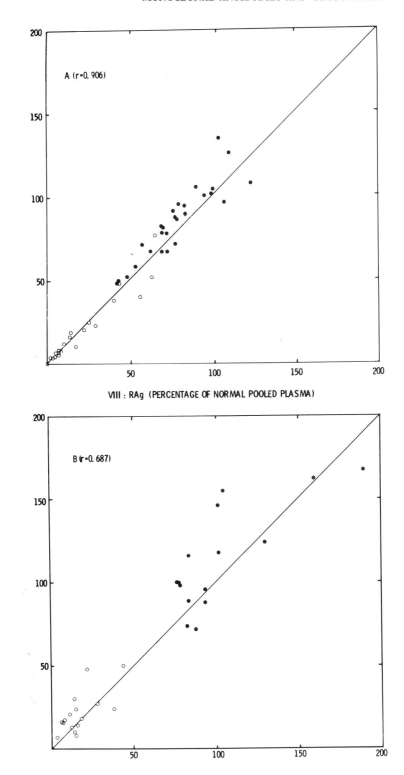

VIII : RAg (PERCENTAGE OF NORMAL POOLED PLASMA)

1984). However, Meyer (Meyer et al, 1981) reports a group of antibodies that have no effect on ristocetin-induced platelet aggregation but inhibit platelet subendothelial adhesion in a Baumgartner perfusion system (Weiss et al, 1978).

By contrast, von Mourik's group have obtained monoclonal antibodies which block both platelet aggregation and adhesion. The effects of several of these antibodies on platelet adhesion have been studied. A preliminary report (Stel et al, 1983c) suggests there are at least two separate regions on the VIII:vWF molecule that are involved in binding, one to the vascular substratum and the other to the adhering platelet.

A recent study (Nokes et al, 1984) has demonstrated two distinct platelet binding sites on the VIII:vWF molecule, by showing that different monoclonal antibodies that inhibit respectively ristocetin-induced and thrombin-induced aggregation can also each block VIII:vWF binding to platelets.

The use of monoclonal antibodies to VIIIR:Ag as immunoabsorbants to bind the factor VIII complex from factor VIII concentrate as part of a purification procedure for obtaining VIII:C has been described by Fulcher & Zimmermann (1982).

Most monoclonals to VIII:vWF that have been examined give the typical pattern of immunolocalisation in vascular endothelial cells in tissues and in isolated cell cultures as shown in Figure 12.4 (Naiem et al, 1982; Stel et al, 1983b; Goodall et al, 1984).

MISCELLANEOUS MONOCLONALS TO OTHER HAEMOSTATIC FACTORS

Monoclonals to human Glu-plasminogen were raised by Ploplis et al (1982). Several of these were shown to bind to specific regions of the plasminogen molecule such as kringle 1–3 or kringle 4. One monoclonal was displaceable by EACA, a significant binding region of plasminogen. The authors anticipate that monoclonals will allow them to '. . . assess the importance of various regions of plasminogen and plasmin in the many functions of these important proteins'.

Nielsen and co-workers (1983) describe a monoclonal to human plasminogen activator derived from melanoma cells. The antibody completely inhibited the plasminogen activator (HPA, 66) and could be used in a one-step purification of HPA, 66 from culture medium yielding homogeneous protein at 79% recovery.

The factor X activator of Russell's viper venom (RVV-X) was used to raise two monoclonal antibodies by Pukrittayakamee et al (1983). One antibody neutralised RVV-X preventing its activation of factor X, the other did not affect the coagulant activity. Both could be used in affinity purification of RVV-X. Clearly these antibodies could have a role as antivenoms if animal model studies give favourable results.

CONCLUDING REMARKS

As we hope this brief survey has adequately demonstrated monoclonal antibodies are now being used to solve scientific problems and overcome technical difficulties across the broad field of haemostasis. It seems inevitable that their scope will widen to include all those factors not yet used as antigens. Their availability through commercial sources will facilitate basic research and diagnostic applications increasingly over the next decade, ultimately replacing heteroantibodies entirely.

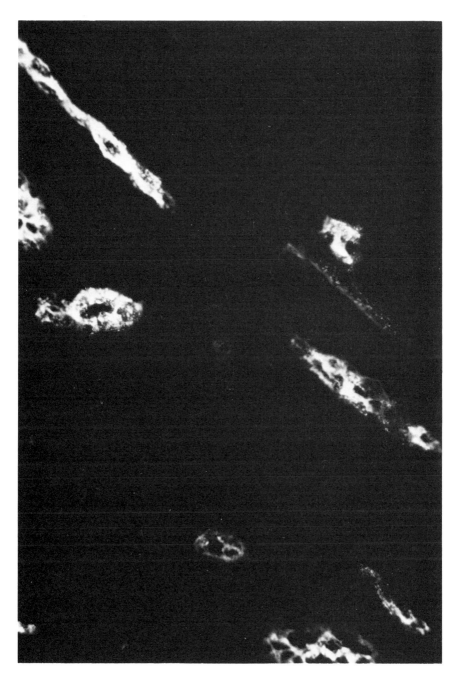

Fig. 12.4   Section of human tonsil stained with a monoclonal antibody against factor VIII-related antigen (RFF VIIIR/2). Blood vessels which have been cut transversely and longitudinally, can be visualised because of positive staining localised to endothelial cells. The granular pattern is typical of the distribution of VIIIR : Ag in these cells.

Ultrasensitive and specific antigen assays will greatly facilitate provision of antenatal diagnosis for the severe haemophilias.

One particularly striking example of the utility of these unique reagents has been their use to complete the purification of VIII:C (Rotblat et al, 1983b; Fass et al, 1982). The extension of this work that will be of the greatest importance in the near future is elucidation of the molecular biology of factor VIII:C with obvious implications for treatment of haemophilia A.

REFERENCES

Bennett J S, Hoxie J A, Leitman S F, Vilaire G, Cines D B 1983 Inhibition of fibrinogen binding to stimulated human platelets by a monoclonal antibody. Proceedings of the National Academy of Sciences of the USA (May) 80(9): 2417–2421

Berndt M C, Phillips D R 1981 Platelet membrane proteins: composition and receptor function. In: Gordon J (ed) Platelets in biology and pathology, vol 2. Elsevier/North Holland Biomedical Press, p 43

Bertina R M, Van der Linden I K 1982 Detection and classification of molecular variants of factor IX. In: Bloom A L (ed) The hemophilias. Methods in hematology. Churchill Livingstone, Edinburgh, ch 9

Bloom A L 1979 The biosynthesis of factor VIII. In: Rizza C R (ed) Congenital coagulation disorders. Clinics in Haematology, vol 8(1). W B Saunders Co Ltd, London, ch 3

Bloom A L, Giddings J C, Wilkes C D 1973 Factor VIII on the vascular intima: possible importance in haemostasis and thrombosis. Nature (London) New Biology 241: 217–221

Bloom A L, Thomas D P (eds) 1981 Haemostasis and Thrombosis. Churchill Livingstone, Edinburgh

Bowie E J, Fass D N, Katzmann J A 1983 Functional studies of Willebrand factor using monoclonal antibodies. Blood (July) 62(1): 146–151

Brown J E, Thuy L P, Carton L P, Hougie C 1983 Studies on a monoclonal antibody to human factor VIII coagulant activity, with a description of a facile two-site factor VIII coagulant antigen assay. Journal of Laboratory and Clinical Medicine (May) 101(5): 793–805

Burnette W N 1981 'Western blotting': electrophoretic transfer of proteins from sodium dodecyl sulfate–polyacrylamide gels to unmodified nitrocellulose and radiographic detection with antibody and radio-iodinated protein A. Analytical Biochemistry 112: 195–203

Coller B S, Peerschke E I, Scudder L E, Sullivan C A 1983a Studies with a murine monoclonal antibody that abolishes ristocetin-induced binding of von Willebrand factor to platelets: additional evidence in support of GP1b as a platelet receptor for von Willebrand factor. Blood 61(1): 99–110

Coller B S, Peerschke E I, Scudder L E, Sullivan C A 1983b A murine monoclonal antibody that completely blocks the binding of fibrinogen to platelets produces a thrombasthenic-like state in normal platelets and binds to glycoproteins IIb and/or IIIa. Journal of Clinical Investigation 72(1): 325–338

Colman R W, Hirsh J, Marder V J, Salzman E W (eds) Hemostasis and thrombosis. Basic principles and clinical practice. J B Lippincott Co, Philadelphia

Damiani G, Zocchi E, Fabbi M, Bargellesi A, Patrone F 1983 A monoclonal antibody to platelet glycoproteins IIb and IIIa complex: its use in purifying human megakaryocytes from sternal bone marrow aspirates for immunofluorescence studies of Ia-like antigens. Experimental Hematology 11(3): 169–177

Di Minno G, Thiagarajan P, Perussia B, Martinez J, Shapiro S, Trinchieri G, Murphy S 1983 Exposure of platelet fibrinogen-binding sites by collagen, arachidonic acid and ADP: inhibition by a monoclonal antibody to the glycoprotein IIb–IIIa complex. Blood 61(1): 140–148

Ehrlich P, Sobel J H, Moustafa Z A, Canfield R E 1983 Monoclonal antibodies to α-chain regions of human fibrinogen that participate in polymer formation. Biochemistry 22: 4184–4192

Elms M J, Bunce I H, Bundesen P G, Rylatt D B, Webber A J, Masci P P, Whitaker A N 1983 Measurement of crosslinked fibrin degradation products — an immunoassay using monoclonal antibodies. Thrombosis and Haemostasis 50: 591–594

Fass D N, Knutson G J, Katzmann J A 1982 Monoclonal antibodies to porcine factor VIII coagulant and their use in the isolation of active coagulant protein. Blood 59(3): 594–600

Foster W B, Katzmann J A, Miller R S, Nesheim M E, Mann K G 1982 Monoclonal antibodies selective for the functional states of bovine factor V and factor Va. Thrombosis Research 28(5): 649–661

Foster W B, Tucker M M, Katzmann J A, Mann K G 1983a Monoclonal antibodies selective for activated factor V. Immunochemical probes for structural transitions occurring during the thrombin-catalyzed activation of the procofactor. Journal of Biological Chemistry 258(9): 5608–5613

Foster W B, Tucker M M, Katzmann J A, Miller R S, Nesheim M E, Mann K G 1983b Monoclonal antibodies to human coagulation factor V and factor Va. Blood 61(6): 1060–1067

Fulcher C A, Zimmerman T S 1982 Characterization of the human factor VIII procoagulant protein with a heterologous precipitating antibody. Proceedings of the National Academy of Sciences of the USA 79(5): 1648–1652

Fulcher C A, Roberts J R, Zimmerman T S 1983 Thrombin proteolysis of purified factor VIII procoagulant protein: correlation of activation with generation of a specific polypeptide. Blood 61(4): 807–811

Galfre G, Milstein C 1981 Preparation of monoclonal antibodies: strategies and procedures. In: Methods in enzymology (immunochemical techniques). Academic Press, London

Goodall A H 1983 The use of monoclonal antibodies in a solid-phase immunoradioactive assay for hepatitis B surface antigen. In: Hunter W M, Comie J E T (eds) Immunoassays in clinical chemistry. Churchill Livingstone, Edinburgh, p 545–556

Goodall A H, O'Brien D P, Rawlings E, Rotblat F, Tuddenham E G D 1982a Affinity depletion and affinity purification of human factor IX by monoclonal antibodies. In: Peeters H (ed) Protides of the biological fluids. Neuroproteins, monoclonal antibodies, separation methods. Pergamon Press, Oxford, p 403–407

Goodall A H, Kemble G, O'Brien D P, Rawlings E, Rotblat F, Russell G C, Janossy G, Tuddenham E G D 1982b Preparation of factor IX deficient human plasma by immunoaffinity chromatography using a monoclonal antibody. Blood 59(3): 664–670

Goodall A H, Meek F L, Waters J A, Miescher G C, Janossy G, Thomas H C 1982c A rapid one-step radiometric assay for hepatitis B surface antigen utilising monoclonal antibodies. Journal of Immunological Methods 52: 167–174

Goodall A H, Jarvis J, Rawlings E, Tuddenham E G D 1983 A specific immunoradiometric assay for VIII: vWF using monoclonal antibodies recognising a functional site on VIIIR: Ag. Thrombosis and Haemostasis 50: 111 (Abs 0327)

Goodall A H, Jarvis J, Chand S, Rawlings E, O'Brien D P, McCraw A, Hutton R, Tuddenham E G D 1985 An immunoradiometric assay for human factor VIII/von Willebrand factor (VIII:vWF) using monoclonal antibodies that define a functional epitope. British Journal of Haematology (in press)

Howard M A, Montgomery D C, Hardisty R M 1974 Factor VIII related antigen in platelets. Thrombosis Research 4: 617

Hoyer L W, de los Santos R P, Hoyer J R 1973 Antihemophilic factor antigen: localisation in endothelial cells by immunofluorescence microscopy. Journal of Clinical Investigation 52: 2737–2744

Jackson C M, Nemerson Y 1980 Blood coagulation. Annual Reviews in Biochemistry 49: 765–811

Jaffe E A 1977 Endothelial cells and the biology of factor VIII. New England Journal of Medicine 296: 377–383

Janossy G (ed) 1982 The lymphocytes. In: Clinics in haematology. W B Saunders Co Ltd, London 11(3)

Katzmann J A, Nesheim M E, Hibbard L S, Mann K G 1981a Isolation of functional human coagulation factor V by using a hybridoma antibody. Proceedings of the National Academy of Sciences of the USA 78(1): 162–166

Katzmann J A, Mujwid D K, Miller R S, Fass D N 1981b Monoclonal antibodies to von Willebrand's factor: reactivity with porcine and human antigens. Blood 58(3): 530–536

Kennel S J, Chen J P, Lankford P K, Foote L J 1981 Monoclonal antibodies from rats immunized with fragment D of human fibrinogen. Thrombosis Research 22(3): 309–320

Kennel S J, Lankford P K 1983 Solid-phase radioimmunoassay of fragment D of human fibrinogen by use of a low-affinity monoclonal antibody. Clinical Chemistry 29(5): 778–781

Kohler G, Milstein C 1975 Continuous cultures of fused cells secreting antibody of predefined specificity. Nature 256: 495–497

Lee H, Martin M, Bezeaud A, Guillin M C 1983 Monoclonal antibodies to prothrombin: A study of their specificities for the different prothrombin activation products. Protides of the Biological Fluids 30: 395–398

Lewis R M, Furie B C, Furie B 1983 Conformation-specific monoclonal antibodies directed against the calcium-stabilized structure of human prothrombin. Biochemistry 22(4): 948–954

McEver R P, Bennett E M, Martin M N 1983 Identification of two structurally and functionally distinct sites on human platelet membrane glycoprotein IIb–IIIa using monoclonal antibodies. Journal of Biological Chemistry. 258(8): 5269–5275

McGregor J L, Brochier J, Wild F, Follea G, Trzeciak M C, James E, Dechavanne M, McGregor L, Clemetson K J 1983 Monoclonal antibodies against platelet membrane glycoproteins. Characterization and effect on platelet function. European Journal of Biochemistry 131(2): 427–436

McMichael A J, Rust N A, Pilch J R, Sochynsky R, Morton J, Mason D Y, Ruan C, Tobelem G, Caen J 1981 Monoclonal antibody to human platelet glycoprotein I. 1. Immunological studies. British Journal of Haematology 49(4): 501–509

McMichael A J, Fabre J (eds) 1982 Monoclonal antibodies in clinical medicine. Academic Press, London

Meyer D, Baumgartner H R, Edgington T S 1981 Effect of hybridoma antibodies to human factor VIII/von Willebrand factor on the adhesion of platelets to the subendothelium. Blood 58: 237a (Abstr)

Miletich J P, Broze G J, Majerus P W 1980 The synthesis of sulfated dextran beads for isolation of human plasma coagulation factors II, IX and X. Analytical Biochemistry 105: 304–310

Montgomery R R, Kunicki T J, Taves C, Pidard D, Corcoran M 1983 Diagnosis of Bernard–Soulier syndrome and Glanzmann's thrombasthenia with a monoclonal assay on whole blood. Journal of Clinical Investigation 71(2): 385–389

Muller H P, van Tilburg N H, Derks J, Klein-Breteler E, Bertina R M 1981 A monoclonal antibody to VIII:C produced by a mouse hybridoma. Blood 58(5): 1000–1006

Nachman R L, Jaffe E A 1975 Subcellular platelet factor VIII antigen and von Willebrand factor. Journal of Experimental Medicine 141: 1101–1113

Nachman R, Levine R, Jaffe E A 1977 Synthesis of factor VIII antigen by cultured guinea pig megakaryocytes. Journal of Clinical Investigation 60: 914–921

Naiem M, Gerdes J, Abdulaziz Z, Sunderland C A, Allington M J, Stein H, Mason D Y 1982 The value of immunohistological screening in the production of monoclonal antibodies. Journal of Immunological Methods 50(2): 145–160

Nielsen L S, Hansen J G, Andreasen P A, Skriver L, Danø K, Zenthen J 1983 Monoclonal antibody to human 66 000 molecular weight plasminogen activator from melanoma cells. Specific enzyme inhibition and one-step affinity purification. The EMBQ Journal, vol 2, no 1: 115–119

Nokes T J C, Mahmoud N A, Savidge G F, Goodall A H, Meyer D, Edgington T, Hardisty R M 1984 Von Willebrand factor has more than one binding site for platelets. Thrombosis Research (submitted)

Ogata K, Saito H, Ratnoff O D 1983 The relationship of the properties of antihemophilic factor (factor VIII) that support ristocetin-induced platelet agglutination (factor VIIIR:RC) and platelet retention by glass beads as demonstrated by a monoclonal antibody. Blood 61(1): 27–35

Ploplis V A, Cummings H S, Castellino F J 1982 Monoclonal antibodies to discrete regions of human Glu$_1$-plasminogen. Biochemistry 21: 5891–5897

Plow E F, Edgington T S 1982 Surface markers of fibrinogen and its physiologic derivatives revealed by antibody probes. Seminars in Hemostasis and Thombosis VIII: 36–56

Pukrittayakamee S, Esnoof P M, McMichael A J 1983 Purification and inactivation of the factor X activator of Russell's viper venom with monoclonal antibodies. Molecular and Biological Medicine 1: 123–135

Rabellino E H, Levene R B, Leung L L K, Nachman R L 1981 Human megakaryocytes: II Expression of platelet proteins in early marrow megakaryocytes. Journal of Experimental Medicine 154: 88–89

Rotblat F, Goodall A H, O'Brien D P, Rawlings E, Middleton S, Tuddenham E G D 1983a Monoclonal antibodies to human procoagulant factor VIII. Journal of Laboratory and Clinical Medicine 101(5): 736–746

Rotblat F, O'Brien D P, Middleton S, Tuddenham E G D 1983b Purification and characterisation of human factor VIII:C. Thrombosis and Haemostasis 50: 108 (Abstr 0319)

Ruan C, Tobelman G, McMichael A J, Drouet L, Legrand Y, Degos L, Kieffer N, Lee H, Caen J P 1981 Monoclonal antibody to human platelet glycoprotein I. II. Effects on human platelet function. British Journal of Haematology 49(4): 511–519

Secher D S, Burke D C 1980 A monoclonal antibody for large-scale purification of human leukocyte interferon. Nature 285: 446–450

Shapiro S S, Hultin M 1975 Acquired inhibitors to the blood coagulation factors. Seminars in Thrombosis and Haemostasis, vol 1, no 4: 336–385

Sola B, Avner P, Sultan Y, Jeanneau C, Maisonneuve P 1982 Monoclonal antibodies against human factor VIII molecular neutralize antihemophilic factor and ristocetin co-factor activities. Proceedings of the National Academy of Sciences of the USA 79(1): 183–187

Sola B, Avner P R, Zilber M T, Connan F, Levy D 1983 Isolation and characterization of a monoclonal antibody specific for fibrinogen and fibrin of human origin. Thrombosis Research 29(6): 643–653

Stel H V, Veerman E C I, Huisman J G, Janssen M C, van Mourik J A 1983a A rapid one step immunoradiometric assay for factor VIII procoagulant antigen utilizing monoclonal antibodies. Thrombosis and Haemostasis 50: 860–863

Stel H V, van der Kwast T H, Veerman E C 1983b Detection of factor VIII/coagulant antigen in human liver tissue. Nature 303(5917): 530–532

Stel H V, Sakariassen K S, de Groot P G, van Mourit J A, Sixma J J 1983c Inhibition of platelet adherence to subendothelium by monoclonal antibodies against FVIII-WF. Thrombosis and Haemostasis 50: 395 (Abstr 1257)

Sultan Y, Avner P, Maisonneuve P 1983 Immunoradiometric assay (IRMA) for FVIII R Ag using two monoclonal antibody classification of von Willebrand's disease (vWD) according to this test. Thrombosis and Haemostasis 50: 105 (Abstr 0308)

Thiagarajan P, Perussia B, De Marco L, Wells K, Trinchieri G 1983 Membrane proteins on human megakaryocytes and platelets identified by monoclonal antibodies. American Journal of Hematology 14(3): 255–269

Thompson A R 1983 Monoclonal antibody to an epitope on the heavy chain of factor IX missing in three hemophilia B patients. Blood 62: 1027–1034

Tobelem G, Ruar C, McMichael A, Kieffer N, Caen J P 1982 Studies with monoclonal antibodies on normal and diseased platelets. In: McMichael A J, Fabre J W (eds) Monoclonal antibodies in clinical medicine. Academic Press (London) Inc, ch 8, p 205–235

Tucker M M, Foster W B, Katzmann J A, Mann K G 1983 A monoclonal antibody which inhibits the factor Va : factor Xa interaction. Journal of Biological Chemistry 258(2): 1210–1214

Vainchenker N, Deschamps J F, Bastin J M, Guichard J, Titeux M, Breton-Gorius J, McMichael A J 1982 Two monoclonal anti-platelet antibodies as markers of human megakaryocyte maturation: immunofluorescent staining and platelet peroxidase detection in megakaryocyte colonies did in in vivo cells from normal and leukaemic patients. Blood 59: 514–521

Weiss H J, Turitto V T, Baumgartner H R 1978 Effect of shear rate on platelet interaction with subendothelium in citrated and native blood. I. Shear rate-dependent increase of adherence in von Willebrand's disease and the Bernard–Soulier syndrome. Blood 53: 244–250

Wilner G D, Mudd M S, Hsieh K, Thomas D W 1982 Monoclonal antibodies to fibrinogen: modulation of determinants expressed in fibrinogen by gamma-chain cross-linking. Biochemistry 21(11): 2687–2692

Zimmerman T S, Ratnoff O D, Powell A E 1971 Immunologic differentiation of classic hemophilia (factor VIII deficiency) and von Willebrand's disease. Journal of Clinical Investigation 50: 244–254

Note added to press proofs

Contributions of monoclonal antibodies to elucidating the structure function and synthesis of factor VIII.

The successful purification to homogeneity of human factor VIII was achieved using a monoclonal affinity column as the final step (Rotblat et al 1983b). This preparation shows up to 10 bands on polyacrylamide gels developed with the ultrasensitive silver stain. Nevertheless by 'Western' blotting using a panel of monoclonal antibodies every subunit could be shown to derive from a single chain precursor of M_r 360 K (Rotblat F et al 1985 Biochemistry, in press).

An epitope map could be constructed relating the binding sites of these monoclonals to functional inhibition.

	360 K		Native chain
★★★	+++	★	
210 K		80 K	Predominant plasma form
★★★	+++	★	
	Thrombin		
90 K		70 K	Species generated
★★★		★	by thrombin proteolysis
55 K 40 K			
★★★			

★ Binding sites of strongly inhibitory monoclonals.
+ Binding sites of weakly or non-inhibitory monoclonals.

In sequential studies of thrombin activation, maximum activity coincided with the presence of M_r 90 K and 80/70 K subunits. Inactivation followed the appearance of M_r 55 K and 40 K breakdown products of the 90 K peptide.

Highly purified factor VIII was partially sequenced and the information used to synthesise oligonucleotide probes which enabled successful cloning, sequencing and expression of the factor VIII gene (Wood et al 1984 Nature 312: 330–336; Vehar et al 1984 Nature 312: 337–342).

Biosynthetically produced factor VIII from hamster kidney cells transfected with an expression plasmid was characterised as resembling the natural product by its ability to bind to and be neutralised by monoclonal antibodies raised against plasma factor VIII.

13. Immune thrombocytopenia and neutropenia

A. H. Waters   R. M. Minchinton

INTRODUCTION

Recent improvements in laboratory techniques for the demonstration of platelet and granulocyte antibodies have led to a better understanding of the aetiology, pathogenesis and management of immune thrombocytopenia and neutropenia.

METHODOLOGY

Methods for the demonstration of antibodies to red cell antigens and lymphocyte antigens, in particular those of the HLA system, are well developed and generally standardised. In contrast, methods for the demonstration of antibodies to platelet and granulocyte antigens are extremely diverse. In fact, new techniques are constantly being introduced, and this reflects a general dissatisfaction with the available methods. It is apparent that no one technique can satisfy the basic requirements of being simple to perform, sensitive, specific, quantitative and adaptable for the detection of both serum and cell-bound antibodies. Technical details and a critical analysis of these methods are given in a recent publication edited by McMillan (1983).

Table 13.1   Patterns of antibody reaction in the immunofluorescence tests and LCT

| | Test | | | |
Antibody	PIFT	GIFT	LIFT	LCT
Platelet specific	+	−	−	−
Granulocyte specific	−	+	−	−
HLA	+	+	+	+

PIFT = platelet immunofluorescence test
GIFT = granulocyte immunoflurescence test
LIFT = lymphocyte immunofluorescence test
LCT = lymphocytotoxicity test

Some techniques are particularly suitable for the detection of alloantibodies and are also readily adapted for the demonstration of drug-dependent antibodies. Complement fixation tests, and more recently, labelled AHG methods using mainly fluorescent and radioactive labels have been widely used for this purpose. Fluorescent AHG techniques are particularly suitable for demonstrating alloantibodies to platelets, granulocytes and lymphocytes. The combination of these tests with the lymphototoxicity test (LCT) may be helpful in differentiating cell-specific antibodies from HLA antibodies (Table 13.1). Positive reactions with all tests indicate the presence of HLA antibodies, as HLA antigens are present on platelets, granulocytes and lymphocytes. Under these circumstances, platelet and granulocyte specific antibodies cannot easily be identified, though they may be present. However, Nordhagen & Flaathen (1983) have shown that chloroquine may selectively strip HLA antigens from platelets leaving them suitable for the demonstration of platelet specific antibodies. This technique can also be used to detect neutrophil specific antibodies (Minchinton & Waters, 1984).

Much of the recent drive to develop new methodology comes from a renewed interest in the demonstration of platelet autoantibodies in idiopathic thrombocytopenic purpura (ITP), as a possible guide to prognosis and treatment. Most of the new techniques are aimed at quantitation of platelet associated IgG (PAIgG) as an indication of autoantibody on the circulating platelets of patients with ITP. The most widely used methods are the quantitative antiglobulin consumption assay (QACA) (Dixon et al, 1975), platelet radioactive antiglobulin test (Soulier et al, 1975; Mueller-Eckhardt et al, 1978) and the enzyme linked immunosorbent assays (ELISA) (Leporrier et al, 1979; Nel & Stevens, 1980; Hegde et al, 1981; Guidino & Miller, 1981).

A major criticism of these PAIgG methods is that they are detecting not only platelet autoantibody, but also non-specifically bound immunoglobulins and immune complexes, and intracellular platelet protein (Helmerhorst et al, 1983; Pfueller et al, 1981; Kelton et al, 1982a; Kelton & Steeves, 1983). Estimates of PAIgG may be increased by platelet fragmentation (Shulman et al, 1982) and a recent method has overcome this problem to a large extent by excluding fragments from the platelet preparation and using ^{125}I-labelled monoclonal antihuman globulin (Lo Buglio et al, 1983) or ^{125}I-staphylococcal protein A (Shaw et al, 1984).

The platelet immunofluorescence test described by Borne et al (1978) avoids, to a large extent, the above problems of non-specific binding by using paraformaldehyde-fixed platelets (Helmerhorst et al, 1983). Furthermore, as the test is read by examination of a platelet suspension using fluorescent microscopy, platelet fragments can be seen and excluded. Although possibly less sensitive, and only semiquantitative, the fluorescent AHG method is widely used for demonstrating platelet autoantibodies. This technique has the further advantage of being suitable for the demonstration of neutrophil auto-antibodies (Verheugt et al, 1978a).

As an adjunct to platelet and granulocyte antibody detection, there has been renewed interest and further developments in methods for studying the survival and sites of destruction of platelets and granulocytes in immune cytopenias. Indium[111]-oxine or tropolonate have replaced ^{51}Cr (sodium chromate) as the label of choice for this purpose. This simple rapid labelling technique ensures that cell function and viability are maintained (Hawker et al, 1980; Danpure et al, 1982), and the higher gamma emission makes ^{111}In more suitable for external organ localisation with a scintillation counter or camera.

PLATELET AND GRANULOCYTE ANTIGENS

In spite of the limitations of available methods for the detection of platelet and granulocyte antibodies, there has been considerable progress in defining the corresponding antigen systems. Antigens on platelets and granulocytes may be considered in terms of those shared with other cells and those exclusive to each cell type.

Shared antigens

Of the shared group, the most important is the HLA system, which is best represented on the lymphocyte. The density of HLA antigens on granulocytes is reported to be lower than on lymphocytes (Thorsby, 1969). Studies in this laboratory and elsewhere (Verheught et al, 1977a), using the granulocyte immunofluoresence test, have shown that the fluorescence obtained with high titre HLA typing sera and granulocytes positive for the corresponding HLA antigen is never as strong as that obtained with granulocyte specific antisera. The HLA A, B and C antigens are represented on platelets, but HLA D/DR antigens do not appear to be present. It has recently been shown that the presence of at least some HLA antigens on platelets is primarily due to their adsorption from the plasma (Lalezari & Driscoll, 1982).

Table 13.2   Platelet and granulocyte-specific antigens

System	Antigen	Gene frequency	Phenotypic frequency
(a) Platelet specific antigens			
Pl^A	Pl^{A1}	0.854	97.6
	Pl^{A2}	0.145	26.8
Ko	Ko^a	0.0745	14.3
	Ko^b	0.9255	99.4
Pl^E	Pl^{E1}	0.975	99.9
	Pl^{E2}	0.025	5.0
Bak	Bak^a	0.685	90.1
Lek	Lek^a	—	98.2
DUZŌ	DUZO	0.094	/22.0
(b) Neutrophil specific antigens			
NA	NA1	0.31	53.9
	NA2	0.69	92.7
NB	NB1	0.72	92.1
NC	NC1	0.80	96.2
ND	ND1	0.88	98.5
NE	NE1	0.12	23.0
9	9^a	0.39	62.6

Data from Central Laboratory of Netherlands Red Cross Blood Transfusion Service; for NE1 Claas et al (1979a); Lek[a], Boizard & Waufier (1984)

Some erythrocyte antigens, such as A, B, H, I, i, P, Le^b may also be present on platelets and granulocytes, although this too may be only by virtue of adsorption of group specific substances from the plasma (Gurner & Coombs, 1958; Lalezari & Murphy, 1967; Kelton et al, 1982b). While the platelet immunofluorescence test readily demonstrates the presence of A and B antigens on platelets, Verheugt et al (1977a) were unable to demonstrate these antigens on granulocytes using the granulocyte immunofluorescence test.

Cell specific antigens

The presently defined cell specific antigens on platelets and granulocytes and the gene and phenotype frequencies in a Caucasian population are shown in Table 13.2.

Antibodies defining platelet specific antigens were first found in the sera of mothers of infants with alloimmune neonatal thrombocytopenia (ANT) and multitransfused patients (Shulman et al, 1964; Weerdt et al, 1963). Similarly, antibodies defining neutrophil specific antigens NA1, NA2, NB1 and NC1 were first discovered in cases of alloimmune neonatal neutropenia (ANN) (Lalezari & Radel, 1974), which are the best source of pure, neutrophil specific antisera. Recently, two new antigens, ND1 and NE1 have been defined with neutrophil specific antibodies from children with autoimmune neutropenia (Verheugt et al, 1978b; Claas et al, 1979a; Sabbe et al, 1983). The clinical significance of neutrophil antigen 9a is uncertain; the antibody defining this system was found in the serum of a multiparous woman (Rood et al, 1965).

CLASSIFICATION OF IMMUNE CYTOPENIAS

Immune thrombocytopenias and neutropenias may be classified as alloimmune, autoimmune and drug-induced (Table 13.3). However, in some situations, an antibody may not fit exactly into one or other of these classes, so that there may be overlap between these groups, especially as more becomes known about the pathogenesis of the immune cytopenias.

Table 13.3   Classification of immune thrombocytopenia and neutropenia

Alloantibodies
1. Decreased post-transfusion survival of platelets and granulocytes
2. Alloimmune neonatal thrombocytopenia and neutropenia
3. Post-transfusion purpura

Autoantibodies
1. Autoimmune thrombocytopenia
    (a) Idiopathic thrombocytopenic purpura
    (b) Autoimmune thrombocytopenia associated with other disorders
2. Autoimmune neutropenia
    (a) Idiopathic neutropenia
    (b) Autoimmune neutropenia associated with other disorders

Drug-induced antibodies
1. Drug adsorption mechanism
2. Immune-complex mechanism
3. Autoantibody mechanism

Alloantibodies

Alloimmunisation to leucocyte and platelet antigens is most commonly due to transfusion or pregnancy. The associated clinical problems depend on the specificity of the antibody, which determines the target cell involved. This has practical implications for transfusion, transplantation and neonatal immunohaematology.

Febrile transfusion reactions due to leucocyte antibodies are a common problem in multitransfused patients. The granulocyte is the main target cell in these reactions, and granulocyte-specific antibodies seem to cause more severe reactions than HLA antibodies reacting with granulocytes (Mollison, 1982; Waters et al, 1981). Other consequences of leucocyte and platelet alloantibodies, excluding transplantation problems, which are not discussed in this chapter, are given in Table 13.3.

1. Immunological aspects of platelet transfusions

Alloimmunisation resulting in unsatisfactory post-transfusion platelet increments is often a problem in patients receiving repeated platelet transfusions from random donors (Grumet & Yankee, 1970; Howard & Perkins, 1978). This can be minimised by restricting the patient's exposure to HLA antigens. The use of leucocyte-poor platelet and red cell concentrates postpones alloimmunisation (Eernisse & Brand, 1981). Plateletpheresis reduces the number of donors required to support each patient, and appears to reduce alloimmunisation (Gmur et al, 1983). Donor selection can also help to minimise alloimmunisation, and for this reason, sibling donors are often used, as they may share at least some antigens with the patient (Yankee et al, 1969; Thorsby et al, 1972). However, siblings are not always available, and should not be used if they may be needed as bone-marrow donors for the patient (Storb & Weiden, 1981).

At the beginning of treatment, it is often most expedient to use random donors until the patient becomes refractory to further platelet support. At this stage, HLA matching for lymphocyte A and B loci will usually improve the survival of transfused platelets (Yankee et al, 1969, 1973). Donor recipient HLA-C compatibility does not appear to influence platelet transfusion effectiveness in refractory patients (Duquesnoy et al, 1977). However, matching for HLA-A and -B loci is not always successful (Thorsby et al, 1972; Bucher et al, 1973; Tosato et al, 1978), and this has led to a more direct approach using donor platelets in a cross-match to predict post-transfusion platelet survival. A number of different methods have been tried (Menitove & Aster, 1983), and so far, the best predictive results have been obtained with labelled indirect antiglobulin techniques, often in association with a lymphocytotoxicity cross-match (Brand et al, 1978; Myers et al, 1981; Waters et al, 1981; Pegels et al, 1982a; Kickler et al, 1983).

The special advantage of the platelet indirect antiglobulin cross-match is that it will detect platelet specific antibodies as well as HLA antibodies active against platelets (Waters et al, 1981). The most common inconsistent cross-match result occurring in leukaemic patients undergoing cytoreductive chemotherapy is a negative cross-match associated with poor platelet recovery. While this may be a 'false' serological result due to failure of the technique to detect significant antibodies, in most cases it appears to be a true negative result associated with poor platelet recovery due to non-immune platelet consumption, e.g. fever, bleeding, sepsis (Pegels et al, 1982a).

The optimal application of platelet cross-matching tests in selecting compatible donors for refractory alloimmunised patients has yet to be defined. In current practice, primary selection is based on HLA matching of related or unrelated donors, the latter requiring an 'on-call' panel of HLA typed donors, or ideally, a bank of viable typed platelets. This will usually restore satisfactory platelet increments. Platelet cross-matching tests may help at this stage to predict compatible donors, or they may be introduced when an HLA matched donor fails to produce satisfactory increments. However, the logistics of finding a compatible donor under these circumstances remains to be established by future prospective studies.

2. Immunological aspects of granulocyte transfusions

Repeated granulocyte transfusions may immunise the recipient against neutrophil specific and HLA antigens (Verheugt et al, 1977b). Alloantibodies reactive with neutrophil antigens may not only cause a severe febrile (non-haemolytic) transfusion reaction, but their presence in a recipient may result in a shortened survival of transfused granulocytes. A granulocyte cross-matching technique, based on the indirect granulocyte immunofluorescence test has been used in this situation to select compatible donors (Dahlke et al, 1982; Chow et al, 1983).

The ability of neutrophil antibodies to affect the fate of transfused neutrophils in vivo has recently been studied using an ^{111}In-labelling technique. Granulocyte agglutinating antibodies, including anti-NA1 and anti-NB1, but not granulocyto-toxins or lymphocytotoxins (HLA antibodies), were associated with reduced intra-vascular survival, increased liver sequestration and failure of the neutrophils to localise at known sites of infection (McCullogh et al, 1981a; Dutcher et al, 1983).

3. Alloimmune neonatal thrombocytopenia and neutropenia

In pregnancy, the mother may be alloimmunised against fetal leucocyte and platelet antigens of paternal origin that cross the placenta. HLA antibodies do not appear to have any harmful effect on the fetus (Borne et al, 1981; Sharon & Amar, 1981), but platelet and granulocyte specific antibodies of IgG class may cause serious neonatal thrombocytopenia and neutropenia in a manner similar to Rhesus haemolytic disease of the newborn (HDN). However, unlike Rhesus HDN, severe clinical manifesta-tions of ANT and ANN may be present in a firstborn infant (Pearson et al, 1964; Verheugt et al, 1979; Borne et al, 1981).

Alloimmune neonatal thrombocytopenia. Thrombocytopenia in the neonate is man-ifest early with signs of bruising and bleeding which may be life-threatening. Alloimmune neonatal thrombocytopenia is estimated to occur in 0.1–0.2% of live births (Shulman et al, 1964), but the true incidence is probably higher than this. As awareness of the problem increases and techniques available for platelet antibody detection become more widely used, it is expected that more cases of ANT will be recognised.

Antibodies to the platelet antigen Pl^{A1} account for most cases of ANT (Shulman et al, 1964; Borne et al, 1981), although antibodies to any of the other platelet antigens may be involved. In fact, mothers of babies with ANT are still the main source of high titre platelet specific typing sera.

The platelet antibody in the mother's serum typically reacts with platelets of the father and the baby, but not with the mother's own platelets. The same antibody may be present in cord serum, and if sufficient circulating platelets are obtainable from the baby, the alloantibody may be demonstrated on their surface. The antigen specificity of the antibody is determined by reactions with a typed platelet panel.

The class and subclass of antibodies causing ANT has been investigated by Borne et al (1981) using FITC-labelled monospecific reagents in the antiglobulin technique. Most maternal sera contained IgG antibodies and in a few weak IgM antibodies were also present. No IgA antibodies were demonstrated. Most IgG antibodies were of the IgG_1 subclass, but a few were either IgG_3 alone or in combination with IgG_1 or IgG_4.

An increased incidence of ANT is not associated with ABO compatibility between mother and child as in Rhesus immunisation (Borne et al, 1981; Taaning et al, 1983), but there appears to be an increased incidence of HLA-B8 (Taaning et al, 1983) and HLA-DR3 (Muller et al, 1983) in the mothers of affected children.

The most effective treatment in severe cases of ANT is the transfusion of platelets lacking the offending antigen. In most cases this would mean using Pl^{A1} negative platelets. These are readily available from the mother by plateletpheresis, or if this is not possible, from a known Pl^{A1} negative donor (McIntosh et al, 1973; Adner et al, 1969).

Maternal autoantibodies in ITP may cross the placenta and cause thrombo-cytopenia in the neonate. The distinction between maternal alloantibodies and autoantibodies can be readily made by testing the maternal serum for the presence of antibody reacting with the mother's own platelets (Kelton et al, 1980a; Leeuwen et al, 1980).

Alloimmune neonatal neutropenia is estimated to occur in about 3% of live births (Verheugt et al, 1979). It often goes unnoticed and the diagnosis is only made when infection becomes a problem in the baby. This usually responds to supportive antibiotic therapy and the neutropenia resolves in a few weeks.

The most commonly occurring antibodies in ANN are anti-NA1 and anti-NB1 with approximately equal frequency, while anti-NA2 and anti-NC1 are less common (Lalezari & Radel, 1974). As expected, these antibodies are IgG, and where tested have been shown to belong to IgG_1 and/or IgG_3 subclasses (Verheugt et al, 1979).

As in the diagnosis of ANT, the serological investigation of a suspected ANN should include reaction of the mother's serum with the neutrophils of the father, the child if possible, and the mother's own neutrophils to exclude the possibility of maternal IgG neutrophil autoantibodies, which could cause a similar condition in the neonate (Leeuwen et al, 1983; see also Table 13.5).

4. Post transfusion purpura

Post transfusion purpura (PTP) is a rare cause of immune thrombocytopenia. It is a bizarre condition in which a Pl^{A1} negative patient develops severe thrombocytopenia from 2–12 days following blood transfusion. The patient is typically female and there is always a prior history of blood transfusion or pregnancy.

The patient's serum contains a high titre anti-Pl^{A1} (Loghem et al, 1959; Shulman et al, 1961); there has been only one reported case of PTP where the antibody was not anti-Pl^{A1} (Zeigler et al, 1975). The severe thrombocytopenia in PTP is due to destruction of the patient's own platelets which are Pl^{A1} negative. The precise mechanism of this destruction is uncertain. It has been suggested that the transfused Pl^{A1} positive platelets release Pl^{A1} antigen which is adsorbed to the patient's circulating Pl^{A1} negative cells, either directly, making them the target for Pl^{A1} antibody or as part of an immune complex (Shulman et al, 1961).

In one case of PTP studied in this laboratory, and in a further two cases studied by Pegels et al (1981), acute phase PTP sera, shown to be Pl^{A1} specific, reacted with the patient's own Pl^{A1} negative platelets after recovery. As an alternative to the above theories, these findings suggest the presence of a platelet autoantibody in the acute phase serum, as demonstrated in an animal (marmoset) model of PTP (Gengozian & McLaughlin, 1980; Gengozian & Annastoby, 1981). In marmosets, the autoantibody was present in low titre and could be found in the serum only when the animals were thrombocytopenic. This was in contrast to the alloantibody to donor platelets which persisted after the thrombocytopenia had resolved.

Morrison & Mollison (1966) have suggested that destruction of the patient's own platelets may be due to a cross-reacting antibody formed during the immunological stimulation caused by transfused alloantigens in PTP.

In the treatment of PTP, platelet transfusion, corticosteroids and exchange transfusion have all been used, but plasmapheresis has proved most effective (Abrahamson et al, 1974). An attempt to treat PTP with platelet transfusions from a Pl^{A1} negative donor was entirely unsuccessful, even though the patient's antibody failed to react in vitro with the transfused Pl^{A1} negative platelets (Gerstner et al, 1979). The prompt response of the platelet count to high dose intravenous immunoglobulin in patients with autoimmune thrombocytopenia (Imbach et al, 1981; Newland et al, 1983) led Mueller-Eckhardt et al (1983) to use this therapy with success in a patient with PTP. Further to this, we have also successfully treated a PTP patient with high dose intravenous IgG. This patient (platelet count $<10 \times 10^9/l$) was refractory to steroids and multiple plasmaphereses, but had a rapid and sustained response to an infusion of IgG (30 g/d for 3 days) (Fig. 13.1).

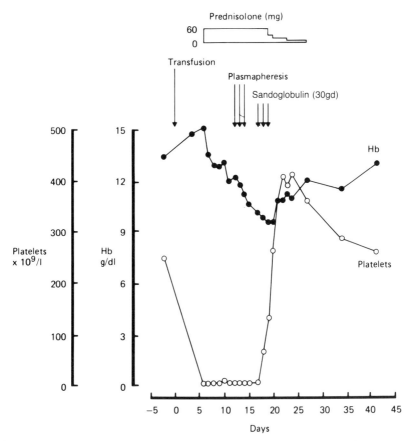

Fig. 13.1   The haematological course of a patient with post-transfusion purpura, showing no response to plasmapheresis and a prompt remission following intravenous IgG.

Autoantibodies

In the past, the diagnosis of autoimmune thrombocytopenia and neutropenia was usually made by the exclusion of other known causes in patients having adequate numbers of megakaryocytes or myeloid precursors in their bone marrow. Confirmation of the diagnosis by laboratory demonstration of the autoantibody responsible was rarely undertaken due to lack of reliable techniques. As these patients are usually severely cytopenic, early methods concentrated on the detection of antibodies in serum alone. This approach often failed to differentiate autoantibodies from alloantibodies to platelets and granulocytes that might be present as a result of previous blood transfusions or pregnancy. To demonstrate the autoimmune nature of the antibody, it must be shown to react with the patient's own cells. However, even with a combination of the more suitable techniques now available, autoantibodies remain elusive in a proportion of patients with conditions where they might be expected to occur.

Autoimmune thrombocytopenia

A. IDIOPATHIC THROMBOCYTOPENIC PURPURA

ITP is a syndrome of unknown aetiology characterised by a reduced peripheral platelet count, megakaryocytes in the bone marrow and a shortened platelet lifespan. There are recent excellent reviews of this subject (Karpatkin, 1980; McMillan, 1981) and this section will concentrate on the platelet autoantibody, compensated thrombocytopenia, and the place of recent novel approaches to treatment.

(i) *Platelet autoantibody*. Although ITP is considered to be an autoimmune condition, platelet autoantibodies are difficult to detect, and estimates of their frequency of occurrence vary according to the method used (Table 13.4). The highest

Table 13.4 Comparison of the incidence of positive results using various methods for demonstrating the platelet autoantibody in ITP

Author	Test	Number of ITP patients tested	% positive results
Dixon et al (1975)	QACA	17	100
Hegde et al (1977)	QACA	28	100
Morse et al (1981)	Single radial immunodiffusion	27	93
Hymes et al (1979)	^{125}I-labelled SPA solid phase	35	92
Kelton et al (1980b)	QACA	37	91
Cines and Schreiber (1979)	PRAT-polyclonal	50	90
Nel and Stevens (1980)	ELISA	9	78
LoBuglio et al (1983)	PRAT-monoclonal	21	71
Borne et al (1980)	PSIFT	80	69
Mueller-Eckhardt et al (1978)	PRAT-polyclonal	18	61
Kelton et al (1980b)	PSIFT	37	46
Waters et al (unpublished)	PSIFT	52	46*

*With the indirect auto test (patient's own cells + patient's serum) the percentage of positive results increased to 65%

incidence of positive results is obtained with quantitative assays measuring the amount of platelet associated IgG (PAIgG) on unfixed washed platelets or platelet lysates. However, as previously discussed, elevated levels of PAIgG are not specific for autoantibody, and may also occur in non-immune thrombocytopenias (Mueller-Eckhardt et al, 1980b; Kelton et al, 1982a).

The involvement of circulating immune complexes (CICs) in the pathogenesis of ITP is controversial. Some patients with ITP have increased levels of CICs either alone or together with platelet autoantibodies, and immune complexes on the platelet surface may result in shortened platelet survival (Trent et al, 1980; Campana et al, 1983). However, methodology for the measurement of CICs is as varied as that for the detection of platelet autoantibodies and this may explain the contrasting findings of Lambert et al (1978) and Ercilla et al (1982) who reported normal levels of CICs in ITP patients.

Another currently controversial topic is the involvement of complement in the pathogenesis of ITP. It has been reported that platelet bound C3 is increased in ITP (Cines & Schreiber, 1979; Hauch & Rosse, 1977), although this could not be confirmed by others (Borne et al, 1980; Nel & Stevens, 1980; Veenhoven et al, 1980; Minchinton & Waters, unpublished observations). Using sensitive quantitative platelet associated IgG and C3 assays, other workers have reported a correlation between the amount of PAIgG and the quantity of C3 bound to ITP platelets (Myers et al, 1982; Kernoff & Malan, 1983). Further studies are needed to confirm that the presence of complement is not an in vitro artefact, and to elucidate the possible role of complement in platelet destruction in ITP.

A major disadvantage of methods measuring PAIgG is that antibody classes other than IgG, which may be significant in ITP, are not demonstrated. Studies using semi-quantitative fluorescent labelled AHG techniques have shown that the platelet autoantibody in ITP is most commonly IgG, but IgM antibodies are also present and may be the only antibody class in some patients (Borne et al, 1980). This has also been confirmed by the ELISA technique (Nel et al, 1983).

The IgG antibody subclasses in ITP have been studied using fluorescein-labelled AHG techniques. IgG1 was found most commonly (94%), often occurring together with IgG3 (49%) or IgG4 (31%), but rarely IgG2 (2%) (Borne et al, 1980). Similar results were reported by Rosse et al (1980), using a modification of the antihuman globulin consumption assay.

The autoantibodies of ITP show no specificity for the known platelet antigens (Donnall et al, 1976), but recent studies suggest that in most cases they react with the platelet membrane glycoproteins IIb and IIIa, which are absent in Glanzmann's thrombasthenia (Leeuwen et al, 1982a).

(ii) *Compensated thrombocytopenia.* From serial studies of patients with ITP, it is possible to define a group with platelet autoantibodies, who have a borderline or normal platelet count. Karpatkin et al (1971) suggest that these patients are part of a larger group of individuals who have compensated autoimmune thrombocytopenia, and that increased platelet destruction is balanced by increased platelet production. This is a vulnerable equilibrium which may be disturbed by a variety of factors, e.g. infection, alcohol or drugs, nutritional deficiency, irradiation or altered physiological conditions, such as pregnancy. We have used ^{111}In-tropolonate to measure platelet survival in a group of such patients and have demonstrated reduced platelet survival in the presence of a platelet autoantibody and a borderline or normal platelet count (Metcalfe et al, 1983, Fig. 13.2). A similar state of compensated immune platelet destruction has been demonstrated in marmosets (Gengozian & McLaughlin, 1980).

Treatment of ITP is based on corticosteroids and splenectomy. Patients refractory to this treatment may respond to immunosuppressive drugs and vinca alkaloids. However, novel approaches to treatment have recently been tried — high dose intravenous IgG, colchicine and Danazol, a synthetic androgen.

Preliminary studies by Imbach et al (1981) showed that some children with ITP responded to large body-weight doses of *intravenous IgG*, and this is confirmed in a recent study of Bussel et al (1983a). High dose intravenous IgG also produced a rapid and predictable rise in the platelet count of adults with acute or chronic autoimmune thrombocytopenia (Newland et al, 1983). Although the initial platelet response was often only transient, there were some prolonged responses when IgG infusions were closely associated with splenectomy, especially early in the course of the disease. The Ig class of the platelet autoantibody, whether IgG or IgM, did not appear to affect the response to intravenous IgG. Similar findings have been reported by others (Fehr et al, 1982; Bussel et al, 1983a).

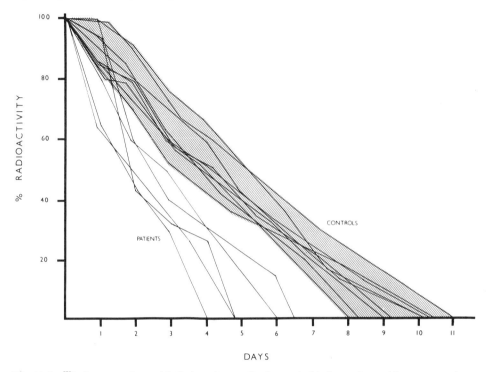

Fig. 13.2 [III]Indium-tropolonate labelled autologous platelet survival in five patients with compensated immune platelet destruction compared with nine normal controls (shaded area).

Various mechansisms have been proposed for the initial platelet response to high dose IgG infusion. Blockade of the macrophage Fc receptors by the high concentration of IgG may reduce the immune clearance of antibody-coated platelets; IgG may also act at the platelet surface blocking the attachment of specific autoantibody (Imbach et al, 1981; Fehr et al, 1982; Newland et al, 1983; Bussel et al, 1983a). It has also been suggested that anti-A and anti-B haemolysins in the IgG preparation, or even non-specific IgG, may coat the patient's autologous red cells resulting in increased, but clinically compensated, sequestration of red cells with subsequent blockade of the mononuclear phagocyte system (Salama et al, 1983).

A different mechanism may be responsible for the long term effect seen in some patients. High dose IgG may have a general immunosuppressive effect, perhaps by activation of T suppressor cells, either non-specifically or via anti-idiotype antibodies in the IgG preparation (Newland et al, 1983).

Whatever the mechanism of action of high dose IgG in immune thrombocytopenia, the rapid and generally predictable response, albeit transient in most cases, makes this therapy a consideration in emergency situations. It has been used with beneficial effect in severe post-transfusion purpura (Mueller-Eckhardt et al, 1983; see also Fig. 13.1), in refractory autoimmune thrombocytopenia following bone-marrow grafting (Min-chinton et al, 1982), and in pregnant women with severe refractory ITP approaching delivery (Morgenstern et al, 1983; Wenske et al, 1983). However, the high cost of intravenous IgG, especially at the doses recommended in adults, limits its wider clinical application.

Colchicine has recently been shown to have a rapid effect in some patients with ITP refractory to steroids and splenectomy (Melo et al, 1981; Strother et al, 1982). Colchicine was tried because of its pharmacological similarity to vincristine, and it is suggested that both drugs may act by disrupting micro-tubule-dependent functions in macrophages, and thereby paralyse their ability to phagocytose antibody-coated platelets. If these preliminary results are confirmed, colchicine would be an important addition to the treatment options for refractory ITP because of its relatively low toxicity, rapid effect in susceptible patients (within 2 weeks) and low cost.

Danazol, a synthetic androgen with reduced virilising effects, has had promising results in a recent clinical trial (Ahn et al, 1983). It produced a response in 15 out of 22 patients with ITP irrespective of previous treatment, and had a beneficial cortico-steroid-sparing effect. It was also associated with a reduction in platelet antibody levels in six out of eight patients tested. The mechanism of action of Danazol in ITP is unknown. Although preliminary results with colchicine and Danazol are promising, the proper place of both drugs in the long-term management of ITP remains to be determined.

B. AUTOIMMUNE THROMBOCYTOPENIA ASSOCIATED WITH OTHER DISORDERS

Platelet autoantibodies causing thrombocytopenia may often be associated with other autoimmune diseases, such as systemic lupus erythematosus (SLE), autoimmune thyroiditis, rheumatoid arthritis (Dixon et al, 1975; Hegde et al, 1977, 1983; Borne et al, 1980; Kelton et al, 1980b; Mueller-Eckhardt et al, 1980b) and autoimmune haemolytic anaemia (Evan's syndrome) (Pegels et al, 1982b). Autoimmune throm-bocytopenia has been reported in patients with chronic lymphatic leukaemia (Kaden et al, 1979; Hegde et al, 1983) and solid tumours (Schwartz et al, 1982).

Thrombocytopenia also occurs in association with viral infections, especially in children, and recent reports suggest that this is due to the production of platelet autoantibodies (Feusner et al, 1979; Chapman et al, 1984). It has been proposed that the platelet autoantibody is in fact an anti-idiotype antibody to the antiviral antibody produced on the wake of a viral infection (Plotz, 1983). The thrombocytopenia associated with malarial infections is due to an IgG malaria antibody reacting with the malaria antigen which is attached to a specific receptor on the platelet surface (Kelton et al, 1983).

Autoimmune thrombocytopenia may also be a feature of the acquired immune deficiency syndrome (AIDS). We have studied three young homosexual men with thrombocytopenia, abnormal T cell helper-suppressor ratios and IgM platelet auto-antibodies (Waters et al, unpublished data). Morris et al (1982) reported eight similar cases in homosexual men, who appeared to have an IgG platelet autoantibody based on increased PAIgG levels. A further seven cases of autoimmune thrombocytopenia have been reported in haemophiliacs receiving factor VIII concentrates; five of these patients also had the abnormal T4/T8 ratios associated with AIDS (Harris et al, 1983; Ratnoff et al, 1983).

C. AUTOIMMUNE CYTOPENIAS FOLLOWING BONE MARROW TRANSPLANTATION

Recent studies carried out in this laboratory provide evidence for an autoimmune basis for unexplained thrombocytopenia and neutropenia occurring after both allogeneic and autologous bone marrow transplantation (Minchinton et al, 1984). Using fluorescent labelled antihuman globulin techniques, a high incidence of antibodies to circulating (donor origin) platelets (52%) and neutrophils (65%) was demonstrated in the early postgraft period. The cell specificity of these antibodies was demonstrated by cross-absorption experiments. Similar observations have been reported by Bierling et al (1983) in a group of allografted patients, and by Plouvier et al (1983) in a patient receiving a bone-marrow autograft for non-Hodgkin's lymphoma. In our own study, such antibodies in the allografted patients were shown, by immunoglobulin allotyping, to be of marrow donor type and were therefore autoantibodies. The antibodies demonstrated after autografting were, by definition, autoantibodies.

The effect of these autoantibodies on the postgraft peripheral cell count varied considerably. In some patients there was no apparent effect, while in others there was a transient sharp fall in a peripheral count that was otherwise recovering or a delayed post-graft platelet or neutrophil recovery. These variable effects probably reflected in vivo activity of the antibody and the ability of the engrafted bone marrow to compensate for antibody mediated cell destruction (Waters et al, 1983).

The investigation did not explain the mechanism of formation of autoantibodies after allogeneic and autologous marrow grafting. It is possible that the underlying malignant condition in the patients studied was itself a reflection of a disturbed immune state. Chemotherapy and radiotherapy used for remission induction or pregraft conditioning were common to both allografts and autografts and may be contributory factors. The engraftment procedure itself may predispose to autoantibody formation. Altered expression of self antigens may result from in vitro stem cell damage or from viral infections. In the early postgraft period, insufficient numbers or inadequate function of suppressor T cells, which normally regulate response to self antigens, may also lead to autoantibody formation. Furthermore, postgraft blood component therapy involving the transfusion of alloantigens sharing determinants (epitopes) with engrafted cells may stimulate autoantibody production.

Without specific investigations on these patients, it was difficult to predict which of the above mechanisms, if any, were responsible for the development of autoantibodies after marrow grafting. However, it is likely that this was due to the interaction of a number of factors during the re-establishment of the normal immune and haemopoietic systems.

2. Autoimmune neutropenia

Autoimmune neutropenia occurring alone or in association with other autoimmune disorders is the least well studied of the autoimmune cytopenias. This is partly because neutrophils, like platelets, are difficult cells to work with in vitro.

A. IDIOPATHIC AUTOIMMUNE NEUTROPENIA

Autoimmune neutropenia occurring alone is uncommon in adults, although chronic 'benign' autoimmune neutropenia is well documented in infants (5–24 months) and is reviewed by Madyastha et al (1983). In a neonate, it is important to differentiate idiopathic autoimmune neutropenia from alloimmune neonatal neutropenia due to maternal neutrophil alloantibodies (see Table 13.5). Furthermore, maternal IgG neutrophil autoantibodies may cross the placenta and cause neonatal neutropenia (Leeuwen et al, 1983).

Table 13.5 Laboratory differentiation of immune neonatal neutropenias

Serum from	Neutrophils from	In vitro reaction	Diagnosis
child	child	positive negative (recovered)	Alloimmune neonatal neutropenia (ANN)
mother	mother	negative	
mother	child	positive	
mother	father	positive	
child	child	positive negative (recovered)	Maternal autoimmune neutropenia (affecting the neonate)
mother	mother	positive	
mother	child	positive	
mother	father	positive or negative	
child	child	positive	Idiopathic autoimmune neonatal neutropenia
mother	mother	negative	
mother	child	positive*	
mother	father	negative	

* Indicating in vivo attachment of autoantibody, i.e. positive direct test.

Neutrophil autoantibodies, unlike platelet autoantibodies, may show specificity for neutrophil specific antigens. Anti-NA1 (Verheugt et al, 1978a; Valbonesi et al, 1979; Priest et al, 1980; Madyastha et al, 1982) anti-NA2 (Lalezari et al, 1975) and anti-NB1 (Verheugt et al, 1978a) neutrophil autoantibodies have been implicated in cases of autoimmune neutropenia. More recently, the investigation of autoimmune neutropenia in infants has led to the identification of two new neutrophil specific antigens—ND1 (Verheugt et al, 1978b) and NE1 (Claas et al, 1979a; Sabbe et al, 1983). Using monospecific antihuman globulin reagents, Verheugt et al (1978a) have shown that neutrophil autoantibodies may be IgG and/or IgM, sometimes with IgA as well.

Most infants with autoimmune neutropenia have a benign course and the condition is self-limited. Steroids are sometimes used to treat those children who have significant infections, but this may further prejudice their immune function, and a recent study by Bussel et al (1983b) suggests that intravenous IgG is more beneficial in this situation.

B.AUTOIMMUNE NEUTROPENIA ASSOCIATED WITH OTHER DISORDERS

In adults, autoimmune neutropenia is usually associated with other autoimmune disorders. These include autoimmune haemolytic anaemia, ITP (Evan's syndrome) (Pegels et al, 1982b), rheumatoid arthritis (Felty's syndrome) (Logue, 1976; Minchinton et al, 1982), systemic lupus erythematosus (SLE) (Verheugt et al, 1978a) and angioimmunoblastic lymphadenopathy with dysproteinaemia (AILD) (Verheugt et al, 1978a; Logue & Schimm, 1980).

The possible involvement of immune complexes in the pathogenesis of secondary neutropenia has yet to be established. Caligaris-Cappio et al (1979) have suggested that the adsorption of immune complexes to neutrophils may cause pulmonary leucostasis with resultant peripheral neutropenia in some patients. In Felty's syndrome, using the granulocyte immunofluorescence test of Verheugt et al (1977a), positive reactions can be demonstrated with the patient's neutrophils but not with the serum. Furthermore, attempts to elute a neutrophil autoantibody from the fluorescent-positive cells have been unsuccessful (Verheugt et al, 1978a; Minchinton et al, 1982). These findings may be due either to the presence of in vivo bound neutrophil autoantibodies with no free serum antibody, or to the presence of in vivo bound immune complexes. Peterson & Wiik (1983) showed that whole IgG fractions of Felty's sera bound strongly to paraformaldehyde fixed and unfixed neutrophils, whereas $(F(ab)_2$ fractions did not. This suggested that specific antibody activity was not present in the sera and supports an immune complex mediated mechanism of neutropenia in Felty's syndrome.

In contrast, absorption and elution experiments in patients with Evan's syndrome have demonstrated the presence of separate, cell-specific autoantibodies responsible for anaemia, thrombocytopenia and neutropenia (Pegels et al, 1982b), and this has also been shown for neutrophil and platelet autoantibodies that may develop after bone marrow transplantation (Minchinton et al, 1984).

C. AUTOIMMUNE NEUTROPENIA DUE TO INHIBITION OF GRANULOPOIESIS

In the previous conditions, autoantibodies reacting with peripheral neutrophils have been demonstrated, but autoantibodies directed against human myeloid progenitors can also result in neutropenia occurring alone or in association with other cytopenias (Fitchen & Cline, 1980; Levitt et al, 1983). It will be important to define the antigenic and cellular specificities of these antibodies, as this will determine the nature of the target cell and the stage of maturity at which the antibody exerts its effect, e.g. bone-marrow precursors and/or mature circulating cells.

Furthermore, neutropenia due to granulopoietic failure may have a cell-mediated immune basis. A recent study by Bagby et al (1983) has demonstrated the importance of a haemopoietic inhibitory T cell (HIT cell) in such patients.

Drug-induced immune thrombocytopenia and neutropenia

In spite of the large number of reported cases of drug-induced immune cytopenias (see reviews: Miescher & Graf, 1980; Young & Vincent, 1980), laboratory confirmation of the immune basis is very sketchy. Linking the in vivo cytopenia to a reliable laboratory demonstration of a drug-dependent antibody has been a task even more difficult than the search for platelet and neutrophil allo- and autoantibodies. However, newly developed tests, such as the platelet and granulocyte immunofluorescence tests, can be expected to elucidate the diagnosis and pathogenesis of drug induced immune cytopenias. This section will deal with specific drugs only in so far as they illustrate presently established mechanisms of in vivo cell destruction.

1. Drug adsorption

Treatment with high dose penicillin may be associated with immune thrombocytopenia and neutropenia (Murphy et al, 1983). In this situation, the drug in high doses appears to be adsorbed onto the cell surface as in penicillin-induced haemolytic anaemia (Petz & Fudenberg, 1966; White et al, 1968). The antibiotic cotrimoxazole has been shown to produce a similar immune thrombocytopenia (Claas et al, 1979b). Demonstration of the cell-antibody interaction in vitro requires the presence of the drug involved.

2. Immune-complex mechanism

This has been well defined for quinine-quinidine thrombocytopenia (Shulman, 1958; Leeuwen et al, 1982b; Christie & Aster, 1982). The antibody is IgG and fixes complement. In the recent study by Leeuwen et al (1982b), all their positive sera contained IgG_1 antibodies, sometimes in combination with IgG_3 or IgM. They also showed that $F(ab)_2$ fragments of the quinine/quinidine antibody did not react with platelets in vitro in the presence of the drug, suggesting that the Fc part of the antibody is essential for attachment of the immune complex to the platelet membrane. Furthermore, they demonstrated variable reactions of different quinine-quinidine antibodies with Bernard–Soulier platelets, suggesting that glycoprotein Ib, which is deficient in these platelets, is an essential receptor for these antibodies, as previously reported by Kunicki et al (1978). However, the membrane defect in Glanzmann's platelets does not appear to affect attachment of the drug-antibody complex (Leeuwen et al, 1982b). The same drugs may also cause neutropenia either alone (Eisner et al, 1977) or in association with thrombocytopenia (Chong et al, 1983; and personal observations) by an immune-complex mechanism.

3. Autoantibody production

Some drugs, e.g. aprindine hydrochloride (Pisciotta & Cronkite, 1983), levamisole (Rosenthal et al, 1977; Thompson et al, 1980), gold (Claas et al, 1983; Borne et al, personal communication) and hydralazine (personal observations) are associated with immune thrombocytopenia or neutropenia and cell specific autoantibodies, which are detectable in vitro in the absence of the drug (Table 13.6). The mechanism of

Table 13.6 Comparison of the serological findings in (A) quinine-induced thrombocytopenia (immune-complex mechanism) and (b) hydralazine neutropenia (autoantibody mechanism)

| | (a) Quinine-induced thrombocytopenia | | | | (b) Hydralazine neutropenia | | | |
| | Patient's platelet | | Normal platelets | | Patient's neutrophils | | Normal neutrophils | |
Drug → Serum ↓	Present	Absent	Present	Absent	Present	Absent	Present	Absent
Patient	+ +	−	+ +*	−	+ +	+ +	+ +	+ +**
Normal	−	−	−	−	−	−	−	−

* IgG++, C+++, IgM−
** IgG++, IgM+++, C+++

antibody formation may be similar to that in α-methyl-dopa (aldomet) induced haemolytic anaemia, where it is suggested that the drug inhibits the function of T suppressor cells which normally suppress autoantibody forming clones of B cells (Kirtland et al, 1980). These patients may also have other signs of immune disturbance, e.g. the above patient who developed neutropenia associated with hydralazine, also had antinuclear antibodies ('hydralazine lupus') which disappeared on withdrawal of the drug.

These mechanisms refer to the immune destruction of mature peripheral cells, but the drug-induced antibody may also affect bone-marrow precursor cells, and this may contribute significantly to the peripheral cytopenia in some cases. This aspect of drug-induced immune cytopenias has been less well studied, but improvements in bone-marrow clonogenic assay techniques now make this feasible.

It is important to test as many different pathogenic mechanisms as possible in each patient. Furthermore, it is essential to test both acute phase and convalescent sera with the patient's own cells; it may, however, be necessary to store the acute phase serum for retrospective testing until the cell count has increased. Tests with the convalescent serum, collected when the drug has been eliminated, may be necessary to demonstrate the essential role of the drug in the in vitro assay system.

Limited data are available on the immunopathology of the drug-induced immune cytopenias. In particular, it is uncertain what determines the target cell for a particular drug antibody. The drug adsorption mechanism (prototype penicillin) appears to be quantitative, and both drug and cell membrane characteristics may determine the critical drug concentration on a particular cell type. In the immune-complex mechanism, there are some pointers towards cell-specific determinants, e.g. the quinine/quinidine antibody reacts poorly or not at all with Bernard–Souilier platelets that lack specific membrane glycoproteins. More recently, Claas et al (1981) have demonstrated familial restriction of certain drug antibody reactions, and suggest that the drug-induced antibody has a dual recognition for the drug and a polymorphic platelet or neutrophil specific membrane determinant. This apparent restriction was not associated with known HLA, platelet specific or neutrophil specific antigens.

Acknowledgements

Personal observations and published work reported in this review are based on studies supported by the Cancer Research Campaign and St Bartholomew's Hospital Joint Research Board. We also thank Mr Paul Metcalfe and Dr Michael Murphy for permission to publish details of collaborative studies in progress, and the many colleagues who have referred patients for investigation.

REFERENCES

Abrahamson N, Eisenberg P D, Aster R H 1974 Post-transfusion purpura: immunological aspects and therapy. New England Journal of Medicine 291: 1163–1166

Adner M M, Fisch G R, Starobin S G, Aster R H 1969 Use of 'compatible' platelet transfusions in treatment of congenital isoimmune thrombocytopenic purpura. New England Journal of Medicine 280: 244–247

Ahn Y S, Harrington W J, Simon S R, Mylvaganam R, Pall L M, So A G 1983 Danazol for the treatment of idiopathic thrombocytopenic purpura. New England Journal of Medicine 308: 1396–1399

Bagby G G, Lawrence H J, Neerhout R C 1983 T-lymphocyte-mediated granulopoietic failure. In vitro identification of prednisone-responsive patients. New England Journal of Medicine 309: 1073–1078

Bierling P H, Vernant J P, Cordonnier C, Rodet M, Maillard J M, Beajean D, Chevallier A M, Duedari N, Rochant H 1983 Platelet associated IgG after BMT for acute leukaemia (abstract). Experimental Haematology 11: Suppl 13: 15

Boizard B, Wautier J-L 1984 Lek^a, a new platelet specific antigen absent in Glanzmann's thrombasthenia. Vox Sanguinis 46: 47–54

Borne A E G Kr von dem, Helmerhorst F M, Leeuwen E F van, Pegels H G, Reisz E von, Engelfriet C P 1980 Autoimmune thrombocytopenia: detection of platelet autoantibodies with the suspension immunofluorescence test. British Journal of Haematology 45: 319–327

Borne A E G Kr von dem, Leeuwen E Fvan, Reisz E von, Boxtel C J van, Engelfriet C P 1981 Neonatal alloimmune thrombocytopenia: detection and characterization of the responsible antibodies by the platelet immunofluorescence test. Blood 57: 649–656

Borne A E G Kr von dem, Verheugt F W A, Oosterhof F, Reisz E von, Brutel de la Riveiere A, Engelfriet C P 1978 A simple immunofluorescence test for the detection of platelet antibodies. British Journal of Haematology 39: 195–207

Brand A, Leeuwen A van, Eernisse J G, Rood J J van 1978 Platelet transfusion therapy. Optimal donor selection with a combination of lymphocytotoxicity and platelet fluorescence tests. Blood 51: 781–788

Bucher U, Weck A de, Spengler H, Tschopp L, Kummer H 1973 Platelet transfusions: shortened survival of HLA identical platelets and failure of in vitro detection of anti-platelet antibodies after multiple transfusions. Vox Sanguinis 25: 187–192

Bussel J B, Kimberly R B, Inman R D, Schulman I, Cunningham-Rundles C, Cheung N, Smithwick E M, O'Malley J, Barandun S, Hilgartner M 1983a Intravenous gammaglobulin treatment of chronic idiopathic thrombocytopenic purpura. Blood 62: 480–486

Bussel J, Lalezari P, Hilgartner M, Partin J, Fikrig S, O'Malley J, Barandun S 1983b Reversal of neutropenia with intravenous gammaglobulin in autoimmune neutropenia of infancy. Blood 62: 398–400

Caligaris-Cappio F, Camussi G, Gavosto F 1979 Idiopathic neutropenia with normocellular bone marrow: an immune-complex disease. British Journal of Haematology 43: 595–605

Campana D, Bergui L, Camussi G, Miniero R, Morgando M P, Sardi A, Novarino A, Caligaris-Cappio F 1983 Immune complexes and antiplatelet antibodies in idiopathic thrombocytopenia purpura. Haematologica 68: 157–166

Chapman J F, Metcalfe P, Murphy M F, Burman J F, Waters A H 1984 Sequential development of platelet, neutrophil and red cell autoantibodies associated with measles infection. Clinical and Laboratory Haematology 6: 219–228

Chong B H, Berndt M C, Koutts J, Robertson T I, Castaldi P A 1983 Quinidine-induced thrombocytopenia and leukopenia: in vitro studies of the quinidine-dependent platelet and granulocyte antibodies (abstract). Pathology 15: 345–352

Chow H S, Alexander D L, Epstein R B 1983 Detection and significance of granulocyte alloimmunization in leukocyte transfusion therapy on neutropenic dogs. Transfusion 23: 15–19

Christie D J, Aster R H 1982 Drug-antibody-platelet interaction in quinine-and quinidine-induced thrombocytopenia. Journal of Clinical Investigation 70: 989–998

Cines D B, Schreiber A D 1979 Immune thrombocytopenia. Use of a Coombs antiglobulin test to detect IgG and C3 on platelets. New England Journal of Medicine 300: 106–111

Claas F H J, Langerak J, Beer L L de, Rood J J van 1981 Drug-induced antibodies: Interaction of the drug with a polymorphic platelet-antigen. Tissue Antigens 17: 64–66

Claas F H J, Langerak J, Sabbe L J M, Rood J J van 1979a NE1: A new neutrophil specific antigen. Tissue Antigens 13: 129–134

Claas F H, Meer J W M van der, Langerak J 1979b Immunological effect of co-trimoxazole on platelets. British Medical Journal ii: 898–899

Claas F, Witvliet M, Timmermans de Jong E, Brand A 1983 Drug-induced thrombocytopenia. Abstract 113. Seventh Meeting, International Society of Haematology, European and African Division, 4–9 September, 1983, Barcelona

Dahlke M B, Keashen M, Alavi J B, Koch P A, Eisenstaedt R 1982 Granulocyte transfusions and outcome of alloimmunized patients with Gram negative sepsis. Transfusion 22: 374–378

Danpure H J, Osman S, Brady F 1982 The labelling of blood cells in plasma with ^{111}In-tropolonate. British Journal of Radiology 55: 247–249

Dixon R, Rosse W, Ebert L 1975 Quantitative determination of antibody in idiopathic thrombocytopenic purpura: correlation of serum and platelet-bound antibody to clinical response. New England Journal of Medicine 292: 230–236

Donnall R L, McMillan R, Yelenosky R J, Longmire R L, Lightsey A L 1976 Different antiplatelet antibody specifiities in immune thrombocytopenic purpura. British Journal of Haematology 34: 147–151

Duquesnoy R J, Filip D J, Rodney G E, Aster R H 1977 Transfusion therapy of refractory thrombocytopenic patients with platelets from donors selectively mismatched for cross-reactive HLA antigens. Transplantation Proceedings 9 Suppl 1: 1827–1828

Dutcher J P, Schiffer C A, Johnston G S, Papenburg D, Daly P A, Aisner J, Wiernik P H 1983 Alloimmunization prevents the migration of transfused indium-111-labelled granulocytes to sites of infection. Blood 62: 354–360

Eisner E V, Carr R M, MacKinney A A 1977 Quinidine-induced agranulocytosis. Journal of the American Medical Association 238: 884–886

Ercilla M G, Borche L, Vives J, Castillo R, Gelabert A, Rozman C 1982 Circulating immune complexes in immune thrombotytopenic purpura (ITP). British Journal of Haematology 52: 679–682

Eernisse J G, Brand A 1981 Prevention of platelet refractoriness due to HLA antibodies by administration of leucocyte-poor blood components. Experimental Haematology 9: 77–83

Fehr J, Hofman V, Kappeler U 1982 Transient reversal of thrombocytopenia in idiopathic thrombocytopenic purpura by high-dose intravenous gamma globulin. New England Journal of Medicine 306: 1254–1258

Feusner J H, Slichter S J, Harker L A 1979 Mechanisms of thrombocytopenia in varicella. American Journal of Hematology 7: 255–264

Fitchen J H, Cline M J 1980 Serum inhibitors of myelopoiesis. British Journal of Haematology 44: 7–16

Gengozian N, Annostby D A 1981 Antibodies selectively reactive to autologous and host-type platelets are obtained following interspecies immunization in marmosets. Clinical and Experimental Immunology 43: 128–143

Gengozian N, McLaughlin C L 1980 IgG + platelets in the marmoset: their induction, maintenance and survival. Blood 55: 885–890

Gerstner J B, Smith M J, Davis K D, Cimo P L, Aster R H 1979 Post-transfusion purpura: therapeutic failure of P1^{A1} negative platelet transfusion. American Journal of Haematology 6: 71–75

Gmur J, Felton A von, Osterwalder B, Honeggar H, Hormann A, Sauter C, Deubelbeiss K, Berchtold W, Metaxas M, Scali G, Frick P 1983 Delayed alloimmunization using random single donor platelet transfusions: a prospective study in thrombocytopenic patients with acute leukemia. Blood 62: 473–479

Grumét F C, Yankee R A 1970 Long term platelet support of patients with aplastic anemia. Effect of splenectomy and steroid therapy. Annals of Internal Medicine 73: 1–7

Guidino M, Miller W V 1981 Application of the enzyme linked immunospecific assay (ELISA) for the detection of platelet antibodies. Blood 57: 32–37

Gurner B S, Coombs R R A 1958 Examination of human leucocytes for the ABO, MN, Rh, Tj^a, Lutheran and Lewis systems of antigens by means of mixed erythrocyte-leucocyte agglutination. Vox Sanguinis 3: 13–22

Harris P J, Kessler C M, Lessin L S 1983 Acquired hemolytic anemia and thrombocytopenia (Evan's syndrome) in hemophilia. New England Journal of Medicine 308: 50

Hauch T W, Rosse W F 1977 Platelet bound complement (C3) in immune thrombocytopenia. Blood 50: 1129–1136

Hawker R J, Hawker L M, Wilkinson A R 1980 Indium (^{111}-In)-labelled human platelets: optimal method. Clinical Science 58: 243–248

Hegde U M, Gordon-Smith E C, Worlledge S 1977 Platelet antibodies in thrombocytopenic patients. British Journal of Haematology 35: 113–122

Hegde U M, Powell D K, Bowes A, Gordon-Smith E C 1981 Enzyme linked immunoassay for the detection of platelet associated IgG. British Journal of Haematology 48: 39–46

Hegde U M, Williams K, Devereux S, Bowes A, Powell D, Fisher D 1983 Platelet associated IgG and immune thrombocytopenia in lympho-proliferative and autoimmune disorders. Clinical and Laboratory Haematology 5: 9–15

Helmerhorst F M, Smeenk R J T, Hack C E, Engelfriet C P, Borne A E G Kr von dem 1983 Interference of IgG, IgG aggregates and immune complexes in tests for platelet autoantibodies. British Journal of Haematology 55: 533–545

Howard J E, Perkins H A 1978 The natural history of alloimmunisation to platelets. Transfusion 18: 496–503

Hymes K, Shulman S, Karpatkin S 1979 A solid-phase radioimmunoassay for bound antiplatelet antibody. Studies on 45 patients with autoimmune platelet disorders. Journal of Laboratory and Clinical Medicine 94: 639–648

Imbach P, Barandun S, d'Apuzzo V, Baumgartner C, Hirt A, Morell A, Rossi E, Schoni M, Vest M and Wagner H P 1981 High dose intravenous gamma-globulin for idiopathic thrombocytopenic purpura in childhood. Lancet i: 1228–1231

Kaden B R, Rosse W F, Hauch T W 1979 Immune thrombocytopenia in lymphoproliferative diseases. Blood 53: 545–551

Karpatkin S 1980 Autoimmune thrombocytopenic purpura. Blood 56: 329–343

Karpatkin S, Garg S K, Siskind G W 1971 Autoimmune thrombocytopenic purpura and the compensated thrombocytolytic state. American Journal of Medicine 51: 1–4

Kelton J G, Blanchette V S, Wilson W E, Powers P, Mohan K R, Effer S B, Barr R D 1980a Neonatal thrombocytopenia due to passive immunisation. Prenatal diagnosis and distinction between maternal platelet alloantibodies and autoantibodies. New England Journal of Medicine 302: 1401–1403

Kelton J G, Giles A R, Neame P B, Powers P, Hageman N, Hirsh J 1980b Comparison of two direct assays for platelet-associated IgG (PAIgG) in assessment of immune and nonimmune thrombocytopenia. Blood 55: 424–429

Kelton J G, Hamid C, Aker S, Blajchman MA 1982b The amount of blood group A substance on platelets is proportional to the amount in plasma. Blood 59: 980–985

Kelton J G, Keystone J, Moore J, Denomme G, Tozman E, Glynn M, Neame P B, Gauldie J, Jensen J 1983 Immune-mediated thrombocytopenia of malaria. Journal of Clinical Investigation 71: 832–836

Kelton J G, Powers P J, Carter C J 1982a A prospective study of the usefulness of the measurement of platelet-associated IgG for the diagnosis of idiopathic thrombocytopenic purpura. Blood 60: 1050–1053

Kelton J G, Steeves K 1983 The amount of platelet-bound albumin parallels the amount of IgG on washed platelets from patients with immune thrombocytopenia. Blood 62: 924–927

Kernoff L M, Malan E 1983 Complement (C3) binding to platelets in autoimmune thrombocytopenia. Clinical and Laboratory Haematology 5: 1–7

Kickler T S, Braine H G, Ness P M, Koester A, Bias W 1983 A radiolabelled antiglobulin test for cross-matching platelet transfusions. Blood 61: 238–242

Kirtland H H, Mohler D N, Horwitz D A 1980 Methyldopa inhibition of suppressor-lymphocyte function. A proposed cause of autoimmune hemolytic anemia. New England Journal of Medicine 302: 825–832

Kunicki T J, Johnson M M, Aster R H 1978 Absence of the platelet receptor for drug-dependent antibodies in the Bernard–Soulier syndrome. Journal of Clinical Investigation 62: 716–719

Lalezari P, Driscoll A M 1982 Ability of thrombocytes to acquire HLA specificity from plasma. Blood 59: 167–170

Lalezari P, Jiang A F, Yegen L, Santorineou M 1975 Chronic autoimmune neutropenia due to anti-NA2 antibody. New England Journal of Medicine 293: 744–747

Lalezari P, Murphy G B 1967 Cold reacting leucocyte agglutinins and their significance. In: Curtoni E S, Mattiuz P L, Tosi R M (eds) Histocompatibility testing. Munksgaard, Copenhagen, Denmark, p 421–427

Lalezari P, Radel E 1974 Neutrophil-specific antigens: Immunology and clinical significance. Seminars in Haematology 11: 281–290

Lambert P H, Dixon F J, Zubler R H, Agnello V, Cambiaso C, Casali P, Clarke J, Cowdery J S, McDuffie F C, Hay F, MacLennan I C M, Masson P, Mueller-Eberhard H I, Penttinen K, Smith M, Tappeiner G, Theofilopoulos A N, Verroust P 1978 A WHO collaborative study for the evaluation of eighteen methods for detecting immune complexes in serum. Journal of Clinical and Laboratory Immunology 1: 1–15

Leeuwen E F van, Borne A E G Kr von dem, Oudesluijs-Murphy A M, Ras-Zeijlmans G J M 1980 Neonatal alloimmune thrombocytopenia complicated by maternal autoimmune thrombocytopenia. British Medical Journal 281: 27

Leeuwen E F van, Engelfriet C P, Borne A E G Kr von dem 1982b Studies on quinine and quinidine dependent antibodies against platelets and their reaction with platelets in the Bernard–Soulier syndrome. British Journal of Haematology 51: 551–560

Leeuwen E F van, Roord J J, Gast G C de, Plas-Van Dalen C van der 1983 Neonatal neutropenia due to maternal autoantibodies against neutrophils. British Medical Journal 287: 94

Leeuwen E F van, Ven J Th M van der, Engelfriet C P, Borne A E G Kr von dem 1982a Specificity of autoantibodies in autoimmune thrombocytopenia. Blood 59: 23–26

Leporrier M, Dighiero G, Auzemery M, Binet J L 1979 Detection and quantification of platelet-bound antibodies with immunoperoxidase. British Journal of Haematology 42: 605–611

Levitt L J, Ries C A, Greenberg P L 1983 Pure white cell aplasia. Antibody-mediated autoimmune inhibition of granulopoiesis. New England Journal of Medicine 308: 1141–1146

LoBuglio A F, Court W S, Vinocur L, Maglott G, Shaw G M 1983 Immune thrombocytopenic purpura. Use of a ^{125}I-labelled antihuman IgG monoclonal antibody to quantify platelet-bound IgG. New England Journal of Medicine 309: 459–463

Loghem J J van, Dorfmeijer H, Hart M van der, Schreuder F 1959 Serological and genetical studies on a platelet antigen (Zw). Vox Sanguinis 4: 161–169

Logue G L 1976 Felty's syndrome: granulocyte-bound immunoglobulin G and splenectomy. Annals of Internal Medicine 85: 437–442

Logue G L, Shimm D S 1980 Autoimmune granulocytopenia. Annual Review of Medicine 31: 191–200

McCullogh J, Weiblen B J, Clay M E, Forstrom L 1981a Effect of leukocyte antibodies on the fate in vivo of indium-III-labelled granulocytes. Blood 58: 164–170

McIntosh S, O'Brien R T, Schwartz A D, Pearson H A 1973 Neonatal isoimmune purpura: response to platelet infusions. Journal of Pediatrics 82: 1020–1027

McMillan R 1981 Chronic idiopathic thrombocytopenic purpura. New England Journal of Medicine 304: 1135–1147

McMillan R 1983 Immune cytopenias. In: Methods in haematology 9. Churchill Livingstone, London

McMillan R, Smith R S, Longmire R L, Velenosky R, Reid R T, Craddock C G 1971 Immunoglobulins associated with human platelets. Blood 37: 316–322

Madyastha P R, Fudenberg H H, Glassman A B, Madyastha K R, Smith C L 1983 Autoimmune neutropenia in early infancy: a review. Annals of Clinical and Laboratory Science 12: 356–367

Madyastha P R, Kyong C U, Darby C P, Genco P V, Madyastha K R, Glassman A B, Fudenberg H H 1982 Role of neutrophil antigen NA1 in an infant with autoimmune netropenia. American Journal of Diseases of Children 136: 718–721

Melo J, Harrington W J, Ahn Y S, Collin A S, Byrnes J J, Pall L M, Mylvaganam R 1981 Colchicine therapy of idiopathic thrombocytopenia (abstract). Blood 58: 200A

Menitove J E, Aster R H 1983 Transfusion of platelets and plasma products. Clinics in Haematology 12: 239–266

Metcalfe P, Murphy M F, Waters A H 1983 The demonstration of immune mediated destruction of platelets in mild (compensated) thrombocytopenia. Abstract 620 Seventh Meeting, International Society of Haematology, European and African Division, 4–9 September, 1983, Barcelona

Miescher J, Graf J 1980 Drug-induced thrombocytopenia. Clinics in Haematology 9: 506–519

Minchinton R M, Doyle D V, Waters A H 1982 Neutrophil surface-bound immunoglobulin — a feature of Felty's syndrome? Clinical and Laboratory Haematology 4: 131–138

Minchinton R M, Waters A H 1984 Chloroquine stripping of HLA antigens from neutrophils without removal of neutrophil specific antigens. British Journal of Haematology 57: 703–706

Minchinton R M, Waters A H, Malpas J S, Starke I, Kendra J, Barrett A J 1984 Platelet and granulocyte specific antibodies after allogeneic and autologous bone marrow grafts. Vox Sanguinis 46: 125–135

Minchinton R M, Waters A H, Kendra J, Barrett A J 1982 Autoimmune thrombocytopenia acquired from an allogeneic bone-marrow graft. Lancet ii: 627–629

Mollison P L 1982 Some unfavourable effects of transfusion. In: Blood transfusion in clinical medicine, 7th edn. Blackwell Scientific Publications, London, p 734

Morgenstern G R, Measday B, Hegde U M 1983 Autoimmune thrombocytopenia in pregnancy: new approach to management. British Medical Journal 287: 584

Morris L, Distenfeld A, Amorosi E, Karpatkin S 1982 Autoimmune thrombocytopenic purpura in homosexual men. Annals of Internal Medicine 96: 714–717

Morrison F S, Mollison P L 1966 Post-transfusion purpura. New England Journal of Medicine 275: 243–248

Morse B S, Giuliani D, Nussbaum M 1981 Quantitation of platelet-associated IgG by radial immunodiffusion. Blood 57: 809–811

Mueller-Eckhardt C, Kayser W, Mersch-Baumert K, Mueller-Eckhardt G, Breidenbach M, Kugel H-G, Graubner M 1980b The clinical significance of platelet-associated IgG: a study on 298 patients with various disorders. British Journal of Haematology 46: 123–131

Mueller-Eckhardt C, Kuenzlen E, Thilo-Korner D, Pralle H 1983 High dose intravenous immunoglobulin for post-transfusion purpura. New England Journal of Medicine 308: 287

Mueller-Eckhardt C, Mahn I, Schulz G, Mueller-Eckhardt G 1978 Detection of platelet autoantibodies by a radioactive anti-immunoglobulin test. Vox Sanguinis 35: 357–365

Muller J Y, Reznikoff-Etievant M F, Patereau C, Lobet R, Pinon F, Soulier J P 1983 Neonatal alloimmune thrombocytopenic purpura. Abstract 111. Seventh Meeting, International Society of Haematology, European and African Division, 4–9 September, 1983, Barcelona

Murphy M F, Riordan T, Minchinton R M, Amess J A L, Shaw E J, Waters A H 1983 Demonstration of an immune-mediated mechanism of penicillin-induced neutropenia and thrombocytopenia. British Journal of Haematology 55: 155–160

Myers T J, Kim B K, Steiner M, Baldini M G 1981 Selection of donor platelets for alloimmunised patients using a platelet-associated IgG assay. Blood: 58: 444–450

Myers T J, Kim B K, Steiner M, Baldini M G 1982 Platelet-associated complement in immune thrombocytopenic purpura. Blood 59: 1023–1028

Nel J D, Stevens K 1980 A new method for the simultaneous quantitation of platelet-bound immunoglobulin (IgG) and complement (C3) employing an enzyme linked immunosorbent assay (ELISA) procedure. British Journal of Haematology 44: 281–290

Nel J D, Stevens K, Mouton A, Pretorius F J 1983 Platelet-bound IgM in autoimmune thrombocytopenia. Blood 61: 119–124

Newland A C, Treleavan J G, Minchinton R M, Waters A H 1983 High dose intravenous IgG in adults with autoimmune thrombocytopenia. Lancet i: 84–87

Nordhagen R, Flaathen S T 1983 Chloroquine stripping of HLA antigens on platelets for the platelet suspension immunofluorescence test. Abstract 618. Seventh Meeting, International Society of Haematology, 4–9 September, 1983, Barcelona

Pearson H A, Shulman N R, Mardar V J, Thomas E C 1964 Isoimmune neonatal thrombocytopenic purpura. Clinical and therapeutic considerations. Blood 23: 154–177

Pegels J G, Bruynes E C E, Engelfriet C P, Borne A E G Kr von dem 1982a Serological studies in patients on platelet — and granulocyte-substitution therapy. British Journal of Haematology 52: 59–68

Pegels J G, Bruynes E C E, Engelfriet C P, Borne A E G Kr von dem 1981 Post-transfusion purpura: a serological and immunochemical study. British Journal of Haematology 49: 521–530

Pegels J G, Helmerhorst F M, Leeuwen E F van, Plas-van Dalen, C. van der, Engelfriet C P, Borne A E G Kr von dem 1982b The Evan's syndrome: characterisation of the responsible autoantibodies. British Journal of Haematology 51: 445–450

Petersen J, Wiik A 1983 Lack of evidence for granulocyte specific membrane-directed autoantibodies in neutropenic cases of rhematoid arthritis and in autoimmune neutropenia. Acta Pathologica, Microbiologica et Immunologica Scandinavica 91C: 15–22

Petz L D, Fudenberg H H 1966 Coombs positive hemolytic anemia caused by penicillin administration. New England Journal of Medicine 274: 171–178

Pfueller S L, Cosgrove L, Firkin B, Tew D 1981 Relationship of raised platelet IgG in thrombocytopenia to total platelet protein content. British Journal of Haematology 49: 293–302

Pisciotta A V, Cronkite C 1983 Aprindine-induced agranulocytosis. Evidence for an immune mechanism. Archives of Internal Medicine 143: 241–243

Plotz P H 1983 Autoantibodies are anti-idiotype antibodies to antiviral antibodies. Lancet ii: 824–826

Plouvier E, Herve P, Faivre L, Noir A 1983 Refractory auto-immune thrombocytopenia following autologous stem cell grafting (abstract). Experimental Haematology 11 Suppl 13: 172

Priest J R, McCullough J J, Clay M E, Krivit W 1980 Neutrophil surface antigen phenotyping: a new way to characterize autoimmune neutropenia. Journal of Paediatrics 96: 164

Ratnoff O D, Menitove J E, Aster R H, Lederman M M 1983 Coincident classic haemophilia and 'idiopathic' thrombocytopenic purpura in patients under treatment with concentrates of antihaemophilic factor (factor VIII). New England Journal of Medicine 308: 439–442

Rood J J van, Leeuwen A van, Schippers A M J, Vooys W H, Frederiks E, Balner H, Eernisse J G 1965 Leukocyte groups, the normal lymphocyte transfer test and homograft sensitivity. In: Balner H (ed) Histocompatibility testing. Munskgaard, Copenhagen, Denmark, p 37–50

Rosenthal M, Breysse Y, Dixon A St J, Franchimont P, Huskisson E C, Schmidt K L, Schuermans Y, Veys E, Vischer T L 1977 Levamisole and agranulocytosis. Lancet i: 904–905

Rosse W F, Adams J P, Yount W J 1980 Subclass of IgG antibodies in immune thrombocytopenic purpura (ITP). British Journal of Haematology 46: 109–114

Sabbe L J M, Claas F H J, Langerak J, Claus G, Smit L W A, Koning J H de, Schreuder C H, Rood J J van 1983 Group specific auto-immune antibodies directed to granulocytes as a cause of chronic benign neutropenia in infants. Acta Haematologica 68: 20–27

Salama A, Mueller-Eckhardt C, Kiefel V 1983 Effect of intravenous immunoglobulin in immune thrombocytopenia. Competitive inhibition of reticuloendothelial system function by sequestration of autologous red blood cells? Lancet ii: 193–195

Schwartz K A, Slichter S J, Harker L A 1982 Immune-mediated platelet destruction and thrombocytopenia in patients with solid tumours. British Journal of Haematology 51: 17–24

Sharon R, Amar A 1981 Maternal anti-HLA antibodies and neonatal thrombocytopenia. Lancet i: 1313

Shaw G M, Axelson J, Maglott J G, LoBuglio A F 1984 Quantification of platelet-bound IgG by ^{125}I-staphylococcal protein A in immune thrombocytopenic purpura and other thrombocytopenic disorders. Blood 63: 154–161

Shulman N R 1958 Immunoreactions involving platelets. I. A steric and kinetic model for formation of a complex from a human antibody, quinidine as haptene, and platelets; and for fixation of complement by the complex. Journal of Experimental Medicine 107: 665–690

Shulman N R, Aster R K, Leitner A, Hiller M C 1961 Immunoreactions involving platelets: V. Post transfusion purpura due to a complement-fixing antibody against a genetically controlled platelet antigen: a proposed mechanism for thrombocytopenia and its relevance in 'autoimmunity'. Journal of Clinical Investigation 40: 1597–1620

Shulman N R, Leissinger C A, Hotchkiss A, Kautz C 1982 An in vivo model demonstrating that elevated platelet-associated IgG is a non-specific consequence of platelet destruction (abstract). Blood 60: 191a

Shulman N R, Marder V J, Hiller M C, Collier E M 1964 Platelet and leucocyte isoantigens and their antibodies: serologic, physiologic and clinical studies. Progress in Haematology 4: 222–304

Soulier J P, Paterean C, Drouet J 1975 Platelet indirect radioactive Coombs test. Its utilization for Pl^{A1} grouping. Vox Sanguinis 29: 253–268

Storb R, Weiden P L 1981 Transfusion problems associated with transplantation. Seminars in Haematology 18: 163–176

Strother S V, Zuckerman K S, LoBuglio A F 1982 Colchicine therapy of refractory immune thrombocytopenia (abstract). Blood 60: Suppl 1, 192a

Taaning E, Antonsen H, Petersen S, Svejgaard A, Thomsen M 1983 HLA antigens and maternal antibodies in allo-immune neonatal thrombocytopenia. Tissue Antigens 21: 351–359

Thompson J S, Herbick J M, Klassen L W, Severson C D, Overlin V L, Blaschke J W, Silverman M A, Vogel C L 1980 Studies on Levamisole-induced agranulocytosis. Blood 56: 388–396

Thorsby E 1969 HLA antigens on human granulocytes studied with isoantisera obtained by skin grafting. Scandinavian Journal of Haematology 6: 119–127

Thorsby E, Helgesen A, Gjemdal T 1972 Repeated platelet transfusions from HLA compatible and unrelated sibling donors. Tissue Antigens 2: 397–404

Tosato G, Applebaum F R, Deisseroth A B 1978 HLA-matched platelet transfusion therapy of severe aplastic anemia. Blood 52: 846–854

Trent R J, Clancy R L, Danis V, Basten A 1980 Immune complexes in thrombocytopenic patients: cause or effect? British Journal of Haematology 44: 645–654

Valbonesi M, Campelli A, Marazzi M G, Cottofava F, Jannuzzi C 1979 Chronic autoimmune neutropenia due to anti-NA1 antibody, Vox Sanguinis 36: 9–12

Veenhoven W A, Sijpestin J A K, Schans G S van der 1980 Platelet antibodies in idiopathic thrombocytopenic purpura. Clinical and Experimental Immunology 39: 645–651

Verheugt F W A, Borne A E G Kr von dem, Decary F, Engelfriet C P 1977a The detection of granulocyte alloantibodies with an indirect immunofluorescence test. British Journal of Haematology 36: 533–544

Verheugt F W A, Borne A E G Kr von dem, Noord-Bokhorst J C, Engelfriet C P 1978a Autoimmune granulocytopenia: the detection of granulocyte autoantibodies with the immunofluorescence test. British Journal of Haematology 39: 339–350

Verheugt F W A, Borne A E G, Noord-Bokhorst J C van, Nijenhuis L E, Engelfriet C P 1978b ND1, a new neutrophil granulocyte antigen. Vox Sanguinis 35: 13–17

Verheugt F W A, Borne A E G Kr von dem, Prins H K, Engelfriet C P 1977b The detection of granulocyte antibodies in relation to granulocyte transfusion. Experimental Haematology 5 Suppl: 151–155

Verheugt F W A, Noord-Bokhurst J C van, Borne A E G Kr von dem, Engelfriet C P 1979 A family with allo-immune neonatal neutropenia: Group-specific pathogenicity of maternal antibodies. Vox Sanguinis 36: 1–8

Waters A H, Metcalfe P, Minchinton R M, Barrett A J, James D C O 1983 Autoimmune thrombocytopenia acquired from an allogeneic bone-marrow graft — demonstration of compensated platelet destruction in both donor and recipient. Lancet ii: 1430

Waters A H, Minchinton R M, Bell R, Ford J M, Lister T A 1981 A cross-matching procedure for the selection of platelet donors for alloimmunized patients. British Journal of Haematology 48: 59–68

Weerdt C M van der, Veenhoven von Reisz L E, Nijenhuis L E, Loghem J J van 1963 The Zw blood group system in platelets. Vox Sanguinis 8: 513–530

Wenske C, Gaedicke E, Kuenzlen E, Heyes H, Mueller-Eckhardt C, Kleihaur E, Lauritzen C 1983 Treatment of idiopathic thrombocytic purpura in pregnancy by high-dose intravenous immunoglobulin. Blut 46: 347–353

White J M, Brown D L, Hepner G W, Worlledge S M 1968 Penicillin-induced haemolytic anaemia. British Medical Journal 3: 26–29

Yankee R A, Graff K S, Dowling R, Henderson E S 1973 Selection of unrelated compatible platelet donors by lymphocyte HLA matching. New England Journal of Medicine 288: 760–764

Yankee R A, Grumet F C, Rogentine G N 1969 Platelet transfusion therapy — the selection of compatible platelet donors for refractory patients by lymphocyte HLA typing. New England Journal of Medicine 281: 1208–1212

Young G R, Vincent P C 1980 Drug induced agranulocytosis. Clinics in Haematology 9: 483–504

Zeigler Z, Murphy S, Gardner F H 1975 Post-transfusion purpura: a heterogeneous syndrome. Blood 45: 529–536

14. Advances in antithrombotic therapy

J. Hirsh   F. Ofosu   J. Cairns

INTRODUCTION

In this chapter five recent advances in antithrombotic therapy are reviewed. These are (1) advances in understanding the antithrombotic and haemorrhagic properties of heparin, (2) the optimal therapeutic range for monitoring long-term anticoagulant therapy in patients with venous thrombosis, (3) current status of drugs which suppress platelet function in the treatment of thromboembolic disease, (4) coronary thrombolysis for the treatment of acute myocardial infarction and (5) the development of a new thrombolytic agent tissue plasminogen activator.

RECENT ADVANCES IN UNDERSTANDING THE ANTITHROMBOTIC AND HAEMORRHAGIC PROPERTIES OF HEPARIN

Heparin is an effective antithrombotic agent, but its clinical use is limited by its major side effect, bleeding (Kelton & Hirsh, 1980). It has generally been assumed that bleeding associated with heparin therapy, like its antithrombotic properties, is directly related to its effect on blood coagulation and, therefore, that this side effect is unavoidable. In this section, recent studies with various heparin fractions and heparinoids are described which demonstrate that the antithrombotic and haemorrhagic effects of heparin can be dissociated (Carter et al, 1982; Henny et al, 1983; Ockelford et al, 1982a,b). These studies also provide to possible explanations for the antithrombotic and haemorrhagic effects of heparin.

Mode of action of heparin

Heparin inhibits blood coagulation by three independent mechanisms; it has an additional effect on haemostasis through its interaction with blood platelets (Fig. 14.1) (Salzman et al, 1980; Zucker, 1977). The major anticoagulant action of heparin when administered at therapeutic concentrations is through its ability to augment the inhibition of a number of activated coagulation factors by antithrombin III. Antithrombin III is a naturally occurring inhibitor of a number of activated clotting factors (factors XIIa, XIa, IXa, Xa and thrombin) which have a serine residue at the enzymatically active centre. Antithrombin III combines with and inactivates these coagulation enzymes in a progressive and irreversible manner by esterification of the susceptible arginyl residue in antithrombin III by the active site serine of the coagulation enzyme. Specific lysyl residues of antithrombin III are required for binding to heparin (Rosenberg & Damus, 1973). Heparin binding markedly accelerates the inhibitory effect of antithrombin III on these activated coagulation factors, by causing a conformational change on the antithrombin III molecule. The heparin then dissociates from the coagulation enzyme antithrombin III complex and can be reutilised (Nesheim, 1983). Recent evidence suggests that factor XIa inactivation by antithrombin III is relatively insensitive to heparin (Scott et al, 1983) and that factor IXa is relatively stable to effects of antithrombin III and heparin (McNeely et al, 1983).

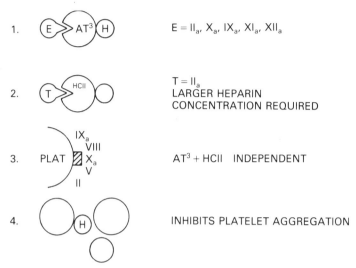

1. $E = II_a, X_a, IX_a, XI_a, XII_a$

2. $T = II_a$
    LARGER HEPARIN
    CONCENTRATION REQUIRED

3. AT^3 + HCII INDEPENDENT

4. INHIBITS PLATELET AGGREGATION

Fig. 14.1 Effect of heparin on haemostasis.

At higher concentrations, heparin has an additional effect on the rate of inhibition of thrombin by a newly described antithrombin known as heparin cofactor II (Tollefsen et al, 1983). Unlike antithrombin III, however, thrombin is the only coagulant protease that has been demonstrated to be inactivated by heparin cofactor II (Tollefsen et al, 1983). The anticoagulant effect of a number of heparinoids including dermatan sulphate (a naturally occurring glycosaminoglycan) and pentosan polysulphate (SP54), a sythetic sulphated polysaccharide, is mediated by heparin cofactor II (Fisher et al, 1982; Tollefsen et al, 1983).

Recently, a third anticoagulant effect of heparin unrelated to antithrombin III and heparin cofactor II has been described. This effect is minor and unlikely to be clinically relevant. Walker & Esmon (1979) reported that heparin inhibits the activation of prothrombin by factor Xa in the absence of antithrombin III. This third anticoagulant effect of heparin has been confirmed by Ofosu and associates (Ofosu et al, 1980; 1982a,b) using three independent experimental systems.

Heparin also interacts with platelets and has been reported to both induce and inhibit platelet aggregation (Huisse et al, 1982; Kelton & Hirsh, 1980). Although it has been suggested that heparin interferes with the inhibitory effect of PGI_2 on platelet aggregation, results of a number of studies indicate that heparin does not act directly with PGI_2 but rather by potentiating platelet aggregation non-specifically (Bertele et al, 1983; McIntyre et al, 1981). Heparin can cause thrombocytopenia which may or may not be accompanied by major arterial thrombosis. Platelets in these patients have been reported to have elevated levels of platelet-associated IGg and the presence of a platelet aggregating factor has been demonstrated in these patients plasma; the mechanisms of heparin induced platelet aggregation and thrombocytopenia are uncertain.

Relationship between the haemorrhagic, antithrombotic and anticoagulant effects of heparin and heparin derivatives

The relationship between heparin dose and the risk of bleeding or recurrent thrombosis has not been properly evaluated because there have been no randomised controlled trials in which either the dose of heparin or the therapeutic range has been the variable under study (Kelton & Hirsh, 1980). In experimental animal studies, the minimum level of heparin which is effective in preventing extension of thrombosis was found to be in the range of 0.3–0.5 units/ml measured by protamine sulphate titration (Chiu et al, 1977). A possible mechanism by which heparin could induce bleeding, unrelated to its anticoagulant effect, has been recently suggested by Salzman and co-workers (1980). They reported that a high molecular weight heparin with low affinity to antithrombin III was more reactive with platelets than the low molecular weight heparin fraction with a high affinity for antithrombin III. They suggested that part of the effect of heparin on haemostasis could be through inhibition of platelet function, an hypothesis which is supported by the observation that heparin, in large doses, prolongs the bleeding time in normal human volunteers.

Some insight into the mechanism of heparin-induced bleeding has been gained from studies with low molecular weight heparins. Low molecular weight fractions can be prepared by a variety of methods. These heparin fractions have reduced antithrombin activity but retain relatively more of their antifactor Xa activity (Barrowcliffe et al, 1979; Ockelford et al, 1982b, Salzman et al, 1980). Very low molecular weight heparin fragments (mol. wt<3000) have no antithrombin activity (Ockelford et al, 1982b; Thomas et al, 1982). This is because potentiation of the inhibitory action of antithrombin III to thrombin apparently requires a heparin molecule large enough to simultaneously bind to thrombin and antithrombin III (Griffith, 1982; Nesheim, 1983). Binding of heparin to ATIII requires a pentasaccharide with a critical saccharide sequence (Ockelford et al, 1982b).

A number of low molecular weight fragments (approximately 6000) and 'heparinoids' have antithrombotic properties in animals and from preliminary studies appear to be antithrombotic in humans (Kakkar et al, 1982; Mueleman et al, 1982; Thomas et al, 1982). Promising results have been reported in studies with these sulphated mucopolysaccharides for the prophylaxis of venous thrombosis, for the treatment of patients during haemodialysis and for the treatment of heparin-induced thrombocytopenia (Harenberg et al, 1983; Henny et al, 1983; Kakkar et al, 1982).

At least two heparinoids have been studied which when compared with standard heparin have a greater ratio of antithrombin to antifactor Xa activity. One of these, pentosan polysulphate (SP54) has antithrombotic effects in experimental animals and possibly also in humans. Pentosan polysulphate potentiates the activities of antithrombin III and heparin cofactor II on thrombin. The other heparinoid is dermatan sulphate which in contrast to standard heparin, only potentiates the action of heparin cofactor II on thrombin (Tollefsen et al, 1983). Dermatan sulphate has antithrombotic effects in experimental animals models (Buchanan et al, 1983). Another heparinoid (ORG 10172), (which is rich in dermatan sulphate) has been reported to prevent fibrin formation in experimental arterial venous shunts as effectively as standard heparin but to have less effect on the adherence of platelets to the thrombus (Mueleman et al, 1982). This heparinoid has been used clinically in patients undergoing renal dialysis and in patients with heparin-induced thrombocytopenia (Harenberg et al, 1983; Henny et al, 1983).

Recently, Mattsson and associates (1983) reported that a low molecular weight heparin fragment (mol. wt approximately 4300) with high affinity to antithrombin III was more effective as an antithrombotic agent in experimental rabbit models when it was covalently coupled to antithrombin III. In addition, the antithrombotic effect of the covalently coupled complex lasted considerably longer as an antithrombotic agent than the uncoupled low molecular high affinity fragment.

We have performed studies in vitro and in vivo with a variety of low molecular weight heparin preparations. In animal models of experimental thrombosis these sulphated mucopolysaccharide had equal antithrombotic activities to standard heparin but consistently produced less haemorrhage. All of these sulphated mucopolysaccharides had antithrombin as well as antifactor Xa activity and all were far less potent than heparin in inhibiting platelet aggregation.

We hypothesised that the antithrombotic effects of heparin were related mainly to its ability to augment antithrombin III-dependent inactivation of activated clotting factors while its haemorrhagic effects were contributed to mechanisms which are antithrombin III-independent (Ofusu et al, 1980, 1982a,b; Salzman et al, 1980).

These concepts are supported by results of experiments which demonstrated: 1) that low molecular weight heparins inhibited platelelet aggregation less than standard heparin, 2) that low molecular weight heparins were poorer inhibitors of the platelet-dependent thrombin and factor Xa generation in antithrombin III-depleted plasma than standard heparin, and 3) that heparin with low affinity to antithrombin III (which did not inhibit antithrombin III dependent coagulation but which did inhibit platelet coagulant activities and platelet aggregation) significantly increased haemorrhage without influencing either in vivo antithrombotic effect or ex vivo anticoagulant activity in animal models (Ockelford et al, 1982a).

The contribution of the antithrombin and antifactor Xa activities to the antithrombotic and anticoagulant actions of heparin

Because low molecular weight heparins have higher antifactor Xa activity than antithrombin activity in plasma, it has been suggested that the higher antifactor Xa activity is responsible for their antithrombotic effects. However, it has been shown that derivatives of heparin of the highest antifactor Xa to antithrombin activity are poor antithrombotic agents in experimental animals (Ockelford et al, 1982b; Thomas et al, 1982).

We investigated the reasons for the relatively weak antithrombic properties of heparins that have predominantly antifactor Xa activity by several approaches. Experiments were performed with three sulphated polysaccharides with a range of ratios of antithrombin to antifactor Xa activities: standard heparin which has equivalent antifactor Xa to antithrombin activities; a heparin octasaccharide that has antifactor Xa activity only; and dermatan sulphate that has antithrombin activity only. The octasaccharide was the weakest antithrombic agent even at very high antifactor Xa levels. Dermatan sulphate was an effective antithrombic agent.

It thus appears that antithrombin activity is required for the antithrombotic effects of heparins and heparinoids.

The effect of heparin on experimental atherosclerosis

Heparin has other effects on the vascular system which are of potential therapeutic value. Clowes & Karnovsky (1977) reported that heparin inhibited intimal smooth muscle cell proliferation in the rat carotid artery which was denuded of endothelium. The results of studies performed more recently indicate that this effect of heparin on smooth muscle cell proliferation is unrelated to its anticoagulant effects since it could be mediated by heparin with low affinity to antithrombin III (Guyton et al, 1980).

Endothelial cells (in vitro) secrete much more heparan sulphate into the medium than do smooth muscle cells and fibroblasts (Gamse et al, 1978). The heparan sulphate secreted by endothelial cells is more 'heparin-like' than the heparan sulphate synthesised by bovine aortic smooth muscle cells.

Recently, Castellot et al (1982) demonstrated that bovine aortic endothelial cells release a heparin-like substance which inhibits growth of smooth muscle cells in vitro. In other studies they demonstrated that heparin blocks the stimulation of cultured aortic smooth muscle cell growth by platelet derived growth factor (Hoover et al, 1980). A serum factor, identified as a platelet heparitinase, is required for the release of heparin-like components from bovine aortic endothelial cells.

In summary, there is now considerable evidence that the antithrombotic and haemorrhagic effects of heparin can be dissociated by using low molecular weight heparins, by using other sulphated mucopolysaccharides, and by using heparin with low affinity to AT III. The findings with low affinity heparin suggest that haemorrhage and other effects on vascular wall function are contributed to by properties of heparin which are independent of AT III binding and thus of their major anticoagulant effect. There is also experimental evidence that 1) the haemorrhagic effect of heparin is contributed to by a reversible platelet functional defect which is relatively less important that its AT III dependent anticoagulant effect for preventing experimental venous thrombosis; and 2) that the antithrombin activity of these mucopolysaccharides is important for their antithrombotic effects. Whether these results which were derived in animals also apply to humans with thromboembolic disease will require careful evaluation with suitably designed clinical trials.

LONG TERM ANTICOAGULANT THERAPY IN PATIENTS WITH VENOUS THROMBOSIS

Patients with venous thrombosis are usually treated with heparin for 7–10 days and then with oral anticoagulants for a period of weeks to months to prevent delayed recurrence of venous thromboembolism. It is common practice to overlap heparin with oral anticoagulant therapy for 4–5 days to provide maximum protection against recurrence during the initial stages of anticoagulant therapy. Until recently, the rationale for overlapping heparin with oral anticoagulants was derived from studies in animals which demonstrated that the antithrombotic effect of vitamin K antagonists lagged behind their anticoagulant effect. More recently a number of additional observations have been made which support this practice. It has been known for some time, that the vitamin K antagonists inhibit the effect of vitamin K on a post-ribosomal carboxylation step in the hepatic synthesis of factors II, VII, IX and X and which results in the synthesis of biologically inactive but immunologically detectable forms of these proteins. More recently, a fifth vitamin K-dependent protein, known, as protein C, has been described (see Ch. 12). Activated protein C inactivates factors Va and VIIIa by a proteolytic step and so is a potentially important anticoagulant. The ability of thrombin to activate protein C is enhanced when it complexes with a newly described endothelial-bound cofactor called thrombomodulin.

Thus the vitamin K antagonists have the potential to be thrombogenic by inhibiting the synthesis of functional protein C as well as antithrombotic by inhibiting the synthesis of factors II, VII, IX and X. When warfarin (or other vitamin K antagonists) is adminstered as a loading dose, it prolongs the prothrombin time within 24 hours by reducing the level of factor VII; however peak anticoagulant activity is delayed for 72–96 hours because of the longer half-lives of factors II, IX and X. Recently, it has been demonstrated that protein C has a similar short half-life to factor VII (6–7 hours) and so for the first 24–48 hours after initiating anticoagulant therapy, the antithrombotic effect is limited to suppression of factor VII while there is a potentially important thrombogenic effect caused by the suppression of protein C activity (Vigano et al, 1983).

The rate of fall of factor VII is dependent on the loading dose but the rate of fall of factors II, IX and X are similar when a large loading dose (for example 40 mg of warfarin) or maintenance daily dose (10 mg of warfarin) is given. The use of a small daily dose tends to avoid overdosage especially in patients who are sensitive to warfarin and this is the preferred approach. Thus the use of a 4–5 day overlap of heparin and warfarin provides the patient with protection against thrombus extension (by heparin) until the levels of factors II, IX and X are reduced into an acceptable range. A brief period of overlap (e.g. 2 days) exposes the patient to the potential thrombogenic effect of low levels of protein C before the levels of factors II, IX and X have time to fall into an acceptable anticoagulant range.

The pattern of practice related to the continued use of anticoagulant therapy after the patient with venous thromboembolism is discharged from hospital varies considerably from centre to centre. In recent years we have performed three randomised clinical trials which have evaluated the need for long-term treatment in patients with acute venous thrombosis (Hull et al, 1982a,b, 1983). The trials were designed to answer two questions: 1) is long-term anticoagulant therapy after an intial course of heparin indicated in patients with acute proximal vein thrombosis and 2) what is the optimal therapeutic range for monitoring oral anticoagulant therapy using the prothrombin time? This second question was addressed because the recommended therapeutic range influences the level of intensity or oral anticoagulant therapy and because in our population of patients with acute proximal vein thrombosis, the use of sodium warfarin monitored at conventional North American levels of anticoagulant control was associated with an appreciable risk of bleeding. The three trials were performed sequentially and the following four anticoagulant regimens for long-term treatment of acute proximal vein thrombosis were evaluated: 1) fixed low dose subcutaneous heparin, 2) adjusted intermediate dose subcutaneous heparin, 3) conventional oral anticoagulant therapy using sodium warfarin with a prothrombin time monitored by rabbit brain thromboplastin (Simplastin) maintained at a level of $1\frac{1}{2}$–2 times control and 4) a less intense anticoagulant regimen using sodium warfarin with a prothrombin time using human brain thromboplastin (Manchester Comparative Reagent) at approximately twice control which is equivalent to a prothrombin time using a rabbit brain thromboplastin of $1\frac{1}{4}$ times the control.

In all three studies patients were treated with an initial course of heparin and were then randomised into one of two forms of long-term therapy which was continued for three months. All patients were assessed for evidence of recurrence using reliable objective endpoints and were assessed for evidence of bleeding. In the first study, the safety and effectiveness of two extreme levels of anticoagulant therapy were compared; high-dose sodium warfarin controlled by a prothrombin time using rabbit brain thromboplastin maintained at $1\frac{1}{2}$–2 times control and low dose subcutaneous heparin (5000 units 12-hourly). An untreated control group was not included for ethical reasons, but if low dose subcutaneous heparin had proven to effective, it was our intention to perform a second study with an untreated control group. Low dose subcutaneous heparin proved to be ineffective (Table 14.1) since there was a 47% frequency of objectively documented recurrent venous thromboembolism compared

Table 14.1 Clinical outcomes per 100 patients treated with the alternative approaches for long-term antiocoagulant therapy

Regimen	Frequency of recurrent venous thromboembolism	Frequency of bleeding complications Major	Minor
Low-dose heparin	47%	0	0
Adjusted-dose heparin	4%	0	2%
Warfarin	2%	4%	18%
Less intense warfarin	2%	4%	0%

to a 2% frequency in patients treated with warfarin sodium therapy monitored in the conventional way. However, the use of sodium warfarin therapy monitored to maintain a prothrombin time using rabbit brain thromboplastin at $1\frac{1}{2}$–2 times control was associated with a high frequency of bleeding (Table 14.1). A second trial was therefore performed in which sodium warfarin was compared with an adjusted dose subcutaneous heparin with the hope that adjusted dose heparin might be associated with a lower risk of haemorrhage without loss of effectiveness. The dose of subcutaneous heparin was adjusted to maintain the mid-interval activated partial thromboplastin time (determined 6 hours after injection) at $1\frac{1}{2}$ times the control value. The dose was then fixed after the initial three days and no further anticoagulant monitoring was performed throughout the three months of long-term therapy. The adjusted dose subcutaneous heparin regimen proved to be effective in preventing recurrent venous thromboembolism and its use was associated with a significantly lower frequency of bleeding than sodium warfarin therapy (Table 14.1).

The adjusted dose subcutaneous heparin regimen was well tolerated by most patients and many preferred self-injection without laboratory monitoring to oral therapy with laboratory monitoring. Nevertheless, oral therapy is preferred by many and the observation made in the second study raised the possibility that a less intense anticoagulant regimen using sodium warfarin might be as effective in preventing recurrent venous thromboembolism but have a lower risk of bleeding than our more conventional dosage regimen.

The optimal therapeutic range for laboratory control of oral anticoagulant therapy has been debated for over 30 years (Loeliger, 1979; Poller & Taberner, 1982) and has remained unresolved because it had never been assessed in properly designed studies. Resolution of this important question can only be achieved by randomising patients into different intensities of anticoagulant effect and by measuring clinically relevant outcomes. In general the thromboplastins used for the prothrombin time test in North America are derived from rabbit brain and those used in the United Kingdom and parts of Europe are derived from human brain. Rabbit brain thromboplastin is less sensitive to the reduction of vitamin K-dependent factors than human brain. The influence of the source of thromboplastin on the response to vitamin K antagonists was clearly shown by Zucker and associates (1970). Similar results have been reported by Pinkerton and associates and Latallo and associates (1981) (Fig. 14.2).

Wright and associates (1948) suggested that the optimal therapeutic range using rabbit brain thromboplastin is obtained with a prothrombin time ratio of 2–2½ times a normal value. By and large this recommendation was accepted (although there was no

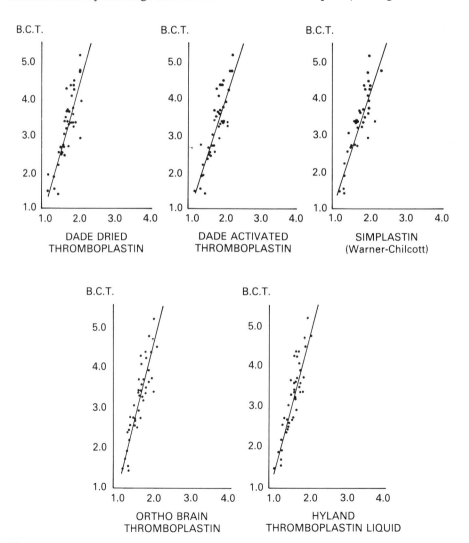

Fig. 14.2   Relationship between the prothrombin time using human brain thromboplastin (ordinate) and five commercially available rabbit brain thromboplastins (abscissa) obtained from plasma samples. From patients heated with dual anticoagulants. Adapted with permission from Pinkerton et al, 1970.

good evidence to support its use) and has been adhered to in North America for the last 30 years (although a number of investigators considered this to be excessive). In 1982, Poller stated that most British hospitals consider that the optimal therapeutic ratio using standardised human brain thromboplastin is 2–4 times the control which is equivalent to a prothrombin time ratio using rabbit brain thromboplastin of $1\frac{1}{4}$–$1\frac{1}{2}$ times normal control. It is clear, therefore, that when the recommended guidelines are followed, patients in North America (monitored by rabbit brain thromboplastin at a ratio of 2–$2\frac{1}{2}$ times normal control) are treated with a more intense anticoagulant regimen than those in Europe (monitored with standardised human brain thromboplastin at a ratio of 2–4 times normal control).

In our first two studies, patients randomised into the sodium warfarin group were monitored to maintain their prothrombin time (using rabbit brain thromboplastin) at $1\frac{1}{2}$–2 times control which is less than the recommended range. Even with our less intense regimen there was a high frequency of bleeding in the sodium warfarin group in both studies. We, therefore, decided to perform a third study to determine whether a less intense regimen using sodium warfarin would retain its effectiveness in preventing recurrent venous thrombosis but be associated with a lower risk of bleeding.

The same therapeutic range using rabbit brain thromboplastin was used in our standard group to provide continuity with our previous two randomised trials and this was compared to a less intense regimen monitored by a human brain thromboplastin (Manchester Comparative Reagent). A human brain thromboplastin was used in our less intensive experimental group because of its greater sensitivity to changes in vitamin K-dependent coagulation factors II, VII and X facilitated the laboratory control of the prothrombin time at the less intense levels of anticoagulant effect that were proposed for this group. We chose a therapeutic range using the human brain thromboplastin of twice control to maximise the difference in the intensity of anticoagulant therapy between the two groups. Our third study demonstrated that sodium warfarin adminstered to provide a less intense anticoagulant effect retained its effectiveness against recurrent venous thromboembolism (the frequency of recurrence was less than 2%, with a greatly reduced bleeding frequency of less than 5%, compared to a frequency of 20% in our conventional warfarin sodium group) (Table 14.1).

Practical recommendations
The findings of these three randomised trials of long-term therapy indicate that 1) low dose heparin therapy (5000 units subcutaneously) following an initial course of intravenous heparin is ineffective and should not be used for long-term therapy in patients with proximal vein thrombosis and 2) the haemorrhagic risk of long-term therapy for venous thrombosis can be substantially reduced by either using an adjusted dose subcutaneous heparin regimen or a less intense oral warfarin sodium.

The adjusted-dose subcutaneous regimen is the treatment of choice in pregnant patients in whom warfarin is contraindicated and in patients who return to geographically remote areas where long-term monitoring is impractical. The less intense oral anticoagulant regimen can be achieved either by maintaining the prothrombin time using a rabbit brain thromboplastin at approximately $1\frac{1}{4}$ times control or by using a more sensitive human brain thromboplastin at approximately twice control

Unresolved issues

Calf vein thrombosis
In the first study (Hull et al, 1979) patients were stratified according to the site of venous thrombosis. Those with calf vein thrombosis were randomised to receive either 6 weeks of conventional sodium warfarin therapy or low-dose subcutaneous heparin therapy (5000 units 12-hourly). There was a very low recurrence rate in both groups suggesting that patients with calf vein thrombosis require much less intense anticoagulant treatment or indeed may not require any long-term therapy although this latter hypothesis must be tested before being applied to clinical practice.

Patients with recurrent venous thrombosis or those with an underlying risk factor
A longer course of therapy is indicated in patients who present with recurrent venous thrombosis or in whom there is a continuing risk factor because of the relatively high recurrence rate in these groups after discontinuing 3 months of anticoagulant therapy. In patients with recurrent venous thrombosis discontinuation of therapy after 3 months is associated with a 20% incidence of recurrence in the next year (Hull et al, 1983). In contrast, recurrence is extremely rare in patients with a first episode of venous thrombosis, except if there is a persistent underlying risk factor.

How long should anticoagulant therapy be continued in these patients? In those with a continuing risk factor which is potentially reversible it would be sensible to continue therapy until the risk factor is reversed, e.g. lower limb fracture. In patients with a history of recurrent venous thrombosis, therapy should probably be continued for at least a year. In patients with an irreversible risk factor, (e.g. antithrombin III deficiency, protein C deficiency) anticoagulant therapy should be continued indefinitely.

ANTITHROMBOTIC EFFECTS OF DRUGS WHICH SUPPRESS PLATELET FUNCTION

Many drugs inhibit platelet function but only a relatively few have been tested as antithrombotic agents and only acetylsalicylic acid (aspirin), sulphinpyrazone, dipyridamole and dextran have been adequately evaluated in well-designed clinical studies. Other drugs which are being tested clinically are ticlopidine, dazoxidine and nafazaprin. In addition, β-adrenergic antagonists, calcium channel blockers and nitrates, drugs which are used in the treatment of coronary heart disease, inhibit platelet function. The proposed mechanisms of action of some of these is summarised in Figure 14.3.

Aspirin
Aspirin is rapidly absorbed in the stomach and upper intestine and has a half-life of absorption of 4–16 minutes. Absorption from enteric coated tablets may be delayed and is sometimes incomplete. Peak plasma levels are obtained 15–20 minutes after aspirin ingestion and the plasma concentration decays in a biexponential manner with a half-life of 15–20 minutes (Orton et al, 1979). Aspirin is rapidly hydrolysed into saliclic acid by esterase enzymes which are found in the gastrointestinal tract in various tissues and in blood. Salicylic acid is inactivated by a number of different

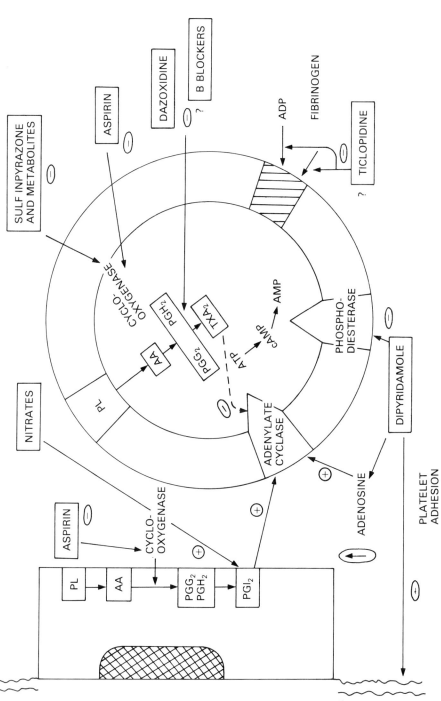

Fig. 14.3 Drugs which suppress platelet function: proposed mechanism of action. *Aspirin*: low dose inhibits platelets cyclo-oxygenase irreversibly for life span of platelet, higher doses inhibit endothelial cyclo-oxygenase but effect transient. *Dipyridamole*: elevates platelet cAMP by inhibiting phospho-diesterase and by inhibiting adenosine uptake by cells; inhibits platelet adhesion to collagen. *Sulphinpyrazone (and metabolite)*: inhibits platelet cyclo-oxygenase (weak and reversible). *Nitrates*: stimulate PGI₂ production. Dazoxidine and ? β-blockers: inhibit thromboxane A₂ production. *Ticlopidine*: ? inhibits affinity of ADP and fibrinogen for platelets.

routes. Aspirin produces gastric erosions and mild dyspepsia in some patients (its most common side-effect) and most individuals receiving aspirin for prolonged periods have an increase in gastrointestinal blood loss (Cohen, 1979).

Effect of aspirin on platelet function
Although aspirin has been described to inhibit platelet adhesion to collagen at low flow rates and at low haematocrit levels, it has no effect on platelet adhesion at physiological rates of shear and at physiological haematocrit levels (Legrand et al, 1979). Aspirin inhibits platelet function by acetylating platelet cyclo-oxygenase. At high concentrations, aspirin acetylates many plasma and tissue proteins but the acetylation reaction of cyclo-oxygenase is saturated at low aspirin concentrations (13 μmol/litre). When aspirin is administered to subjects in doses as low as 40–160 mg, it inhibits platelet cyclo-oxygenase activity by more than 80% (Burch et al, 1978). As a consequence of this effect, aspirin inhibits the oxidation of arachidonic acid to the endoperoxides PGG_2 and PGH_2 and, therefore, inhibits thromboxane A_2 production. Aspirinised platelets (obtained either by adding aspirin to platelet rich plasma in vitro or by preparing platelet-rich plasma from subjects who have ingested aspirin) show impaired aggregation with adrenaline, collagen, adenosine diphosphate (second wave) and very weak concentrations of thrombin. This inhibitory effect can be overcome by increasing the concentration of collagen or thrombin and is due mainly, or perhaps entirely, to the PGG_2, PGH_2 and thromboxane A_2 production. Aspirin, in therapeutic doses, does not inhibit the thromboxane A_2 independent release reaction and aggregation induced by collagen or thrombin and does not inhibit the primary wave of aggregation with adenosine diphosphate.

The effect of aspirin on platelet function is maintained for the life-span of the platelet and there is evidence that aspirin also acetylates platelets before they are released into the circulation and while they are still within megakaryocytes (Burch et al, 1978).

Effect of aspirin on vascular wall prostaglandin synthesis
When the prostaglandin synthetic pathway is activated in vessel wall cells (endothelial cells and smooth muscle cells), prostacyclin (prostaglandin I_2) is formed. This prostaglandin is a powerful inhibitor of platelet aggregation and a vasodilator and so has opposing effects to thromboxane A_2. When arachidonic acid is incubated with cultured endothelial cells, it is oxidised to PGG_2 and PGH_2 by the enzyme cyclo-oxygenase. PGH_2 is then converted into prostaglandin I_2. The synthesis of PGI_2 by vascular wall cells is inhibited by aspirin but, compared to the platelet, this effect is relatively short-lived and requires slightly larger doses of aspirin (Patrignani et al, 1982). In vivo studies in rabbits indicate that very high doses of aspirin are thrombogenic (Buchanan, 1981; Zimmerman et al, 1979). This thrombogenic effect is short-lived, presumably because de novo synthesis of cyclo-oxygenase can occur in vascular wall cells, and it lasts longer in arteries than veins (Buchanan et al, 1980, 1981). Paradoxically, the thrombogenic effect occurs only with aspirin concentrations which are in excess of those which inhibit PGI_2 synthesis, raising the possibility that it is contributed to by an additional effect of aspirin. Salicylate inhibits the lipoxygenase pathway of vascular wall cells and there is evidence that lipoxygenase products inhibit platelet adhesion to endothelial cells. It is possible, therefore, that the thrombogenic

effect of high doses of aspirin observed experimentally is contributed to by inhibition of synthesis of lipoxygenase products by endothelial cells induced by the salicylate moiety of aspirin.

The optimal antithrombotic dose of aspirin has not yet been determined. Clinically the most impressive results have been obtained with low doses (165 mg/day in patients undergoing haemodialysis and 320 mg/day in patients with unstable angina) but no differences in effectiveness have been found between 300 mg/day and 1500 mg/day in postmyocardial infarction patients. Partignani et al (1982) reported that a daily dose of 0.45 mg/kg (approximately 30 mg to a 70 kg person) given for 7 days produced virtually complete inhibition of thromboxane B_2 production without significantly inhibiting PGI_2 synthesis. If the antithrombotic effect of aspirin is due only to the inhibition of thromboxane A_2 synthesis, and if inhibition of PGI_2 is important in thrombogenesis , then very low doses of aspirin of 30–50 mg/day would be optimal. If, however, the antithrombotic effect of aspirin is contributed to by its effect on platelet lipoxygenase pathway, then higher doses may be required to obtain an optimal antithrombotic effect.

Effect of aspirin on haemostasis

Aspirin prolongs the bleeding time in normal volunteers over a dosage range of 300 mg and 3.6 g/day. This effect is exaggerated in patients with associated haemostatic abnormalities. A number of studies have demonstrated that aspirin does not normalise the reduced platelet survival seen in patients with prosthetic heart valves but that it has a potentiating effect on dipyridamole in achieving this effect (Ritchie & Harker, 1977). High doses of aspirin have been reported to prolong the prothrombin time (Lowe & Vinazzer, 1976). The mechanism of this effect is unclear but the prolongation is corrected by the administration of vitamin K (Goldsweig, 1976). Sodium salicylate has been reported to increase blood fibrinolytic activity, an effect which is thought to be independent of the plasminogen/plasmin system and related to an increase in cellular fibrinolysis (Moroz, 1977).

Effect of aspirin on animal models of thrombosis

Aspirin prevents thrombosis in a variety of experimental animal models. It has been reported to inhibit arterial thrombosis. Aspirin has also been reported to reduce injury-induced experimental venous thrombosis but the results have been less consistent (Gertz et al, 1979; Honour et al, 1977a,b). Kelton and associates (1978) reported that aspirin reduced the size of thrombi only in male rabbits, an observation which has not been consistently found in all clinical studies of the antithrombotic effect of aspirin (Bousser et al 1983; Canadian Cooperative Study Group, 1978; Harris et al, 1977).

Aspirin has been reported to have a variable effect on the bleeding time in experimental animal models (Dejana et al, 1979). A number of investigators have demonstrated that in very high doses, aspirin shortens the bleeding time, presumably by inhibiting vascular wall PGI_2 formation (Blajchman et al, 1979; Buchanan et al, 1979). Aspirin decreases adrenalin-induced myocardial necrosis in dogs and it has an anti-arrhythmic effect in these animals (Moschos et al, 1978). Verrier and colleagues (1982) also reported that the salicylates moiety of aspirin has anti-arrhythmic effects when animal hearts are perfused with platelet-free fluids.

Sulphinpyrazone

Sulphinpyrazone had been used as a uricose uric agent for a number of years before it was found by chance to lengthen the reduced platelet survival seen in patients with hyperuricaemia. Sulphinpyrazone lengthens the reduced platelet survival associated with a variety of thrombovascular disorders (Harker et al, 1979; Wilkinson et al, 1979).

Sulphinpyrazone is derived from phenylbutazone by sulphoxide substitution. Its absorption after oral administration is rapid and complete and peak plasma concentrations are reached at 1–2 hours. It is extensively protein bound and has a plasma half-life of 2–3 hours. Over 50% of sulphinpyrazone is excreted unchanged or as the glucuronide conjugate and the remainder is metabolically transformed by oxidation and reduction. When given in doses of 800 mg/day (200 mg QID), plasma concentrations of 30–40 mg/ml are obtained.

Side effects of sulphinpyrazone are minimal and consist of gastrointestinal intolerance and gastrointestinal bleeding in patients with peptic ulcer disease (Canadian Cooperative Study Group, 1978).

The effects of sulphinpyrazone on platelet function
Sulphinpyrazone is a weak cyclo-oxygenase inhibitor; its suphide metabolite is a more potent cyclo-xygenase inhibitor (Buchanan et al, 1978; Butler et al, 1979; Pederson & Jakobsen, 1979, 1981; Wiley et al, 1979). The sulphide metabolite inhibits sodium arachidonate induced platelet aggregation, collagen induced platelet aggregation, thromboxane B_2 synthesis, and thrombin induced malondialdehyde in rabbit platelets. Neither the sulphide metabolite nor sulphinpyrazone inhibit ADP induced primary aggregation (Buchanan et al, 1978; Pedersen & Jakobsen, 1981). Sulphinpyrazone does not prolong the bleeding time in patients (Canadian Cooperative Study Group, 1978). A number of reports have appeared indicating that reduced platelet survival time is lengthened by sulphinpyrazone in patients with valvular heart disease, ischaemic heart disease and transient cerebral ischaemia.

The effect of sulphinpyrazone on vascular wall and other cells
Sulphinpyrazone has been reported to protect endothelium from damage (Hladovec, 1979). It has also been reported to protect dogs from ischaemic death possibly by protecting the myocardium from the effects of ischaemia (Beamish et al 1981; Goldstein et al, 1980).

Effect of sulphinpyrazone on animal models of thrombosis
Sulphinpyrazone reduces experimental arterial thrombus (Hladovec, 1979; Philp et al, 1978) prevent death from disseminated platelet thrombi produced by arachidonic acid infusion (Kohler et al, 1976).

Sulphinpyrazone normalises the reduced platelet survival associated with implantation of arteriovenous cannulae in rabbits and baboons (Harker et al, 1979) and of dacron arterial prostheses in dogs (Wilkinson et al, 1979).

Antithrombotic action of sulphinpyrazone
The mechanism for the antithrombotic effect(s) of sulphinpyrazone is unlikely to be due to the reversible inhibition of prostaglandin synthesis alone (Buchanan, 1982).

Dipyridamole

Dipyridamole is a pyrimido-pyrimidine compound that was initially used clinically as a vasodilator. Following oral adminstration in therapeutic doses, a blood level of 1–3 μmol per litre of dipyridamole is achieved. The major route of dipyridamole metabolism is through hepatic transformation to a glucuronide metabolite which is excreted in the bile. The half-life of dipyridamole is approximately 12 hours. The major side effects of dipyridamole are nausea, vomiting, diarrhoea and occasionally headaches and vertigo.

Effect of dipyridamole on platelet function

Dipyridamole acts in a number of ways to inhibit platelet function. It is a potent inhibitor of platelet cyclic AMP phosphoiesterase. It potentiates adenosine inhibition of platelet function by blocking the reuptake of adenosine by vascular and blood cells; and it may potentiate the anti-aggregatory activity of PGI_2 (Moncada & Korburt, 1978).

An increase in platelet cyclic-AMP level is induced by inhibition of phosphodiesterase and indirectly by stimulation of adenyl-cyclase by adenosine. The elevated cyclic-AMP level potentiates the anti-aggregatory action of PGI_2 (DiMinno et al, 1978; Moncada & Korburt, 1978).

Dipyridamole has been reported to inhibit platelet adhesion to rabbit aortas both in vitro and in vivo, to inhibit the ADP induced platelet aggregation, and to inhibit adrenaline and collagen induced serotonin release. Dipyridamole is bound to an acid glycoprotein which limits its availability to platelets (Subbarao et al, 1977). Comparatively high concentrations of dipyridamole are required to modify platelet function in vitro. Dipyridamole has a greater antiplatelet effect in vivo than in vitro. There has been a report that dipyridamole inhibits prostaglandin synthesis (Ally et al, 1977) but this has been challenged (Moncada & Korburt, 1978).

Dipyridamole does not prolong the bleeding time in normal volunteers. Harker et al (1977) have reported that dipyridamole normalises reduced platelet survival in a dose dependent manner in a variety of thrombovascular disorders. Aspirin (1 g/day) which when used alone has no effect on the shortened platelet survival augments the effect of dipyridamole (100 mg/day) on normalising platelet survival.

Effect of dipyridamole on animal models of thrombosis

The reported effects of dipyridamole on inhibiting experimental thrombosis in animals have been variable. In most experimental models of arterial thrombosis, it has been effective but there have been notable exceptions. A synergistic antithrombotic effect betwen aspirin and dipyridamole has been reported (Honour et al, 1977b).

Dextran

Dextran is a branched polysaccharide which is hydrolysed and fractionated into polymers of variable molecular weight. It is adminstered by intravenous infusion either as a solution with a mean molecular weight of 70 000 (dextran 70) or 40 000 (dextran 40). Dextran was initially introduced as a plasma expander and was subsequently shown to affect haemostasis and thrombosis (3306). Dextran, with a molecular weight of less than 50 000 is predominantly excreted in the urine. Dextran infusion may be complicated by allergic reactions which are more frequent with dextran 70 than dextran 40 preparation. Other adverse effects include volume overload and oliguric renal failure.

Effect of dextran on haemostasis
Dextran has effects on fibrinolysis, blood viscosity and platelet function.

Fibrin clots formed in the presence of dextran are more susceptible to lysis by plasmin. Dextran expands plasma volume and so decreases blood viscosity. The effect of dextran on platelets is complex. Weiss (1967) reported that dextran 70 inhibited ADP-induced platelet aggregation ex vivo at concentrations that had no effect in vitro. This inhibitory effect of dextran was delayed for a number of hours after infusion suggesting that the effects may be due either to a metabolite of dextran or to a time-dependent effect on either platelets or plasma proteins. Dextran has also been reported to inhibit platelet adhesion (Aberg et al, 1979a) and to both potentiate and inhibit platelet aggregation by ADP and collagen. The infusion of dextran 70 into volunteers or patients decreases the level of factor VIII antigen and ristocetin cofactor activity (Aberg et al, 1979b). This effect is maximal several hours after infusion and was not observed when dextran was added to platelet suspensions in vitro. Dextran produces only minimal or no prolongation of the bleeding time in normal individuals (Weiss, 1967) but significantly prolongs the bleeding time in patients with von Willebrand's disease.

Effect of dextran on animal models of thrombosis
Dextran has been shown to inhibit thrombosis in experimental models of venous and arterial thrombosis. It is also effective in reducing arteriovenous shunt thrombi in rhesus monkeys (Mason et al, 1976).

Ticlopidine

Ticlopidine, a newly developed antiplatelet agent (Bruno & Molony, 1982), inhibits platelet aggregation induced by ADP and other aggregating agents (Johnson et al, 1977). Ticlopidine has much greater antiplatelet effects ex vivo than in vitro and the maximum platelet inhibitory activity develops after a number of days of adminstration. The antiplatelet effect persists for 5–7 days after the drug is discontinued (Ellis et al, 1981; Thebault et al, 1975). There is preliminary evidence that prolonged use of ticlopidine may produce leucopenia.

Oral adminstration of ticlopidine to animals or man results in a dose and time dependent increase in platelet inhibiting activity and a parallel increase in template bleeding time (Ellis et al, 1981). With a dose of 500 mg per day in humans maximum activity develops in 5–8 days as demonstrated by the inhibition of platelet aggregation with thrombin, collagen, epinephrine, arachidonic acid, ristocetin, platelet activating factor and ADP (Abe et al, 1980; Brommer, 1981; Conard et al, 1980; Johnson et al, 1977; O' Brien et al, 1978). The drug does not inhibit thromboxane synthetase (Ebihara et al, 1978).

Ticlopidine irreversibly alters the platelet membrane for a number of days after oral ingestion (Ashida & Abiko, 1978; Lips et al, 1980). There is evidence that treatment with ticlopidine results in a loss of low affinity binding sites for ADP on human platelets and in reduced affinity of fibrinogen for the platelet membrane (Bruno, 1983).

Nafazatrom

Nafazatrom has been shown to be an effective antithrombotic agent in experimental animals (Buchanan et al, 1982; Seuter et al, 1979). Nafazatrom normalises reduced platelet survival induced in rabbits with an aortic catheter and this antithrombotic effect is associated with inhibition of ADP and collagen-induced platelet aggregation ex vivo (Buchanan et al, 1982). In addition, in vivo platelet aggregation is significantly inhibited (Ambrus et al, 1982; Buchanan et al, 1982). Vermylen et al (1979) reported that nafazatrom induced PGI_2 stimulation by vascular wall cells.

Dazoxidine

Dazoxidine is a substituted imidazole which in vitro inhibits the formation of thromboxane A_2 from the endoperoxide PGH_2 (Randall et al, 1981). It inhibits collagen induced aggregation in vitro and ex vivo but does not inhibit high dose collagen aggregation or primary aggregation of ADP (Vermylen et al, 1981). It does not inhibit arachidonic induced platelet aggregation in vitro presumably because some aggregation is induced by PGG_2 and PGH_2 (Heptinstall et al, 1980). The drug has been shown to effective in experimental thrombosis in some animal models (Heiss et al, 1982) for example, it inhibits the deposition of radiolabelled platelets onto injured vessels (Randall & Wilding, 1982) but had little effect on thrombus formation on prosthetic surfaces in baboons even though there was a modest prolongation of the bleeding time (Hanson & Harker, 1983).

Cardiac active drugs

A number of agents which are commonly used to treat patients with coronary artery disease inhibit platelet function.

Nitrates

Nitroglycerine stimulates PGI_2 production either when added to bovine coronary arteries, rabbit arteries or human cultured endothelial cells (Levin et al, 1981; Shror et al, 1981). This effect is seen at clinically attainable concentrations and is associated with a mild prolongation of the bleeding time and with inhibition of platelet aggregation when endothelial cells supernant is added to a platelet suspension.

Calcium channel-blocking agents

Nifedipine, verapamil and diliazen inhibit platelet aggregation in vitro (Coeffier et al, 1983; Johnsson, 1981) but the clinical significance of these effects is unknown. Han et al (1983) demonstrated that the calcium entry blocking agents nifedipine and verapamil inhibit the formation of thromboxane B_2 from endogenous arachidonate and also inhibit the release of arachidonate from platelets by phosopholipases.

Beta adrenergic blocking agents

The β adrenergic blocking agents, timilol, propanolol and metoprolol have been reported to inhibit the second phase of aggregation induced by adenosine diphosphate and other aggregating agents, possibly by inhibiting the synthesis of thromboxane A_2 from arachidonic acid (Frishman, 1978).

Evidence that antiplatelet drugs are antithrombotic in man (Table 14.2)
The antithrombotic effects of drugs which suppress platelet function have been evaluated in well-designed clinical trials in patients with arterial venous shunts, following aorta-coronary by pass surgery, in patients with valvular heart disease, in patients with ischaemic heart disease (myocardial infarction and unstable argina), in patients with cerebral vascular disease and in patients with venous thrombosis.

Table 14.2   Results of published randomized trials with drugs which suppress platelet function

	Positive	Uncertain	Negative
Art-venous shunts	ASA SULF	—	—
Unstable angina	ASA	—	—
Myocardial infarction	?ASA		—
		SULF	
Aort-cor by-pass	ASA + DIP	—	—
Cer. vas. dis (TIA)	ASA	—	SULF DIP
Venous thrombosis	DEX	ASA	SULF DIP
Valvular heart disease	DIP + WARF ASA + WARF ?SULF		?ASA

ASA = acetylsalicylic acid
SULF = sulfinpyrazone
DIP = dipyridamole
DEX = dextran
WARF = warfarin

Arterial venous shunt thrombosis
Studies with aspirin (Harter et al, 1979; Hennkens et al, 1978) and sulphinpyrazone (Kaegi et al, 1975) have convincingly demonstrated that these drugs prevent thrombosis in arterial venous shunts in patients undergoing chronic haemodialysis. The study with aspirin was particularly important since a dose of 160 mg daily was used.

Aortocoronary bypass surgery
A number of studies have been performed evaluating the effects of antiplatelet drugs in patients undergoing aortocoronary bypass surgery. In two studies (McEnany et al, 1982; Pantley et al, 1979) using aspirin and dipyridamole, medications were begun on the third postoperative day and no significant difference in the frequency of graft thrombosis was found between the aspirin and placebo groups. In a third study (Chesebro et al, 1982) which was a double-blind trial, dipyridamole plus aspirin was compared with placebo in 407 patients. Dipyridamole was commenced 2 days preoperatively and aspirin commenced on the first postoperative day and there was a significant and impressive reduction in the frequency of graft thrombosis in patients randomised into aspirin and dipyridamole.

Valvular heart disease
Both dipyridamole and sulphinpyrazone are effective in normalising the reduced

platelet survival in patients with prosthetic heart valves. The combination of either aspirin (Dale et al, 1977) or dipyridamole (Sullivan et al, 1977) with oral anticoagulants is more effective than oral anticoagulants alone in preventing systemic embolism in patients with prosthetic heart valves. There is also suggestive evidence that aspirin alone does not offer adequate protection against systemic embolism in these patients. Chesebro and associates (1982) reported results of non-randomised trials comparing warfarin with warfarin plus aspirin and warfarin plus dipyridamole in patients with prosthetic heart valve replacement. They concluded that systemic thromboembolic events were reduced in the group treated with warfarin and dipyridamole and that there was an increase in intracranial bleeding in the warfarin plus aspirin group. Although sulphinpyrazone and dipyridamole normalise the reduced platelet survival seen in patients with prosthetic heart valves, there is no firm evidence that they are clinically effective when used without anticoagulants. However, in the only randomised study of patients with rheumatic valvular heart disease, Steel & Rainwater (1980) reported a significant reduction in the incidence of systematic embolism from 20% in the control group to 2.5% in the sulphinpyrazone group.

Coronary artery disease — rationale for using antiplatelet drugs
There is considerable evidence that platelets play an important role in the pathogenesis of complications of coronary heart disease (Chandler, 1982). Patients who die suddenly usually have severe coronary atheroma but in the majority of these an occlusive thrombus is not present at autopsy. In contrast patients who die with pathological evidence of myocardial infarction usually have an occlusive thrombus in the artery supplying the region of infarct. Recent studies of coronary angiography in patients admitted to hospital soon after suffering acute myocardial infarction indicate that 70–80% of these patients have an occlusive thrombus in the coronary arteries subtended by the infarct (De Wood et al, 1980).

Most patients who die suddenly have a ventricular arrhythmia (Hindle, 1982). A number of theories have been proposed to explain the mechanism of sudden death. Experimentally, fatal arrhythmia is produced in animals by embolising the coronary microcirculation with platelet aggregates and this mechanism has been proposed by some to be responsible for some of the fatal arrhythmias in patients with ischaemic heart disease (Haerem, 1978). Other suggested mechanisms include an effect of catecholamines on a scarred myocardium which is electrically unstable (Fitzgerald, 1983), and reversible ischaemia caused by coronary spasm (Maseri et al, 1978).

Postmyocardial infarction
Three drugs have been evaluated in postmyocardial infarction patients — aspirin, sulphinpyrazone dipyridamole and a combination of aspirin and dipyridamole.

Six long-term secondary prevention studies have been performed with aspirin (Aspirin Myocardial Infarction Study Research Group, 1980; Breddein, 1977; Coronary Drug Project Research Group, 1976; Elwood & Sweetnam, 1979; Elwood & Williams, 1979; Persantine–Aspirin Reinfarction Study Group, 1980). None of these six individual studies observed differences in mortality which was statistically significant but there was a strong trend in five of these six studies. Details of these studies have been published in a number of reviews. If the results are pooled, the risk reduction with aspirin is 16% for cardiovascular deaths and for the outcome of reinfarction, fatal or non-fatal, the pooled estimate of risk reduction with aspirin is 21% (Editorial, 1980a).

Peto has pointed out that very large trials including 5000–10 000 patients per group would be required to ensure that an actual risk reduction of 10–20% can be observed with confidence. Lacking such large trials he has suggested that data from a number of properly randomised trials should be pooled to provide the best guide to the true effects of any therapeutic agent. Not all clinical epidemiologists agree with this approach (Goldman & Feinstein, 1979).

There have been two studies with sulphinpyrazone (Anturane Reinfarction Trial Policy Committee, 1982; Report from the Anturane Reinfarction Italian Study, 1982). One performed in North America and one in Italy. The analysis of North American study the Anturane Myocardial Reinfarction Study has been criticised on two grounds: the protocol departures and the classification of sudden death. Patients were excluded from the analysis after randomisation on the basis of a number of prospectively defined criteria. If the analysis had been performed on the basis of an intention to treat, there would have been 60 deaths in the placebo group and 41 in the sulphinpyrazone, a difference which is not statistically significant. The second problem related to the definition of sudden death versus myocardial infarction. Questions were raised that some of the patients classified into the sudden death category should have been classified into the myocardial infarction group. Since the differences found between the sulphinpyrazone and placebo groups were almost exclusively in the sudden death category, reclassifying patients from the sudden death category into the myocardial infarction group could remove part of the impressive difference found for anturane using sudden death as the endpoint.

The Food and Drug Administration did not approve the claim by the pharmaceutical company that sulphinpyrazone is effective in preventing sudden death in the first six months after infarction (Editorial, 1980b, 1978a). The principal criticisms of the FDA report were that the criteria for classifying the causes of death were illogical and that they were applied inconsistently. The FDA was also concerned about two potential sources of bias, namely, the exclusion from the primary analysis of patients who had been considered to be improperly enrolled because they were ineligible and the practice of classifying certain deaths as non-analysable particularly after the deaths had occurred. Because of this, the Policy Committee decided to check both the consistency and the objectivity of the original classification by external and independent reviewers (Anticoagulants in acute myocardial infarction, 1973). Since the Policy Committee had remained blinded with respect to treatment assignment, it also undertook a complete reclassification of all deaths using the same material as that used by the external reviewers. Essentially, similar results were obtained.

A second Anturane Reinfarction Trial was reported by an Italian group (Matsuo et al, 1981b). This was a study of 727 patients randomised in a double-blind trial of sulphinpyrazone and placebo. The design was similar to the Anturane Reinfarction Trial except that patients were withdrawn from the study if any thromboembolic event occurred. A thromboembolic event was defined as a myocardial infarction, stroke, or transient ischaemic attack. Treatment with sulphinpyrazone did not affect the total mortality or the sudden death rate, but it did reduce the incidence of reinfarction and of all thromboembolic events over an average period of 19 months. The effect did not show the pattern of early benefit in the Anturane Reinfarction

Study. Thus, although the two trials of sulphinpyrazone showed beneficial effects, these effects were not consistent.

Unstable angina
Lewis and associates (1983) reported on a multicentre, double-blind placebo control-led randomised trial of aspirin treatment (324 mg daily) in 1266 men with unstable angina. Six hundred and twenty-five subjects took aspirin and 641 took placebo for 12 weeks. Aspirin was commenced on an average of 51 hours after presentation. The principle endpoints were death from acute myocardial infarction. The incidence of death or acute myocardial infarction was 50% lower in the aspirin group than the placebo group of 31 patients (5%) compared to 65 (10.1%) (P = 0.0005). Non-fatal acute myocardial infarction was 51% lower in the aspirin group and there was a 51% reduction in mortality in the aspirin group. There was no significant side effects from aspirin. The protective effect from aspirin on acute myocardial infarction and death was maintained over a 12-month follow-up period. These results strongly suggest that one aspirin tablet a day (324 mg) is effective in preventing the major complications of unstable angina.

Cerebrovascular disease
Stroke is a common cause of death in the Western world and accounts for approximately one death in five. Many patients identify themselves as being at especially high risk for having a stroke by having a transient ischaemic attack (TIA). Platelets are important in the pathogenesis of TIAs and stroke. In 1977, Fields and co-workers reported the results of a double-blind trial in which 189 patients received aspirin (1.3 g/day) or placebo. All entrants had a history of transient cerebral ischaemia and were followed for two years. Aspirin produced a non-significant benefit but subgroup analysis demonstrated a significant reduction in TIAs, stroke or death in those patients who had multiple episodes of transient cerebral ischaemia prior to admission in those who had a carotid lesion appropriate for their symptoms.

The Canadian Cooperative Study Group (1978) was a multicentre trial in which patients with a transient ischaemic episode occurrring within the previous three months were randomised to receive aspirin (1.3 g/day), sulphinpyrazone (800 mg/day), aspirin plus sulphinpyrazone, or placebo. There were 649 patients originally entered into the study of whom 64 were later disqualified for not having met entry requirements. No statistical interaction was demonstrated between aspirin and sulphinpyrazone and therefore the results of all patients receiving either aspirin of sulphinpyrazone were compared with those not receiving that drug. The aspirin-treated patients had a significant reduction in the incidence of transient ischaemia, stroke, or death. Subgroup analysis indicated that the benefit was limited to the males. Sulphinpyrazone was not shown to be effective.

In the French study, 604 patients with cerebral ischaemic events (both transient and completed) in the distribution of either the carotid or vertebral-basilar circulation were randomly allocated to receive one capsule three times per day of either aspirin (330 mg per capsule) placebo or 330 mg of aspirin plus 75 mg of dipryridamole. The primary end point was defined as fatal or non-fatal cerebral infarction and the patients were followed for 3 years. There were 31 fatal and non-fatal cerebral infarctions in the placebo group, 17 in the aspirin group and 18 in the aspirin dipyridamole group. The difference between aspirin and placebo was statistically significant. There was no difference between the aspirin and the aspirin and dipyridamole group. It is of interest that there was also a significant difference in the incidence of myocardial infarction in the two treatment groups ($p < 0.05$). Subgroup analysis did not show a significant sex difference in the efficacy of aspirin.

Venous thrombosis

Three antiplatelet drugs, aspirin, dextran, and sulphinpyrazone, have been evaluated in the prophylaxis of venous thrombosis (Gallus, 1979; McKenna et al, 1980). The results with dextran have been positive for major venous thrombosis and pulmonary embolism. The results with aspirin have been mixed and the results with sulphin-pyrazone have been negative.

CORONARY THROMBOLYSIS FOR THE TREATMENT OF ACUTE MYOCARDIAL INFARCTION

The renewed interest in thrombolytic therapy of acute myocardial infarction has been stimulated by three main factors:

1. The recognition of a high frequency of occlusive coronary thrombosis in the early hours of acute myocardial infarction.

2. The recognition of the importance of myocardial infarct size as an important determinant of early and late prognosis.

3. The experimental evidence that infarct size can be modified by early reperfusion.

Interest in reperfusion as a technique for infarct size limitation has been rekindled by the recognition of the central role of occlusive thrombosis in acute myocardial infarction. DeWood et al (1980) noted complete occlusion of the expected coronary artery in over 85% of patients who underwent coronary angiography within 6 hours of onset of infarction. This high frequency of coronary thrombosis has been confirmed by reports of other early angiographic studies (Kenny & Registry Committee, 1983; Mason, 1981).

Studies of reperfusion of the ischaemic myocardium in the dog circumflex ligation model indicate that considerable salvage is possible with reperfusion at 40 minutes, but little when reperfusion is delayed for 3 hours (Jennings & Reimer, 1982). The time constraints in humans with ischaemic heart disease may be less rigid but the available limited information indicate that early therapy is important to obtain maximum success.

Thrombolytic therapy of acute myocardial infarction was first reported in 1959 (Fletcher et al, 1959). During the next 15 years, a large number of trials of intravenous thrombolytic therapy were conducted, in most instances, employing streptokinase. Most of the trials were instituted before the importance of the time constraints upon infarct size limitation were fully recognised. Patients were often entered up to 72 hours after the onset of acute myocardial infarction and most of the studies failed to demonstrate a significant benefit. Recently, Stampfer et al (1982) reviewed trials which met acceptable criteria of good study design. Statistically significant reduction of mortality by streptokinase was reported in three of the six trials in which therapy was begun within 24 hours of the onset of symptoms. A pooled risk ratio was calculated and on the basis of this it was suggested that intravenous streptokinase therapy initiated within the first 24 hours of acute myocardial infarction may reduce mortality over the subseqent weeks by 20–25%. Although the technique of pooling the results a number of relatively small well designed studies has been advocated by some biostatisticians (Stampfer et al, 1982), others have pointed out the weaknesses inherent in this approach (Goldman & Feinstein, 1979).

Many studies of intracoronary thrombolysis had been reported, and reviews of experience are available (Kennedy & Registry Committee, 1983; Limitation of infarct size with thrombolytic agents, 1982; Proceedings of the symposium on intracoronary thrombolysis in acute myocardial infarction, 1981). Current experience indicates that in patients undergoing coronary angiography within 6 hours of pain onset, about 80–85% will have an occlusive thrombus in the infarct vessel. The current infusion regimes generally deliver a dose of about 250 000 units of streptokinase at an initial rate of about 4000 i.u./min clot lysis is observed, often followed by a slower infusion rate for an arbitrary time period, usually about 1 hour (Cowley, 1982). Lysis is achieved in 60–80% of cases, normally within 30 minutes (Cowley, 1982; Jutzy et al, 1983; Mason, 1981). Urokinase has not been widely employed as an agent for coronary thrombolysis, although in appropriate doses it appears to have equal efficacy to streptokinase in clot lysis.

A number of potentially serious complications of thrombolytic therapy may occur, although fatal outcomes appear to be rare and most deaths have been attributed to extensive evolving infarction in patients whose clot could not be lysed (Kennedy & Registry Committee, 1983; Mason, 1981; Weinstein, 1982). Ventricular tachyarrhythmias are commonly observed, occurring as reperfusion is achieved (Rey et al, 1983; Westveer et al, 1983). Bradyarrhythmias and hypotension are also observed, particularly with reperfusion of inferior infarcts (Wei et al, 1983). A few instances of bleeding are reported in most trials, but with appropriate precautions in the incidence is low (Mason, 1981; Weinstein, 1982). A few allergic and/or febrile reactions are generally noted in each reported trial.

There is no question that streptokinase can rapidly lyse coronary thrombi. The critical question is whether or not patient benefit occurs. This problem has been addressed by evaluating the effect of streptokinase on infarct size, on myocardial function and more recently on mortality. To the present there is little evidence that infarct size is limited as a result of streptokinase reperfusion. Some authors note improvement in myocardial function (Anderson et al, 1983) whereas others do not. Segmental rather than global analysis of myocardial function may be required to detect differences (Sheehan et al, 1983). Within patient comparisons indicate that with successful reperfusion, the uptake of [201]Thallium by the affected myocardium is improved, indicative of restoration of function rather than simply perfusion (Schofer et al, 1983; Schuler et al, 1982). However, in the only large controlled study available, there was no significant group difference of [201]Thallium defect size between treated and untreated patients (Ritchie et al, 1983).

The Western Washington Trial provides the strongest evidence for the efficacy of intracoronary streptokinase (Kennedy et al, 1983). In this study, 250 patients were randomly allocated to streptokinase or conventional therapy following coronary angiography, completed a mean of $4\frac{1}{2}$ hours after onset of acute myocardial infarction. Thirty-day mortality was 3.7% in the SK treated group and 11.2% in the control group (p < 0.02). This differences was slightly greater by 6 months follow-up. There were no differences in radionuclide ejection fraction or [201]Thallium perfusion defect size (Ritchie et al, 1983).

Few hospitals are equipped to provide cardiac chatheterisation on a 24-hour basis. Even in those which can, there are likely to be significant delays when the potential for infarct size limitation is critically time dependent. For these reasons there has been a reawakening of interest in the intravenous adminstration of streptokinase to patients with AMI. The focus has been on rapid lysis of the coronary thrombus with the hope of achieving rapid reperfusion and infarct size limitation. Several trials conducted in Europe indicate that the infusion of 0.5 to 1.5×10^6 i.u. of streptokinase over 1 hour results in coronary artery patency in about 60% of patients evaluated by coronary angiography at 1 hour postinfusion (Schroder, 1983). The largest published series is that of Schroder et al (Schroder et al, 1983) in which 97 patients received intravenous streptokinase. Of the 75 patients having angiography at 4 weeks, 84% had a patent infarct vessel, and of those beginning treatment within 3 hours of pain onset, all were patent. There are now available a few small trials comparing intravenous to intracoronary streptokinase. As intravenous doses have been increased and infusion regimes shortened, the success rates have begun to approach those achieved by the intracoronary injection. The greater simplicity of intravenous therapy may permit earlier initiation of therapy and consequently earlier reperfusion than is possible with intracoronary administration. A large randomised trial of high dose, short duration intravenous streptokinase is currently underway in Europe and is expected to prove whether or not significant reduction of mortality may be achieved by this approach.

TISSUE PLASMINOGEN ACTIVATOR: A PROMISING NEW THROMBOLYTIC AGENT

The major side effect of thrombolytic therapy with the two plasminogen activators, streptokinase and urokinase, is haemorrhage. This occurs as a consequence of hyperplasminaemia which impairs haemostasis by at least three mechanisms. These are: 1) the direct lysis by plasmin of fibrin in haemostatic plugs, 2) the production of a generalised coagulation abnormality characterised by hypofibrinogenaemia and reduction levels of factors V, VIII and an increase in fibrin-split products, and 3) by the direct effect of plasmin on platelet membrane glycoproteins which produces defective platelet function (Adelman et al, 1983).

In recent years, a new plasminogen activator, extrinsic plasminogen activator t-PA has been developed which has potential advantages over streptokinase and urokinase because it induces fibrinolysis without producing hyperplasminaemia and the associated haemostatic defects caused by the proteolytic effects of circulating plasmin. Extrinsic plasminogen activator (t-PA) is a serine protease which has been isolated from a human melanoma cell line, and has been purified and characterised and is now being produced for clinical use by recombinant DNA technology. Tissue activator is distinct from urokinase and has been called tissue type plasminogen activator (t-PA). It has a molecular weight of about 72 000. Recently the gene of the human tissue type plasminogen activator (rt-PA) has been successfully cloned and expressed to produce a glycosylated protein indistinguishable from melanoma derived t-PA (mt-PA) (Pennica et al, 1983). The t-PA derived from melanoma cell culture and recombinant DNA in mammalian cells appear to be identical in terms of kinetics of plasminogen activation both in the presence and absence of fibrin (Collen et al, 1985). They are also identical in terms of their ability to lyse I-125 fibrin-labelled clots in vitro (Collen et al, 1985, Matsuo et al, 1981a). In these studies, non-crosslinked clots lyse more extensively crosslinked clots (Korninger & Collen, 1981).

Purified t-PA is inactive in human plasma in vitro with a half-life of 90–105 minutes by α-2-antiplasmin and to a lesser extent by α-2-macroglobulin. Recently, an additional rapid inhibitor to tissue plasminogen activator has been described in plasma (Korninger et al, 1981).

Following intravenous injection in rabbits, both mt-PA and rt-PA have a very short half-life (2–3 minutes). Labelled t-PA was shown to rapidly accumulate in the liver with release of degradation products in the blood. An experimental hepatectomy markedly prolonged the half-life of mt-PA in blood (Collen et al, 1985; Korninger et al, 1981). Tissue plasminogen activator is unique because unlike urokinase and streptokinase it is a relatively poor plasminogen activator in plasma but its enzymatic activity is strikingly increased after binding to fibrin (Collen et al, 1985). Tissue activator has high affinity for fibrin to which it binds resulting in a complex which has a high affinity for circulating plasminogen (Collen et al, 1985; Hoylaerts et al, 1982).

The plasmin which is produced by the interaction of t-PA with fibrin-bound plasminogen is protected from interaction with α-2-antiplasmin because it is bound to fibrin through lysine binding sites which are required for binding with α-2-antiplasmin (Fig. 14.4).

Studies by Collen and associates (1983, 1984) in animals and more recently in humans have demonstrated that the infusion of t-PA produces thrombolysis of venous thrombi without inducing a significant generalised haemostatic defect. Both mt-PA and rt-PA produced lysis of experimental jugular vein thrombi in rabbits. Mt-PA has also been demonstrated to induce thrombolysis of experimental pulmonary emboli in rabbits without extensive plasminogen activation and without the production of a systemic fibrinolytic state (Matsuo et al, 1981b). The clinical studies have been performed with rt-PA and although promising are limited to case reports.

In a recent study (Collen et al, 1983a) of experimental coronary artery thrombosis, dogs were randomised to receive intracoronary or intravenous streptokinase or intracoronary or intravenous tissue plasminogen activator. Tissue plasminogen activator given either intravenously or by the intracoronary route produced thrombolysis in less than 10 minutes. While streptokinase produced thrombolysis in approximately 30 minutes when administered by the intracoronary route and in 80 minutes following intravenous injection.

We have recently demonstrated that for an equivalent thrombolytic effect, t-PA produces significantly less bleeding from standardised wounds in rabbits than streptokinase. Indeed in our studies, there was no increase in blood loss from rabbit ear wounds over 4-hour period of infusion when animals treated with tissue plasminogen activator were compared with saline-treated control animals. In contrast, there was a marked and progressive increase in blood loss in animals treated with streptokinase. These results confirm previous impressions that t-PA is able to produce effective thrombolysis without inducing a haemorrhagic state and raise an important fundamental issue that bleeding during thrombolytic therapy is largely caused by the consequences of hyperplasminaemia.

FIBRINOGEN ⟶ FIBRIN

THIS IS LINKED WITH THREE KEY REACTIONS

1. PLASMINOGEN ACTIVATOR t-PA (●) BINDS TO
FIBRIN ( ) AND t-PA IS THEN
ACTIVATED (◗).

2. PLASMINOGEN ◯ BINDS TO THE
BIMOLECULAR COMPLEX OF t-PA AND FIBRIN AND IS
CONVERTED TO PLASMIN ◯

ANTIPLASMIN SUSCEPTIBLE
SITE

3. α_2-ANTIPLASMIN (◯) BINDS TO CROSS-
LINKED FIBRIN BUT PLASMIN IS PROTECTED
THROUGH ITS BINDING TO FIBRIN FROM BEING
INACTIVATED

4. WHEN FIBRINOLYSIS OCCURS PLASMIN IS RELEASED
INTO THE BLOOD AND IS RAPIDLY NEUTRALIZED BY
ANTIPLASMIN.

FIBRINOLYSIS

Fig. 14.4 Physiological fibrinolysis and thrombolysis.

REFERENCES

Abe T, Kazama M, Naito I et al 1980 Clinical evaluation of ticlopidine in the inhibition of platelet function — a multiclinic double-blind study in comparison with aspirin. Blood Vessel 11: 142–151

Aberg M, Hedner U, Bergentz S-E 1979a The antithrobotic effect of dextran. Scandinavian Journal of Haematology 34: 61

Aberg M, Hedner U, Bergentz S-E 1979b Effect of dextran on factor VIII (antihaemophilic factor and platelet function). Annals of Surgery 189: 243–247

Adams G F, Merrett J D, Hutchinson W M, Pollock A M 1974 Cerebral embolism and mitral stenosis: survival with and without anticoagulants. Journal of Neurology, Neurosurgery and Psychiatry 37: 378–383

Adar R, Salzman E W 1975 Treatment of thrombosis of veins of the lower extremities. New England Journal of Medicine 292: 348–350

Adelman B, Loscalzo J, Michelson A D, Handin R I 1983 Fibrinolytic therapy inhibits platelet/von Willebrand factor interactions. Blood (Suppl. 1) 62: 296a

Aggeler P M, Kosmin M 1969 Anticoagulant prophylaxis and treatment of venous thromboembolic disease, In: Sherry S, Brinkhous K M, Genton E et al (eds) Thrombosis. National Academic Science, Washington DC, p 639–689

Ally A I, Manku M S, Horrobin D F, Morgan R O, Karmazin M, Karmali R A 1977 Dipyridamole: A possible potent inhibitor of thromboxane A_2 sythetase in vascular smooth muscle. Prostaglandins 14: 607–609

Ambrus J L, Ambrus C M, Gastpar H, Williams P 1982 Study of platelet aggregation in vivo. IX. Effect of nafazatrom on in vivo platelet aggregation and spontaneous tumor metastasis. Journal of Medicine 13: 35–47

Anderson J L, Marshall H W, Bray B E et al 1983 A randomized trial of intracoronary streptokinase in the treatment of acute myocardial infarction. New England Journal of Medicine 308: 1312–1318

Anticoagulants in acute myocardial infarction 1973 Results of a cooperative clinical trial. Journal of the American Medical Association 225: 724–729

Anturane Reinfarction Trial Policy Committee 1982 The Anturane Reinfarction Trial: re-evaluation of outcome. New England Journal of Medicine 306: 1005–1008

Arfors K-E, Bergqvist D, Tangen O 1975 The effect of platelet function inhibitors on experimental venous thrombosis formation in rabbits. Acta Chirurgica Scandinavica 141: 40–42

Ashida S, Abiko Y 1978 Effect of ticlopidine and acetylsalicylic acid on generation of prostaglandin I_2-like substance in rat arterial tissue. Thrombosis Research 13: 901–908

Ashida S, Abiko Y 1979 Inhibition of platelet aggregation by a new agent, ticlopidine. Thrombosis and Haemostatis 40: 542–550

Aspirin Myocardial Infarction Study Research Group 1980 A randomized controlled trial of aspirin in persons recovered from myocardial infarction. Journal of the American Medical Association 243: 661–669

Barritt D W, Jordon S C 1960 Anticoagulant drugs in the treatment of pulmonary embolism: a controlled trial. Lancet i: 1309–1312

Barrowcliffe T W, Johnson E A, Eggleton C A, Kemball-Cook G, Thomas D P 1979 Anticoagulant activities of high and low molecular weight heparin fractions. British Journal of Haematology 41: 573–583

Beamish R E, Shillon K S, Singal P K, Dhalla N S 1981 Protective effect of sulfinpyrazone against catecholamine metabolite adrenochrome-induced arrhythmias. American Heart Journal 102(2): 149–152

Bell R G 1978 Metabolism of vitamin K and prothrombin synthesis: anticoagulants and the vitamin K-epoxide cycle. Federal Proceedings 37: 2599–2604

Bender F, Aronson L, Hougie C et al 1980 Bioequivalence of subcutaneous calcium and sodium heparins. Clinical Pharmacolology Therapy 27: 224–229

Berte L E, Jutzy K R, Alderman E L et al 1983 Randomised comparison of intravenous and intracoronary streptokinase early post-myocardial infarction. Circulation 68(Suppl III): III–119

Bertele V, Roncaglioni M C, Donarti M B, Dgatano G 1983 Heparin counteracts the antiaggregating effects of prostacyclin by potentiating platelet aggregation. Thrombosis and Hemostasis 49: 81–83

Bjerkelund C J, Orning O M 1969 The efficacy of anticoagulant therapy in preventing embolism related to DC electrical conversion of atrial fibrillation. American Journal of Cardiology 23: 208–216

Blajchman M A, Senyi A F, Hirsh J, Surya Y, Buchanan M, Mustard J F 1979 Shortening of the bleeding time in rabbits by hydrocortisone due to inhibition of prostacyclin (PGI_2) generation by the vessel wall. Journal of Clinical Investigation 63: 1026–1035

Borgstrom S, Greitz T, Van der Linden W et al 1965 Anticoagulant prophylaxis of venous thrombosis in patients with fractured neck of the femur. A controlled clinical trial using venous phlebography. Acta Chirurgica Scandinavica 129: 500–509

Boston Collaborative Drug Surveillance Group 1974. Regular aspirin intake and acute myocardial infarction. British Medical Journal 1: 440–443

Bousser M G, Eschwege E, Haguenau M et al 1983 'AICLA' controlled trial of aspirin and dipyridamole in the secondary prevention of athero-thrombotic cerebral ischemia. Stroke 14: 5–14

Bream M L, Philip R B, Ferguson G G 1976 Intravenous arachidonate in the mouse a model for the evaluation of antithrombotic drugs. Thrombosis Research 9: 67–80

Breckenridge A 1978 Oral anticoagulant drugs: pharmacokinetic aspects. Seminars in Hematology 15(1): 19–26

Breckenridge A M 1977 Interindividual differences in the response of oral anticoagulants. Drugs 14: 367–375

Breddein K 1977 Multicenter two-year prospective study on the prevention of secondary myocardial infarction by ASA in comparison with phenprocoumon and placebo. In: Buissell J P, Klimt C R (eds) Multicenter controlled trials: principles and problems. INSERM, Paris, p 77–92

Brommer E J P 1981 The effect of ticlopidine upon platelet function, haemorrhage and post-operative thrombosis in patients undergoing suprapubic prostatectomy. Journal of International Medical Research 9: 203–210

Brown B G, Cukingnan R A, Goede L et al 1981 Improved graft patency with antiplatelet drugs in patients treated for one year following coronary artery bypass surgery. American Journal of Cardiology 47: 494 (abstract)

Bruno J J 1983 The mechanisms of action of ticlopidine. Thrombosis Research (Suppl IV): 59–67

Bruno J J, Molony B A 1982 Ticlopidine hydrochloride: A new antithrombotic agent. In: Scriabine A (ed) New drug annual, vol 1. Raven Press, New York

Buchanan M R 1982 The effect of platelet-active drugs on platelets, vessel-wall cells, and their interactions: a preliminary report. In: Hirsh J, Steele P, Verrier R L (eds) Effects of platelet active drugs on the cardiovascular system. Proceedings of a Symposium, University of Colorado Health Science Center, Denver

Buchanan M R, Rosenfel J, Hirsh J 1978 The prolonged effect of sulphinpyrazone on collagen-induced platelet aggregation in vivo. Thrombosis Research 13: 883–892

Buchanan M R, Blajchman M A, Dejana E, Mustard J F, Senyi A F, Hirsh J 1979 Shortening of the bleeding time in thrombocytopenic rabbits after exposure of jugular vein to high aspirin concentration. Prostaglandins Medicine 3: 333–342

Buchanan M R, Dejana E, Cazenave J-P, Richardson M, Mustard J F, Hirsh J 1980 Differences in inhibition of PGI_2 production by aspirin in rabbit artery and vein segments. Thrombosis Research 20: 447–460

Buchanan M R, Dejana E, Gent M, Mustard J F, Hirsh J 1981 Enhanced platelet accumulation onto injured carotid arteries in rabbits following aspirin treatment. Journal of Clinical Investigation 67: 403–508

Buchanan M R, Blajchman M, Hirsh J 1982 Inhibition of arterial thrombosis and platelet function by nafazatrom. Thrombosis Research 28: 157–170

Buchanan M R, Boneu B, Cerskus A L, Hirsh J 1983 The relative importance of anti-II and anti-X activities in thrombus prevention in rabbits. Blood 62 Suppl 1: 298a

Buchanan M R, Boneu B, Cerskus A L, Ofosu, F, Hirsh J 1984 The anticoagulant and antithrombotic effects of heparin: 2) The relative importance of thrombin inhibition and factor Xa inhibition. Blood (in press)

Burch J W, Stanford N, Majerus P W 1978 Inhibition of platelet prostaglandin synthetase by oral aspirin. Journal of Clinical Investigation 61: 314–319

Butler K D, Dieterle W, Maguire E, Pay G F, Wallis R B, White A M 1979 Sustained effects of sulfinpyrazone. In: Oliver M F, Sherry S (eds) Cardiovascular actions of sulfinpyrazone: basic and clinical research. Symposia Specialists Inc., Florida, p 17–35

Campbell W B, Johnson A R, Callahan K S, Graham R M 1981 Anti-platelet activity of beta-adrenergic antagonists: inhibition of thromboxane synthesis and platelet aggregation in patients receiving long-term propranolol treatment. Lancet ii: 1382–1384

Canadian Cooperative Study Group 1978 A randomized trial of aspirin and sulfinpyrazone in threatened stroke. New England Journal of Medicine 299: 53–59

Capurro N L, Kipson L C, Bonow R O, Goldstein R E, Shulman N R, Epstein S E 1980 Relative effects of aspirin on platelet aggregation and prostaglandin-mediated coronary vasodilation in the dog. Circulation 62: 1221–1227

Carter C J, Kelton J G, Hirsh J, Cerskus A, Santos A V, Gent M 1982 The relationship between the hemorrhagic and antithrombotic properties of low molecular weight heparin in rabbits. Blood 59(6): 1239–1245

Castellot J J, Favreau L V, Karnovsky M J, Rosenberg R D 1982 Inhibition of vascular smooth muscle cell growth by endothelial cell derived heparin. Possible role of platelet endoglycosidase. Journal of Biological Chemistry 257: 11256–11260

Chandler A B 1982 Thrombotic processes in coronary disease. In: Colman R W, Hirsh J, Marder V J, Salzman E W (eds) Hemostasis and Thrombosis. Lippincott, Philadelphia

Chesebro J H, Clements I P, Fuster V et al 1982 A platelet-inhibitor-drug trial in coronary-artery bypass operations. Benefit of periperative dipyridamole and aspirin therapy on early postoperative vein-graft patency. New England Journal of Medicine 307: 73–78

Chesebro J H, Fuster V, Elveback L R et al 1983 Trial of combined warfarin plus dipyridamole or aspirin therapy in prosthetic heart valve replacement: danger of aspirin compared with dipyridamole. American Journal of Cardiology 51: 1537–1541

Chiu H M, Hirsh J, Yung W L 197 Relationship between the anticoagulant and antithrombotic effects of heparin in experimental venous thrombosis. Blood 49: 171–184

Clagett G P, Salzman E W 1975 Prevention of venous thromboembolism. Progress in Cardiovascular Diseases 17: 345–366

Coeffier E, Cerrina J, Jouvin-Marche E, Benveniste J 1983 Inhibition of rabbit platelet aggregation by Ca^{2+}-antagonists verapamil and diltiazem and by trifluoperazine. Thrombosis Research 31: 565–576

Cohen A 1979 Fecal blood loss and plasma salicylate study of salicylic and aspirin. Journal of Clinical Pharmacology 19(4): 242–247

Collen D 1980 On the regulation and control of fibrinolysis. Thrombosis and Haemostatis 43: 77

Collen D, Bergmann S R, Fox K A A, Ter-JPogossian M M, Sobel B E 1983a Clot-selective coronary thrombolysis with tissue-type plasminogen activator. Science 220: 1181–1183

Collen D, Stassen J M, Verstraete M 1983b Thrombolysis with human extrinsic (tissue-type) plasminogen activator in rabbits with experimental jugular vein thrombosis. Journal of Clinical Investigation 71: 368

Collen D, Stassen J M, Marafino B et al 1985 Biological properties of human tissue-type plasminogen activator obtained by expression of recombinant DNA in mammalian cells. J. Pharm. Exp. Ther (in press)

Conard J, LeCrubier C, Scarabin P Y, Horellou M H, Samama M, Bousser M G Effects of long term administration of ticlopidine on platelet function and hemostatic variables. Thrombosis Research 20(1): 143–148

Coronary Drug Project Research Group 1976 Aspirin in coronary heart disease. Journal of Chronic Diseases 29: 625–642

Cowley M J 1982 Methodological aspects of intracoronary thrombolysis. Drugs, dosage and duration. Circulation 68(Suppl I): I-90–97

Dale J, Myhre E, Storstein O, Stormorken H, Efskind L 1977 Prevention of arterial thrombo-embolism with acetylsalicylic acid. A controlled clinical study in patients with aortic ball valves. American Heart Journal 94(1): 101–111

Dejana E, Quintana A, Callioni A, de Gaetano G 1979 Bleeding time in laboratory animals. III. Do tail bleeding times in rats only measure a platelet defect? (The aspirin puzzle). Thrombosis Research 15: 199–207

De Wood M A et al 1980 Prevalence of total coronary occlusion during the early hours of transmural myocardial infarction. New England Journal of Medicine 303: 897–902

Deykin D 1970a Warfarin therapy. I. New England Journal of Medicine 283: 691–694

Deykin D 1970b Warfarin therapy. II. New England Journal of Medicine 283: 801–803

DiMinno G, de Gaetano G, Garattini S 1978 Dipyridamole and platelet function. Lancet ii: 1258–1259

Douglas A S 1971 Management of thrombotic diseases. Seminars in Hematology 8: 95–139

Dyken M L, Kolar O J, Jones F H 1973 Differences in the occurrence of carotid transient ischemic attacks associated with antiplatelet aggregation therapy. Stroke 4: 732–736

Ebihara A, Aoki N, Yoshida N, Sano M, Matsubayashi K, Suzuki T 1978 Clinical pharmacology of a new antithrombotic agent, ticlopidine. Japanese Journal of Clinical Pharmacology 9(4): 395–402

Editorial 1980a Aspirin after myocardial infarction. Lancet 1: 1172–1173

Editorial 1980b FDA says no to Anturane. Science 208: 1130–1132

Editorial 1978a Sulfinpyrazone and prevention of myocardial infarction. Food and Drug Administration Drug Bulletin 8: 3

Editorial 1978b Sulfinpyrazone, cardiac infarction, and the prevention of death: a successful trial or another tribulation? British Medical Journal 1: 941–942

Ellis D J, Roe R L, Bruno J J, Carnston B J, McSpadden M M 1981 The effects of ticlopidine hydrochloride on bleeding time and platelet function in man. Thrombosis and Haemostasis 46(1): 176 (0543)

Elwood P C, Sweetnam P M 1979 Aspirin and secondary mortality after myocardial infarction. Lancet ii: 1313–1315

Elwood P C, Williams W O 1979 A randomized controlled trial of aspirin in the prevention of early mortality in myocardial infarction. Journal of the Royal College of General Practitioners 29: 413–416

Fields W S, Lemak N A, Frankowski R F, Hardy R J 1977 Controlled trial of aspirin in cerebral ischemia. Stroke 8: 301–316

Fields W S, Lemak N A, Frankowski R F, Hardy R J 1978 Controlled trial of aspirin in cerebral ischemia. Part II, Surgical group. Stroke 9: 309–319

Fisher A M, Morton R E, Marsh N A, Williams S, Gaffney P J, Barrowcliffe T W 1982 A comparison of pentosan polysulphate and heparin. II. Effects of subcutaneous injection. Thrombosis and Haemostasis 47: 109–113

Fisher C M 1959 Observations of the fundus oculi in transient monocular blindness. Neurology 9: 333–347

Fitzgerald J D 1983 The action of beta antagonists in prolonging survival after myocardial infarction. In: Kulbertus H E, Wellens H J J (eds) The first year after a myocardial infarction. Futura Publishing Company Inc, New York, p 267–288

Fletcher A P, Sherry S, Alkjaeisy N et al 1959 The maintenance of a sustained thrombolytic state in man II. Clinical observations on patients with myocardial infarction and other thrombo-embolic disorders. Journal of Clinical Investigation 38: 1111

Freeman I, Wexler J, Howard F 1963 Anticoagulants for treatment of atrial fibrillation. Journal of the American Medical Association 184: 1007–1010

Frishman W H, Christodoulou J, Weksler B B et al 1978 Abrupt propranolol withdrawal in angina pectoris: effects on platelet aggregation and exercise tolerance. American Heart Journal 95: 169–179

Gallus A S 1979 Antiplatelet drugs: clinical pharmacology and therapeutic use. Drugs 18: 439–477

Gallus A S, Hirsh J 1976 Treatment of venous thromboembolic disease. Seminars in Thrombosis and Haemostasis 2: 291–331

Gamse G, Fromm H G, Kresse H 1978 Metabolism of sulfated glycosam inoglycans in cultured endothelial cells and smooth muscle cells from bovine aorta. Biochemical et Biophysica Acta 544: 514–528

Ganz W, Geft I, Maddahi J et al 1983 Non-surgical reperfusion in evolving myocardial infarction. Journal of American College of Cardiology 1: 1247–1253

Gent Ae, Brook C G D, Foley T H, Miller T N 1968 Dipyridamole: a controlled trial of its effect in myocardial infarction. British Medical Journal 4: 366–368

Gertz S D, Kurgan A, Wajnberg R S, Nelson E 1979 Endothelial cell damage and thrombus formation following temporary arterial occlusion. Journal of Neurosurgery 50: 578–586

Goldman L, Feinstein A R 1979 Anticoagulants and myocardial infarction: the problems of pooling, drowning, and floating. Annals of Internal Medicine 90: 92–94

Goldstein R E, Davenport N J, Capurro N L et al 1980 Relative effects of sulfinpyrazone and ibuprofen on canine platelet function and prostaglandin-mediated coronary vasodilation. Journal of Cardiovascular Research 2: 339

Goldsweig H G, Kapusta M, Schwartz J 1976 Bleeding, salicylates and prolonged prothrombin time. Three case reports and a review of the literature. Journal of Rheumatology 3: 37–42

Griffith M J 1982 Kinetics of the heparin-enhanced antithrombin III thrombin reaction. Journal of Biological Chemistry 257: 7360–7365

Gunning A J, Pickering G W, Robb-Smith A H T, Russell R R 1964 Mural thrombosis of the internal carotid artery and subsequent embolism. Quarterly Journal of Medicine 129: 155–195

Guyton J R, Rosenberg R D, Clowes A W, Karnovsky M J 1980 Inhibition of rat arterial smooth muscle cell proliferation by heparin: in vivo studies with anticoagulant and non-anticoagulant heparin. Circulation Research 46: 625–634

Haerem J W 1978 Sudden, unexpected coronary death. Acta Pathologica et Microbiologica Scandinavica Sect A (Suppl) 265: 1

Han P, Boatwright C, Ardlie N G 1983 Effect of the calcium-entry blocking agent nifedipine on activation of human platelets and comparison with verapamil. Thrombosis and Haemostasis 50: 513–517

Hanson S R, Harker L A 1983 Effect of dazoxiben on arterial graft thrombosis in the baboon. British Journal and Clinical Pharmacology (Suppl) Vol 15, Suppl 575–605

Harker L A, Slichter S J, Sauvage L R 1977 Platelet consumption by arterial prostheses: the effect of endothelialization and pharmacologic inhibition of platelet function. Annals of Surgery 186: 594–601

Harker L A, Hanson S R, Kirkham T R 1979 Experimental arterial thromboembolism in baboons: mechanism, quantitation and pharmacologic prevention. Journal of Clinical Investigation 64: 559–569

Harenberg J, Zimmerman R, Schwarz F, Kubler W 1983 Treatment of heparin induced thrombocytopenia by new heparinoids. Lancet i: 986–987

Harris W H, Salzman E W, Athansoulis C A, Waltman A C, DeSanctis R W 1977 Aspirin prophylaxis of venous thromboembolism after total hip replacement. New England Journal of Medicine 297: 1246–1248

Harrison M J G, Marshall J, Meadows J C, Russel R W R 1971 Effect of aspirin in amaurosis fugax. Lancet ii: 743–744

Harter H R, Burch J W, Majerus P W et al 1979 Prevention of thrombosis in patients on hemodialysis by low dose aspirin. New England Journal of Medicine 301: 577–579

Heiss M, Haas S, Blumel G 1982 The antithrombotic effect of a new thromboxane-synthetase inhibitor (UK–37,248) in comparison with acetylsalicylic acid (ASA) in experimental thrombosis. Haemostasis 12: 102

Hennkens C H, Karison L K, Rosner B 1978 A case-control study of regular aspirin use and coronary deaths. Circulation 58: 35–38

Henny C P, Ten Cate J W, van Bronswijk H et al 1983 Use of a new heparinoid as anticoagulant during acute haemodialysis of patients with bleeding complications. Lancet i: 890–893

Heptinstall S, Bevan J, Cockbill S R, Hanley S P, Parry M J 1980 Effects of selective inhibitor of thromboxane synthetase on human blood platelet behaviours. Thrombosis Research 20: 219–230

Hindle L E Jr 1982 Short-term risk factors for sudden-death. In: Greenberg H M, Dwyer M Jr (eds) Sudden coronary death. New York, Annals of the New York Academy of Sciences

Hirsh J, Genton E, Gent M 1975 Low dose heparin prophylaxis for venous thromboembolism. In: Fratantoni J (ed) Prophylactic therapy for deep venous thrombosis and pulmonary embolism. Government Printing Office, Publication No (NIH) 76–866, Washington DC, p 254

Hirsh J, Genton E, Hull R 1981 Management of suspected venous thromboembolism in pregnancy. In:

Hirsh J, Genton E, Hull R (eds) Venous thromboembolism, Grune & Stratton, New York, p 145–151

Hladovec J 1979 Is the antithrombotic activity of 'antiplatelet' drugs based on protection of endothelium? Thrombosis and Haemostasis (Stuttg) 41: 774–778

Honour A J, Carter R D, Mann J I 1977a The effects of treatment with aspirin and an antithrombotic agent SH1117 upon platelet thrombus formation in living blood vessels. British Journal of Experimental Pathology 58: 474–477

Honour A J, Hockaday T D R, Mann J I 1977b The synergistic effect of aspirin and dipyridamole upon platelet thrombi in living blood vessels. British Journal of Experimental Pathology 58: 268–272

Hoover R L, Rosenberg R, Haering W, Karnovsky M J 1980 Circulation Research 47:578–583

Hoylaerts M, Rijken D C, Lijen H P, Collen D 1982 Kinetics of the activation of plasminogen by human tissue plasminogen activator. Role of fibrin. Journal of Biochemistry 257: 2912–2919

Huisse M-G, Guillin M C, Bezeaud A, Toulemonde F, Kitzis M, Andreassian B 1982 Heparin-associated thrombocytopenia. In vitro effects of different molecular weight heparin fractions. Thrombosis Research 27: 485–490

Hull R, Hirsh J 1979 Prevention of venous thrombosis and pulmonary embolism with particular reference to the surgical patient. In Joist J H, Sherman L A (eds) Venous and arterial thrombosis. Grune & Stratton, New York, p 93–122

Hull J H, Murray W J, Brown H S et al 1978 Potential anticoagulant drug interactions in ambulatory patients. Clinical Pharmacology Therapy 24: 644–649

Hull R, Delmore T, Genton E et al 1979 Warfarin sodium versus low-dose heparin in the long-term treatment of venous thrombosis. New England Journal of Medicine 301: 855–858

Hull R, Delmore T, Carter C et al 1982a Adjusted subcutaneous heparin vs. warfarin sodium in the long-term treatment of venous thrombosis. New England Journal of Medicine 306: 189–194

Hull R, Hirsh J, Jay R et al 1982b Different intensities of anticoagulation in the long term treatment of proximal vein thrombosis. New England Journal of Medicine 307: 1676–1681

Hull R, Carter C, Jay R et al 1983 The diagnosis of acute recurrent deep vein thrombosis. A diagnostic challenge. Circulation 67: 901–906

International Multicentre Trial 1975 Prevention of fatal postoperative pulmonary embolism by low doses of heparin. Lancet ii: 45–51

Jennings R B, Reimer K A 1982 Factors involved in salvaging ischemic myocardium: effect of reperfusion of arterial blood. Circulation 68(suppl I): I-25–36

Johnson M, Walton P L, Cotton R C, Strachan C J L 1977 Pharmacological evaluation of ticlopidine, a novel inhibitor of platelet function. Thrombosis and Haemostasis 38(1): 64–66

Johnson H 1981 Effects by nifedipine (adalat R) on platelet function in vitro and in vivo. Thrombosis Research 21: 523–528

Jutzy K R, Berte L E, Alderman E L, Miller R G, Friedman J P 1983 Relation of systemic fibrinolytic state with route of streptokinase adminstration and recanalization. Circulation 68(Suppl III): III–39

Kaegi A, Pineo G F, Shimizu A, Trivedi H, Hirsh J, Gent M 1975 The role of sulphinpyrazone in the prevention of arteriovenous shunt thrombosis. Circulation 52: 497–499

Kakkar V V, Djazaeri B, Fok K, Fletcher M, Scully M G, Westwick J 1982 Low molecular-weight heparin and prevention of post-operative deep vein thrombosis. British Medical Journal 284: 375–379

Kelly J G, O'Malley K 1979 Clinical pharmacokinetics of oral anticoagulants. Clinical Pharmacokinet 4: 1

Kelton J G, Hirsh J 1980 Bleeding associated with antithrombotic therapy. Seminars in Hematology 17: 375–379

Kennedy J W and the Registry Committee, Society for Cardiac Angiography 1983 Intracoronary streptokinase in acute MI: report from the society for cardiac angiography registry. Circulation 68(Suppl III): III–121

Kennedy J W, Ritchie J L, Davis K B, Fritz J K 1983 Western Washington randomized trial of intracoronary streptokinase in acute myocardial infarction. New England Journal of Medicine 309: 1477–1482

Koch-Weser J 1968 Coumarin necrosis. Annals of Internal Medicine 68: 1365–1367

Koch-Weser J, Sellers E M 1971 Drug interactions with coumarin anticoagulants. New England Journal of Medicine 285: 547–558

Kohler C, Wooding W, Ellenbogen L 1976 Intravenous arachidonate in the mouse: a model for the evaluation of antithrombotic drugs. Thrombosis Research 9: 67–80

Korninger C, Collen D 1981 Studies on the specific fibrinolytic effect of human extrinsic (tissue-type) plasminogen activator in human blood and in various animal species in vitro. Thrombosis and Haemostasis 46: 561

Korninger C, Stassen J M, Collen D 1981 Turnover of human extrinsic (tissue-type) plasminogen activator in rabbits. Thrombosis and Haemostasis 46: 658

Lam-Po-Tang P R L C, Poller L 1975 Oral anticoagulant therapy and its control: an international survey. Thrombosis et Diathesis Haemorrhagica 34: 419–425

Latallo Z S, Thomson J M, Poller L 1981 An evaluation of chromogenic substrates in the control of oral anticoagulant therapy. British Journal of Haematology 47: 307–318

Legrand Y J, Fauvel F, Kartalis G et al 1979 Specific and quantitative method for estimation of platelet adhesion to fibrillar collagen. Journal of Laboratory and Clinical Medicine 94: 438–446

Levin R I Jaffe E A, Weksler B B, Tack-Goldman K 1981 Nitroglycerin stimulates synthesis of prostacyclin by cultured human endothelial cells. Journal of Clinical Investigation 67: 762–769

Lewis H D, Davis J W, Archibald D G et al 1983 Protective effects of aspirin against acute myocardial infarction and death in men with unstable angina: results of veterans administration cooperative study. New England Journal of Medicine 309: 396–403

Lips J P M, Sixma J J, Schiphorst M E 1980 The effect of ticlopidine administration to humans on the binding of adenosine disphosphate to blood platelets. Thrombosis Research 17(1–2): 19–27

Loeliger E A 1979 The optimal therapeutic range in oral anticoagulation history and proposal. Thrombosis Haemostasis 42: 1141–1152

Loew D, Vinazzer H 1976 Dose-dependent influence of acetylsalicylic acid on platelet functions and plasmatic coagulation factors. Haemostasis 5: 239–249

Maseri A et al 1978 Coronary vasospasm as a possible cause of myocardial infarction: a conclusion derived from the study of preinfarction angina. New England Journal of Medicine 299: 1271

Mason D T 1981 International experience with percutaneous transluminal coronary recanalization by streptokinase — thrombolysis reperfusion in acute myocardial infarction: New, safe, landmark therapeutic approach salvaging ischemic muscle and improving ventricular function. American Heart Journal 102: 1126–1133

Mason R G, Wolf R H, Zucker W H, Shimoda B A Mohammad S F 1976 Effects of antithrombotic agents evaluated in a nonhuman primate vascular shunt model. American Journal of Pathology 83: 557–563

Mathey D G, Kuck K, Tilsner V et al 1981 Non-surgical coronary artery recanalization in acute transmural myocardial infarction. Circulation 63: 489–497

Matsuo O, Rijken D C, Collen D 1981a Comparison of the relative fibrinogenolytic, fibrinolytic and thrombolytic properties of tissue plasminogen activator and urokinase in vitro. Thrombosis and Haemostasis 45: 225

Matsuo O, Rikjen D C, Collen D 1981b Thrombolysis by human tissue plasminogen activator and urokinase in rabbits with experimental pulmonary embolism. Nature 291: 590

Mattsson C H, Homer E, Uthne T, Hoylaerts M, Collen D 1983 Antithrombotic effect of high affinity heparin fragment covalently coupled to antithrombin III. Thrombosis and Hemostasis 50: 224 (abstract)

McEnany M T, Salzman E W, MKUNDTH E D et al 1982 The effect of antithrombotic therapy on patency rates of saphenous vein coronary artery bypass grafts. Journal of Thoracic Cardiovascular Surgery 83: 81–89

McIntyre D, Handin R I, Rosenberg R, Salzman E W 1981 Heparin opposes prostanoid and non-prostanoid platelet inhibitors by direct enhancement of aggregation. Thrombosis Research 22: 167–175

McKenna R, Glanante J, Bachmann F, Wallace D L, Kaushal S P, Meredith P 1980 Prevention of venous thromboembolism after total knee replacement by high-dose aspirin or intermittent calf and thigh compression. British Medical Journal I: 514–517

McNeely T, Roberts H R, Griffith M J 1983 Heparin's effect on the activation of factor IX and factor X in whole plasma. Blood 62: 305(a) (abstract)

Meuleman D G, Hobbelan P M J, von Dedem G, Moelker H C T 1982 A novel antithrombotic heparinoid (Org 10172) devoid of bleeding inducing capacity. A survey of its pharmacological properties in experimental animal models. Thrombosis Research 27: 353–363

Mitchell J R A 1981 Anticoagulants in coronary heart disease — retrospect and prospect. Lancet i: 257–262

Moncada S, Korburt R 1978 Dipyridamole and other phosphodiesterase inhibitors act as antithrombotic agent by potentiating endogenous prostacyclin. Lancet i: 1286–1289

Moroz L A 1977 Increased blood fibrinolytic activity after aspirin ingestion. New England Journal of Medicine 296: 525–529

Morris G K, Mitchell J R 1976 Warfarin sodium in the prevention of deep venous thrombosis and pulmonary embolism in patients with fractured neck of femur. Lancet ii: 869–872

Moschos C B, Haider B, Khan V, Lyons M M, Regan T J 1978 Relation of platelets to catecholamine induced myocardial injury. Cardiovascular Research 12: 243–246

Mundall J, Qunitero P, Von Kualla K N, Harmon R, Austin J 1972 Transient monocular blindness and increased platelet aggregability treated with aspirin. Neurology 22: 280–285

Nalbandian R M, Beller F K, Kamp A K et al 1971 Coumarin necrosis of skin treated successfully with heparin. Obstetrics and Gynecology 38: 395–399

Nesheim M E 1983 A simple rate law that describes the kinetics of heparin catalysed reaction of antithrombin III and thrombin. Journal of Biological Chemistry 258: 14708–14717

Ockelford P, Carter C J, Cerskus A, Smith C A, Hirsh J 1982a Comparison of the in vivo haemorrhagic and antithrombotic effects of a low antithrombin III affinity heparin fractions. Thrombosis Research 27: 679–690

Ockelford P, Carter C J, Mitchell L, Hirsh J 1982b Discordance between the anti-Xa activity and the antithrombotic activity of an ultra-low molecular weight heparin fraction. Thrombosis Research 28: 401–409

O'Brien J R, Etherington M D, Shuttleworth R D 1978 Ticlopidine — an antiplatelet drug: Effects in human volunteers. Thrombosis Research 13: 245–254

Ofosu F A, Blajchman M A, Hirsh J 1980 The inhibition of heparin of the intrinsic pathway activation of factor X in the absence of antithrombin III. Thrombosis Research 20: 391–403

Ofosu F A, Modi G, Cerksus A, Hirsh J, Blajchman M A 1982a Heparin with low affinity to antithrombin III inhibits the activation of prothrombin in normal plasma. Thrombosis Research 28: 487–497

Ofosu F A, Blajchman M, Modi G, Cerskus A L, Hirsh J 1982b Activation of Factor X and prothrombin in antithrombin III-depleted plasma. Thrombosis Research 23: 331–345

Ofosu F A, Modi G J, Smith L M, Cerksus A L, Hirsh J, Blajchman M A 1984 Heparin sulfate and dermatan sulfate inhibit thrombin generation in plasma by complementary pathway. Blood 64(3): 727–747

Orton D, Jones R T, Kaspi T et al 1979 Plasma salicylate levels after soluble and effervescent aspirin. British Journal of Clinical Pharmacology 7: 410–412

Pantley G S, Goodnight S H Jr, Rahimtoola S H et al 1979 Failure of antiplatelet and anticoagulant therapy to improve patency of grafts after coronary-artery bypass. A controlled, randomized study. New England Journal of Medicine 301: 962–966

Patrignani P, Fiblabozzi P, Patrono C 1982 Selective cumulative inhibition of platelet thromboxane production by low-dose aspirin in healthy subjects. Journal of Clinical Investigation 69: 1366–1372

Pederson A K, Jakobsen P 1979 Two new metabolites of sulphinpyrazone in the rabbit: a possible cause of the prolonged in vivo effect. Thrombosis Research 16: 871–876

Pederson A K, Jakobsen P 1981 Sulphinpyrazone metabolism during long-term therapy. British Journal of Clinical Pharmacology 11: 597–603

Pennica D, Holmes W E, Kohn W J et al 1983 Cloning and expression of human tissue-type plasminogen activator cDNA in E. coli. Nature 301: 214

Persantine–Aspirin Reinfarction Study Group 1980 Persantine and aspirin in coronary heart disease. Circulation 62: 449–461

Philp R B, Francy I, Warren B A 1978 Comparison of antithrombotic activity of heparin, ASA, sulphinpyrazone and VK 744 in a rat model of arterial thrombosis. Haemostasis 7: 282–293

Poller L 1976 British comparative thromboplastin therapeutic range. Thrombosis and Haemostasis 36: 485 (abstract)

Poller L, Taberner D A 1982 Dosage and control of oral anticoagulants: an international collaborative survey. British Journal of Haematology 51: 479–485

Proceedings of the symposium on intracoronary thrombolysis in acute myocardial infarction. 1981 American Heart Journal 102: 1123–1208

Randall M J, Parry M J, Hawkeswood E, Cross P E, Dickinson R P 1981 UK–37 248, a novel, selective thromboxane synthetase inhibitor with platelet anti-aggregatory and antithrombotic activity. Thrombosis Research 23: 145–162

Randall M J, Wilding R I R 1982 Acute arterial thrombosis in rabbits: reduced platelet accumulation after treatment with thromboxane synthetase inhibitor dazoxiben hydrochloride (UK–37 248–01). Thrombosis Research 28: 607–616

Report from the Anturane Reinfarction Italian Study 1982 Sulphinpyrazone in post-myocardial infarction. Lancet i: 237–242

Report of the Working Party on Anticoagulant Therapy in Coronary Thrombosis to the Medical Research Council 1969 Assessment of short-term anticoagulant adminstration after cardiac infarction. British Medical Journal 1: 335–342

Rey M, Siegel S, Feit F et al 1983 Late ventricular ectopy in the Mt Sinai NYU myocardial infarct reperfusion trial. Circulation 68(Suppl III): III–410

Rijken D C, Hoylaerts M, Collen D 1982 Fibrinolytic properties of one-chain and two-chain human extrinsic (tissue-type) plasminogen activator. Journal of Biological Chemistry 257: 2920

Ritchie J L, Harker L A 1977 Platelet and fibrinogen survival in coronary atherosclerosis. American Journal of Cardiology 39: 595–598

Ritchie J L, Davis K A, Williams D L, Harp G D, Kennedy J W 1983 Radionuclide EF and tomographic 201–TI defect size: Western Washington randomized intracoronary streptokinase trial (WWIST). Circulation 68(Suppl III): III–121

Rosenberg R D 1976 Actions and interactions of antithrombin and heparin. New England Journal of Medicine 292: 146–151

Rosenberg R D 1982 Heparin–antithrombin system. In: Coleman R W, Hirsh J, Marder V, Salzman E W (eds) Thrombosis and hemostasis: basic principles and clinical practice. Lippincott, Philadelphia

Rosenberg R D, Damus P S 1973 The purification and mechanism of action of human antithrombin — heparin cofactor. Journal of Biological Chemistry 248: 6490–6505

Ross John Jr 1982 Limitation of infarct size with thrombolytic agents. Circulation 68 (Suppl I): I-1–109

Salzman E W, Deykin D, Shapiro R M 1980 Effect of heparin and heparin fractions on platelet aggregation. Journal of Clinical Investigation 65: 64–73

Schofer J, Mathey D G, Montz R, Bleifeld W, Stritzke P 1983 Use of dual intracoronary scintigraphy with thallium–201 and technetium–99 m pyrophosphate to predict improvement in left ventricular wall motion immediately after intracoronary thrombolysis in acute myocardial infarction. Journal of American College of Cardiology 2: 737–744

Schroder R 1983 Systemic versus intracoronary streptokinase infusion in the treatment of acute myocardial infarction. Journal of American College of Cardiology 1: 1254–1261

Schroder R, Biamino G, Leitner E-R et al 1983 Intravenous short-term infusion of streptokinase in acute myocardial infarction. Circulation 67: 536–548

Schuler G, Schwartz F, Hofman M et al 1982 Thrombolysis in acute myocardial infarction using intracoronary streptokinase: assessment by thallium–201 scintigraphy. Circulation 66: 658–664

Scott C F, Schapiro M, Colman R W 1983 Effect of heparin on the inactivation rate of factor XIa by antithrombin III. Blood 60: 940–947

Second Report of the Sixty Plus Reinfarction Study Research Group 1982 Risks of long-term oral anticoagulant therapy in elderly patients after myocardial infarction. Lancet i: 64–68

Seifert R M 1979 Analysis of vitamin K_1 in some green leafy vegetables by gas chromatography. Journal of Agriculture and Food Chemistry 27: 301

Seuter F, Busse W D, Meng K, Hoffmeister F, Moller E, Horstmann H 1979 The antithrombotic activity of BAY G 6575. Arzneim–Forsch/Drug Research 29(I), 1: 54–59

Sevitt S, Gallagher N G 1959 Prevention of venous thrombosis and pulmonary embolism in injured patients. Lancet ii: 981–989

Sheehan F H, Mathey D G, Schofer J, Krebber H-J, Dodge H T 1983 Effect of interventions in salvaging left ventricular function in acute myocardial infarction: a study of intracoronary streptokinase. American Journal of Cardiology 52: 431–438

Shror K, Grodzinska L, Darius H 1981 Stimulation of coronary vascular prostacyclin and inhibition of human platelet thromboxane A_2 after low-dose nitroglycerin. Thrombosis Research 23: 59–67

Sixty Plus Reinfarction Study Research Group 1980 Oral anticoagulant therapy in elderly patients after myocardial infarction. Lancet ii: 989–994

Skinner D B, Salzman E W 1967 Anticoagulant prophylaxis in surgical patients. Surgery Gynecology and Obstetrics 125: 741–746

Stampfer M J, Goldhaber S Z, Yusuf S, Peto R, Hennekens C H 1982 Effect of intravenous streptokinase on acute myocardial infarction. New England Journal of Medicine 307: 1180–1182

Steele P, Rainwater J 1980 Favourable effect of sulfinpyrazone on thromboembolism in patients with rheumatic heart disease. Circulation 62(3) 462–465

Stenflo J, Suttie J W 1977 Vitamin K dependent formation of carboxyglutamic acid. Annals Revue of Biochemistry 4: 157–172

Subbarao K, Ruckinski B, Rausch M A, Schmid K, Niewiarowski S 1977 Binding of dipyridamole to human platelets and to an acid glycoprotein and its significance for the inhibition of adenosine uptake. Journal of Clinical Investigation 60: 936–943

Sullivan J M, Harken D E, Gorlin R 1971 Pharmacologic control of thromboembolic complications of cardiac-valve replacement. New England Journal of Medicine 284(25): 1391–1394

Suttie J W 1979 How coumarin anticoagulants work. Drug Therapy 9: 63

Szekely P 1964 Systemic embolism and anticoagulant prophylaxis in rheumatic heart. British Medical Journal 1209–1212

Taberner D A, Poller L, Burslem R W et al 1978 Oral anticoagulants controlled by the British comparative thromboplastin versus low-dose heparin in prophylaxis of deep-vein thrombosis. British Medical Journal 1: 272–274

Taylor G J, Mikell F L, Moses H W et al 1983 Intravenous and intracoronary streptokinase for MI. Circulation 68(Suppl III): III–314

Thebault J J, Blatrix C E, Blanchard J F, Panak E A 1975 Effects of ticlopidine, a new platelet aggregation inhibitor in man. Clinical Pharmacology Therapy 18(4): 485–490

Thomas D P, Merton R E, Barrowscliffe T W, Thunberg L, Lindahl U 1982 Effects of heparin oligosaccharides with high affinity for antithrombin III in experimental venous thrombosis. Thrombosis and Haemostasis 47(3): 244–248

Tollefsen D M, Blank M K 1981 Detection of a new heparin-dependent inhibitor of thrombin in human plasma. Journal of Clinical Investigation 68: 589–596

Tollefsen D M, Petska C A, Monafo W J 1983 Activation of heparin cofactor II by dermatan sulfate. Journal of Biological Chemistry 258: 6713–6717

Vaughan E D, Moore R A, Warren H et al 1969 Skin necrosis of genitalia and warfarin therapy. Journal of American Medical Association 210: 2282

Vermylen J, Chamone D A F, Verstraete M 1979 Stimulation of prostacyclin release from vessel wall by BAY G 6575, and antithrombotic compound. Lancet i: 518–520

Vermylen J, Carreras L O, Schaeren J V, Defreyn G, Machin S J, Verstraete M 1981 Thromboxane synthetase inhibition as antithrombotic strategy. Lancet 1: 1073–1075

Verrier R L, Radder E, Lown B 1982 Comparative effects of sodium salicylate and sulphinpyrazone on ventricular vulnerability in the normal and ischemic heart. In: The effect of platelet-active drugs on the cardiovascular system. Edited by University of Colorado Health Sciences, Denver

Vigano S, Mannucci P M, Solinas S, Bottasso B, D'Angelo A, Mariani G 1983 Early fall of C during short-term anticoagulant treatment. Thrombosis and Haemastasis 50(1): 310 (abstract)

Wei J Y, Markis J E, Malagold M et al 1983 Cardiovascular reflexes stimulated by reperfusion of ischemic myocardium. Circulation 67: 796

Weinstein J 1982 The international registry to support approval of intracoronary streptokinase thrombolysis in the treatment of myocardial infarction. Assessment of safety and efficacy. Circulation 68(Suppl I): I-61–66

Weiss H J 1967 The effect of clinical dextran on platelet aggregation, adhesion and ADP release in man: in vivo and in vitro studies. Journal of Laboratory and Clinical Medicine 69: 37–46

Westveer D C, Steward J, Hauser A M et al 1983 The significance of reperfusion arrhythmias with thrombolytic coronary recanalization. Circulation 68(Suppl III): III–410

Whitlon D S, Sadowski J A, Suttie J W 1978 Mechanism of coumarin action: significance of vitamin K epoxide reductase inhibition. Biochemistry 17: 1371–1377

Wiley J S, Chesterman C N, Morgan F J, Castaldi P A 1979 The effect of sulphinpyrazone on the aggregation and release reactions of human platelets. Thrombosis Research 14: 23–33

Wilkinson A R, Hawker R J, Hawker L M 1979 The influence of antiplatelet drugs on platelet survival after aortic damage or implantation of a dacron arterial prosthesis. Thrombosis Research 15: 181–189

Wright I S, Marple C D, Beck D F 1948 Anticoagulant therapy of coronary thrombosis with myocardial infarction. Journal of the American Medical Association 138: 1074–1079

Zimmerman R, Thiessen M, Morl H, Weckesser G 1979 The paradoxical thrombogenic effect of aspirin in experimental thrombosis. Thrombosis Research 16: 843–846

Zucker M G 1977 Heparin and platelet function. Federal Proceedings 36: 47

Zucker M B, Rothwell K G 1978 Differential influences of salicylate compounds on platelet aggregation and serotonin release. Current Therapy Press 23: 194–199

Zweifler A J 1962 Relation of prothrombin concentration to bleeding oral anticoagulant therapy. New England Journal of Medicine 267: 283–285

15. The acquired immunodeficiency syndrome (AIDS)

J. E. Groopman

INTRODUCTION

Nearly four years ago, four young, previously healthy men presented to the University of California Los Angeles Medical Center with fever and interstitial pneumonia. They proved to have *Pneumocystis carinii* as the cause of their pulmonary infection, a distinctly unusual protozoal pathogen in individuals with no underlying cause of immunosuppression. What began as an unusual cluster of cases in Los Angeles is now known to be an epidemic of worldwide concern. This chapter is a comprehensive presentation of the 'state of the art' in acquired immunodeficiency syndrome (AIDS). The epidemiology, clinical and laboratory features, therapeutic options, and current research on aetiology of AIDS will be discussed. AIDS is a complex disorder that spans the disciplines of immunology, molecular biology, public health, haematology, oncology, infectious disease and psychiatry. It is a deeply tragic epidemic with profound morbidity and possibly uniform fatality of its victims. AIDS also poses a formidable challenge to clinician and researcher alike in the search for its prevention and treatment. The discovery of the primary etiologic agent of AIDS, a retrovirus termed human T-lymphotropic virus type III (HTLV-III) or lymphadeno-pathy-associated virus (LAV) provides the scientific substrate upon which the disease may be conquered.

EPIDEMIOLOGY

AIDS was defined for purposes of epidemiological surveillance in 1981 as (1) the presence of a reliably diagnosed disease at least moderately predictive of cellular immunodeficiency and (2) the absence of an underlying cause for the immune deficiency or of any defined cause for reduced resistance to disease (Centers for Disease Control, 1981). Included under 'diseases at least moderately predictive of cellular immune deficiency' are two neoplasms, Kaposi's sarcoma and primary lymphoma of brain, and a wide spectrum of opportunistic infections. Currently, three-and-a-half years after surveillance for AIDS was initiated by the Centers for Disease Control (CDC), over 7000 cases that satisfied the surveillance definition have been diagnosed and reported in the US. Over half of these cases have been diagnosed during the first 10 months of 1984. Despite the difficulties in obtaining accurate data on a disease associated with lifestyles outside the mainstream of society, a concerted and co-ordinated effort among public health officials, physicians, and community leaders of high-risk groups has provided us with reasonably accurate data. A recent review by Allen (1984) details current epidemiologic trends. Nonetheless, it is likely that the current statistics underestimate the true prevalence of AIDS.

It is often asked whether AIDS is a new disease. The CDC reviewed all requests for pentamidine isoethionate, the only therapy for *Pneumocystis carinii* pneumonia prior to the licensing of trimethoprim-sulfamethoxazole in the US, and only available via the CDC. They determined that no cases of *Pneumocystis carinii* pneumonia occurred in the US prior to 1979 in an individual who did not have a well-recognised disorder of cellular immunodeficiency. Similarly, tumour registries have been reviewed for diagnoses of Kaposi's sarcoma and/or primary non-Hodgkins lymphoma of central nervous system, and no cases clinically suggestive of AIDS have been uncovered. For these reasons, as well as the clinically obvious features of opportunistic infections in previously healthy individuals, it may be concluded that AIDS did not exist in the US prior to 1979.

Although the aetiology of the disease has recently been identified, no single laboratory test or combination of tests is yet verified as a diagnostic standard, so that patients are still characterised as having AIDS on the basis of the opportunistic infections and neoplasms they develop. The surveillance definition of AIDS is both stringent and restrictive and fails to include a wide range of clinical conditions and laboratory abnormalities that appear to be associated with AIDS. These associated conditions are now termed AIDS-related complex (ARC). The clinical features of ARC include prolonged generalised unexplained lymphadenopathy, fever, oral candida, herpes zoster, unexplained weight loss, night sweats, and constitutional symptoms such as malaise, fatigue and myalgia (CDC, 1982; Gottlieb et al, 1983). Laboratory abnormalities in ARC are similar to those in AIDS, particularly an absolute lymphopenia, leukopenia, thrombocytopenia, and cellular immunologic abnormalities. It is estimated that there are 2–5 times as many individuals with ARC as those with AIDS. Because the CDC adopted a restricted surveillance definition of AIDS in 1981, there are very few epidemiologic data on ARC patients. It appears that ARC is appearing in the same risk groups as AIDS, specifically homosexually active men, haemophiliacs (Davis et al, 1983; Ragni et al, 1983), Haitian immigrants (Vieira, 1983), intravenous drug abusers, female sexual partners of AIDS patients (Harris et al, 1983), children of high-risk parents (Oleske et al, 1983; Rubinstein et al, 1983), and prisoners (Womser et al, 1983) The high-risk groups outside the continental US are similar to those reported to CDC from the US. There is an outbreak of AIDS on the island of Haiti (Moskowitz et al, 1983). Interestingly, AIDS is not particularly prevalent in the Dominican Republic, a country that is geographically contiguous with Haiti on the island of Hispaniola. Also of interest is the occurrence of AIDS in Africans from Zaire and Chad. The prevalence of cases of AIDS in Kinshasha, capital city of Zaire, may be the highest in the world. Preliminary serological studies for antibody to HTLV-III/LAV in rural Zaire indicate that nearly half of the asymptomatic adult population may be infected with the agent (Saxinger et al, unpublished; Groopman & Gottlieb, 1983). The occurrence of AIDS in Haitians and Central Africans is unexplained, and may provide important clues to the origin and spread of the disease.

The AIDS epidemic in the US has shown an exponential curve with few cases occurring during the early years and then a sharp rise, typical of the spread of an infectious agent with a long incubation period in a highly susceptible population. Although certain public health officials in New York City have recently claimed that there has been a plateau in this curve, analysis of the most recent surveillance data is not sufficiently reliable to determine whether indeed this exponential increase is tapering in the most highly affected areas. It is reasonable to predict that within the near future flattening of the total curve may be seen due either to a decline in the number of susceptible persons being exposed, 'saturation' of the vulnerable populations with the agent, or due to the effect of preventive measures that have been initiated during the last year. It is of note that asymptomatic healthy homosexually active men between the ages of 20 and 45 in areas of the US where the disease is most prevalent show many immunological abnormalities seen in AIDS (Kornfeld et al, 1982). Testing of such asymptomatic persons for HTLV-III/LAV shows a high degree of seropositivity (Groopman et al, 1985). Similar data has been obtained on healthy asymptomatic haemophiliacs (de Shazo et al, 1983; Kitchen et al, 1984).

The distribution of AIDS cases within the high-risk groups has remained relatively stable since the reporting of additional cases. Seventy-two per cent of all AIDS cases have occurred in homosexual or bisexual men, 17% in intravenous drug abusers, about 5% in fairly recent Haitian immigrants to the USA, and 0.6% in men with haemophilia. Six per cent of AIDS cases reported to the CDC do not belong to one of the well-recognised risk groups. Of these, about half have been patients for whom sufficient information to allow classification into a risk group was not available due to early death or other reasons. Approximately 10% of cases with known risk factors occur in individuals with Kaposi's sarcoma and normal immunologic parameters; it is unclear whether these represent 'background' or sporadic cases of the neoplasm in young individuals as opposed to the development of the neoplasm secondary to the immunosuppression of AIDS. Of the remainder of this clinical subgroup, about 17% are patients who have received blood transfusions during the 5 years prior to the onset of AIDS, and 15% are patients who have had heterosexual relations with persons with AIDS or with persons who are in a group with an increased incidence of AIDS. Of the probable transfusion cases of AIDS, the first four were diagnosed in 1982, suggesting that more cases with this risk factor will probably be diagnosed during the forthcoming years. The relative risk of acquiring AIDS by random blood transfusion is likely to remain small in comparison with the risk of acquiring it by sexual contact, shared unsterile needles, and clotting factor concentrates, since more than 3 million patients in the US receive blood transfusions each year, and there have been only 62 cases of transfusion-related AIDS. These cases yield important information on apparent incubation period (median 25 months) and the possibility of an asymptomatic carrier state ('suspicious' donor in a high-risk group alive and asymptomatic while transfusion recipient developed AIDS). In addition to the adult patients with AIDS, approximately 70 infants and young children have been reported with a constellation of opportunistic infections highly suggestive of AIDS (Oleske et al, 1983; Rubinstein et al, 1983). Recognised causes of congenital immune deficiency in these children have been ruled out. The probable means of transmission of AIDS to such infant cases have included blood transfusion and being born to parents, usually mothers, who are in a high-risk group for AIDS.

The age distribution of AIDS cases has been striking in that over 90% of patients are only 20–49 years of age, with over 45% being 30–39 years of age. Among homosexual AIDS cases the median age is 35 years, which is comparable for intravenous drug abusers and Haitians; the median age for haemophiliacs with AIDS is 47 years. Adult patients who develop AIDS after receiving random blood products tended to be older than those with other risk factors, possibly because of the preponderance of cardiac by-pass patients in this group. The age distribution and diagnosis of patients with AIDS in the major high-risk groups has not changed significantly in the last 3 years.

The sex distribution is also remarkably constant in that over 93% of cases have occurred among men. Women comprise 41% of the drug user cases, 13% of the Haitians, 87% of the heterosexual contact cases, and 50% of random blood transfusion cases. Finally, the racial distribution of cases has reflected the racial composition of those geographic areas of the US with a high prevalence of the disease: 59% of cases are in whites, 26% in blacks, and 14% in individuals of Hispanic origin. Homosexual cases have occurred more frequently in whites, and drug user cases in blacks and Hispanics. There does not appear to be an adherent racial susceptibility or protection against AIDS. There have been very few (only 6) cases among Asians but this may reflect the paucity of Asians in the major risk groups.

The geographic clustering of AIDS is striking. Over four-fifths of cases have been reported from only five States: New York, California, New Jersey, Florida and Texas. Over 60% of cases have been reported from four cities, New York, San Francisco, Los Angeles and Miami. New York City alone has reported 1700 cases. There has been some change in the distribution of cases by State since the initial recognition of AIDS. The proportion of cases from New York has dropped from over 50% initially to 38% of the last 500 cases reported. California, Florida, and New Jersey have maintained relatively constant proportions of the total AIDS cases in the US. Currently, reports have been received from 45 States, the District of Columbia, and Puerto Rico. Interestingly, 85% of the drug user cases have occurred in New York or New Jersey. The majority of Haitian cases have occurred in Florida or New York, and three-quarters of the haemophiliac cases have occurred in residents of States other than New York, Florida, New Jersey and Texas.

AIDS has been recognised outside the US and appears to be increasing in Europe. The outbreak of AIDS among Central African immigrants to Belgium and France has already been mentioned. European cities with large homosexual populations such as Paris, London, Amsterdam, and Copenhagen, have all reported cases. Recently, a European task force to monitor AIDS has been established. Surveillance from Africa indicate that AIDS is very frequent in Zaire. The epidemiology of AIDS in Africa differs from that in the United States (Clumeck et al, 1984). About half of the African cases are women and the factors of homosexuality, blood products, drug abuse do not appear to be operative in the occurrence of the disorder. Given the high prevalence of HTLV-III/LAV seropositivity in Central Africa, these cases may represent emergence of the pathogen in the general heterosexual population. Similarly, ARC has been recognised in Europe. Many of the early cases of AIDS or ARC among Europeans could be epidemiologically linked to sexual or illicit drug contacts in the USA.

It is of note that the opportunistic infections and neoplasms seen in AIDS are not uniformly distributed in the high-risk populations. Almost 44% of homosexual men with AIDS have Kaposi's sarcoma. Kaposi's sarcoma is very unusual (less than 5%) among intravenous drug users, heterosexual contacts, or transfusion recipients. The neoplasm occurs in about 24% of patients without identified risk factors and in about 12% of Haitians. Thus, the relative risk of Kaposi's sarcoma in an AIDS patient who is a homosexual man is greater than five times that of an AIDS patient from all other groups. The reason for clustering of this neoplasm in male homosexuals with AIDS is not known, but is probably related to the prevalence of cytomegalovirus in the male homosexual population (see below).

The protozoal pneumonia with *Pneumocystis carinii* has occurred in over half of all patients with AIDS. It is the single most common opportunistic infection in AIDS and has been documented in nearly three-quarters of intravenous drug addicts with the disease, 94% of haemophiliacs, and 87% of heterosexual contact and transfusion-related cases. It has occurred in less than 43% of Haitians in whom other opportunistic infections such as central nervous system toxoplasmosis occur more frequently. The prognosis for AIDS patients with *Pneumocystis carinii* is much less favourable than those with Kaposi's sarcoma.

AIDS is clearly an infectious disease. The means of transmission appear to be multiple, and include sexual contact, sharing unsterile needles, blood products, and possible vertical transmission to infants. This epidemiology of AIDS closely resembles that of hepatitis type-B. The 'AIDS agent' (HTLV-III/LAV) is present in blood, semen, and saliva (Groopman et al, 1984c,d). It is unclear whether a specific sexual practice facilitates the transmission of the disease or is simply a marker for large numbers of different sexual partners and thus a statistically greater chance to contract the disease. Nonetheless, rectal intercourse, insertion of the fist into the partner's rectum, and anal lingus have been reported as prevalent sexual practices among homosexual men with the disease compared to case controls (Jaffe et al, 1983). Because AIDS has occurred in heterosexual contacts of individuals with the disease, it can be assumed that this type of sexual contact was sufficient for transmission of the disease. Similarly, it is unclear whether different blood products are more likely to transmit AIDS. Because factor VIII concentrates are prepared from several thousand different donors, the occurrence of the disease among haemophiliacs may reflect their exposure to tens of thousands of different persons. There is no evidence to date implicating transmission of AIDS through products such as hepatitis-B immune globulin, other immune globulins, or the hepatitis-B vaccine. Indeed, the incidence of AIDS in cohorts of homosexual men who were vaccinated for hepatitis-B in 1981–2 appears to be slightly lower than among those individuals who did not receive vaccine.

Although it has been suggested that recognised modes of transmission such as homosexual activity and intravenous drug abuse may account for some of the Haitian AIDS cases, these lifestyle factors clearly do not explain many of the cases. Since the majority of Haitian cases occur among individuals who have recently entered the US, it is possible, given the long incubation time of this disease, that these persons contracted the syndrome while still in Haiti. It is possible that AIDS has been transmitted on the island of Haiti through the use of unsterile needles and injection equipment used by unlicensed pharmacists and healers.

No cases of AIDS have occurred among health care personnel due to exposure to a hospitalised AIDS patient. Seroconversion for antibody to HTLV-III has occurred in a nurse after needlestick injury. The only large group of health care workers with AIDS has been homosexual men, and development of the disease in that group is presumed to be through sexual activity rather than occupation.

AETIOLOGY

The aetiology of AIDS has recently been discovered (Gallo et al, 1984; Barre-Sinoussi et al, 1983). It was clear from the epidemiology of the disease that AIDS is caused by a transmissible agent. Several ubiquitous DNA viruses, such as Epstein–Barr virus, cytomegalovirus, and hepatitis-B virus, had been considered as candidates for the cause of AIDS (Groopman & Gottlieb, 1982, 1983; Gottlieb ct al, 1983). Cyto-megalovirus was proposed as the cause of AIDS since it is recognised as a cause of transient immunosuppression, has circumstantial epidemiologic associa-tions with Kaposi's sarcoma, is very prevalent in the homosexual community, and is transmissible by blood products. Epstein–Barr virus is associated with immunosup-pression as well during acute infectious mononucleosis, is also epidemiologically linked to a neoplasm seen with increased frequency in AIDS, non-Hodgkin's lymphoma of the Burkitt's type, and is a potent B-cell stimulant which could lead to some of the clinical and laboratory manifestations of AIDS (see below). Hepatitis-B virus is also very prevalent among the male homosexual community, is a well-known pathogen associated with blood products, and may function synergistically with the delta agent in the pathogenesis of chronic liver disease and/or hepatoma. These reasons for considering such viruses as the cause of AIDS were intriguing but still far from forceful. More importantly, one must explain the dramatic appearance of this disorder in 1979/80 in the US despite the well-recognised existence of such viruses among high-risk cohorts prior to that period. Overwhelming data based on recovery of HTLV-III/LAV and antibodies to this virus from patients with AIDS, ARC, and at risk cohorts indicate that this virus is the primary pathogen Koch's postulates have been most closely approximated by studies of HTLV-III in transfusion-AIDS (Groopman et al, 1984c). HTLV-III appears able to cause AIDS as the sole infecting virus in such cases, since no evidence was present for injection with Epstein-Barr virus hepatitis-B virus and cytomegalovirus. Some of the biological properties of HTLV-III are detailed in Chapter 9.
virus in such cases, since no evidence was present for infection with Epstein-Barr virus, hepatitis-B virus and cytomegalovirus.

This virus belongs to the larger family of human T-cell leukaemia viruses. Some of the biological properties of HTLV are detailed in Chapter 9. HTLV-III does not appear capable of transforming cells, but rather is cytopathic and ultimately leads to cell lysis. HTLV-III has a tropism for the OK T4 positive helper inducer subset of lymphocytes and appears to be transmissible via sexual, blood-borne and needle routes. Seroepidemiologic studies indicate that nearly all patients with AIDS and ARC have been infected with HTLV-III. Furthermore, the virus can be readily re-covered from the majority of ARC patients and at least a third of AIDS patients. A similar, if not identical virus has been identified in a small number of pre-AIDS and AIDS patients in France (Barre-Sinoussi et al, 1983; Vilmer et al, 1984). Although HTLV-III infection may be sufficient for the ultimate clinical outcome of opportunistic infections and/or Kaposi's sarcoma, co-factors such as cytomegalovirus, Epstein-Barr virus, or alloantigen stimulation with factor VIII concentrate may enhance the host susceptibility to HTLV-III and its clinically virulent effects. A diagnostic test for AIDS and ARC is under development based on antibody to the major antigens of HTLV-III. Certainly understanding the pathobiology of this virus should ultimately lead to rationale therapy of the syndrome.

IMMUNOLOGICAL DYSFUNCTION IN AIDS

AIDS is unique among primary immunodeficiency disorders because of its trans-missible nature. The pattern of opportunistic infections recognised in AIDS patients implicates a deficiency in cell-mediated immunity since this is the limb of the immune system that chiefly responds to the obligate and facultative intracellular pathogens such as protozoa, viruses, mycobacteria and fungi. Although AIDS appears to be a new disease, two conditions of immunodeficiency previously studied resemble AIDS. They are iatrogenic immunosuppression prior to organ transplantation with agents such as cyclosporine, steroids, and azathioprine, and a rare congenital immunodeficiency disorder, purine nucleosidase phosphorylase deficiency. These will not be discussed here but have recently been reviewed (Rosen, 1984).

Although it is clinically apparent that there is a profound defect in cell-mediated immune function in AIDS, defective antibody production in response to challenge with new antigens also occurs in AIDS patients (Lane et al, 1983). Despite the failure of the humoral immune system in this context, infections with pathogens such as *Salmonella*, *Pneumococcus*, and *Haemophilus*, are unusual in AIDS. Therefore, the B-lymphocyte dysfunction is not a major clinical problem in these patients.

The central problem is to dissect out the primary defect or defects of immunity in AIDS that lead to the clinical manifestations. It is clear that the immune system is a complex network of interacting cells so that a primary defect in one cell type may be reflected in secondary dysfunction of other cells. Identifying the primary part of the immune system that is abnormal may focus research on that particular lineage of cells and more rapidly lead to isolation of the transmissible agent that causes AIDS.

Cell-mediated immunity against intracellular organisms occurs via interaction of microbial antigens with T-lymphocytes which recruit and activate monocyte–macrophages through soluble products (lymphokines), lead to effective intracellular killing, infiltrates of round cells and granuloma formation (Bodmer, 1981; Finberg & Benacerraf, 1981). It is clear this is a simplistic picture of the process because dendritic lymphoid cells, macrophages, and perhaps B-lymphocytes (all bearing the Ia antigen on the cell surface) may be involved in presentation of antigen to the T-cell. In addition, interactions among suppressor/cytotoxic T-cells, helper/inducer T-cells, and their soluble products such as gamma interferon, interleukin 2, etc., constitute an adaptive part of the cellular host defense. In addition, antibodies, which are generally thought of as involved in humoral host defence such as opsonisation, are also involved in immunity against viruses not only through neutralisation but probably through antibody-dependent cellular cytotoxicity wherein virus encoated cell surface neo-antigens characteristic of affected host cells are recognised. It has recently been appreciated that the class of large granular lymphocytes previously included among 'null' lymphoid cells contribute to cellular host defence. Classification of these large granular lymphocytes is not complete, but it includes populations involved in pro-duction of alpha interferon, antibody-dependent cellular cytotoxicity and some forms of natural cytotoxicity such as natural killer (NK) cells. Alpha interferon appears to participate in the activation of macrophages, maturation of cytotoxic T-lympho-cytes, and augmentation of NK cell activity (Stiehm et al, 1982). The difficulties in dissecting out the complex interactions in this network of cells are apparent. Such difficulties are increased by the limitations in sensitivity and specificity of our in vitro assays of cell functions as well as the only partial biochemical characterisation of many of the soluble mediators of immunity. Despite these limitations, it is clear that the major clinical problem in AIDS involves a failure of cell-mediated immunity and consequent infection with opportunistic pathogens normally handled by T-lympho-cytes (Gottlieb et al, 1982).

Immunity may be tested in vivo to a certain extent as well. AIDS patients are generally anergic by skin test to common recall antigens. This anergy demonstrates that in vivo there is a defect in some part of the process from antigen recognition through recruitment of inflammatory cells. Such skin test anergy is not a uniform finding among AIDS patients. About 10–15% of patients in large series of AIDS patients preserve skin test reactivity, occasionally with microbial antigens derived from pathogens causing active infection (such as positivity to *Candida* skin test during oral oesophageal candidiasis) (Siegal, 1984). The significance of this finding is not yet clear, but suggests that cellular activities involved in skin test hypersensitivity are not a major defect in host defence in AIDS or that there is heterogeneity in the cellular populations that react to antigens of such pathogens, and that preservation of the clone reacting to certain antigens and thereby providing a positive skin test need not correlate with actual body defence against infection. Primary immunisation designed to elicit skin test reactivity via delayed hypersensitivity generally employs haptens such as 2,4-dinitrochlorobenzene (DNCB) or 2,4-dinitroflurobenzene (DNFB). Such haptens bind to skin proteins, or perhaps bind directly to antigen-presenting, Ia-bearing cells with subsequent clonal selection and expansion of antigen-reactive T-lymphocytes. Development of a contact dermatitis upon challenge 1 month later with DNCB or DNFB suggests intact cellular immunity. Generally, primary immunisation to elicit such skin test reactivity is defective in AIDS patients and they cannot be sensitised to such haptens.

A striking histopathologic finding in a large number of AIDS patients is the failure to produce granulomas. Inflammatory responses are abnormal in AIDS, and one often finds large numbers of micro-organisms in infected tissues that do not elicit an expected inflammatory reaction. This observation is clinically important in that special stains for micro-organisms should be performed on tissue in the absence of those histopathologic changes that typically alert a physician to a particular type of infection.

Both leukopenia and lymphopenia are common in AIDS patients as well as in AIDS-related complex (ARC) (Gottlieb et al, 1983). Asymptomatic leukopenia often is an early marker for development of AIDS. The pathophysiology of leukopenia in AIDS in the absence of complicating factors such as opportunistic infection, myelosuppressant drugs, or chemotherapy, is not known. True antineutrophil antibodies have not yet been demonstrated. The high titres of circulating immune complexes may bind to the neutrophil Fc receptor leading to premature phagocytosis. Preliminary studies of bone marrow progenitors have demonstrated a reduced number of myeloid colony-forming units (CFU-GM) which appears to be related to an adherent cell population and not a circulating inhibitor (Siegal, 1984).

Polyclonal hypergammaglobulinaemia, chiefly involving IgG and IgA, are usually present in the disease. Serum IgD is also raised and may be a marker of the disease. Monoclonal immunoglobulins have not yet been described in AIDS. The aetiology of the polyclonal hypergammaglobulinaemia has not yet been determined, but in light of the high antibody titres to the Epstein–Barr virus, it has been suggested that reactivation of this virus known to be a potent stimulus for antibody production, non-specifically 'turns on' the B cells. Increased antibody production is not a uniform finding in AIDS, particularly upon challenge with new antigens. It is of note that most patients with AIDS lack serum antibodies to toxoplasmosis in the face of active infection and that IgM antibodies do not appear during cytomegalovirus infection. Lane et al (1983) have demonstrated that AIDS patients do not form appropriate antibodies upon deliberate sensitisation with keyhole limpet haemocyanin (KLH) or with pneumococcal vaccine.

The major histocompatibility locus is found on chromosome 6 and codes for a number of cell surface antigens of HLA, A, B, C, D and DR types. A number of disorders of the immune system appear to be linked to certain HLA genotypes. It appears that Kaposi's sarcoma is linked to HLA/DR5 in that this HLA type occurs two to three times more frequently among AIDS patients with Kaposi's sarcoma than in the general Caucasian population (Rubinstein et al, 1983). ARC may also be linked to the DR5 locus. The immunogenetics of AIDS is a subject under intensive investigation and may provide important clues to those components of the immune system that determine susceptibility to the transmissible AIDS agent.

Monoclonal antibodies have proven to be useful tools in identifying subpopulations of T-lymphocytes (Kung et al, 1979). Although it is now recognised that correlation of surface phenotype with presumed function is complex, the ability to identify 'a helper/inducer' and 'suppressor/cytotoxic' subsets of circulating T-cells has greatly assisted AIDS research. There is generally an absolute decrease in the number of OKT4/Leu3 ('helper/inducer') T-cells with a variable decrease in OKT8/Leu4 ('suppressor/cytotoxic') T-lymphocytes. It is now clear that the OKT4/Leu3 population is heterogeneous with respect to other surface antigens as well as function in that OKT4-positive cells can function to suppress antibody production. Determination of other surface antigens such as Leu8 and TQ1 may help identify that class of the OKT4/Leu3 population which is functionally impaired in AIDS. Much has been made of the ratio between the OKT4 and OKT8 populations. Normally the ratio of these two T-cell populations is 1.5–2.5 while in AIDS the ratio is inverted and is often below 1.0. It is clear that one change in each population can result in the same inversion of ratio and is far from specific for AIDS. A number of viral disorders are marked by a similar inversion in ratio. For example, self-limited Epstein–Barr virus acute infectious mononucleosis in an immunocompetent host will result in an inverted T helper/T suppressor ratio. The cause of this inverted ratio is generally an increase in the suppressor (OKT8) subset and not a decrease in the helper (OKT4) population. Therefore, an absolute decrease in the OKT4/Leu3 population is highly suggestive of AIDS. This occurs in 70–90% of AIDS patients at time of diagnosis. Dalgleish et al (1984) and Klatzmann et al (1984) have shown that the T4 molecule behaves as a receptor for the AIDS virus. There are clearly individuals with clinical AIDS who have normal numbers of T lymphocytes and normal proportions of subsets. This is perhaps the best example that the clinical immunodeficiency of AIDS relates not only to quantitative but also qualitative abnormalities in the T-cell system.

Nonetheless, T-cell subset imbalance with an inverted ratio is a rough guideline to the severity of AIDS. Individuals with overwhelming opportunistic infections generally have ratios below 0.5, while patients with Kaposi's sarcoma who tend to be clinically healthier early in their course often have ratios between 0.5 and 1.0. Patients with ARC also have T-cell subset imbalance but tend to have ratios greater than 0.5. It is of note that studies done on asymptomatic, healthy high-risk groups have demonstrated T-cell subset imbalance in a significant proportion of the study population (Kornfeld et al, 1982; de Shazo et al, 1983; Rogers et al, 1983). Specifically, 50–80% of young sexually active male homosexuals in cities such as New York, Los Angeles, and San Francisco have T-cell subset ratios significantly below the normal mean. Some of this T-cell subset imbalance is due to an increase in the suppressor cell population without any perturbation of the helper cells and may reflect the frequent and repeated exposure through sexual contact to a number of viruses such as cytomegalovirus (Detels et al, 1983). The T-cell subset studies may fluctuate on repeated determination, particularly in the asymptomatic healthy homosexual cohorts. These abnormalities on T-cell testing may signify widespread exposure of the gay population to HTLV-III/LAV. Haemophiliacs when similarly studied demonstrate an inverted T-cell subset ratio in 30–50% of the population. This, by and large, is related to an increase in the suppressor cell population and may again reflect the frequent exposure to herpes viruses and hepatitis-B in blood products. Nonetheless, it appears that greater than three-fourths of asymptomatic haemophiliacs treated with factor VIII concentrates have antibody to HTLV-III (Kitchen et al, 1984). Of note is that preliminary studies of asymptomatic healthy Haitians in the US do not demonstrate such T-cell subset imbalance (Nicholas et al, 1983). This further emphasises the difficulty in dissecting out the epidemiologic factors that have led to the disproportionate prevalence of AIDS among Haitians in the US.

It is of interest that monoclonal antibody studies of lymphocytic infiltrates in Kaposi's sarcoma lesions as well as of lymphocytes in lymph nodes in patients with AIDS or ARC demonstrate similar changes in subset distribution to that found in peripheral blood (Cochran et al, 1983; Modlin et al, 1983). Thus there does not appear to be any gross difference between distribution of lymphocyte populations in the circulation and in tissue.

Other changes in T-cell surface phenotypes have been noted in AIDS, including the appearance of activation-associated antigens determined by OKT10 and HLA DR (Ia). There may also be reduced expression of the TAC antigen, an antigen closely associated with the interleukin 2 receptor.

Peripheral blood mononuclear cells normally proliferate in response to a variety of plant-derived lectins, microbial antigens, and allogeneic and autologous cell antigens. In the majority of AIDS patients, the proliferative response is markedly decreased upon challenge with these antigens (Siegal et al, 1982). These systems generally test the integrity of the T-cell and monocyte populations. B-cell proliferation in vitro to *Staphylococcal* protein (Cowan strain) is also decreased. Several investigators have reported on soluble serum factors present in AIDS which are inhibitory to normal proliferative responses. Generation of 'help' by T-lymphocytes of B-cell antibody production appears to be deranged in AIDS. In contrast, there does not appear to be excessive suppressor T-cell activity in AIDS as measured in coculture assays. Thus, the polyclonal hypergammaglobulinaemia in AIDS may be multifactorial, with B cells 'driven' by independent mitogens such as Epstein–Barr virus as well as the failure of suppressor T cells to limit the antibody response. Currently, despite the quantitative and qualitative study of T-cell function in AIDS, the immune dysregulation is not understood. If in vivo there were important failure of T-cell-mediated 'help' of antibody production, and if indeed there is clinical significance to the failure in AIDS to produce antibody upon challenge with a variety of antigens, one might expect clinical infection with encapsulated organisms such as *Pneumococcus* and *Salmonella* to be a prominent manifestation of this disorder. Infection with such bacteria is rare until the latest stages of the disease.

Attention has focused on abnormalities in lymphokine production and response in AIDS. Only limited data are available. Gamma interferon production by T cells in vitro appears to be normal or increased while production of interleukin 2 (T-cell growth factor) may be decreased (Siegal, 1984). The expression of receptors for interleukin 2 as measured by TAC antigen on activated T cells appears to be decreased but the responses to exogenous highly purified interleukin 2 is adequate in vitro, suggesting that receptors are adequately displayed on sufficient numbers of responding cells (Rook et al, 1983). Interleukin 2 appears to stimulate both NK cells and cytotoxic T cells (that are HLA restricted against CMV-infected targets) in vitro. Alpha interferon is produced by myeloid cells such as monocytes–macrophages and much attention has recently been focused on apparently aberrant form of α interferon in AIDS. Alpha interferon serum levels are elevated in AIDS patients (Eyster et al, 1983). Alpha interferon is normally resistant to acid treatment and maintains its antiviral activity at pH 2. Patients with AIDS have been noted to have an acid-labile form of α interferon and indeed this has been suggested as a putative diagnostic marker of the disease (Eyster et al, 1983). In several instances, an elevation in the serum level of acid-labile interferon occurred several months prior to clinical onset of AIDS. Further study is required to validate the utility of the test. The biologic significance of this unusual form of α interferon is unclear. High levels of serum interferon in AIDS patients may simply reflect the frequent and persistent viral infections associated with the immunodeficiency or may reflect a physiologic response to the aetiologic agent of AIDS.

The levels of thymic hormones have similarly been measured in AIDS. Facteur Thymique Serique (FTS) is depressed in the majority of AIDS patients (Dardenne & Safai, 1983). The thymus has recently been studied in AIDS. Of note, in one case, Hassall's corpuscles were noted to be absent in the thymus. This finding of disappearance of Hassal's corpuscles is quite unusual since thymic involution does not usually involve loss of such structures. One group has attempted to reconstitute the immune system in AIDS by thymic transplantation, but without apparent efficacy (Dwyer, 1983).

Studies of phagocytosis and microbial killing by neutrophils and monocytes–macrophages have not yet been performed. There may be some element of neutrophil dysfunction in very advanced stages of AIDS since infections with Gram-negative bacilli, *Staphylococcus aureus*, and *Mucormycosis*, suggesting neutrophil dysfunction, have occurred. Both serum and urine lysozyme have been known to be elevated in AIDS which may reflect rapid turnover in monocytes involved in inflammatory responses. An absolute neutropenia often occurs in conjunction with the lymphopenia seen in AIDS. Studies have recently been reported on bone marrow myeloid progenitors in AIDS. The colony forming unit/granulocyte macrophage (CFU-GM) is decreased; similarly, T-lymphocyte colonies in semi-cell media (CFU/TL) also appear depressed when bone marrow from these patients is cultured (Mitsuyasu,

1984). The cause of a low proliferative rate in vitro of these bone marrow stem cells is not yet determined.

INFECTIOUS COMPLICATIONS OF AIDS

About two-thirds of AIDS patients have opportunistic infections without Kaposi's sarcoma. Clinical onset of such infections generally occurs 1–6 months after a non-specific illness of variable severity (Gottlieb et al, 1983). Many patients report a prodrome of low-grade fevers, night sweats, a non-productive cough, intermittent diarrhoea, and pruritus. Fevers of unknown origin can occasionally be quite prolonged (greater than 12 months' duration) and may represent reactivation of certain viruses such as cytomegalovirus and Epstein–Barr virus. Weight loss of 10–15% of body weight is a striking early clinical feature in many patients who eventually develop opportunistic infections. Patients with AIDS are clinically 'catabolic' and, despite aggressive caloric supplementation, including parenteral hyperalimentation, often are unable to gain or maintain weight. This weight loss may occur in the absence of gastrointestinal dysfunction with associated diarrhoea. Enteric pathogens are frequent among some of the groups at risk for AIDS, such as homosexually active men, and may explain some of the episodes of diarrhoea. Nonetheless, in the majority of individuals with either AIDS or ARC, no cause is demonstrated for the diarrhoea.

Many patients report painful generalised lymphadenopathy of minimal to moderate degree during the first weeks to months of this febrile prodrome that often subsides by the time of onset of severe opportunistic infections. Several investigators have documented the 'burnout' pathologically in lymph nodes as individuals have progressed from the prodromal condition with intense follicular hyperplasia in enlarged nodes to a paucity of lymphadenopathy with histopathologic 'dropout' of germinal centres.

Certain unusual and unexplained clinical findings occur in the AIDS prodrome. Alopecia is a common finding particularly in patients with fever of unknown origin. A non-specific seborrhoeic or eczematous dermatitis with diffuse facial erythema has also been noted. Arthralgia, myalgia, sinusitis, and decreased libido are all reported symptoms in the prodromal state.

There is a wide spectrum of opportunistic infections in AIDS which are often multiple, recurrent, and eventually fatal. These are listed in Table 15.1. Patients presenting with Kaposi's sarcoma are susceptible to the same array of pathogens but infections generally occur later in the clinical course. The most frequent initial infections are *Pneumocystis carinii* pneumonia and oesophageal candidiasis. Less commonly, disseminated cytomegalovirus, severe perianal herpes simplex, cerebral toxoplasmosis, cryptosporidial enteritis, cryptococcal meningitis, and disseminated histoplasmosis occur. Mycobacterium avium–intracellulare, an atypical mycobacterium, has been recognised as a frequent cause of hectic fevers and hepatosplenomegaly in AIDS patients. This mycobacterium is generally non-pathogenic for immunocompetent individuals. Mycobacterium tuberculosis, generally disseminated, has occurred in a large portion of Haitian patients with AIDS. It is of note that mycobacteria are easily found in involved organs and proliferate without eliciting granulomata. Demonstration of mycobacterium avium intracellulare infection re-

Table 15.1 Infectious complications of acquired immunodeficiency syndrome

Viral	Fungal	Protozoal	Mycobacterial	Others
Cytomegalovirus	*Candida albicans*	*Pneumocystis carinii*	*Mycobacterium*	*Nocardia*
Disseminated	Oral thrush	Pneumonia	*avium intracellulare*	*Legionella*
Pneumonia	Oesophagitis	Retinal infection	Disseminated	
Retinitis	Disseminated	*Toxoplasma gondii*	*Mycobacterium tuberculosis*	
Encephalitis	*Cryptococcus neoformans*	Encephalitis	Disseminated	
Herpes simplex	Meningitis	*Cryptosporidium*		
Progressive	Disseminated	Enteritis		
Herpes zoster	*Histoplasma capsulatum*	*Isospora belli*		
Limited cutaneous	Disseminated	Enteritis		
Progressive multifocal	*Petriellidium boydii*			
leukoencephalopathy	Pneumonia			
	Aspergillus			
	Pulmonary			

quires recovery of the organism from tissues other than lung since this atypical mycobacteria may be a saprophyte in the bronchial tree.

In the majority of cases of *Pneumocystis carinii* pneumonia associated with AIDS the chest X-ray reveals diffuse interstitial infiltrates. However, it has been amply documented that AIDS patients may have significant pulmonary infection with *Pneumocystis carinii* and have a perfectly normal chest X-ray. Symptoms of cough, dyspnoea, fever and either hypoxaemia at rest or with exercise, as well as an abnormally elevated alveolar/arterial oxygen concentration gradient occur in patients with abnormal or normal chest X-ray. Pulmonary function tests in *Pneumocystis carinii* pneumonia generally reveal a restrictive defect, a low diffusing capacity, and rarely improvement of these parameters with bronchodilators. The gallium scan of lung is often positive. Definitive diagnosis is made by silver methenamine stain of bronchial brushings and/or transbronchial lung biopsy.

Toxoplasma gondii is a well-recognised cause of central nervous system infection in AIDS. CNS toxoplasmosis appears to occur in a disproportionate number of Haitian AIDS cases for unknown reasons. Toxoplasmosis of the central nervous system most commonly presents the symptoms of headache, mental status deterioration or seizures (Horowitz et al, 1983). A CT scan reveals single or multiple abscesses with an apparent predeliction for location in the basal ganglia. Examination of the spinal fluid in patients with CNS toxoplasmosis was remarkable for elevated protein, low glucose, and absence of cells. Lack of specific IgM antibody or rise in titre of IgG antibody to *Toxoplasma gondii* certainly does not exclude the diagnosis. Brain biopsy if feasible or empiric antitoxoplasma therapy is indicated in this clinical setting. CNS infection with toxoplasmosis gives a different CT scan finding from individuals with AIDS who have CMV encephalitis. CMV encephalitis manifests as a progressive dementia.

Many of the non-specific constitutional symptoms of AIDS such as fever, malaise, anorexia and myalgia may be caused by infection with CMV. Because CMV can often be cultured from urine and particularly semen from asymptomatic high-risk individuals, such as homosexually active men, attributing these non-specific symptoms to CMV infection is clinically difficult (Mintz et al, 1983). Demonstration of CMV in lung, liver, or funduscopic evidence of CMV retinitis certainly are highly suggestive of disseminated infection. Serum IgG antibody to CMV is often elevated and is not a reliable laboratory marker for significant infection.

LYMPHADENOPATHY AND AIDS

AIDS related complex (ARC) has previously been discussed. Much attention has recently focused on the histology of the lymph node in such patients (Modlin et al, 1983; Metroka et al, 1983). Three distinct histopathologic patterns have been described: 1) explosive follicular hyperplasia with focal coalescence of follicles; 2) follicular involution with hypocellular germinal centres, paracortical hyperplasia and plasma cells in the medullary cords, and 3) a mixed pattern of follicular hyperplasia and follicular involution. Preliminary data indicate a high rate of conversion of ARC to AIDS, the latter diagnosed by appearance of Kaposi's sarcoma or non-Hodgkin's lymphoma, over 3–18 months in patients with the second (follicular involution) pattern. Development histologically of follicular involution is generally associated with clinical deterioration with 'B' symptoms such as fever, weight loss, night sweats and diarrhoea. Cachexia and weight loss are cardinal symptoms and signs of this progression of ARC to AIDS. Clinical management of lymphadenopathy in high-risk individuals is still a controversial matter. Lymph nodes in these patients may wax and wane in size and a thorough evaluation for intercurrent illness associated with lymphadenopathy, such as viral (CMV or EBV) mononucleosis, toxoplasmosis, etc. should be performed. Which lymph nodes should be biopsied, how many should be biopsied, and how frequently should biopsies be repeated are unanswered questions. Every investigator who has cared for large numbers of such patients can attest to the infrequent occurrence of Kaposi's sarcoma or lymphoma serendipitously discovered by lymph-node biopsy in an otherwise asymptomatic individual.

Patients with ARC who have such 'B symptoms' or chronic oral candida or an episode of herpes zoster should be carefully followed since they appear to have a greater likelihood of progression to AIDS. Oral candida and herpes zoster are not included among the list of opportunistic infections required by the CDC for the definition of AIDS. This arbitrary definition of AIDS clearly reveals its limitations in this context.

IDIOPATHIC THROMBOCYTOPENIC PURPURA (ITP)

Morris et al (1982) described the syndrome of 'autoimmune' thrombocytopenic purpura in homosexual men with associated T-lymphocyte abnormalities. Although these investigators reported complete responses to corticosteroid therapy, this has been criticised by many because of the concern of potentiation of opportunistic infection in such high-risk individuals. Both CMV, which is prevalent in healthy homosexual men, and candida are clearly recognised to disseminate in individuals further immunosuppressed by such iatrogenic intervention. Kaposi's sarcoma prior to the AIDS epidemic was well recognised in association with immunosuppressive (corticosteroid and azathioprine) therapy in renal transplant patients and it is possible that steroid therapy would enhance or accelerate the appearance of Kaposi's sarcoma in patients at risk for AIDS. Furthermore, it appears that the thrombocytopenic purpura is not 'autoimmune' in that the antibodies are not specifically directed against platelet-associated antigens. The mechanism of thrombocytopenia appears to be premature phagocytosis of platelets coated by non-specific immunoglobulins. There are very high titres of circulating immune complexes in AIDS patients as well as frequent viral diseases such as CMV which are associated with thrombocytopenia. Since the majority of patients with ITP in such higher-risk groups are asymptomatic and do not have clinical bleeding, it is judicious to simply follow them without intervention. Significant bleeding could be managed temporarily with steroids and then with vincristine and/or splenectomy. A similar recent occurrence of ITP among haemophiliacs receiving factor VIII concentrate may also indicate that this population has had exposure to HTLV-III/LAV.

KAPOSI'S SARCOMA AND OTHER NEOPLASMS

Kaposi's sarcoma was a relatively rare neoplasm in North America prior to the AIDS epidemic (Safai & Good, 1981). The neoplasm appears to be of endothelial origin (Guarda et al, 1981). Kaposi's sarcoma was seen in two different Western hosts before

1979: elderly men of Ashkenazic Jewish or Mediterranean descent and patients with cellular immune dysfunction secondary to renal transplantation or prior lymphoma. The natural history of Kaposi's sarcoma in elderly men is that of an indolent dermal neoplasm often confined to the lower extremities and rarely a cause of significant morbidity for the patient. Kaposi's sarcoma is more aggressive in the setting of renal transplantation with rapidly advancing dermal lesions and frequent visceral involvement. Interestingly, some renal transplant patients with Kaposi's sarcoma had spontaneous regression of their neoplastic lesions when immunosuppressive therapy was discontinued (Groopman et al, 1984b). There was thus circumstantial evidence of a relationship between Kaposi's sarcoma and the immune system prior to AIDS. Kaposi's sarcoma is a common neoplasm in Africa, comprising up to 10% of all cancers in Kenya and Uganda (Kungu & Gatei, 1981). Kaposi's sarcoma in Africa generally affects young men with involvement of lymph nodes and viscera in addition to skin.

Giraldo and colleagues (Giraldo et al, 1971, 1975, 1980) have provided considerable evidence of a link between Kaposi's sarcoma and the cytomegalovirus prior to the advent of AIDS. Patients with Kaposi's sarcoma in North America and Europe have an elevated prevalence and titre of antibody to cytomegalovirus (Giraldo et al, 1975). Kaposi's sarcoma lesions may have DNA and RNA related to cytomegalovirus suggesting a role for the virus in its pathogenesis.

The prevalence of this previously rare neoplasm in AIDS is striking and again points to the relationship between Kaposi's sarcoma and the immune system. The clinical manifestations of Kaposi's sarcoma associated with AIDS resemble the African form more than the classic Western form, with early involvement of lymph nodes and viscera and an aggressive course (Gottlieb et al, 1983). Nearly half of AIDS patients with the neoplasm have gastrointestinal involvement, which is often asymptomatic. Other favoured sites of Kaposi's sarcoma in AIDS patients include lung, brain and oropharynx.

Non-Hodgkin's lymphoma of the Burkitt's type appears to occur in a disproportionate number of AIDS patients (Groopman & Gottlieb, 1982). There are preliminary data that these lymphomas contain DNA sequences related to the Epstein–Barr virus (Ziegler et al, 1982). Such non-Hodgkin's lymphomas occur in the head and neck and central nervous system as well as abdomen in the setting of AIDS.

A simplistic model of the genesis of Kaposi's sarcoma or non-Hodgkin's lymphoma in AIDS postulates the concerted action of two distinct 'agents' or viruses: the first is HTLV-III/LAV which results in profound and persistent immune deficiency, and the second is an ubiquitous DNA virus such as cytomegalovirus or the Epstein–Barr virus which is oncogenic only in a milieu of cellular immune deficiency (Groopman & Gottlieb, 1982). If this is true, then reconstitution of the cellular immune system could lead to 'spontaneous' regression of the neoplasms, analogous to the cases in renal transplantation.

THERAPY OF AIDS AND KAPOSI'S SARCOMA

There is no therapy of AIDS. A number of experimental approaches to immune reconstitution, including syngeneic bone marrow transplantation (Mitsuyasu et al, 1983), thymic transplantation (Dwyer et al, 1983), α-2 interferon (Gottlieb et al, unpublished data), plasmapheresis, thymopoietin, thymosin, cimetidine, procaine-amide, transfer factor, and isoprinosine have been attempted and unsuccessful. It is possible that immune injury is so severe as to obviate reconstitution. It is also possible that HTLV-III persists in affected patients and definitive therapy requires oblitera-tion of this virus. Because of the apparent transmission of AIDS by asymptomatic persons or those with ARC (Allen, 1984) and the advanced clinical and immunological status of patients with AIDS, the therapeutic intervention may be more successful in the former rather than latter cases. Lacking any treatment, the most rational medical intervention is directed at changes in lifestyle and blood product procurement to limit spread of the disease. Meanwhile, pilot trials of interleukin-2 or γ interferon are underway. Kaposi's sarcoma is responsive to radiotherapy (Holcek & Harwood, 1978) or chemotherapy, particularly vinca alkaloids such as vinblastine (Groopman & Mitsuyasu, 1984). Unfortunately, regression of lesions is meaningless in such patients without immune reconstitution. Recombinant α-2 interferon has been success-ful in achieving complete and partial remissions of Kaposi's sarcoma in AIDS (Krown et al, 1983; Groopman et al, 1984). Again, α-2 interferon does not appear to augment immune function in these patients despite its antineoplastic effects and will probably be of limited value.

CONCLUSION

AIDS is a complex disorder of the immune system that is manifested as opportunistic infections and neoplasms. It results from infection with a T-lymphotropic retrovirus, HTLV-III/LAV, with a long incubation period that may reflect host susceptibility. The therapy of AIDS is unknown, but the impact of the disorder in North America and now Europe and Africa is profound. Both the tragedy of a generally fatal disorder affecting mainly young adults and the importance of the syndrome with regard to the pathogenesis of neoplasia impels the scientific community to persist in making AIDS a research field of highest priority.

REFERENCES

Allen J 1984 Epidemiology of the Acquired Immunodeficiency Syndrome. Seminars in Oncology 11: 1–11.
Barre-Sinoussi F, Chermann J C, Dey F et al 1983 Isolation of a T-lymphotropic retro virus from a patient at risk for acquired immune deficiency syndrome (AIDS). Science 220: 868–870
Boldogh I, Beth E, Huang E S, Kyalwazi S K, Giraldo G 1981 Kaposi's sarcoma: IV. Detection of CMV DNA, CMV RNA, and CMNA in tumor biopsies. International Journal of Cancer 28: 469–474
Bodmer W F 1981 Structure and function: A contemporary view. Tissue Antigen 17: 9–20
Centers for Disease Control 1981 Kaposi's sarcoma and Pneumocystis pneumonia among homosexual men — New York City and California. Morbidity and Mortality Weekly Report 30: 305–308
Centers for Disease Control 1982 Diffuse, undifferentiated non-Hodgkins lymphoma among homosexual males — United States. Morbidity and Mortality Weekly Report 31: 277–279
Clumeck N 1984 AIDS in African Patients. New England Journal of Medicine 310: 492–495
Cochran A J, Nestor M S, Groopman J E, Ahmed A R 1983 Tumour infiltrates in Acquired Immunodeficiency Syndrome patients with Kaposi's sarcoma. Lancet i: 416
Dalgleish A G, Beverley P C L, Clapham P R et al 1984 The CD antigen is an essential component of the receptor for the AIDS retrovirus. Nature 312: 763–767
Davis K C, Horsburgh C R Jr, Hasiba U, Schocket A L, Kirkpatrick C H 1983 Acquired

Immunodeficiency Syndrome in a patient with hemophilia. Annals of Internal Medicine 98: 284–286

Dardenne M, Safai B 1983 Low Serum Thymic Hormone Levels in Patients with Acquired Immunodeficiency Syndrome. New England Journal of Medicine 309(1): 48–49

Detels R, Fahey J L, Schwartz K, Greene R K, Visscher B R, Gottlieb M S 1982 Relation between sexual practices and T-cell subsets in homosexually active men. Lancet i: 609–611

Dwyer J 1983 Thymus transplantation in AIDS. Presented at Conference on Aquired Immunodeficiency Syndrome November 14–17, 1983. New York, New York

Eyster M E, Goldert J J, Poon M-C, Preble O T 1983 Acid-labile alpha interferon: a possible preclinical marker for the acquired immunodeficiency syndrome in hemophilia. New England Journal of Medicine 309(10): 583–586

Finberg R, Benacerraf B 1981 Induction, control and consequences of virus specific cytotoxic T cells. Immunology Review 58: 157–180

Gallo R C 1984 Frequent detection and isolation of cytopathic retroviruses (HTLV-III) from patients with AIDS and at risk of AIDS. Science 224: 500–502

Giraldo G, Beth E, Haguenau F 1971 Herpes-type virus particles in tissue culture of Kaposi's sarcoma from different geographic retions. Journal of the National Cancer Institute 49: 1509–1526

Giraldo G, Beth E, Kourilsky F M, Henle W, Henle G, Mike V et al 1975 Antibody patterns to herpes viruses in Kaposi's sarcoma: serological association of European Kaposi's sarcoma with cytomegalovirus. International Journal of Cancer 15: 839–848

Giraldo G, Beth E, Huang E S 1980 Kaposi's sarcoma and its relationship to cytomegalovirus (CMV): III. CMV DNA and CMV early antigens in Kaposi's sarcoma. International Journal of Cancer 26: 23–29

Gottlieb M S, Schroff, Schanker J M, Weisman J D, Fan P T, Wolf R A et al 1981 Pneumocystis carinii pneumonia and mucosal candidiasis in previously healthy homosexual men: evidence of a new acquired cellular immunodeficiency. New England Journal of Medicine 305: 1425–1431

Gottlieb M S, Groopman J E, Weinstein W M, Fahey J L, Detels R 1983 The Acquired Immunodeficiency Syndrome. Annals of Internal Medicine 99: 208–220

Groopman J E, Gottlieb M S, Goodman J, Rothman J, Rudnick S 1984a Recombinant alpha-2 interferon therapy of Kaposi's sarcoma associated with the acquired immunodeficiency syndrome. Annals of Internal Medicine 100: 671–677

Groopman J E, Mitsuyasu R T 1984b Therapy of Kaposi's sarcoma/AIDS. Seminars in Oncology 11: 53–59

Groopman J E et al 1984c Virologic studies in transfusion-related acquired immunodeficiency syndrome. New England Journal of Medicine 311: 1419–1422

Groopman J E, Salahuddin S Z, Sarngadharan M G et al, 1984d HTLV-III in saliva of people with AIDS-related complex and at risk for AIDS. Science 226: 447–449

Groopman J E, Mayer K H, Sarngadharan M G, Ayotle D, Devico A, Finberg R, Allan J B, Gallo R C 1985 Seroepidemiology of HTLV-III among homosexual men with AIDS, generalized lymphadenopathy and asymptomatic controls in Boston. Annals Internal Medicine (in press)

Guarda L G, Silva E G, Ordonez N G, Smith J L Jr 1981 Factor VIII in Kaposi's sarcoma. American Journal of Clinical Pathology 76: 197–200

Harris C, Small C B, Klein R S, Friedland G H, Moll B et al 1983 Immunodeficiency in female sexual partners of men with the acquired immunodeficiency syndrome. New England Journal of Medicine 308: 1181–1184

Holecek M J, Harwood A R 1978 Radiotherapy of Kaposi's sarcoma. Cancer 41: 1733–1738

Horowitz S L, Bentson J R, Benson D F, Davos I, Pressman B, Gottlieb M S 1983 CNS toxoplasmosis in a new acquired cellular immunodeficiency syndrome. Archives of Neurology 40: 649–652

Jaffe H W, Choi K, Thomas P A, Haverkos H W, Auerbach D M, Guinan M E et al 1983 National case-control study of Kaposi's sarcoma and Pneumocystis carinii pneumonia in homosexual men: part 1, epidemiologic results. Annals of Internal Medicine 99: 145–151

Kitchen L W, Baun F, Sullivan J L, McLane N F, Brettler D B, Levine P H, Essex M 1984 Aetiology of AIDS-antibodies to human T-Cell leukaemia virus (type III) in haemophiliacs. Nature 312: 367–369

Klatzmann D, Champagne E, Chamaret S et al 1984 T-lymphocyte T4 molecule behaves as the receptor for human retrovirus LAV. Nature 312: 767–768

Kornfeld H, Vanda Stouwe R A, Lange M, Reddy M, Grieco M 1982 T-lymphphocyte subpopulations in homosexual men. New England Journal of Medicine 397: 729–731

Krown S E, Real F X, Cunningham-Rundles S, Myskowski P L, Koziner B, Fein S et al 1983 Preliminary observations on the effect of recombinant leukocyte A interferon in homosexual men with Kaposi's sarcoma. New England Journal of Medicine 308: 1071–1076

Kung P C, Goldstein C, Reinherz E L, Schlossman S F 1979 Monoclonal antibodies defining distinctive human T cells surface antigens. Science 206: 347–349

Kungu A, Gatei D G 1981 Kaposi's sarcoma in Kenya: a retrospective clinicopathological study. Antibiotics & Chemotherapy 29: 38–55

Lane H C, Masur H, Edgar L C, Whalen G, Rook A H, Fauci A S 1983 Abnormalities of B-cell activation and immunoregulation in patients with the acquired immunodeficiency syndrome. New England Journal of Medicine 309(8): 453–458

Metroka C E, Cunningham-Rundles S, Pollack M S, Sonnabend J A, Davis J M, Gordon G et al 1983 Generalized lymphadenopathy in homosexual men. Annals of Internal Medicine 99: 585–591

Mintz L, Drew W L, Miner R C, Braff E H 1983 Cytomegalovirus infections in homosexual men: an epidemiological study. Annals of Internal Medicine 99(3): 326–329

Mitsuyasu R T 1984 T-lymphocyte colony formation in vitro in AIDS. Presented at the Schering-UCLA Symposium on AIDS, February 5–10, 1984, Park City, Utah

Modlin R L, Hofman F M, Meyer P R, Vaccaro S A, Ammann A J, Conant M A et al 1983 Altered distribution of B and T lymphocytes in lymph-nodes from homosexual men with Kaposi's sarcoma. Lancet ii(8353): 768–771

Morris L, Distenfeld A, Amorosi E, Karpatkin S 1982 Autoimmune thrombocytopenic purpura in homosexual men. Annals of Internal Medicine 96(6 Pt 1): 714–717

Moskowitz L B, Kory P, Chan J C, Haverkos H W, Conley F K, Hensley G T 1983 Unusual causes of death in Haitians residing in Miami. High prevalence of opportunistic infections. Journal of the American Medical Association 250(9): 1187–1191

Nicholas P, Masci J, deCatalogne J, Solomon S, Bekesi J G, Selikoff I J 1983 Immune competence in Haitians living in New York. New England Journal of Medicine 309(19): 1187–1188

Oleske J, Minnefor A, Cooper R Jr, Thomas K, dela Cruz A, Ahdieh H et al 1983 Immune Deficiency Syndrome in Children. Journal of the American Medical Association 249(17): 2345–2349

Popovic M, Sarngadharan M G, Read E, Gallo R C 1984 Detection, isolation and continuous production of cytopathic retroviruses (HYLV-III) from patients with AIDS and pre-AIDS. Science 224: 497–500

Ragni M V, Spero J A, Lewis J H, Bontempo F A 1983 Acquired immunodeficiency-like syndrome in two haemophiliacs. Lancet i: 213–214

Rogers M F, Morens D M, Stewart J A, Kaminiski R M, Spira T J, Feorino P M et al 1983 National case-control study of Kaposi's sarcoma and *Pneumocystis carinii* pneumonia in homosexual men: part 2, laboratory results. Annals of Internal Medicine 99: 151–158

Rook A H, Masur H, Lane H C, Frederick W, Kasahara T et al 1983 Interleukin-2 enhances the depressed natural killer and cytomegalovirus-specific cytotoxic activities of lymphocytes from patients with the acquired immune deficiency syndrome. Journal of Clinical Investigation 72: 398–403

Rosen F 1984 Immunodeficiency syndromes. New England Journal of Medicine 311: 300–310

Rubinstein A, Sicklick M, Gupta A, Bernstein L, Klein N, Rubinstein E et al 1983 Acquired immunodeficiency with reversed T_4/T_8 ratios in infants born to promiscuous and drug-addicted mothers. Journal of the American Medical Association 249(17): 2350–2356

Sarngadharan M G, Popovic M, Bruch L, Schupbach J, Gallo R C 1984 Antibodies reactive with human T-lymphotropic retroviruses (HTL-III) in the serum of patients with AIDS. Science 224: 506–508

Safai B, Good R A 1981 Kaposi's sarcoma: a review and recent developments. Cancer 31: 2–12

Schupbach J, Popovic M, Gilden R V, Gond M A, Sarngadharan M G, Gallo R C 1984 Serological analysis of a subgroup of human T-lymphotropic retroviruses (HTLV-III) associated with AIDS. Science 224: 503–505

deShazo R D, Andes W A, Nordberg J, Newton J, Daul C, Bozelka B 1983 An immunologic evaluation of hemophiliac patients and their wives: relationships to the acquired immunodeficiency syndrome. Annals of Internal Medicine 99: 159–164

Siegal F P, Lopez C, Hammer G S, Brown A E, Kornfeld S J, Gold J et al 1981 Severe acquired immunodeficiency in male homosexuals, manifested by chronic perianal ulcerative herpes simplex lesions. New England Journal of Medicine 305: 1439–1444

Siegal F P 1984 Immune function and dysfunction in AIDS. Seminars in Oncology 11: 29–39

Stiehm E R, Kronenberg L H, Rosenblatt H M, Bryson Y, Merigan T C 1982 Interferon: Immunology and clinical significance. Annals of Internal Medicine 96: 80–93

Vilmer E, Barre-Sinoussi F, Rouzioux C et al 1984 Isolation of a new lymphotropic retrovirus from two siblings with haemophila A, one with AIDS. Lancet i: 753–764

Wormser G P, Krupp L B, Hanrahan J P, Gavis G, Spira T J, Cunningham-Rundles S 1983 Acquired immunodeficiency syndrome in male prisoners: new insights into an emerging syndrome. Annals of Internal Medicine 98: 297–303

Ziegler J L, Drew W L, Miner R C, Mintz L, Rosenbaum E, Gershow J et al 1982 Outbreak of Burkitt's-like lymphoma in homosexual men. Lancet ii: 631–633

Index

Abortion, indications, in sickle cell disease, 91
Acquired immunodeficiency syndrome (AIDS), 369–385
  aetiology, 373–375
    T-cell lymphotropic retrovirus, 374, 379
    virologic evidence, 374
  epidemiology, 369–373
    age distribution, 371
    asymptomatic carrier state, 371
    incubation period, 371
    related complex, 370
    sex distribution, 371–372
    transmissibility, 373
  idiopathic thrombocytopenic purpura, 383
  immunological dysfunction, 375–378
    B-lymphocyte dysfunction, 375
    iatrogenic immunosuppression, 375
    granuloma production failure, 376
    Kaposi's sarcoma, 377–378
  infectious complications, 380–382
    opportunistic infections and weight loss, 380
    Pneumonocystis carinii pneumonia, 369, 382
    toxoplasmosis in the central nervous system, 382
  Kaposi's sarcoma and other neoplasms, 384
  lymphadenopathy, 382–383
  therapy and conclusions, 385
Acute non-lymphocytic leukaemia *see* Bone marrow transplantation
Acyclovir
  against cytomegalovirus, 208, 215
  against herpes simplex, 208
Adipocytes
  insulin requirement, 3
  production in mouse chimeras by total lymphoid radiation, 6
Adult T-cell leukaemia/lymphoma, 222, 223
Agarose gel electrophoresis, after restriction enzyme analysis, 37
Agnogenic myeloid metaplasia, fibroblast proliferation, 19
AHG techniques, demonstration of allo antibodies, 309
AIDS *see* Acquired immunodeficiency syndrome
Allo-antibodies, practical implications, 312–315
  see also Immune thrombocytopenia
Allogenic donors *see* Bone marrow
Allo-immune neonatal thrombocytopenia, 311, 314
  alloimmune neonatal neutropenia, 314
  post-transfusion purpura, 315–316

Alpha interferon, in acquired immunodeficiency syndrome aetiology, 376
Alu repeats, intergenic regions, α globin gene cluster, 65
Aminoglycosides
  nephrotoxic agents, 214
  therapy, in neutropenia, 209–211
Amniocentesis, in prenatal diagnosis, 82–83, 90
Amphotericin B, myths and toxophobia, 214
Anaemia
  aplastic, 171, 173
  malarial, 115–118
    acute infection, 118
    chronic infection, 116
    defective red cell production, 117
    murine genetic strains, bone marrow culture, 1, 4
    see also Aplastic anaemia: Bone marrow transplantation: Human T-cell virus
Androgen therapy, aplastic anaemia, 173, 174
Antibiotic(s)
  cephalosporins, 209
  empirical use, 203–205, 209
  in gastrointestinal decontamination, 204–205
  in persistent pyrexia, 210–212
  specific therapies, bone marrow transplantation, 212–214
  synergism, 209
  see also Penicillin
Antibodies, monoclonal *see* Monoclonal antibodies
Antibody reaction, immunofluorescence tests, 309
Anticoagulant therapy
  and protein C deficiency, 277
  sodium warfarin, bleeding risk, 338–340
  see also Antithrombotic therapy
Antifactor Xa *see* Antithrombotic therapy
Antithrombin III
  deficiency, specific molecular defect, 60
  heparin, affinity, and haemostasis, 335–337
  inhibition of activated coagulation factors, 333–334
Antithrombotic therapy
  antiplatelet drugs, evidence of antithrombotic effects, 350–354
    aortocoronary bypass surgery, 350
    arterial venous shunt thrombosis, 350
    cerebrovascular disease, 353
    coronary artery disease, 351
    postmyocardial infarction, 351–353
    unstable angina, 353
    valvular heart disease, 350
    venous thrombosis, 354

Antithrombotic therapy (*contd*)
  coronary thrombolysis in myocardial infarction, 354–356
  drug suppression of platelet function, 342–354
    see also specific agents
  heparin, 333–337
    antifactor Xa, 336
    effect on experimental atherosclerosis, 337
    haemorrhagic and antithrombotic effects, 335
    mode of action, 333
    long term anticoagulant therapy, in venous thrombosis, 337–342
      clinical outcomes, 339
      practical recommendations, 341–342
    tissue plasminogen activator, t-PA, 356–358
      physiological fibrinolysis and thrombolysis, 358
Antiviral therapy in bone marrow failure, 215
  acycloguanosine, 215
  adenine arabinoside, 215
APAAP [immunoalkaline phosphatase technique], 133
Aplastic anaemia
  and microenvironmental failure, 19
  severe, allogeneic transplantation, 173
    immunosuppressive therapy, 174
    syngeneic transplantation, 174
Aprindine hydrochloride, immune thrombocytopenia, 324
Aspergillosis and amphotericin, 214
Aspergillus sp, 200, 203, 205, 211
Aspiration
  percutaneous thoracic, closed needle, 214
  transtracheal, 214
Aspirin, 342–345
  effects on haemostasis, 345
  inhibition of arterial thrombosis, 345, 350
  effects on platelets, 344, 350, 351
  effects on prostaglandins, 344
  unstable angina, 353
Atherosclerosis, experimental, effect of heparin, 337
Autoantibody, spontaneous appearance, 291
Autoimmune thrombocytopenia, 317–321
  autoimmune neutropenia, 321–323
  compensated thrombocytopenia, 318
  following marrow transplant, 321
  idiopathic thrombocytopenic purpura, 317–320
  and other disorders, 320
Autologous transplants *see* Bone marrow transplantation
Autoprothrombin IIa *see* Protein C
Avian
  leukaemia-virus-induced B-cell lymphoma, 224
  leukosis virus, 231, 233
  myeloblastosis virus, *c-myb*, 227, *228*
  myelocytomatosis, *c-myc*, 227, *228*
5-Azacytidine, in demethylation of globin genes, 58, *59*, 83–84

B-cell chronic lymphocytic leukaemia, Jamaica, 222
Bacillus cereus, 200, 212

Bacteraemias
  diagnosis, in neutropenia, 208–210
  Gram negative, therapy, 207
Bacterial infections *see* Pathogens, major: names of individual organisms
Bacteriophage
  genomic library, *Plasmodium*, 123
  production of cloning vectors, 41–43
Bacteroides sp., infection in neutropenia, 200, 209
Barts' hydrops syndrome, 67, 70–71
  see also Thalassaemia, alpha
Bdellovibrio bacteriovorus in *E. coli*, specific membrane proteins, 115
Beta blockers and inhibition of aggregation, 349
Beta-lactam, combinations with minoglycoside, 210
Bilirubin levels in sickle cell disease, reduction with medroxyprogesterone, 101
Biopsies, immunohistological typing, 133
'Blackwater fever', haemolysis with haemoglobinuria, 116
'Blanket cell', haematopoiesis, 2
Blood clotting factors *see* Antithrombotic therapy: Heparin
B-*lym* genes, 232–234
Bone marrow
  depletion of progenitor cells, 5–6
  ectopic implants and haematopoiesis, 1
  necrosis, painful crisis, 97
    cyanate therapy, 97
    vasopressin analogue, 97–98
  stromal cells *see* Haematopoiesis
Bone marrow failure, infections
  antibiotic therapy, length of course, 212
  factors predisposing to infection, 199
    breakdown of physical barriers, 201
    cell mediated immunity, 201
    loss of colonisation resistance, 202
    malnutrition, 202
    splenectomy, 202
  host defences, manoeuvres to enhance, 206–208
    acceleration of myeloid regeneration following chemotherapy, 207
    active immunisation, 206
    'catheter related' infections, 206
    immunomodualtion, 208
    latent infection, protection against, 208
    mucous membrane and skin, 206
    neutralization of endotoxaemia, 206
    passive immunisation, 207
    prophylactic granulocytes, 206
    reactivation of latent organisms, protection against, 208
  introduction, 199
  major pathogens, 212–215
    clinical correlates, 200
  neutropenic patients, empirical and specific therapy, 208–210
  persistent pyrexia, 210–212
  prophylaxis of infection, 203–206
    decontamination of patients, 204–205
    environmental studies and diet, 205
  pyrexia, persistent, management, 210–212

Bone marrow failure, infections
  pyrexia (*contd*)
    granulocytopenia, 210–212
  sources of infection and surveillance cultures,
      202–203
  specific therapy, 208–210, 212
    antiviral therapy, 215
    catheter-related organisms, 212–213
    cephalosporins, 209
    fungal infections, 214
    Legionella pneumonia, 213
    protozoan infection, 213
Bone marrow transplantation
  acute lymphocytic leukaemia, 177–178
    allogenic transplantation, 177
    chronic myelogenous leukaemia, 178
    other haematologic malignancies, 178
  acute non-lymphocytic leukaemia, 175–176
    allogeneic transplantation, 175
    comparison, conventional chemotherapy, 176
    importance of age on outcome, 176
    second or greater remission, 176
  allogeneic bone marrow transplantation, 188–189
    mismatched, related donors, 188
    unrelated donors, 189
  autoimmune cytopenias, 321
  autologous transplantation, 179–180
  clinical applications, 171
  graft versus host disease, 180–186
    acute, clinical presentation, 180
    chronic, clinical presentation, 181
    ex vivo removal of T-lymphocytes from donor
        marrow as prophylaxis, 184–186
    immune system, 182
    in vivo T-lymphocyte modification as
        prophylaxis, 182–184
    therapy, 186
  immunodeficiency disorders, 172
  infection, defence against, 186–188
    after first 3 months, 187
    early granulocytic period, 186
    protozoan and viral infections, 186
  for inherited disorders, 180
  severe aplastic anaemia, 173–174
    allogeneic, 7, 173
    immunosuppressive therapy, 174
    syngeneic, 174
Bromovinyl deoxyuridine, 215
Bronchial lavage, in pneumocystic pneumonia, 214
Burkitt type lymphoma, 136–142, *137*, *139*
  human cell lines, 227
BYDU *see* Bromovinyl deoxyuridine

Calcium channel-blocking agents and aggregation
    inhibition, 349
Calf vein thrombosis, warfarin thrombosis, 342
CALLA-positive lymphomas, 138, 141
Candida sp, *200*, 203, 204
  and acquired immunodeficiency syndrome, 381,
      383
Candidiasis, and amphotericin B, 214
  catheter related, 212

Carcinomas, NIH 3T3 transforming assay, 232
Catheters, intravenous, and infection, 201–202
Cell membrane antigens *see* Monoclonal antibodies
Cellular *onc* genes, amplification in human
      leukaemias, 230
  and chromosomes, 230
  expression in human haematopoietic cells, *229*
  expression in human lymphomas, 230
  onc gene cooperation and neoplastic
      transformation, 233–234
  properties of viral *onc* genes, *228*
  ras onc gene family and B lym genes, *232*
  retroviral-related cellular response, 226–227
  transforming genes, DNA-mediated transfer,
      223, 232
Cephalosporins, therapy in neutropenia, 209–210
Cetiedil, trials, in sickle-cell disease, 98
C-group trisomy and acute leukaemia, fibroblast
    cultures, 9
Chediak-Higashi syndrome, bone marrow
    transplantation, 172
Chloroquine resistance, malaria, 122
Chloroquinone, demonstration of platelet specific
    antibodies, 310
Chromosomal markers, use in CFU-F studies, 6
Chromosomes
  aberrations, 230–231
    acute promyelocytic leukaemia, 231
    Burkitt's lymphomas, 230–231, 233
    Philadelphia, 230–231
  abnormally banded region, 230
  double minute, 230
  homogeneously staining regions, 230
  mapping of *onc* genes, 230–231
  rearrangement within an immunoglobulin locus,
      60
Chronic myeloid leukaemia, Human T-cell
    proviruses, 223
Circulating immune complexes, idiopathic
    thrombocytopenic purpura, pathogenesis, 317
Clonal neoplasia, origin of stromal cells, and G6PD,
    7
Cloning *see* Molecular cloning
Clostridium difficile, 200, 210
Coagulation assays *see* Monoclonal antibodies
Colchicine, in refractory idiopathic
    thrombocytopenic purpura, 320
Collagen synthesis by marrow stromal cells, 12
  classification, 2
Colony forming cells (CFU) *see* Haematopoeisis
Common acute lymphocyte leukaemia antigen, 11
Common variable immunodeficiency, bone marrow
    transplantation, 172
Complement activation in erythrocytes, 116
C-*onc* genes see Retroviruses
Congenital neutrophil dysfunction, bone marrow
    transplantation, 172
Contraception, indications in sickle cell disease, 101
Coombs test, erratic results in acute malaria, 116
Cooperative Study of Sickle Cell Disease, National
    Institute of Health, 101
Corynebacteria, 200, 202, 212

Cosmids, in molecular cloning, 43
Cotrimoxazole
  immune thrombocytopenia, 324
  pneumocystic pneumonia, 213–214
Cryptococcus, 200
Cyclophosphamide, bone marrow transplantation
  acute non-lymphoblastic leukaemia, 175
  severe aplastic anaemia, 173
Cyclosporin A, post-grafting immunosuppressive in
    bone marrow transplantation, 174
Cystitis, haemorrhagic, complication of
    cyclophosphamide therapy, 176
Cytomegalovirus, 199, 200
  acyclovir therapy, 208, 215
  prophylaxis, 203
  transfer in bone marrow recipients, 206, 215
Cytoreductive therapy, high-dose, malignancy, 171
Cytoskeletal proteins, monoclonal antibodies, 12

Danazol, in refractory idiopathic thrombocytopenic
    purpura, 320
Dazoxidine, inhibition of collagen induced
    aggregation, 349
Decontamination, patient, 204–205
Dexter culture (long-term marrow culture), 4
Dextran, effect on thrombosis, 347, 354
Differential hybridisation, in gene cloning, 48
8-(1,3-Dihydroxy-2-proloxymethyl) guanine
    (DHPG), 215
Dipyridamole inhibition of platelet function, 346,
    350, 351
DNA, RNA
  analysis, 53–56
  complementary DNA (cDNA), 38, *39*
  functional anatomy, β globin gene, *31, 32*
  gene expression, 30–33
  molecular cloning *see* Gene isolation
  molecular hybridisation, 33–34
  sequencing techniques, 52–56
  structure, 25–28
  transcription, 28–30, 31
DNA transfection techniques, 221
  see also Transforming genes
Double minute chromosome *see* Chromosomes
Drosophila genome, cellular *onc* genes, 227
Drug-induced immune cytopenias, 323–325

Electrophoresis, haemoglobin, in sickle-cell disease
    diagnosis, 90
  in malarial parasite cycle, 113
Endonucleases *see* Restriction endonucleases
Endothelial cell markers, specific, 11
Endothelium, denudation, inhibition of smooth
    muscle by heparin, 337
Endotoxaemia, and polymixin B, 207
Enterobacteria, in neutropenia, 209–211
Enterobacteriaceae, 200
EORTC trials, infection in neutropenia, 208–212
Erythropoiesis, ineffective, in malaria, 118
Escherichia coli, 200, 201, 203
  J5, 207
Expression vectors, in bacterial translation,
    eukaryotic genes, 47

Eye disease, in sickle cell haemoglobin C anaemia,
    98, 99

Factor V deficiency, and protein C, 272–274
  monoclonal antibodies, 294–296
Factor Va, human coagulant, and protein C, 272–
    274
Factor VIII, associated antigen, human stromal
    cells, 11
  deficiency and protein C, 272–274
  monoclonal antibodies, 287, 294–296, 304
Factor IX, 296
Factor Xa, protection of factor Va, and
    prothrombin, 273
Feline sarcoma virus, *c-fes*, 227, 228
Fetal haemoglobin in anaemic baboons, 82–83
  see also Hereditary persistence (HPFH)
Fibreoptic brush bronchoscopy, 214
Fibrinogen, monoclonal antibodies derived from
    mouse-mouse hybridomas, 291–292
Fibrinolysis and thrombolysis, 358
Fibroblasts
  excessive proliferation in myelofibrosis, 19
  mouse, transfection of human genomic DNA, 51
  NIH 3T3, aneuplid murine line, 232
  as receptors for platelet-derived growth factor, 19
  see also Haematopoieosis
Fluorescein angiograms in proliferative sickle cell
    retinopathy, 99
2'Fluoro-5-iodo arabinosyl cytosine, 215
Folic acid
  malaria-related haemolysis, 117
  routine supplementation in sickle-cell disease,
    96–97
Fungal infections, in bone marrow transplantation,
    211, 214–215
  see also name of organisms

Gastrointestinal decontamination, 204
Gene amplification, in *onc* gene activation, 230
Gene blotting analysis, diagnostic methods, 53–57
  antenatal diagnosis, sickle cell anaemia, 57
  thalassaemia, 58
  use of 5-azacytidine, *in vivo* gene manipualtion,
    58, 59
Gene deletion
  Bart's hydrops syndrome, 67, 70–71
  Constant Spring mutation, 70
  in delta-beta and gamma delta beta thalassaemia,
    79-82
  haemoglobin H disease, 67, 69–70
  and homozygous β thalassaemia, 77–78
  and non deletion in thalassaemia, 67–71
  J. Tongariki and other α chain variants, 71
Gene expression
  functional boundaries of the gene, 30
  human β globin gene, 30, 31, 32
  oligonucleotide signals (splicing signals), 33
Gene isolation, 34–51
  applications of recombinant DNA techniques,
    56–60
  cloned genes, study of structure and expression, 51
  nucleic acid sequencing, 51–52

Gene isolation (*contd*)
  DNA, RNA analysis, 53–56
  blotting techniques, 53–54, 59
  S1 nuclease analysis, 54–56
  enzymatic *in vitro* manipulation, bacteriophage, 41–43
    cloning vehicles — plasmids, 40
    cosmids, 43
    protypical experiment, 41
    restriction endonucleases and DNA ligases, 35–37
  reverse transcriptase and DNA synthesis, 38
  hybrid selected translation screening, 45–47
    isolation of cDNA clone by subculture, 46
  identification of specific genes (screening), 43–45
    immunochemical purification, 45
  immunochemical identification of bacterial recombinant proteins, 47–51
    'cloning phenotypes' into foreign host cells, 49–51
    screening by differential molecular hybridisation, 47–48
    by use of synthetic oligonucleotides, 48–49
Glanzmann's platelets, membrane defect, 324
Glioblastomas
  c-*sis* expression, 227
  isolation of transforming genes, 232
α-Globin genes, associated with various sickle-cell disease groups, *103*
Globin genes, in molecular cloning, 44–45
  human β globin gene, 30–32
Globulin, anti-thymocyte, in bone marrow transplantation, 174
Gluathionine mechanism, G6PD deficiency, 121
Glucose-6-phosphatase dehydrogenase
  in clonality determinations, 7, 8
  malaria as selective agent, 121–122
  world wide prevalence, 121
Glycoproteins, membrane, and inhibition of cell invasion
  glycophorin, 112
  specific parasite proteins, *Bdellovibrio*, 115
  syaloglycoprotein, 112
Glycosaminoglycans *see* Proteoglycans
Gold, autoantibody production, 324
Graft versus host disease
  aplastic anaemia transplant, 205
  granulocytopenia with PUO, 211–212
  hyposplenism, functional, penicillin therapy, 207
  see also Bone marrow transplantation
Gram positive bacteria, 200–201, 209–211
  see also species names
Granular lymphocytes, 'null' lymphoid cells, 375–376
Granulocyte antibodies *see* Immune thrombocytopenia and neutropenia
Granulocyte transfusion therapy, 210–211
  cross matching technique, 313
Granulocytopenia
  decontamination of patient, 204–205
  impaired neutrophil function, 201
  management, 210–211

Granulocytopenia (*contd*)
  myeloid regeneration, 207
  pathogens, specific therapy, 212–214
  prophylaxis of infection, 203
  PUO after antibiotic therapy, 211–212
  total replacement therapy, 206
  transfusion therapy, 210–211
Granulopoiesis, and cerebrospinal fluid, murine, 18

Haematopoiesis, 1–20
  biosynthetic functions, marrow stromal cells, 12–18
    collagen, 12
    colony-stimulating factor, 18
    defective haematopoiesis, proteoglycan changes, 14
    interferon, 18
    prostaglandins, 18
    proteoglycans, 12–16, *13*
  characterisation with antibodies, 11
    common acute lymphocyte leukaemia antigen, 11
    cytoskeletal proteins, 12
    factor VIII associated antigen, 11
  and human disease, 18–20
    aplastic anaemia, 19
    myelofibrosis, 19
    myeloproliferative disorders, 20
  in vitro systems, colony formation, 3–5
    fibroblastic cell cultures, 3
    long term marrow culture, 4
  in vivo observations, 1
  origin of stromal component, 6–10
    antigenic and physical characteristics, 9
    in clonal neoplasia, 7–9
    transplantation studies, 6
  stromal cells, long term effects, human and murine, 5–6
  definition, 2
  regulation, 10
  terminology, 2
Haematopoietic malignancies, 221
  see also Human T-cell leukaemia virus
Haemoglobin F synthesis
  deficit in β globin production, 79
  heterocellular persistence, genetic hypothesis, 104
  increase associated with medroxyprogesterone, 101
  levels in sickle-cell disease, associated with retinopathy, 98
Haemoglobin S, polymer structure, 91
  see also Sickle cell disease
Haemoglobinopathies, beta chain, use of 5 azacytidine, *in vivo* gene manipulation, 58, 59
Haemoglobinuria, associated with intravascular haemolysis, 116
Haemophilia, and thrombocytopenia, 320
Haemophilia B, 60
Haemophilus influenzae, 210
Haemorrhagic effects, heparin, 335–337

Haemostasis, effect of heparin, 334
Hairy-cell leukaemia, 223
Heart disease, ischaemic, antithrombotic drugs, 350–354
    aortocoronary bypass, 350
    aterial venous shunt thrombosis, 350
    cerebrovascular disease, 353
    coronary artery disease, 351
    post-myocardial infarction, 351–353
    unstable angina, 353
    valvular heart disease, 350
Heparin
    pneumococcal disease, 93
    prophylactic, pregnancy in sickle cell disease, 100
    see also Antithrombotic therapy
Hepatic disease and protein C deficiency, 279
Hepatosplenomegaly, T-cell malignancies, 222
Hereditary persistence of fetal haemoglobin (HPFH), 79–83
herpes simplex, 200, 202, 208
Herpes zoster, 200, 203, 208
    and acquired immunodeficiency syndrome, 381, 383
Histology, lymphoma, 130–132
    frozen sections, 131
    labelling procedures, immunoperoxidase, 131
    preparation of tissue for sectioning, 130
HL 60, human promyelocytic cell line, 227, 229, 230
HLA antibodies, lymphocytotoxicity test, 309
    shared antigens, 311
HLA-A, B, C and DR determinants see Bone marrow transplantation, clinical applications
Hodgkin's disease, 134, 157–159
Human T-cell leukaemia/lymphoma virus
    antibodies, 222
    epidemiology, 221
        molecular survey, 222
        serological survey, 222
    genome, 221
    Japan, 222–223
    leukaemogenesis by retroviruses, 224–226
    properties, 223
    T-LCL Caribbean, 222–223
    viral and cellular genes, 225
Humoral immunity, defects, 201
Hybrid selected translation, immunoprecipitation of protein, 45–47
Hybridomas see Monoclonal antibodies
Hydralazine neutropenia (lupus), 324
Hypercalcaemia, T-cell malignancies, 222
Hyperplasminaemia, 356
Hypokalaemia, length of antibiotic therapy, 212
Hyponatraemia, use in reduction of painful crises, 97
Hypoprothrombinaemia, and cephalosporins, 210

Idiopathic thrombocytopenic purpura, 310, 312, 317–320
Immune complex mechanism quinine-quinidine thrombocytopenia, 324

Immune cytopenias, drug induced see Immune thrombocytopenia and neutropenia
Immune thrombocytopenia and neutropenia
    classification of immune cytopenias, 315–323
        alloantibodies, 312–315
            alloimmune neonatal thrombocytopenia, 314
            granulocyte transfusions, 313
            platelet transfusions, 312
            post-transfusion purpura, 315
        autoantibodies, 316–323
            autoimmune thrombocytopenia, other disorders, 320
            and acquired immunodeficiency syndrome, 320
            autoimmune neutropenia, 321
            following bone marrow transplant, 321
            idiopathic autoimmune neutropenia, 321–322
            idiopathic thrombocytopenic purpura, 317–320
            inhibition of granulopoiesis, 323
            with other disorders, 322
        drug-induced immune thrombocytopenia and neutropenia, 323–325
            autoantibody production, 324
            drug adsorption, 323–324
            immune-complex mechanism, 324
        methodology, platelet and granulocyte antibody detection, 309–310
        platelet and granulocyte antigens, 310–312
            cell specific, 311–312
            shared (HLA group), 311
Immunisation, 206–207
    active, in patients with impaired immunity, 206
    passive, viral infections, 207
Immunoassays, detection of monoclonal antibodies, 286, 290
Immunochemical methods, in cloning specific mRNAs, 45
Immunodeficiency disorders, primary, bone marrow transplantation, 172
Immunofluorescent labelling, neoplastic lymphoid cells, 130
Immunosuppressive therapy
    allogeneic bone marrow transplantation, 173–174
    severe aplastic anaemia, 174
    syngeneic bone marrow transplantation, 174
    Wiskott-Aldrich syndrome, 172
Impotence and sickle-cell disease, 100
111In-labelling technique, transfusion of neutrophils, 313
Infection, exogenous sources, 203
Interferon, 18, 215
Interleukin, 2, 225, 226
Intravascular coagulation, disseminated, and protein C deficiency, 278–279
125Iodine-labelled monoclonal antihuman globulin, platelet autoantibodies, 310
Ion exchange chromatography, analysis of proteoglycans, 15
Iron deficiency
    in SS disease, 96

Iron deficiency (*contd*)
  treatment, and malaria, 117
Isouramil, inhibition of *Plasmodium* growth, 121

Kaposi's sarcoma, incidence in acquired
    immunodeficiency syndrome patients, 377,
    383
Klebsiella, 200, 201, 203
Kostmann's syndrome, 172

Laminar air flow, in reverse barrier isolation, 205
Laser, argon, in proliferative sickle retinopathy, 98
latent micro-organisms, reactivation, 208
Legionella pneumonia, 200, 213
Leg ulceration, chronic, in sickle cell disease, 102
Leukaemia
  acute non-lymphocytic, use of anti-CALLA
      antibody, 11
    microenvironmental abnormalities, 20
  chronic myelogenous, fibroblast proliferation,
      19–20
    Philadelphia chromosome, and G6PD marker,
        7–8, 60
  chronic myeloid, human T-cell proviruses, 223
  common acute lymphoblastic antigen, 9
  hairy cell, 223
    see also Lymphoma
  lymphoblastic, co-trimoxazole therapy, 208
  multipotent stem cell, G6PD heterozygotes, 8
Leukaemogenesis *see* Human T-cell
    Leukaemia/lymphoma virus
Levamisole, autoantibody production, 324
Ligases, DNA, in gene cloning, 36
Lithium carbonate, and granylocyte elevation, 207
Lymphoblastic leukaemia, co-trimoxazole therapy,
    208
Lymphocytes
  donor, in immunodeficiency disorders, 172
  pleomorphic multinucleated, circulating, 222
Lymphoma, immunological analysis, 127–164
  classification, 127
    malignant lymphomas, distinction from non-
        lymphoid neoplasms, 133
    by monoclonal antibodies, 128–130
    tissue sections versus cell suspensions, 130
      immunohistology, 130–133
  Hodgkin's disease, 134, 157–159
  large cell lymphomas resembling true histiocytic
      neoplasms, 159–160
  malignant lymphomas, B cell, 136–149
    centroblastic/centrocytic lymphoma, 144
    centroblastic lymphoma, 148
    centrocytic lymphoma, 146
    chronic lymphocytic leukaemia, B cell, 142
    of early B cells, 138
    hairy cell leukaemia, 142
    immunoblastic lymphoma, 148
    lymphoplasmacytic/cytoid lymphoma, 149
    multilobated lymphomas of B cell type, 149
    prolymphocytic leukaemia, B cell, 142
  malignant lymphomas, T-cell, 149–156
    of plasmacytoid T-cells, 156

Lymphoma
  malignant lymphomas (*contd*)
    peripheral T-cell lymphomas/leukaemias, 153
    pleomorphic T-cell lymphoma, 155
    prethymic asnd thymic, 152
    Sezary syndrome, 155
    T-immunoblastic lymphoma, 156
  National Cancer Institute, classification, 127–128
  non-Hodgkin's lymphomas, immunohistological
      identification, 160–164
Lymphopenia, and lymphocyte dysfunction, 201
Lysozyme, marker of histiocytes, 160

Major histocompatibility loci *see* Bone marrow
    transplantation, allogenic transplantation
Malaria, 109–123
  genetic factors, 118
    other abnormal haemoglobins, 119
    glucose-6-phosphatase dehydrogenase
        deficiency, 121–122
    haemoglobin S, 118
    ovalocytosis, 119–121
    thalassaemia genes, 119
  haemolytic anaemia, 115–118
    chronic malaria, 115
    famine conditions, 118
    haemoglobinuria, 117
    immune status, 117
  intraerythrocytic development, 113
    gametocytogenesis, 114
    maturation changes, 114–115
  invasion of red cells, 112
  schizogonic cycle, 109–111
  schizogony, 115
  and thrombocytopenia, 320
  vaccine, 123
Malignancy
  isolation of transforming genes, 232
  second, incidence in bone marrow
      transplantation patients, 172
Malnutrition
  bone marrow failure, 202
  risk of *Pneumocystis carnii*, 202
Marrow buffy coat cells, long term cultures, 9
Marrow fibroblast colony forming cells (CFU-F)
    assay, 2
  evidence for haematopoietic function, 3
Mean cell volume and sickle cell thalassaemia, 102
Measles, 200
Medroxyprogesterone, and increase of
    haemoglobin, 101
Megaloblastic anaemia and folate deficiency, 96–97,
    117
Meningitis, incidence in sickle cell disease, 93
Mitogenic response
  measurement by tritiated thymidine, 10
  platelet-derived growth factor and regulation of
      haematopoiesis, 10
Molecular cloning
  cloning vehicles, 40
    bacteriophage, 41–43
    cosmids and single strand bacteriophage, 43

Molecular cloning
  cloning vehicles (*contd*)
    plasmids, 40–41
  hairpin loop formation, 38–39
  primer extension techniques, 39
  reverse transcriptase synthesis of cDNA, 38
  see also Gene isolation
Monoclonal antibodies
  coagulation factors, antibody production, 286–288
    applications, 288
    functional studies, 288
    immunoaffinity purification, 288
    immunoassays, 289, 290
    immunohistology, 290
    screening of hybridomas, 287
    therapeutic applications, 291
  factor VIII : C, 287, 294–296, 304
  factor VIII R : Ag, 286
  factor III — von Willebrand factor, 299–302
  factor IX, 287, 289, 296–297
  fibrinogen, 291–292
  haemostasis, 285
  hybridoma-derived antibodies, 285–286
  in lymphoma, classification, 128–129
  miscellaneous monoclonals, 302
  platelets, 297–299
  prothrombin, 292–294
  Workshops on Leukocyte Differentiation Antigens, 128
Moxalactam, empirical therapy, 209
Mucopolysaccharidase, deficiency, 171
Mucopolysaccharides, acid, acid, 12–16
Mucormycosis and amphotericin B, 214
Mucous membranes
  chemo/radiotherapy, induced damage, 201
  in immunocompromised patients, 206
Murine leukaemia virus, rat thymoma, 224
Mycobacteria, 200, 204
Myelodysplastic syndromes, 239–248
  acute leukaemia, relationship, 242–243
  clinical features, 240–241
  conclusions, 261
  differentiation inducing agents, 250
  haematological features, 243
    chronic myelomonocytic leukaemia, 247
    prognosis, 248
    idiopathic acquired sideroblastic anaemia, 246
    refractory anaemia, 245–246
    refractory anaemia with excess of blasts, 247
      in transformation, 247
    secondary, 247
  in vitro studies, 251
    blast cell colonies, 253
    defective maturation, *in vitro*, 254
    erythroid bursts and colonies, 253
    gm-CSA and other regulators, 255–256
    granulocyte-macrophage colonies, 252–253
    long term marrow cultures, 254
    mixed lineage colonies, 253
    role of lymphocytes, 256
  incidence, *244*

Myelodysplastic syndromes (*contd*)
  karyotypic abnormalities, 257–261
    common abnormalities, 258–260
    incidence, 258, *259*
    relation to findings in AML, 260
    secondary, and acute myeloid leukaemia, 260–261
  pre-leukaemic syndrome, diagnostic criteria, 239
  terminology, 240, 241
  treatment, 248–250
Myelofibrosis, fibroblast proliferation, 19–20

Nafazatrom, antithrombotic agent, 349
National Cancer Institute (1982), classification of lymphoma, 127–128
Neonatal screening, sickle cell disease, 101
Neoplasms, derived from true histiocytes, 134
  see also Lymphoma
Neoplastic cells, labelling reactions
  onc-gene cooperation, neoplastic transformation, 233
  T-antigens and CALLA, 153
  T-cell lymphoma, *150*
  see also Lymphoma
Nephrotoxicity, length of antibiotic therapy, 212
Neuroblastoma, isolation of transforming genes, 232
Neutropenia, specific therapy, 199–201, 208–210
  see also Granulocytopenia
Neutrophil dysfunction, congenital, 172
Neutrophil specific antibodies, detection, 310
NIH 3T3 cells, aneuplid murine fibroblast line, transforming assay, 232
Nitroglycerine, inhibition of platelet function, 349
Nuclear magnetic resonance, in HbS polymer formation, 91
'Null' lymphoid cells, cellular host defence, 375–376

Oligonucleotide probes, use in first trimester diagnosis, 83
Oligonucleotides (splicing signals), 33
  commercially available synthetic primer, 38, 48–49, 50
onc-genes see Cellular *onc*-genes
Oncogenes, association with immunoglobulin gene and CHL, 60
Oral mucositis, side effect of cyclophosphamide, 176
Oralocytosis, resistance to *Plasmodium* infection, 119–121
Ototoxicity, length of antibiotic therapy, 212

Parasite-host, membrane junctions, ATP and spectrin phosphorylation, 112
Parvovirus infection, implication in aplastic crisis of SS disease, 96
Pathogens, major, and clinical correlates in bone marrow failure, 200
Penicillin, prophylactic use, sickle-cell disease, 94–95
  empirical therapy, neutropenia, neutropenia, 208–210

Penicillin (*contd*)
  length of therapy, 212
  lifelong, prior to splenectomy, 206–207
Peroxidase conjugated anti-rabbit Ig, 131
Phage lambda *see* Bacteriophage
Philadelphia chromosome *see* Chronic myelogenous
    leukaemia
Phosphonoformic acid, cytomegalovirus
    pneumonia, 215
Pittsburgh pneumonia agent, 200, 213
Plasmids, in molecular cloning, 40–41
Plasminogen activators *see* Tissue plasminogen
    activator
Plasmodium see Malaria
Platelet
  aggregation *see* Antithrombotic therapy, heparin
  antibodies *see* Immune thrombocytopenia
  associated immunoglobulin G in idiopathic
    thrombocytopenic purpura, 310
  cross matching tests, HLA matching of donors,
    313
  derived growth factor (PDGF), marrow stromal
    cell proliferation, 10
  function, cephalosporin therapy, 210
Pneumococcal septicaemia, in sickle cell disease,
    93–95, 102
Pneumocystis carinii, 200, 201, 202
  association with acquired immunodeficiency
    syndrome, 369, 381–382
  in children, 213
  and cytomegalovirus, 213
Pneumonia, 208
  and AIDS, 369, 381–382
  clinical correlates, 199
  febrile syndromes, 213
  Legionella, 213
  Pittsburgh pneumonia agent, 213
  pneumocystic, 213–214
Pneumonitis *see* Cytomegalovirus pneumonitis
Post transfusion purpura, 315–316
  see also Immune thrombocytopenia
Pregnancy, risks, in sickle cell disease, 101
Prenatal diagnosis
  abortion, indications, 91
  fetal blood sampling, timing, 82
  fetal DNA from trophoblastic villi, first
    trimester, 82–83, 90
Priapism, in sickle cell anaemia, 100
Procarbazine and antithymocyte globin, in bone
    marrow transplantation, 174
Proliferative sickle retinopathy, 98, *99*
Prostaglandin, and haematopoiesis, 18
Prostaglandin synthesis, effect of aspirin, 344–345
Protein C (serine protease zymogen), 269–279
  activation, 270–272
    co-factor thrombomodulin, 270
    schematic model, *271*
  anticoagulant, 338
  anticoagulant properties, 273
    factor Va, 273
    factor VIII : C, 274
  biochemistry, 269–270

Protein (*contd*)
  deficiency of protein C, 275–279
    disseminated intravascular coagulation, 278
    hereditary thrombotic disease, 275–277
    purpura fulminans, 277
    skin necrosis, 277
  fibrinolytic properties, 274
  inhibition of activation, 272
  regulation of haemostasis, model, *279*
Protein S, and activated protein C, 274
Proteoglycans (acid mucopolysaccharide), 12–16,
    13
  analytical methods, *15, 16*
  electron microscopy, *17*
  mouse long term marrow culture, 14
  suppression of haematopoiesis, 14
Prothrombin, monoclonal antibodies, 292–293
Pseudomonas sp, 200, 201, 209
  aeruginosa, 203, 208
Pulmonary embolism
  and contraception, 101
  in sickle cell pregnancy, 100
Purpura fulminans syndrome, 277
pX protein, HTLV, 221, 224, 226
Pyrexia, management, in neutropenia, 210–212

Quantitative antiglobulin consumption assay, 310
Quinine, quinidine thrombocytopenia, immune
    complex mechanism, 324

Rabbit brain thromboplastin venous thrombosis,
    randomised trials, 338–341
Radioimmunoprecipitation, serological survey, T-
    cell Malignancies, 222
Radiolabelling
  differential molecular hybridisation, 47
  relative rates of globin chain synthesis, 82
ras-onc gene family, 232–233
Rat thymoma, murine leukaemia virus, 224
Recombinant DNA technology
  genetic library, *Plasmodium*, 23
in haematologic disease, isolation of thalassaemic
    genes, 56
  prenatal diagnosis, sickle cell disease, 90–91
  see also Gene isolation
Red cell heterogeneity, in sickle cell disease, 92
Restriction endonucleases
  Dde I sickle mutation, 90
  Hpa I, restriction site, HbS gene, 90
  recognition sequences, *35*
Restriction enzyme mapping, 82
Restriction fragment length polymorphisms linkage
    markers, 82–83
Reticulocytes, serial counting, and defective
    erythrocyte production, 117
Retinopathy, proliferative, in sickle cell
    haemoglobin C disease, 98, 99
Retroviral transforming genes (v-oncs), 221
Retroviruses
  cloning, human cellular homologues, 227
  human T-cell leukaemia/lymphoma virus, 221–
    223, 224–226

Retroviruses (*contd*)
  onc genes transduced in different species, 226, 228
Reverse barrier isolation, 205
Reverse transcriptase (RNA-dependent DNA polymerase) *see* Molecular cloning
Rhabdomyosarcomas, 232
RNA *see* DNA

S1 nuclease analysis maps, 54–56
Schwartzmann reactions, passive immunisation, 207
Sephacel *see* Ion exchange chromatography
Serial passage of parasites, loss of competence, 114
Serratia sp., 200
Serum screening, anti-HTLV antibodies, 221–222
  serological survey, 222
Severe aplastic anaemia *see* Aplastic anaemia
Severe combined immunodeficiency disease, transplants, 172
Sexual function, and priapism, sickle cell disease, 100
Sickle cell disease, 89–104
  clinical aspects, 92—95
    acute splenic sequestration, 92
    aplastic crisis, 95
    contraceptive advice, 101
    folate deficiency, 96
    iron deficiency, 96
    painful crisis, 97
    pneumococcal disease and prevention, 93–95
    pneumococcal vaccine, 95
    pregnancy, 100
    priapism, 100
    proliferative retinopathy, 98
    splenomegaly, 93
  genotypes, 89
  haemoglobin C, 89, 98
  natural history, 101–104
    α thalassaemia, 102
    environmental factors, 104
    heterocellular persistence of fetal haemoglobin, 104
    spectrum, 104
    three subgroups, haematological comparison, 103
  pathophysiology, 91
    endothelial adherence, 92
    polymer formation, 91
    red cell heterogeneity, 92
  prenatal diagnosis, 57, 90–91
Simian sarcoma virus
  c-*sis* cloning, 227, 228
  sequence homology with platelet derived growth factor, 11
Simplastin anticoagulant therapy, 338–339, *340*
Skin hyperpigmentation, side effect of cyclophosphamide, 176
Skin necrosis, protein C deficiency, 277
Southern blotting technique, 53–55, 59
Spleen, erythropoietic suppression, in mice, 14
Splenectomy, and risk of infection, 202, 206–207

Splenic sequestration, acute, in sickle cell disease, 92–93
Splenomegaly, 93–94
Staphylococcus aureus, 200, 201, 208
Staphylococcus epidermidis, 200, 202, 212
Starvation, prolonged, and proteoglycans, 14
Stem cells
  in clonal neoplasia, 7
  donor peripheral blood, source, 174
  human and murine, *in vitro* culture, 4–6
Stractan gradients, in quantitation of red cell heterogeneity, 92
Streptococcus pneumoniae, 200, 202
Streptokinase, myocardial infarction, 354–357
Stromal cells *see* Haematopoiesis
Strongyloides, 200
Sulphinpyrazone, lengthening of platelet survival, 346, 351–353
Syngeneic donors *see* Bone marrow

T-cell growth factor, 225, 226
T-cell malignancies *see* Human T-cell leukaemia/lymphoma virus
T-lymphocytes in acquired immunodeficiency syndrome
  failure of cell-mediated immunity, 376
  gamma interferon production, 379
  monoclonal antibodies, use in identification, 377
  sub-set imbalance, inverted ratio, 378
  see also Human T-cell leukaemia: Lymphoma: T-cells
Thalassaemia, molecular pathology
  α thalassaemias, 66–72, 102
    carrier states, 71
    genotype/phenotype relationships, 70
    interactions with sickling disorders, 71
    nomenclature, 66–70
    triplicated alpha gene arrangement, 72
  β thalassaemias, 73–77
    mutation sites, *74, 75*
    normal and abnormal splicing, 76
  classification, 66
  deficiency of globin mRNA, 56
  delta-beta and gamma-delta-beta forms, 79–83
    classification, 79–81
    hereditary persistence of fetal haemoglobin, 79–83
  genetic control, 63–66
    arrangement of genes, 63
    α globin gene cluster, *64*
    β globin gene cluster, 65–66
  identification of mutations, 56
  'mild' β, 78–79
  malaria as selective agent in polymorphism, 119
  prenatal diagnosis, 82–83
  thalassaemia intermedia, 77–79
    association of α- and homozygous β in Cypriots, 77–78
    with heterozygous β, 78–79
Thoraco-abdominal irradiation, bone marrow transplantation, 173

Thrombocytopenia, immune *see* Immune thrombocytopenia
Thromboembolic disease, and protein C deficiency, 275–277
see also Venous thrombosis
Thrombomodulin, cofactor in the activation of protein C, 270-272
Thymoma, rat, murine leukaemia virus, 224
Ticlopidine, inhibition of platelet aggregation, 348
Tissue plasminogen activator, 356–358
Torulopsis, 200
Total body irradiation
  acute non-lymphocytic leukaemia, 175
  Wiskott-Aldrich syndrome, 172
Total lymphoid irradiation, and cyclophosphamide, bone marrow transplantation, 173, 174
Toxoplasma gondii, 200
  central nervous system infection in acquired immunodeficiency syndrome, 381–382
Transforming genes, isolated by DNA-mediated transfer, tumorigenesis, 223, 226, 232–233
  see also Human T-cell leukaemia: Retroviruses
Transfusion
  repeated platelet, random donors, 312–313
  in sickle cell pregnancy, 100
5-Trifluorothymidine, 215
Trimoxazole therapy, pneumocystic pneumonia, 213–214
Trophoblast biopsy, in first trimester diagnosis, 83
Tuberculosis, reactivation following immunosuppression, 208
Tumorigenesis, 221
  T-cell malignancies, 221
  transforming assay, 232

Varicella/zoster therapy, 215
Vaso-occlusion, in sickle-cell disease
  endothelial adherence, 92
  first year of life, 102
  high levels of HbF, 104
  pneumococcal disease, 93
  priapism, 100
  proliferative retinopathy, 98
Vasopressin analogue, and painful crisis in sickle cell disease, 97
Venous thrombosis, anticoagulant therapy, 337–341
  practical recommendations, 341–342
Virus, therapy, *see* Antiviral therapy
Vitamin K
  antagonists, anticoagulant effect, 337–338
  and bleeding, 210
  dependent serine protease zymogens *see* Protein C
  and Protein C, 270
V-onc genes *see* Retroviruses

Warfarin, thrombogenesis, 338
Waterhouse-Friedrichsen syndrome, pneumococcal septicaemia, 93
Wiskott-Aldrich syndrome, immunosuppressive therapy, 172
World Health Organisation, malaria, 122

X-linked dysfunction of lymphocytes, 172

Y bodies, fluorescent, long term marrow cultures, 6

Zygomycoses, 200